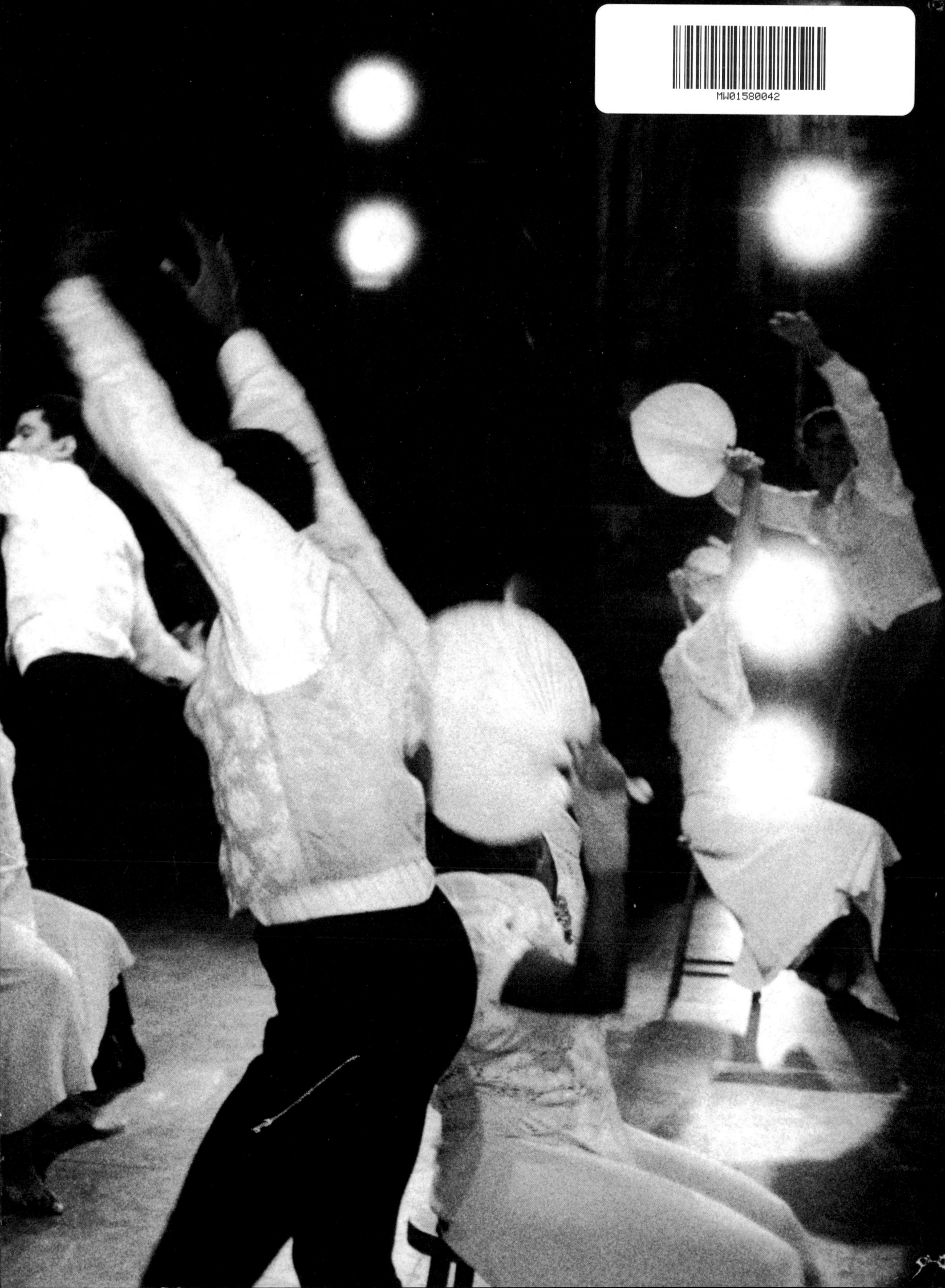

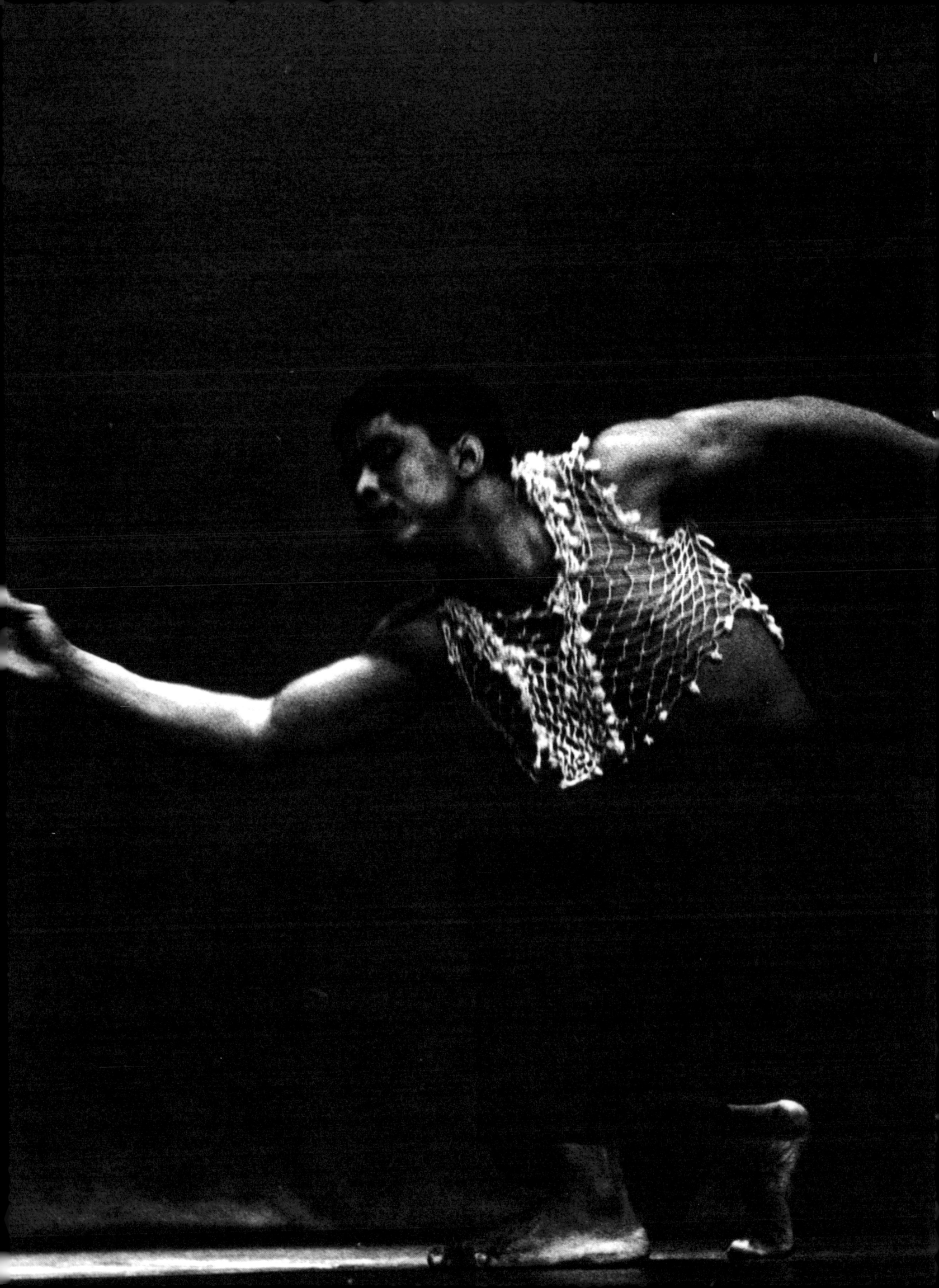

EDGES OF AILEY

EDGES OF AILEY

Edited by Adrienne Edwards

With essays by Horace D. Ballard, Harmony Bench and Kate Elswit, Aimee Meredith Cox, Thomas F. DeFrantz, Adrienne Edwards, Malik Gaines, Jasmine Johnson, Joshua Lubin-Levy, Uri McMillan, Ariel Osterweis, and J Wortham, and conversations with Kyle Abraham, Claire Bishop, Masazumi Chaya, Aimee Meredith Cox, Brenda Dixon-Gottschild, Adrienne Edwards, Jennifer Homans, Judith Jamison, Sylvia Waters, Jamila Wignot, and Jawole Willa Jo Zollar, with a chronology by CJ Salapare

Whitney Museum of American Art, New York
Distributed by Yale University Press, New Haven and London

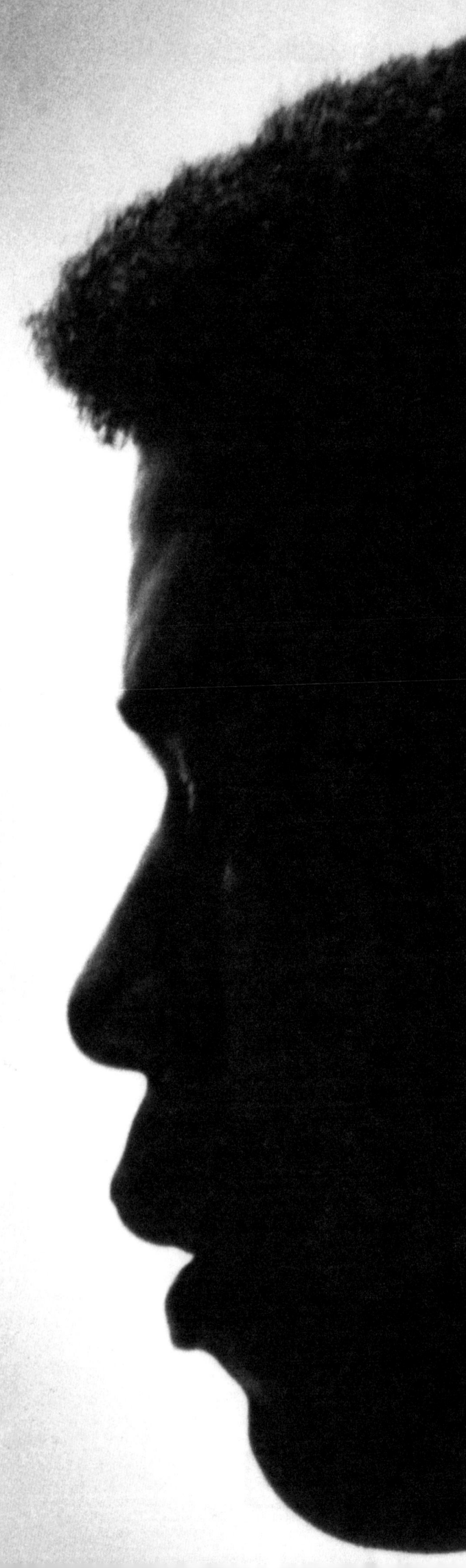

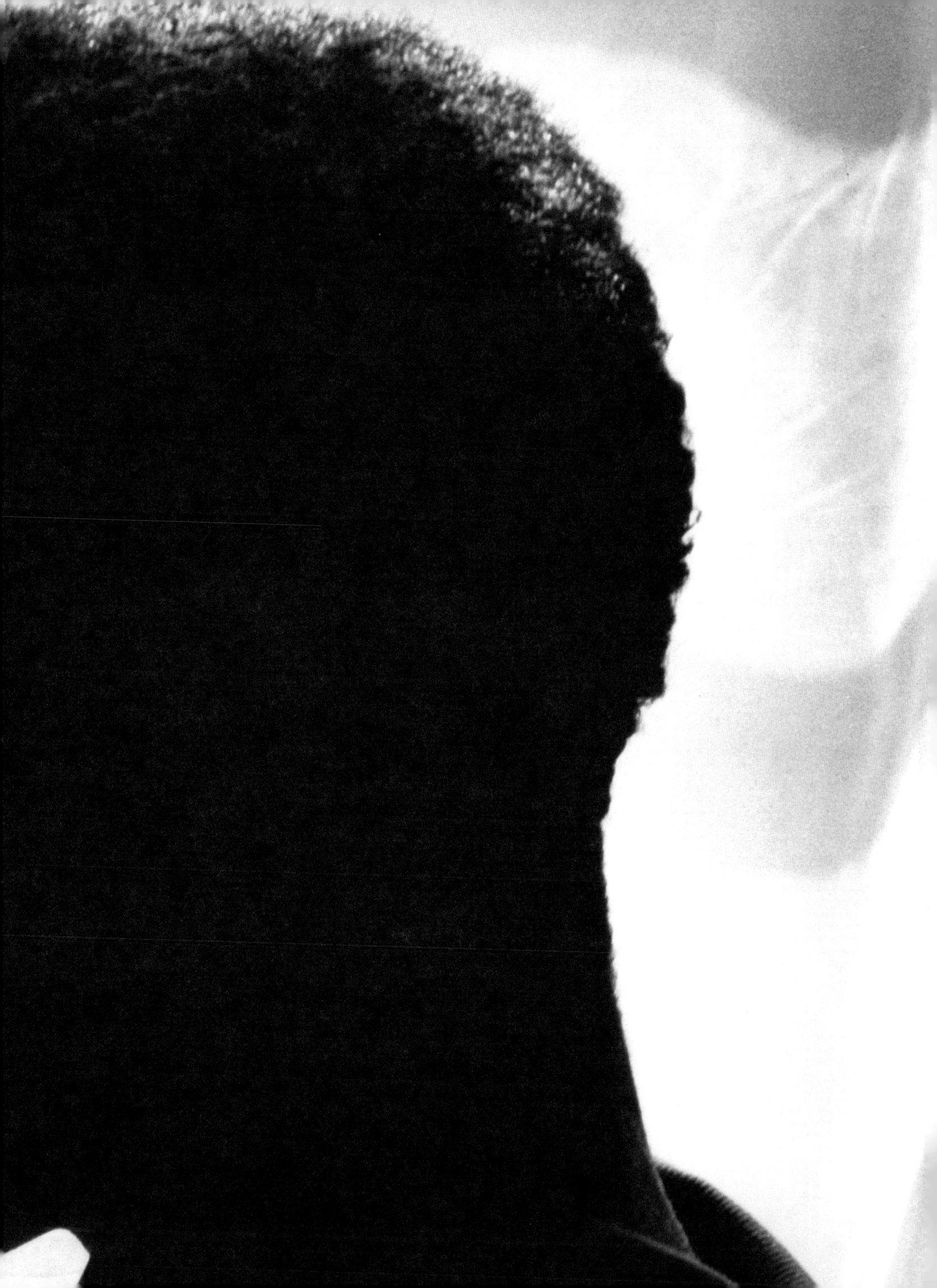

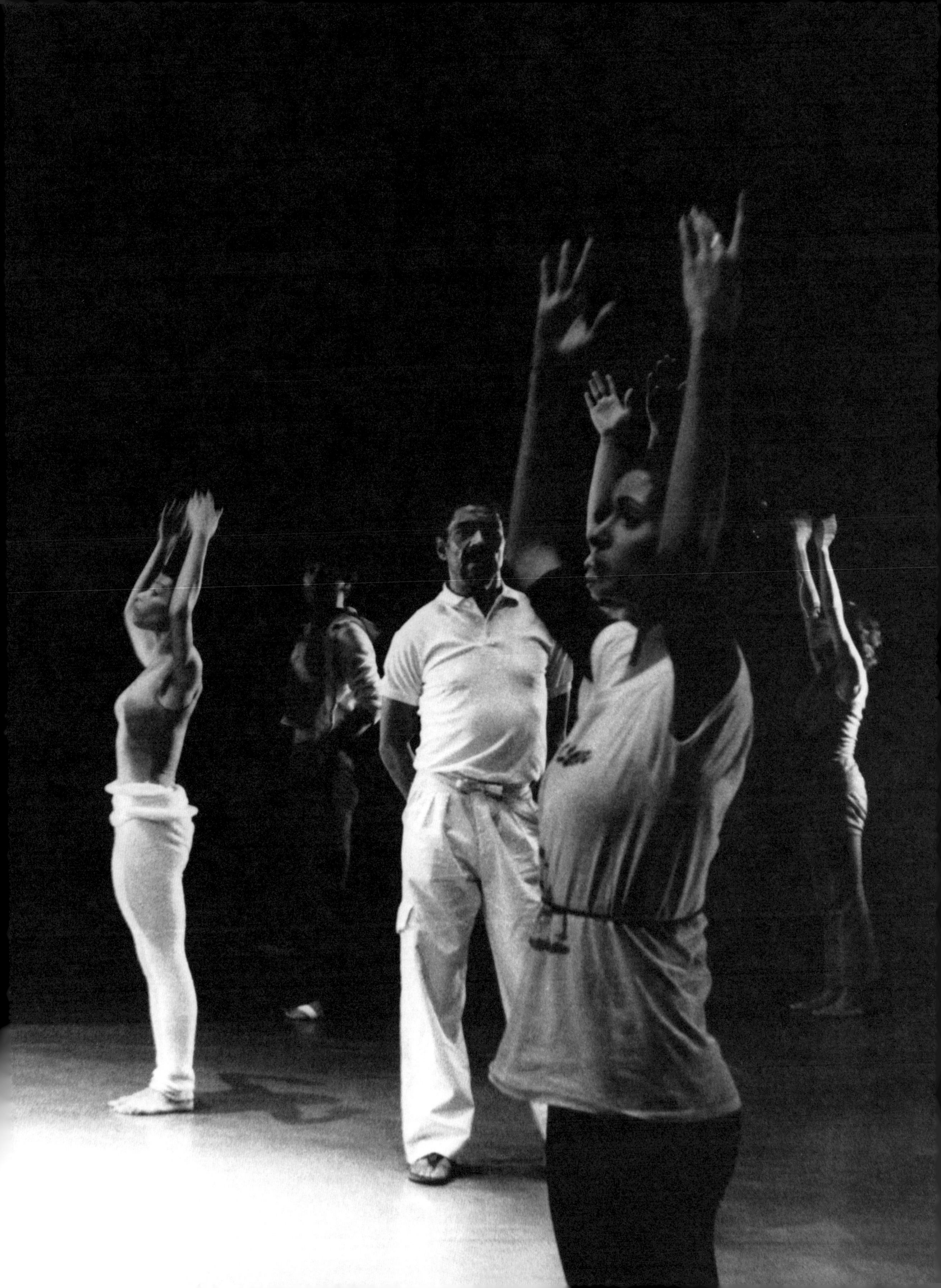

6	**Foreword** Scott Rothkopf	121	# Chronology CJ Salapare
8	**Acknowledgments** Adrienne Edwards		
11	**Such Sweet Thunder: On the Edges of Ailey** Adrienne Edwards	151	# Choreography
29	**Show Who You Are: Reflecting on Alvin Ailey** Masazumi Chaya, Adrienne Edwards, Judith Jamison, Sylvia Waters	275	# Archives
39	**How to Play Drums** Malik Gaines		
47	**Alive with Ailey** Jasmine Johnson	321	# Performances
53	**Beyond Culture and Somewhere between Starshine and Clay: Dancing with Alvin Ailey's Commitment to Black Study** Aimee Meredith Cox	329	# Artworks
59	**Elegant Mutinies** Horace D. Ballard		
67	**The Rhythm of Life: Alvin Ailey's Queer Gesture** Uri McMillan		
73	**Take Me to the Water** J Wortham		
77	**Virtuosity's Blood Memories** Ariel Osterweis		
85	**At the Edge of Each Other: Reading with Alvin Ailey's Archives** Joshua Lubin-Levy		
93	**Radical Accounting and the Edges of Archives: Alvin Ailey American Dance Theater's Historical Data** Harmony Bench and Kate Elswit		
101	**dear alvin** Thomas F. DeFrantz		
109	**After Ailey: A Conversation** Kyle Abraham, Claire Bishop, Aimee Meredith Cox, Brenda Dixon- Gottschild, Adrienne Edwards, Jennifer Homans, Jamila Wignot, Jawole Willa Jo Zollar	366	Appendix: Choreography and Dancers
		370	Checklist of the Exhibition
		376	Lenders to the Exhibition
		380	Index

Foreword

Performance may not be new to museums, but Alvin Ailey largely is. At least since the 1960s, art museums have been alive with music, dance, theater, and other forms of performance art—a development in which the Whitney Museum of American Art has long played a leading role. Yet for all its multiplicity, dance in the context of contemporary art museums has hewed primarily to two creative streams, as noted in this volume by *Edges of Ailey* curator Adrienne Edwards, the Whitney's Engell Speyer Family Senior Curator and Associate Director of Curatorial Programs. One line descends from the legacy of impresario Lincoln Kirstein, who not only founded the New York City Ballet with George Balanchine but also cut a wide swath across the worlds of art, fashion, and design. The other more prominent narrative begins with the seismic invention of Merce Cunningham and continues through the choreography of figures such as Trisha Brown and Yvonne Rainer to the likes of Ralph Lemon and Sarah Michelson today. While Ailey was certainly aware of and known to the key practitioners of both these modes, his work has never received institutional recognition commensurate with theirs nor with his broad popular appeal. Indeed, the latter may have hindered the former, along with a host of other biases against Ailey, not least of all his race.

Now is Ailey's time. Or rather, now is the museum's time to recognize belatedly this titanic creative force not simply as one of the twentieth century's greatest American choreographers, nor as its greatest Black choreographer, but as one of the greatest artists working in any medium anywhere in the world. This exhibition situates Ailey—and those he drew on and inspired—smack in the middle of twentieth-century avant-garde thought, right where he and they belong. And in so doing, it pressures and even redefines that trajectory by making it contend with stories and forms it had once all but ignored. Ailey, quite simply, forged a capacious new mode for "expressing the Black experience," in his words. Today we might question the presumptive universality of that phrase by making it either plural, "Black *experiences*," or singular, "*his* Black experience," as Edwards contends in these pages. Yet even thus qualified, Ailey's experience contained multitudes. His genius was to make the unique observations of his eye, his ear, his mind, and his body coalesce in an art that seemed to speak for so many to so many more.

Ailey got around. He made it from segregated rural Texas to Los Angeles and then New York; from the Black Church to Soul Train; from sold-out venues across the United States to performance halls around the globe. He made it to Broadway, to the gay clubs of Times Square, and to Lyndon B. Johnson's White House. He established one of the very few dance companies in history that has long survived its founder, still training future talent, while stewarding Ailey's repertory and commissioning new productions in his wake. He had a life full of love and sex with other men at a time when it was far more difficult to be entirely open about such things, especially if you were a Black man whose mother went to church and whose company at times counted on the US State Department for support. The title *Edges of Ailey* draws our attention to the edges of the man and his work, but also to the many edges he pushed and those he danced along and across.

A topic as sprawling as *Ailey*—both the creator and the corpus—does not readily lend itself to museological treatment. Yet the instant Edwards mentioned this kernel of an idea at our very first meeting in 2017, I immediately knew the Whitney had to take it on, whatever it might be. Since opening downtown two years prior, the Museum had vigorously redoubled its commitment both to performance and to innovative modes of exhibition making. This was evident in the work of Edwards's predecessor, Jay Sanders, the Museum's former curator of performance, whether inviting MPA and her collaborators to live ant-farm style between two panes of glass in our theater or staging the last concerts of Cecil Taylor in the vast empty expanse of the Whitney's fifth floor. Since joining the curatorial team in 2018, Edwards aimed to integrate performance even more squarely within the Museum's gallery spaces and, importantly, within the art histories it tells. This did not necessarily mean foregrounding visual artists "working in performance," but rather unspooling the cross-disciplinary dialogues between a jazz composer like Jason Moran and his visual-arts collaborators; or rethreading the fabric of connections between the photography of Every Ocean Hughes and her theatrical and filmic projects; or chronicling decades of performance by My Barbarian in a compact yet kaleidoscopic installation within a single gallery. Building on all these precedents, *Edges of Ailey* represents a kind of climax of the Whitney's and Edwards's own journeys in and through performance.

Edges of Ailey is one of—if not *the*—most ambitious and complex exhibitions undertaken in the Museum's history. It surveys Ailey's choreography through an immersive multichannel video installation of documentary footage in the Neil Bluhm Family Galleries and through a multipart residency of the Alvin Ailey American Dance Theater in the Susan and John Hess Family Theater. Throughout the run of the exhibition, the Whitney's theater will also host ten new commissions made by choreographers working in response to Ailey's legacy, while the galleries will feature archival material from Ailey's life in the context of a panorama of artworks that inspired Ailey, expound on themes related to his work, or are freshly made in relation to it. This wondrous constellation is Edwards's brilliant brainchild, and I am immeasurably grateful for her curatorial vision and her perseverance in orchestrating so complex a polyphony in the face of many obstacles, including a global pandemic. Her work would not have been possible without the expert curatorial collaboration of Joshua Lubin-Levy, Curatorial Research Associate, and CJ Salapare, Curatorial Assistant. And, above all, the endeavor owes to the Whitney's entire staff whose immense talents and dedication time and again make the most daunting ideas a beautiful reality.

Such a challenging and expansive undertaking would not have been possible without the support of visionary donors who were generous with both their funds and their belief in *Edges of Ailey*. I am enormously grateful to the Jerome L. Greene Foundation for understanding the importance of this groundbreaking exhibition—even before we understood what it might become—and in so doing launching our project as lead sponsor. Great thanks also go to Bank of America and Delta for sponsoring this project and for their longstanding support of the Whitney. The Ford Foundation's essential leadership contribution allowed us to realize the full curatorial ambition of the exhibition. I owe tremendous gratitude to the following individuals and foundations for recognizing the significance of this endeavor with incredible generosity: Judy Hart Angelo, the Arnhold Family | Arnhold Foundation, the Barbara Haskell American Fellows Legacy Fund, the Horace W. Goldsmith Foundation, Anne-Cecilie Engell Speyer and Rob Speyer, the Whitney's National Committee, and Clara Wu Tsai. I am extremely grateful to the Holly Peterson Foundation, the Keith Haring Foundation Exhibition Fund, the National Endowment for the Arts, A4 Arts Charitable Trust, the Adam D. Weinberg Artists First Fund, Candace and Rick Beinecke, Kevin Gan and Benjamin Blad, Elizabeth Marsteller Gordon, the Harkness Foundation for Dance, Sharon and John Hoffman, Nancy Magoon, and an anonymous donor. The extensive research for the exhibition was made possible by an endowment from Rosina Lee Yue and the late Bert A. Lies, Jr. The Marshall Weinberg Fund for Performance, endowed in honor of his parents, Anna and Harold Weinberg, provides crucial support for the performance program. This exhibition catalogue, which offers an unprecedented look at Ailey's life and work from multiple perspectives, would not have been possible without the generosity of the Mellon Foundation. Although many of the artworks in the exhibition are drawn from the Whitney's collection, numerous institutions and individuals graciously lent important art works to complement our own holdings. As always, I am indebted to the Whitney's entire Board of Trustees for their unwavering commitment to the Whitney's mission and pathbreaking exhibitions such as this one.

    Finally, I wish to express my deepest gratitude to the Whitney's collaborators at the Alvin Ailey American Dance Theater and Foundation, including Executive Director Bennett Rink and its staff, dancers, and choreographers past and present. Their care for Mr. Ailey—as he is affectionately and reverently known in their midst—has sustained this project, as well as generations of creators and devoted audiences around the globe. We at the Whitney could not be more grateful for their trust and partnership in honoring a legacy that they have long nurtured with intellect, sweat, and love.

                Scott Rothkopf
                Alice Pratt Brown Director

Acknowledgments

Edges of Ailey is bigger than any one person, dance company, or museum. I have been deeply moved by the life and choreography of Alvin Ailey. Even though he is not among us in the flesh, it feels important to express how significantly I have been altered by his example—not only how generously and with great curiosity he lived, loved, and danced but equally from what he left behind so that we might know the stakes of what he has done. In assembling this extravaganza over the last six years, I have kept close to Mr. Ailey and abided by his ways of being and doing, which has been profoundly rewarding. I am forever changed as a curator and scholar because of him.

Being able to experiment and innovate what an exhibition about performance in a museum might be was possible because of the imaginative and relentless research, outreach, and organization undertaken by the core team for this project. They culled through thousands of pages and hours of archival footage, responded to countless emails, attended innumerable meetings, and instinctively realized a question was really a wish and made it a reality. CJ Salapare, Joshua Lubin-Levy, Lynn Schatz, Elisabeth Skjaervold, and Jared Huggins, as well as Josh Begley and Kya Lou: thank you for being alongside me in the most generous, generative, wonderous, and rigorous ways. This really would not have happened without you.

My sincere gratitude goes to Scott Rothkopf, the Whitney's Alice Pratt Brown Director, who has consistently shown endless support and trust for my work in general and championed this ambitious project since its earliest days in his previous role as chief curator. I am also immensely grateful to Adam D. Weinberg, the Whitney's former director, who encouraged and thoroughly understood the combinatory aims of the exhibition and created an institution that could realize it, having made interdisciplinary art and performance a hallmark of his vision for and legacy at the Museum.

This tribute to Mr. Ailey would not have been possible if not for the unwavering trust and sustained collaboration between the Whitney and the Alvin Ailey American Dance Theater (AAADT) and Foundation. I am grateful to the Ailey leadership, many of whom served on our Dance Advisory Committee, and to the entire staff for their eagerness and steadfast support. I would like to thank Bennett Rink and Robert Battle for their guidance and enthusiasm, along with the other members of the committee: Ronni Favors, Marion Koltun, Melanie Person, Matthew Rushing, and Eric Wright. A special acknowledgment goes to Dominique Singer and Sylvia Waters for their openness and wealth of knowledge, which greatly enriched this book and the exhibition.

Allan Gray and Carmaletta Williams generously opened Mr. Ailey's personal papers at the Black Archives of Mid-America, enabling a fuller presentation of Mr. Ailey, the man himself.

An exhibition of this scope and groundbreaking format would not have been possible without the expertise, flexibility, grit, and imagination of the Museum's exhibition team. I am deeply grateful to the following colleagues for meeting the demands of a show filled with innumerable challenges and for rising to the occasion at every turn. I thank Maura Heffner, Joshua Rosenblatt, Michael Gibbons and everyone in AV, Emilie Sullivan, Diana Carvajal, Paula Bauer, Susan Steinfield, Elissa Medina, and Greg Reynolds. Katie Fong as well as interns Beza Lulseged, Maria Wilson Nuñez, and Jaiha Lee supported this project in endless ways. Nicole Bradbury and Kristopher Pourzal also contributed their essential research.

The pendant performances are an immense undertaking, and I thank the Whitney's performance team for realizing its complex vision: Elisabeth Skjaervold, Andreas Huang, Alex Zylka, and all those involved with staging performances at the Museum. I greatly appreciate everyone involved with Ailey's robust weeks-in-residence at the Whitney: the AAADT, Ailey II, Ailey Extension, the Ailey School, and Ailey Arts In Education and Community Programs. I am grateful to the choreographers who agreed to imagine and present new work on the occasion of the show and were inspired by Ailey's own repertory model: Kyle Abraham, Ronald K. Brown, Trajal Harrell, Bill T. Jones, Ralph Lemon and Kevin Beasley, Sarah Michelson, Okwui Okpokwasili with Peter Born, Will Rawls, Matthew Rushing, Yusha-Marie Sorzano, and Jawole Willa Jo Zollar.

Two essential components of the exhibition—the video surround and the data visualizations—have enlivened Mr. Ailey's life and legacy in inventive ways. The former materialized thanks to the vision, talent, commitment, and openness of Josh Begley and Kya Lou, with the assistance of Jocelyn Brown, Henoch Moore, Aaron Igler and Matt Suib of Greenhouse Media, Rebecca Kent, Alessandra Bellizia, Eileen Pierce, and Sascha von Oertzen. The latter was engineered and brought to fruition through the expertise of Harmony Bench and Kate Elswit together with their research team.

This expansive publication serves not only as a crucial component and extension of the exhibition but as a landmark contribution to the scholarship surrounding the life, work, and legacy of Mr. Ailey. I extend endless gratitude to designer Garrick Gott, editor Sarah Noreika, production specialists Nerissa Dominguez Vales and Sue Medlicott, and the Whitney's Director of Publications Beth Huseman. I am also grateful to Monica Adame Davis, Jacob Horn, Beth Turk, and Audrey Warne for their assistance at various stages. The publication is greatly enriched by essays that thoughtfully contextualize and amplify themes from Mr. Ailey's life and dances. I am indebted to Horace Ballard, Harmony Bench and Kate Elswit, Aimee Meredith Cox, Thomas F. DeFrantz, Malik Gaines, Jasmine Johnson, Joshua Lubin-Levy, Uri McMillan, Ariel Osterweis, J Wortham, and CJ Salapare for their contributions. I am also grateful for the insightful conversations I had with Masazumi Chaya, Judith Jamison, and Sylvia Waters, contemporaries of Mr. Ailey and legends in their own right, along with those contemplating Mr. Ailey's legacy today: Kyle Abraham, Claire Bishop, Aimee Meredith Cox, Brenda Dixon-Gottschild, Jennifer Homans, Jamila Wignot, and Jawole Willa Jo Zollar.

The ideas for this exhibition were refined in the spring 2023 Mellon Seminar "Alvin Ailey and Beyond" at the City University of New York's Graduate Center. I am grateful to the inimitable Claire Bishop for serving as my co-leader and interlocutor. The thinking behind *Edges of Ailey* was enriched by the brilliance of everyone in the class: Ian Anderson, Anna Cahn, Sasha Dobos-Czarnocha, Jasmine François, Emily Furlich, Alicia Gallant, Naiomy Guerrero, Alyssa Hanley,

Catherine Jijón, Leah Newman, Alexandra Rego, Laura Suárez Rodriguez, and Quinn Schoen.

An undertaking such as this one requires tremendous efforts from everyone at the Museum. My gratitude extends to the following individuals and their stellar teams: I.D. Aruede, Amy Roth, and Alex Tonetta in Administration; Marilou Aquino, Morgan Arenson, Nicky Combs, and Eunice Lee in Advancement; Angela Montefinise, Ashley Reese, and Nora Gomez-Strauss in Communications and Content; Jane Carey in Community; Matt Skopek in Conservation; Cris Scorza, Anne Byrd, Megan Heuer, and Dyeemah Simmons in Education; Peter Scott and David Selimoski in Facilities; Sunil Chaddha and Dan Nascimento in Finance and Accounting; Hilary Greenbaum in Graphic Design; Gregg Bordowitz at the Independent Study Program; Nick Holmes in Legal; Bri O'Brien Lowndes in Marketing; Maria Nielson in the Office of People and Culture; Julie Rega in Membership; Barbi Spieler in Registration; Farris Wahbeh in Research Resources; Larry DeBlasio in Security; Andrew Cone in Strategic Planning; Bridget Mendoza in Technology; and Wendy Barbee-Lowell in Visitor and Member Experience.

A special thanks goes to my colleagues in the Curatorial department who supported this project in many ways. I offer gratitude to Kim Conaty, Elisabeth Sussman, Chrissie Iles, Barbara Haskell, Christiane Paul, Marcela Guerrero, Drew Sawyer, Meg Onli, Rujeko Hockley, Jennie Goldstein, and Laura Phipps. In addition, I appreciate the collegiality of Kelly Long, Roxanne Smith, Nakai Falcón, Scout Hutchinson, Caroline Webb, Ophelia Deng, Joanna Epstein, Beatriz Cifuentes, Angelica Arbelaez, David Lisbon, Rose Pallone, Mary Creed, Rowan Diaz-Toth, and Araceli Bremauntz-Enriquez.

My gratitude goes to the Whitney's Trustees and also to the lenders and those who facilitated loans: the Alvin Ailey Dance Foundation; the Antonio Archives and Devon Caranicas; the Art Institute of Chicago and Sarah Oehler; Autograph; the Estate of Romare Bearden; the Black Archives of Mid-America, Allan Gray, Carmaletta Williams, and Laura Darnell; the Beinecke Rare Book and Manuscript Library and Melissa Barton; the Brooklyn Museum; the Langston Hughes Estate and Sarah Yake; the Carl Van Vechten Trust, the late Edward Burns, and Logan Esdail; the Cameron Art Museum; Casey Kaplan Gallery and Kevin Beasley; the Chapin Library and Anne Peale; the Cincinnati Museum Center and Elizabeth Pierce; the Currier Museum of Art and Kurt Sundstrom; Corvi-Mora, Tommaso Corvi-Mora, and Lynette Yiadom-Boakye; the Danforth Art Museum, Jessica Roscio, and Rachel Passannante; DC Moore Gallery, Kate Larkin, and Edward De Luca; Beth Rudin DeWoody and Jen Chisholm; Eric Firestone Gallery and Jennifer Samet; Jeff and Leslie Fischer; the Gordon Parks Foundation; Hales Gallery; halley k harrisburg and Michael Rosenfeld; the High Museum of Art and Katherine Jentleson; the Hood Museum of Art and Michael Hartman; the Howard University Gallery of Art and Kathryn Coney; Hudgins Family; Jack Shainman Gallery, Tamsen Greene, and Lynette Yiadom-Boakye; Jacob's Pillow Archives, Norton Owen, and Patsy Gay; Jenkins Johnson Gallery; the Johnson Collection and Sarah Tignor; Rashid Johnson and Alexandra Ernst; Ralph Lemon; the Library of Congress, Rachel Waldron, David Mandel, and Libby Smigel; the Los Angeles County Museum of Art; Crystal McCrary and Raymond McGuire; the Metropolitan Museum of Art, David Breslin, and Alisa LaGamma; the Metropolitan Opera; Michael Rosenfeld Gallery; Leslie Miller and Richard Worley; the Mohn Family Collection; the Museum of Contemporary Art, Los Angeles; the Museum of Modern Art, Ann Temkin, Lily Goldberg, Stuart Comer, and Josh Siegel; the Museum of the City of New York and Elizabeth Randolph; the National AIDS Memorial and Brian Holman; the National Gallery of Art, Harry Cooper, and Molly Donovan; the Nevada Museum of Art; the New York Public Library and the Schomburg Center for Research in Black Culture, LaTanya Autry, Alexander Garcia, Linda Murray, Phil Karg Cosgrove, Annemarie van Roessel, and Doug Reside; Jennifer Packer; Paula Cooper Gallery; Jordan Roth, Richie Jackson, and Alexis Johnson; Ryan Lee Gallery, Jeffrey Lee, and Daisy Fornengo; Salon 94, Jeanne Greenberg Rohatyn, and Karon Davis; Lorna Simpson; the Smithsonian American Art Museum, Randall Griffey, and Melissa Ho; the Solomon R. Guggenheim Museum; the Souls Grown Deep Foundation and Raina Lampkins-Fielder; the Stuart A. Rose Manuscript, Archives, and Rare Book Library and Gabrielle Dudley; the Studio Museum in Harlem and Thelma Golden; Mickalene Thomas; Blaise Tobia; the Virginia Museum of Fine Arts and Leo Mazow; and those who wish to remain anonymous.

Thank you to Zita Allen, Jennifer Dunning, Thomas F. DeFrantz, Brenda Dixon-Gottschild, and Susan Manning for your immense contributions to the field of dance and our understanding of Mr. Ailey's momentum in it. Dunning and DeFrantz's work was foundational for the chronology in this volume.

The following lodestars have sustained me as I have imagined and made this motley project; they have my heartfelt gratitude for their dedication, honesty, fortitude, generosity, and presence: Cecilia Alemani, Elizabeth Alexander, Hilton Als, Jody and Paul Arnhold, Kevin Beasley, David Breslin and Emily Blanchard, Barbara Browning, Deborah Cullen-Morales, Donna De Salvo, Anne-Cecilie Engell Speyer, Eleonora Fabião, Malik Gaines, RoseLee Goldberg, Thelma Golden, Deana Haggag, Kathy Halbreich, Trajal Harrell, Pati Hertling, Leo Holder, Eungie Joo, Bill T. Jones and Bjorn Amelan, Koyo Kouoh, Robin D. G. Kelley, Ralph Lemon, André Lepecki, Glenn Ligon, Dave McKenzie, James McKnight, Rodney McMillian, Julie Mehretu, Sarah Michelson, Sophie Mörner, Fred Moten, Wangechi Mutu, Alexandro Segade, Lorna Simpson, Olga Viso, Darren Walker, Simone White, Catherine Wood, and Clara Wu Tsai. Heartfelt appreciation goes to Kevin Gan and Ben Blad and their Oberon Foundation for the Arts for lending the time and space to develop this project and imagine and write sections of this book.

Among the themes important to Mr. Ailey are Black spirituality, migration, and liberation—that is the question of sustenance, movement, and freedom of whoever has an intimacy with the set of conditions that are given to Blackness; what Ralph Ellison distinguished as the "blackness of blackness." *Edges of Ailey* unfolds at a time of unimaginable death, violence, precarity, and uncertainty. As Toni Morrison has written: "This is precisely the time when artists go to work. There is no time for despair, no place for self-pity, no need for silence, no room for fear. We speak, we write, we do language. That is how civilizations heal." Following Mr. Ailey as a vital example, art has the capacity to hold the moment or at least question it, to foreground compassion, survival, and humanity to those of us who need it at this dark horizon. May we rise out of the disaster that already prevails to meet one another with open hearts to the suffering of the world in a way that honors our inherent sacredness, for as W.E.B. Du Bois warns us: "The cost of liberty is less than the price of repression."

For my family, my teacher José Esteban Muñoz, and my beloved Natalie Diaz without whom . . . .

Adrienne Edwards
Engell Speyer Family Senior Curator and
Associate Director of Curatorial Programs

* SUCH SWEET THUNDER

"WORLD III" – party atmosphere –
UNISEX   hand greetings – black –
  DISCOTHEQUE – REAL PEOPLE

CREATE ATMOSPHERE OF JARDIN, GALLERY,
Huppert. P.R. dress – block dress –
daring dress – * identify strongly with
what young people are wearing today
when they party –

At end chord point to character
    who starts next work
credits for two panels
    over ptg group + frozen figure.
    who starts next ballet – stage as true
    form the post in white – almost
    lightly –

Adrienne Edwards

Such Sweet Thunder

On the Edges of Ailey

Edges of Ailey is the culmination of six years of research, reflecting upon, planning, and imagining nothing less than an interdisciplinary extravaganza about the life, dances, adjacencies, and legacy of the choreographer Alvin Ailey (1931–1989). This three-part project comprises an exhibition in the Neil Bluhm Family Galleries on the fifth floor of the Whitney Museum of American Art, a pendant performance program in the Susan and John Hess Family Theater, and this accompanying scholarly catalogue. Up to now most exhibitions about dance presented in art museums revolved around two approaches: the world of Lincoln Kirstein, cofounder of the New York City Ballet and the School of American Ballet; and the unconventional movement methods of the dancers involved with the Judson Dance Theater and artists aligned with it, namely Merce Cunningham. While I did not know what "material" existed from which to evolve an exhibition, I knew the repertory well from my nearly lifelong, repeated sojourns to performing arts venues in Atlanta and New York to see the Alvin Ailey American Dance Theater (AAADT) perform. In some ways, I have been thinking about Ailey for almost my entire life. From the very start of exploring the possibility of this show, there was a prevailing feeling that while many people were aware of the Ailey company's high-profile, internationally renowned brand, few knew about the icon who started it, the man himself. Therefore, the exhibition focuses on and, in true Ailey style, constellates a multiverse around Mr. Ailey, and what he achieved during his lifetime.[1] As a staging of history, it encompasses not only his choreography for his eponymous company, but also the full range of his obsessions, curiosities, and creative output—from before he founded the AAADT and with other institutions while leading it— deeply and attentively tracing and expanding from the rich moving-image archive, composed of recordings and footage of interviews, performances for the camera, dances, choreographic methods, and rehearsals dating back to as early as 1962, as well as from a trove of personal notebooks, drawings, letters and postcards, and other ephemera. It asks, if his shining were not for us, then for whom?[2]

    My arrival to and unfolding of this project are situated precisely along the lines poet Dionne Brand offers in her luminous, genre-defying book *A Map to the Door of No Return*: "One enters a room and history follows; one enters a room and history precedes. History is already seated in the chair in the empty room when one arrives. Where one stands in a society seems always related to this historical experience. Where one can be observed is relative to that history. All human effort seems to emanate from this door. How do I know this? Only by self-observation, only by looking. Only by feeling. Only by being a part,

fig. 1

Alvin Ailey, page from Loose Notes #11 [755], ca. 1974, Allan Gray Family Personal Papers of Alvin Ailey (AC10), Series 3: Notebooks, folder 175, Black Archives of Mid-America, Kansas City, Missouri sitting in the room with history."³ In approaching the history of Mr. Ailey, I find myself in the circuit of his own concern for history, for that which preceded him, which is represented in the exhibition through the gathering of a surprising and generative range of influences on his work and his interests. What I have learned throughout the process of organizing this project is that what we think we know about Mr. Ailey and his art, indeed even what he told us about it—that imperative of "expressing the black experience" and "putting the black experience out there in a meaningful, beautiful way"—was a meta-framework or an animating force for why he did what he did, but it certainly was not the entire story.⁴ For the archive would reveal his contingencies of existence through a far more complex set of references and scenes, a multitude of histories in dance, literature, visual art, music, gay life, entertainment, spirituality, the movements in and of the Black diaspora, and Black sociality, which he coalesced and folded into his dances and are represented in various ways in this volume. His Black history, his Black experience, his Black motility, was varied, multiplicitous, and polyvocal, and in each he was an instigator and a threshold.

The archive is a question of the future itself, of what happens upon our arrival to it, as much as a means of understanding what is an adequate response to the promise the archive offers us in the midst of the possibilities and responsibilities it holds forth for us today, the impossible future for Mr. Ailey, and for tomorrow, which is our own horizon.⁵ As Jacques Derrida reminds us in his writings on the archive, "[W]e want to know what that will have meant, we will only know in times to come. Perhaps. Not tomorrow but in times to come, later on or perhaps never . . . a very singular experience of the promise."⁶ Such a promise is only ever situated on the other side of the threshold, and what we can glean from it is entirely conditional—this is to say, tentative, dependent, and contingent upon our own present experience (how our world and experience of it contour our reading of the archive and what we know of history and historical subjects, with the sleight and benefit of hindsight).⁷ Archival work is ghost work; history is there, as Brand reminds us, seated as the specter of a future perfect history. It is an " imaginary world, in which spirits and ghosts are given reality."⁸ Mr. Ailey's archive, a volume of material that ranges in the thousands of pages, dwells between the records of the AAADT and his personal effects, the former held by the Library of Congress in Washington, DC, and the latter in the personal papers of the Allan Gray family at the Black Archives of Mid-America in Kansas City, Missouri; in reading them alongside each other, the complexities and contradictions of this famously private individual make a clear assessment difficult. As we see in the exhibition and in this catalogue, his notebooks (he consistently journaled over many years) reveal a total life, making no separation between his choreographic notes; rules for, measure of, and love of the AAADT dancers; to-do lists; or reflections on his lovers and his own life, for they often sit across the page from one another, indicating their inextricability. Yet, since they frequently appear as taxonomies or missives, there can be little explication about their deeper relation beyond their intense proximity; they contain a fundamental characteristic of the archive—that it is in itself distinguished by the difficulty of translation.⁹ Derrida redirects our expectations: "[T]he structure of the archive is *spectral*," reminding us that "the truth is spectral."¹⁰ What a person's archive does do is to allow us to glimpse "what he thinks in truth secretly."¹¹ The very impulse to retain and hand over for posterity the records of one's life, by moving them from private to public, Derrida observes as a drive—namely, in Freudian psychoanalytic terms, a death drive, a drive against and also for loss, a "gathering together of signs," which is consigned by a desire that "operates in silence."¹² The unification, identification, and classification of these life holdings are a political act, an insistence on the control and location of history and memory, placed in reserve and thus into the possibility of a circuit of repetition since "the archive produces as much as it records the event."¹³ Mr. Ailey's archive is evidence of "a having been here," that there was a life and what such a life entailed, and to that extent the archive is "marked in his body"; it is also a body, that precarious flesh now held in a range of ephemera, as a wager for the future, against the potential for absolute finitude and forgetfulness.¹⁴ The archive is not merely a collection of what will have been but rather a movement toward what is possible, and that holding out for the possible is the theatrical potential of the material itself, it is the figure of possibility as and at the precipice of history and the future.

Mr. Ailey's archive, a multivalent, dynamic archaeology of histories, exists not only in the material repository of objects and images but most famously in his choreography, particularly that of the company's repertory. As part of the robust live performance aspect of

figs. 2a–i

Carl Van Vechten, *Alvin Ailey*, 1955. Beinecke Rare Book and Manuscript Library, Yale University, New Haven, Connecticut

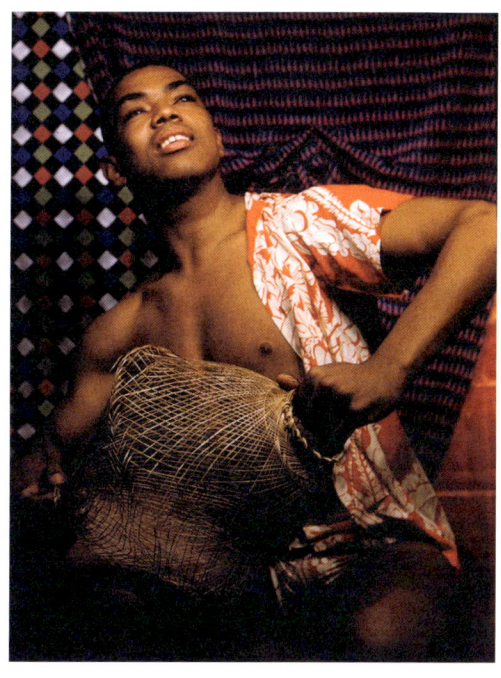
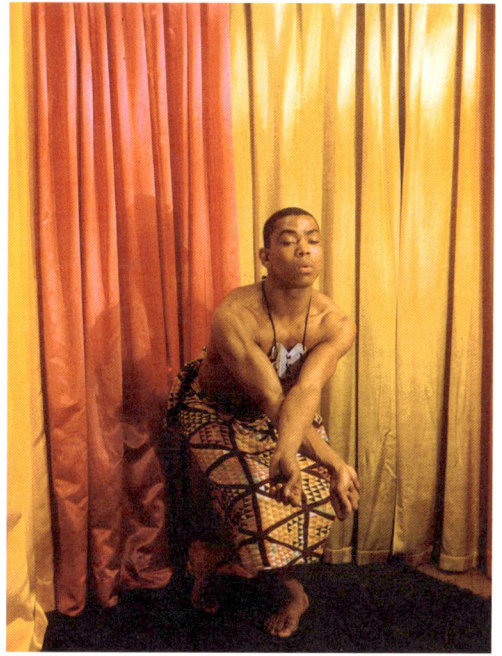
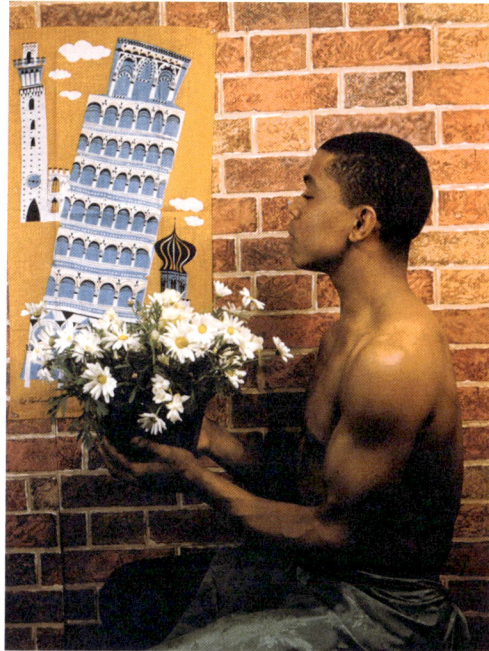
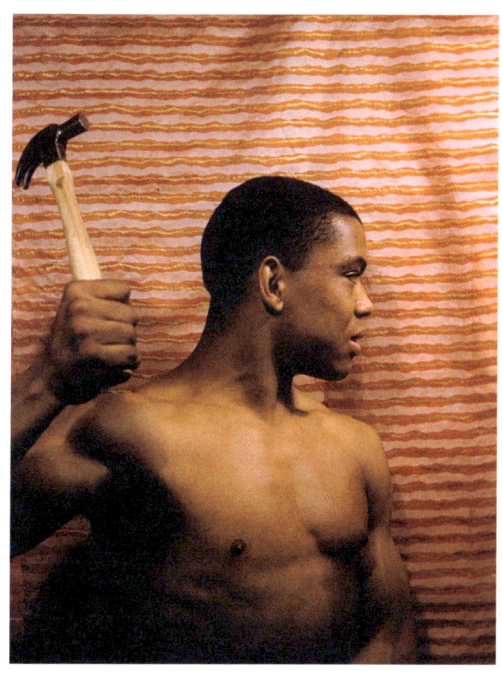
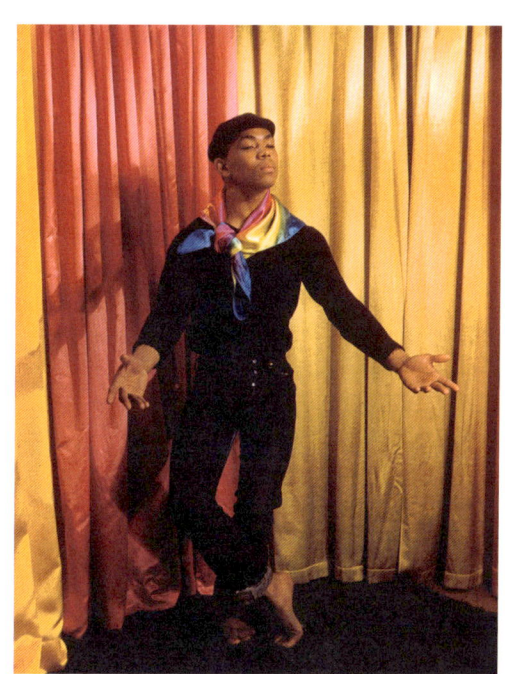
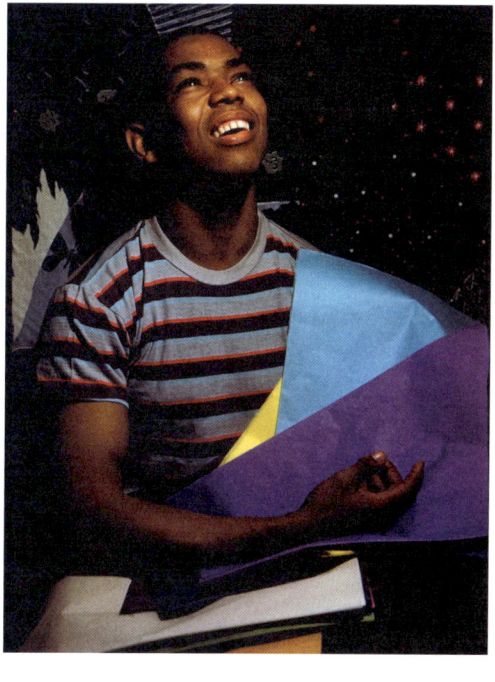
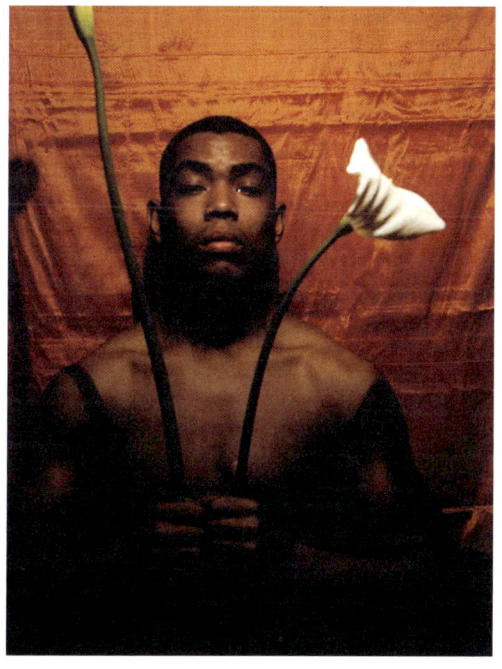
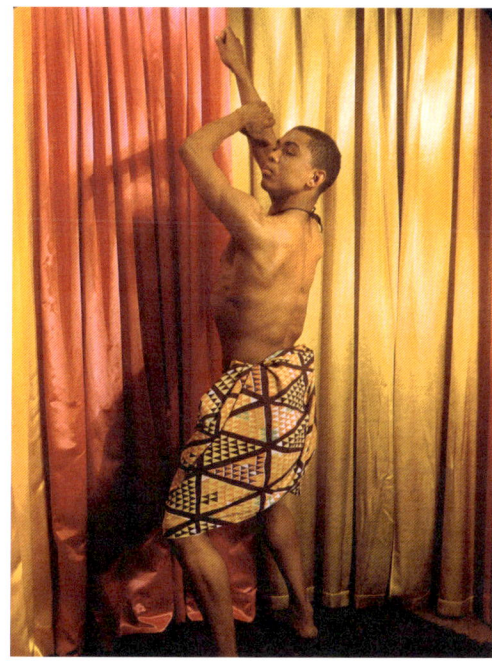
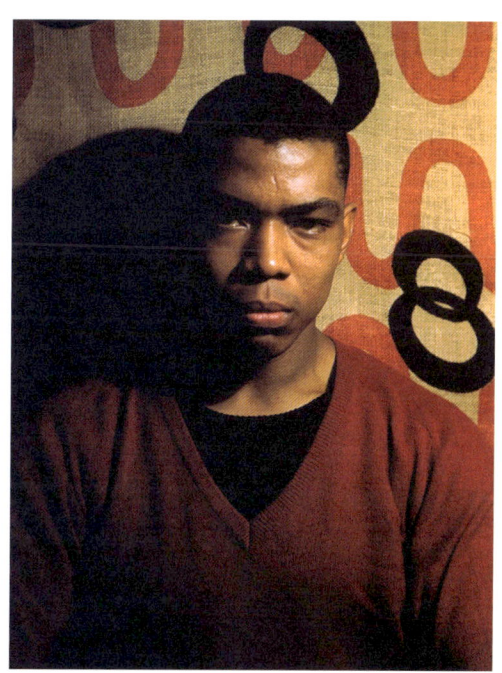

Such Sweet Thunder

the exhibition, the AAADT is in residence at the Whitney for one week each month during the run of the show, for a total of five weeks, essentially bringing to the Museum the full complement of their programming, from performances by the first company and Ailey II, a troupe of emergent dancers founded in 1974, to the Ailey School, a dance training platform established in 1969, and the Ailey Extension program, which offers classes to the public, as well as its arts education initiatives. Their residence at the Museum is accompanied by dance commissions by a group of choreographers and their collaborators, including Kyle Abraham, Ronald K. Brown, Trajal Harrell, Bill T. Jones, Ralph Lemon and Kevin Beasley, Sarah Michelson, Okwui Okpokwasili and Peter Born, Will Rawls, Matthew Rushing, Yusha-Marie Sorzano, and Jawole Willa Jo Zollar. These artists were selected with the members of the Dance Advisory Group—Robert Battle, Ronni Favors, Marion Koltun, Melanie Person, Bennett Rink, Matthew Rushing, and Eric Wright—who began convening in October 2022 and met over eight months to discuss and identify the contributors. Among the group's guiding principles was the way Mr. Ailey himself was curious about and invested in a range of choreographic styles, from narrative-driven dances to abstract, interdisciplinary performance art. We were also mindful of the fact that whatever a Black dancer's artistic sensibility might be, they all must contend in one way or another, whether they want to or not, with dance in Mr. Ailey's wake or, to put it another way, dance after Ailey.

The Ailey repertory, or the archive of dances, is also presented in the Museum's fifth-floor exhibition gallery through a surround of eighteen screens that wrap the perimeter of the space. Dynamically imagined with filmmakers Josh Begley and Kya Lou, a video montage of recorded material sourced from the Ailey archive, dating from 1962 to 1989, supplemented by contextual footage of cultural, social, historical, and political events of the times, unfolds across this multimedia installation. An inherent problem in making exhibitions about dance is the near impossibility of reproducing the dynamics and sensuality of live performance in almost any other media, yet this is precisely the necessary work at hand, not only to tell the history of dance but also for the future of the form and those committed to it.

It is worth revisiting the debates on the nature of dance and the problem of the archive in representing it. Scholar Peggy Phelan is emphatic about such an impossibility when she states, "Performance cannot be saved, recorded, documented, or otherwise participate in the circulation of representations *of* representations. . . . Performance's being . . . becomes itself through disappearance."[15] Her position falls in the camp of "you had to be there," and while there is indeed an undeniable aspect of the specific experience of live dance—the valences of its ephemerality, the irreplicable sense of being in the moment—this stance elides and delimits the fullness of the ways dance can and has appeared to us. By performance historian Joseph Roach's reasoning, there resides within the very fundamental tenets of performance a kind of "record," one that is indexical, instructional, ideogrammatic, and even lexical: "Performance genealogies draw on the idea of expressive movements as mnemonic reserves, including patterned movements made and remembered by bodies, residual movements retained implicitly in images or words (or in the silences between them), and imaginary movements dreamed in minds, not prior to language but constitutive of it."[16] Beyond the necessity and act of preserving choreography, the question of the archive is one of who can be in the room, who can arrive to the occasion, and who is at the event. This is nothing less than a question of knowledge and access, an interrogative Mr. Ailey was keenly aware of. In fact, I was struck by two letters he retained in his archive, one from a professor at Howard University and the other from a public-school teacher, each asking him why there were not more Black people at the Ailey company's shows they attended. In addition to recording rehearsals with dancers from the earliest days of the company, Mr. Ailey made and revised dances for the camera, particularly for television. His refusal to allow the dance to disappear and his efforts to ensure its broad circulation were as much political as they were brand-building. His declared intention to make dances about the Black experience, his "blood memories" as he described it, was a refusal to allow these memories, traditions, and innovations to evanesce as well as a vow to use the archive of recorded dance as a mechanism to transmit vital knowledge.[17]

Mr. Ailey seems to have been as much concerned with "you had to be there" as he was with who could not be there, especially those who needed to be there—that is, those whom the dances concerned. The richness of his archive—the documents, notebooks, short stories, letters, drawings, and videos—is an emphatic statement that he

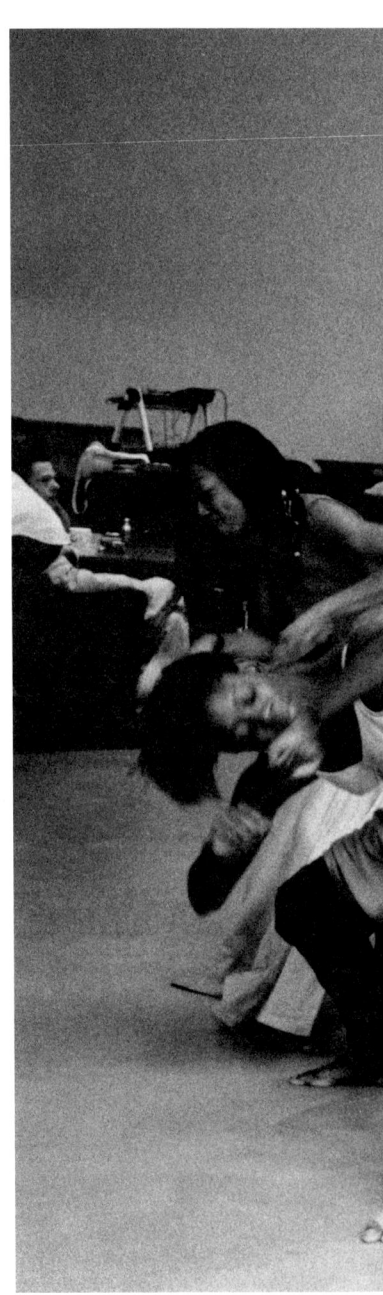

fig. 3

Rehearsal for *The Magic of Katherine Dunham*, ca. 1987–88

was here. Together, these objects and the embodied archive—the repertory of dances that is the treasury and inventory of gestures, stories, movement, singing—endure as two halves of an inextricable whole.[18] It is not live performance, with its choreographic structures shifting depending upon who embodies them, that is transmitted through the archive, but rather its connotation, implication, and signification. The video document or dance notation does not replace the live performance itself; instead, it is "part of the archive; what it represents is part of the repertoire."[19] In the exhibition, live performance and the repertory as recorded moving images are presented in tandem, as two necessary means of transmission, reflecting the various circuits in which dance manifests.

Mr. Ailey's notebooks, particularly his outlines for lecture demonstrations he gave while on tour, illuminate the constellation of influences and references in his dances that is not immediately obvious when seeing his works. His choreographies are shaped by a range of embodied archives in innumerable ways. Noted influences include, in dance, Lester Horton, Katherine Dunham, Carmen de Lavallade, Pearl Primus, Ted Shawn, Jack Cole, Martha Graham, and Merce Cunningham; and in music, Duke Ellington, Marian Anderson, Bessie Smith, Billie Holiday, Roberta Flack, Donny Hathaway, Charlie Parker, Leontyne Price, and Jimi Hendrix. He was a voracious reader, citing James Baldwin, Langston Hughes, Hart Crane, Tennessee Williams, Countee Cullen, and Lorraine Hansberry, and we are publishing and exhibiting Mr. Ailey's own short stories and poems for the first time. In 1961 he studied acting with Stella Adler, an experience that fundamentally changed him as an artist; years later, he credited Adler with "fir[ing] my imagination as a choreographer.

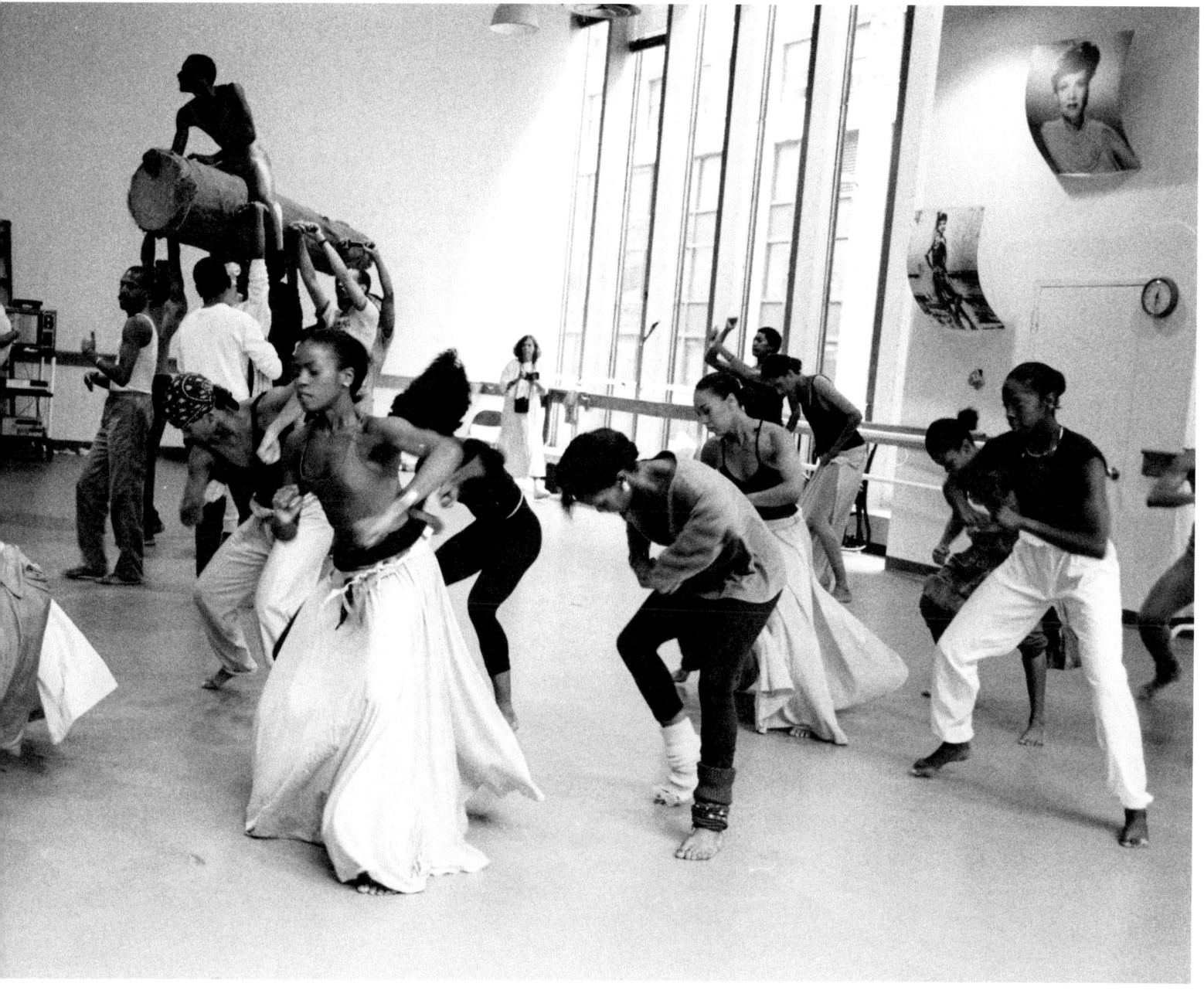

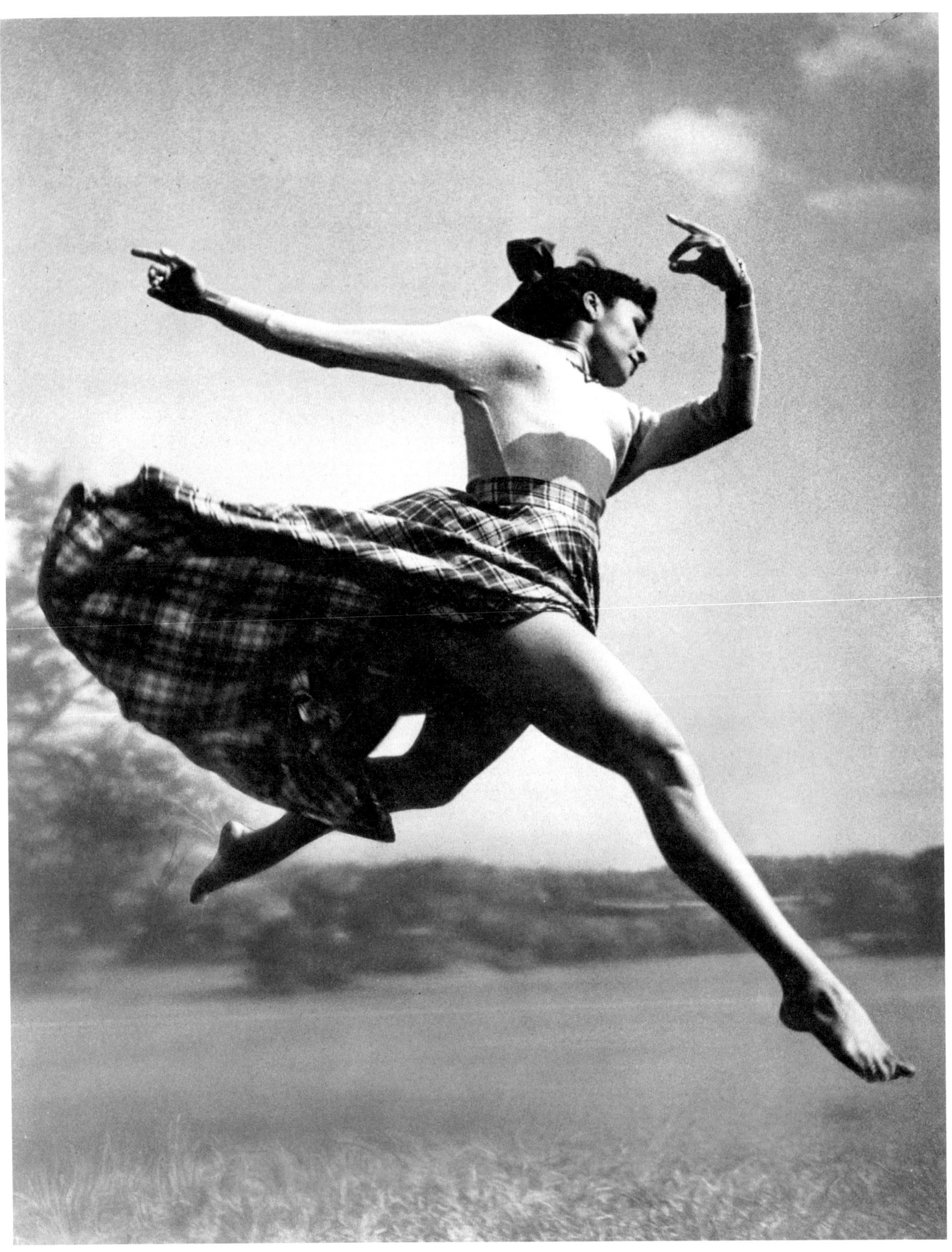

Adrienne Edwards

fig. 4

Katherine Dunham at Villa I Tatti, Florence, 1949

She taught me how to look inside myself as a black person also. My experience as a black person was valid, theatrically."[20] The total effect of all these things was enfolded into his work. As he explained it, "Modern dance seemed to encapsulate all of my ideas. . . . [T]here was movement, there was color, there was painting, there was sculpture, and there was the putting it all together into a kind of meaningful, expressive art form. . . . Dance could be that expressive thing for me."[21]

While Mr. Ailey often referenced his childhood in rural Texas, rife with experiences of rituals of the Black church, the nightlife of juke joints, racial violence, and hard labor, he was also profoundly moved by his early exposures to live dance, music, and theater, including a performance by the Ballet Russe de Monte Carlo, a Duke Ellington concert, and Dunham's *Tropical Revue*, all of which he saw in 1945 in Los Angeles, where he had moved with his mother in 1942. Mr. Ailey described Dunham's show, with its all-Black cast, as a "transcendent experience."[22] On the arm of his friend de Lavallade, Mr. Ailey visited Horton's studio in 1947 and eventually enrolled in classes there. If, as Pierre Nora argues, performance comprises "real environments of memory" that embody "gestures and habits, in skills passed down by unspoken traditions, in the body's inherent self-knowledge, in unstudied reflexes and ingrained memories," outlining Mr. Ailey's entrée to dance provides an early indication of the range of styles, histories, and cultures that shaped him and is ultimately embedded in his own choreographies.[23] *Edges of Ailey* features a section showcasing these influences, some articulated herein, through archival materials and reproductions, performance documentation, dance films, photographs, correspondence, dance programs, and other objects to illustrate the sheer breadth of voices sieved into and the myriad scenes charted through his works.

The artistic context in which Mr. Ailey arrives to choreography is shaped, in dance, visual art, and music, by a tendency that "the non-Western is the raw material to be reworked and made 'original' in the West," and is an important formulation in which to understand the sites and citations of African and Caribbean culture in the artists who would influence the development of dance in the United States and, indeed, his own ideas.[24] Dunham, who was also an anthropologist, attaining a doctorate in the field, wrote extensively about her travels and studies of ritual dances in the Caribbean, particularly in Haiti and Jamaica, as well as Brazil. She gave Mr. Ailey a blueprint for employing an auto-ethnographic methodology in his creative process, heightening the inherent theatricality of quotidian life and cultural and spiritual practices. While Dunham turned away from the United States for sources of inspiration, seeking to combine her findings with European and Native American forms of expression, Ailey was ultimately and primarily directed toward the everyday life of Black Americans and, later, in Brazil. For Dunham, "a direct retention of African forms in North America is certainly the exception rather than the rule, and the West Indies are still a more fertile field for the analysis of the survival of the dance in its shift from tribal to folk culture."[25] With her ethnographic training, Dunham traces the relationship between dance and West African–derived spiritual practices that had been transformed in the Americas, which incorporated not only specifically reimagined religious life but also all aspects of cultural existence, from spiritual dances to seasonal and social dances. In these amalgamated practices, Dunham notes that their African retentions are obscured and subsumed, under the veil of Catholicism, which is made to hold vodou, as well as in home life and rum shops. She remarks upon the role of migration in further hybridizing cultural life throughout the African diaspora, the fusing of social dances such as the Lindy Hop, and the music of Jamaican mento and jazz.

Horton, whose technique is still taught at the AAADT, founded, together with dancer Bella Lewitzky, the first interracial modern dance company in the United States.[26] Known for its "vividly theatrical and dramatic style," the company, with which Mr. Ailey danced from 1949 to 1954, was another lodestar for the emergent choreographer.[27] A contemporary of Dunham, Horton appropriated non-Western forms, including Native American, Caribbean, Japanese, Javanese, and Balinese, for his choreographies, theatricalizing them for the concert stage and commercial contexts, such as film. His dances sometimes concerned political events, specifically in 1935 and 1937, when he created two dances about Nazism. At Horton's studio, Mr. Ailey met dancer James Truitte, who would become an important figure in the AAADT, and he came to understand the significance of all aspects of the performance experience: costumes, set design, lighting, music, and so on. When Horton died unexpectedly from a heart attack in 1953, Ailey became artistic director of the dance group.

The fusion of European and African forms was also prevalent in the dances of Graham, Shawn, Doris Humphrey, and Helen Tamiris in the 1930s and '40s. From late 1928 to the early 1940s, Tamiris created a suite of nine dances, mostly composed of a cycle of solos called *Negro Spirituals*; Ted Shawn and His Men Dancers, Shawn's all-male troupe, performed concerts of the same name from 1933 to 1936 and again in 1938. Perhaps *Revelations* (1960; see pp. 160–73), Mr. Ailey's most renowned dance, was a response to the prevalence of white dancers who made works set to music that arose from and sustained Black life. It is worth noting that other Black choreographers—including Talley Beatty, in his *Southern Landscape* (1947), and Donald McKayle, in his *Rainbow Round My Shoulder* (1959), which is in the AAADT's repertory—made dances concerning similar themes.

In a program note, Shawn explained the inspiration for his *Negro Spirituals*: "These three dances draw their substance from one of the richest emotional fields of all—the American Negro and his songs."[28] As dance historian Susan Manning writes, he associated Blackness in dance with "emotionalism and physicalized religiosity," and as Shawn himself wrote in *The American Ballet* in 1926, "Anglo-Saxon history" was "more truly" American.[29] Mr. Ailey's archive reveals an ongoing correspondence with Shawn, who despite his limiting beliefs, performed at the historically Black Hampton Institute (now Hampton University) in 1925 while on tour with the Denishawn company, a portmanteau of the last names of the group's founders, Ruth St. Denis and Shawn, and again with His Men Dancers in 1933, 1935, and 1938.[30] As a founder of Jacob's Pillow, a vitally important incubator of dance that he established in 1931 in the Berkshires, in western Massachusetts, Shawn invited Mr. Ailey and his new company, which he founded in 1958, to perform there in 1959; Mr. Ailey had previously danced at Jacob's Pillow, with the Horton group, in 1953 shortly before Horton's death.

The tendency toward amalgamation was not solely relegated to the hybridity of African and European aesthetics but also extended to combinatory beings, human and animal. Specifically, mythological figures, such as the Minotaur and the faun, recur in the choreographic ideas and short stories we find in Mr. Ailey's archive, and sometimes we can glimpse that these figures are self-referential. We can situate this interest in myth not only in ballet but also in the dances of Graham, whose autobiography coincidentally is titled *Blood Memory* (1991), a concept that she describes as such: "There are always ancestral footsteps behind me, pushing me, when I am creating a new dance, and gestures flowing through me. Whether good or bad, they are ancestral. You get to the point where your body is something else and it takes on a world of cultures from the past."[31] Whereas Ailey explained that his "blood memories" reference Black life and culture and the music of rural Texas, he and Graham are both clearly animating ancestral forces in their dances.

For choreographers of the postwar era, commercial scenes, namely Hollywood and Broadway, were financially necessary places in which to work in order to continue to make and present their dances and sustain their companies; at the time, Broadway paid more in wages than other performing arts presenters.[32] Mr. Ailey, like Dunham and Horton, performed in many theatrical and television productions. Indeed, in 1954 he moved from Los Angeles to New York to perform in the Broadway musical *House of Flowers*; that same year, he was part of the dance corps in the film version of *Carmen Jones*. Three years later, while performing in the Broadway production of *Jamaica*, he assembled a group of Black dancers and began to choreograph again. Jack Cole, the impresario of the form of jazz dance that is theatricalized for the mainstream stage, is a name that shows up repeatedly as a reference and collaborator throughout Ailey's career as a choreographer. The distinct theatrical "sparkle" with which Mr. Ailey's choreography in general and his company in particular are associated is fundamentally imbued with the aesthetics of his time in the bright lights.

In tracing some of the choreographic inspirations for Mr. Ailey, I want to suggest that his "blood memories" are far more multivalent than indeed he himself stated, even from the very beginning of his imaginings of what might be possible for him through dance. In an interview with a Brazilian news outlet, Mr. Ailey said: "I don't have any method. I don't have any real way of doing it. I don't have any rules. For me, choreography is a spontaneous act."[33] Although he may not have created a codified choreographic method as did classical ballet, Cunningham, Dunham, and Graham, what he did do was ensure his dancers were trained in a wide range of methods, to be used as foundations, and he choreographed in the spaces between those systems. There are innumerable ways and a broad spectrum of approaches to make a dance: some choreographers draft scores that evolve from elaborate notation systems, while others work purely in an improvisational manner. Mr. Ailey did a little of both. His notebooks include detailed plans in the form of lists of different choreographers and selections from their works that he then arranged and incorporated into his dances as his own. Mr. Ailey's approach started with selecting a piece of music that he then set directly on dancers, and he was known for changing sections of the dances and even the performers themselves right before the event. As he said, "Black people have a great sense of what happens between the movements."[34] His selection of dancers was in and of itself a kind of choreography—he knew what each artist could bring to the systems and structures, and how a body that moves in a certain way might animate the spaces between them. In rehearsal footage, we can hear him placing a dance on someone, emphatically instructing, "We can flavor those a little more.... Cut through the space... like an animal licking its wounds... like a searchlight.... Whatever it is you can't reach it."[35]

Dunham was one of the earliest figures to carve out a way for someone with Mr. Ailey's ambition to be recognized as a dancer; an invaluable part of her work was to attain status for Black dancers in the dance world, something Mr. Ailey would continue with the AAADT.[36] McKayle, a contemporary of Mr. Ailey, who in addition to his own company made dances for the AAADT, searingly observed in 1966 that "the Negro as an artist is recognized rather than the artist as a Negro."[37] Continuing, he critiques the limiting roles for Black performers as "the hand-clapping, I-got-rhythm stereotype so dearly beloved of yesterday," with a pointed reference to the history of minstrels in theater in the United States. In conclusion, he asserts that the stakes for Black artists needed to be different at that pivotal moment of the Black Arts Movement, insisting that the sociopolitical context in which Black artists make work is inseparable from their artistry: "As to the future of the Negro artist in American dance, it must be stressed that it cannot be viewed outside of the whole seething, shifting social scene." Such concerns were echoed by Mr. Ailey, who followed three imperatives in founding his company, as dance and Ailey scholar Thomas DeFrantz elucidates: "to employ the scores of excellent black dancers in New York who had no performing homes, to give artistic voice to African American experience in terms of concert dance, and to assemble a racially integrated repertory company that could perform both modern dance classics and new works by Ailey and other young choreographers."[38] Ailey integrated his company in 1961 with the addition of the white female dancer Connie Greco, who joined the troupe ahead of its first tour in Australia and Southeast Asia. The company has since remained multiracial, thereby demonstrating what Mr. Ailey characterized as universalizing the Black experience and what I might describe as testing the affective potentialities of Blackness across bodies and dance styles.[39]

Mr. Ailey's choreographic audacity aligns with what Black studies scholar Kevin Quashie has described as the "delicate work of trying to call blackness into formation."[40] Despite and also because of the accumulation and sedimentation of events against Black life that preceded Mr. Ailey's arrival—namely, enslavement and its afterlives, Jim Crow apartheid, and lynching—his necessarily romantic, virile, and virtuosic insistence upon the beauty of Blackness in dance was a fragile revelation of the need of its very possibility, a possibility that is nothing less than a claim of Black life. The proscenium stage frames while also structuring an important distance that Black studies scholar Daphne Brooks has articulated as a critical position in which to navigate Black alienation.[41] Quashie describes "looking as a constitutive act of black being," and I would add "appearing" and "witnessing" as equally essential aspects of this dynamic.[42] Here I mark the positionality of the Black dancer and choreographer on the stage or in the wings, and that of the audiences who are Black seeing themselves and their stories presented before them. What Mr. Ailey's work suggests is that a void of love toward Blackness does not confine or undermine what Blackness is and how it might be presented; and that although racist sentiments and acts are prevalent in the world, indeed constituent parts of the Western capitalist structure, they do not overwhelm how we make our worlds and revel in them. We instead, and Mr. Ailey is an exemplar of this, cast our "subject into the suspension of an imaginary."[43] For Black feminist scholar Terrion L. Williamson, "[T]he register of black experience... is not reducible to the terror that calls it into existence but is the rich remainder, the multifaceted artifact of black communal resistance and resilience that is expressed in black idioms, cultural forms, traditions, and ways of being."[44] The "remainder" of which Williamson speaks recalls Mr. Ailey's sense of his choreographic methodology, in absence of what his technique might be, that peculiar feeling of what is situated between the systems and their structures, and it is where we might come to know what a body can do. Take, for example, the directive that Amiri Baraka (as LeRoi Jones) espoused in his 1965 essay "The Revolutionary Theatre": "What is called the imagination (from image, magi, magic, magician, etc.) is a practical vector from the soul. It stores all data, and can be called on to solve all our 'problems.' The imagination is the projection of ourselves past our sense of ourselves as 'things.' Imagination (image) is all possibility, because from the image, the initial circumscribed energy, any use (idea) is possible. And so begins that image's use in the world. Possibility is what moves us."[45] The imagination is an unfolding of the profoundest intimacy; it is the way through which we dramatize, unfurl, project, and bloom being in life, making and remaking ourselves.

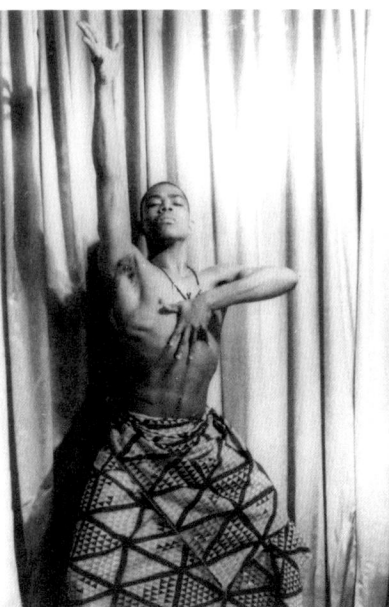

As were many queer people of his generation and of preceding ones, Mr. Ailey was known for being a "private person," two words that sit at the precipice of an individual's sexuality and the question of who needs to know about it or who can speak of it as a witness. These words work to indicate a difference and to create enough of a gap in knowledge that this difference need not be specified. Looking back on Mr. Ailey's life after the many hard-fought and well-earned equal rights for LGBTQI+ people in this country, it has been vital to refrain from approaching the question of his gayness and the extent to which it might have informed his choreography from the perspective of today's social and political reality for queer people, no matter how precarious some of those advances might seem in the current political climate. For me and other queer scholars, thinking, writing, or art making that considers gay life and culture during the time in which Mr. Ailey lived necessitates a difficult displacement of our current reality and a generous and generative vulnerability toward "the open secret." In *Epistemology of the Closet*, published a year after Mr. Ailey's death, queer studies scholar Eve Kosofsky Sedgwick contends, "'Closetedness' itself is a performance initiated as such by the speech act of a silence—not a particular silence, but a silence that accrues particularity by fits and starts."[46] Having combed through Mr. Ailey's personal archive, the matter of the extent of his "being in the life" begs the question: closeted to whom? His notebooks are filled with references to his gay life and interests, from his research in homosexual psychology to his short stories resplendent with same-sex desire, to letters between him and his therapist that evince him grappling with his sexuality, to a clear interest in the art of queer writers and musicians, to notes weighing the positive and negative qualities of his lovers, to notations of movement and clothing styles seen on the dance floor of gay clubs to be used in his choreographies, to musings on non-binary gender, "drag queens," and a range of types of love and sex. Sedgwick explains that we live in "a culture where same-sex desire is still structured by its distinctive public/private status, at once marginal and central, as *the* open secret. . . . [I]t's only being shameless about risking the obvious that we happen into the vicinity of the transformative."[47] Following this, I want to suggest that Mr. Ailey embedded within his dances clear and distinct references to gay life; we need approach them only in light of what he has left behind, his archive. The "sparkle" of gayness is undeniable in *Quintet* (1968; see p. 193), with its women dancers performing a drag show about women; in *Night Creature* (1974; 237–39), with its reference to Duke Ellington's music and to "the people who are themselves at night"; and in the decadence of Mr. Ailey's staging of the 1977 opening night performance for Studio 54.[48] If Mr. Ailey was closeted, his dances and notebooks were the escape hatch and vehicles through which he could veil as he revealed the embeddedness of sexual difference.

When Mr. Ailey remarked in an interview, "The success of the dance has always seemed to me to depend upon how personal it is," requiring that "some part of yourself" be exposed, he was allowing that as much as his work concerns Blackness, it also concerns gayness, for the two are folded into each other in his choreography; they enter the stage together.[49] As the field of queer studies has grown, among the important opportunities of this exhibition and catalogue is to invite scholars to contemplate this aspect of Mr. Ailey's dances, to consider what Sedgwick has described as the "aboriginal maw of darkness" from which to "wrestle facts, insights, freedoms, progress, perhaps there exists instead a plethora of *ignorances*."[50] With this knowledge, we can mobilize a more multivalent understanding of Mr. Ailey's dances—their desires, emanations, opacities, collusions, and meanings.

The innumerable interlocutors of Mr. Ailey's dances have also helped form our collective interpretation of their meanings. As this relates to Black queer people today, it is vitally

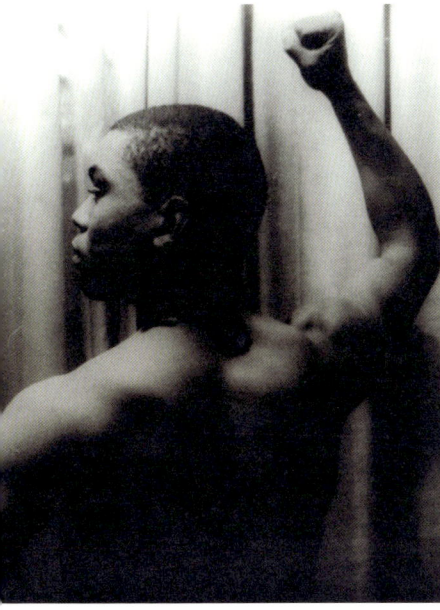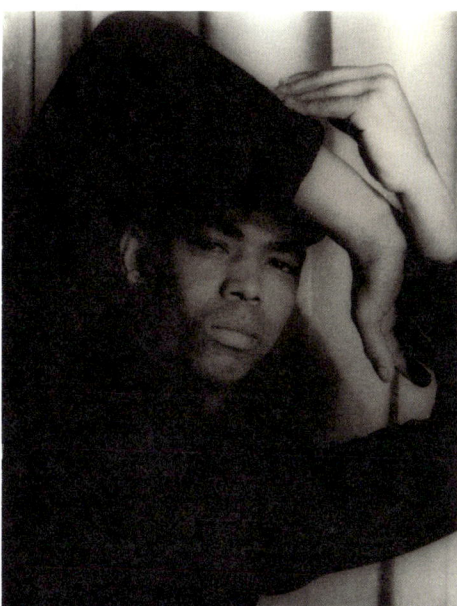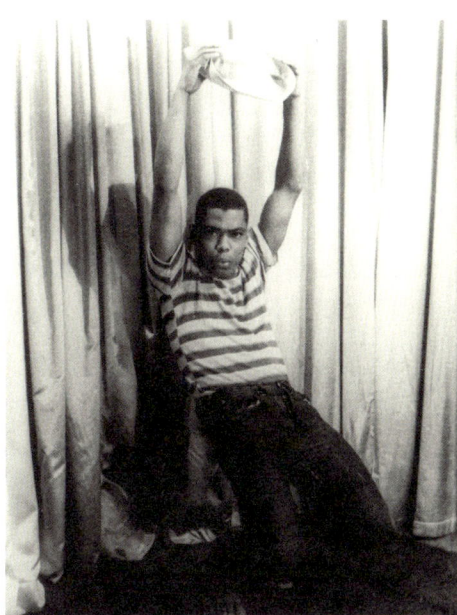

figs. 5a–d

Carl Van Vechten, *Alvin Ailey*, 1955. Beinecke Rare Book and Manuscript Library, Yale University, New Haven, Connecticut

necessary for us to chart this aspect of Mr. Ailey's creativity, which he left in the archive for us to receive in the future. As Sedgwick clarifies, "It is probably people with the experience of oppression or subordination who have most *need* to know it."[51] In Mr. Ailey, as a figure, we see a range of various oppressions comingled and our need for these injustices to be identified and acknowledged, because in understanding and specifying the full dimensions of his life, we can better know the intersecting complexities embodied in his dances, their shaping presence. This is to say that we need to speak of Mr. Ailey in the genealogy of Black gay people before and alongside him, from figures in the Harlem Renaissance, especially Hughes; to the civil rights era, including Baldwin, Hansberry, and Bayard Rustin; to the creative scene of the 1980s with Julius Eastman, Essex Hemphill, and Marlon Riggs. We have to meet the imperative that historian Kevin Mumford sets forth around the cost of disclosure—that is, to acknowledge one's queerness in the wake of the movement for Black equality on the one hand and in the context of Black sexuality's history as a site of "domination and terrorism" on the other.[52] Lest we forget that Mr. Ailey founded his company in 1958, in the midst of the Cold War and Civil Rights Movement, which presented an "image of respectability" as proof of our worthiness of full citizenship; "ultra-civility" was a strategy and comportment in Black social and political advancement, making for a "legacy of sexual reticence" and an assertion of "normalcy of the black family," which "resulted in the erasure of black homosexuality," with "the closet becoming the site of a necessary sacrifice in the project towards black advancement and equality."[53] In the mid-twentieth century, successful Black figures such as Mr. Ailey, Baldwin, Hansberry, and Rustin were required to make a choice between the two aspects of themselves that shaped their lives so profoundly. For Mr. Ailey and Hansberry, the complexity of these forces of and external to themselves, intertwined with the success of their artistry and the fame that followed, was tangled within their diaries and left to the archive. Meanwhile, inside the Black Power movement, with its hypermasculine revolutionaries, some felt that queer people were questionable for not upholding traditional aspects of Black culture, as if being gay undermined a family structure already pressured, to put it mildly, for centuries. Huey P. Newton was relatively singular in his belief that gay people "could be the most revolutionary" and that "the terms 'faggot' and 'punk' should be deleted from our vocabulary."[54] We must remember that homosexuality was not declassified as a mental illness by the American Psychiatric Association until 1973. Gay sociality flourished during the 1970s, only to retreat in the 1980s with the AIDS crisis. First reported in 1981, the syndrome overwhelmed queer worlds with its absolute uncertainty, sheer scale, and insurmountable devastation, which Mr. Ailey did not escape, dying from AIDS-related complications in 1989. At Baldwin's funeral, as was true of Ailey's, none of the eulogies, by Baraka, Maya Angelou, and Toni Morrison, spoke of the writer's gayness. As Black lesbian feminist scholar Barbara Smith observed, "Although Baldwin's funeral completely reinforced our Blackness, it tragically rendered his and our homosexuality completely invisible," resulting in the loss of "the challenging impact that telling the whole truth . . . could have had . . . and nobody knew his full name."[55] At Mr. Ailey's funeral, Dudley Williams's performance of "A Song for You" held and offered glimpses of the unremarked upon, the sidelong glances weighted by this reality while also alight in a movement, caring, loving. In Mr. Ailey, his unspoken yet acknowledged queerness arrives in the fold of Blackness, which it destabilizes while buttressing, and renders a sense of ambivalence about his gayness precisely because of its unspoken, undeniable presence, instantiating itself even as it is nevertheless seemingly cloaked. Such tension produces multiple positions—a faceting, a constructedness—as manifold styles of expression coalesce in his dances.

I return to the final element in the structure of the exhibition, that of how it is staged and the amplifying visual artworks that are enveloped by the Ailey archival surround. Typically exhibitions that feature performance present live art as an addendum or special program to contextualize the visual art. Here the choreographer, his dances, and archives envelop, indeed surround, the other artworks in the show, a framing through which dance is foregrounded in what is a broader and deeper cultural history. The result is an exhibition as art installation that instigates a layered, cross-viewing experience—a staging ground meant to hold and reflect the dynamics of the choreography itself—which disrupts complacencies. Recalling Mr. Ailey's "blood memories," as well as the curtains and seats of the majority of proscenium stages (particularly opera houses and ballet theaters) and the carpet and pews of many Black churches, the entirety of the Museum's fifth floor is covered in a deep crimson. There are nearly no walls constructed in the space; rather, there is an archipelago of island structures in the center of the gallery that holds three systems of display: a cable suspension system, a set of pyramidal structures, and half walls. Installed on them and between the moving-image installation and archival vitrines are paintings, sculptures, prints, photographs, drawings, and a video that amplify themes in Mr. Ailey's dances. In a televised interview, he explained, "I wanted to paint... I made watercolors. I wanted to sculpt. I wrote poetry. I wanted to write the great American novel."[56] His notebooks and letters further evince and elaborate his curiosity for and explorations in a range of art forms, with lists of visual artists and art catalogues he wished to secure. Ailey company dancers have remarked upon how he encouraged them to visit museums during their tours. Following Ailey's own methodology, *Edges of Ailey* inevitably brings other stories into view, and other creative and communal visions into relief.

In the course of reflecting upon his life and legacy, we learned a lot about the way he did things, and his special approach to commissioning, supporting, and fostering the work of other choreographers has informed the selection of artworks. The visual art has been made before, during, and after Mr. Ailey's lifetime. The earliest is Robert Duncanson's *View of Cincinnati, Ohio from Covington, Kentucky* (ca. 1851), which, depending on where you stood at the time it was made, concerned a question of being free or not for a Black person. Five of the most recent works have been made on the occasion of the exhibition, homages to Mr. Ailey by Jennifer Packer, Dunham by Mickalene Thomas, Judith Jamison in *Cry* by Karon Davis, and the Black dancing body more generally by Lynette Yiadom-Boakye. While some artists and subjects are directly connected to Ailey, such as Baldwin, de Lavallade, Dunham, Marian Anderson, Romare Bearden, Geoffrey Holder, and Hector Hyppolite, the vast majority share, echo, and amplify the subjects found in Ailey's dances, what he described as "movements full of images."[57]

The artworks are assembled thematically around the most persistent ideas in Ailey's choreography—namely, a southern imaginary spanning the American South, Brazil, the Caribbean, and West Africa; Black spirituality from candomblé to vodou to the Black Baptist and Pentecostal traditions; the conditions that instigated Black migration to the western and northern United States and the ensuing experiences; the necessity for and resilience of an intersectional Black liberation; the prominence of Black women in Ailey's life and work; the remarkable breadth, innovation, and experimentation of Black music; the myriad forms of Blackness in dance; and meditations on dance after Ailey. Taken together, it is evident that such ideas have been a preoccupation for many Black artists for nearly two centuries. I am especially proud to highlight artworks from the Whitney's collection. These expansive and generative artistic juxtapositions, across genres and subjects, illuminate and unfold their complexity as they constellate. Blackness *appears* as foundational and inextricable from any American narrative. As for Ailey himself—whether through his life, his enduring concerns, or his creative throughlines—serves as the staging ground for these artworks: the reason for their communion and their very means of concatenation.

The importance and requisite sensuality of Quashie's notion of Black aliveness and performance studies scholar Joshua Chambers-Letson's call for "More Life" has performance, in general, and dance, in particular, as vectors where Blackness produces a fury and flurry of possibilities, wherein one makes what one feels and wherein queerness and Blackness intertwine symbolically as a rupture and a solidarity.[58] As Chambers-Letson argues, art invokes the appearance, just the appearance, of possibility; this is its promise—a dawning.[59] That horizon of the morning is nothing less than a liberation in which dance is a rehearsal for the possible. For, as he writes:

> We don't know what freedom is and don't remotely have the conditions through which we could know what freedom would be *except* as vision. Vision: sense, aesthetic encounter.... [W]e might yet have the capacity to experience freedom as sense, materializing it in and on the body through performance. This sense of freedom is not located in the future, but in the present. Though ephemeral, when this sense of freedom is generated across the body through performance, the body becomes aware that the rest of the time *something's* missing, *something* better than this is possible, and that *something* must be done. This kind of freedom is not used on or against us, but is something we put to work against those forces that dull and diminish us, making it impossible to even wish for the knowledge of what freedom *would* feel like. Or at least, it's something we put to work as we try to survive those forces.[60]

Mr. Ailey's choreography and life pivoted, to quote poet and theoretician Fred Moten, on the "freedom drive that animates Black performance."[61] Mr. Ailey entered the room, summoning all the specters required to foment his imagination—a beacon, a warning, and a celebration, illuminating that, in the words of literary scholar and cultural historian Saidiya Hartman, "we are coeval with the dead."[62] The romanticism, beauty, and virtuosity of his makings show us what art can do in spite of and because of our conditions, necessarily a yearning, a plurality, a future.

When my brother fell
I picked up his weapons
and never once questioned
whether I could carry
the weight and grief,
the responsibility he shouldered.
I never questioned whether I
could aim
or be as precise as he.
He had fallen,
and the passing ceremonies
marking his death
did not stop the war.

Standing at the front lines
flanked by able brothers
who miss his eloquent courage,
his insistent voice
urging us to rebel,
urging us to not fear embracing
for more than sex,
for more than kisses
and notches in our belts.

Our loss is greater
than all the space we fill with
prayers
and praise.

He burned out his pure life force
to bring us dignity,
to bring us a chance
to love ourselves
with commitment.

. . .

Every night
a light blazes for you
in one of our hearts.

—Essex Hemphill, excerpt from
"When My Brother Fell" (1992)

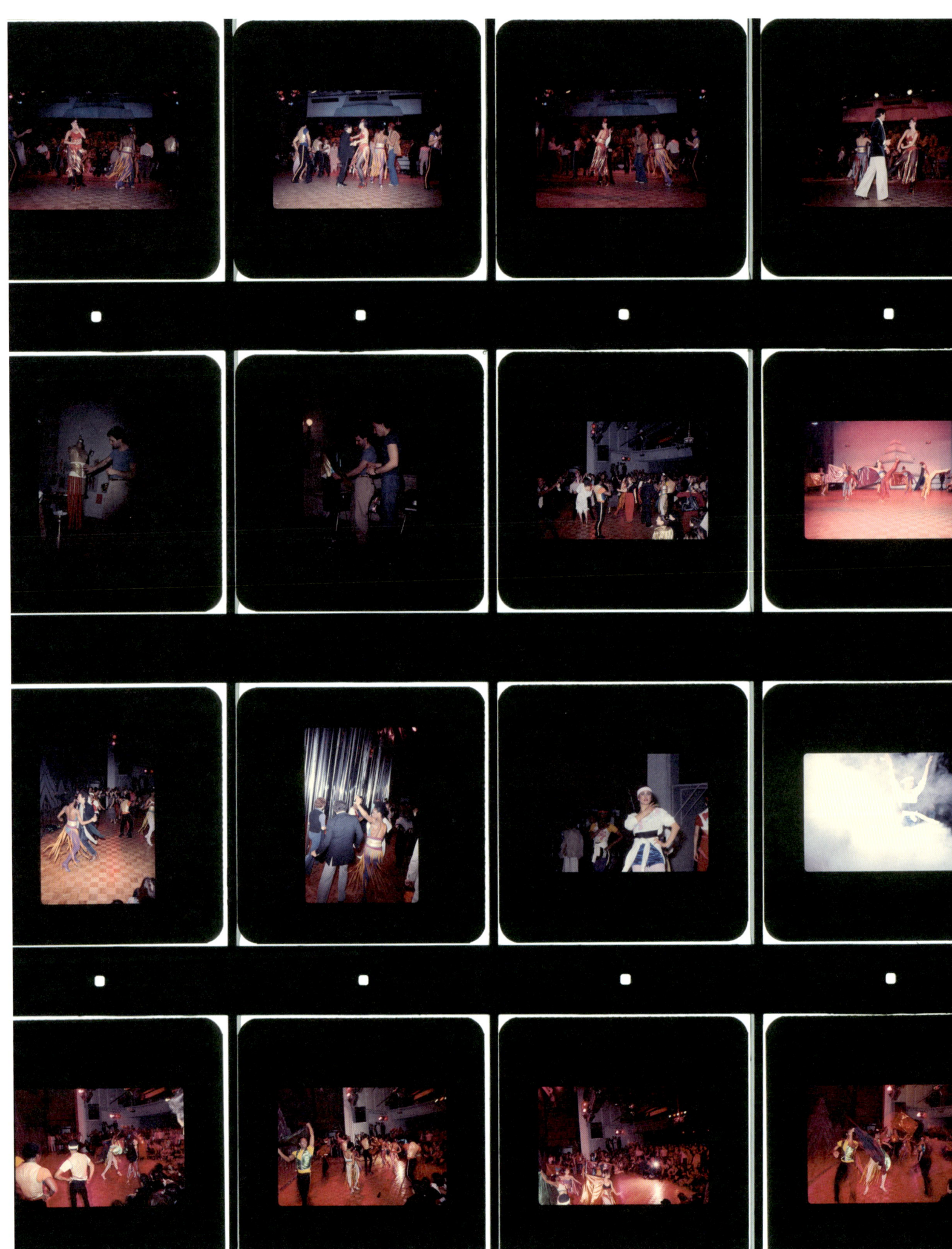

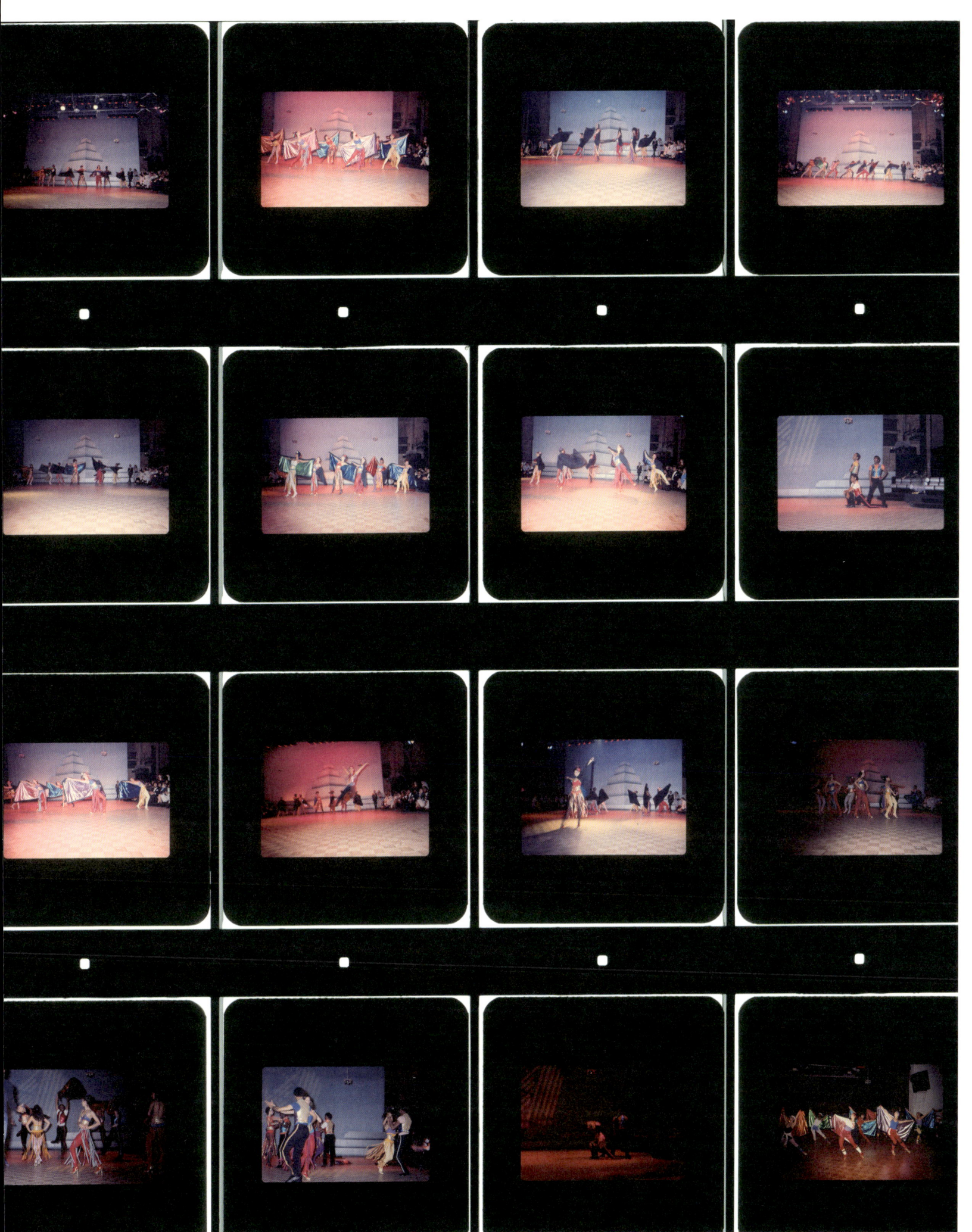

Such Sweet Thunder

fig. 6
Studio 54, 1977. Color slides, 2 × 2 in. (5.1 × 5.1 cm) each.
The Antonio Archives

NOTES

1   With regard to the concept of the multiverse and its relationship to Blackness, queerness, and performance, see Malik Gaines, *Black Performance on the Outskirts of the Left: A History of the Impossible* (New York: New York University Press, 2017).

2   See Toni Morrison, *Beloved* (1987; repr., New York: Vintage, 2004). "But if her shining was not for him, who then?"

3   Dionne Brand, *A Map to the Door of No Return: Notes to Belonging*, (Toronto: Vintage Books, 2001), 24–25.

4   Alvin Ailey, interview, *Essence*, WNBC-TV, New York, September 18, 1984.

5   Jacques Derrida, *Archive Fever: A Freudian Impression*, trans. Eric Prenowitz (1996; Chicago: University of Chicago Press, 2017), 36.

6   Derrida, 36.

7   Derrida, 37.

8   Sigmund Freud, "Delusion and Dream in Jensen's Gradiva," in *The Standard Edition of the Complete Psychological Works of Sigmund Freud*, trans. James Strachey (London: Hogarth, 1953–74), 17.

9   Derrida, *Archive Fever*, 90.

10 Derrida, 84 (emphasis in original), 87.

11 Derrida, 47.

12 Derrida, 3, 10.

13 Derrida, 4, 17.

14 Derrida, 41.

15 Peggy Phelan, *Unmarked: The Politics of Performance* (1993; repr., New York: Routledge, 2001), 146 (emphasis in original).

16 Joseph Roach, *Cities of the Dead: Circum-Atlantic Performance* (New York: Columbia University Press, 2021), 26.

17 Alvin Ailey, quoted in Brenda Dixon-Gottschild, *The Black Dancing Body: A Geography from Coon to Cool* (New York: Palgrave Macmillan, 2003), 279.

18 Diana Taylor, *The Archive and the Repertoire: Performing Cultural Memory in the Americas* (Durham, NC: Duke University Press, 2003), 20.

19 Taylor, 20.

20 Alvin Ailey, interview by Celia Ipiotis, *Eye on Dance*, PBS, October 7, 1989.

21 Ailey, *Essence*.

22 Alvin Ailey, quoted in Susan Manning, *Modern Dance, Negro Dance: Race in Motion* (Minneapolis: University of Minnesota Press, 2006), 210.

23 Pierre Nora, "Between Memory and History: Les Lieux de Mémoire," in *History and Memory in African American Culture*, ed. Geneviève Fabre and Robert O'Meally (New York: Oxford University Press, 1994), 284, 289.

24 Taylor, *Archive and the Repertoire*, 9.

25 Katherine Dunham, "The Negro Dance" (1941), in *Kaiso! Writings by and about Katherine Dunham*, ed. VèVè A. Clark and Sara E. Johnson (Madison: University of Wisconsin Press, 2005), 219; for the discussion of Dunham that follows, see esp. pp. 220–25.

26 The Lester Horton Dance Group was founded in 1932, evolving from his growing interest in choreography and classes taught at Norma Gould's Los Angeles–based studio. Lewitzky, who trained there, eventually became a close artistic partner to Horton from 1934 to 1950, and in 1948 she cofounded the Lester Horton Dance Theater, with Horton, dancer William Bowne, and her husband, Newell Reynolds. Following Horton's sudden death in 1953, Ailey assumed the role of director of the company, until his move to New York in late 1954. The company continued to operate under the leadership of Frank Eng, who had been Horton's partner, until 1960.

27 Manning, *Modern Dance*, 210; the discussion that follows is drawn from this source, see esp. 21, 26, 212–13.

28 Ted Shawn and His Men Dancers, souvenir program for *Negro Spirituals*, 1936–37, Jerome Robbins Dance Division, New York Public Library for the Performing Arts; quoted in Manning, 26.

29 Manning, 27–28.

30 Manning, 29.

31 Martha Graham, *Blood Memory* (New York: Doubleday, 1991), 13; quoted in Manning, 179.

32 Manning, 185.

33 Alvin Ailey, interview by Dias Leme, Worldnet, March 18, 1987.

34 Ailey, *Eye on Dance*.

35 Alvin Ailey, in rehearsal footage broadcast as part of Ailey, *Eye on Dance*.

36 Manning, *Modern Dance*, xiv.

37 Donald McKayle, "The Negro Dancer in Our Time" (1966), in *The Dance Has Many Faces*, ed. Walter Sorell, 3rd ed. (Chicago: Chicago Review Press, 1992), 75.

38 Thomas F. DeFrantz, *Dancing Many Drums: Excavations in African American Dance* (Madison: University of Wisconsin Press, 2002), 9.

39 Manning, *Modern Dance*, 183.

40 Kevin Quashie, *Black Aliveness, or a Poetics of Being* (Durham, NC: Duke University Press, 2021),

41 See Daphne A. Brooks, *Bodies in Dissent: Spectacular Performances of Race and Freedom, 1850–1910* (Durham: Duke University Press, 2006).

42 Quashie, *Black Aliveness*, 4.

43 Quashie, 59.

44 Terrion L. Williamson, *Scandalize My Name: Black Feminist Practice and the Making of Black Social Life* (New York: Fordham University Press, 2016), 9.

45 LeRoi Jones [Amiri Baraka], "The Revolutionary Theatre," *Liberator*, July 1965, repr. in National Humanities Center, *The Making of African American Identity*, vol. 3, *1917–1968* (Research Triangle Park, NC: National Humanities Center, 2007), accessed April 29, 2024, https://nationalhumanitiescenter.org/pds/maaiii3/protest/text12/barakatheatre.pdf.

46 Eve Kosofsky Sedgwick, *Epistemology of the Closet*, rev. ed. (1990; Berkeley: University of California Press, 2008), 3.

47 Sedgwick, 22 (emphasis in original).

48 Alvin Ailey, notebook, Allan Gray Family Personal Papers of Alvin Ailey, Black Archives of Mid-America in Kansas City, MO.

49 Alvin Ailey, interview, *Best Talk in Town*, WPIX, New York, December 8, 1987.

50 Sedgwick, *Epistemology*, 8 (emphasis in original).

51 Sedgwick, 23 (emphasis in original).

52 Kevin Mumford, *Not Straight, Not White: Black Gay Men from the March on Washington to the AIDS Crisis* (Chapel Hill: University of North Carolina Press, 2016), 23, 3, respectively.

53 Mumford, 3.

54 Huey P. Newton, "The Women's Liberation and Gay Liberation Movements," August 15, 1970, New York; quoted in Mumford, 90.

55 Barbara Smith, "We Must Always Bury Our Dead Twice: A Tribute to James Baldwin," in *The Truth that Never Hurts: Writings on Race, Gender, and Freedom* (New Brunswick, NJ: Rutgers University Press, ca. 1998); quoted in Mumford, 182–83.

56 Alvin Ailey, interview by Harry Belafonte, *In the Company of Alvin Ailey*, WNET, November 10, 1978.

57 Ailey, notes for a lecture, Notebook #88, Gray Papers.

58 Joshua Chambers-Letson, *After the Party: A Manifesto for Queer of Color Life* (New York: New York University Press, 2018), 4–5.

59 Chambers-Letson, 23.

60 Chambers-Letson, 7 (emphasis in original).

61 Fred Moten, *In the Break: The Aesthetics of the Black Radical Tradition* (Minneapolis: University of Minnesota, 2003), 12.

62 Saidiya Hartman, "The Time of Slavery," *South Atlantic Quarterly* 101, no. 4 (Fall 2002): 759.

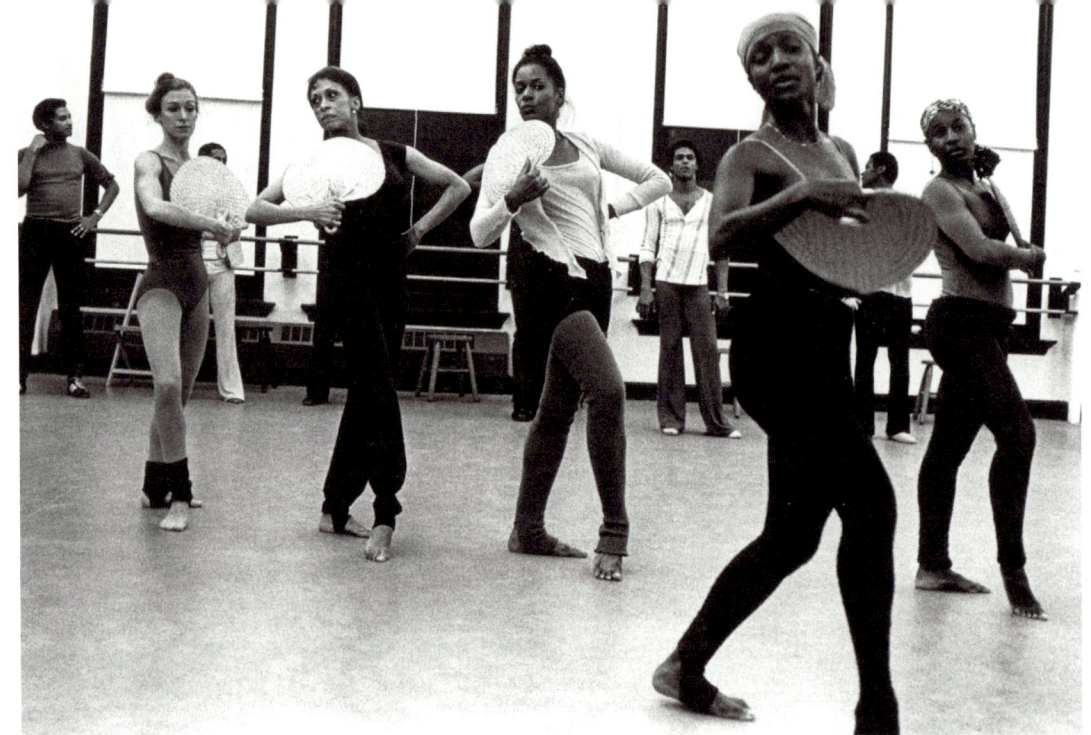

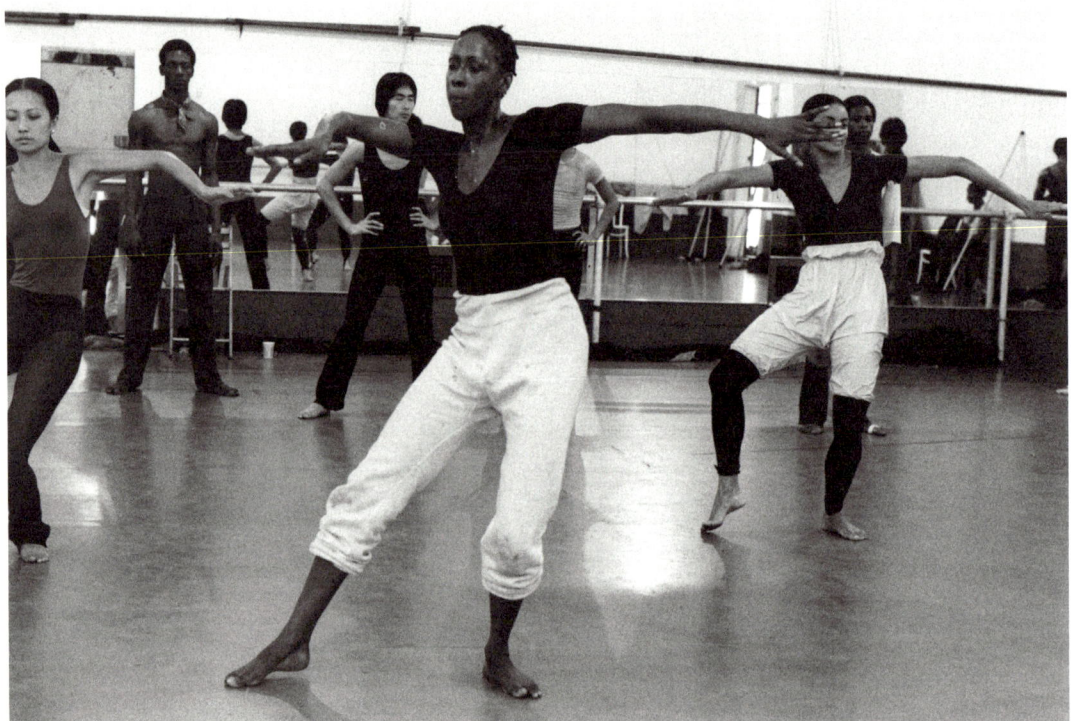

fig. 1

Sylvia Waters (front), 1978

fig. 2

Judith Jamison (center), n.d.

fig. 3

Masazumi Chaya (front left), 1975–76

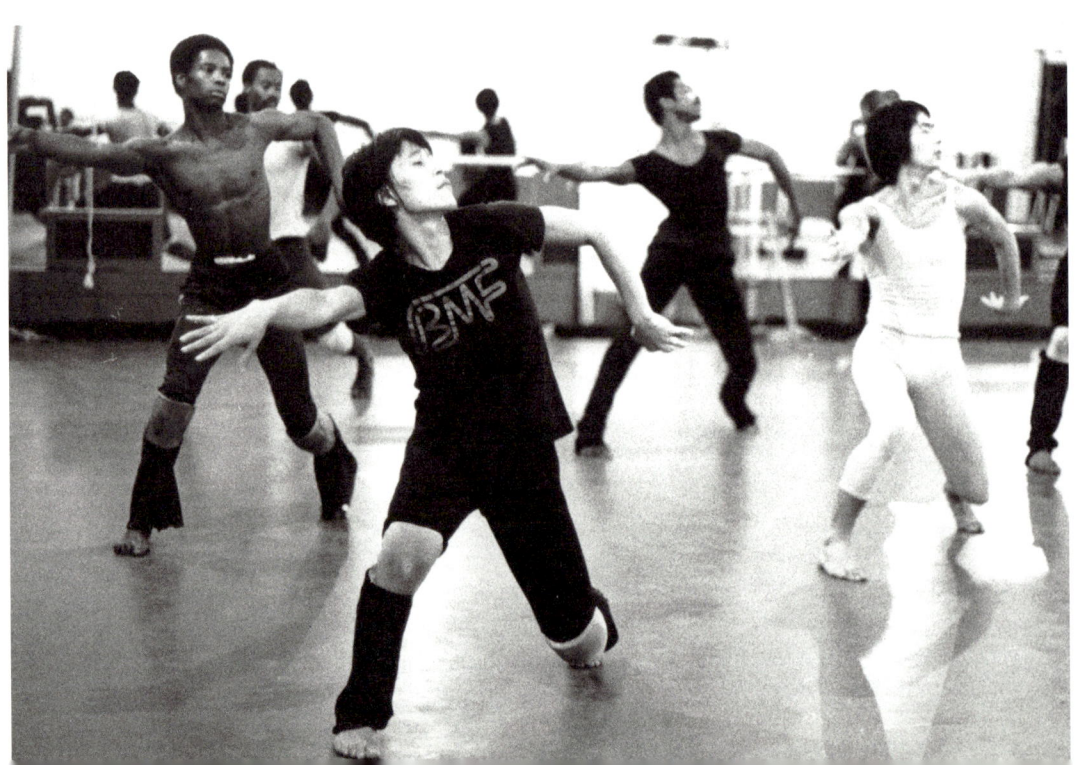

Masazumi Chaya
Adrienne Edwards
Judith Jamison
Sylvia Waters

Show Who You Are

Reflecting on Alvin Ailey

Judith Jamison

Sylvia, you should start, because you were among the first to have seen the company perform.

Sylvia Waters

Yes, but prior to seeing the company, I had my first sighting of Alvin Ailey. It was in 1954; I was a teenager. My girlfriend and I were walking along Fifty-Seventh Street, and this absolutely gorgeous man, wearing a peacoat and a watch cap, came along between Park and Lexington. I remember exactly where it was. We looked at him, smiling, and he smiled back at us. Not lasciviously, just a friendly smile that we weren't accustomed to from strangers in New York. When we passed by him, we turned around and looked back, and he turned around too, still smiling. Two weeks later, as I was waiting outside the studio for my class at the New Dance Group, the same man walked in, and he said, "Hi," as if he knew me. It turned out that Alvin was the substitute teacher for Charles Blackwell that day. I realized years later that this was the first time I was taught Lester Horton technique; it was before I knew what that was. After that, I began to see Alvin at concerts or occasionally teaching at the New Dance Group. I never got to see him act, however.

In 1958, I saw the first-ever performance of the Ailey company, at the 92nd Street YM-YWHA. Alvin shared the program with another dancer-choreographer, Ernest Parham. The Ailey company performed *Blues Suite*, and it was an absolutely, totally impactful evening. This first concert was followed by several others, all of which Alvin paid for with his own money. I'm not sure that the dancers got paid, but they rehearsed incessantly—day, night, and in between matinee and evenings shows of *Jamaica*, which Alvin was in at the time.

In 1960, I saw the first performance of *Revelations*, which was an hour long. But I hadn't remembered that detail, because I was just so enthralled and bowled over by what I saw. It was a very, very special time in modern dance history, and certainly in my personal history. From there, it was kismet. I worked with Donald McKayle, who was a colleague of Alvin's, a number of times, and I performed in *Black Nativity* in Europe. It was there that I ran into Alvin and his company again, and I saw their performances in London and Copenhagen. At that point, I knew I wanted to join the Ailey company, but that didn't happen for another four or five years.

Judith Jamison

I didn't realize *Revelations* was originally an hour long. By the time I joined the company in 1965, I learned the half-hour version. Do you know what was edited out?

Sylvia Waters

I have it written down, but off the top of my head, I don't remember all the songs that were cut. One was "Elijah Rock"; another was "Mary, Don't You Weep." By the time I saw *Revelations* again, in 1964, I would say that was the definitive version. That's the version we know.

Judith Jamison

I believe the first time I saw the company perform was in 1963, while I was a student at the University of the Arts in Philadelphia. I don't remember anything else on the program that day, because I was numb after seeing the Ailey company's performance. At the time, Alvin was still dancing, and I didn't appreciate how amazing it was to have seen him dance until I joined the company in 1965. By then, he wasn't dancing or performing anymore.

I later realized that I had previously seen him dance, with the great Carmen de Lavallade, on the television series *Lamp unto My Feet*. John Butler was usually the choreographer of the dances on that show. It was a religious program, and they would dance the stories of the Old Testament, such as that of David and Goliath.

But seeing the Ailey company in person—seeing Alvin himself and Minnie Marshall and James Truitte perform "Fix Me, Jesus"—just tore me up. That's what I remember most. I also recall that for "Wade in the Water," they carried regular umbrellas; they weren't the golf umbrellas that the company uses now. And the fans in the "yellow" section of *Revelations* were bigger than those used today.

I think the performance was at the Walnut Street Theatre in Philadelphia; it was a small theater. After the show, I remember going backstage with some of my fellow classmates and looking into the dressing rooms. The doors were open, and we saw the dancers packing wicker baskets. All the costumes were carried in those baskets, and when I joined the company, we still used them. Today there are garment racks that go into huge, wheeled containers that are loaded onto airplanes. But it started with those wicker baskets. It was all so wonderful to see.

After this experience, my classmates and I were so impressed by what we had witnessed that we became not very creative; we began just imitating what we had seen. Everybody was doing "I Been 'Buked," with the incredible static arms at the end. We had experienced our own revelation.

Adrienne Edwards

Ms. Jamison, how did you begin to dance for Ailey?

Judith Jamison

He invited me. I had moved to New York by the end of 1964 or the beginning of 1965. I was working with the American Ballet Theatre (ABT), and Carmen de Lavallade and the great Geoffrey Holder took me under their wings. In 1965, Carmen and I were in an Agnes de Mille piece called *The Four Marys*; each of us was one of the Marys. After that, I worked at the New York World's Fair, pushing buttons at the log flume ride. I hadn't danced for a while. Martha Johnson, who was the pianist at the ABT, told me that Donald McKayle was holding an audition. I went to it, and I was terrible. As I left, there was a man—Alvin Ailey—sitting on the steps, and about two days later, he called me and asked if I would like to join his company.

When I walked into the YWCA at Eighth Avenue and Fifty-First Street for my first rehearsal with the company, I entered a dreamland. As I looked around at the people, my jaw dropped. I had seen some of them on stage. I mean, my first partner in the company was James "Jimmy" Truitte, who was an amazing man and an incredible dancer. But Alvin abruptly got rid of my wonderment. He said, "Hello, come on down. Learn this." Boom! That was it. We had to learn so much material so fast, something like six or seven ballets in two or three weeks. And they were important works, by Mr. Ailey and by Talley Beatty, Louis Johnson—choreographers whom Alvin had invited to share the stage with him. How generous is that? So, we'd learn all these dances, and then, boom, we were on. Those were the days of traveling by bus, not by airplane. Everywhere we went was by bus.

    Masazumi Chaya

While I was dancing with Richard Englund's repertory company in New York, my teacher Benjamin Harkarvy told me to go see the Ailey company at City Center and not to miss the dance called *Cry*. I didn't have enough money to buy a ticket, so one evening, I waited until intermission and then I quietly entered the theater with the crowd. I saw Judy in *Cry*. After that, I wanted to see the company perform again, but that time I bought a ticket so I could sit closer to the stage. It was then that I saw the company's entire performance, including the powerful *Revelations*.

    Adrienne Edwards

What year was that?

    Masazumi Chaya

It was 1971. The following year, I joined the Ailey company. I will never forget those first experiences of seeing the Ailey company. Other than in Broadway shows, I had never witnessed so many different types of dancers on a stage. Sometimes they danced together; other times, it wasn't together but the dancers were so individually beautiful. I had never seen dance like that. I wanted to join the company, but I had a contract with Richard Englund so I stayed there. When I heard that the Ailey company was holding auditions, however, I went to one with Michihiko Oka. Actually, Oka had already auditioned for the company, and he had been asked to return for a callback and to bring someone who could help translate his contract. So, I went with him, and I was in the office with Ivy Clarke, who was the Ailey company's general manager. She asked me my name, and then she opened a drawer and there was a copy of the *New York Times*, with Clive Barnes's nice review of a performance of mine with the Englund company. Ivy asked, "Is this you?" I said it was, and she told me to return for a callback audition. When I came back, Judy and Alvin were there, and Dudley Williams demonstrated the "yellow" section of *Revelations*.

    Sylvia Waters

I was there, too.

    Masazumi Chaya

That's right. I was hired then. Oka was, too. That was my first experience with Alvin himself.

    Adrienne Edwards

I'm wondering about the context of when each of you joined the company. Ms. Waters mentioned the New Dance Group, and Ms. Jamison talked about studying dance in Philadelphia and then coming to New York. What was the dance scene in New York like at the time?

    Sylvia Waters

The dance world to me was a new and strange and wonderful and incredible community of people whom I looked up to. When I was studying at the New Dance Group, there were so many fantastic teachers and dancers from the High School of Performing Arts. Donald McKayle, Geoffrey Holder, Anneliese Widman, and Carmen de Lavallade were all teaching. Alvin was mostly substitute teaching, so I took only that one class with him. I then enrolled at the Juilliard School, the same year Dudley Williams did. In the summer, I would see Alvin at concerts. He asked me what I was up to, and I told him that I was going to City College and attending summer school, and that I wanted to finish Juilliard in four years, not five. I next heard he was doing a production of *West Side Story* somewhere in New Jersey, and I thought, "Oh my God, why didn't I keep my mouth shut?"

    By then, Alvin had begun to put together a dance company. I heard that they were going on tour in Europe; that was in 1964. At the time, I was working at Bloomingdale's, because I couldn't use my scholarship at the Martha Graham School or anywhere else. I was then invited to perform in *Black Nativity*, which would be touring in Europe for seven months. After I signed the contract for the show, I went over to the Clark Center, where Alvin and his company, which included many of my dancer friends, were rehearsing. He again asked me what I was doing, and I told him that I had just signed a contract for *Black Nativity*. Without missing a beat, he said, "Well, do you have Takako's number?" Takako Asakawa was another dancer.

Black Nativity and the Ailey company had the same management, and that's why I ran into Alvin and his company so often in Europe. When I finally came back to New York after being away for a while and working with other companies, including Maurice Béjart's and McKayle's, I still lusted to be part of the Ailey company. I went to a performance at the Brooklyn Academy of Music, and I ran into Alvin and Nick Cernovitch, an incredible lighting designer. Alvin once again asked me, "Sylvia, what are you doing?" I said, "Nothing," and he replied, "Well, I need a girl." And that's when I joined the company. It was 1968.

On the way to my first rehearsal, I ran into Judith, whom I'd met a couple of years earlier and whom I originally knew as Judith, not Judy. She was walking up Eighth Avenue from the Port Authority, and she was wearing this fantastic turban wrap. At rehearsal, we prepared for the company's first Broadway season at the Billy Rose Theatre. We had ten weeks, I believe, to get ready for it. We were learning ballets in all four corners of the studio, different sections of different ballets. It was madness, but it was incredible. I was in such pain that first week, but still it was amazing. Dudley was there; Judy was there. We learned ballets by Talley Beatty, Louis Johnson, and Alvin, of course.

I had never toured with a company in the United States, only in Europe. We traveled by bus, as Judy mentioned, riding along with the ladders, the stools, the fans, the costumes. We ate at diners and truck stops. I hated the mashed potatoes at these places, and I would get on the servers' nerves by asking if the mashed potatoes were made from real or dehydrated potatoes. I went to the original McDonald's while traveling with the company; I'd never seen anything like that. I talk about all this in dance history classes and whatnot, but dancers today can't imagine it.

Masazumi Chaya

When I joined the company in 1972, we were getting ready for the Connecticut Dance Festival. We had two weeks to learn seven dances, I believe. We were learning *The Lark Ascending, Streams, Revelations, Blues Suite, Rainbow Round My Shoulder*—all these dances. One day, Alvin asked me to come to the hallway in front of the men's room, and he began teaching me a dance. I didn't know which dance it was. Right before departing for Connecticut, we had a run-through at the studio, and people kept wondering, "When are we going to dance that ballet that Alvin taught us?" It turned out that what he taught us was the women's choreography of the "yellow" section, with the hand clap and jump. We went to Connecticut, and we danced *Streams, The Lark Ascending, Revelations*. I don't remember if we did *Rainbow Round My Shoulder*, but we danced almost everything we had learned. I had a great time.

Judith Jamison

When did we perform at the Palais des Sports in Paris? 1974? We had to do the same ballets for four weeks. One was *Carmina Burana*, which had so many lifts in it. I felt so badly for the men because they were doing all the lifting. The Palais des Sports is a sports stadium, like a small Madison Square Garden. Such wonderful people came to see us while we were there. James Baldwin came to see us.

What I found remarkable when we toured is how hard Alvin fought for us to perform at every venue possible. That really made an impression on me. Unfortunately, he passed away before we performed at the Paris Opera House, which he had worked so hard to get us into. When we finally did, we sold out our week of performances, and then we never went back.

To this day, the company still performs in as many venues as possible. Ailey II now picks up a lot of the slack, but the second company didn't exist back in our day. It was us who played at all these venues.

Sylvia Waters

We are leaving out whole chapters: the Brooklyn Academy of Music, North Africa, the Soviet Union, Leonard Bernstein's *Mass*. In 1969, the company was one of five constituent companies at the Brooklyn Academy, along with those of Merce Cunningham, Paul Taylor, and Eliot Feld, and an acting company and an opera or musical theater company. Even though we filled the seats to the rafters when we performed there, we weren't making any money, and the academy did not provide us with rehearsal or storage space. Really, they didn't provide anything at all.

    Adrienne Edwards

What did you get for the Brooklyn residency, then? Just the ability to perform there?

    Sylvia Waters

I'm sure there was something. I don't know what the box office was or how it was distributed. This was also when the company dancers unionized with AGMA, the American Guild of Musical Artists. Our weekly salaries went from maybe $128 to $129; that's the difference that made! But at the end of the second season, which was in the spring of 1970, Alvin announced he was closing down the company. We were shocked, horrified: "How could you do that? What do you mean? Look at the success we have everywhere we go!" He said, "Well, you can't have a company if you don't have money. You can't have a company if you don't have a home. We don't have either, so I'm closing it down. I'm tired. I can't ask you to work for nothing. I can't ask you to rehearse for nothing." We replied, "What do you mean? We rehearse for nothing. We get unemployment. What's the difference? What are you doing?"

    We left there very disenchanted. Weeks went by, and some of us had little gigs and others had no gigs. I worked with Fred Benjamin for a hot minute. One day in April or May, I ran into Bill Hammond, the Ailey company manager, on West Eleventh Street. He had a huge smile on his face, and he asked me if I could keep a secret: the company was going to North Africa in July, and that tour would pay for our rehearsal period to go to the Soviet Union for six weeks, which would be followed by tours in Paris and London. I asked him if he was serious, and he told me he was and reminded me that it was a secret. When I next saw Judy, I said, "Can you keep a secret?"

    Judith Jamison

It's so interesting how I repressed that stuff about Alvin saying he was going to end the company. I suppose that's how I survived. I took all that negative information, pressed it down, and kept my head down.

    Sylvia Waters

Some years later, I learned—I don't remember if it was from Alvin or someone else— that the whole shutting down thing was a ploy Alvin used to get attention, to fundraise, to encourage his friends at the State Department to help him out. When he announced that he was going to dissolve the company, there was a lot of press about it. People were aghast. But the outcome, of course, was positive. The Soviet Union tour was one of the hardest we ever did, but in retrospect, I have no regrets.

    Judith Jamison

Neither do I, but it was *the* hardest tour. And I really would have liked to have had some *morozhenoye* (ice cream) that wasn't melted and not had mystery meat.

    But the people! Some had never seen a Black person, some had seen us perform, and others had never seen a Black person before they saw us perform. It was an overwhelming experience. I remember people running down the street after us. They didn't speak a word of English, but they would have a little bottle of vodka or something for us, or they had these big smiles on their faces because they had just come from seeing us perform. When we returned to Russia twenty years later, the people remembered us. It was the USSR when we first went, and it was Russia when we came back in 1990.

    Sylvia Waters

To think of the horror of what is happening today in Ukraine, in Kiev—that's what we knew it as, not Kyiv. The Soviet tour actually began in Ukraine.

    Judith Jamison

We were there. That's amazing.

      Sylvia Waters

Following on what Judy said, on that tour we ate a lot of mystery meat with an egg on top, different kinds of borscht, and chicken with hardly any meat on it.

      Judith Jamison

And served cold.

      Sylvia Waters

Yes, and as the days got colder, vegetables became hard to get. We used to play this game of sorts, thinking about the foods we missed: roast beef, Parker House rolls. I believe it was in the fifth week of the tour that we were in Moscow, and the US Embassy there held a party for us. They had a spread: fried chicken, baked chicken, roasted chicken, steak—

      Judith Jamison

Caviar, potatoes, everything.

      Sylvia Waters

Coca-Cola. Even though some of us didn't drink alcohol, there was Scotch, there was rye. Some of us even stayed over and had pancakes and eggs for breakfast.

      Judith Jamison

That tour was six weeks long, and we went to a different city each week. We traveled on small propeller planes, the kind that sits at an angle when parked.

      Sylvia Waters

There were gun turrets on the front of those planes.

      Judith Jamison

I don't think I noticed that. They resembled World War II planes. I love those types of planes, though not to tour in. But every Monday we would get on one and fly to the next city.

      Sylvia Waters

We took a train once into what was then Leningrad, now Saint Petersburg. To be able to visit a place such as the Hermitage, in the days before it was renovated, and see all these paintings that I knew only from books, was an incredible experience.

      Judith Jamison

Chaya, you went to Russia in 1990, right?

      Masazumi Chaya

Yes, and there was still no food. But Judy, you found a Pizza Hut, and you ordered pizza for the crew and dancers. The minute it arrived, everyone dove right in.

      Judith Jamison

That was tough. But you were there, and that's the thing: there are places we went to that now have different names and that we can no longer go back to.

      Masazumi Chaya

True. I remember in Russia not being able to go into some of the stores. Instead, we had to go through one of the young men who were always hanging around us. I mentioned to one of them that I missed sushi, and the next day sushi arrived. It was flown in from Denmark or someplace like that. Those men hanging around, listening to our conversations, were KGB agents.

      Judith Jamison

We would go to our hotel rooms and talk to the lampshades or the walls.

Sylvia Waters

If you complained about something, maybe that you needed another blanket, you'd suddenly get a knock on the door, and somebody would have brought you a blanket. How did they know? You could be very paranoid.

Masazumi Chaya

To go back to the company's financial situation, Alvin was struggling. When we moved from the Minskoff Building to 211 West Sixty-First Street, I found a book that contained payroll records. Jimmy was getting forty dollars, Dudley was getting thirty dollars, but every page I went through, Alvin was marked as zero.

Sylvia Waters

I've seen some records in the archives showing that Alvin would pay everyone but himself. When there were live musicians accompanying a performance, they were always paid first.

Judith Jamison

Dancers today should know about the sacrifices Alvin made in order for them to be where they are now. Actually, they often do know, but sometimes they don't appreciate it or they put it away in a little compartment and forget it. But just think of what he did to allow all of us to be able to tell these tales and to have generations of dancers in a space they can call their own. He was a remarkable person. There are no words for it.

Adrienne Edwards

That's extraordinary. I wanted to go back to when Ms. Jamison mentioned Mr. Ailey's generosity. He was using the company almost like a commissioning vehicle to support other choreographers. Where do you think that impulse came from?

Sylvia Waters

I think it relates to his having come up when dancers didn't consistently work in a company like they do now, with contracts. Instead, there were pickup companies, and works were set on whichever dancers were available. Out of this lineage came incredible ballets, some masterworks even, including ones by Talley Beatty, José Limón, Donald McKayle, and Anna Sokolow. Alvin's idea—which was a very unique idea and remained so for a long time—was to have a repertory company so these works wouldn't be performed only once or twice, at the YMHA or at Hunter College or the like. He wanted them to be performed for broader audiences all over, and he invited Talley, Donald, Anna, Louis Johnson, and others to set their works on his company. The list goes on because almost every company at the time was a single-choreographer company. Alvin wanted his to be like the mixed-repertory ballet companies that use choreography by many different choreographers. That remained a unique ideology until maybe ten years ago.

Judith Jamison

Then people suddenly caught on that having a repertory company worked.

Sylvia Waters

Alvin's was really the first, and I would say that his was one of the few integrated companies at the time. That reflects his background with Lester Horton. Lester took dancers of every stripe because many weren't allowed to be in the white ballet schools. Alvin carried that with him.

Adrienne Edwards

Ms. Jamison, you said that it tore you up when you first saw Mr. Ailey's choreography, that you were numb after seeing it. How would you describe his style of dance, and what made it different? If you can articulate it, what was it that moved you, and how do you teach that?

Judith Jamison

Well, you have to have talent, and you have to come in with something for the choreographer. You have to meet them halfway. This is why I feel that rehearsal space is sacred, and that's why I don't like visitors at rehearsals. When people are creating, the air is different; it's not the same air that we breathe. You keep doing things over and over and over again, and over and over and over again, and something—maybe a look—will tell you exactly what direction you need to go. It's intangible. I'm not great at articulating what that is because it's very spiritual to me. It's as if some kind of combustion occurs, and at that point, you know if something is working or if it isn't.

Sylvia Waters

As Judy said, Alvin tried to get you to bring something of yourself to the step. A step is never just a step; it has to have you behind it. He would ask you to use your imaginings and your experience, and that came from his acting background. I describe Alvin as a hybrid choreographer. Yes, he used Horton technique, but he loved an arabesque and the classical line. Many of his ballets are inhabited by people with feelings and emotions. He wasn't afraid to explore that on a very profound level.

Masazumi Chaya

Alvin would tell me to use my step and show myself. Sometimes I would worry, "What should I do? Why can't I dance like that?" But Alvin would tell me that I wasn't being myself because I was focused on what someone else was doing. He'd say, "You know what the step is. Use it and show who you are." This ideology was part of what made the company successful, and Judy, as director, you maintained that idea. Whenever dancers doubt themselves, they are told that they have everything, but they're just not showing themselves.

Judith Jamison

Alvin could be very blunt. If a dancer asked him, "Why did so-and-so get that part and not me?," he would respond with something like, "Can you do an arabesque like that? Then go away." And that would be the end of that.

Sylvia Waters

I think we all had those experiences with Alvin. When I first started working with him, it was terrifying because he was telling me that I was the most unique individual. There I was trying to pull stuff from myself and not worry about the arabesque itself but rather worry about what that arabesque meant. It was a different way for me to work. Most choreographers will give you the steps and tell you how high, how low, how wide, how far. But they don't necessarily tell you about the character, your character. They may not ask you to participate in that way or collaborate with them in that way. Alvin was as much a theatrical director as he was a movement director. He liked when you moved between the steps, and he called this "rubato." What happens between the movements is important.

Judith Jamison

Absolutely, and that's hard to teach. You have to know about it already. Alvin gave you so much that sometimes there was no explanation needed, or if he did explain something, then it would make all the sense in the world. When we gave lecture demonstrations at schools, we would listen to him introduce the company. To hear him speak to the audience about what they were about to see and who the participants were, and tell the audience that they had the freedom to take away from the performance whatever they took from it—my goodness, that was an education in itself!

But if any of us began to feel too big for our britches, he would remind us that while we were educating people, we were also entertainers. He would knock us down a bit and say, "Look, come on now. You're in front of an audience. They need to be entertained."

Sylvia Waters

Often when he was working on a new piece, he would give us images but he wouldn't necessarily tell us what they were about. He didn't talk a lot during rehearsal. You could go through a whole rehearsal period wondering about the story, but by being so physically engaged with the piece, its meaning would become clearer to you toward the end.

Adrienne Edwards

I was really struck in the archive and in the notebooks by all the different people Mr. Ailey was reading or thinking about or whose work he was looking at. It was such a diverse group. He seemed to have a genuine curiosity, which I think relates a bit to something Ms. Jamison said, about that thing you couldn't quite pinpoint or articulate.

Sylvia Waters

He was a prolific reader.

Masazumi Chaya

In each city we went to, Alvin would buy every newspaper on the stand. He would go through them on the bus, and then he would toss them to me. A pile of newspapers every day. He really wanted to understand what humans do and what they go through. Everything is so technical now, but young dancers can still relate to *Blues Suite* or *Revelations* because of what goes on inside the soul. Alvin always had that at the front of his mind.

Judith Jamison

Wherever we toured, Alvin wanted us to understand that the world doesn't revolve around us or dance, that there's a world outside. He encouraged us to visit museums and see whatever else there was to offer, and to talk to people who were not in dance. He wanted each of us to make a whole human being out of our experience.

Online conversation held February 8, 2024

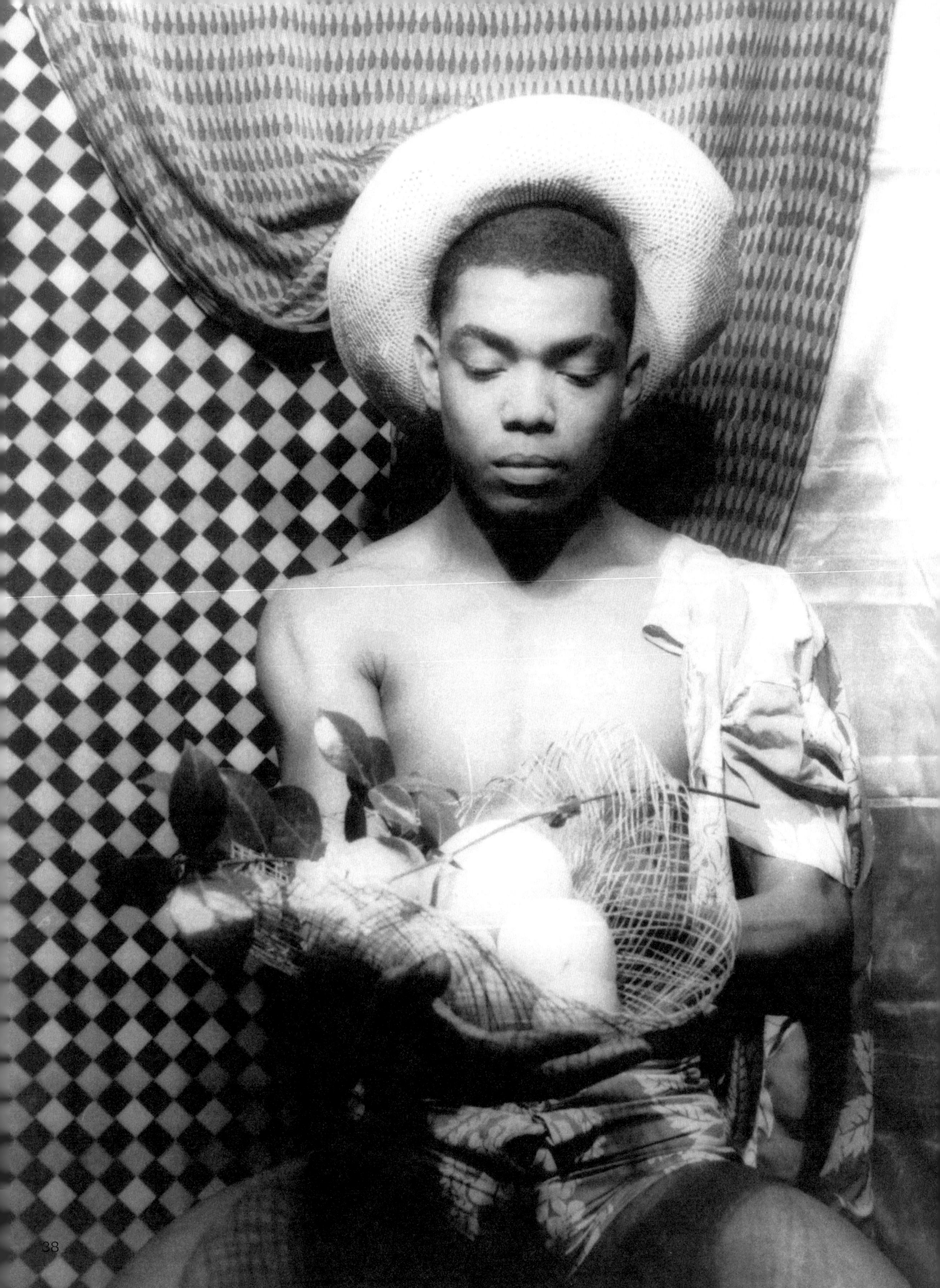

Malik Gaines

How to Play Drums

There are so many remarkable things about Alvin Ailey. Two in particular cast a certain light on the contours of his virtuosity and on his contribution to the very idea of expression. First, Ailey was beautiful. Stunning. The radiant boyishness captured by Carl Van Vechten's camera (fig. 1); the star dancer's muscular bundle of human curves and angles moving in modern shapes; the handsomely mature Mr. Ailey, company man, ambassador, honoree, and troubled custodian of a visionary responsibility—all so beautiful. However, he was said to have grown thin and drawn toward the end. He apparently did not look well when bumped into on the street. Ailey's gorgeousness had aligned with an "it" quality that, along with giant talent and discipline, carried him far. That feature is one of life, which stands in contrast with his death from AIDS-related illness on December 1, 1989. Ailey was not the only beautiful, talented, physically disciplined person who died of AIDS complications in that period; there were many. But of those, he certainly was among the most celebrated and internationally recognized figures. It is notable for a Black gay man to have been this successful, as in other situations being Black and gay would contribute to overwhelming isolation, marginalization, and diminishment of achievement. Ailey's virtuosity catapulted him through those limitations, which pressed against his legacy but have never overcome it. We attend to this legacy decades after his death, as we have done for other dance luminaries, including Merce Cunningham, Katherine Dunham, Martha Graham, and Arthur Mitchell. Ailey's is a name that fills in the very idea of dance. Body after body has moved with intention, athleticism, and spirit in the school he invented and named. On this very day, someone is likely holding the shapes of his *Revelations* in their living, magic form. *Revelations*, the most exhaustively seen of his dances, takes up the symbolization of Black experience through a reaching and yearning choreography, as Ailey's own achievements extend the already wondrous vocabularies of the Black arts. Ailey offers much to the study of virtuosity.

Studying performance and reflecting on the aptitudes of its impressive contributors are processes that orient themselves around the more abundant forms of presence: around exertion, action, and extension of technique. To keep those expenditures in context, it is sometimes useful to reflect on an idea Fred Moten mentioned, that of "nonperformance."[1] Moten tends to look to etymology to remind us of what we are actually talking about when we use the words we have been given. Performance suggests a bringing into being, an instantiating of form. But here we have a history. There are the flows of compulsory labor whose rhythms remain in motion. Those include a requirement

fig. 1
Carl Van Vechten, *Alvin Ailey*, 1955. Beinecke Rare Book and Manuscript Library, Yale University, New Haven, Connecticut

to appear. To appear distorted. To appear as a distorted negation of one's disappearance. To exceed one's own disappearance, to demand representation. To be overrepresented. To be represented to death. To be represented as death. To refuse, to work-stop. To produce refusal. To reproduce refusal. To bring into nonbeing. These requirements activate performance. The body that appears as a virtuoso is animated by choreography that was already in motion. The negative form of nonperformance acknowledges that the contracts written to conscript the labor of Black performance will fully employ its virtuosity, but at the same time run a counterbalance of penalties levied against the virtuoso for never—despite ever more inventive and effective expressions—meeting the unfulfillable terms of being. These are difficult grounds on which to instantiate. Godlike powers of invention are demanded of the performer. Ailey nearly attained them. No wonder his mother, Lula Cooper (née Cliff), was so proud of him. One way to imagine nonperformance in relation to Ailey is in the speculative performances of his post-death, the performances that could not be made after 1989. He was very close with his mother, and he did not want to upset her. This is one of the reasons his death was attributed, at the time, to a blood disorder. Another, as the next-generation choreographer Bill T. Jones has commented, was that Ailey had no community of gay men or others struggling through the AIDS crisis.[2] He was isolated, marginalized, diminished. As his illness progressed and he became increasingly weak, his company brought a couch into the rehearsal room for him to rest on. But his dances continue today.

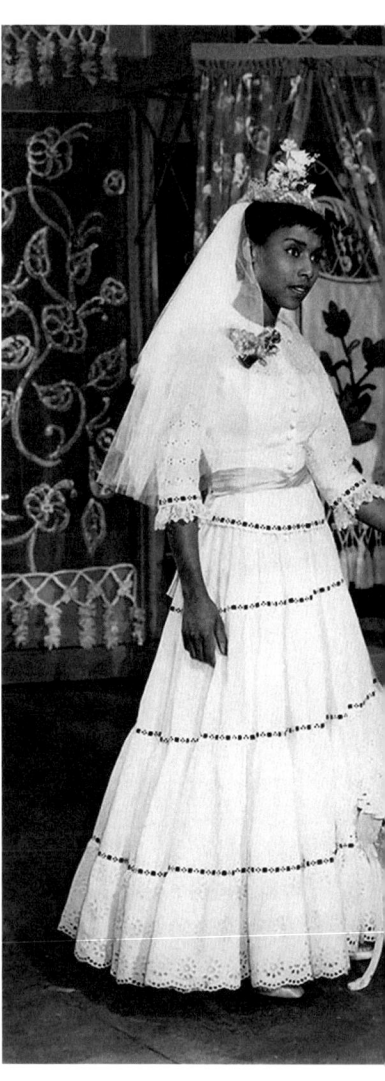

In the mid-1950s, Ailey, then in his early twenties, moved from Los Angeles to New York, where he landed in a crucible of Black creativity. Already excellent, experienced, and responsible performers, he and Carmen de Lavallade, his friend and comrade from Lester Horton's dance company, were ringers brought in to perform in the remarkable Broadway musical *House of Flowers* (fig. 2). Set in a Caribbean brothel and channeling its writers' homosexual and leftist feelings around Black tropical life, the show was a labor of icons. Diahann Carroll, in her Broadway debut, sang "I Never Has Seen Snow," an elegant jazz-tinged ballad using stilted white-stage Black vernacular, with a pristineness that nearly rights the song's failures. Pearl Bailey headlined the show and belted "One Man Ain't Quite Enough" with her indefatigable bravura and élan. Everyone involved was a big deal, up to the white creative team: writer Truman Capote collaborated with composer Harold Arlen on the lyrics for Arlen's score, and Peter Brook was the director. The process was difficult, as Bailey found Brook disrespectful and made her findings known. Yet the show gave Ailey and de Lavallade, who performed a big dance number, the opportunity to meet a chorus of performers who would continue to populate their lives. An anecdote from Ailey biographer Jennifer Dunning captures the milieu, recalling an "elegant woman with long, tapered legs and a familiar face who haunted the show."[3] It was Marlene Dietrich, Arlen's lover, who would "sew and chat with the wardrobe staff" and who "tirelessly ran errands for performers," having had a "special affinity for the dancers, drawing them out and listening to them talk about their lives."[4] This setting was an amazing conjunction of forces from which a new generation of Black actors, dancers, and musicians would transform their world. Black performers' appearances very often were arranged within the systems offered by white writers, producers, and venues, presenting a chic modernist aesthetic of desegregation but also a lot of actual contact among different people that was still prohibited elsewhere in US life. Ailey was suddenly in a prismatic section of New York history, studying dance with legends past, dancing at parties with future legends, and getting cast in shows—not only as a dancer but also, based on his appeal, as an actor. He appeared on Broadway with Lena Horne in *Jamaica* (fig. 3); in the musical *Sing, Man, Sing!* with Harry Belafonte; in the play *Tiger Tiger Burning Bright* with Claudia McNeil, shortly after her career-defining role in Lorraine Hansberry's *A Raisin in the Sun*. The elder McNeil supposedly lorded her seniority over the young cast, lamenting that she, unlike her younger colleagues, had limited opportunities in her early career, having had to spend so much time stuck in Langston Hughes's plays.[5] A luminary for sure, Hughes, like James Baldwin after him, is not known for his plays. Whereas their elders had hoofed their way through vaudeville and profound indignities, up-and-comers now were gaining experience on the legitimate stage, in unprecedented appearances. Ailey, for one, leapt across Broadway in the company of tremendous Black performers whose names still inspire awe and pride.

Ailey was twenty-three when he arrived in New York, and he was already an experienced choreographer and administrator, having previously led the Los Angeles dance company of his mentor, Lester Horton. Ailey, along with de Lavallade, was an ambassador

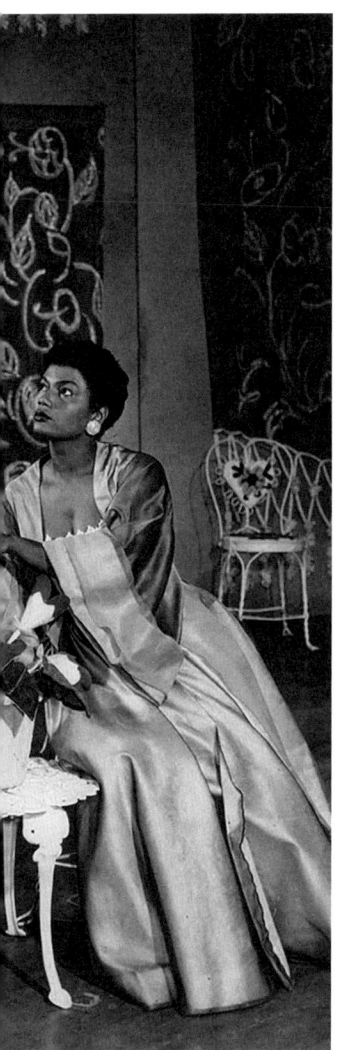
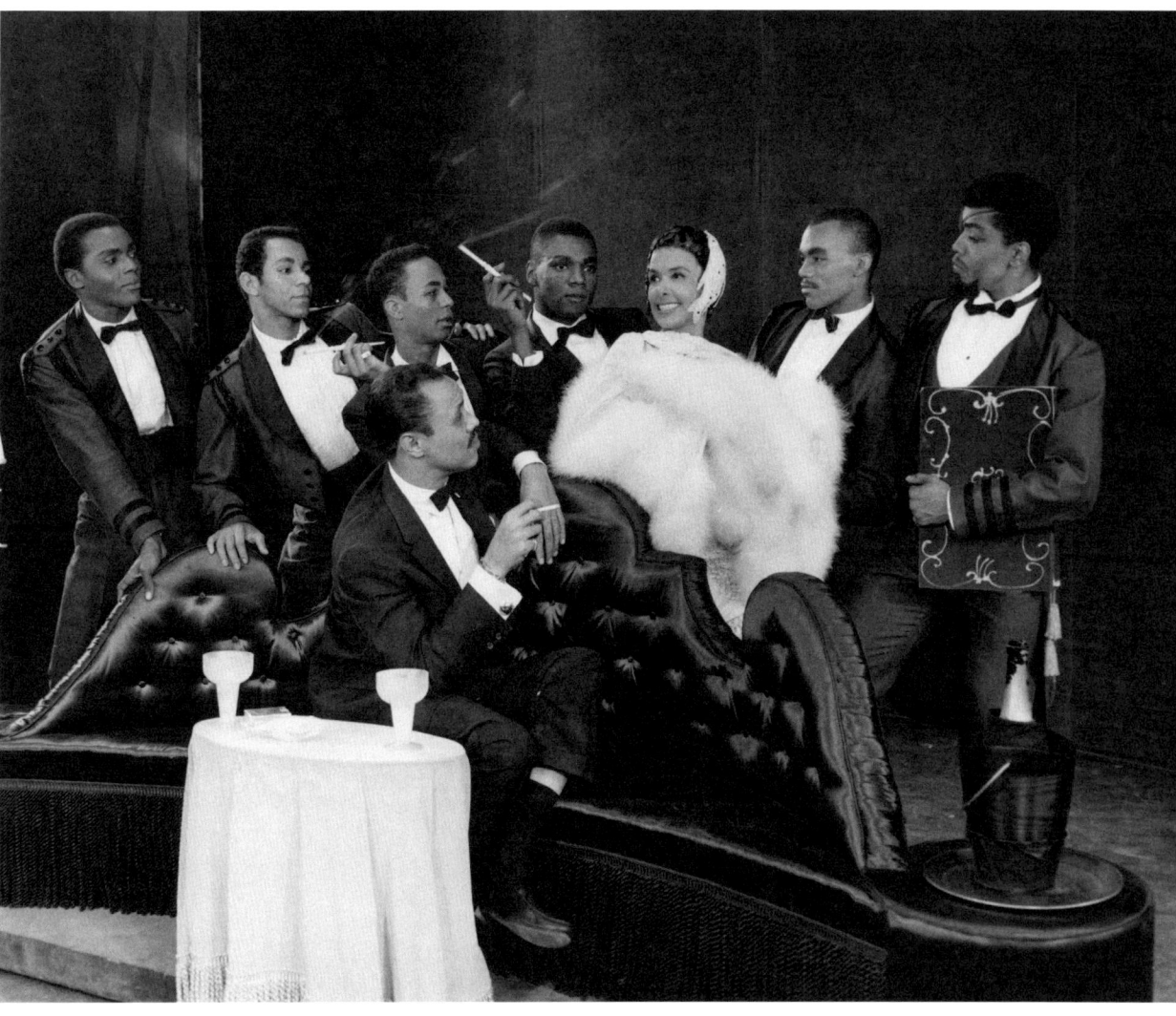

fig. 2

Diahann Carroll (left) and Pearl Bailey (right) in *House of Flowers*, Alvin Theatre, New York, 1954. Photograph by Zinn Arthur

fig. 3

Lena Horne (third from right) and Alvin Ailey (far right) in *Jamaica*, Imperial Theatre, New York, 1957. Photograph by Friedman-Abeles. Billy Rose Theatre Division, The New York Public Library for the Performing Arts

of Horton's technique, which was syncretic, incorporating various cultural sources, and big on lyrical expression. Ailey came to this technique as a teenager in Los Angeles, and his body grew into it. This sense of body had accumulated what Ailey had absorbed as a young person, newly arrived in Southern California from rural Texas and soaking in the shows that would pass through the grand theaters of downtown LA. There Ailey saw a wide range of performances, from Dunham in *Tropical Revue* to the Ballet Russe de Monte Carlo. Ailey too was syncretic. He made his body available to all this energy and carried it around the globe. It is a long way from rural Texas to the Soviet Union, where, in 1970, Ailey's was the first modern US dance company to visit. In what by the early 1960s became near constant travels for his company, with substantial sponsorship by the US Department of State in its attempt to promote the free-expression brand, Ailey delivered an image of US Black virtuosity to the world, exporting and expertly delivering one of our most precious resources.

The perpetual, durable signature of Ailey's work, *Revelations* (1960; see pp. 160–73) was the culmination of his amazing trajectory of experience, from Texas to dance with a capital D. *Revelations* was carried away on a sea of demand from its first appearance, which kept the company on the road. This elegant, elongated, and precisely coordinated depiction of the Black American struggle is something for which there was no shortage of appetite. The beautiful redemptive-ness of the gorgeous bodies' efforts has continued to stir audiences to their feet for decades. Many people identify with the dance and recognize real things in it, like the praise-dancing of some Christian churches that offers a physical continuity with mothers and ancestors. The spiritual "Wade in the Water," which accompanies a crucial section of the work, conveys a familiar doubleness, as one of those traditional songs that speaks of biblical imagery but also of potential escape routes. *Revelations* has a unified integrity but conveys mixed knowledge. Its authenticity is its multiplicity. It played in New York, in the American South, in Leningrad (Saint Petersburg), and at the First World Festival of Negro Arts in Dakar, Senegal. The dance and its production conjoin rootedness with an endless migratory flow.

William Greaves's 1966 documentary film on the festival in Dakar captures the scene there:[6] Léopold Sédar Senghor, Senegal's first president, arrives from an airplane and gives a stirring speech to those assembled from around the world, followed by a performance by Louis Armstrong's band. Senghor opened the festival during a wave of African independence, situated in attendant ideologies, that called for the urgent reformation of the arts as a foundation of a reemergent culture after those forms of expression and communication had been disparaged, disallowed, and dismantled by colonial authorities. Like others of his head-of-state peers from the time, Senghor had to invent a nation in the space left by colonization, and drew on local African and diasporic ideas and practices to invest that statehood with identity, community, and a redistribution of natural resources, including human ones. Senghor was particularly connected to Francophonic Black diasporic thought, having spent time in France between the World Wars along with Aimé Césaire, Jeanne and Paulette Nardal, and others from France, the Caribbean, and Africa who were astutely connecting art, ideas, political liberation, and transnational movement. Greaves's film conveys some of the headiness of this liberation moment, as it is introduced by Marpessa Dawn, Duke Ellington, and Hughes, who are shown strolling around an arts exhibition and comparing their faces to African masks. Diasporic Blacks, including US Americans who faced racist reprisals where they stayed, were essential figures in the scene of African independence.

Greaves's film includes a montage of dance presentations that sets a scene of reconciliation. Arranged under modern national categories rather than more specific tribal or ethnic names, groups of dancers take the stage to offer examples of African movement. In Africa, there is no precolonial history of concert dance on a stage in front of a seated audience; that is a very European formation. Rather, these amazing dances correspond with different rites or masquerade traditions: episodes of festivity, the marking of transitions, and modes of ancestral communication. But this moment called for formal syncretism. In this context, *Revelations* takes the stage (figs. 4a–d). Ailey's company, which had been on tour in Europe, was brought in as a last-minute replacement to represent the United States at the Dakar festival. Arms arc in formation, reaching and striving. Modernity and its aesthetic, modernism, are thorny problems in the afterlife of the colony. That problematization is the intrinsic material of Ailey's work. The very modern *Revelations* demonstrated what Ghanaian President Kwame Nkrumah said about the push for original African arts, that US Blacks have already been doing so for three hundred years.[7] In this time, a strong sense of shared origins endured, as in Ailey's poem from the mid-1960s, "Instruction: How to Play Drums," which offers his orientation toward this vision in its first line: "Be Born in Africa."[8] Although the act of representing this vision in Dakar ironically directed Ailey's work toward the frontal gaze of the concert stage, in his work, Ailey was able to carefully manage the difference between authentic feeling and stage performance. He seemed especially aware of their potential tensions when he choreographed *Quintet* in 1968 for five women in his company (see p. 193). The dance partitions inner and outer experience, using costume and popular showiness to accentuate the artificial side of life. The women appear in campy blond wigs and gowns reminiscent of Marilyn Monroe, and their routines resemble girl-group ensembles delivered frontally, until they break off into solos and other formations that seem to reveal more personal, interior dramas. Costumes fall away. After much alienating feeling, the group returns to formation, charming its audience with a synchronized femininity. All this is done to a sequence of songs by the singer-songwriter Laura Nyro, whose fantastic work of this time experimented with popular soul sounds and delivered a clear and unique voice that was both theatrical and diaristic. On her early albums, driving piano rhythms rise and break as emphatic declarations give way to moody grooves. Tempos and intensities shift, emotions change but are fully felt, and Black musical influences swirl in a young white musician's powerful experimentalism. The dance and the music place Black people and Black expressive materials in contingent, and sometimes attenuated, relations. Ailey's choreography tends to be both dynamically showy and deeply symbolic, offering a lot of range for its subjects to move in. While *Revelations* consistently appears to represent a real experience, in *Quintet*, experience appears as a series of inconsistent representations of realness.

Did Nyro ever see *Quintet*? Biographers do not mention it. One presumes she was elsewhere in 1968 when *Quintet* debuted at the Edinburgh International Festival in Scotland, as Nyro's radiant breakthrough album, *Eli and the Thirteenth Confession*, was

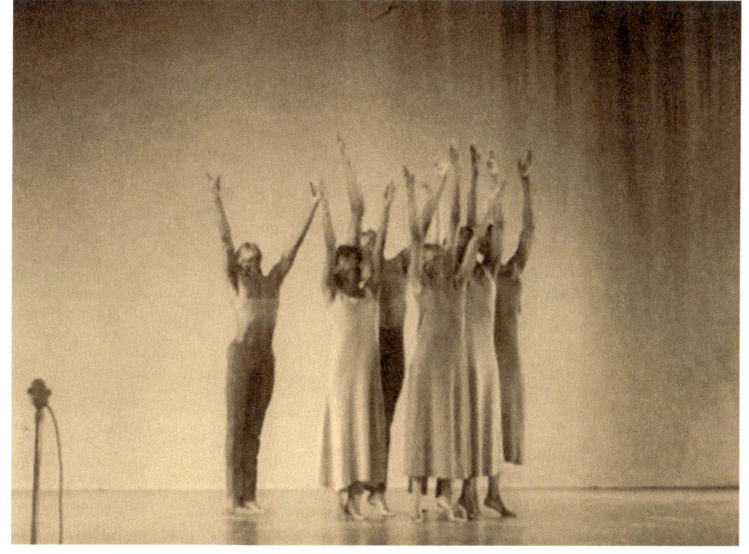
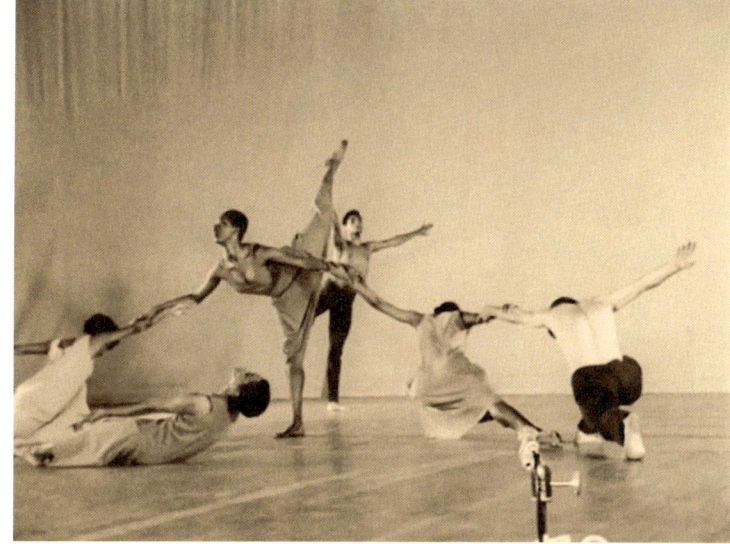
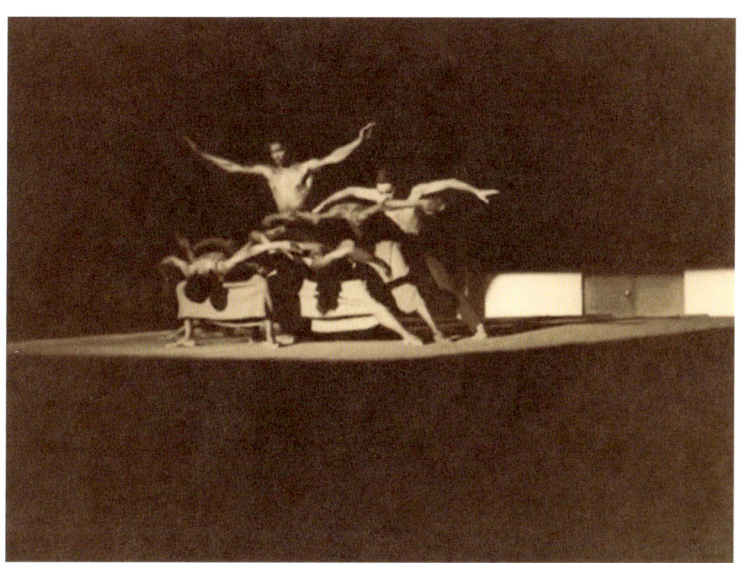
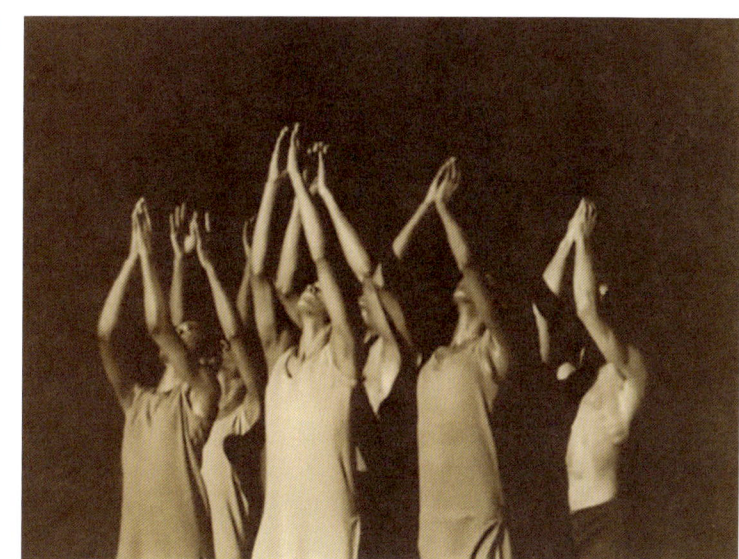

figs. 4a–d

Revelations in William Greaves's documentary film *First World Festival of Negro Arts* (1966)

newly circulating. She would spend nights in 1968 recording her most acclaimed album, *New York Tendaberry*, which was released the following year. When Ailey's renowned work *Cry*, which uses Nyro's haunting "Been on a Train" as a central score element, premiered at New York City Center in May 1971, Nyro was in a studio in Philadelphia recording *Gonna Take a Miracle*, her album of 1960s soul and rhythm and blues covers, with members of the band Labelle—Patti LaBelle, Nona Hendryx, and Sarah Dash—as backing vocalists. The success of *Cry* made it a staple of the Ailey repertory, so it is not impossible that Nyro saw it somewhere. The singer died of cancer in 1997, eight years after Ailey's death. It is an interesting scene to imagine: the genius singer-songwriter, a bisexual New Yorker of Eastern European Jewish and Italian descent who had changed her name from Nigro to Nyro for professional reasons, absorbing this exhaustive symbolization of the struggles of Black womanhood, choreographed by a gay man in honor of his mother, to Nyro's bluesy song. Real, but more complicated than it looks.

Of performing the extraordinary and expressive *Cry*, its brilliant original star dancer Judith Jamison has said: "You survive inside what [Ailey's] giving you and what the music is telling you. You live in those moments."[9] All these artificial structures were armatures for what Ailey and Jamison were really after—life. An intensely demanding solo, *Cry* takes its mover on a journey from servitude to exaltation, mapped against music of Alice Coltrane and Pharoah Sanders, Nyro, and the Voices of East Harlem, a choir of young people whose grainy and glorious "Right On Be Free" sets the pace for the work's dizzying freedom-dream finale. Jamison's premiere brought down the house, offering seemingly supernatural powers of movement, as she stretched, leapt, spun, and lunged into every space of the stage, with a buoyant white skirt blossoming and blowing around her (see pp. 216–19). This was actually a skirt previously used in *Revelations*, where it was meant to

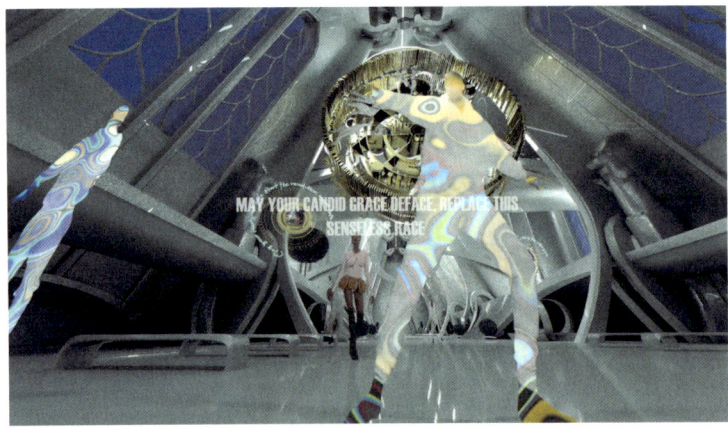
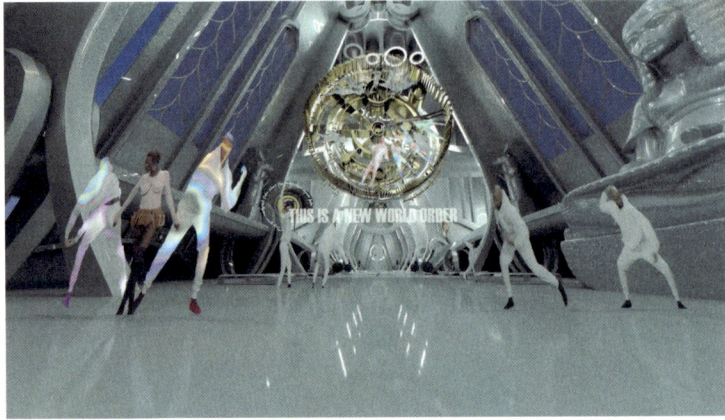
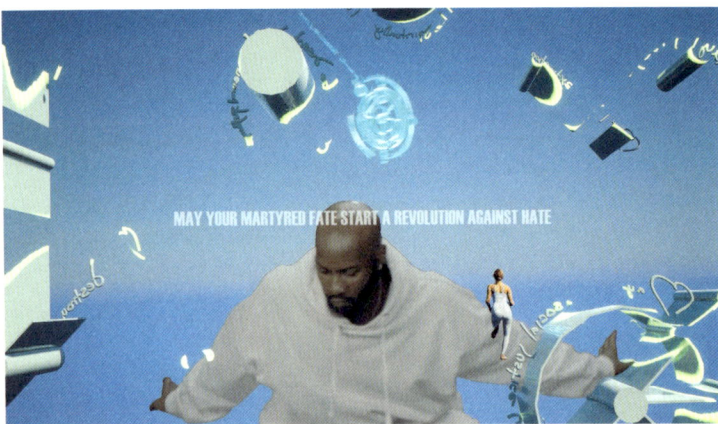
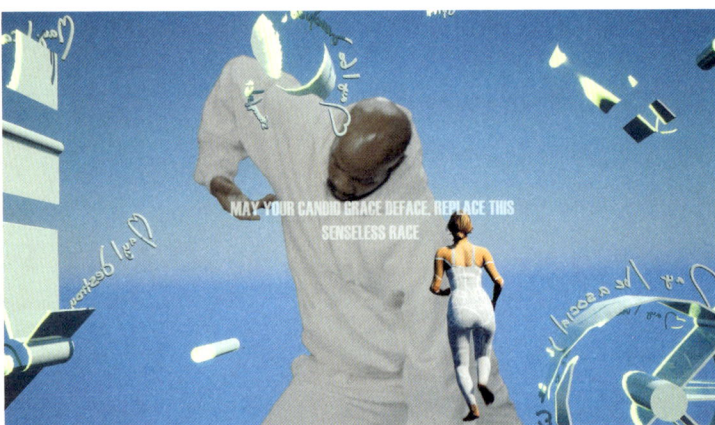

give a sense of enslavement, repurposed when the planned *Cry* costume could not endure the choreography's velocities. Jamison's sleek and narrow 1970s silhouette—including a long-sleeve white leotard with that skirt billowing to the floor, crowned with the dancer's cropped natural hair—offered an iconic Black femininity that was chic, poised, and capable of miracles, an image that may in fact have been a historical necessity. Describing the mental preparation for the piece, through which the dancer not only moves in space but assumes symbolic roles, Jamison stated: "I was to be a woman who did the most servile of work but was never defeated by it. I was a mother protecting her children. I was a queen who'd come from Africa."[10] Africa circulates in the work's imagination. Some of the choreography was inspired by African events, including movements from a dance demonstration by countryside performers that the company had seen in a local bar in Zaire (Democratic Republic of the Congo), and a photograph of a starving woman with outstretched arms and a baby in her lap that was taken during the Nigerian civil war. This elsewhere provides a difficult source and a fantastic future for all this agility.

A critic's 1972 review of *Cry* contextualizes the work's expression, which was by then out of favor with the white avant-garde: "The concept of the star vehicle is one that is difficult for modern-dance, the mere display of performing élan being always regarded as suspect. Thankfully, Ailey doesn't subscribe to the aversion. Miss Jamison has more of that élan than most and her audience obviously revels in it. The solo is a long, exhausting tour de force.... It is a miniature epic that accumulates its energy with great effect."[11] This work was required to achieve an instance of Black power that had not yet been offered. While wildly popular, it was out of step with dominant tastes in dance, including those of downtown artists such as Yvonne Rainer, who were saying no to all the coercive drama and its punishing bodily demands. Dancers in the Ailey company who have undertaken *Cry* have spoken of specific physical syndromes they must monitor in their knees, backs, and heads, the consequence of the dance's nearly impossible choreography.[12] There is violence in this freedom. Although the movement's "energy" produces "great effect," it is also "exhausting."[13] This likewise sums up Ailey's life and work, propelled from somewhere within and suspended in a vortex of representation that will very often indifferently subsume those who are strong enough to appear.

Yes, Ailey was given a giant medallion with a rainbow ribbon by US President Ronald Reagan and his wife, Nancy, at the choreographer's Kennedy Center Honors. But he was also beaten by police on the street in New York for no good reason. These gestures are

figs. 5a–d

O'Shae Sibley in Jacolby Satterwhite's *A Metta Prayer* (2023)

counterparts. They frame the command performance of Black virtuosity. While Ailey's work can help support an upright vision of excellence, it also attests to the cost of such valuation. Nevertheless, our need for Ailey remains strong. So many Black contemporary dancers have continued to pass through some form of Ailey's training. From practitioner-scholars such as Aimee Meredith Cox to experimental movers like Will Rawls to concert-dance inheritors such as Kyle Abraham. Dancer O'Shae Sibley was an active participant in classes at the Ailey School. You can see the confidence and complexity in his solos captured by Jacolby Satterwhite for the artist's 2023–24 animated installation *A Metta Prayer* in the lobby of the Metropolitan Museum of Art. Sibley's projected form stretched and flowed amid pharaonic statues and other artifacts (figs. 5a–d). Sibley was dancing to Beyoncé when he was murdered at a gas station in an anti-Black and anti-queer attack. The extremes are intolerable. The motion in the passage between life and death is what our most powerful choreographies are bound to present. As Ailey knew, that motion can be the most moving.

NOTES

1. Fred Moten, "Blackness and Nonperformance" (lecture, The Museum of Modern Art, New York, September 25, 2015).

2. Bill T. Jones, in *Ailey*, directed by Jamila Wignot (New York: Neon, 2021), DVD.

3. Jennifer Dunning, *Alvin Ailey: A Life in Dance* (Reading, MA: Addison-Wesley, 1996), 83.

4. Dunning, 84.

5. Alvin Ailey and A. Peter Bailey, *Revelations: The Autobiography of Alvin Ailey* (Secaucus, NJ: Carol Publishing Group, 1995), 86.

6. *The First World Festival of Negro Arts*, directed by William Greaves (New York: William Greaves Productions, 1966), film, 40 min.

7. J. H. Kwabena Nketia, "Kwame Nkrumah and the Arts," in *Gender: Evolving Roles and Perceptions*, ed. Ghana Academy of Arts and Sciences (Accra: Ghana Academy of Arts and Sciences, 2006), 144–45.

8. Alvin Ailey, "Instructions: How to Play Drums," box 150, folder 3, Alvin Ailey Dance Foundation Collection, Music Division, Library of Congress, Washington, DC.

9. Judith Jamison, in Wignot, *Ailey*.

10. Judith Jamison, quoted in Valerie Gladstone, "Dance: The Long Shadow of Ailey's Great 'Cry,'" *New York Times*, November 26, 2000.

11. Don McDonagh, "A Dance Solo, 'Cry,' Given Special Élan by Judith Jamison," *New York Times*, November 23, 1972.

12. Gladstone, "Long Shadow."

13. Gladstone.

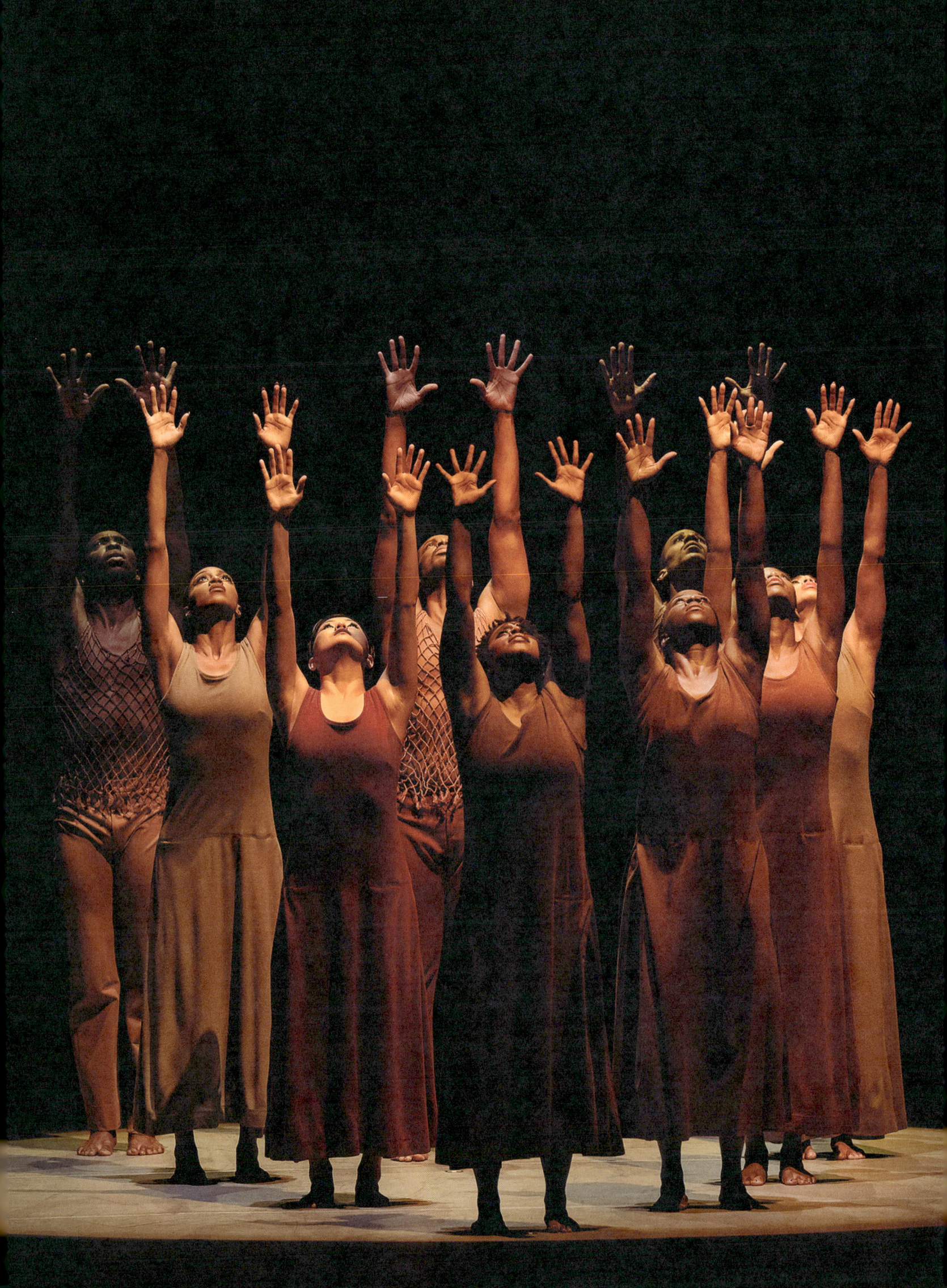

Jasmine Johnson

Alive with Ailey

I. Teaching Ailey

At its first moment, there is applause. Dancers, dressed in shades of chocolate, rust, sepia, and caramel, stand clustered at center stage, forming an oblong diamond. Chins lift upward, making space for lengthened necks. Throats peer straight ahead. Arms stretch down. The fleshy part of hands shines forward. Chests lift as if raised toward the heavens. Bare feet root the dancers' bodies. This vision alone—stilled dancers perched, grounded, readied—compels applause.

"I Been 'Buked" rolls in and the dancers sink into a squat, positioning their heads and right arms down, as left hands trace up and down that side of the body. The dancers lift up and over to the opposite side. Right hands slide up that side of body, eventually finding their ascent. "Childrennn," the gospel carries. With a slow, deliberate pace as if moving through water, the dancers rise from their lowered positions. Arms lifted, fingers spread, palms proud: a garden of hands in bloom (fig. 1).

I show Alvin Ailey's canonical *Revelations* as part of a seminar I am teaching on Black dance. Following the design of the class, we watch one iteration of the performance together as a group. Before our next session, we (re)read a number of writings on Ailey and the Alvin Ailey American Dance Theater (AAADT) in addition to interviews and primary sources that trace the mattering and changing shape of the company across its towering life. In that following class—with readings in tow and having completed viewings of additional works choreographed by Ailey as well as pieces by others—we witness *Revelations* again to see what affirmed, changed, or italicized grammars might have come forth. A practice of layered study: the invitation is for the class to engage Ailey's work through our existing vocabularies, the research produced from a field we might call Black Dance Studies, and the collective wisdom of the conversation.

When I offer courses on histories and theories of Black dance, students have more familiarity with Ailey, by and large, than any other choreographer or company with which we engage throughout the semester. Students have seen AAADT performances in person more than those by any other choreographer or company included on the syllabus. Early conversations often begin with tracing how *Revelations* might map onto a history of Black American subjugation, or how the dance speaks to anti-Blackness and Black spiritual resolution. This is an indexical practice that sometimes trades in the politics of authenticity: that Ailey is choreographing a findable and singular Black American history. There is often also language on the extraordinary talents of the AAADT company members. Indeed, as

fig. 1

Revelations, n.d.

Thomas F. DeFrantz has written, "For many African American audiences, the Ailey company operates as far more than a modern dance troupe. It represents the standard by which to gauge excellence in the performing arts."[1] This is true for my predominantly Black students, who often speak of Ailey through the language of beauty and virtuosity. Some have attended Ailey dance camps or were inspired to commit to a life of professional dance by way of seeing, and being taken by, the AAADT.

For many of them, the company was part of the fabric of their family's social lives. Every year, they saw the AAADT perform, as a Christmas, New Year's, or spring tradition. Many students shared the joy of attending an Ailey performance, around which they assembled with their parent, aunties, or siblings, everyone donning their sartorial best. The company's annual tour provided an opportunity for adornment, gathering, and collective witnessing. The personal traced the early edges of our conversations, and I listened to students' stories of familiarity, the stage for which the AAADT made possible.

The event of Ailey was draped in animated retelling, even while discussion around the textures of the program was short and often made synonymous with *Revelations* itself. No doubt there was respect for the canonical work. And I picked up a kind of disposition that folks had arrived on regarding what *Revelations* is "about." Like a *Jeopardy!* question made known by a singular clue, I became curious about the challenges and possibilities of Black-danced iconicity.

An emblematic challenge in teaching about the AAADT is having to work against an overconfidence in knowing *Revelations* insofar as the work is presumed to "speak" Black resistance and linear progress up out of slavery. Elsewhere I have written about gendered Black hypervisibility and the kind of astigmatism, or blurred vision, that repetitious ocular consumption can produce.[2] Here, though, I want to think through how the experience of teaching the AAADT has resulted, and necessarily so, in a vital regard for the company and its founder. How might we work toward a critical beholding that allows for complication and careful readings of the choreographic registers, resonances, and literacies inside a particular piece? How might we make room for an ongoing curiosity around the study of Black dance without being attached to mastering it, pinning it down, or producing a single story about it?

I am asking how study can cultivate unknowing.

II. Unknowing Ailey

I might argue that the profound iconicity of a work such as *Revelations* can potentially iron out intricate textures of relations—relations that, for example, engender applause even before full witnessing. Working against the formality to hold applause until the end of a production, this early ovation upends the implicit conventions of white proscenium audiences to be inactive, instead instantiating a call-and-response rhythm that is characteristic of Black diasporic embodied traditions. What, I wonder, are we affirming through applause at the sight of those epochal bloomed hands?

I assign the study of Ailey in courses that center the choreographic and embodied work of Black dance as well as those that, at face value, are presumed to not do so (Introduction to Black Studies, for example). In each circumstance, I have found Ailey to be a powerful means through which we think about the utility of movement to negotiate our relationship to history, and a way to explore Blackness as heterogenous, unstable, aesthetic, and presentist. Blackness is a surplus expressed through dance. Through the AAADT, students who come to Black studies, often without an explicit interest in dance, get a sense of "how concert dance performance conveys meaning to its audience" and "consider[s] bodily communication and the expressivity of gesture."[3]

There are no neat arrivals, despite the inevitable ending and sometimes crisp landing of a dance. A seemingly straightforward performance—rehearsed, set, polished, marked—is itself a bundle of questions. Drawing from Stuart Hall's language on the substance of Black popular culture, I argue that Black dance itself "is a contradictory space. It is a site of strategic contestation. But it can never be simplified or explained in terms of the simple binary oppositions that are habitually used to map it out: high and low; resistance versus incorporation; authentic versus unauthentic; experiential versus formal; opposition versus homogenization."[4]

The AAADT's continually expanding repertory embodies/indexes Black aesthetics and sensibilities while also hailing new ones. This is especially significant given that, despite the company's historic Blackness, neither "Black" nor "African American" is in its name. As dance scholar Clare Croft asserts, "Ailey rejected being pigeonholed as a black company and insisted that all his work, including the State Department tour, represented American dance more broadly. In essence, Ailey used the intertwined logic of Americanness and universalism to his own ends."[5] Therefore, when I evoke "Black dance," I do so knowing the instability and failures of the term, even while I embrace the distinct histories of Africanist aesthetics that it importantly signifies.[6] DeFrantz expounds on some of the labors and complications of the Ailey company's expansion and growing popularity over time:

> How does the company, securely positioned in the multicultural global arts economy we all share, stay "black"?
>
> Some answers lie in the strategies Ailey enacted to bring dance to the widest possible public. In large part, his carefully groomed, nonconfrontational troupe presented work that represented black experience to cultural outsiders. Without the benefit of wealthy patrons who might have funded his early explorations of dance form, Ailey built his company's success from the committed labor of his dancing collaborators, a "devoted band of friends, men and women whose professional lives were, in effect, a work of hopeful activism," from his own affable, articulate persona, which normalized American race relations for an international audience, and from a repository chosen to showcase an accessible and glamorous vision of dancing black bodies in several theatrical milieux.[7]

Across the conversations with my class, we move from articulating the AAADT through its representational or indexical registers (how it speaks "past," or speaks anything, really), as well as through its status as aesthetic producer, corporation, and school, toward a discussion of Ailey, including moments like the one that inaugurates this essay, as messy in its seeming straightforwardness. So too there is this important connection that DeFrantz relates: that the AAADT's global reception depended on a number of factors, including, among others, community support, a savvy financial vision, and charisma.

The company produces textures of feeling and Black presence.

I want to suggest that teaching Ailey is to engage in a practice of critical reading that is in service of the project of Black Studies (a discrete academic interdiscipline) and in the practice of Black study (a critical mode of Black being that predates, and spills over, the institutionalization of the field). Dance, in its capacity to not only express but iterate, imbues itself with an ability to speak of past, sure, but also and perhaps more urgently, instantiate a now. Following bell hooks, we know that "theory is not inherently healing, liberatory, or revolutionary. It fulfills this function only when we ask that it do so and direct our theorizing toward this end."[8] This applies to Black dance, a capacious and unsingular world of movements and embodiments within which Ailey might belong while he and the company ongoingly reshape its meanings.

Unknowing Ailey is an openness to study, one that disabuses any notions of neat personhood and makes space for the range, contradictions, and marvels of Black queer humanness. It is an investment in historiographies of the man and the company—not to arrive at a singular meaning of their lives and worlds, but to make room for the infinite existence and necessary complication upon which choreographic innovation can and does root.

Our ambition as a class is not to know Ailey; it is to pursue the always unfinished work of getting to know him, made possible by being with dance.

III. Alive with Ailey

Unknowing allows for Black aliveness with Ailey.

When my students and I watch Ailey together, for the second time—with the writings of Ailey, DeFrantz, Brenda Dixon-Gottschild, and others, and Ailey interviews, diary entries, and playbills in mind—we move toward a different set of conversations. We are excited by readings that include marveling at the virtuosity on display while also inviting something else. What choreographic strategies did Ailey employ in making *Revelations*? What drove his decision to slice its run time in half?[9] What framing machinations and danced rigor have come to make the piece the company's jewel and showpiece? How can a distinctly Africanist suite of choreographies lend itself to American universalism and broad, international reverence?

When my students and I rewatch Ailey, we name our own presence as audience members who are not merely consuming modern dance but who are invited into new feeling and presence. In this sense I (re)recognize myself, embodied. That I not only am watching but am being constituted by this danced presence. This might have something to do with what Kevin Quashie describes as aliveness. Quashie takes special interest in the aesthetic world-making possibilities of the poem and the essay, "for what they tell us about our being: about how we are and about how we can be."[10] This emphasis on encounter, regard, and possibilities of copresence ushers forward space to hold Black living "compassed by being alive, where aliveness sets the parameters for understanding loss, pain, belonging, for countenancing love, grace, healing."[11] He continues: "*Aliveness is of and in the one who is alive. . . .* [W]hat I am trying to do is to write about aliveness in a black world rather than life in the world as we know it—to write about aliveness in the aesthetic imaginary of black thought, which might help us attend to the poetic aliveness inevitable in each black human being. Again, I mean aliveness as instance(s) of being."[12]

Although Quashie's prerogative is the poem and the essay, I believe movement might find a home in his language and feeling. Black dance votes for a now, one predicated on shared encounter and loving witness. In this light, the audience's immediate applause is recognition of the magnum opus that is *Revelations* and an ovation for our Black selves. An anticipation of what we know or imagine is to come, and a vote for how we want to feel. We might anticipate the exceptional skill of the company members who "are able to give the impression that they are deeply in their bodies as they transcend it," as Aimee Meredith Cox writes, "carving stories, meanings, memories, and images in space that surely emanate from the physical being, but somehow appear to make the body irrelevant, despite its virtuosity."[13]

The significance of *Revelations* is not that the work "express[es] what we already know we are," to evoke Hall again. Rather, it is through dance that "we represent and *imagine* ourselves 'and' come to know how we are constituted and who we are."[14] In this vein, we might understand ourselves as being seen as beautiful by the AAADT. Recognizing the glory in us as them, we might applaud to say, "I love seeing you and being seen by you."

A legacy of Ailey's masterwork is not that it gives access to a neat, predictable Blackness lying there for us to point to (and own). Blackness is being newly uttered while it simultaneously rehearses a repertoire that previously exists. One of the many bounties of Ailey the choreographer is a necessary opacity that snuggles next to an international recognizability. The goal is not to know him entirely (a disposition upon which presumptions of contained or encased personhood hinge). A gift that comes with teaching Ailey is the possibility of exploring the vastness of Black life iterated through an evening's program that, by Ailey's design, includes *Revelations* and much more.

We return where we began. What some of us might be applauding in those first moments of *Revelations*—in that initial sprouting of open hands—is an anticipated encounter with a remarkable history of Black religious faith uttered through Africanist modern dance. What we see in an Ailey performance is expansive Blackness being newly conferred each time it is expressed. We applaud the encounter between a historic performance we anticipate and an aliveness made possible by the deep regard for Black (danced) presence that we feel in the now.

NOTES

1. Thomas F. DeFrantz, *Dancing Revelations: Alvin Ailey's Embodiment of African American Culture* (New York: Oxford University Press, 2004), 72.

2. Jasmine Johnson, "Flesh Dance: Black Women from Behind," in *Futures of Dance Studies*, ed. Susan Manning, Janice Ross, and Rebecca Schneider (Madison: University of Wisconsin Press, 2020), 154–69.

3. DeFrantz, *Dancing Revelations*, xv.

4. Stuart Hall, "What Is This 'Black' in Black Popular Culture?," *Social Justice* 20, nos. 1–2: 108.

5. Clare Croft, *Dancers as Diplomats: American Choreography in Cultural Exchange* (New York: Oxford University Press, 2015), 70.

6. By "Africanist," I mean to evoke the work of scholars such as Robert Farris Thompson and Brenda Dixon-Gottschild. As Dixon-Gottschild writes, "Africanist dance idioms show a democratic equality of body parts. The spine is just one of many possible movement centers; it rarely remains static. The Africanist dancing body is polycentric. . . . It is also polyrhythmic . . . and privileges flexible, bent-legged postures that reaffirm contact with the earth." Dixon-Gottschild, *Digging the Africanist Presence in American Performance: Dance and Other Contexts* (Westport, CT: Praeger, 1998), 8.

7. DeFrantz, *Dancing Revelations*, 69–70. DeFrantz quotes from Jennifer Dunning, *Alvin Ailey: A Life in Dance* (Reading, MA: Addison-Wesley, 1996), 52.

8. bell hooks, *Teaching to Transgress: Education as the Practice of Freedom* (New York: Routledge, 1994), 61.

9. When it premiered in 1960, *Revelations* was an hour long. Ailey subsequently revised the ballet, editing it down to about thirty minutes, which is the version we know today.

10. Kevin Quashie, *Black Aliveness, or a Poetics of Being* (Durham, NC: Duke University Press, 2021), 2.

11. Quashie, 10.

12. Quashie, 19–20 (emphasis in original).

13. Aimee Meredith Cox, *Shapeshifters: Black Girls and the Choreography of Citizenship* (Durham, NC: Duke University Press, 2015), 29.

14. Hall, "What Is This 'Black'?," 111 (my emphasis).

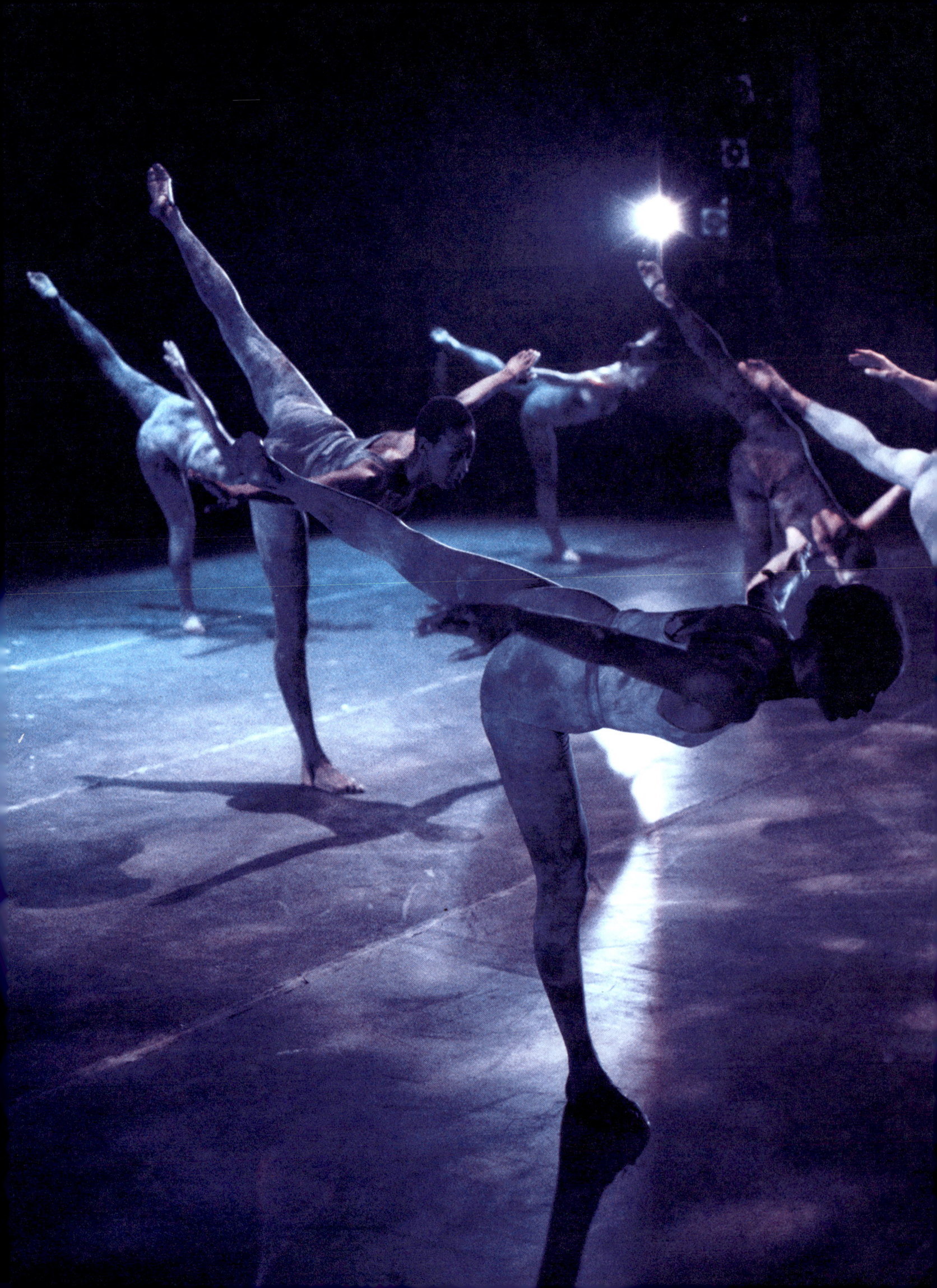

Aimee Meredith Cox

Beyond Culture and Somewhere between Starshine and Clay

Dancing with Alvin Ailey's Commitment to Black Study

It was 1994, during my first season with Ailey II, then known as the Alvin Ailey Repertory Ensemble. We were on tour, traveling by bus through the southern and southwestern United States, where we performed at small colleges and regional theaters by night and taught classes in high-school gymnasiums and community centers by day. On this particular evening, I had just finished performing in *Revelations* in front of an audience for the first time, and I now sat in the back of the bus, ruminating on every one of my missteps. As the other dancers made their way down the aisle, I sank low in my seat, waiting for the moment I knew I couldn't avoid. Sylvia Waters, the company's artistic director, came over to me, her face revealing her exasperation: "If you don't figure out how to use that fan, I am going to take you out of the 'yellow' section." I nodded my understanding. The choreography for the "yellow" section of *Revelations* (1960; see pp. 160–73) was by far the simplest we had learned that year in terms of the actual steps and the fact that most of it was performed in unison. But, as anyone who has witnessed a performance of *Revelations* knows, the steps in and of themselves are not the point; they are the vehicle used to convey certain parts of the cultural context of Black life. In this section, the context is the Black southern church. Within the canon of literature on Alvin Ailey and the Alvin Ailey American Dance Theater, much space has been given to the making of *Revelations* and the aspects of Ailey's childhood in Black communities in rural Texas that shaped the ballet.[1] Ailey used the term "blood memories" to give name to the process of cultural memory encoded on and within the body[2]—the parts of our history that flow through our veins and ride our breath, showing up in our unconscious thought, informing our ways of relating, and inflecting every move we make. As dancers in the second company, this history was passed down to us and offered as cultural nourishment to encourage movements that were about more than achieving beautiful lines or technical virtuosity. Our movements held the possibility of expressing a landscape of experience beyond ourselves.

The ballet *Streams* (fig. 1) premiered in 1970 during the Ailey company's residency at the Brooklyn Academy of Music. On the surface, *Streams* and *Revelations* are very different, particularly with regard to the latter's "yellow" section. The costumes for the women in that section are oversize yellow dresses (hence the name) made from heavy fabric that pulls the dancers closer to the earth. The outlines of my and the other women's bodies were hidden under the weight of the fabric, which moved around us with a rhythmic delay. Sometimes the dress felt as if I were dancing with a slightly lethargic partner. The matte, light gray Lycra of our *Streams* unitards, on the other hand, covered and held us like the

fig. 1

Streams, n.d.

thinnest glove. Nothing went unseen on our bodies or in our steps. We learned the choreography for *Revelations* before that of *Streams*, as every company member had a role in the former and it was our most requested piece on tour. Although as a young dancer it was unclear to me if the audience was aware that both ballets called upon the same movement vocabulary of Horton shapes, Graham contractions, and classical lines, as well as a grounded emphasis in Africanist aesthetics, I was trained to recognize that the two dances expressed a common technical language. Even with their shared choreographic reference points, I was better able to find myself in the *Streams* choreography than in that of *Revelations*. In *Streams*, I felt less like I was performing and more like I was dancing, whereas in *Revelations*, it seemed as if I had to step into a character I was not sure I was prepared to portray. The history and cultural references to Ailey's experience growing up Black in rural Texas were the starting points that I should have been able to access through my own Black female body and familial history, particularly through the stories conveyed by my elders, whose bodies held and moved from this history. Yet, I sensed that the richness of this history somehow escaped me, and the idea of Ailey's blood memories as being inaccessible overwhelmed me with shame. I thought to myself, "This is who I am. It shouldn't be so hard."

Until . . . I found my way into *Revelations* and, more significantly, into a new understanding of blood memories through *Streams*.

From the opening processional of *Streams*, in which every body is essential for completing the moving tableau, through all the following sections of the ballet, I realized that a meditative quality pervaded the quieter as well as the more overtly dramatic, faster-paced moments. Each step felt ceremonial—both modern and primordial. Although the work's demanding technical aspects of the choreography left nothing for individual dancers to hide behind, and we worried about our ability to execute the steps with the precision they required, we never felt alone on stage. The movement made sense only in the context of the collective. Emerging from the wings in a soaring grand jeté then landing at center stage in a deep crouching position to open the "Danza" section of *Streams* was one of my most exhilarating moments in the ballet—second only to when three women dancers ran onto the stage after me and assumed the same crouching position. I could, in a very literal sense, feel that they had my back as we moved diagonally across the stage with the sharp, focused precision of warriors ready for battle. Toward the end of the ballet, we danced in languid duets—men and women, and men and men—moving as if we were underwater. Our bodies leaned against each other, pressing inward to help hold ourselves up, then falling into each other's arms and spiraling to the floor at our partner's feet. These pairs of dancers ask the viewer to understand partnership by conveying it through an embodiment of trust and connection that defies the socially constructed bind of gender. With these expressions of the tenderness and ferocity of moving in community, I was able to feel my way back to *Revelations* without the weight of a predetermined narrative of Black life that was not yet my experience. Although one critic proclaimed that the unison movement of the "Coda" in *Streams* "could be annoying," moving together with the charge of finding coordinated breath and steps was a balm for the dancer, such as myself, who finds the feeling of relationality often difficult to access off stage; we were building community as we danced.[3] Perhaps this is why Dudley Williams, a long-time Ailey company dancer, described the *Streams* choreography as "good good good good movement." It was "sink-your-teeth-into movement" that was "trying to say something."[4]

Reading Williams's commentary on *Streams* almost thirty years after I joined the second company, I find the last part of his statement—"trying to say something"—compelling. I receive his words with the hindsight of the dancer I once was along with the ethnographic perspective from my decades of training as an anthropologist. What is this "something" that Ailey's work is trying to say? And how might an ethnographic reflection on the multiple meanings of blood memories aid in understanding how this effort in expression reflects the complexity of Black life? The canon of written work on Ailey is overwhelmed by writing that explores the ways in which the Ailey repertory reflects his cultural experience of growing up in the rural Black South.[5] This is important work, for sure, and it makes explicit how everyday gestures, ways of life, acts of communal solidarity and intimacy, and the imprint of labor and love can be articulated on the moving body.

I would like to consider the transference of the Black southern cultural archive to choreography meant for the concert stage as foundational to a long and varied history of performance ethnography. In this case, I mean performance ethnography in the sense of curated embodied acts that gain form and meaning by calling on cultural reference points. In this process, every detail signifies. The use of the fan in the "yellow" section of *Revelations* is not simply the gesture of cooling oneself on a hot day; rather, it is connected to an embodied archive that holds the personal history of the person fanning along with the collective history of their cultural landscape. In this way, how the fan is held, the tempo of the fanning, and the tilt of the dancer's head as it receives cooler air mark the distinction between waving a prop and signaling from where and from whom the movement comes. I never heard the word "ethnographic" used during my time at Ailey, but an ethos of organic research tied to a specific place, time, and people infused the pedagogy in our rehearsals.

The teaching moments in rehearsals for *Revelations* assumed that, in addition to our modern dance and ballet training, we were well versed in the comportment of the Black South. This cultural training, like dance training, develops certain skills, even if the ability to execute a seamless pirouette and that of navigating life with a distinct worldview seem wildly unrelated. My struggles with the choreography of the "yellow" section made me feel as if I somehow had failed at being in my Black-American-female body, and later as if I were a failed ethnographer unable to immerse myself in a culture presented to me as my own. *Streams* offered the possibility of expanding the definition of culture and ethnography. If many of the shapes I was asked to make with my body were the same across the two ballets but felt so different under my skin, could it be that I had more space to realize my own narrative in *Streams*? The abstraction of *Streams* provided a wider landscape in which I could locate myself, allowing me to see and feel what I was unable, at first, to grasp in the cultural specificity of *Revelations*.

I realized this expanded territory could include not only what I witnessed and learned growing up in Cincinnati, but also all that I had been exposed to after leaving home and living in a world outside my family and local community. In many ways, I understood "my culture" at this juncture to include the Black Midwest and the collective of young Black artists and students of which I now considered myself a part. Thus, my culture, as I experienced it, broadened to encompass the predominantly Black communities I was living among in New York City. I was in the process of self-making, and the language, aesthetic inspiration, and way of moving through the streets that I was learning were forms of socialization, providing a new blueprint for locating myself in the world. Black migration from the South to the North, from the South to the West, and from the Midwest to the East, and remigrations back and forth along any number of axes in the US have always involved cultural exchange and synthesis. Similar to ethnography, such movement requires immersion in a new place while remaining anchored in an older, more familiar location through which everything else is filtered. Like ethnographers, both Ailey and I discovered worlds and ways of being that we witnessed through the lens of our own geographic and cultural points of origin while marveling at how these new worlds offered the possibility for other ways of life.

Ailey left Texas for the West Coast in 1942, joining his mother, who had moved to Los Angeles in search of better work opportunities and life chances for herself and her son. A little more than a decade later, Ailey landed in New York City, where the Alvin Ailey American Dance Theater would eventually take root. Along his journey, he met choreographers and teachers who would play critical roles in his technical training and aesthetic exposure as a dance artist. This is visible in his choreographic works in which the techniques of Merce Cunningham, Katherine Dunham, Martha Graham, and, of course, Lester Horton can be tracked in the dancers' moving bodies. Another type of training, which could be called cultural training, is recognizable in works, such as *Blues Suite* and *Revelations*, that reflect Black southern life in leisure and worship, respectively. What I am curious about, however, is yet another type of training, one that is largely self-directed rather than emergent through the passing on of a technical skill for embodied mastery or through processes of enculturation. It is grounded in self-making and takes up as its methodology the tenets of Black study, as defined by Fred Moten and Stefano Harney:

> We are committed to the idea that study is what you do with other people. It's talking and walking around with other people, working, dancing, suffering, some irreducible

convergence of all three, held under the name of speculative practice. The notion of a rehearsal—being in a kind of workshop, playing in a band, in a jam session, or old men sitting on a porch, or people working together in a factory—there are these various modes of activity. The point of calling it "study" is to mark that the incessant and irreversible intellectuality of these activities is already present.[6]

The practice of Black study thus respects the fact of our speculative being in this world, where curiosity is the greatest teacher and training happens through ever-unfolding acts of relationality. Our selfhood takes shape in multiple contexts and in relationship to all life forms in the natural and built environment. Ailey's immersion in everyday acts with other beings—in his backyard in Rogers, Texas; in dance studios in Los Angeles and New York; in the homes of close and newly acquainted friends; in alleys; on dance-club floors; in bars; and in the space of his thoughts and feelings in his Black queer body—nourished his artistry. Ailey was the embodiment of Black study, and his creative legacy is a testament to the complexity of Black life and Black aliveness. We can identify and list the evidence of technical dance training and cultural history that has already been ranked and codified in Black dance.[7] The type of training that comes from living in the world with the sensibility of Black study, however, is not necessarily as legible since it reflects a personal interiority that may never be fully seen or touched. Desire, preference, passion, wonder, or the urgency of a will to experience life at both the socially constructed center and the resiliently innovative edges does not neatly map onto cultural patterns or familiar movement vocabularies. Skill means something different in the space of Black study, where the closest things to the concept of individual mastery are found in reciprocity, the humility of being a student, and a yearning to be with others. The training that requires Black study is preparation for a life that exists beyond performance, even as performance tries to replicate that life.

Ailey offers a challenge to the concepts of culture and the purely ethnographic when intersected by Black life. In fact, as a Black woman and anthropologist, I have come to understand the practice of ethnography to be, at its core, Black study. All the places Ailey called home and all the people he encountered left an enduring impact on him that accumulated to form the bricolage of his creative life. Bricolage, the process of making something out of what is available to you, is a technique of Black life—especially when that something is your existence in an anti-Black world. Ailey offers us the Black body as a bricolaged, living artifact—a combination of histories known and unknown, strategies for survival and innovation, practices of life affirmation and ecstasy, and the radiant residue of those who came before and left the essence of their aliveness on our bodies. But there are also the grooves we create and deepen as we make our way through the world in Black bodies that carry the past but also establish new cultural, embodied, and neurological pathways guided by our desire to make lives for ourselves. Our bodies hold the stories of self-exploration and all forms of training required for self-articulation. In true bricolage form, we make ourselves up. We draw from what has been handed to us and what has moved through us, along with what we seek and chase after, to craft a version of ourselves as a stay against all that has been socially preconfigured and politically orchestrated. I imagine Ailey and the poet Lucille Clifton (1936–2010) would have been great friends had they ever had the chance to spend time together. In arguably her most frequently recited poem, Clifton asks, "won't you celebrate with me / what i have shaped into / a kind of life?," and then later, "what did i see to be except myself? / i made it up / here on this bridge between / starshine and clay."[8]

Self-making or making ourselves up occurs within the multiple cultures we cross and requires an auto-ethnographic sensibility reliant on Black study. I found an ease of movement in *Streams*, despite it sharing much of the same dance vocabulary with *Revelations*, because its steps felt as if I were dancing on the bridge between starshine and clay. *Streams* resonated as the link between who I was and the possibilities for how I might shape myself. It was from this anchoring in my body that I was able to make my way back to *Revelations* and move from a lived experience that did not rely on the obligation to perform a legible version of Black culture.

NOTES

1. See, for example, Thomas F. DeFrantz, *Dancing Revelations: Alvin Ailey's Embodiment of African American Culture* (New York: Oxford University Press, 2004); and Brenda Dixon-Gottschild, *The Black Dancing Body: A Geography from Coon to Cool* (New York: Palgrave Macmillan, 2003).

2. Alvin Ailey, quoted in Dixon-Gottschild, *Black Dancing Body*, 279.

3. The critique of the unison choreography in *Streams* came from Deborah Jowitt, dance critic for the *Village Voice*. She went on to say that "*Streams* leaves an unpleasant taste—a sock-it-to-'em Broadway chorus that shamelessly wraps up the dance and bats it across the pit to make the crowd howl." Jowitt, quoted in Jennifer Dunning, *Alvin Ailey: A Life in Dance* (Cambridge, MA: Da Capo, 1996), 251.

4. Dudley Williams, quoted in Dunning, 251.

5. For less-referenced examples, see Joe Edward Hatfield, "Dancing Southern Diaspora: Alvin Ailey's Blood and the Backwardness of Quare Disidentification," *Text and Performance Quarterly* 37, no. 1 (June 2017): 51–67; and Lynne Fauley Emery, *Black Dance from 1619 to Today* (Trenton, NJ: Princeton Book Company, 1989).

6. Fred Moten and Stefano Harney, *The Undercommons: Fugitive Planning and Black Study* (New York: Minor Compositions, 2013), 110.

7. Brenda Dixon-Gottschild is an excellent reference in this regard; see her aforementioned *The Black Dancing Body* and *Digging the Africanist Presence in American Performance: Dance and Other Contexts* (Westport, CT: Praeger, 1998).

8. Lucille Clifton, "won't you celebrate with me," in *Collected Poems of Lucille Clifton, 1965–2010*, ed. Kevin Young and Michael S. Glaser (Rochester, NY: BOA Editions, 2012), 427. The full poem reads:

   won't you celebrate with me
   what i have shaped into
   a kind of life? i had no model.
   born in babylon
   both nonwhite and woman
   what did i see to be except myself?
   i made it up
   here on this bridge between
   starshine and clay,
   my one hand holding tight
   my other hand; come celebrate
   with me that everyday
   something has tried to kill me
   and has failed.

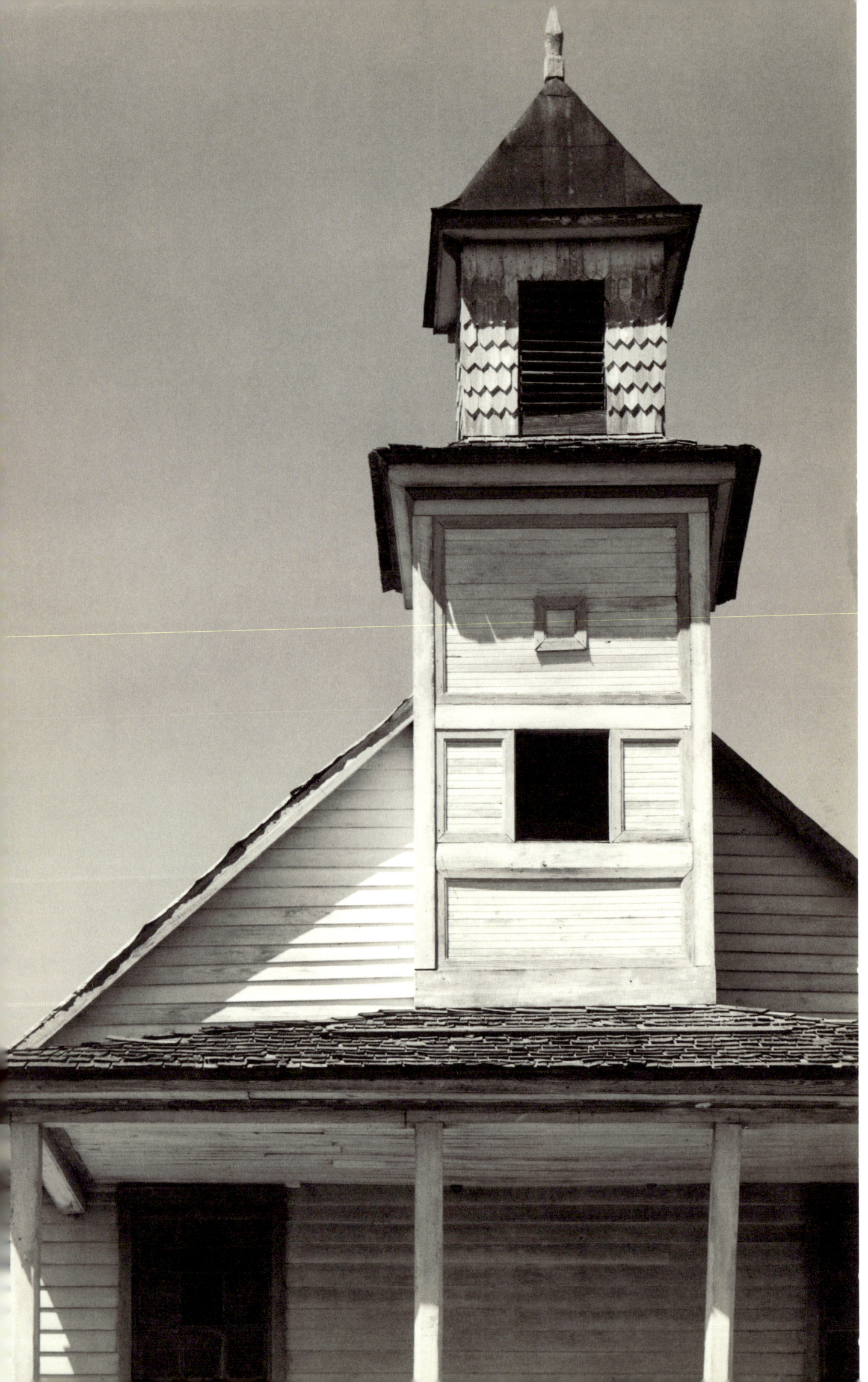

Horace D. Ballard

Elegant Mutinies

We learn about metaphor in grade school. We learn that metaphors are countable and uncountable nouns that name a relationship between states of being or things. We learn that metaphors are figures of speech without the use of the preposition "like" or the conjunction "as."

When we are older—perhaps crying to a friend on the telephone after heartbreak or listening to a sports announcer erupt into lyrical denouement over a goal—we learn about good metaphors. Good metaphors are semiotic rodeos that cleave us on the bone of that joint where the mind ends but our lives begin to see. No mere witty remark or observant quip, a good metaphor is the purposive magic of transfiguration. A good metaphor is a (dis)orientation or an elegant theft, a mutiny that helps us imagine our lives differently. Dance is a good metaphor for life as dance is breath adorned.

Susan Sontag surmised that "one cannot think without metaphors,"[1] and I find her certitude helpful. Thinking through metaphor aids an interpretation of Alvin Ailey as a conceptual practitioner in the field of Black aesthetics and in the ever-broadening field of American dance. The singular Adrienne Edwards has called us together in these pages. It is from the well of her rigorous example I draw. For as Edwards reminds us, "blackness is not simply matter for the expression of an artwork. Rather, blackness is a conceptual paradigm" that is at turns inherent, infiltrative, and rich with immanence.[2] Her articulation guides my rumination around the chief metaphor from which Ailey drew inspiration: the Black Church tradition.

There are innumerable good metaphors for calling forth and acknowledging divine power and numinous experience in the African diaspora. In the Americas, we often speak of "Black Church": a metonym that refers to the ethos and traditions of predominantly Black, mainline Protestant congregations, denominations, and liturgies in Canada, the Caribbean, South America, and the United States (fig. 1). These spaces formed in parallel to the Protestant and Catholic congregations that excluded and/or segregated Black parishioners in the eighteenth and nineteenth centuries.

The Black Church traditions Ailey knew emerged out of the Christian *doxa* used to justify colonialism and plantation economies. After collective actions for liberation in the late eighteenth and early nineteenth centuries threatened regional and global systems of production, the enslaved were forbidden from reading the Bible or gathering in worship. It was then that the land found a way to give back to those who labored and suffered for its abundance. Campfire and secret meetings and mud-scummed and wooden prayer

fig. 1

Walker Evans, *Negro Church*, 1936. Gelatin silver print, 5 7/16 × 3 7/16 in. (13.8 × 8.7 cm). Whitney Museum of American Art, New York; purchase, with funds from the Photography Committee, 97.68

houses in fallow pastures and marshy recesses became the tabernacles of the enslaved-elect. "Operat[ing] in the shadows," these surreptitious spaces staked out from red clay and black loam under evening air scented with swamp oak, pine, and magnolia became "resilient sites of resistance to various forms of white supremacy."[3] Processions, sorrow songs or spirituals, praise dancing, baptismal rites, revival, and glossolalia (speaking in tongues) all have their roots in the clandestine worship of enslaved believers. Central to these meetings and these practices we now call traditions was the collective voice of the people in song and the voice of the pastor, delivering the Word.

One of the signature attributes of Ailey's ballets was the music he chose—often pre-recorded and often a rendition of a Negro spiritual or its modern, jazz-age tessellation. As products of Second Great Awakening fervor and coded resistance, the spirituals are spells of metaphorical transfiguration for a context of longing, belonging, and (dis)place-ment (fig. 2). They operate through riff and reformulation of the seventeenth-century syntax of the King James Bible to bend time and transpose the "nation within a nation" of the enslaved into biblical forebears with ancient resolve. By "focusing on the power and martyrdom of such mighty figures of transcendence as Moses, David, and Jesus,"[4] Black Church emphasizes the embodied yearning for liberation and "great works" of justice, retribution, redemption, sorrow, joy, hope, and faith both in the pew and in the street. As Henry Louis Gates Jr. makes plain, amid a milieu of consistent and continuous "instability where African American families could be torn apart at a moment's notice, the enslaved found a rock in the religion and practices they developed in communion with one another."[5] These histories and their remembrance in performance counsel, command, and expect that God intervenes in individual lives and in the world as a healer, deliverer, and sustainer. Amid the quotidian trials and sociopolitical tribulations that befall individuals, multiple generations of a familial unit, or a community, a Black God is "a delivering God."[6] In fixing the eternal character of God, Black Church serves as a kind of semiotic mutiny of religious presence.

As Edwards contends, "Blackness, in the fullest sense of the word, has a seemingly unlimited usefulness in the history of modern art."[7] What Ailey accomplished in returning to Black Church semiotics is to provide us with an "aesthetic counterpoint" within the pieties of modernism; "an experience in which to feel-think about how we have arrived at this moment and with this insight consider where we might go."[8] In a similar vein, I wish to underscore the living, ever-present existence of these metaphors in our contemporary moment. In my designation of Black Church as a metonym, I am calling attention to at least four operative metaphors, which could also be described as assemblies of relation that we must hold concomitantly. All these Ailey experienced (as do many of us Black Protestants of faith) as metaphorical and mutinous contingencies—a repertoire of possible opportunities, resists, and affects to be drawn upon.

The first concerns Black Church as an operative, extended metaphor that encompasses the sense of communion, family, and fellowship that endures across shared histories of displacement, enslaved labor, violence, and courage within and beyond the wake of the Plantationocene. Second, Black Church functions as a cradle for the multi-sited yet collective birthplace(s) of soul performance—what W. E. B. Du Bois called "the most beautiful expression of human experience born this side the seas."[9] Third, we must acknowledge the ways in which Black respectability politics around binary gender expression and patrician gender performances of dress, gesture, mannerisms, participation, and voice are still felt to be synonymous with Black Church spaces. Cisgender, heterosexual, masc voices maintain a compounded privilege and prominence in Black Church that stem from systemic male privilege and misogyny in society, as well as much-researched eviscerations of Black familial units and the preponderance of mortal violence on the bodies of Black men. However, all cisgender, masc voices are not equal. The elevation of "pastor" to the father figure of the community and the quiet assignment or overt demotion of other masc persons, especially those involved in the artistic auxiliaries of the church, to subservient roles (what Langston Hughes termed in a short story, the audacious musical work in the church of the "brilliant queer"[10]) have deep roots and lasting ramifications. I urge us to hold Marlon Rachquel Moore's incisive consideration of the "cluttered" metaphors, contradictions, and ironies at play in "the triangulated relationship between [queers], black patriarchy and the historic institution of the black church."[11]

Fourth, Black Church is a facet of a larger, gothic architectonic of relationality that cannot be defined. We call this relationality the South. Multiple, co-constitutive discourses collide, rupture, and ultimately demarcate in their junctive and disjunctive

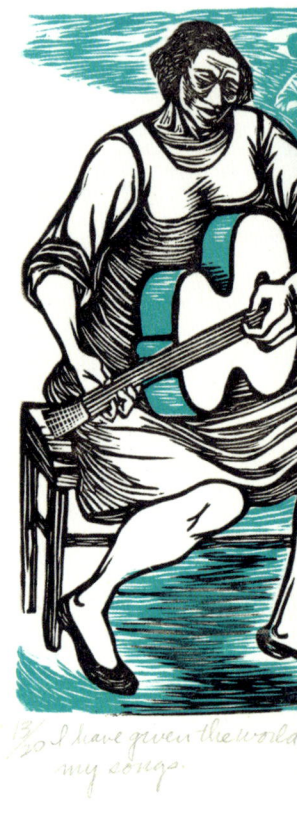

fig. 2

Elizabeth Catlett, *I have given the world my songs*, 1947, printed 1989. Linoleum cut, 10 1/16 × 7 1/4 in. (25.6 × 18.4 cm). Printed by Robert Blackburn Printmaking Workshop, ed. no. 13/20. Whitney Museum of American Art, New York; purchase, with funds from the Print Committee, 95.193

tension that landscape of imagined home and factual exile that cannot be satisfactorily charted, but can be claimed (as I do) as home. Since the physical borders of the South are disputed, if unmappable, the region functions more as an ideological territory than a physical place. As such, its heartland and peripheries can be framed only through critical discourses that are themselves mutable. Some of these discourses include addiction, climate precarity, evangelicalism, migration, speech patterns and patois, carceral colonies, mining, ecological fecundity, river deltas, music, cinema, respectability politics, real and perceived racial violence, demographics around education and health, and the meta-narratives of historical fact, historical memory, and myth that overlay and compound their inextricable binds.

As some began to migrate away from the unmappable, yet real conditions and infiltrations of land and labor and into new but still uncertain lives at the end of the nineteenth century, the rural idioms of Black Church migrated with them. We see this most clearly in the annual occurrence of revival that still takes place in the "waiting season" of August and early September before cash crops are ready to be harvested, even though few communities remain solely structured around agrarian labor. The migratory diasporas and the reformulated, communal nodes that remained in the Black Belt became aesthetic sites of becoming and disjuncture. A dispersed people newly settled began to consider having a "church home," a marker of Black respectability and proxy-permanence.

The blues emerged in this tumultuous period. The Greek-chorus collectivity of Gospel under bondage began to walk in concert with a vanguard expressionism attuned to soliloquy. As artist Ja'Tovia Gary describes, the blues constitute "a new social order: the ideas being expressed became those of the individual" in their experience of deliverance, hardships, physical and psychological pain, labor, love, unrequited love, and the spirit.[12] The intervention of the divine was still expected; the presence of the ancestors to provide strength and intuition remained close. "Provocative, transgressive and often queer," the blues transmigrated communal pain into the living bodies of "solo performance figures ... primarily Black women, backed by an ensemble of musicians." In the blues we see the "new reality of sexual agency that was previously denied Black women during the period of enslavement" in concert with the growing use of euphemism and metaphor to treat the complexities of religious expression, sensuality, and upheaval under Jim Crow.[13] As in Black Church, the blues operate by amplifying the body to the place of high altar: the body is an organizing site of multiple and competing signifiers of experience. It is also true that the emergence of the blues marked the emergence of Black spirituality being commodified into cultural spectacle. It was also a moment of metamorphosis for the Holy Spirit. That which was once deliverer migrated into the role of confidant and companion.

History makes plain how our grandparents and great-grandparents needed these romantic metaphors and embodied performances of recycled and reclaimed witness for survival. Even after the de jure end of enslavement, the terror did not cease. The devaluing of Black life did not cease. The need for deliverance of self and community did not cease. Black existence has always been, and remains, precarious in the hemisphere. From the last decades of the nineteenth century into the modern era, the divine has remained an active participant in all aspects of Black life, from the juke joint to the bedroom, from the emergency room or the prison cell to the pulpit. It is out of this precarity and preciousness of life that the "holy profane" dichotomy of Black experience arises. The metaphor we have to name this co-constitutive alliance between the sacred and the secular in individual and collective Black lives is called *soul*.

The Negro spirituals tell us that soul is a physiological positioning in the presence of God that is *just like fire, shut up in the bones*. In the first stanza of her poem "Parable," Louise Glück (1943–2023) yokes soul to bodily movement when her speaker greets readers with:

> First divesting ourselves of worldly goods, as St. Francis teaches,
> in order that our souls not be distracted
> by gain and loss, and in order also
> that our bodies be free to move
> easily ...[14]

Du Bois mordantly called the moans, leaps, and flutterings of soul "the frenzy" of the spirit.[15] James Brown insists you either have it or you don't. But you need it and can get it, because you

> Know we need it (soul power)
> We got to have it (soul power)
> Know we want it (soul power)
> Got to have it (soul power)[16]

Soul, according to Brown, equals a kind of power via self-possession. A broken body, a weary mother, an abandoned lover in the dark—all cry out and sing forth, with soul. The prophetic power of Brown's painterly call-and-response foments the co-constitutive relationship between body and spirit, as in

> Let your body pop
> And let your feelings flow
> Raise up, get yourself together
> And drive that funky soul![17]

Soul is an errant, uncountable metaphor that names the holy/profane relationship between body and spirit. Soulfulness becomes the quality of alignment between the two. Hymn, myth, and parable across cultures foretell and warn that to catch a god or to be caught, clutched, or raptured by a spirit is to burn, to be outraged, and sometimes to incur the wrath of other gods. (One can also undergo a metamorphosis and be turned into birds, bats, flowers, maritime calamities, or, once in a while, stars, but I digress.) The point is that spirit changes the body. And in the process of the body *popping*, the bones *burning*, and the feelings *flowing*, soul is hailed as a conveyance toward an interactive, sensate, and spectacular self. To be soulful is to have a body, in Daphne Brooks's words, "in dissent": a self-alert to the spectacular ways of "the experience of 'double-consciousness'—this feeling of two-ness,' of being both 'an American' and 'a Negro,'" and of how the leveraging or leaning into this "dissonant condition" can be used "to forge discursive as well as embodied insurgency."[18]

Ailey was born in 1931 in rural East Texas, only two generations from the muscle memory of enslavement. Three years before his death, Ailey reflected in an interview:

> The first ballets [that I choreographed] were ballets about my black roots. I lived in Texas . . . until I was 12 . . . so I have lots of what I call blood memories . . . about Texas, blues and spirituals and gospel music, ragtime music . . . And I had very intense feelings about all those things. So the first ballets that I made when I came to New York were based on those feelings . . . all of this is a part of my blood memory: my uncles, my family, my mother, all were in these churches . . . very intense, very personal.[19]

Ailey's kenning, his "blood memories," is an utterance of soul. The expression gestures toward the ravel of family and the sense of home/place. His archive of specificities ("my uncles, my family, my mother") and incomprehension ("very intense feelings," "all those things") saturates his sonic and muscle memory, providing a mixtape of colors, instrumentations, tonal shifts, and vibes that incapsulate a life. Today, the Alvin Ailey American Dance Theater bears the weight of memory, as "nearly all of [Ailey's] dances had some basis in a relationship, feeling or event that he experienced."[20] From Ailey's words, we can glean a facet of his process, which is not, for example, a question of how the blues function in his choreography but rather a question of how *memories of* "Texas, blues, and spirituals and gospel" function in his body. As distinct yet interrelated sites of soul music, these genres emerged from the painterly and textural metaphors of Black Church even as they abstract and center "questions of value and that ever-elusive, peculiarly American notion of freedom—life, liberty, and the pursuit of happiness—that always somehow escapes us."[21] As such, the phrase "blood memories" is itself a metaphor: one that foments a kind of integral, or perhaps soulful, correspondence between experience, memory, ritual, and spirit, which Ailey channels through the lexicon of dance.

◇

Here is something I hold, fashioned from equal parts memory and metaphor. It is the miracle of Dudley Williams (figs. 3a,b) in "A Song for You," the first variation from Ailey's solo ballet *Love Songs* (1972). Permit me to describe what my heart recalls.

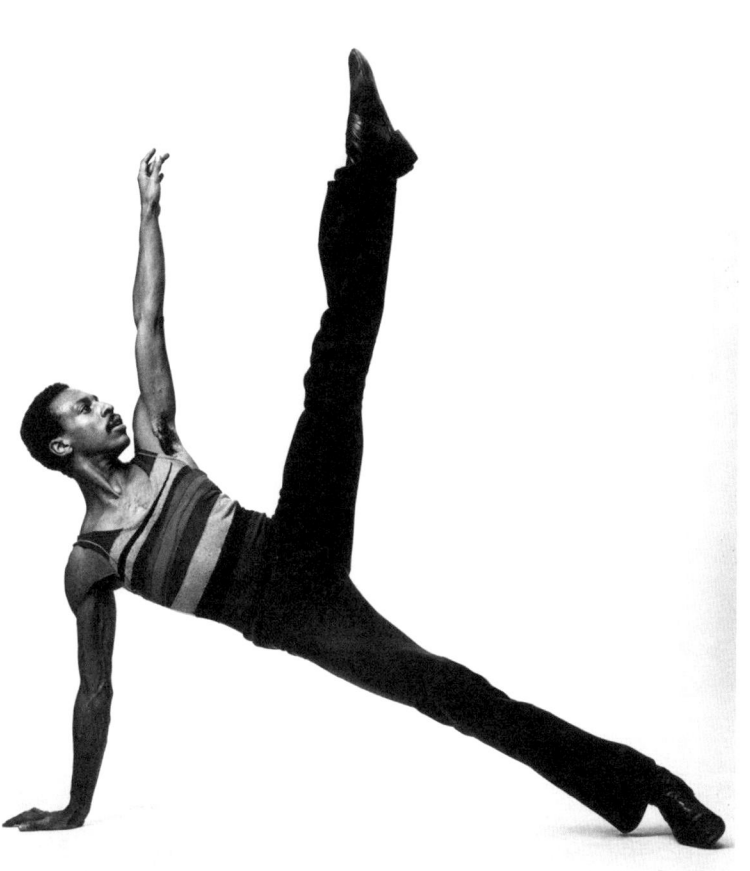
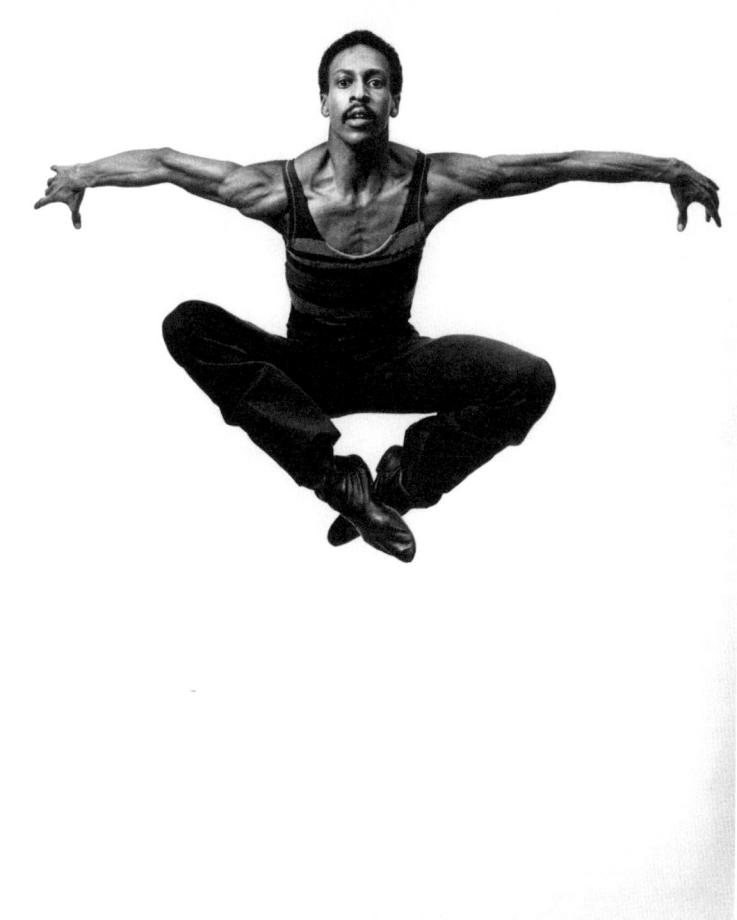

But we're alone now
And I'm singing this song to you [22]

figs. 3a,b

Jack Mitchell, "*The Road of the Phoebe Snow*": Dudley Williams, 1969. National Museum of African American History and Culture, Washington, DC. Jack Mitchell Photography of the Alvin Ailey American Dance Theater Collection

With eyes trained on a vision beyond the audience, Williams revolves from the *fouetté* into *écarté derrière* with the leg *en l'air*, and slowly cantilevers the thigh down into a high lunge, his arms in second position wrapping across his torso as the turn crests, his collarbone through spine luxuriating with the bass line into *passé en relevé* then *tendu passé*. Williams then sweeps the leg to reset the stance to *developpé front*. Breath. The feet for a moment are rooted, the toes spread wide on the boards.

His torso quivers: an isolation of the upper line from the hips. The air sparkles. The downstage leg brushes into an arc that lifts toward the sky, moving into *tendu derrière* from a closed second position rather than the open fifth! (Like, dude, how?!) So human and impossible and miraculous. It is only now that one's eye notices Williams is wearing the color blue. As his body arcs into an arabesque, there is the sustaining susurrus of breath. His torso begins to lift upupup ever so slowly through the sternum and up through the throat as he becomes parabolic: a blue ship with a black mast, tossed, pitching in the molecular sea of hushed space.

Then, a rush of air as he exits the breath and collapses inward, into a closed *plié*, his torso twisted forward, opposite the hips. In the most sumptuous six count, Williams then begins to rise. As he lifts, his head begins to pour back, so that as he rises, he releases, pantomiming falling. And then (with what possible capacity, except grace?) Williams extends his arms in a vertical extension so slowly that you think your brain broke and time itself has been bewitched by those arms, longer than any highway ever traveled, growing more golden the further they recede into Leonardo da Vinci's theory of landscape . . . Breath. He h-o-l-d-s this slow-motion somersault of an inversion for the two-beat resolution of the phrase.

Elegant Mutinies

> I love you in a place
> Where there's no space or time
> I love you for my life
> You're a friend of mine
> And when my life is over
> Remember when we were together
> We were alone
> And I was singing this song to you[23]

The heaven of love. And its loss. This is Ailey's theme and Williams's testimony. This is how God stepped out and made a universe from discarded parts of God's self. This is Lucifer, pleading and petulant, as the former beloved star surveys the black expanse of a new dimension not yet named. In the conceptual diptych of a choreographer's idea and a dancer's act—a pairing of simulacra and approbated theft—Ailey and Williams provide us with the wondrous, visible metaphor of metamorphoses. A human becoming avian before our eyes.

I began ballet and gymnastics when I was three years old (fig. 4). Ailey—his bearded, leonine image, his mercurial nature, his body of work (fig. 5)—has been a source of (dis)orientation for me since childhood. His autobiography was the first memoir I ever owned, and to this day, my favorite ballet is Ailey's *Cry* (1971; see pp. 216–21). Although I no longer dance, I remain curious about the network of ideas and metaphors behind Ailey's impetus to create. I am specifically interested in his conceptual relationship to romanticism, which is itself an existential stance toward history, metaphor, and memory. Can Ailey's attentiveness to the working and reworking of metaphor be a kind of conceptual act? I think so.

Ailey lived, fretted, ghosted, spun out, loved, made, and worked in the blessed assurance of the tangibility of metaphors and metamorphosis. He was drawn to French and Spanish language and literature as a child, and he studied Romance languages and comparative literature at the University of California, Los Angeles, while beginning his training with the American dancer and choreographer Lester Horton.[24] I think it is plausible that an education in textual analysis and semantics is never lost, only transferred into an exploration of other semiotic modes. Ailey choreographed the way so many of us read and write—that is, to understand one another, and ourselves, in relation to history and the world.

In Ailey's pluralistic return to Black Church as a site from which to excavate and shape an affective oeuvre, we glean a foretaste of art practices in our current era. Ailey, like many contemporary artists today, navigated the entangled, often asynchronous possibilities of what Edwards has termed a "lush conceptualism." As Edwards explains, "In lush conceptualist works, the object is thick, dense, multivalent, and polyvocal rather than dematerialized. Such a move reflects the conceptual complexity of the context in which the artist exists and the works arise, particularly when it concerns questions of belonging, identity, history, and sociopolitical systems, while simultaneously expressing an ambivalence about maneuvering, circumnavigating, and reimagining them."[25]

In Joseph Kosuth's essay "1975," the artist writes, "What began in the mid-sixties as an analysis of the context of specific objects (or propositions) and correspondingly the questions of function, has forced us now, ten years later, to focus our attentions on the society and/or culture in which that specific object operates."[26] Terming this shift in the explorations and interrogations of conceptualism a "radicalization," Kosuth acknowledges the need for art to stand in relation to the varied cultural contexts of its materials and its time.[27] Moreover, scholarly interventions over the past twenty years by Edwards—as well as Torkwase Dyson, Darby English, Ashley James, Kellie Jones, Naima J. Keith, Fred Moten, Valerie Cassel Oliver, Legacy Russell, Franklin Sirmans, Zoé Whitley, and others—have demonstrated that Black artists were on the vanguard of abstract and conceptual practices and were some of the first to be interested in questions and propositions of function and affective intensity. Unlike their white counterparts in the conceptual discipline, Black makers could not afford to disentangle analysis from political liberation, and thus, they worked at the porous and slippery intersection of form and politics. Conceptual tools of abstraction and repetition, per Edwards, "offer in a durational fashion everything representation obscures—the fact of our destabilization, the hard edge of our precarity."[28]

Coming to prominence as the monomyths of modernism crumbled, Ailey's artistry was at the fore of the turn Kosuth articulates. Moreover, as Ailey's attentions emerged out of the metaphors of memory, which are already revisited, reworked, redacted, and

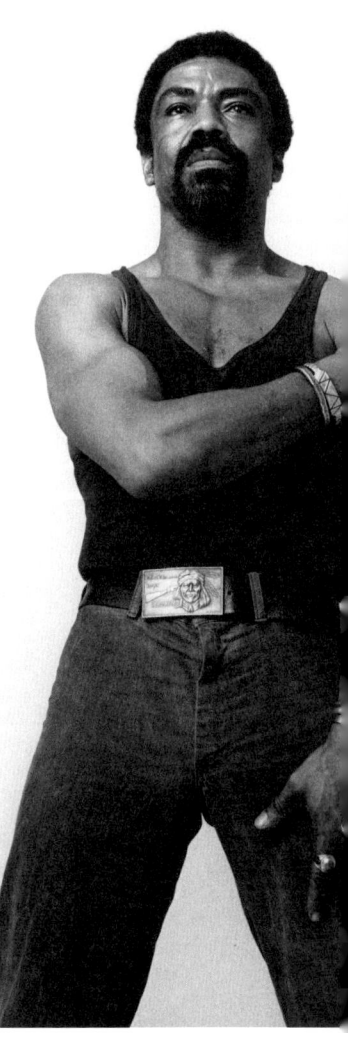

fig. 4

The author's dance shoes, ca. 2007. Courtesy the author

fig. 5

Jack Mitchell, *Portrait of Alvin Ailey*, 1975. National Museum of African American History and Culture, Washington, DC. Jack Mitchell Photography of the Alvin Ailey American Dance Theater Collection

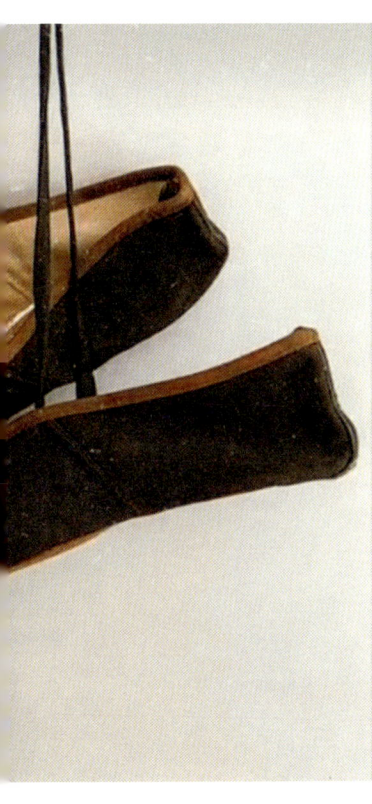

distilled propositions toward individual and collective experience, his unremitting excavation and testing of constraints, forms, motifs, patterns, rules, and structures of classical dance place him in dialogue with contemporary expressions of conceptual practice. The adorned breath of the bodies inhabiting Ailey's dances flows along a continuous ridge at the apex of conceptual and metaphorical acts. Conceiving of Ailey's practice as a conceptual one renders him perhaps more clearly to our estimations in hindsight. We can set aside the commercial and commodified aspects of racial representation and glimpse the man in the studio, turning before a mirror, gleaning from his cultural past tactics for negotiating the critical realities of his present.

Dance emphasizes the distinctions of reception between looking/learning and reading/performing, between dance as a visual phenomenon and dance as a vehicle for the communication of content. A useful pathway to exploring Ailey's conceptual practice might be to look at the alphabet of movements that became the basis for what we might call "Ailey technique." From Horton á la the Denishawn School of Dancing and Related Arts founded in 1915 by Ruth St. Denis and Ted Shawn, Ailey gleaned a toolkit of movements found in the ecstatic, sacred rituals of the Eurasiatic diasporas. These include cantilevered or lateral extensions, lunges and off-center balances, and flat backs that when swung upward, propel the upper torso into full revolutions. From Katherine Dunham, Ailey refined a syntax derived from African-diasporic and Indigenous Caribbean knowledge. Perhaps most apparent is an emphasis on grounded, supported strength that roots itself in the earth and radiates up through the heels into the spine and then branches out into polycentric movements or isolations. As the earth is the giver of strength, the language of release, of fall and recovery, is central, as is the reliance on collective, passed energy among members of a group of dancers.

All these components are present in Ailey's repertory, although they perhaps are most recognizable in the ballets Ailey himself built and circulated in and out of as a dramatis persona during his lifetime: *Blues Suite* (1958; see pp. 156–59), *Revelations* (1960; see pp. 160–73), and *Hermit Songs* (1961; see pp. 180–82). As the enslaved mutinied against the invective not to praise, Ailey resisted the abstracted, if ironic, strictures of what expressions should be the subject of modern dance. The economical and unique orientations drawn from Dunham and Horton that essentialize a global accounting of the sacred are leveraged as part of Ailey's lexicon of propositions that convey emotion in ballets centered around imparting Negro soul. In this translation of ethnomusicological specificities into expressions of Black Church, Ailey's individual memory becomes universal metaphor, and that metaphor becomes a visible performance, a love gift for the audience to interpret. This mutinous metamorphosis reminds one of traditions of ekphrasis—the metaphorical sleight of hand in which one art form answers or stands in for another. When ethnocentric movements are removed from their sites of discourse, they become impressionistic and modular orientations, which must be reconceived, reworked, and then deployed as metaphor. Ailey's choreography thus becomes a kind of *sacra scriptura*: what is written on the heart is manifest in the breath, and thus, the capacity of the body to expand into line.

In her review of Ailey's *Memoria* (1979; see p. 255) in the *New York Times*, Anna Kisselgoff reflected: "'Write about what you know,' young writers are told. Choreographers have had more difficulty taking the same lesson to heart. This is not because they are bereft of words but because they are untrammeled by words.... The great legends of the world beckon for reinterpretation, the universal themes lend themselves to restatement.... [A]s Alvin Ailey has just shown in his latest premiere, . . . a choreographer's best work is frequently his most personal. . . . It is a dance of both exultation and quiet but deep feeling."[29]

Kisselgoff recognizes *soul* at work. The dancers in *Memoria*, as in Ailey's other seventy-nine repertory ballets, are figures of speech, serving as linguistic possibilities in the expression of a relationship, feeling, or event that he experienced. As Nizan Shaked reminds us, "[C]onceptualists expanded their dialogue with a modernist avant-garde" through the late 1960s and into the 1970s, drawing on civil rights– and Vietnam-era debates and public actions to employ "a range of conceptualist typologies that focused on the politics of the art object, its circulation, context, and other ideological frameworks that gave it meaning, and expanded it into a broad set of practices."[30] Ailey infused the rising tide of abstraction during this era with an expressionistic, sculptural profundity that circles around the mystical nature of everyday life. In this vein, Ailey walked a different path than Merce Cunningham (although it is important to note that he was influenced by Cunningham's ethos of complex, intellectual games of precision in which music, audience, and the physical limits of the stage were all up for renegotiation in the moment and at the site of performance).[31] Rather than an imaginative construction zone or playground with assorted components and modalities, Ailey imagined a theater—a forum as old as human civilization in which the dancer(s) makes visible the emotional truth and witness of the congregation and the audience is polis and chorus, in witness to the truth of the stories unfolding. In this way, Ailey offers a different form of conceptual practice than the *doxa* of advanced, prescriptive measures that question the very nature of art. Ailey gives us a kind of romantic conceptualism around composition and emotive transcription that dissects and synthesizes the semiotic systems of Black Church and ballet.

Years on, I realize that what we have been gifted in Ailey's oeuvre is the elegant mutiny of metaphor. By means cultural, intellectual, physical, and psychological, Ailey's great ballets and variations offer unruly, abstracted slippages of analogy between embodied acts, his personal ghosts, and the histories and tropes of the Black Church tradition. What we can locate in Ailey's work is not a corrective of conceptual practice but an antithesis that aimed to bring "blood memory"/soul and the intersectional politics of race, gender, sexuality, and faith into the discipline of conceptual practice to be analyzed, reworked, and remade. It is this tradition—and Ailey's incisive, visual extractions from it as a means of providing the audience with a form of poetic truth, informed by experience and imagination—that I have tried to engage. To get at Ailey we must attend to the metaphor of Black Church as a palimpsest of Black identity. We must attend to the elegant, righteous, and lush mutiny of making art in a broken world.

NOTES

1. Susan Sontag, *AIDS and Its Metaphors* (New York: Farrar, Straus, and Giroux, 1989), 5.

2. Adrienne Edwards, *Blackness in Abstraction*, exh. cat. (London: Pace Gallery, 2016), n.p.

3. Henry Louis Gates Jr., *The Black Church: This Is Our Story, This Is Our Song* (New York: Penguin, 2021), 65.

4. Gates, 69–70.

5. Gates, 68–69.

6. Quoted by Larry G. Murphy in Gates, 65.

7. Edwards, *Blackness in Abstraction*.

8. Adrienne Edwards, "The Alchemy of Issues," in *Whitney Biennial 2022: Quiet As It's Kept*, ed. David Breslin and Adrienne Edwards, exh. cat. (New York: Whitney Museum of American Art, 2022), 106.

9. W. E. B. Du Bois, *The Souls of Black Folk* (1903; New York: Bantam, 1989), 178.

10. Langston Hughes, "Blessed Assurance" (1963), in *Short Stories [of] Langston Hughes*, ed. Akiba Sullivan Harper (New York: Hill & Wang, 1996), 231–36.

11. Marlon Rachquel Moore, "Black Church, Black Patriarchy, and the 'Brilliant Queer': Competing Masculinities in Langston Hughes's 'Blessed Assurance,'" *African American Review* 42, nos. 3–4 (Fall–Winter 2008): 501.

12. Ja'Tovia Gary, "Artist's Questionnaire: Ja'Tovia Gary Sets Her Sights on Love," interview by Yasmina Price, *New York Times*, August 30, 2023, nytimes.com/2023/08/30/t-magazine/jatovia-gary-moma.html.

13. Gary, "Artist's Questionnaire."

14. Louise Glück, "Parable," in *Faithful and Virtuous Night* (New York: Farrar, Straus and Giroux, 2014), 3.

15. Du Bois, *Souls of Black Folk*, 134.

16. James Brown, vocalist, "Soul Power," by James Brown, recorded January 26, 1971, with the J.B.'s and Fred Wesley, on the album *Soul Classics*, King Records, 1972.

17. James Brown, vocalist, "People Get Up and Drive Your Funky Soul," by Charles Bobbit, James Brown, St. Clair Pinckney, and Fred Wesley, recorded between 1967 and 1973, on the *Slaughter's Big Rip-Off* soundtrack, Polydor Records, 1973.

18. Daphne A. Brooks, *Bodies in Dissent: Spectacular Performances of Race and Freedom, 1850–1910* (Durham, NC: Duke University Press, 2006), 3.

19. Alvin Ailey, quoted in Brenda Dixon-Gottschild, *The Black Dancing Body: A Geography from Coon to Cool* (New York: Palgrave Macmillan, 2003), 279.

20. "Memoria," Repertory, Alvin Ailey American Dance Theater, accessed August 24, 2023, https://www.alvinailey.org/performances/repertory/memoria.

21. Edwards, "Alchemy of Issues," 104.

22. Donny Hathaway, vocalist, "A Song for You," by Leon Russell, recorded 1971, on the album *Donny Hathaway*, Atco, 1971.

23. Hathaway, "A Song for You."

24. See Jennifer Dunning, *Alvin Ailey: A Life in Dance* (Reading, MA: Addison-Wesley, 1996), 35, 43; see also Alvin Ailey and A. Peter Bailey, *Revelations: The Autobiography of Alvin Ailey*, 2nd ed. (New York: Citadel, 1997), 35–39, 44–45.

25. Edwards, "Alchemy of Issues," 105.

26. Joseph Kosuth, "1975," *The Fox*, no. 2 (1975): 89.

27. Kosuth, 89.

28. Edwards, "Alchemy of Issues," 106.

29. Anna Kisselgoff, "Dance View: Alvin Ailey's Homage to Joyce Trisler," review of *Memoria*, choreographed by Alvin Ailey, New York City Center, *New York Times*, December 16, 1979.

30. Nizan Shaked, *The Synthetic Proposition: Conceptualism and the Political Referent in Contemporary Art* (Manchester, UK: Manchester University Press, 2017), 149.

31. At the same moment that Jerome Robbins was putting the idioms of immigrant social halls and tenement streets on view in film and in Broadway houses, the same movements criticized and feared in real life, applauded in the dark hush; at the same moment that Cunningham was concurrently serving an abstracted sense of movement, one aligned with chance and near misses, a dance rigorous and learned in imperfection; and at the same moment that the New York City Ballet—the juggernaut established by Lincoln Kirstein and George Balanchine to bring concert dance to its modernist pinnacle in the postwar rise of New York—was coming into flower, this is the moment Ailey is giving church. Each of these figures were "brilliant queers." Yet, only Ailey and Robbins actively called upon the audience to bring their everyday lives into the auditorium and serve as denizen and witness to the ways high art is a heightened but insistent metaphor for the struggles and mercies of the quotidian.

Uri McMillan

The Rhythm of Life

Alvin Ailey's Queer Gesture

This essay reconsiders choreographer Alvin Ailey and his eponymous company in the context of the late 1970s, specifically during the glossy halcyon days of disco—a polarizing cultural phenomenon rarely discussed alongside Ailey's soulful repertory. I turn to two legendary spatial sites in New York City: the funky Nuyorican Poets Café on the Lower East Side and the posh Midtown nightclub Studio 54. Admittedly, both venues could not be further apart in their social purpose and attendant cultural memory. The former began in 1973 as a living room salon in the East Village apartment of Puerto Rican poet Miguel Algarín (1941–2020); it eventually became a vital theatrical forum for poets, playwrights, and musicians of color, particularly Black and Puerto Rican artists, even as its queerness was subsumed for masculinist cultural imperatives.[1] Studio 54, in contrast, was a glitzy nightclub that opened in a former television studio in 1977. It immediately became known for its hedonistic, sexually charged atmosphere, a heady cocktail-like mixture of fashion, music, and celebrity where queerness circulated freely and often extravagantly. Despite the two venues' divergence, Ailey's ghosting presence on *both* is a remarkable historical occurrence that has largely gone unnoticed, virtually elided in the cultural genealogies surrounding them.

I utilize a performance-studies methodological approach to examine these disparate scenes, primarily because such an analytical lens recognizes the ultimate disappearance of embodied acts, not as a so-called lack, but as fundamental to how we study them. Instead of privileging the liveness that comes with firsthand viewing of such events, now an impossibility in both cases, I attend to the lingering traces accompanying these acts, including textual and visual supplements.[2] However, I also read outside that official documentation by imagining how audiences in that historical milieu absorbed those dances and, by extension, how the latter rematerialize in the present moment. In doing so, I concur with theorist José Esteban Muñoz that "for queers, the gesture and its aftermath, the ephemeral trace, matter more than traditional modes of evidencing lives and politics."[3] Thus, this essay reconceives Ailey's disco-inflected gestural lexicon as a portal that connects a prismatic queer past to its illuminating and ever-unfolding future.

In the late 1970s, Ailey began a friendship with Algarín, cofounder of the Nuyorican Poets Café. Both men frequented the Blarney Stone, a bar near the Port Authority Bus Terminal, and this likely is where they initially met. At first, they may seem an improbable pair, given their differences. Ailey, for example, was a gay man, even if he was not able to be fully "out" as one, and at times, he was sexually adventurous. Algarín's sexuality remains less transparent, more a matter of speculation than fact. Ailey was born in rural Rogers, Texas; he moved to Los Angeles with his mother when he was eleven, eventually encountering dance as an art form. Algarín was born in Santurce, Puerto Rico, migrating with his family at nine to the Lower East Side of Manhattan. Ailey briefly enrolled in college, first at the University of California, Los Angeles (UCLA), to study languages, and considered becoming a teacher before leaving to pursue dance fully. Algarín, in contrast, earned a doctorate in comparative literature at Rutgers University in New Brunswick, New Jersey, where he eventually taught for three decades. And yet, despite their dissimilar upbringings and career trajectories, they undoubtedly shared a mutual appreciation of their respective roles as highly visible artistic ambassadors—Ailey for Black modern dance and Algarín for the Nuyorican movement. Both were cultural emissaries attempting to translate specific vernacular and embodied forms into digestible works that celebrated diasporic traditions while appealing to broad audiences. And we can imagine that part of what they bonded over—while sipping liquor in a dimly lit dive bar where no one recognized them—was navigating the psychological (and financial) duress accompanying such a mandate.

After all, for the Alvin Ailey American Dance Theater and Ailey himself, the late 1970s—specifically 1977 to 1979—were both a celebratory time and one of fiscal and personal hardship that put immense pressure on both. The company's budget had tripled to $3 million from 1973 to 1978, a testament perhaps to the popularity of the company and, concomitantly, the heightened ambition and scale of its compelling performances. Yet the company had a "worrisome deficit" in 1977 that forced it to cancel a two-week engagement that June.[4] Nevertheless, the increasingly recognized cultural institution hit an important milestone in 1978, celebrating its twentieth anniversary. And on October 18, 1979, a ribbon-cutting ceremony was held for its new theater-district headquarters in the Minskoff Building on Broadway, between Forty-Fourth and Forty-Fifth Streets, a three-story complex replete with four large studios, a corner office for Ailey, and "long-awaited showers!"[5] Ailey was also embraced as a purveyor of modern dance by his peers, earning the prestigious Capezio Dance Award in 1979, one of the three major prizes in American dance at the time. Indeed, that year's tour schedule confirmed the company's local *and* global stature: in addition to performing two seasons at New York City Center, the company embarked on a two-month, eleven-city tour of Europe that summer. However, while on tour with the company in Luxembourg in October of that year, Ailey learned of the tragic death of his friend and fellow dancer Joyce Trisler.[6] While processing his grief, he developed the elegiac piece *Memoria* (1979; see p. 255) as a tribute to "the joy … the beauty …

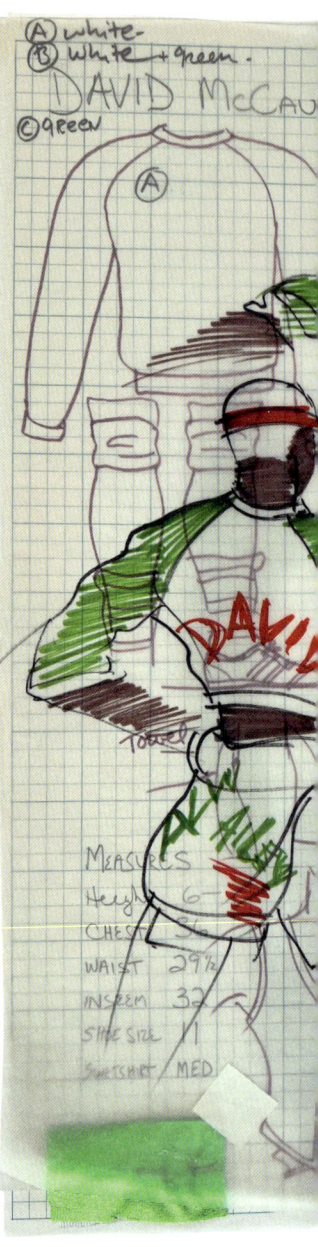

fig. 1

Allan Tannenbaum, *Fiorucci Dancers at Studio 54*, April 26, 1977

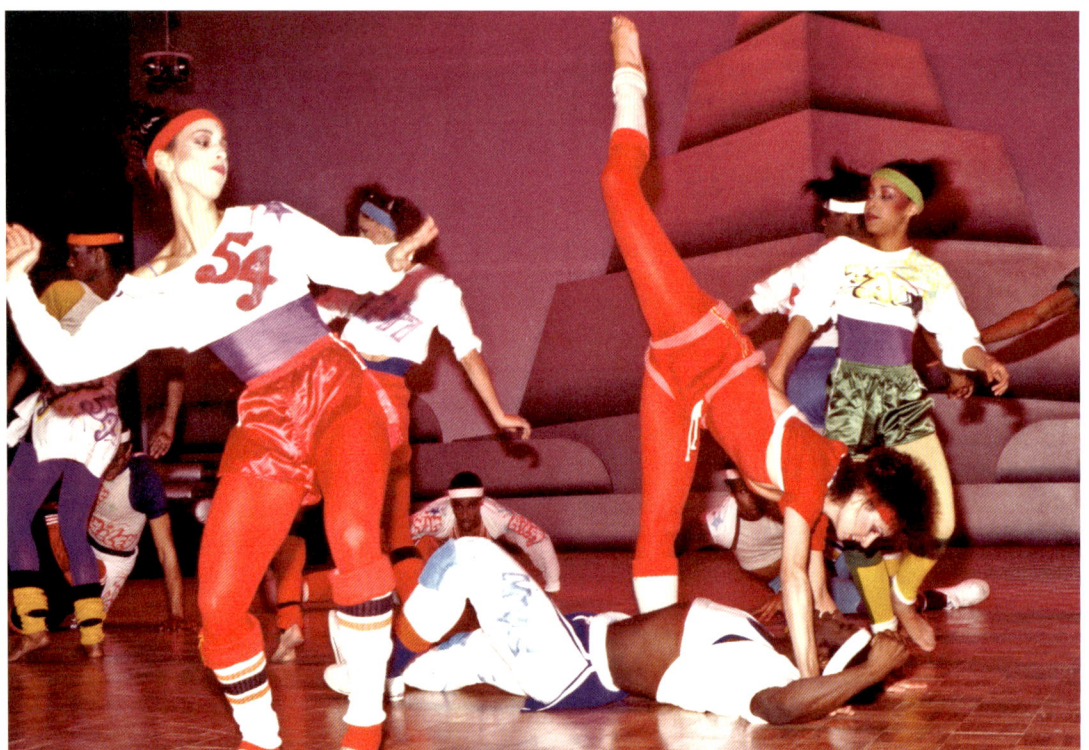

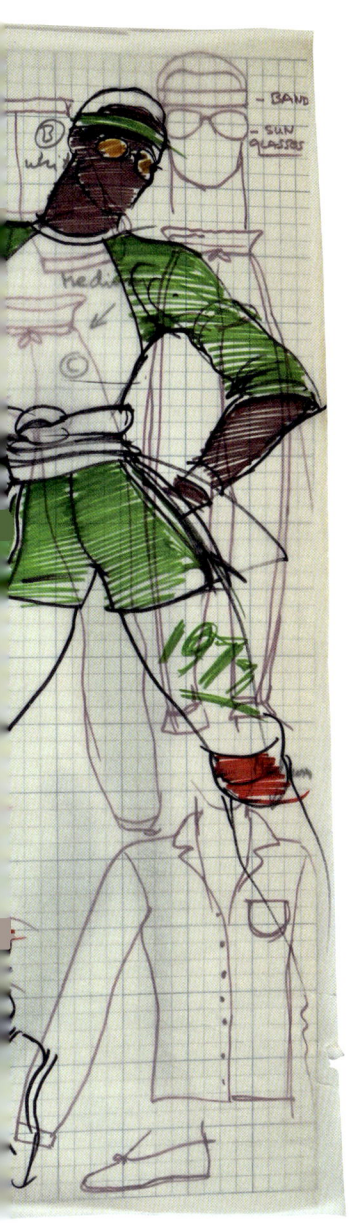

fig. 2

Antonio Lopez, *David*, 1977. Ink on vellum, approx. 18 × 11 in. (45.7 × 27.9 cm). The Antonio Archives

the creativity . . . and the wild spirit" of his friend, according to the program notes.[7] Set to a score by pianist Keith Jarrett incorporating "cool jazz, rock, [and] a touch of postmodern trance music," the piece premiered at City Center on November 29, 1979.[8]

A frequent destination for Ailey and Algarín was the Nuyorican Poets Café; here, we catch a fascinating glimpse of Ailey's acumen in engineering a kind of social choreography outside the rarefied domain of concert dance. As Algarín recalled, Ailey would "watch the crowd of young people who stayed on to dance after the [café's] shows, pushing the chairs to the side to make a disco floor." And sometimes Ailey would participate, gliding "incognito onto the dance floor" while moving "the dancers through choreographed disco moves, with none of them suspecting who he was."[9] This brief anecdote illuminates how gesture operated for Ailey: it was a form of intercommunicative exchange shaped by the kinetic energies that pinballed back and forth between bodies in exquisite motion. As Muñoz reminds us, it is less critical what queer gesture means than what it *does*, what it performs into being, in its generative capacity to conjure something more significant than its individual atomized movements.[10]

This is made more explicit in Ailey's experimentation with transforming the café from a spoken-word venue into a sizzling disco, albeit through the mechanism of light. Specifically, Ailey discovered Algarín's flimsy secondhand light board on a balcony overlooking the café's theater. Ever inventive, Ailey adeptly wielded it, producing, according to Algarín, "a lush play of colored lights across the dancing bodies, light that was in throbbing symbiosis with the music's beat." Annoyed by Ailey's actions, Algarín continued with a cruder description: "Alvin would stand there yanking the goddamn lights and as the beat went he went with it. Bam bam bam bam."[11] But eventually, as this went on for several nights (Ailey locking an increasingly irritated Algarín out of the balcony), Algarín suddenly developed a different comprehension of what his friend was orchestrating:

> Alvin was letting the mood of the music move him, and so it wasn't just some kind of madman crazed with buttons. It was lyrical manipulation of light, as if he were doing dance movement on the light. Here was a bunch of ghetto kids dancing, but now it wasn't only the music. The lights had taken them too. Willie the soundman cut the sound for a moment, because it seemed the lights were doing a magical reproduction of the sound and he wanted to see if it were true. And Alvin continued the lights, and this room erupted in cheers, screaming, and everyone danced more intensely. There was no music. So he had pulled it off. From that day on, I let him destroy the board, without complaining. Which he did. Totally.[12]

In other words, Ailey understood how the multisensorial environment of the disco produced an ecstatic interplay of the ocular, sonic, and kinesthetic. This embodied knowledge, unsurprisingly, was partly the result of the discos he and his students frequented together during the 1970s.[13] Ailey's perception, gleaned from personal experience, also shaped his expansive notion of choreography. His tutelage extended past rote notions of teaching trained professional dancers how to lengthen and contort their bodies in precise coordination with musical accompaniment. As evinced above, the skill of choreography was also about inciting movement through more visceral means, such as chromatic stimuli, or more precisely an ever-mutating assortment of vivid pink, blue, and purple lights seemingly dancing of their own accord. Ailey did not simply use the dilapidated and eventually ruined light board to mimic the swirling rhythms engulfing the Nuyorican Poets Café. He cleverly employed light as a choreographic and affective instrument through which he danced and, in turn, guided an assemblage of quotidian others in how to feel *and* get down.[14]

I privilege Ailey's sustained attention to the technique of lighting because it, again, hints at how differently he perceived dance and its social utility. In contrast to some of his peers' more restrained and classical approaches, Ailey idealized dance as closer to an immersive experience, not unlike Algarín's café-turned-disco, rather than as simply technique. While seemingly divergent from his role as a choreographer, Ailey envisioned lighting, a seemingly innocuous element, as intrinsic to how spectators should experience dance. "I have always called my company a dance theater because I believe that bringing together the elements of music, costumes, lights, movement, and themes creates a totality that the word *dance* alone does not encompass," he remarked in his autobiography.[15] Ailey's signature gestural vocabulary (a blend of ballet-Broadway-modern dance) and his Lester Horton–influenced focus on costumes contributed to this egalitarian theatrical

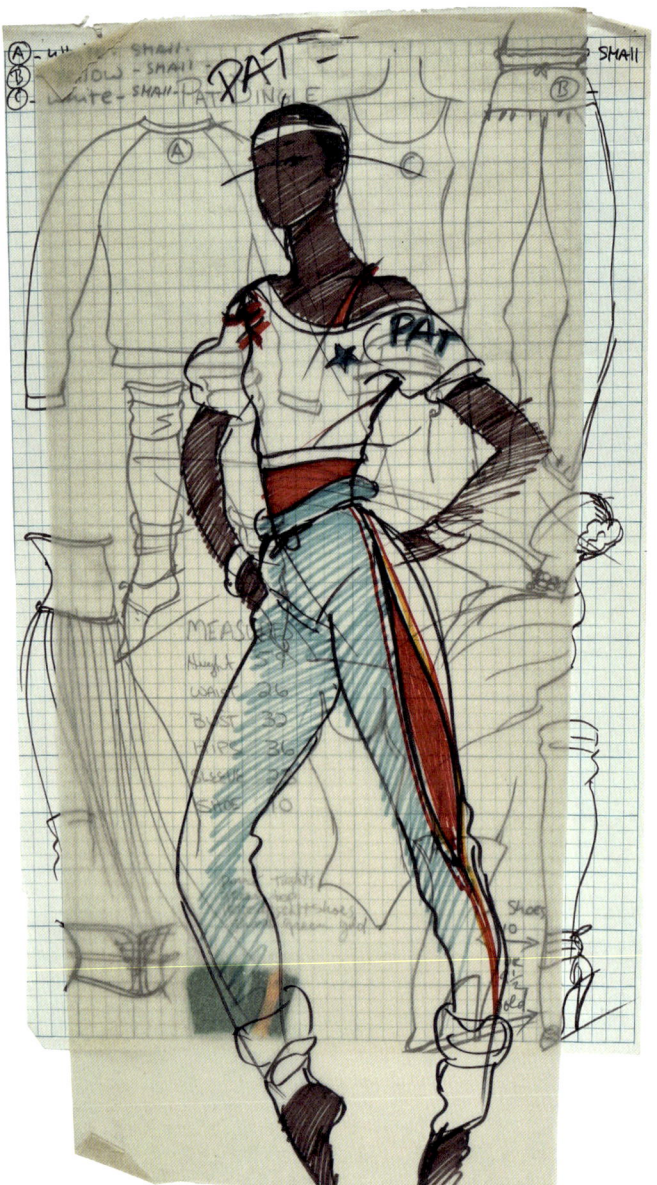
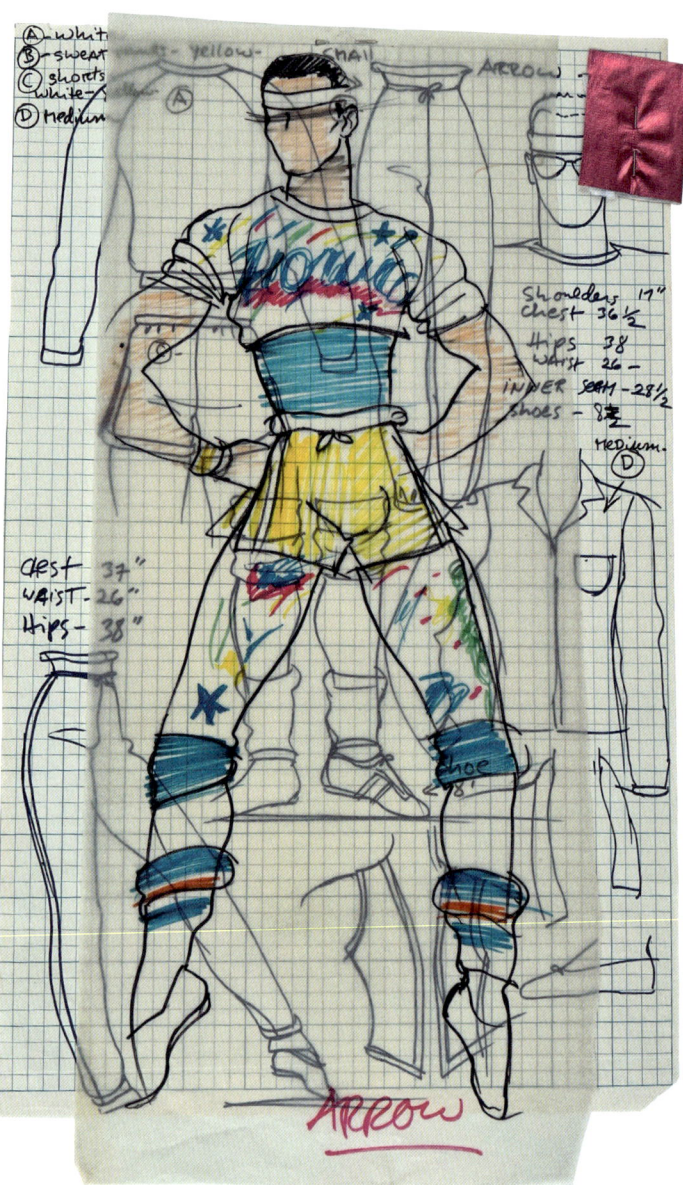

experience that some critics derided as too commercial; it also dovetailed with Ailey's hopes of creating "a company with appeal to the people who went to movies and rock concerts and theater in general"—specifically Black people "who do not feel so welcome in the elite halls of City Center and Lincoln Center, who do not go downtown."[16]

The tension between the critical appraisal of dance critics and the enthusiasm of Ailey's courted masses was especially apparent when the Ailey company performed disco-inspired pieces. A 1979 *New York Times* review of *Tilt*, for instance, showcased evident disdain for disco music and the company's specific take on it.[17] A new work at the time, choreographed by George Faison (who also designed the costumes and "delectably tasteless stage décor"), *Tilt* was characterized as a high-energy "workout" for a trio of "mugging" female disco dancers who "strut, bob and generally shake it up in an unvarnished disco idiom that reveals the numbing lack of invention in our newest American art form." However, while decrying the lack of "an ounce of subtlety in any of it," the writer begrudgingly acknowledged that the "audience's cheers attested to the indisputable power of this manic and maniacal bit of dance." These comments reveal Ailey's ability to capture the zeitgeist in his modern dance interpretation of disco, a unique sonic form fostered in New York City–based loft parties, juice bars, and subterranean nightclubs earlier in the decade that was cresting a wave of mainstream popularity by 1979. This same embrace of popular dance music seemingly came at the cost of "nuanced choreography" and ostensibly traded high art for the dreadfully banal, echoing common accusations lobbed at Ailey. Yet the drift to the popular may have been the exact point since

fig. 3

Antonio Lopez, *Pat*, 1977. Ink on vellum, approx. 18 × 11 in. (45.7 × 27.9 cm). The Antonio Archives

fig. 4

Antonio Lopez, *Arrow*, 1977. Ink on vellum, approx. 18 × 11 in. (45.7 × 27.9 cm). The Antonio Archives

Ailey was less interested in dance as an elite, Eurocentric art form. Instead, to quote Juana María Rodríguez's words in another context, Ailey perceived dance as more of an "embodied social practice" that highlighted the "collective possibilities of sociality" and the "social laws and limits that also structure these exchanges."[18]

Consequently, Ailey's company may have found the perfect environment when they performed at the glamorous (and decidedly commercial) Studio 54 on opening night, April 26, 1977. The nightclub was housed in a former opera house and CBS television studio on West Fifty-Fourth Street (thus the name), and its owners, Steve Rubell and Ian Schrager, redesigned the building's interior extensively before the club's much-publicized opening. They hired experts to produce a mix of high-end interior design, elaborate floral arrangements, and state-of-the-art audio equipment. And, in contrast to Algarín's rinky-dink light board, Rubell and Schrager paid particular attention to the lighting, which included pulsing light poles above the polished parquet floor. The Ailey costumes for the Studio 54 performance were designed by Nuyorican fashion illustrator Antonio Lopez (1943–1987), an in-house consultant for the hip Midtown clothing store Fiorucci, affectionately dubbed the "daytime Studio 54." Extant sketches and photographs from the night illustrate a brightly colored hybrid of sportswear and dance clothes: for example, blue leg warmers with contrasting red kneepads, cropped sweatshirts spray-painted with "54" and worn over purple leotards, ribbon skirts worn over swimsuits and tights in contrasting colors (figs. 1–4).[19]

Despite their different fields of expertise, the pairing of Lopez's and Ailey's artistry makes sense given that both emphasized bringing out the personalities of their specific muses, be it models (for Lopez) or dancers (for Ailey). Moreover, Ailey's attention to "how the fabric moves" and costumes that were "artistic, that frame the dancers beautifully—and more practically, that will endure and be washable" seems to have been in line with Lopez's fabric choices, colors, and overall design for each dancer's sporty attire.[20] Although we can surmise that the dancers gesticulated to a disco soundtrack, no surviving video documentation of the performance exists. The startling lack of other information—such as specific songs or the testimony of dancers or spectators—treats it as a mere prelude to the widely mythologized main event, Studio 54 itself.[21]

Only in time traveling to the contemporary moment (and relocating to the prototypical art museum) is this dynamic flipped, repositioning Ailey-inflected disco as the star attraction. In celebration of the opening of the Brooklyn Museum's 2020 exhibition *Studio 54: Night Magic*, six young dancers of color from Ailey II, the junior company founded in 1974, were invited to dance inside the museum. The brief video clip, recorded on March 13, 2020, shows the dancers exuberantly and defiantly dancing together amid a global pandemic (figs. 5a–c).[22] Set to the Trammps 1976 hit "Disco Inferno," the piece is choreographed to appear as if disco is wildly contagious. Seemingly random participants (including a museum guard) are suddenly converted into disco dancers, growing from one lead dancer to a small ensemble. Gliding between galleries, they eventually dance in unison in the atrium (the same one used in the first episode of the FX television show *POSE* [2018–21]), showcasing classic Ailey-ballet-meets-Broadway movements. The video ends with a shot of the charismatic lead dancer in a sunny gallery, elegantly enacting improvised disco moves, her warm dynamism contrasting with the cold stasis of the sculpture next to her. This performance gestures to the larger history of presenting dance inside museums, partly acknowledging visual art's long-standing relationship with dance.[23] But it ultimately suggests that Ailey's queer gesture is a potent insurgent force that can render the imaginative real even in the face of historical erasure.

figs. 5a–c

Ailey II dancers performing at the Brooklyn Museum for the exhibition *Studio 54: Night Magic*, March 13, 2020

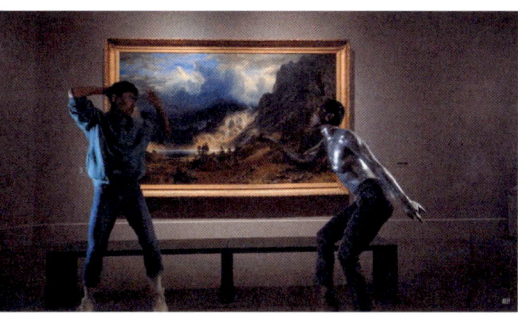
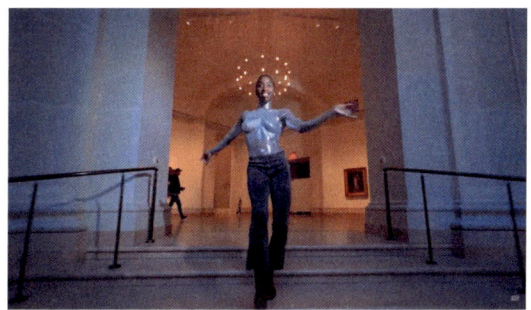
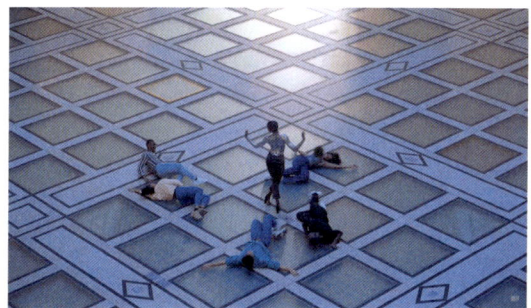

NOTES

1. See Karen Jaime, *The Queer Nuyorican: Racialized Sexualities and Aesthetics in Loisaida* (New York: New York University Press, 2021).

2. See Amelia Jones, "'Presence' in Absentia: Experiencing Performance as Documentation," *Art Journal* 56, no. 4 (Winter 1997): 11–18.

3. José Esteban Muñoz, *Cruising Utopia: The Then and There of Queer Futurity* (New York: New York University Press, 2009), 81.

4. These details are paraphrased from Jennifer Dunning, *Alvin Ailey: A Life in Dance* (Boston: Da Capo, 1998), 311–12.

5. Tom Stevens [the Ailey company's administrative director], quoted in "Alvin Ailey Gets New Headquarters," *New York Times*, October 19, 1979.

6. Trisler, a UCLA graduate, was a dancer and choreographer who met and performed with Ailey at the Lester Horton Dance Theater in Los Angeles; they both became known as protégés of the eponymous West Coast modern-dance innovator. Upon moving to New York City in 1954, she danced with the Juilliard Dance Theater from 1955 to 1959 and with Ailey during his company's first European tour in 1964. She was also on the teaching staff at the company, and her works are part of its repertory.

7. Program notes quoted from "*Memoria*," Repertory, Alvin Ailey American Dance Theater (website), accessed December 1, 2023, https://www.alvinailey.org/performances/repertory/memoria.

8. Jennifer Dunning, "Dance: Ailey Homage to Joyce Trisler," *New York Times*, December 3, 1979.

9. Miguel Algarín, quoted in Dunning, *Alvin Ailey*, 327.

10. Muñoz, *Cruising Utopia*, 67.

11. Algarín, quoted in Dunning, *Alvin Ailey*, 327.

12. Algarín, quoted in Dunning, 127–28.

13. See Tim Lawrence, *Love Saves the Day: A History of American Dance Music Culture, 1970–1979* (Durham, NC: Duke University Press, 2004).

14. Ailey's belief that "the entire body registers the emotion of the dance, not just the face," is also a clue; it suggests that he manipulated light as a conduit for producing this emotional expressiveness via the body. Quoted in Dunning, *Alvin Ailey*, 301.

15. Alvin Ailey and A. Peter Bailey, *Revelations: The Autobiography of Alvin Ailey* (Secaucus, NJ: Carol Publishing Group, 1997), 95.

16. Alvin Ailey, quoted in Jennifer Dunning, "The Alvin Ailey Blend—Ballet, Modern and Broadway," *New York Times*, November 26, 1978.

17. Jennifer Dunning, "Dance: Faison's 'Tilt,' in Disco Idiom, at the Ailey," *New York Times*, May 6, 1979.

18. Juana María Rodríguez, *Sexual Futures, Queer Gestures, and Other Latina Longings* (New York: New York University Press, 2014), 100.

19. Specifically, I am referring to photographs by Juan Ramos and Allan Tannenbaum. For their photographs of the event and fittings, see Matthew Yokobosky, *Studio 54: Night Magic* (New York: Rizzoli Electa, 2020).

20. Ailey and Bailey, *Revelations*, 95.

21. The company also performed at Studio 54 on November 19, 1979, in a benefit concert titled *Young Friends of Alvin Ailey*. A copy of the program lists an honorary committee, chaired by Nick Ashford and Valerie Simpson, of the duo Ashford and Simpson, that included two Ailey dancers (Judith Jamison and Dudley Williams) as well as singers Stephanie Mills, Teddy Pendergrass, and Grace Jones, who receives a special thanks. There seems to be no video documentation of the event.

22. The video was recorded on the same day that the Brooklyn Museum closed due to the COVID-19 pandemic. The museum and the exhibition would reopen that September, with social distancing and mask restrictions in place. "Ailey II Discos at the Brooklyn Museum," posted April 26, 2020, https://www.youtube.com/watch?v=AmdgceZTF4c.

23. See Claire Bishop, "The Perils and Possibilities of Dance in the Museum: Tate, MoMA, and Whitney," *Dance Research Journal* 46, no. 3 (December 2014): 63–76.

J Wortham

Take Me to the Water

"Waaaaade." Even before you hear the rest of the song, you understand its meaning. You *feel* it: all those voices weighed down by their collective bass have the power to enter your cells through osmosis. The song is so layered—in meaning, voices, history—that it can require some wading of its own to make the words legible. But perhaps that superimposition of sound is a cloaking device, one of the many deployments of Black technologies meant to protect the transmission of precious information. The spiritual "Wade in the Water" first emerged in the 1800s, sung to remind freedom seekers to cover their tracks by traveling through bodies of water. It is heavy, intentionally. As the song comes into its efflorescence, it becomes more knowing and premonitory: God is going to trouble these waters.

Alvin Ailey's life mission was also to trouble those waters. So much so that when he choreographed a dance to "Wade in the Water" for his iconic 1960 work *Revelations*, he chose the version sung by Ella Jenkins, a children's musician, which is underwritten with a syncopated calypso beat that has the ability to roll the song forward a few centuries without losing its threads to the past. In 1945, as a teenager, Ailey caught a glimpse of dance that would forever transform his relationship to it: the legendary Katherine Dunham's *Tropical Revue*, at the Biltmore Theatre in Los Angeles. Ailey went to see the production again and again, absorbing the mesmerizing movements and smoldering catharsis of the routines. He was captivated by Dunham's reverence for Caribbean and African cultures and the way she folded polyrhythmic dance with perpetual motion into the framework of European-style ballets. In an interview, Dunham described the way her technique allows the axis of the body to be fluid and polycentric, providing multiple points of grounding that orient from the spine, the limbs, the palms.[1] Her influence can be felt in *Revelations*, particularly in the limbic undulation of the dancers and their ability to defy gravity with kicks and half dips, archiving the ritual of refusing to succumb.

Ailey hinges past to the present, moving the tense and coiled exigency of the song's origins into a new dimensionality. There is no reification of suffering, sorrow, or violence. Only the possibility of transmuting it, which does not mean burying it. The architecture of dance, of bodies and movement, is aligned with water, the medium of passage and cleansing, momentum and motion, divisions between freedom and unfreedom. Many memorials to the past rely on Black suffering as a pathway to knowledge, as Black studies scholar Christina Sharpe remarks in her astounding memoir *Ordinary Notes*. And yet, as she observes, "spectacle is not repair."[2] Ailey is the embodiment of this cellular respiration—Toni Morrison's practice of rememory that locates itself in creating a new collective memory that does not require exhuming collective trauma to fortify and sustain itself.

Witness this in the first act of *Revelations*. The dancers start huddled together, draped in the language of the earth—ocher, sandstone, terra-cotta, burnt ocher—representing the complex ecologies of time, shaped by the metamorphic agent of history. Ailey wanted to invoke the image of people coming up out of the ground, stretching toward the sun, blooming (see p. 46, fig. 1). Coming from the earth into the ether. The second act is called "Take Me to the Water." Ailey imagined it as a purification rite, the healing suture between the first act (emergence) and the final act (jubilation). It features "Wade into the Water" about twelve minutes into the production.

In one of Ailey's production notebooks, he sketched out a rough vision of the stage. He specified that it should be "crossed by enormous pieces of water-colored silk" to create the impression of "shadows of water on the stage."[3] Dancers wear all white and carry umbrellas as they move between the silk sea waves (fig. 1). It is a muscular dance, the transmission of strength visible in the quilt of thousands of woven fibers, stretching and pressing together to move the bodies on stage. As a song, "Wade" contains multiple strategies—for evasion of capture, for liberation—and Jenkins's funky version reminds viewers that the lessons encrypted in the song are still needed today.

Water figures into all of Ailey's work because it shaped his entire life. He was baptized in a pond behind the True Vine Baptist Church in Rogers, Texas, where he grew up. He remembered hearing "Wade in the Water" sung during those rituals of naming and belonging, and he sought to memorialize them in ballet. Water was the conduit through which Ailey conducted his research, his work of translating somatic memories into dance. Memory made flesh. "All of this is a part of my blood memory: my uncles, my family, my mother, all were in these churches . . . very intense, very personal," he said in an interview.[4] Later, many of the journals he kept in adulthood are rich with references to the Caribbean, including musings on when he could next travel there for the winter or holidays. Water has the highest surface tension of all liquids except mercury. Surface tension is another way to say energy, another way to say strength, another way of holding. It is formed by the hydrogen bonds in water molecules, and the stronger the intermolecular interactions, the greater the surface tension. It can become strong enough to float items, defying notions of possibility. All of *Revelations* lives up to this promise: a poetic flurry of beauty that still manages to startle, to surprise, no matter when or how often you see it. To watch the performance is to be reminded of the line in the poem "Wade in the Water" by Tracy K. Smith: "Is this love the trouble you promised?"[5] For what else are we seeing crystallized in this cosmic relationship to time, our memories, our bodies, each other, but love?

In an article published in 1989, Melva Wilson Costen, a professor of worship and hymnologist, noted that traditional spirituals never cease their work. Emancipation as perpetual motion. "God works to free God's people in any age," she wrote.[6] The taproot first planted by spirituals continues to grow and bear new fruit. *Revelations*, a show that accretes power as it ages, offers a spell for shaking free of possession, of anything that isn't yours, and moving forward, unequivocally, toward freedom.

Notice this in how the dancers' movements impart the song's origins, which is to say, they embody the product of their ancestors' intentions. Freedom, or at least a version of it, as made available by that passage through water. Their movements are a new response to that song's old call. The lines made by their bodies, muscles contracting around bone to carry the dancers across the stage. The dancers fling their arms out, as if to say, "*Go, go, you go, now.*" They are still walking the path of liberation, even as they arrive on this stage, and they invite us to join them.

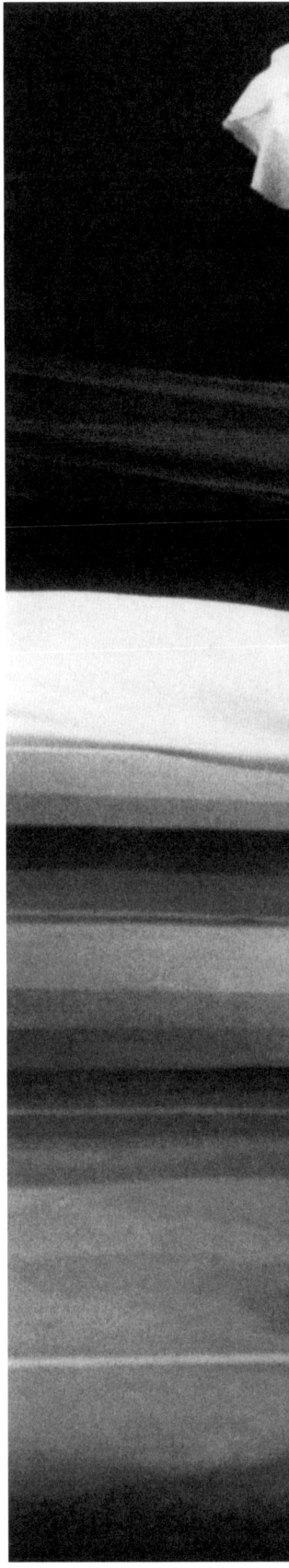

fig. 1

Revelations, ca. 1970

NOTES

1. Katherine Dunham, in *Katherine Dunham on the "Pole through the Body" in Dunham Technique*, produced by Vicky Risner, September 2002, video, 1:26, https://www.loc.gov/item/ihas.200003848/.

2. Christina Sharpe, *Ordinary Notes* (New York: Farrar, Straus and Giroux, 2023), n23.

3. Alvin Ailey, "Crane Reflections—Britten," box 140, folder 12, Alvin Ailey Dance Foundation Collection, Music Division, Library of Congress, Washington, DC.

4. Alvin Ailey, quoted in *An Evening with the Alvin Ailey American Dance Theater*, directed by Thomas Grimm (1986; Chatsworth, CA: Image Entertainment, 2000), DVD.

5. Tracy K. Smith, "Wade in the Water," in *Wade in the Water: Poems* (Minneapolis: Graywolf, 2018), 15.

6. Melva Wilson Costen, "Published Hymnals in the Afro-American Tradition," *The Hymn* 40, no. 1 (January 1989): 7.

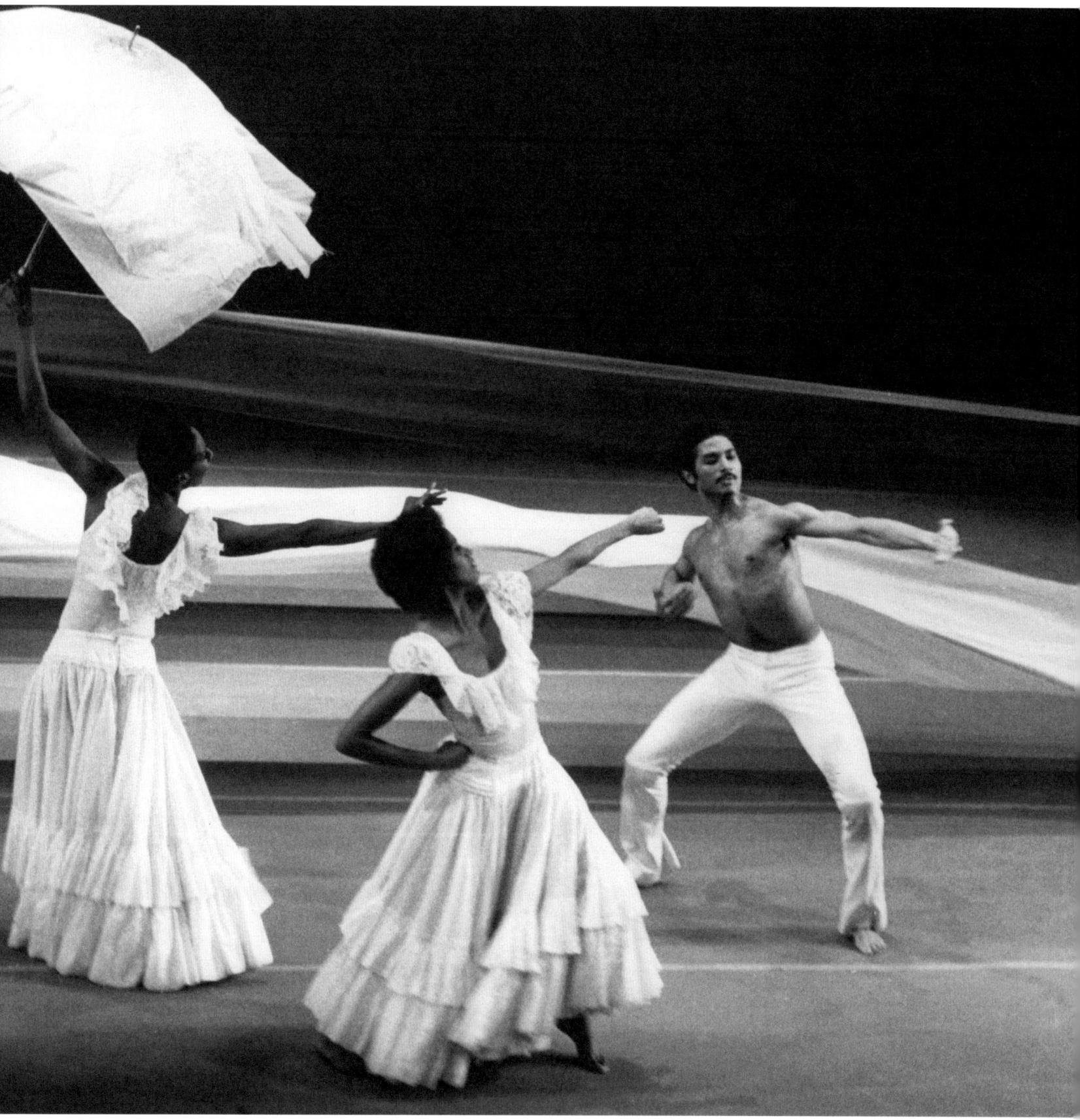

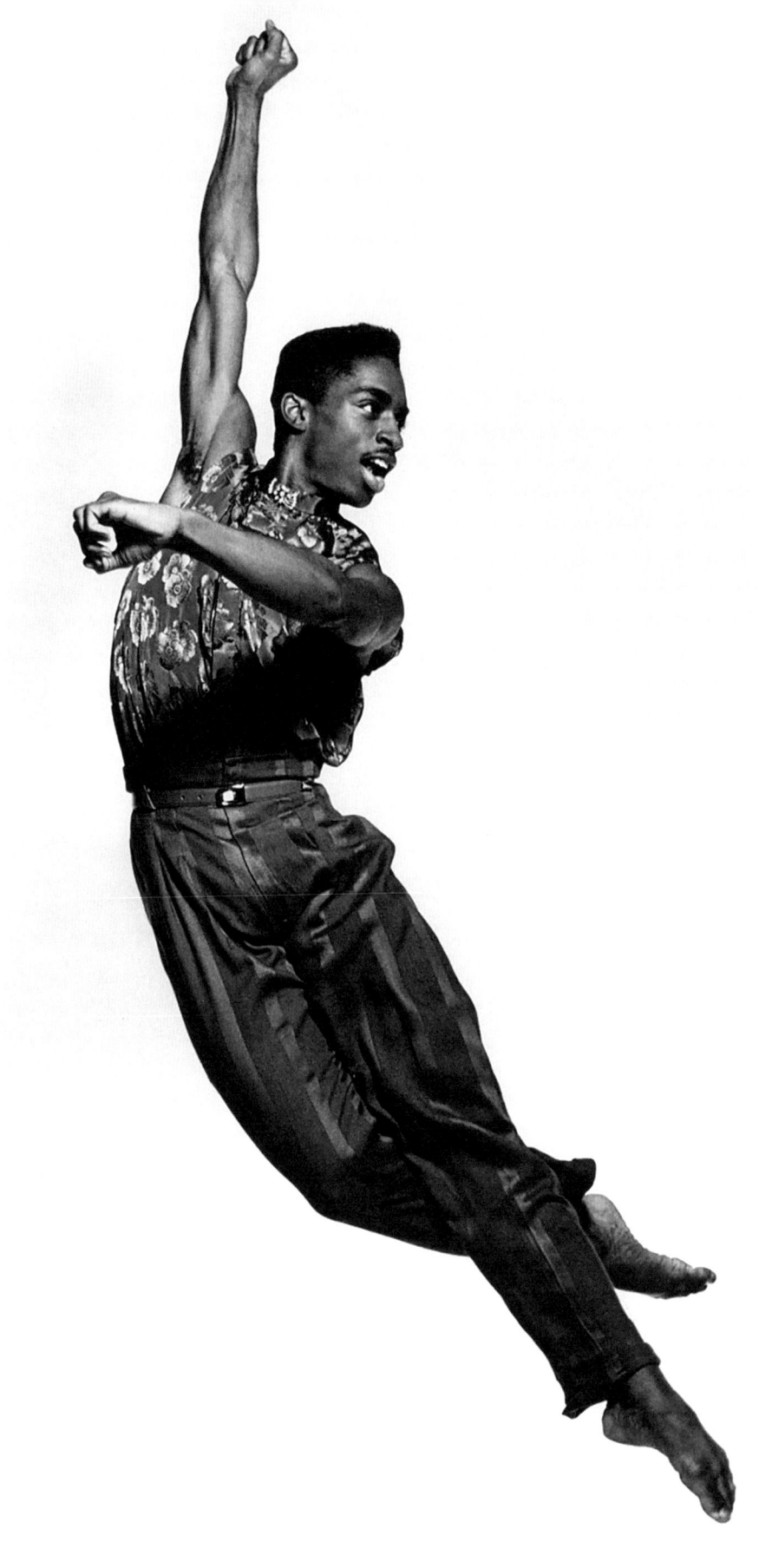

Ariel Osterweis

Virtuosity's Blood Memories

Being in the Diaspora braces itself in virtuosity or despair.
   —Dionne Brand[1]

I had these creative sides bubbling inside . . . dark, deep things, beautiful things inside me. . . . my blood memories—the memories of my parents, uncles, and aunts, the blues and the gospel songs that I knew from Texas.
   —Alvin Ailey[2]

There's the idea that with one shard of a shattered mirror, what's imprinted in the shard is the last thing the mirror saw. The mirror can see all kinds of things, but in this case it's the "Rose Adagio" from the ballet *Sleeping Beauty* or the clump of dancers in "I Been 'Buked" [in *Revelations*].
   —Donald Byrd[3]

I did [*Episodes*] after a very dear friend of mine died from AIDS. . . . I really wish that I had five more minutes with him.
   —Ulysses Dove[4]

What is virtuosity, if not a kind of mourning? Such embodied yearning, such outstretching of spirit could only ever find its urgency in a desire to recover from loss. "*Being* in the Diaspora," writes poet Dionne Brand, "braces itself in virtuosity or despair."[5] In the late 1980s, the way Ailey dancers so fervently committed to the difficulty of choreographic virtuosity came of a practice of both lamentation and ambition in the face of inescapable mortality. By examining the artistry behind two works from this time created for the Alvin Ailey American Dance Theater (AAADT)—Donald Byrd's *Shards* (1988) and Ulysses Dove's *Episodes* (1989)—I will describe how, in its unrelenting excess, the virtuosity emerging out of the company betrayed a kind of recuperation of spirit through muscular rigor amid so much grieving during the devastating effects of the AIDS epidemic on the Black gay community and on the AAADT itself.

Let us recall that the period in question was defined by Reaganism, the culture wars,[6] and what Michelle Alexander has called the New Jim Crow.[7] In 1986, US President Ronald Reagan signed the Anti-Drug Abuse Act. That same year, photographer Robert Mapplethorpe published *Black Book*, comprising ninety-six photographs of Black male

fig. 1

Jack Mitchell, *"Shards": Desmond Richardson*, n.d. National Museum of African American History and Culture, Washington, DC. Jack Mitchell Photography of the Alvin Ailey American Dance Theater Collection nudes. These images quickly became implicated in the culture wars, inciting numerous national debates on obscenity, fetishism, classicism, sexuality, religion, and Blackness. Senator Jesse Helms of North Carolina criticized Mapplethorpe's photographs as obscene, claiming they upset religious morality and so-called family values. Three years later, in 1989, Mapplethorpe's images once again were at the center of controversy, when the National Endowment for the Arts—an organization that President Reagan had vowed to abolish during his first presidential campaign, in 1980—was involved in a scandal for providing funding for exhibitions of Mapplethorpe's photography and Andres Serrano's *Piss Christ* (1987).

It was in 1986 that eighteen-year-old and soon-to-be Ailey virtuoso Desmond Richardson (who would figure prominently in both *Shards* and *Episodes*) (fig. 1) was named a Presidential Scholar in the Arts, an honor presented to him by President Reagan, at the precise moment that the Reagan administration was stripping arts funding and choosing to ignore the AIDS crisis. All this anti-Black and sexualized violence, epitomizing the New Jim Crow, had a direct effect on the Ailey dance community.[8] The embodied urgency of the Ailey dancers' virtuosity during this moment cannot be underestimated.

In its liveness, ephemerality, and physicality, no art form eludes the traditional Western museological archive more than dance. And after film, video, photography, and re-performance, writing is perhaps the least adept modality for containing dance's afterlives. If dance exceeds the limits of the written word, virtuosity is the mode of dance that most exceeds its form. To that end, alongside the Whitney Museum of American Art's archival assemblage for this exhibition and catalogue, this essay about the emergence of virtuosity in the AAADT mobilizes dance's least likely archival device (writing) in an attempt to re-enliven a moment in the company's history most resistant to classification. This exhibition's insistence on live dance performances in a museum in a retelling and reframing of dance history is significant at the level of reinvigorating dance and performance studies' contributions to the concept of the embodied archive.[9] It also creates space for audiences to return to Ailey's "blood memories," including those that may have been suppressed decades ago when certain freedoms of expression were not afforded.

During the late 1980s and early 1990s, dance—noticeably in the work of the Ailey company's virtuosos—expressed what words could not. At that time, in a move largely attributable to the inclusion of Byrd's and Dove's choreography in the company's repertory, many Ailey dancers started pushing the boundaries of technique in concert dance, inaugurating what I call the "virtuosic turn" in contemporary dance.[10] Both Byrd and Dove are known for having propelled Ailey dancers beyond former limits, toward extremes: while Byrd demanded of the dancers mathematical intricacy, angularity, and brisk directional shifts, Dove encouraged heightened emotional engagement, connecting feeling to form (fig. 2). Their choreography created virtuosic opportunities for Ailey dancers who were eager to bring together classical ballet and African diasporic forms in a way that reflected the culturally charged velocity of American life at the time—its speed, momentum, and ambition—while offering glimpses of emotional weight and the tense glitches inherent to invention.

Virtuosity, however, falls prey to both celebratory and derogatory connotations, pulled into a range of associations, from the mechanical to the soulful. Because the term as utilized in Europeanist discourse came about with the advent of the printing press in the fifteenth century and journalism as a tool of judgment, virtuosity as a designation has traditionally been tied to systems of valuation. The practice and reception of virtuosity function within and across historical temporalities, when differently educated audiences diverge in their experience of a work. As such, the term is rendered unstable. A virtuosic aesthetic experiences a period of emergence but can then become vulnerable to emulation and imitation over time. A style of dance may eventually become recognizable or over-rehearsed, or may be misunderstood or experienced as illegible, if a viewer lacks the cultural knowledge to perceive creative invention as opposed to superficial excess.

Although virtuosity is often a celebratory term, its intermittent pejorative undertone in Eurocentric journalistic contexts tends to reflect broader sociocultural anxieties about technology's potential subsumption of the human. Easy correlations between the "soulless" and the "mechanical" are undone by taking into consideration virtuosity within Black dance aesthetics. In *The Black Dancing Body*, dance scholar Brenda Dixon-Gottschild writes: "Soul represents that attribute of the body/mind that mediates *between* flesh and spirit. It is manifested in the *feel* of a performance. It has a sensual, visceral connotation of connectedness with the earth (and the earth-centered religions that distinguish West

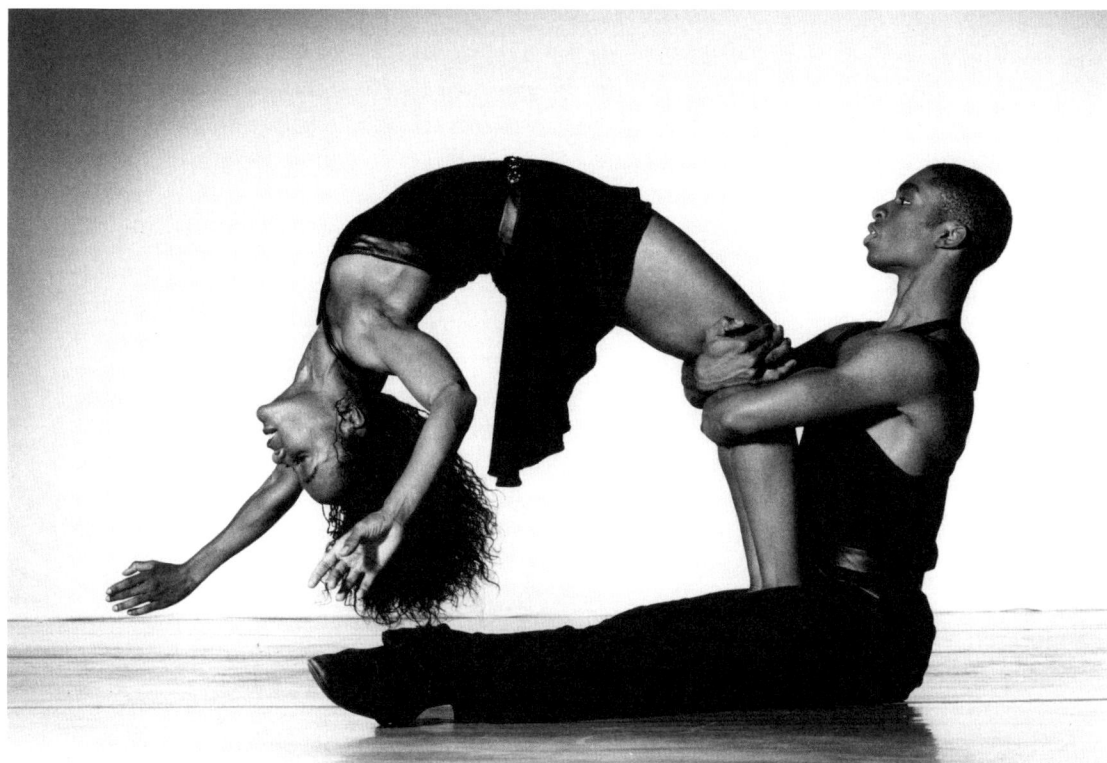

fig. 2

Jack Mitchell, *"Episodes": Renee Robinson and Desmond Richardson*, 1991. National Museum of African American History and Culture, Washington, DC. Jack Mitchell Photography of the Alvin Ailey American Dance Theater Collection

and Central African cultures) and, concomitantly, a reaching for the spirit."[11] If Byrd's choreographic vocabulary brought heightened attention to the dancer's potential for technical inventiveness while subtly pointing to Ailey's ever-soulful *Revelations*, Dove delivered an aesthetics of soul against a backdrop of razor-sharp technique. In their virtuosic rigor, Byrd and Dove presented us with choreography that invalidated any presumed binary opposition between virtuosity's mechanical and soulful qualities. Both choreographers deconstructed classical ballet technique, placing it into conversation with postmodern styles coming out of street dance and Merce Cunningham's approaches, as well as American modern dance and African diasporic techniques.

Ailey nurtured stylistic and technical versatility in his dancers, and the company's repertory insists upon skill in ballet, modern dance, jazz, and Katherine Dunham technique; Ailey dancers have to be ready for anything. Dancers entering the company, especially those who trained at the school—where all styles named here are taught—have trained in ballet; the techniques of Dunham, Martha Graham, and Lester Horton; jazz; and sometimes West African or street dance (including hip-hop styles). One could make the case that any dance form is inherently hybrid in its stylistic influences, although some dance cultures value the appearance of purity more than others. Classical ballet tends to fall into the former, while modern dance and the even broader and ever historically inclusive category of "contemporary" dance more readily acknowledge their accumulating heterogeneity. Thus, when a choreographer such as Byrd entered an Ailey studio, he knew he could call upon a multitude of vocabularies and even collaboratively create new ones with the dancers.

Most often, the American choreographer William Forsythe (b. 1949), who directed Ballett Frankfurt for two decades starting in 1983, is credited—after George Balanchine—with almost single-handedly deconstructing ballet. Although it is not inaccurate to ascribe much of ballet's punk, avant-garde deconstruction in the 1980s to Forsythe, there were other significant American and British choreographers of the same generation engaging in similar explorations. They include Byrd and Dove, as well as Michael Clark and Alonzo King (and later, Wayne McGregor and Dwight Rhoden). With the exception of Forsythe, and Clark and McGregor (both of whom are from the UK), the aforementioned choreographers are African American, and each uniquely developed an aesthetic of Black queer experience, working in what poet and scholar Fred Moten calls "the break."[12] Moten has written about "the break" as related to the improvisatory imperative of Black life, and Ailey's work certainly emerges from such inventiveness. In aesthetic terms as applied to concert dance choreography, I tend to think of "the break" (and its association with the Black

Virtuosity's Blood Memories

radical tradition) as a concept more relevant to choreographers, such as Byrd (especially) and Dove, who reject narrative and revel in abstraction as formal deconstruction and fracture, call upon methodologies such as retrograde and insertion, and embrace the inventive potential of error and glitch. In other words, while Ailey lived in "the break," Byrd and Dove made dances that played in actual breaks in the movement, resulting in Black radical choreography that refused resolution and instead offered up the opacity of abstraction. Such audacity of complexity was something of a novelty aesthetically for the Ailey company up until the late 1980s.

Forsythe and his choreographic contemporaries shared a rootedness in ballet along with a simultaneous investment in Black dance and club culture. It is not so much that the insertion of Black dance into ballet is where we locate "the break"; instead, I am pointing to the ensuing choreographies' Black aesthetics of abstraction and illegibility as themselves embodying "the break." In the Ailey repertory, "the break" is located in and through Africanist aesthetics, and the two ideas cannot be thought of apart in regard to the AAADT. Dixon-Gottschild's concept of Africanist aesthetics in American dance suggests that Balanchine's contribution to American ballet was such that he incorporated an Africanist aesthetic, influenced by Black dance and music in Harlem. Such influences are found, according to Dixon-Gottschild, in jazzy hip thrusts, the inversion of turned-out legs to parallel, the play with syncopation, and the embrace of speed. Africanist aesthetics in dance embrace soul and posit that "the universe is in a dynamic process-in-motion, not a static entity."[13] If the Africanist elements in Balanchine's work need to be more explicitly excavated and revealed, one could argue that Ailey's own choreography is more overtly Africanist.

"The break," according to Moten, defines the space of much Black performance and, like Moten's writing, embraces opacity and resists analysis. In other words, "the break" is not a gap that is devoid of content; instead, Moten has described it as a disruption or invagination. For Moten the "rich nonfullness" of the "articulation" of Blackness takes place "by and through an infinitesimal and unbridgeable break."[14] Moten's concept of "the break" tends to describe artistry that resists legibility or dramatic resolution, and often does not find itself paired with studies of the Ailey repertory. But Byrd's and Dove's postmodern investments in formal experimentation put pressure on the limits of classicism and modern dance while insisting on Blackness, and demand consideration through the lenses of "the break" and Africanist aesthetics—as well as queer of color critique. American studies scholar Roderick Ferguson's elaboration on "queer of color analysis" takes its cue from Mikhail Bakhtin in suggesting that "material heterogeneity resists canonizing heterogeneity, opting instead to expose the gender and sexual diversity within racial formations."[15] In other words, according to Ferguson, "queer of color analysis has to debunk the idea that race, class, gender, and sexuality are discrete formations, insulated from one another."[16] Explorations of choreography such as Byrd's and Dove's engage what Ferguson describes as "inquir[ies] into the nonnormative components of racial formations," thus challenging "restrictions of normative epistemes" and moving "beyond identity politics."[17] We cannot think through Byrd's and Dove's contributions to American dance outside a queer of color framework, no matter how comparatively subtle their queer messaging may seem to the contemporary viewer. Albeit differently, both choreographers insisted on the thrust of virtuosity—in its excess and inherently queer and often racialized mode—precisely during the historical moment of Reagan's violent disregard for the AIDS epidemic. That Byrd and Dove were choreographing within the context of a predominantly African American company that enthusiastically employed gay dancers and was, in that very moment, losing some of those dancers, including Ailey himself, to AIDS, the specter of death was ever present in the rehearsal studio during the creation of *Shards* and *Episodes*. With palpable urgency, Byrd and Dove necessarily called upon Africanist aesthetics and "the break" to generate a shared aesthetics of queer of color virtuosity—an insistence on endurance in the presence of mortality and sociopolitical negligence.

Byrd bridged the potential distance between Balanchine's and Ailey's approaches to Africanist aesthetics by exaggerating the Africanist elements Balanchine called upon in the service of ballet and abstracting those found in Ailey's *Revelations*. According to the AAADT:

> Back in 1988, Donald Byrd originally created *Shards* for the Alvin Ailey Repertory Ensemble (now called Ailey II). But the Ensemble's director, Sylvia Waters, gave Mr. Ailey a peek at Byrd's work, and Ailey decided to premiere it with his main company instead.

To create this abstract work, Byrd looked at both classic ballets like *Sleeping Beauty* and influential modern dance by major African-American choreographers of the time—Mr. Ailey, Talley Beatty, and Donald McKayle—and deconstructed the language these choreographers used and recombined it with his own sensibility as a rising young artist.[18]

Influenced by Ailey, Balanchine, Beatty, Cunningham, and McKayle, among others, Byrd asked his dancers to perform with both force and detachment. In the rehearsal studio and in technique classes, Byrd challenged dancers to retrograde movement, tracing phrases back to front, allowing the motion to embrace otherwise awkward jolts created by kinesthetic reversals, thus generating moments of effortful tension (fig. 3). As he explained in a 2011 interview:

> If you think of shards in a kind of genetic way, the inside of each gene—a shard perhaps of the body—has the capacity to reproduce the whole organism again. You clone from the cell. And so there's the idea that with one shard of a shattered mirror, what's imprinted in the shard is the last thing the mirror saw. The mirror can see all kinds of things, but in this case it's the "Rose Adagio" from the ballet *Sleeping Beauty* or the clump of dancers in "I Been 'Buked" [in *Revelations*]. It's an Escher-like way of thinking about it, that things kind of turn in on themselves and create a kind of infinity.[19]

While the stylistic dialogism of choreographers such as Byrd and Dove (and even Ailey in the past and then Rhoden starting in the 1990s) tends to be overlooked by critics, Lewis Segal of the *Los Angeles Times* was attuned to the tension *Shards* staged between ballet and "other movement forms":

> [*Shards*] fractures and reassembles the components of Ailey-style in rigorous neo-minimalist terms, with an emphasis on startling contrasts in dynamics. A dancer's arm abruptly shoots forward and then is slowly, softly pulled back to graze the face. Formal, balletic turns-in-extension dissolve in wiggly colloquial motion. Gestural statements that resemble streamlined postmodernizations of Ailey's powerful, recurrent "Buked and Scorned" motif from *Revelations* alternate with sleek passages of dance-as-pure-design. Such sharp push/pull oppositions become a major rhythm in

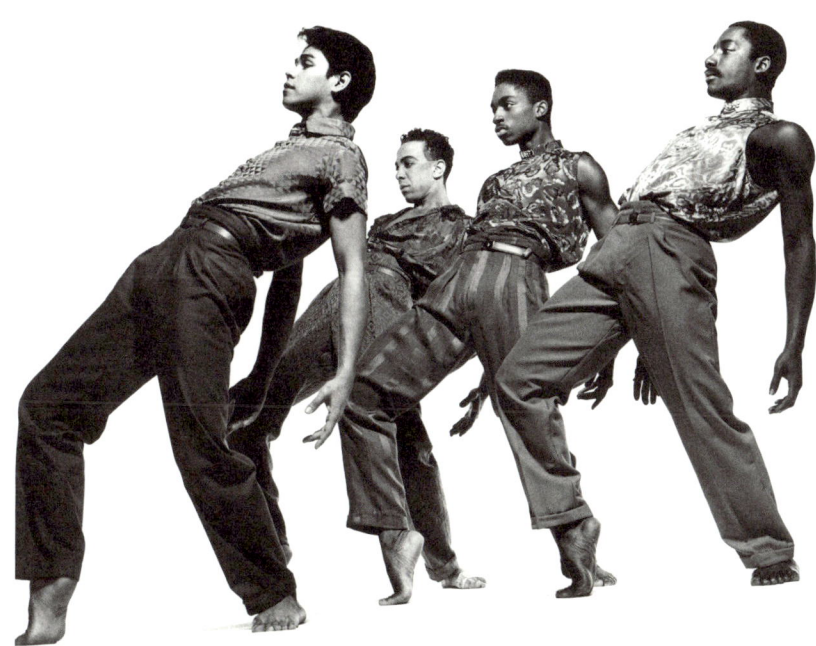

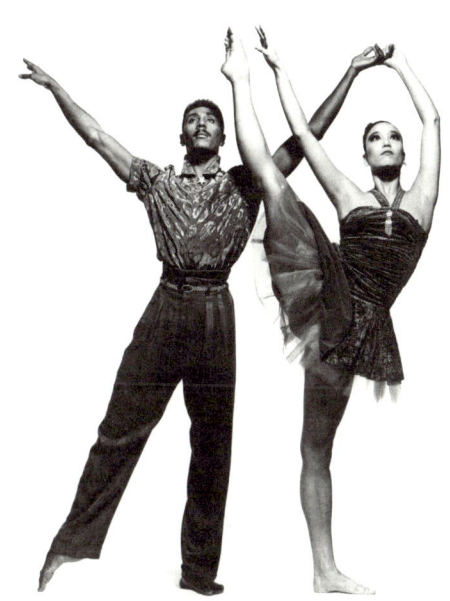

fig. 3

Jack Mitchell, *"Shards": Max Luna, Dwight Rhoden, Desmond Richardson, and Dereque Whiturs*, 1988. National Museum of African American History and Culture, Washington, DC. Jack Mitchell Photography of the Alvin Ailey American Dance Theater Collection

fig. 4

Jack Mitchell, *"Shards": André Tyson and Dana Hash*, n.d. National Museum of African American History and Culture, Washington, DC. Jack Mitchell Photography of the Alvin Ailey American Dance Theater Collection

Shards, underpinning the moody wash of sound provided by Mio Morales. But it is classical ballet that increasingly becomes Byrd's preoccupation (just as it has sometimes been Ailey's): All the playoffs with other movement forms only heighten the centrality of the ballet vocabulary, repertory and even hierarchy. It's as if he's trying to define his own place in the continuity of dance tradition by investigating links to Ailey, to Balanchine and to the street. Byrd is best known as a dance rebel, outrageous and fearless. But *Shards* explores his influences and inspirations while transforming them for dancers of his own generation.[20]

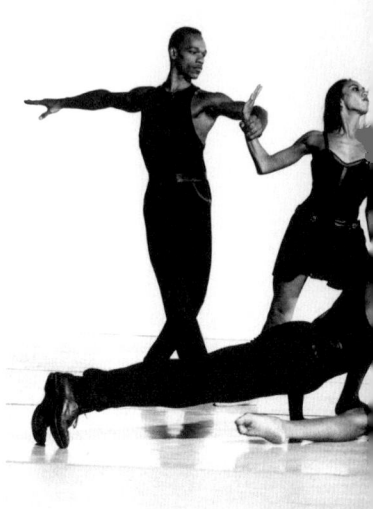

Supported by the propulsion of Morales's percussive electronic score, the dancers in *Shards* betrayed a kind of tense inexhaustibility. To view archival videos of a 1988 rehearsal and a 1990 performance is to discern the meeting point of trained effortlessness and the struggle of the new, the dancers' inevitable inability to conceal the totality of their labor: in Byrd's choreography, we witness the slight strain of his angular imperative to strike the air with pointed foot, swiftly traveling the longest path possible as opposed to taking a curved shortcut (fig. 4).[21] Byrd's insistence on a subtle exposure of laboring through a corporeal path perhaps never before taken impelled the audience to kinesthetically think with the dancers, a possibility that is made more available when the recognizable is interrupted by the strange. In other words, novelty often emerges out of the act of combining existing forms. This is where virtuosity enters. Albeit unconsciously, an audience senses a dancer's virtuosity when their dancing is in excess of the composition, when form fails to contain that which exceeds technical excellence and definable charisma.

Thus, the choreography of Byrd's *Shards* provided the ideal opportunity for a dancer such as Richardson to experiment and excel at a new kind of virtuosity. Upon reflection, we find that what we deem virtuosic in 1988 may become subsequently mimicked by more mainstream performance cultures and later appear less virtuosic or unique, or may suffer from dilution and a diminishment of charge. Virtuosity exists in relation to temporality and historicity. In rehearsal, Richardson and his fellow dancers were performing Byrd's difficult passages with aplomb, and the viewer was also privy to some trial and error, as the material was newer to the dancers in rehearsal than it was in performance after hours of repetition. Virtuosity is most often the mode of a soloist. A soloist (think, concerto) is given an exceptionally challenging passage to execute on their own while the group is silent or still (or otherwise layered beneath the soloist's performance). Or one detects a virtuoso while observing them perform with a group: the virtuoso stands out, they give their performance a little more umph than the next dancer—executing the same steps but moving through them with more attenuation, holding a balance one millisecond longer, adding a flourish, or jumping higher (see fig. 1).

Above and beyond his refinement of a certain kind of charisma—the ability to connect with his audience affectively through gaze, focus, phrasing, and a personal mode of initiating movement with force and following through with flow—it is no surprise that Richardson is the Ailey-trained dancer most commented upon as the embodiment of virtuosity,[22] for not only is he continually asked to perform works composed of hybrid techniques and demands, but he is expertly versed in street dance (specifically popping) in addition to ballet and modern dance. In other words, when Richardson is called upon to either improvise or make choreography "his own" (as a dancer is often told in rehearsal), he is able to pull from the carbonated dynamics of popping as much as the connective tissue of ballet. African American dancers such as Richardson have carried out a crucial role in generating a mode of virtuosity born of a heterogeneous coalescence of street, classical, and modern dance forms, from popping, locking, and breaking to ballet, jazz, and Horton.[23] Beginning in the AAADT in the 1980s and extending to both Forsythe's and Rhoden's rehearsals in the 1990s, Richardson has worked in the space of "the break," drawing on improvisatory skills of inserting popping moves into ballet and contemporary dance-informed phrases. Such virtuosic transgression and invention in the 1990s emerged out of the particularly formalistic AAADT repertory unfolding in the late 1980s and epitomized by Byrd and Dove.

Many of the dancers from the original cast of Byrd's *Shards* (including Rhoden and Richardson) also danced in Dove's *Episodes* (fig. 5). Dove shared:

> I did [*Episodes*] after a very dear friend of mine died from AIDS. . . . I really wish that I had five more minutes with him to say things like, "I really appreciated the time we spent together." . . . yet I didn't have five minutes. . . . What would life be like if everybody lived

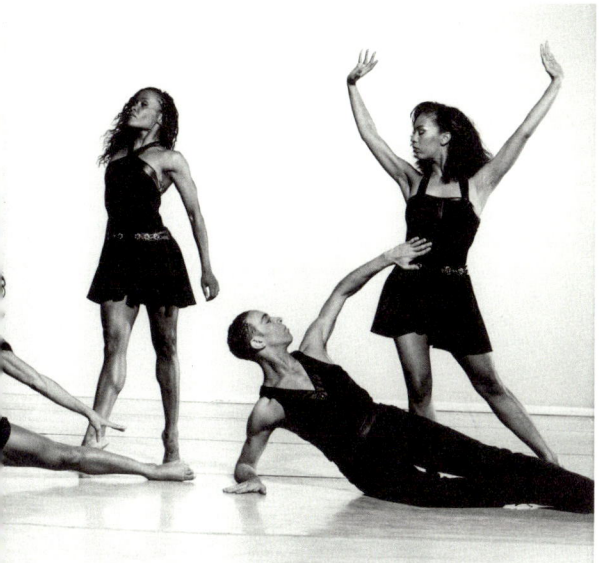
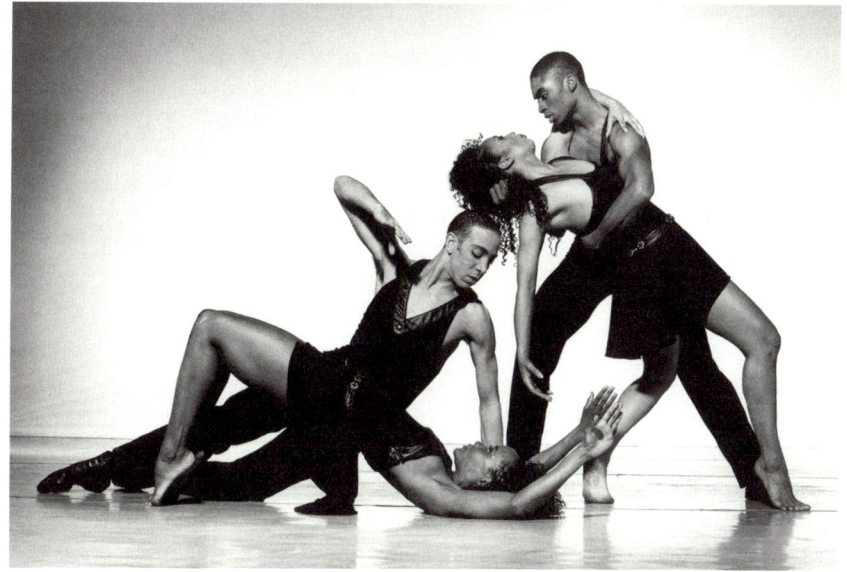

fig. 5
Jack Mitchell, *"Episodes": The Company*, n.d. National Museum of African American History and Culture, Washington, DC. Jack Mitchell Photography of the Alvin Ailey American Dance Theater Collection

fig. 6
Jack Mitchell, *"Episodes": Dwight Rhoden, Renee Robinson, Desmond Richardson, and Debora Chase*, n.d. National Museum of African American History and Culture, Washington, DC. Jack Mitchell Photography of the Alvin Ailey American Dance Theater Collection

every single moment so at the end of life we didn't need five minutes with anybody—that life was so fully lived that each episode of life was complete and the only thing we could hope for was to have more episodes, but not to go back and think that there was any episode that was incomplete. . . . In the crux of life, if you're learning all the time, you're really always going forward. . . . A major part of the issue was the forwardness and direction of a diagonal, and the choice that's inherent in an X when two diagonals cross: there's always the idea of choice—that you can go one way or you can go another way.[24]

If *Shards* began and ended in what Byrd described as a "clump of dancers [as] in 'I Been 'Buked' [in *Revelations*]," Dove's *Episodes* was structured around an X created by diagonal lighting, ever charged by the crux of its center, where a dancer could make a "choice." In *Episodes*, Dove took us on a distilled journey of starkly defined couplings, escapes, convergences, and abandonments. The audience could sense the visceral charge of romantic and sexual attractions and dramaturgies, as both heterosexual and homosexual couples, and even trios, came together (fig. 6). Dancers caught each other midair, as if out of nowhere. In perhaps the most memorable portion of the piece, Rhoden and Richardson, two dancers who were romantically entangled in the late 1980s and early 1990s, and later went on to cofound Complexions Contemporary Ballet in New York, ran onto stage one after the other, leaping over each other with such urgency and lush technical prowess as if to announce virtuosity's undeniable hold on this new era in contemporary dance. Although not explicit by any means, their 1989 duet has often been read as the most unabashed example of Black gay love in the Ailey repertory up until this moment. Needless to say, queer of color viewers will seek representation and recognition however possible, through repeated viewings, archival research, choreographers' interviews, and even gossip. While the AAADT, a company that often functioned as a US national cultural export, could not afford to stage much LGBTQI+ content, dancers' virtuosity, gendered casting choices, and abstraction provided conduits for queer of color aesthetics.

With so much racist, homophobic emphasis at the time on AIDS as a blood "contagion," dance audiences had the opportunity to kinesthetically experience Ailey's ethos of dancing from blood memories, from complex fabrics of individual and collective African American histories. As Ailey shared, his blood memories included everything from family memories to blues and gospel songs. Ultimately, he described them as "creative sides," and Byrd and Dove rigorously and daringly embraced the creativity of choreographing from blood memory. By calling upon Ailey dancers to carry out such creativity, signaled by one dancer's hyperextended leg or another dancer's incessant speed (perhaps an exaggeration of ballet, perhaps a blood memory of a hip-hop dance from childhood), they eschewed the feigned category of purity and instead insisted on the heterogeneity of culture, form, gender, and sexuality. Ultimately, in its unrelenting excess, virtuosity in the AAADT's late-1980s choreographic imaginary functioned as productive mourning—yearning ambition as a response to needless death. In its melancholic joy, the pursuit of virtuosity emanating from this era of Ailey history continues to move—and be reshaped by—subsequent generations of dancers and choreographers.

NOTES

1. Dionne Brand, *A Map to the Door of No Return* (Toronto: Vintage Canada, 2023), 27, e-book (emphasis in original).

2. Alvin Ailey, in *Ailey*, directed by Jamila Wignot (New York: Neon, 2021), film.

3. Donald Byrd, "An Interview with Choreographer Donald Byrd," by Jamal Story, Features, Dance Consortium (website), published August 23, 2011, https://danceconsortium.com/features/interview/an-interview-with-choreographer-donald-byrd/.

4. Ulysses Dove, in *Episodes*, directed by Thomas Grimm, choreography by Ulysses Dove, performed by Debora Chase, Wesley Johnson, Dwight Rhoden, Desmond Richardson, Renee Robinson, Elizabeth Roxas, Stephen Smith, Desire Vlad, and Dereque Whiturs, set design by Douglas Grekin, costumes by Jorge Gallardo, produced by Thomas Grimm (ArtHaus Musik, 1990), eVideo, 24 min.

5. Brand, *A Map to the Door*, 27.

6. At the 1992 Republican National Convention in Houston, Patrick Buchanan, who had sought that year's Republican presidential nomination, stated, "There is a religious war going on in this country. It is a cultural war, as critical to the kind of nation we shall be as was the Cold War itself, for this war is for the soul of America." Patrick Joseph Buchanan, "Culture War Speech: Address to the Republican National Convention," August 17, 1992. The full speech appears on the website Voices of Democracy: The U.S. Oratory Project, accessed April 16, 2024, https://voicesofdemocracy.umd.edu/buchanan-culture-war-speech-speech-text/. Buchanan's speech uses "soul" to indicate conservative Christianity, not Black soul. I discuss African American "soul" in relation to Desmond Richardson's virtuosity in my book *Body Impossible: Desmond Richardson and the Politics of Virtuosity* (New York: Oxford University Press, 2024), chap. 3.

7. Michelle Alexander, *The New Jim Crow: Mass Incarceration in the Age of Colorblindness* (New York: New Press, 2010), eBook, Kindle.

8. The New Jim Crow extended President Richard Nixon's war on drugs via such troubling initiatives as the school-to-prison pipeline; see Alexander, 6.

9. For more reading on this topic, see André Lepecki, "The Body as Archive: Will to Re-Enact and the Afterlives of Dances," *Dance Research Journal* 42, no. 2 (Winter 2010): 28–48; José Esteban Muñoz, "Ephemera as Evidence: Introductory Notes to Queer Acts," *Women and Performance: A Journal of Feminist Theory* 8, no. 2 (1996): 5–16; and Diana Taylor, *The Archive and the Repertoire: Performing Cultural Memory in the Americas* (Durham, NC: Duke University Press, 2003).

10. Ariel Osterweis, "Virtuosity: I Know It When I See It," introduction to *Body Impossible*, 1–24.

11. Brenda Dixon-Gottschild, *The Black Dancing Body: A Geography from Coon to Cool* (New York: Palgrave Macmillan, 2003), 223 (emphasis in original).

12. Fred Moten, *In the Break: The Aesthetics of the Black Radical Tradition* (Minneapolis: University of Minnesota Press, 2003).

13. Brenda Dixon-Gottschild, *Digging the Africanist Presence in American Performance: Dance and Other Contexts* (Westport, CT: Praeger, 1996), 11.

14. Moten, *In the Break*, 255n1.

15. Roderick A. Ferguson, *Aberrations in Black: Toward a Queer of Color Critique* (Minneapolis: University of Minnesota Press, 2004), 21.

16. Ferguson, 4.

17. Ferguson, 29.

18. "*Shards*," Repertory, Alvin Ailey American Dance Theater (website), accessed December 11, 2023, https://www.alvinailey.org/performances/repertory/shards.

19. Byrd, "An Interview."

20. Lewis Segal, "Dance Review: Alvin Ailey Introduces 'Shards,'" *Los Angeles Times*, March 16, 1989.

21. *Shards*, AAADT performance video, England, October 19, 1990; *Shards* rehearsal video, AAADT (1515 Broadway), August 5, 1988; both accessed September 2023, Alvin Ailey American Dance Theater Archives, New York.

22. The *New York Times* dance critic Jennifer Dunning has referred to Richardson as "one of the great virtuoso dancers of his generation."; Dunning, "Dance Review: The Many Aspects of Complexions," *New York Times*, August 1, 1995.

23. On this, see my extended discussion in Osterweis, *Body Impossible*, 1–23.

24. See note 4, above.

Joshua Lubin-Levy

At the Edge of Each Other

Reading with Alvin Ailey's Archives

> I think my best works are personal. The ones that endure seem to be the ones that come out of my guts—the hardest ones, that reveal some part of self.
> —Alvin Ailey[1]

In the countless pages of writing in Alvin Ailey's archives, his handwriting shifts shape. Hastily scrawled missives suggest a hand trying to keep up with the speed at which his mind and body worked. Then, neatly spaced lists in capital letters repeat his thinking, as though he were attempting to solidify fleeting thoughts into a lasting form. His marks move, sometimes with but more often against, the ruled lines of the page. Reading through his archive, I have wondered if Ailey encountered the page less as a routine exercise in writing and more like an open stage on which to plot words like dancers. Or, more simply, when his handwriting crosses the ruled line, is it an indication he was writing amid a rehearsal and did not want to take his eyes off the dancers? One must be careful not to over-ascribe meaning to the smallest gesture when conducting archival research. But where should one draw the line, especially with an artist such as Ailey, who himself so often blurred the boundary between his life and his work? Certainly, there are some items that were never meant to be read by anyone other than the author. Knowing that Ailey frequently pulled from his own lived experience to make work relevant to the lives of his audiences—using his biography to find a framework for dances that conveyed a collective Black, American experience—even the most intimate details buzz with the potential of becoming choreography.

Following the way Ailey's writing pushes and pulls across this threshold, enumerating a rich psychic interior and developing choreography that aspired to "celebrate the beauty of mankind . . . its roots germinating in Black America,"[2] this essay leans into the blurry relationship between the individual and the collective, the self and the social, and the personal and the political, closely reading the way Ailey choreographed in the precipice between these seemingly binarized positions. What I am asking is nothing like how the personal becomes political in Ailey's practice—which, in any case, should be obvious given that, from its inception in 1958, his company emphasized the importance of elevating the history of Black dance and music as the foundation of American art. Rather, it is a question of how one might understand the centrality of the personal and the self as a conduit to broader social and political aspirations in Ailey's practice. To do so, I stay close to fragments in Ailey's archive, specifically the draft of a program for a ballet titled *Au Bord*

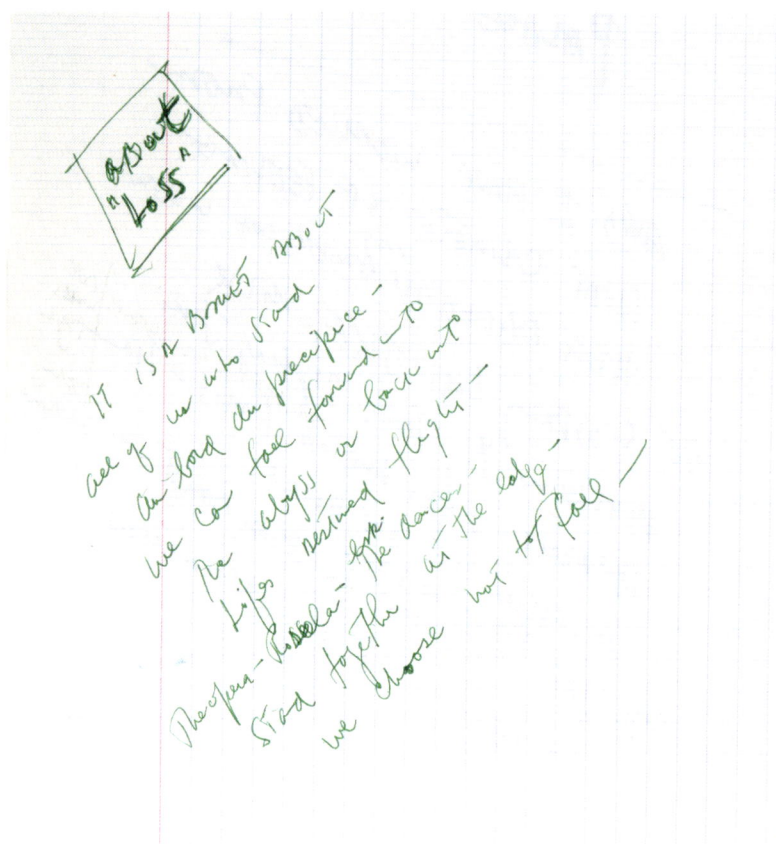

fig. 1

Alvin Ailey, page from Notebook #102 [734], "Untitled," n.d., Allan Gray Family Personal Papers of Alvin Ailey (AC10), Series 3: Notebooks, folder 131, Black Archives of Mid-America in Kansas City, Missouri. All pages illustrated in this essay are from this notebook.

du Précipice (1983). The choreography for this ballet, like much of Ailey's work, draws from personal experience. What the writing in his archive illuminates, I argue, is how Ailey worked to make choreographic intent public.

The centrality of individual, even personal, forms of expression in Ailey's practice can be tied back to his staunch commitment to the tradition of modern dance. Ailey claimed modernism as a central tenet of his work and celebrated modern dance as a "revolt against ballet" that prioritized the "individuality of expression" through formal invention.[3] Dance scholars such as Clare Croft have highlighted the ways in which Black dance artists at mid-century, Ailey perhaps chief among them, used modernism's universalizing tendency (toward formal innovation) to create a politics of self-determination through performance.[4]

Given modernism's celebration of newness and originality, Ailey expressed his love for modern dance contradictorily by curating the work of other modern choreographers into his company's repertory. In a letter granting Ailey's request to perform a work by Lester Horton, Frank Eng (Horton's partner and business manager) snidely responded: "I was under the impression that in leaving us you were seeking pastures greener than Horton's. I am certain Martha Graham, nor [José] Limon, nor Anna Sokolow would permit dancers outside their groups to dance their choreographies."[5] Personal expression is evident in much of Ailey's own choreography and is rooted in what he called "blood memories," which he elaborated as not only the memories themselves but also his "intense feelings about them"—the feelings connected to the memories being as much a source of creative drive as perhaps the memories themselves.[6] But there is also a degree of personal expression in the careful selection of work by others that Ailey used to create context in which to embed his own original dances. More than the articulation of a single artist's vision, the Ailey company was and continues to be a different way of assembling dance history—part of its mission is to make "one arm of ourselves a museum of classic American works."[7]

In this sense, Ailey's approach to modern dance, and to dance in general, differed from many of his colleagues. Reflecting on his career in notes for a 1985 lecture, Ailey articulated the difference thus: "Each MD (Modern Dance) Choreographer, I Myself, Invents language relating to what he or she has to say—but not all have invented a technique, nor have I . . . Total Dancer Concept because of the use of many choreographers, because of creative challenge, and my repertory system to develop teachers, choreographers, movements full of images."[8] Inventing his own language (with and through the body) but not his own technique, Ailey refused the terms of authorship claimed by so many other modern choreographers. One need only think of those dancers whose surnames are stand-ins for a particular dance method: (Lester) Horton, (Martha) Graham, (Katherine) Dunham, among many others. These were techniques that Ailey adored, trained in, studied, and brought into the pedagogy of his company and, later, the Ailey School's curriculum. Their work is the etymology of the language he would create. His interest was less in the individual's capacity for unique expression than in the individual dancing body as an expression of totality (what he called the *total dancer concept*), as one who *uses many choreographers* to create *movements full of images*. This modality of accumulation is further reflected, on another page from Ailey's lecture notes, in his recognition of modern dance as a "rich gathering of historical forces"[9]—a celebration not of the originality of modern choreographers but of their opening up of the discipline to a broad array of influences dealing with the human condition and reflection on the world. In a similar vein, Ailey's own language pulled together strands of pedagogy from multiple modern dance techniques, combining these with influences from the music and dance forms rooted in Black American folk tradition, and eventually expanding to include influences accumulated through the company's years of international travel and the important feedback of new generations of dancers. It was a language that continually expanded its vocabulary, aspiring to prepare the dancing body to contain and express this multitude.

The total dancer concept points to what dance made possible for Ailey: an awareness of the body as a medium of absorption and accretion, and a container for this melting pot of historical forces that was different from other externally imposed frameworks of belonging. These forces include not only those that the Ailey company intentionally took in (such as the work by other choreographers curated into the repertory) but also ones discovered within the company's own work and methods. As Sylvia Waters observes: "At times Alvin would 'individualize' a movement from one of his most classic works (such as 'Sinner Man' or 'I Want to Be Ready' from *Revelations*), further challenging the abilities and still untapped strengths of the Ensemble, helping each dancer to make the transition from technician to performer to artist."[10] Waters's comment again positions Ailey with a desire to transcend technique, to go beyond mere acuity or skill in order to frame dance as a process of discovery, particularly attuned to what remains unrealized in the forms (and works) in existence. Thus, when Ailey wrote of his company, as he did in 1962, that "we have in our programs the history of American dance going all the way back to Isadora Duncan + before," referring to it as "truly an American Dance Co.,"[11] one might imagine this relationship to history not as staid and knowable but as a horizon of possibilities yet to be uncovered. What it meant to be *truly American* remained an open question, a sense of being under continual rehearsal.

I stress this searching, open-ended relation to being an "American" dance theater to highlight Ailey's intervention in claiming the nation-state (in addition to modernism). Creating "movements full of images" that center Black American experience, Ailey deliberately contended with the broader imperative in modern America to hunt down what Albert Murray calls the "illusive Black image"—the preponderance of attempts to narrativize, document, survey, disclose, and thereby "fix" the meaning of the so-called Black Experience.[12] Image, here, refers not only to photographs but, of course, to the broader media sphere or published studies, reports, journalism, and literature. Murray, whom Ailey read in depth, vociferously criticizes the "jargon of social science," which, despite its intention, creates and circulates images that become definitive of Blackness in the popular imaginary and that tend to focus on immiseration and misery.[13] Against this imperative, Murray and Ailey both argued that art—especially the blues, as both a genre and a method—was an "antidote" capable of making "sense of the ambiguities and absurdities inherent in all human experience."[14]

If art in general afforded a more nuanced representation of Black American history and culture, dance offered Ailey another level of engagement with a legacy of Black culture he was determined to capture. In a note on his pedagogy, he expressed the need to train dancers physically and mentally, not only in technical skill but also "to use things to induce word[s] into oneself"—as though dance offered a means of contending with the boundary between the material body and its discursive construction.[15] Indeed, Ailey developed his

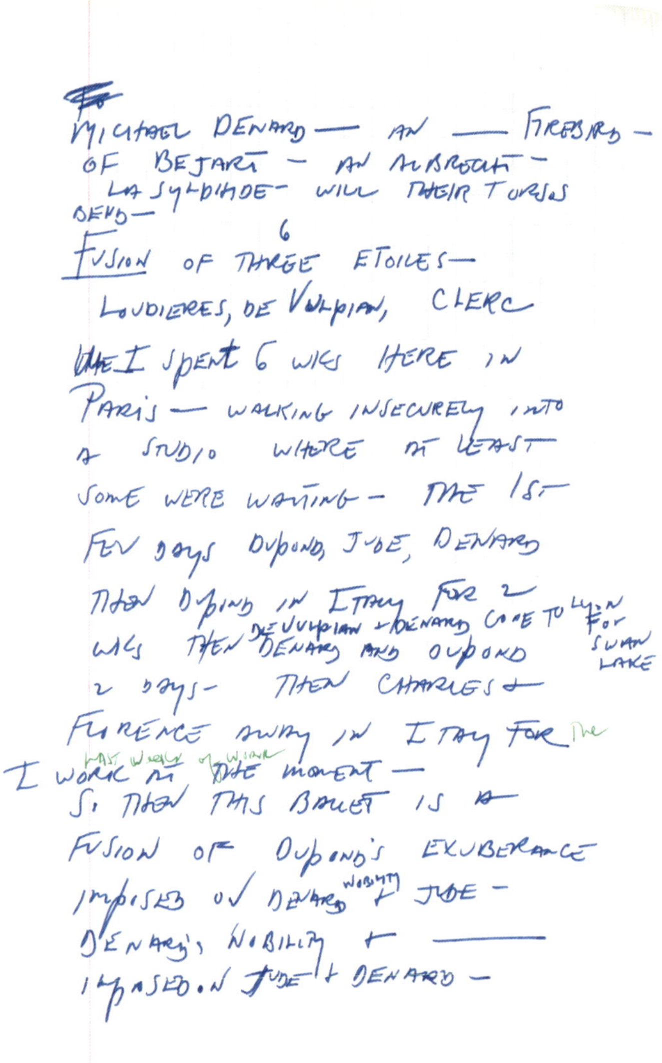

fig. 2

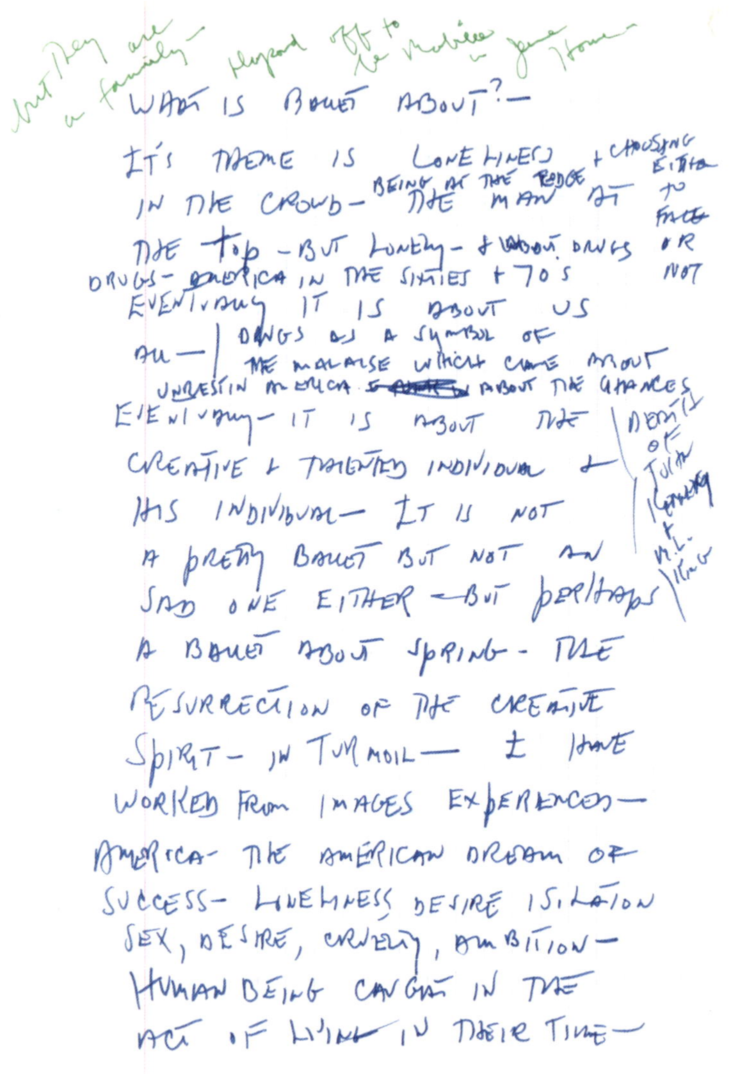

fig. 3

(modern dance) language both on the page and through the body. Even his process of choreographing "at the moment" (fig. 2), building choreography on his dancers rather than in advance, suggests a particular attunement to working at the threshold between embodiment and the body's signification, uncovering ways to use the body that both articulate and evade its attempted capture.

Au Bord du Précipice is seemingly about an artist's vexed relationship with separating his life from his work, particularly given the demands of his adoring public, whose obsession seems to drive him mad, pushing him deeper and deeper into a state of isolation and abandonment.[16] The plot is a quintessentially modernist trope of, according to Ailey, "[t]he creative + talented individual … caught in the act of living in their time" (fig. 3). The theme recurs across Ailey's body of work; as Thomas DeFrantz notes, "the most severe criticisms of [*Précipice*] centered on its obvious, conventional narrative of decay, barely transformed from earlier Ailey works like *Quintet* and *Flowers*."[17] Choreographed not for his own company but for the Paris Opera Ballet, *Precipice* (as it was later retitled) starred Patrick Dupond in the role of "He." While He is a familiar figure in Ailey's choreography, the dance would have had particular resonance when it debuted in 1983, only three years after Ailey himself suffered a rather public breakdown, owing to a combination of professional pressure, drug addiction, and a tumultuous relationship. It is almost too easy, in other words, to imagine He as a figure of autobiography.

Several handwritten pages in one of Ailey's notebooks outline his intention for the ballet, highlighting that despite its appearance as a story about an ill-fated star, the work was meant (at least for Ailey) to capture a distinctly American sentiment: "all of us who stand au bord du precipice" (see fig. 1). He labeled these pages *affiche* (fig. 4), the French term

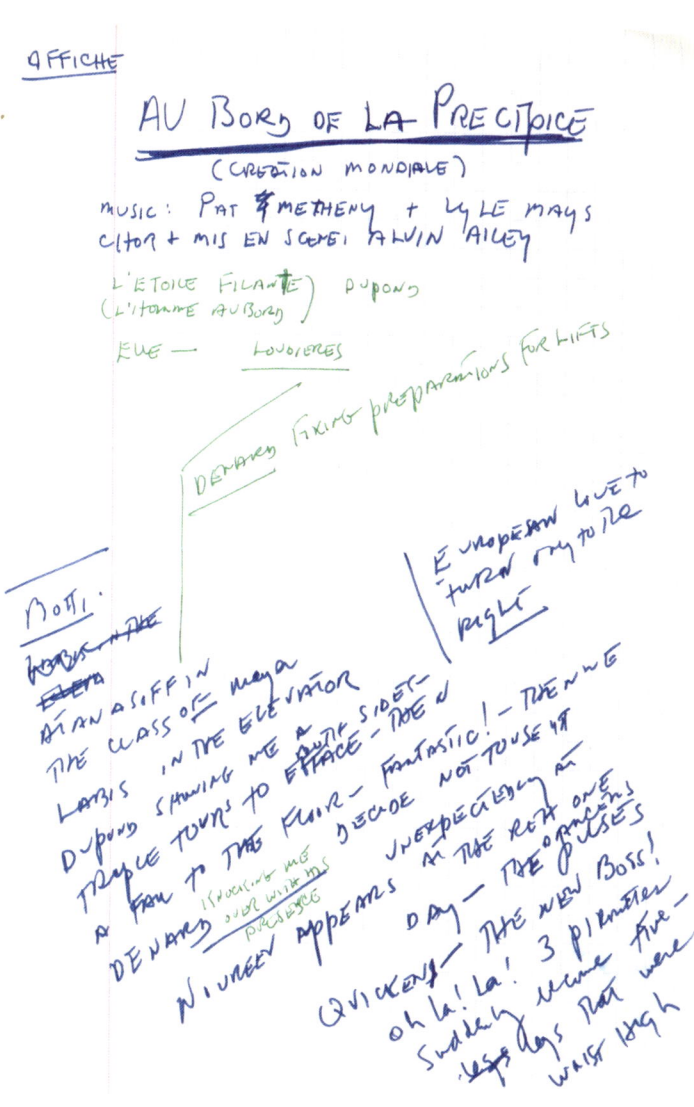

fig. 4

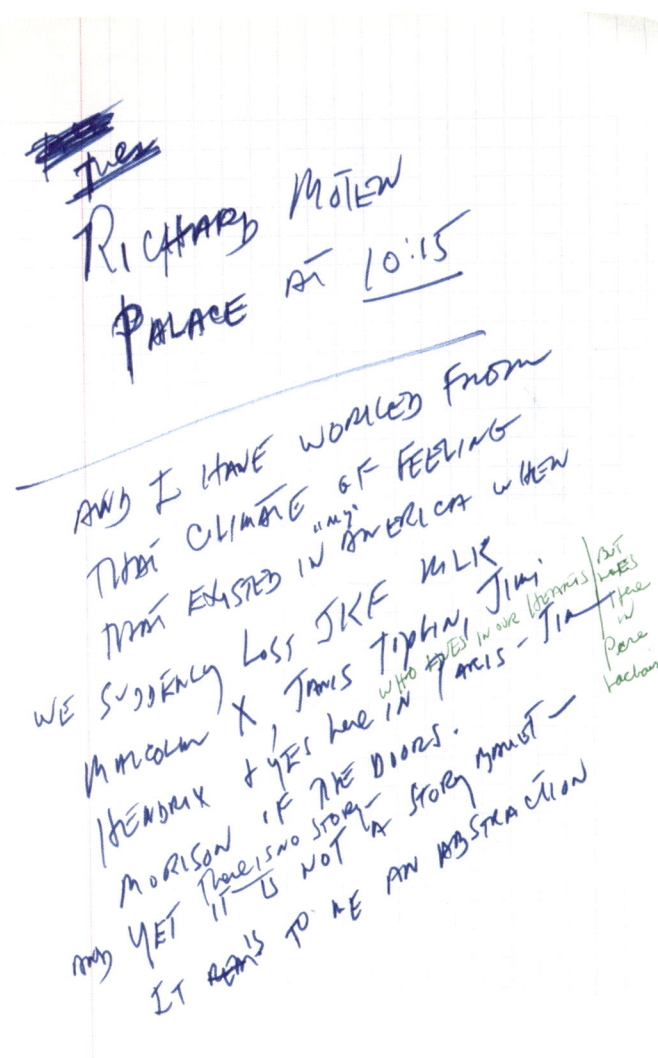

fig. 5

for poster, with its resonance with the word *affix* and roots in the French verb *ficher* (to fasten, fix, settle in)—all of which Ailey may have been attuned to as an expert in multiple languages. His affiche, however, becomes particularly useful as a tool of unfixing what might otherwise be a straightforward (auto)biographical reading of the dance. Curiously, Ailey denied the work's reference to biography by employing a highly personal tone of reflection and observation, one that draws attention to the artist not as an icon in public life but rather as tangled in the affective relations of the creative process.

After an extended discussion of the creative process, Ailey's affiche describes the ballet as being about "loneliness in the crowd," situating this concept in the historical moment of America in the 1960s and '70s and in relation to American ideology: "images experienced—America—the American dream of success" (see fig. 3). At the end of the 1960s, the failed promise of the American Dream was particularly pronounced. The utopianism of the countercultural movement waned, a booming postwar economy began a downward turn, and rising forms of violence abroad and at home all undermined the sense of hope in progressive politics that characterized the prior years. Capturing this context, Ailey's description of *Precipice* continues: "I have worked from that climate of feeling that existed in 'my' America when we suddenly lost JFK, MLK, Malcolm X, Janis Joplin, Jimi Hendrix + yes here in Paris—Jim Morison [sic] of the Doors. And yet there is no story—it is not a story ballet—it is to me an abstraction" (fig. 5). Not only did the figures Ailey listed embody the utopianism of an early counterculture movement but their deaths have often been used to emblematize the end of that earlier era. Still, critical reception of *Precipice* has tended to emphasize the reference to rock stars, especially noting the physical resemblance between Dupond and Morrison, both lithe young white men with thick manes of wavy brown hair. But if the figure of He has a reference point at all, wouldn't it be the strange synthesis of the six figures Ailey names and who stretch across the political and pop culture spectrums? They suture together a complex matrix of not only art and politics but also gendered and racial identity. They figure a range of cultural transformation, as their collective existence (much like their loss) suggests something more like a "climate of feeling" than a reducible political or identitarian position. This sense of *Precipice* as a group portrait, rather than the story of an individual protagonist, is certainly more aligned with the post-1968 turn away from faith in the heroic individuals toward collective politics.

Situating the work in relation to the political climate of the late 1960s, Ailey's affiche pays equal attention to the process of making the ballet. Prior to introducing the "climate of feeling" in America as a theme, Ailey wrote personal observations of his experience of working with the Paris Opera Ballet. His notes open with an implicit power struggle between two stars of the dance world, suggesting a comparison between himself and the ballet company's newly appointed director, Rudolf Nureyev. Ailey described his difficulty in assembling the dancers, whereas when Nureyev entered the rehearsal room unexpectedly, Ailey observed that "[t]he dancers' pulses quicken—the new boss! oh la! la! 3 pirouettes suddenly become five" (see fig. 4). By contrast, Ailey expressed his insecurity and "frustration beyond my normal torment" in working with a company that is not his own (fig. 6).

Ailey went on to attribute his anguish to the misalignment between his own method of working ("at the moment") and that of the ballet company. The Paris company members are never available when he is ready to work—the reader learns that they are busy creating other works, maintaining the repertory, and leading their own personal lives—such that Ailey must make dance with whatever bodies show up to rehearsal, crafting movement on one dancer to eventually give to another. The result is a ballet that he described as a "fusion of three étoiles [stars]," first citing Monique Loudières, Claude de Vulpian, and Florence Clerc, but then returning to the original notion, referring to the work as "a fusion of Dupond's exuberance imposed on [Michaël] Denard's nobility + [Charles] Jude—Denard's nobility + ____ imposed on Jude + Denard" (see fig. 2). The description of the fusion remains unresolved. On this synthesis of dancing bodies Ailey further remarked that "perhaps the most important has been the extraordinary collaboration in this venture of Ulysses Dove—who spent 7 years as a [dancer] of my own co[mpany]" (fig. 7), but who, at the time, was assistant director of the choreographic research group of the Paris Opera Ballet. Ailey described Dove as "my <u>voice</u>—arms—legs." This porous relation between the dancers reflects the breakdown of individualism and the icon similarly articulated in the chain of celebrities lost. It is almost as though they are dissipating into each other, as Ailey's writing in broken and cut-off fragments suggests difficulty in capturing the two dancers' unique quality.

More than an obsession with celebrity, whether his own or others, Ailey was arguably fascinated with the pathos surrounding the exceptional individual, the one not only faced with public scrutiny but situated at the fulcrum of collective attachments and desires. The process of creating *Precipice* suggests this by pulling together a multiplicity of bodies—figures from the past, dancers who keep missing one another in the rehearsal room, the ensemble that undulates around Dupond, the audience to whom the cast often directs attention as equally complicit in the disintegration of the star. *Precipice*, in other words, might be less a story of the central protagonist and more a ballet about the series of longings and adoration—the collective attachments—held together through the figure of He. Reading Ailey, this is the climate of feeling he sought to conjure, but it is also the precipice where he leaves the contemporary reader. Artists often stop at the edge of their audience, unsure of how a work will be received, of what will be made of so much desire and intention to communicate. Ailey's archives foreground his own attempt to grapple with the chasm between himself and all the others he sought to connect with through dance. In a page titled "artistry," he wrote in the imperative, "[L]earn what your body is doing so you can communicate feeling . . . expand your bodies into space and create a mysterious and poetic vapor-light around yourself."[18] Commanding his reader, Ailey called into being a future action, a slippage no less from "body" to "bodies," which through dance does not just capture but creates a climate of vapor-light. In the haze of this ether, one can imagine, bodies blur between one and another, emerging and receding through a fog that fills the precipice between the dancer and the audience.

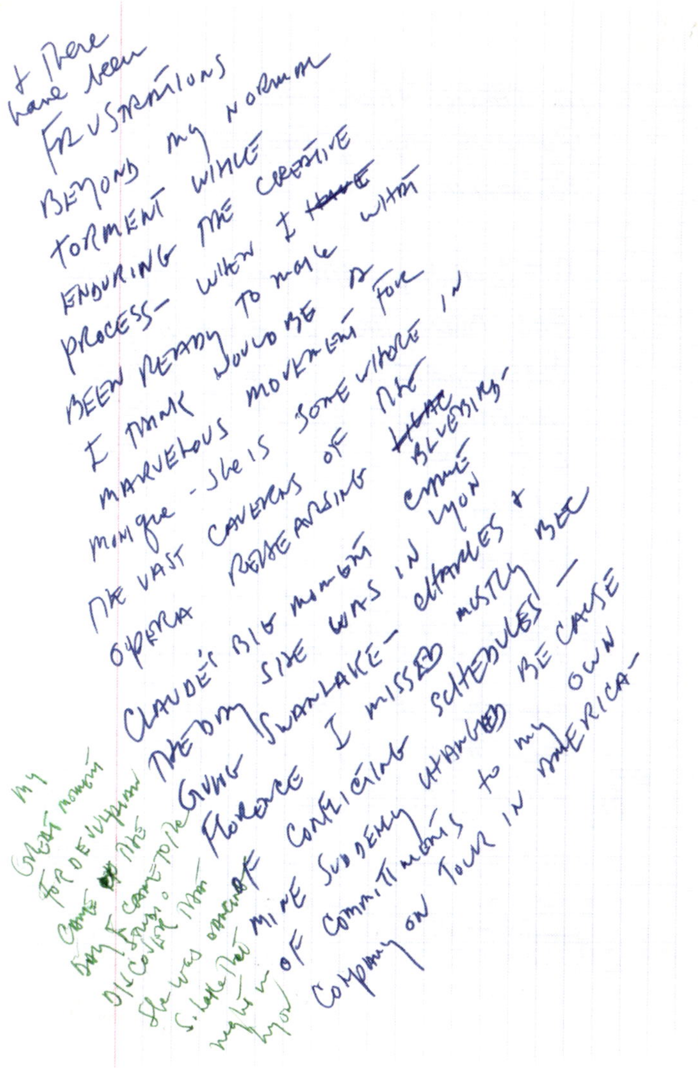

& there have been FRUSTRATIONS BEYOND my norm of TORMENT while ENDURING the CREATIVE process— when I have been ready to note with MARVELOUS MOVEMENT for MONIQUE — she is someone in the VAST CAVERNS of the OPERA REHEARSING the BLUEBIRD

CLAUDE'S BIG NUMBER — she was in LYON
my greatest moment for developing the DAY Gave SWANLAKE— CHARLES +
came of this Christophe FLORENCE I missed mostly BEC
barry I can't to be discussed that mine suddenly changed because
S. Lake Noh she was opening of conflicting schedules —
my view of commitments to my own
you company on tour in AMERICA —

fig. 6

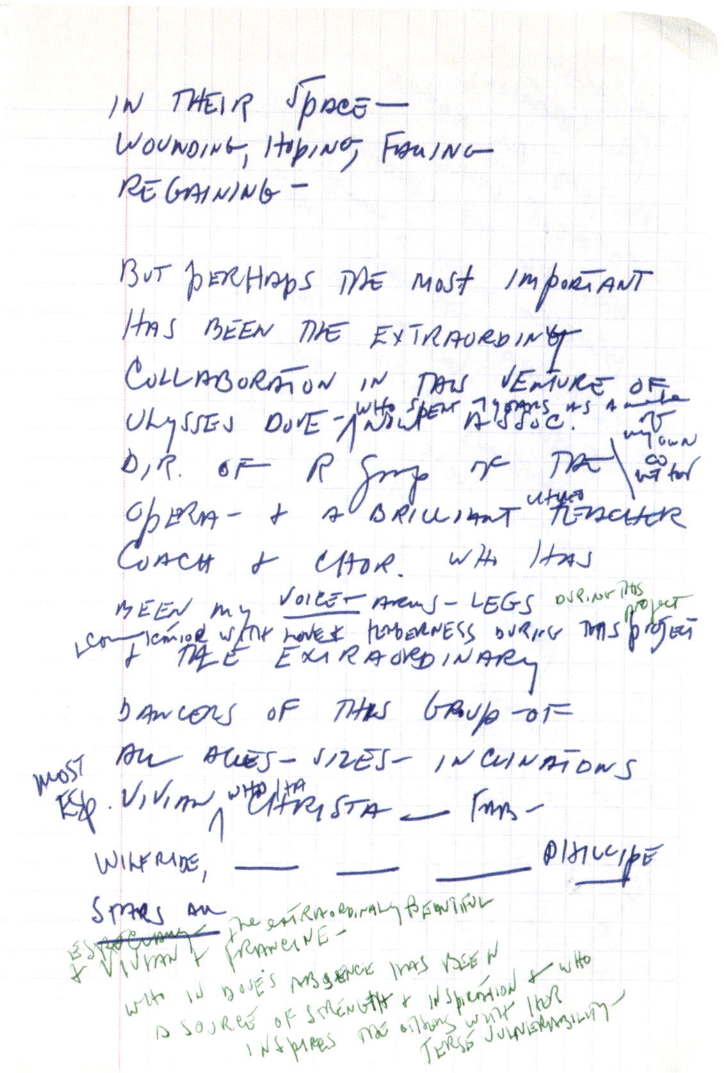

IN THEIR SPACE —
WOUNDING, HOPING, FAILING —
REGAINING —

BUT PERHAPS THE MOST IMPORTANT HAS BEEN THE EXTRAORDINARY COLLABORATION IN THIS VENTURE OF ULYSSES DOVE — who spent 7 years as a writer assoc. DIR. OF R group of the 8 water OPERA — & A BRILLIANT teacher COACH & CHOR. WHO HAS BEEN MY VOICE ARMS — LEGS during this leaning senior with love & tenderness during this project & THE EXTRAORDINARY DANCERS OF THIS GROUP OF MOST ALL AGES — SIZES — INCLINATIONS
ESP. VIVIAN, with it CHRISTA — TMR —
WILFRIDE, ————— @ PHILIPPE
STAYS on
the extraordinarily beautiful
& VIVIAN & FRANCINE —
who in Dove's absence has been
a source of strength & inspiration & who
inspires the others with her terse vulnerability

fig. 7

At the Edge of Each Other

NOTES

1. Alvin Ailey, quoted in *Celebrating "Revelations" at Fifty*, directed by Judy Kinberg (2010), https://youtu.be/44nqeAXLS-k?si=na27MZpEUTQwUlmn.

2. Alvin Ailey, "The Philosophy of the Company," Dance Theater Foundation, Inc., Request to the Ford Foundation for Cash Reserve Grant, 1974, box 138, folder 8, Alvin Ailey Dance Foundation Collection, Music Division, Library of Congress, Washington, DC (hereafter AADFC).

3. Alvin Ailey, notes for a lecture delivered in 1985, Notebook #88, "Untitled," n.d., Allan Gray Family Personal Papers of Alvin Ailey (AC10), Series 3: Notebooks, folder 117, Black Archives of Mid-America in Kansas City, MO (hereafter Gray Papers).

4. See, for example, Clare Croft, *Dancers as Diplomats: American Choreography in Cultural Exchange* (New York: Oxford University Press, 2015).

5. Frank Eng to Alvin Ailey, n.d., box 18, folder 3, "Ailey, Alvin, to Frank Eng, 1955–1976," Lester Horton Dance Theater Collection, Music Division, Library of Congress, Washington, DC.

6. Alvin Ailey and A. Peter Bailey, *Revelations: The Autobiography of Alvin Ailey* (New York: Birch Lane, 1995), 12. The full quote reads "blood memories, blood memories about Texas, the blues, spirituals, gospel, work songs, all those things going on in Texas in the 1930s during the depression. I have intense feelings about them."

7. Ailey, "Philosophy of the Company," AADFC.

8. Ailey, notes for a lecture, Notebook #88, Gray Papers.

9. Ailey, notes for a lecture.

10. Sylvia Waters, "The Alvin Ailey Repertory Ensemble," in "Alvin Ailey: An American Visionary," ed. Muriel Topaz, special issue, *Choreography and Dance* 4, no. 1 (1996): 30.

11. Alvin Ailey, "Saturday, 27 January, 1962," National Diary for 1962, folder 189, Series 3: Notebooks, Gray Papers.

12. Albert Murray, *The Omni-Americans: New Perspectives on Black Experience and American Culture* (New York: Outerbridge & Dienstfrey, 1970), esp. "The Illusive Black Image," 69–170.

13. Murray, 12.

14. Murray, 5.

15. Alvin Ailey, "What I will expect of dancers," Dance Theater Foundation, Inc., box 150, folder 8, AADFC.

16. The title is a French phrase that, literally translated, means "at the edge of the precipice," though it is often used metaphorically to describe being on the verge of a decisive or consequential moment.

17. Thomas F. DeFrantz, *Dancing Revelations: Alvin Ailey's Embodiment of African American Culture* (Oxford, UK: Oxford University Press, 2006), 216.

18. Alvin Ailey, "artistry," Notebook #81 [707], "Untitled," n.d., Gray Papers.

Harmony Bench and Kate Elswit[1]

Radical Accounting and the Edges of Archives

Alvin Ailey American Dance Theater's Historical Data

The work of accounting for dance's histories most often relies on anecdotes on privileged works and exemplary biographical moments. By contrast, we propose a radical accounting of dance history that represents the complexity of dance landscapes, including all the contributing artists, all the dance works that they made and performed, and all the places where those performers and performances were seen. Our manually curated datasets transform archival materials into data-driven designs that make visible the interconnections of performance history across time, space, and bodies. This intentional data curation and its visualization demand close proximity to historical evidence to grapple with the meaningful messiness of archives and construct a framework for historical imagination.[2] We pull together methods from dance scholarship to draw movement out of static records, from critical data studies to humanize data through an ethics of care, and from experimental visualization to surface new interpretations of the past.

Applying our radical accounting process to the many archives that hold the history of the Alvin Ailey American Dance Theater (AAADT)[3] in the context of this exhibition, we have built and visualized datasets that locate 4,122 concert performances in 505 cities in sixty-six countries and 158 repertory pieces that appeared in 2,050 program permutations, from the founding of the company in 1958 to Alvin Ailey's death in 1989; as well as the trajectories of the company's 335 artists from 1958 to 2023. Cumulatively, the data and visualizations trace the retention and transmission of embodied knowledge across generations of dancers, and the ways in which individual artists became vectors within a broader performing arts ecosystem. They particularize the daily activities through which the AAADT grew from a small touring company to a global phenomenon. And they help us understand the importance of Ailey not only as a choreographer but also as a dance historian, who shared dance as a living history with audiences around the United States and the world.

We have long been guided by the question: what makes curation, analysis, and visualization of data meaningful for the study of dance history? Our project *Dunham's Data: Katherine Dunham and Digital Methods for Dance Historical Inquiry* focused on the case study of one of the twentieth century's major African American choreographers.[4] Katherine Dunham (1909–2006) inspired generations of dance artists, including Ailey, by the way she inextricably embedded African diasporic practices into American modern dance. Ailey described an early formative experience of seeing Dunham perform in Los Angeles when he was a teenager: "What Miss Dunham was doing was Afro-Caribbean.

It was blues; it was spirituals; it touched something of the Texas in me."[5] Across three decades of Dunham's daily itinerary, including the performances that Ailey saw,[6] we crafted an argument about the circulation of Dunham, her dancers, and her work through the world, and the physical toll of maintaining a transnational career as a Black female performer over many decades. Tracing the comings and goings of her dancers, drummers, and singers from 1937 to 1962 and the interconnections of her repertory allowed us to make a case for potential pathways of body-to-body transmission as well as the ways in which dance works themselves connected artists who might never have shared time and space. The "everyday" perspective in *Dunham's Data* laid the groundwork for radical accounting by grappling with how we might look across data points to evidence and elaborate dance history as transnational, intergenerational, and collective.

The AAADT archives already document many examples of the company's history in data form, from handwritten attempts of tour histories recorded on yellow legal paper to typed lists of company membership by season.[7] To audit and expand on these, our team worked with the Ailey archives at the AAADT and the Library of Congress, and conducted further research at other collections including those of dancer Dudley Williams at the New York Public Library for the Performing Arts; the Allan Gray Family Personal Papers of Alvin Ailey at the Black Archives of Mid-America in Kansas City, Missouri; the Bureau of Educational and Cultural Affairs Historical Collection at the University of Arkansas, Fayetteville; and many smaller public and private collections. We also consulted periodicals ranging from small town and local college presses to large international newspapers. Among the materials analyzed were programs, critical reviews and previews, advance advertising, casting sheets, datebooks, contracts, tour reports sent to government agencies, and company travel itineraries. Artist personalities and useful data points often merge in annotations on these documents. Williams, for example, weaves together accounts of dancing in the AAADT's repertory and during nights on the town, as he counts down the number of performances left on tour. And dancer Donna Wood's comments assessing particular performances document last-minute changes to the program.

Whereas Ailey later described fitting six performers plus all the costumes and scenery—including "stools, ladders, and fans"[8]— for early tours into a single station wagon, figure 1a shows how the company grew. Here, we represent the company from 1958 to 2023 with reference to its dancers and artistic directors, based on the AAADT's records of company membership.[9] Each segment, or stream, represents an artist's presence in the company season by season, and grows taller the longer they stay. The height of the total graph at a given moment is formed by the number of dance artists and the duration of their individual tenure at the company. Dancers are depicted in blue; leadership roles, including rehearsal directors, in purple; and artistic directors in magenta, with each shaded by the season in which they joined, from dark to light. As an example, Williams is represented at the center of the graph as a dark blue stream, and when he retired from the stage in the 2004 season after dancing with Ailey for decades, the total height of the graph contracts significantly, but temporarily. This figure visualizes the contribution of each artist to the company's total body of knowledge, at the same time as it offers a sense of how the company exceeds any one individual—even its creator. Figures 1b–d pick up on this sense of continuity and rupture by representing each of the company's artistic directors (Ailey, Judith Jamison, and Robert Battle) in the context of the dance artists who performed under their leadership.[10]

When dance histories highlight only individual creators and star performers, as is most common, we lose the larger ecosystem—the dense network of connections through which dance-based knowledge is developed and transmitted within a community of artists, each of whom moves through different companies, shows, and other relationships. The emergence of Ailey's company coincided with the final years of Dunham's company, which gave its last performances in early 1963. Joining our dataset on Dunham's performers with that of Ailey's dancers and choreographers revealed ten overlapping artists.[11] With the addition of data from two mid-century Broadway Caribbean musicals in which Ailey himself performed, *House of Flowers* (1954–55) and *Jamaica* (1957–59), further connections appeared, such as Dunham dancer and teacher Pearl Reynolds, who performed in both productions alongside Ailey and later taught at the Ailey School.[12] The matinee that is recognized as the first performance of the Ailey company took place on March 30, 1958, in the middle of the *Jamaica* run on a Sunday, when Broadway theaters were dark. It was a shared bill with choreographer and former Dunham dancer Ernest Parham at the Dance Center of

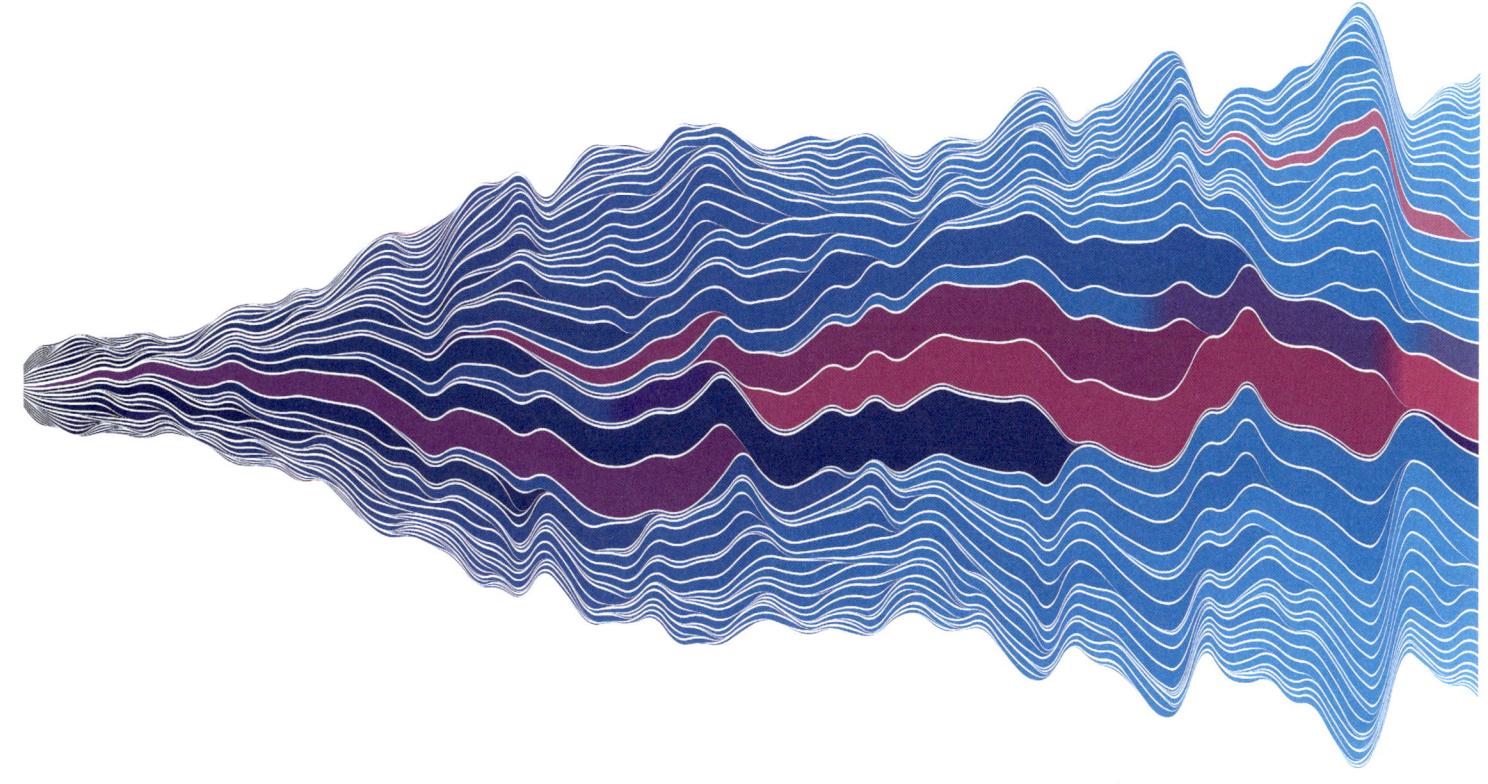

fig. 1a

AAADT Company Membership Flow by Season, 1958–2023. Each stream represents an artist's trajectory, growing taller with the duration of their membership. Years as dancers are depicted in blue; leadership roles, including rehearsal directors, in purple; and artistic and associate artistic directors in magenta, with the shading of each artist's stream set by the first season that they were employed by the company, from dark to light. Cumulatively, the number of dance artists and their individual tenures with the company determine the height of the graph for a given season.

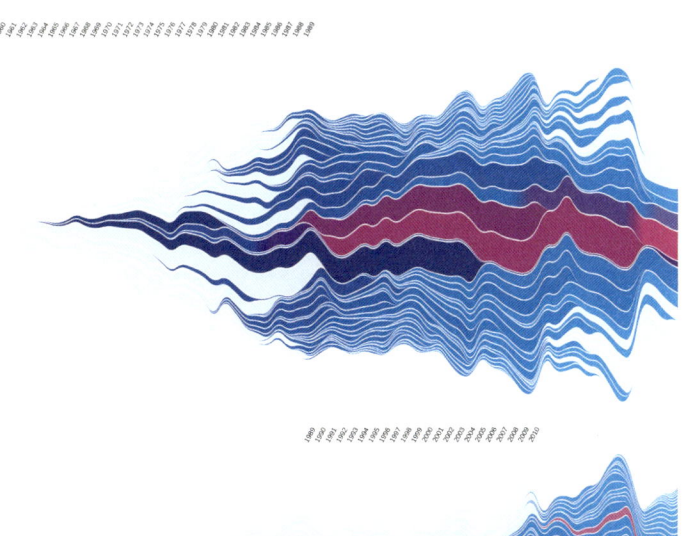

figs. 1b–d

AAADT Company Membership Flow by Season and Artistic Director, 1958–2023. Triptych representing AAADT under the artistic directorship of Alvin Ailey (1b. 1958–89), Judith Jamison (1c. 1989–2011), and Robert Battle (1d. 2011–23) respectively, which shows both continuity and generational shifts in the company.

Radical Accounting and the Edges of Archives

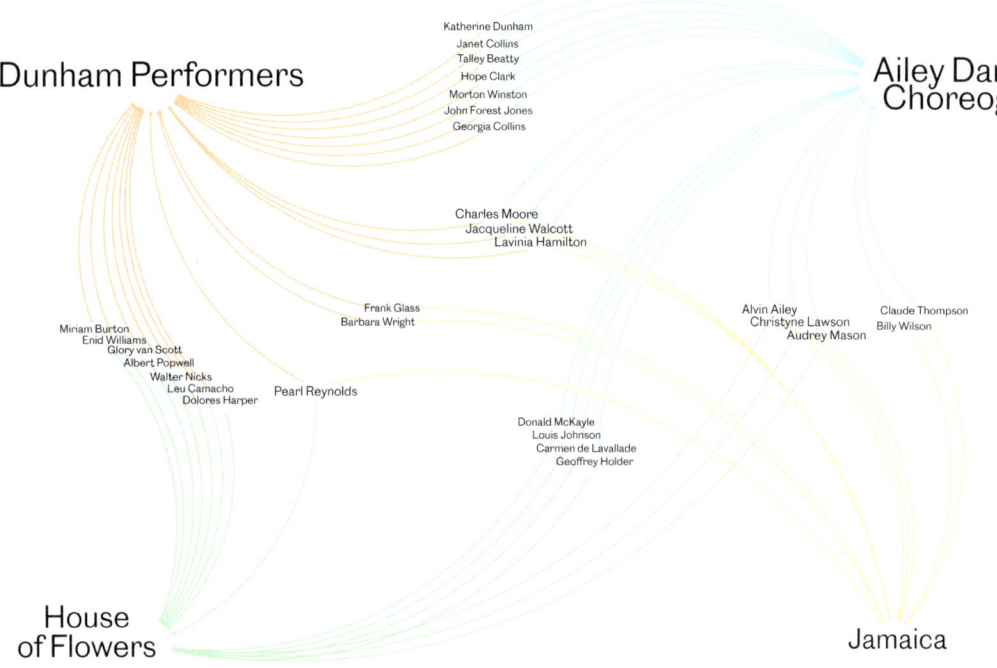

fig. 2

Ailey Artists and Beyond: Toward an Indicative Ecosystem. Four mid-century performance contexts that featured Black performers are located at the corners. The twenty-nine individuals who appear in two or more of these contexts are identified, suggesting the dense network of connections that emerged between Katherine Dunham's performers (orange), individuals who danced with and choreographed for Ailey's company (blue), and the two Broadway Caribbeana musicals in which Ailey performed: *Jamaica* (yellow) and *House of Flowers* (green).

fig. 3

AAADT Manhattan Performance Locations, 1958–89. Venues in which the Ailey company performed in Manhattan during his lifetime, plotted on a photograph taken by Fairchild Aerial Surveys in the 1950s. The image has been transformed to align with map coordinates for geo-referencing. Every venue has a unique pole on which each performance run is represented by a sphere, with those lowest on the pole occurring earliest in time. While there are forty-three venues on this visualization of Manhattan, our full data set from the New York Metropolitan Area includes 106 venues.

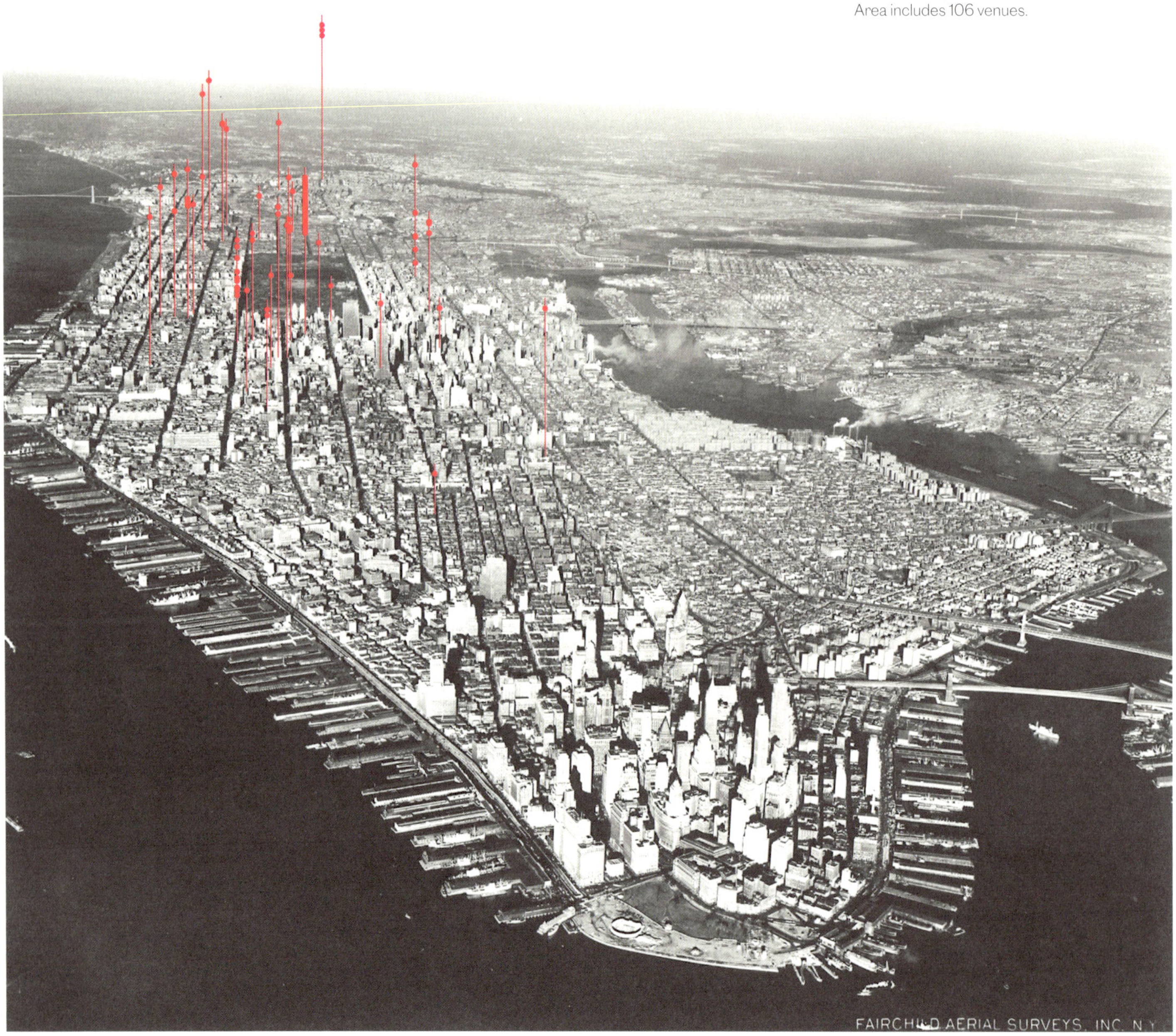

figs. 4a–d

Three-Dimensional Architecture of AAADT Touring, 1958–89. The company's touring across 505 cities over Ailey's lifetime is shown as three-dimensional architectures. Time is represented as elevation and color gradient, from 1958 in yellow near the basemap to 1989 in purple at the highest point. Images with spheres on poles highlight individual runs in each city (figs. 4b, 4c), while the other images focus on travel by connecting cities in their chronological sequence (figs. 4a, 4d).

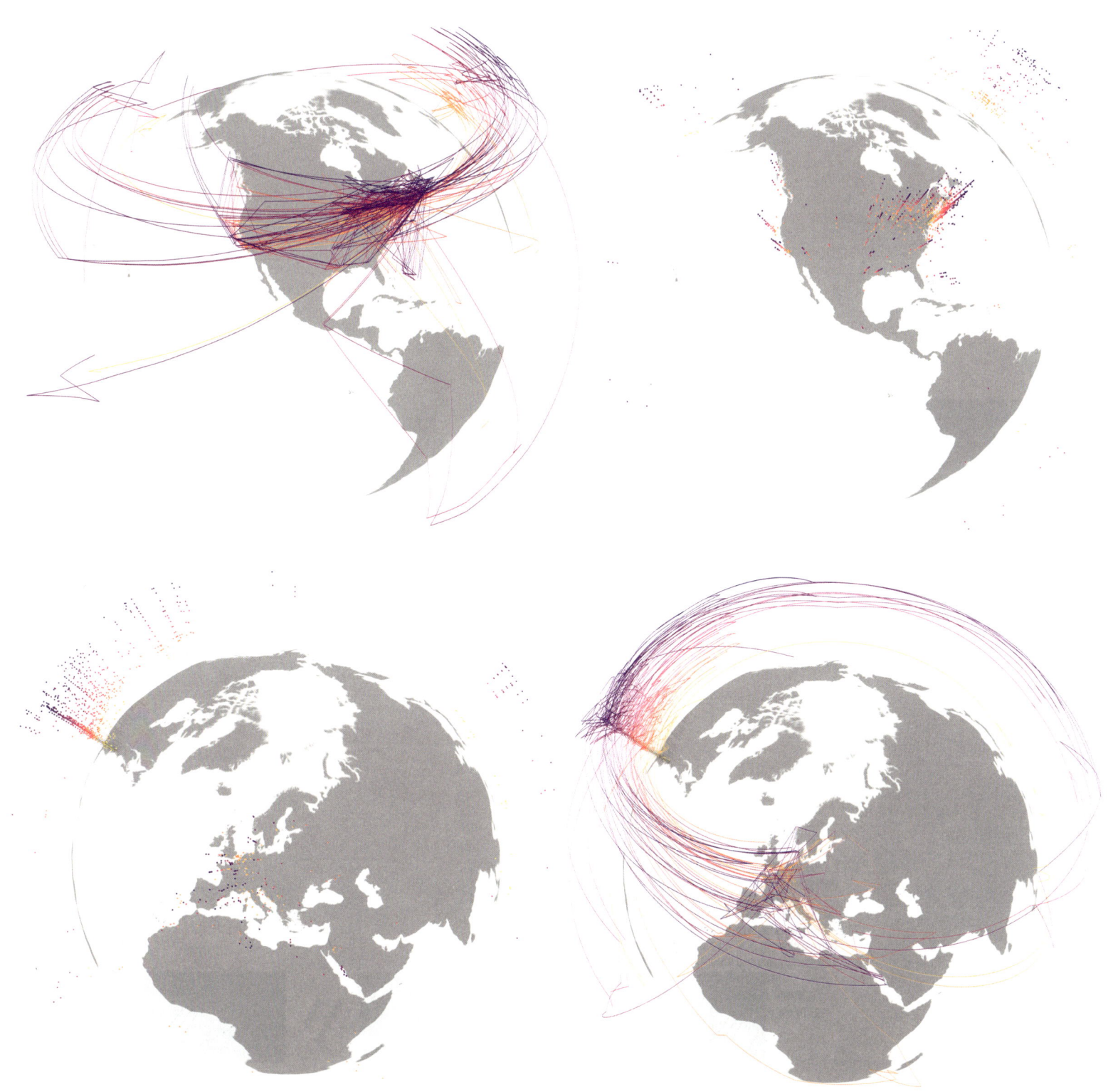

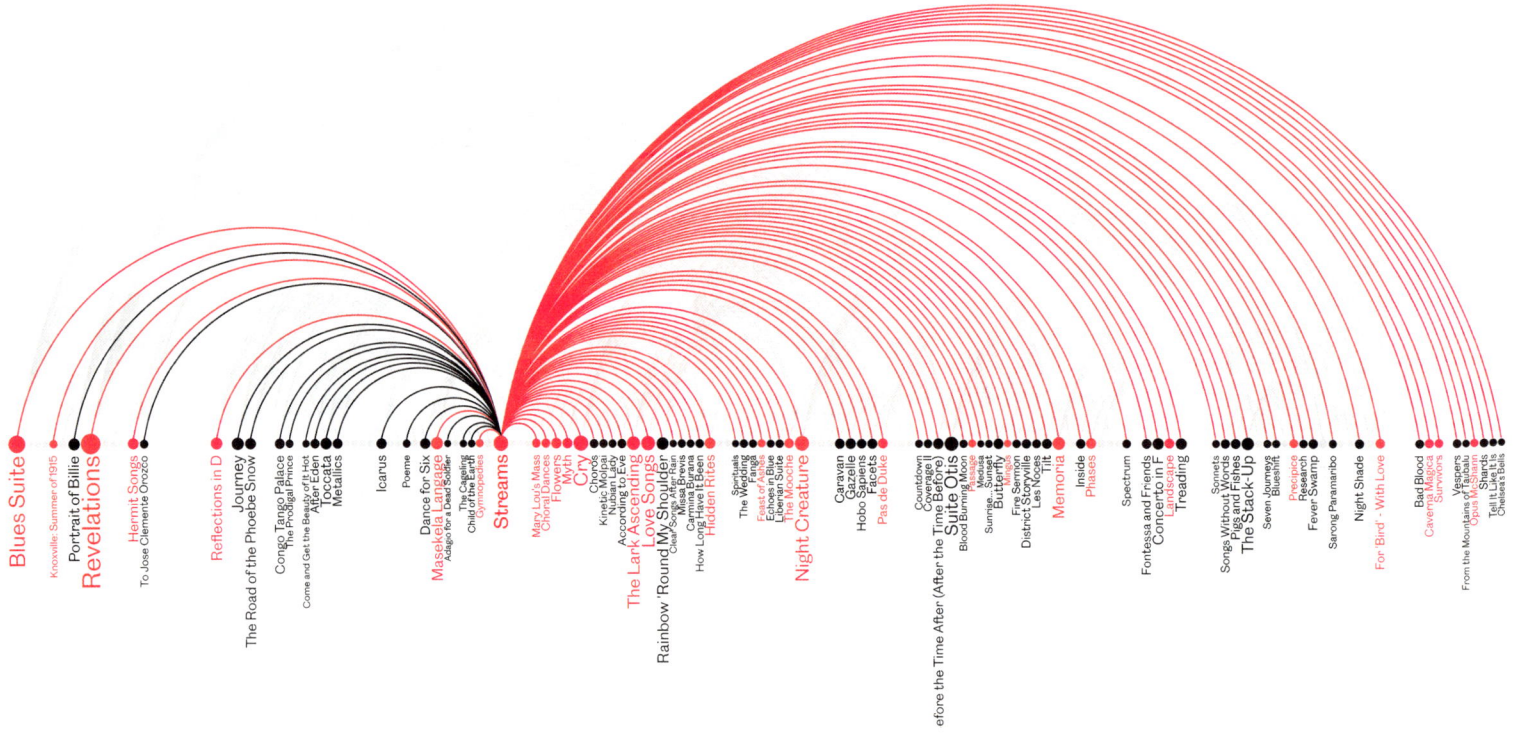

figs. 6a–b

AAADT Repertory Relationships, 1958–89. Repertory is arranged chronologically by first AAADT performance, with the arcs representing connections between the 158 works across 2,050 distinct programs. Figure 6a represents Ailey choreographies in the company's signature fuchsia, while non-Ailey works are in black to show the overall balance of repertory between 1958 and 1989. Figure 6b offers a detail of *Streams*, highlighting its connections to all the other works alongside which it was programmed during that time.

the YM-YWHA on East Ninety-Second Street. In total, twenty-nine artists appear in two or more constellations formed by the interconnections of Ailey's artists (as dancers, choreographers, or both), Dunham's company, and those two Broadway shows (fig. 2).

In this way, data can be suggestive, like gossip; we do not know the exact nature of the relationships signaled by crossovers between casts, but we can place these artists together in history through the traces of connection they left behind. In doing so, we open possibilities to speculate on what might have passed between them to create the shared vocabularies and literacies of their arts landscape. There are many more vectors of Ailey that are beyond the scope of our data—including those that move outward into the world, such as Jamison's numerous independent guest performances of *Cry*, as well as those that move inward, such as dancers' pathways through the Ailey School or the Alvin Ailey Repertory Ensemble (founded in 1974; now called Ailey II) into the main company. There are also family relationships: for example, Ailey dancer Sara Yarborough is the daughter of Dunham dancer Lavinia Williams. As the stream graph representing the Ailey company's body of knowledge suggests, the AAADT exists in relation to so many other dimensions of history.

We have extended this project of tracing complex ecosystems of practice across performance venues as well. In the New York metropolitan area alone, we counted 106 distinct sites at which the Ailey company performed 1,147 shows and lecture demonstrations between 1958 and 1989.[13] Forty-three of these venues are identified geographically on an aerial photograph of Manhattan from about 1950 (fig. 3). The process of identifying individual performance venues prompted us to think more closely about their specificity, from educational spaces such as Canarsie High School in Brooklyn and Staten Island Community College to public spaces such as Van Cortlandt Park in the Bronx, as well as community venues like the Church of the Master in Harlem and the Clark Center for the Performing Arts in the West Side YWCA, where the company was in residence from 1960 to 1969. Pedagogical institutions, including high schools, community colleges, and universities, played particularly important roles as sites of support in the emergence and consolidation of the Ailey company across these years; roughly a quarter of the performance dates in our full dataset include events located at or sponsored by high schools or colleges. The data underscores Ailey's commitment to these sites even after 1971 when the AAADT established an annual performance season at City Center.[14]

The contours of the AAADT's network of support emerge further in relation to the company's national and international touring, which is indicated on a series of globes in figures 4a–d. Each performance run is represented by a sphere on the pole for the corresponding city, arranged chronologically (figs. 4b, 4c); these are also connected as sequential pathways that create an architecture of the company's travel (figs. 4a, 4d). As was the case for Dunham's company, the AAADT's most regular international performances took place in Paris (166 shows across many trips from 1964 on), but whereas Dunham traveled the world without government sponsorship, Ailey benefited from repeated support from the US cultural diplomacy program.[15] The AAADT's first such tour was to Asia in 1962 before the company had even engaged in a national tour. The company regularly returned to cities across the US and beyond that demarcated broader Black geographies of the era, from Historically Black Colleges and Universities in the South to cities that developed substantial Black urban communities following the Great Migration. By 1989, they had performed over one hundred shows in cities such as Washington, DC; Boston; Detroit; and Chicago. At the same time, the company also built pathways from US suburbs to global cities, including Sydney, Tokyo, and Copenhagen, where reviewers remarked upon the unfamiliar themes.[16] Figure 5 represents the 160 cities where the company performed four or more shows, often across multiple visits in Ailey's lifetime, highlighting the establishment of touring patterns that became vital for the company's sustainability. Programs often include premiere dates associated with New York City for all choreographies in the company's repertory, and while our datasets show that seventy-three pieces do appear for the first time in New York between 1958 and 1989, the remaining eighty-five are spread across thirty-nine other cities. For example, the first documented performances of ten pieces took place in Kansas City, Missouri, which became an important residency site for the company.

Just as this process of radical accounting makes visible the AAADT's national and transnational networks of support, it also elaborates connections across the company's repertory. Most Ailey shows consisted of four or five works, and the company averaged twenty-two pieces in active repertory each year during Ailey's lifetime. The arc diagrams in figures 6a and 6b visualize the repertory from the relational perspective of program data by connecting each work to every other work alongside which it was presented in company programs between 1958 and 1989. We have found evidence for 2,177 performances of *Revelations* (1960); 873 of *Blues Suite* (1958), plus an additional sixty-eight of another incarnation, *Roots of the Blues* (1961); and 781 of *Cry* (1971). Of the programs we have documented, 69 percent include one or more of those pieces, all choreographed by Ailey (fig. 6a). Although it is not unexpected to find that *Cry* is the fourth most connected work in the AAADT's repertory in terms of its staging alongside other pieces, what is surprising is that it is surpassed by the plotless dance *Streams*, which has received significantly less critical attention (fig. 6b).

As a repertory company, the AAADT also serves as a platform that supports both established and emerging choreographic voices. During his lifetime, Ailey-choreographed works constituted just over one-third of the company's repertory, which includes his works that first premiered with other dance companies. Figure 6a uses color to differentiate between works choreographed by Ailey versus those by others, demonstrating the overall mix of creators. Many of the works created by someone other than Ailey still held ties to the AAADT; a quarter were choreographed by then-current or former company members. The non-Ailey works were split between new commissions and restagings, with the time between a world premiere and the first performance by the Ailey company ranging from mere weeks to multiple decades—marking another way that the programming drew connections across eras.[17] Beyond these full-scale performances, audiences further encountered the AAADT repertory through events including lecture demonstrations, workshops, and master classes. On the company's 1985 China tour, for example, lecture demonstrations provided an avenue to share active repertory "whose steamy sensuality would not pass censorship for a regular public performance."[18]

If data approaches lend themselves to thinking about how the repertory company model exceeds the individual choreographer in favor of the full company oeuvre, they simultaneously call attention to how Ailey functioned as mentor and curator. Figure 7 presents a visual timeline of the works that audiences might have encountered through the company's repertory, year by year from 1958 to 1989, showing how Ailey built and circulated dance history in what he described as his desire "to become a museum of classical American modern dance works that should be seen."[19] He oversaw the incorporation of already canonical works by Dunham and many other choreographers such as Talley Beatty, Lester Horton, Pearl Primus, Ted Shawn, and Anna Sokolow within his company's repertory and, by extension, within the embodied memory of his dancers. For example, the company performed Dunham's *Choros* from 1972 to 1974 and then in 1987 presented the evening-length show *The Magic of Katherine Dunham,* which reprised some of Dunham's most significant choreography as well as aspects of her technique. As mentor, Ailey provided a platform for both established and emerging choreographers to share their work, extending this opportunity not only to then-current and former company members, including Ulysses Dove and George Faison, but also choreographers from outside the company, such as Donald Byrd, Bill T. Jones, and Rudy Perez.

Eulogizing Ailey, early company member James Truitte lamented that Ailey did not bring the "[B]lack experience into more of his work, as was his original intention," but proposed that Ailey did so by championing other Black choreographers, including Geoffrey Holder, Louis Johnson, and Donald McKayle.[20] To return to the ecosystem with which we began, all three choreographers that Truitte names performed in *House of Flowers* with Ailey. The relationships implicit in so much of Ailey's programming were also made explicit through the many works he made for or dedicated to other artists, including *Love Songs* (1972), which showcased Williams; *Cry*, made for Jamison and dedicated to "all Black women everywhere—especially our mothers";[21] and *Memoria* (1979), which marked the death of dancer Joyce Trisler. This body of commemorations and remembrances took on a new valence amid the pervasiveness of AIDS-related deaths that permeate dance's archives from the 1980s. These projects not only participate in telling formal dance history from Ailey's vantage point but also serve as a reminder of how choreography is a form of memory keeping.

The archives that surround the AAADT exemplify how dance histories may foreground singular figures and yet be undeniably collective. Radical accounting draws together the edges from such archives by bringing each person, place, and piece into view that may otherwise have stayed on the periphery, and in so doing makes further connections available across time, space, and bodies. Our intentional data process aligns with commitments to develop "methodologies that draw insight from the subjective, embodied, contingent, political, and affective in ways that transcend traditional boundaries between qualitative and quantitative."[22] This is interconnected with the practices of care we have sometimes described as "visceral" approaches to data,[23] which include centering dance-based knowledge practices in data curation and exploring visual forms that can attune us to feeling with and alongside the traces of bodily experience that slip through the gaps of dance's archives. Graphic forms can bring forth new knowledge by "modeling interpretation" rather than re-presenting what is already known.[24] Visualizations such as those in this essay provide structures through which to imagine the past, taking their shape from the individuals and stories that gather in our datasets, while leaving space for new historical encounters to emerge.

NOTES

1. This text is equally coauthored by Harmony Bench and Kate Elswit; the name order is alphabetical. All datasets and visualizations have been created by Moving Data, led by Bench and Elswit, with project team members Antonio Jiménez-Mavillard and Tia-Monique Uzor, and additional archival collection research supported by assistants, primarily Amy Schofield and Wanda Hernández.

2. See Katie Rawson and Trevor Muñoz, "Against Cleaning," in *Debates in the Digital Humanities 2019*, ed. Matthew K. Gold and Lauren F. Klein (Minneapolis: University of Minnesota Press, 2019), https://dhdebates.gc.cuny.edu/read/4805e692-0823-4073-b431-5a684250a82d/section/07154de9-4903-428e-9c61-7a92a6f22e51#ch23; Harmony Bench and Kate Elswit, "Mapping Movement on the Move: Dance Touring and Digital Methods," *Theatre Journal* 68, no. 4 (December 2016): 575–96, https://doi.org/10.1353/tj.2016.0107; and Harmony Bench and Kate Elswit, "Visceral Data for Dance Histories: Katherine Dunham's People, Places, and Pieces," *TDR* 66, no. 1 (Spring 2022): 39–63.

3. Although the company performed under various names prior to settling consistently on the Alvin Ailey American Dance Theater, we use both "AAADT" and "Ailey company" throughout to reference all iterations of the company since 1958, including the De Lavallade-Ailey American Dance Company, Alvin Ailey and Company, the Alvin Ailey Dance Theater, and the Alvin Ailey City Center Dance Theater.

4. *Dunham's Data* was funded by the Arts and Humanities Research Council (AHRC AH/R012989/1, 2018–22) and supported by postdoctoral assistants Antonio Jiménez-Mavillard and Tia-Monique Uzor.

5. Alvin Ailey and A. Peter Bailey, *Revelations: The Autobiography of Alvin Ailey* (New York: Birch Lane, 1995), 41.

6. Ailey's comment refers to a performance of *Tropical Revue* at the Biltmore Theatre in Los Angeles, where, according to *Dunham's Data*, the production ran from April 8 to 15, 1945—marking one stop of Dunham's extensive domestic and international touring throughout the mid-twentieth century. See Harmony Bench and Kate Elswit, "Dunham's Data: Katherine Dunham and Digital Methods for Dance Historical Inquiry, Everyday Itinerary, 1947–60" ([Ann Arbor, MI]: Inter-university Consortium for Political and Social Research, 2024), https://doi.org/10.3886/ICPSR37698. See also Jacqueline Quinn Moore Latham, "A Biographical Study of the Lives and Contributions of Two Selected Contemporary Black Male Dance Artists—Arthur Mitchell and Alvin Ailey—in the Idioms of Ballet and Modern Dance, Respectively" (PhD diss., Texas Woman's University, 1973), 454.

7. We are grateful to Ailey archivist Dominique Singer for her generosity in gathering and sharing these preliminary datasets and many other archival holdings.

8. Alvin Ailey, notebook 75 [673], transcription of diary of Russia trip, 1970, Allan Gray Family Personal Papers of Alvin Ailey (AC10), Series 3: Notebooks, ca. 1964–ca. 1988, box 10, folder 103, Black Archives of Mid-America in Kansas City, MO.

9. Information about company membership was adapted from materials provided by the AAADT and has generally not been modified from the original.

10. These visualizations reflect Battle's resignation in the 2023–24 season, but do not include his successor.

11. Harmony Bench and Kate Elswit, "Dunham's Data: Katherine Dunham and Digital Methods for Dance Historical Inquiry, Personnel Check-In, 1947–1960" ([Ann Arbor, MI]: Inter-university Consortium for Political and Social Research, 2024), https://doi.org/10.3886/ICPSR38544. Latham suggests Leu Camacho as also connected to Ailey.

12. Internet Broadway Database (entries on *Jamaica* and *House of Flowers*; accessed October 1, 2023), https://www.ibdb.com; Dan Dietz, *The Complete Book of 1950s Broadway Musicals* (Lanham, MD: Rowman & Littlefield, 2014). On *House of Flowers* and particularly *Jamaica* as "mock transnational" performances of the Caribbean, see Shane Vogel, "Surfacing the Caribbean: Black Broadway and Mock Transnational Performance," chap. 4 in *Stolen Time: Black Fad Performance and the Calypso Craze* (Chicago: University of Chicago Press, 2018).

13. The New York metropolitan area includes New York City and its suburbs in Connecticut, New Jersey, and Pennsylvania.

14. Beginning in the mid-1970s, some of the venues at high schools and other community performance spaces shifted toward presenting the Repertory Ensemble and the Alvin Ailey Student Workshop, while the main company maintained annual performance seasons at various colleges and universities.

15. On Ailey and US cultural diplomacy, see Clare Croft, "Refusing Modernist Formulas of Second-Class Citizenship: Arthur Mitchell and the Alvin Ailey American Dance Theater," chap. 2 in *Dancers as Diplomats: American Choreography in Cultural Exchange* (New York: Oxford University Press, 2015).

16. A 1970 newspaper review opened with the observation that an Ailey program "in the suburbs looks and feels different than it does in New York City, where viewers are more accustomed to social protest than they may be at Newark State College." Joseph Gale, "Dance Program at Newark State," *Newark News*, March 17, 1970, Alvin Ailey Dance Foundation Collection, box 63, folder 4, Music Division, Library of Congress, Washington, DC (hereafter AADFC).

17. For an account of the AAADT's diverse repertory as staging "composite bodies that reveal aesthetic affinities and political connections among disparate dance techniques and histories," see Thomas DeFrantz, "Composite Bodies of Dance: The Repertory of the Alvin Ailey American Dance Theater," *Theatre Journal* 57, no. 4 (December 2005): 660, https://doi.org/10.1353/tj.2006.0012.

18. Gerald Stryker, "Report on China Tour of Alvin Ailey American Dance Theater, October 27–November 11, 1985," AADFC, box 128, folder 5.

19. Alvin Ailey, quoted in Ken Sandler, "Alvin Ailey's Company Draws the World," *Newsday*, November 26, 1978, AADFC, box 73.

20. James Truitte, "Dear Alvin," *Choreography and Dance* 4, no. 1 (1996): 10.

21. AAADT performance program for August 2, 6, and 7, 1971, AADFC, box 126, folder 1.

22. Marika Cifor, Patricia Garcia, T. L. Cowan, Jasmine Rault, Tonia Sutherland, Anita Say Chan, Jennifer Rode, Anna Lauren Hoffmann, Niloufar Salehi, and Lisa Nakamura, "Feminist Data Manifest-No," 2019, https://www.manifestno.com/home.

23. Bench and Elswit, "Visceral Data for Dance Histories."

24. Johanna Drucker, *Visualization and Interpretation: Humanistic Approaches to Display* (Cambridge, MA: MIT Press, 2020), 2.

Thomas F. DeFrantz

dear alvin

Where to begin? So much has changed since the time when we never met, LOL. You had already left this earthly plane when I began thinking about your work carefully, in order to produce an academic study and a book—and a life in dance, TBH. Your presence has never wavered though, for me or some 8.5 million New Yorkers who see your name each year throughout the boroughs, as they wonder what culture might look like. It's funny, you created the gathering pool for strangers to imagine dance and excellence as something available through our Black presence in its rampant diversity. You did that, and it still endures, and that is why I write to you now, for this exhibition catalogue, and with you too, I guess, to wonder with the reversionings and the shifts and the shittiness of so much of it now. And, Alvin, it did get a lot shittier than many of us thought it could . . .

Oh, Alvin, you created an event horizon—an open summation that spills outward toward any manner of Black possibility realized through embodied gesture. None of us working in dance or Black visual cultures or maybe even music moves without relationship to what you created, as strange as that surely sounds. We all belong to you somehow; we are among your edges and your legacies as people who wonder about dance. We think of you and the most famous images of your form from the 1960s onward: beautiful of body and an unflappable integrity of commitment to give dance back to the people. **We people**. Maybe this is the event horizon for professional artistry: to create structures that encourage people to see themselves among the movingness of dance. We might not want this all the time; sometimes we want to see otherworldly visions of sylphs and sirens or lockstep J-sette. But you reminded us to look for ourselves on the stage; our families and the stories we heard somehow made manifest through dancing. You never wavered in your belief in this, and your resolve proved right through all the ridiculousnesses that continue. You believed in Black people, and here we are, keepin' on keepin' on.

Alvin, we never met, but I'm one of those queer kids from the Midwest, a fluorescent-beige gay Black boy who learned to love dance after seeing your company on tour. We are legion, of course, and you believed in us, placing us and our desires front and center in your operations and your creations. Gay Black boys loving our mothers. Fuck, you believed in your mother the way we all have to think twice or three times before we do a misdeed she won't like. She had all those hesitations that church life brings forward for us queers and the suspicion that God don't like gay. She was strong, in the ways that Black femmes always seem to move way beyond the possible to make space for us. It surely isn't fair that they bear so much pressure no matter what. Your mother, Lula Cooper (née Cliff, of course, of course), told us that her grandfather was a white man from Washington state. That's how our Blackness moves, through all manner of combinatory formations, desired or not; your great-grandfather, though, cared for his Black family in some ways. This probably helped your mother teach you not to race-hate even when that would be the obvious response to white supremacy. She made a way for you to become you and committed to a multiracial assembly. You never forgot her or denied her place in your imagination. We both know that being gay means thinking about Mama in a certain sort of way; she just knows so much more than the other dolls and she belongs to *us* somehow. So, when your mother famously slapped you backstage for wearing makeup and something like *prancing onstage*, you forgave her and brought her closer in some ways. We gay sons try to do this; we forgive because we're trying to fit in when we know that our queerness pushes us out, at least a little bit. Maybe this is an edge of you, your gay essence, but being gay reminds us all the time that it's not an edge but a center of daily desire to be mitigated and explored with caution. Caution, that we don't disappoint Mother. Well, maybe just not *too* much . . .

Alvin, you made a dozen beautiful dances. We should all be so lucky, we who slog away in the studio and try to align ambition and desire to movement and music and design. You made many more works than that dozen, of course, but these twelve or so capture my imagination whenever I hear their music or think of their performances. A dozen, then: *Night Creature, Cry, The Lark Ascending, Quintet, Survivors, The River, Pas de Duke, Memoria, Blues Suite, Masekela Langage, Hidden Rites*, and of course, *Revelations*. In some ways, I understand how you did it. You worked with the music as your companion in creating the structure for dancing; loving the blues or gospel music or the spirituals in a terrific arrangement, or Laura Nyro or Abbey Lincoln and Max Roach or Ralph Vaughan Williams. Your great musical taste: sophisticated and relatable at once, now available to anyone with an internet connection and the patience to listen along with Duke Ellington or Keith Jarrett. You allowed music to guide your creations, and the notebooks that we found after you passed offer glimpses of how you thought with the musical structures. Music catapulting us toward destiny, always; and when the music was "just okay," your dance was a little bit better than that somehow. Today only a few choreographers work with music as the guiding light for performance in this way; it has to do with copyright and royalty rates and control and the ability to edit the sounds and transform them somehow. It's all good; it's just how things are now. But we can depend on your dances to allow us to hear and feel the music you've chosen in all its affective evidentiary. It's an important reliability that you brought to the theater. In your dances, the music *means*, and respecting it allows us to grow collectively . . .

Alvin, you hit your full stride right when US Black culture turned to hip-hop. That must've smarted for you a lot; seeing the Black world turn its attentions to music and dance that didn't need a concert stage but thrived in nightclubs, basements, street corners. Early hip-hop changed how we thought about dance and expertise in Black gesture, rendering modern dance and its descendants old-fashioned. By then, you had made a school and method for helping us move into careers as professional artists, and to explore concert dance as a way to express aspects of Black life. But hip-hop told us all something else about being Black and young and embedded in global capital; it unleashed political possibility in a way that museums and opera houses never could. You watched that happen, but you weren't here long enough to witness how some artists eventually made space within your dance company to allow for house, disco, and hip-hop to land on your stages. OMG, you would so love Rennie and the things that Kyle and Ron K. have made for the company. Still, hip-hop moves with a lurch through the concert hall: some publics resist it because its politics are obvious even when they seem to be only the noize of sonic dissent. But Black worlds without hip-hop are unimaginable now, so its gestures arrive in fragments everywhere you were and in many of the dances you made, performed now by artists who have grown up entirely imbricated in this culture. I wonder what dances you would make now. You made a funk-disco dance at the very end of your career, but I don't think you cared for it much, and WIGIG . . .

You also worked when the idea of a *dance company* appealed. That's all changed. Companies became recognized as hotbeds of power abuses and any manner of sexual assault; in the last decade, we went through a long-delayed reckoning that finally shifted the ability of a dance company to operate in hierarchical lockstep. This also means that dance companies don't hold a general appeal for many young dancers; I mean, not every artist wants to be told what to do and how to do it. You worked outside of that model, even as you did "make dances"; you coordinated the vision of music and lighting and design and casting and the moves and movement of people on the stage, often in elaboration of what you remembered from the Lester Horton studio. You also tried to allow the interpretive artists—the dancers—to be some version of themselves inside your dances, encouraging us to extend and stretch the material toward portrayals that made sense to each of us along the way. So, over time, the actual materials of the dances change. Tempos become faster, more turns are added, emphases alter. Your method, which is entirely Black, demands that the dancers *interpret* the movement; it's never enough to just "do the steps." You've gotta feel it, care for it, wonder with it, design its engagement. **Aileydancers**, as we call them these days, figure out how to craft performance and a life as an artist because of the structures of your choreography. But that vision of a company is generally gone for most folx. Somehow, THE AILEY stands as a singularity of sorts, an actual dance company that employs dozens of artists for a consistent itinerary of performances throughout the year. You know, your company still performs more than any other in terms of actual dance engagements. Hard work ain't no stranger here . . .

Alvin, by now, most dance artists are engaged in *projects*. It's a weird sort of structure, TBH; we gather to make a thing with rehearsals and preparation stretching across several years. We focus on a few ideas and build out discrete worlds of dance theater performed in hour-long creations. This is the standard for "interesting" dance now, a certain specialization that invites the audience to think together through the exploration of ideas. Some of us focus on Black femme living and trauma; some of us focus on Igbo and candomblé spiritual practices; many of us focus on queer possibilities. These performances are smaller-scale than the things you made, and they don't try to **be for everyone**, in that often-quoted way you said that dance could be. I'm talking specifically about dances for Black adults, though; for the children, we still go to Debbie Allen's show and school recitals, and we watch reality dance competitions on television. And we go to see the Ailey company, when we can afford it. It got really expensive, as you always knew it would. The opera houses and large stages where your company performs now aren't always so welcoming to those of us struggling with the rent and getting the kids to school. But when we can afford it, we go see your Ailey people in order to *feel*. Alvin, I think that's a *project* too; this dancing out ways to *feel* that get shared with an audience in your work. SMH. It's confusing, but this idea of relatable dance that encourages us to *feel* among one another is not considered to be valuable or necessary culture by some social elites. The *projects* that traffic in more obscure formations are what we usually see in museums and live-art dance theaters. Of course, I think there's room for all of it, for the familiar and the strange, if we could manage to recognize our different ways of being in the world and their amazingnesses . . .

You operated as a RACE MAN, something we don't even have anymore, and something lots of people can't even imagine. You did things that could help *glorify the race* and move a moral compass toward an obvious inevitable triumph of Black being-in-motion. That's shitass hard work, of course, forcing people to acknowledge something obvious about our collective Black concern for embodied artistry and performance. Our music and dance run this world, and you knew that all along, but you held yourself back so that the race could move forward. We don't even call Black a race anymore all the time; being post-racial nowadays, we acknowledge our mixedness as often as not. Still, lots of us just plain Black, and that's cool. If you want to be a race, there's more of them to pick from now. But you had only one race to join, and you stayed in even when it wasn't convenient at all (as race seldom tends to be). Because that sort of thing has disappeared now—there's not even an Oprah anymore, not really—it's nearly impossible to understand what that was. An actual commitment to Black people whom you would never meet or know, most of us struggling just to get through the bullshit day? Yah, we don't have that anymore; it's just not available . . .

Watching your dances again and again, I think, man, you loved the ladies. I know it wasn't a playa mentality you were chasing, like some of the other guy choreographers of your day, LOL; it was more like, you respected these femmes and wanted them to lead us forward. Makes sense, and it also managed to keep the dudes coming into the room, these fine Black women dancing like you can't believe. The women work hard in your dances, even if the guys usually steal the spotlight. So many of the women who have interpreted your *Cry* tailor-made for the original OG Judith Jamison: Donna Wood, Briana Reed, Barbara Pouncie, Debora Chase-Hicks, Nasha Thomas, Dwana Adiaha Smallwood, Bahiyah Sayyed-Gaines, Renee Robinson, Deborah Manning, Linda-Denise Evans, Linda Celeste Sims, Jacqueline Green, Constance Stamatiou, Jacquelin Harris, so many more. It's totally unfair to make a list when so many must be left off; there are so many, many more . . . Exquisite performances each unlike the others. To consider how the women work in your dances, all we have to do is watch "Fix Me, Jesus" or "Wade in the Water" or "The Day Is Past and Gone" from *Rev*, and we get it: the femmes guide, protect, care, decide. You didn't make winsomes who need someone else to walk, turn, or balance; you showed us again and again that femme forward is the only Black way. TY4that.

But, Alvin, the queer space is the most important space that you cultivated, even if it remains fairly closeted. You had lesbians and gays in your company from the beginning, and you brought in the queers from the start. Why wouldn't you have? We gain by proximity and being near one another allows us to know something more than we thought before. Meaning, by centering the gays in the large company operations, you created a space that would not disavow our rampant same-sex desire as it led us to the dance classes, to the auditions and performances, to the bathhouses and "women's-only" soirees. We gays always have pride of place in Ailey, even if we don't trumpet it too loudly, lest some Adam Clayton Powell sense of propriety derails your company's preeminence. Bayard Rustin had to be on the sidelines, and you opted to keep yourself straight enough for the normativities that were funding large-scale culture in the 1960s. But you never stopped loving us and our loving, and the queer marquee-stars of Ailey are legendary. WAP as we want to be, telling the essential stories of Black creativity on big-ass opera-house stages. Yaaaaaaasssssssss.

But then, it's probably this closeted respectability that turns some of the too-cool afro-fools away from Ailey operations. It's too bad, of course, that we have to *turn to you* now, as if you weren't doing your work all along. For you, believing in dance meant believing in Black people moving, and people gotta move; our movements are magnificent. Other artists wonder through variations of obscurity or critical theory, but you rendered the cosmos with a plié and a shoulder roll, a tilt and a turn with a contraction. One example I'm thinking of is from the beginning of *Memoria*, the work you made in a rush of emotion to remember your white dance-party girlfriend-confidante Joyce Trisler. *To the sound of quiet, thought-ridden piano arpeggios supported by a bed of strings trembling in an ambivalent dissonance, two women dance together, mirroring each other and consecrating the ground below with fluttering gestures of hands passing up and down the body. And then, a striking image of mutual support: one woman in a deep penché arabesque, the other in a high-extension side balance. Each supporting the other; an unexpected held pose that suggests a place of momentary rest activated by the connection between the two women*. In this brief moment, we witness femmes caring gorgeously, one for the other. This lasts a second at most. And it can last forever in our memory. How could we all not value that possibility in dance on a stage? Your method as a choreographer is infinitely relatable even when people think they want something else. There's nothing like witnessing Black excellence no matter its container; only a fool would deny the cumulative power of Ailey. Still, we don't all pay attention all the time, it's true.

Alvin, you never got to live out loud as a gay man in a loving public relationship, in the ways we try to now. Today it's sort of possible to be gay, queer, non-binary, trans, or figuring-it-all-out in public on the socials and still be holding up some big old arts institution. You didn't get that opportunity though, and you had to live in a terrible shadow all the time, barely supported when you did find someone to love or become infatuated with. I saw those photographs of you in the archive years ago, of that super-handsome white guy you hung out with when you two were smoking hot and young. Weren't we all smoking hot just because we were young, somehow? Anyway, he has kind eyes and a great body in those pictures; a few times some of the OGs told me a little bit about you and him, and how you were able to soften some when you had each other's gaze. That was before everything blew up completely, though, toward THE AILEY, when it was still a fairly itinerant, small dance company in the early 1960s. He was a good-looking foil for you, and I vaguely recall one snapshot with the two of you, probably on a beach. Maybe I'm inventing that part because I wanted it so much for you. Later, when the newspapers reported on your calling out to the young man ¿Abdullah? in a Manhattan building, near the end of your life, we were all super sad that your gayness had been turned tawdry in public without the balancing narratives of respect and reconciliation. You never got to be gay or queer or even homosexual from THE AILEY point of view, which is still a terrible thing. Fuck, by now even the POPE is willing to bless same-sex relationships; shit has changed. I'm really sorry you missed this moment—well, at least that part of this moment . . .

Alvin, so much of the dance you made yearns to solve fragments of time in life. Movements that stir the air somehow, making it different than it was. Like booze, I guess. God, we like our stuff, don't we? The cocaine, the Molly, the oxy, and the shrooms, the sex and the Sunday service, the dancing all night. The bad relationships and the fighting, the petty disavowals and dismissals, the jealousies and the hurt of feelings overlooked. Sex with strangers destined to always stay strangers. We love our stuff; it keeps us going. It helps us recognize ourselves within the chaos. You staged this in your dances sometimes: the abusive power relationships that melt into tender embraces; the literal shooting up junk before dancing into an otherworld. It's really hard to be a *public Negro* and not need some sort of addiction to get through the week; the pressures are just beyond the beyond. It's probably part of why there are so few "race people" now; it's just too much work, and now there are more Black people on the planet anyway so maybe we can share the load. No one has to be an Alvin Ailey anymore, happily, and we're willing to give our Beyoncés a year or two out of the spotlight. But the pressure still lands on whoever is in the driver's seat, we know that, and we try to care as a group toward that responsibility as best we can. We're not very good at it though, and we left you out to dry in some ways. I hope we can do better caring for future leaders of your amazing company; supporting them so that they don't overwork. Work is another addiction fed by the marketplace, and none of us seems to know how to get beyond that . . .

And then, some dance critics won't give up on trying to hold down your ambition and achievement; their musings on what makes Black art insufficient spill into how too many people think about our creativity. It's surely too bad that ideas move in these ways, but they do. As some warn that your imagination was too small, they prove again and again that they know nothing of how artistry spreads. It matters beyond measure that space emerges for the banal, for the magnificent, for the entirely expected and preordained, for the experimental, and for the exceptional. Of course, a celebration of Mary Lou Williams or a demonstration of training techniques turned into a dance phrase; in time, an entire dance of continual motion will lead us forward to the destinies of exquisite Black theater. While critics get caught up on the bumps in the road, we artists understand the long haul, past the slave ships and the auction block, past Congo Square and the Civil War, past the Summer of Soul and the eternal Black uprisings screaming for justice. Your vision arises as a balm, offering respite to the anti-Black weather. And yah, BAE.

And your belief in the spirit. Not Christian, but *spirit*; the thing that can happen when we are encouraged to dance and witness beyond the form. You helped us be with spirit as we performed in concert dance, in *Revelations* of course but also in moments in most of your works. The moments in the choreography when you encourage us to dance beyond the moment, the movement, the stage, the story: to dance into the unknown. Alvin, it's still hard for folx to acknowledge all that you built. It's a challenge to focus in on what makes *something incredibly important to so many people* valuable or interesting; it's easy to be dismissive and call it entertainment in opposition to thinking-in-motion. Today we make work about our impossible Black pasts, the inheritance gap, and the challenges of global capital and climate change, and we bring in cultural theorists to buoy our inventions. Alvin, there are so many Black cultural theorists now writing stupendous analyses of how none of it is working; we read their formations and wonder at the worlds they can help us build in dance. We try to make these worlds and sometimes we manage okay. But these works are not usually sustainable or for the ages, in the way that your modern dances can be. You didn't have this twenty-first-century explosion in Black critical theory. You worked with what you had, and you worked with it well. It's hard to talk about how relationships between Black people matter when they are played out with clarity on a dance stage. It's hard to witness Black people agreeing about how to move, as we do nearly all the time in your dances and in the dances that your company stages. Well, that's hard only because we are so used to seeing Black people in turmoil, in trouble, in pain, in trauma. You had a different vision for us; one where we are magnificent and gorgeously capable among one another. The other Black choreographers of the 1960s and '70s agreed, and their work has mostly disappeared by now too. We're left with Black artists who demonstrate their discomfort at being in the public eye, which is fine of course; it's all fine and it's all whatever the moment needs. But see … well, there was this moment when young Black femmes (including the queers and queens, of course) focused in on Black Joy and Black Girl Magic, but your work was rarely thought about in those contexts. You patented that shit back in the day; Black Joy as a sovereignty, **moving with others** toward a goal of Black expression. SMH. Somehow you got relegated to the old school. Alvin, we need your art, danced with the understanding of its caring heart of exhilaration. To do that, and to witness its essences, we need to believe in Black *[queerfemme]* possibility, which has never been easy. As if Black Joy would be easy to maintain. You did that, of course. You maintained Black Joy as an aspect of professional artistry in dances that demonstrated how to work through the pain and come out on the other side. Your dances always end with the very necessary applause at the achievement of the dancing; the joy of calling forth recognition of embodied expertise. But then, times changed …

So now we have a museum show about you and your edges—how lucky is that? It's an opportunity to put some more sweet into the sauce and invite people who never gave you a second thought the chance to do better. Act like you know: there are so many reasons THE AILEY continues while others fall off. It's about Black excellence, yes, but also about your ability to push Black Dance beyond any uncanny valley of critical obscurity to the place where dancing continually matters. Doing that populist work, you paid the price of the ticket for us all. You know, that thing Jimmy Baldwin wrote about—the price of the ticket as the demand for a song to justify our shared captivity in the agon of race. Alvin, you took it to another level, and made our dancing capacity *obvious*, for all to witness. The clarity of your approach stuns us, even now, when some young Blax can be quick to judge and accuse the elders of having been facile and too easily understood. We all become captive to the thinking that obscurity is better than clarity, forgetting that joy in motion holds a source code of collective futurity as an aspect of shared critical dissatisfaction. We might all be captive in an inability to recognize Black dance as its own end, without need for justification or elaboration or revision. Huh. Well, then. Let's see here. Alvin, what did you teach us?

> **We dance because whyTF wouldn't we? There are no limits to what a body in motion can do; our great distinction is to believe in that and to exercise that on the daily in pretty much every context there could ever be. We dance because we believe in dance and its multiplicities; we don't need others to explain to us why the dancing matters; we understand this on a cellular level. Truly. We. Get. It.** *getit getit getit!*

But it's all okay; it gives me this chance to think toward you and rant and lament and wonder. None of that maybe from my life now decidedly in the middle. My little life in dance, also built on the bridge of your underappreciated back. I've gained so very much in the world from my willingness to care about your work and by extension my fantasy idea of you. We can all be this lucky, expressing gratitude toward you and holding up the sturdy vision of Black excellence that you propose.

Okay, so Alvin, here's a proper ending to a commissioned essay about you for a catalogue about your edges:

OF COURSE, the Alvin Ailey American Dance Theater belongs in a museum, as well as on the stage and even in the streets. The 1988 film *Jazz City* featured Ailey dancers performing his choreography around New York, with *Cry* performed on a street in Harlem; the workingmen of *Blues Suite* dancing underneath a bridge to Brooklyn; the moves of *Night Creature* realized in a nightclub; the pas de deux of *Survivors* worked through in a prison; and *Revelations* offered up in a church sanctuary. Ailey's organization was able to do that because Ailey had crafted something so incredibly rare: a site of dance where Blackness can flourish toward its own creative ends, animated by the edgy gestures of gays and queers and lesbians and straights, all of us concerned with telling compelling stories of Black life.

But Alvin, here's what I really want to say to you:

I wonder how you are. I wonder if you would recognize yourself today. I wonder if you would make dances now. I wonder if you would rather be in public love and fucking on the daily. I wonder if you would become Catholic or move to Colombia—anything to get out of the USA. I wonder if you would rest more. I wonder if you would tell people how tired you are all the time. I wonder if you would write it all down, if you had the time and the place to think it all through. I wonder if you could be any more beautiful to me.

yours, in motion,

tommy

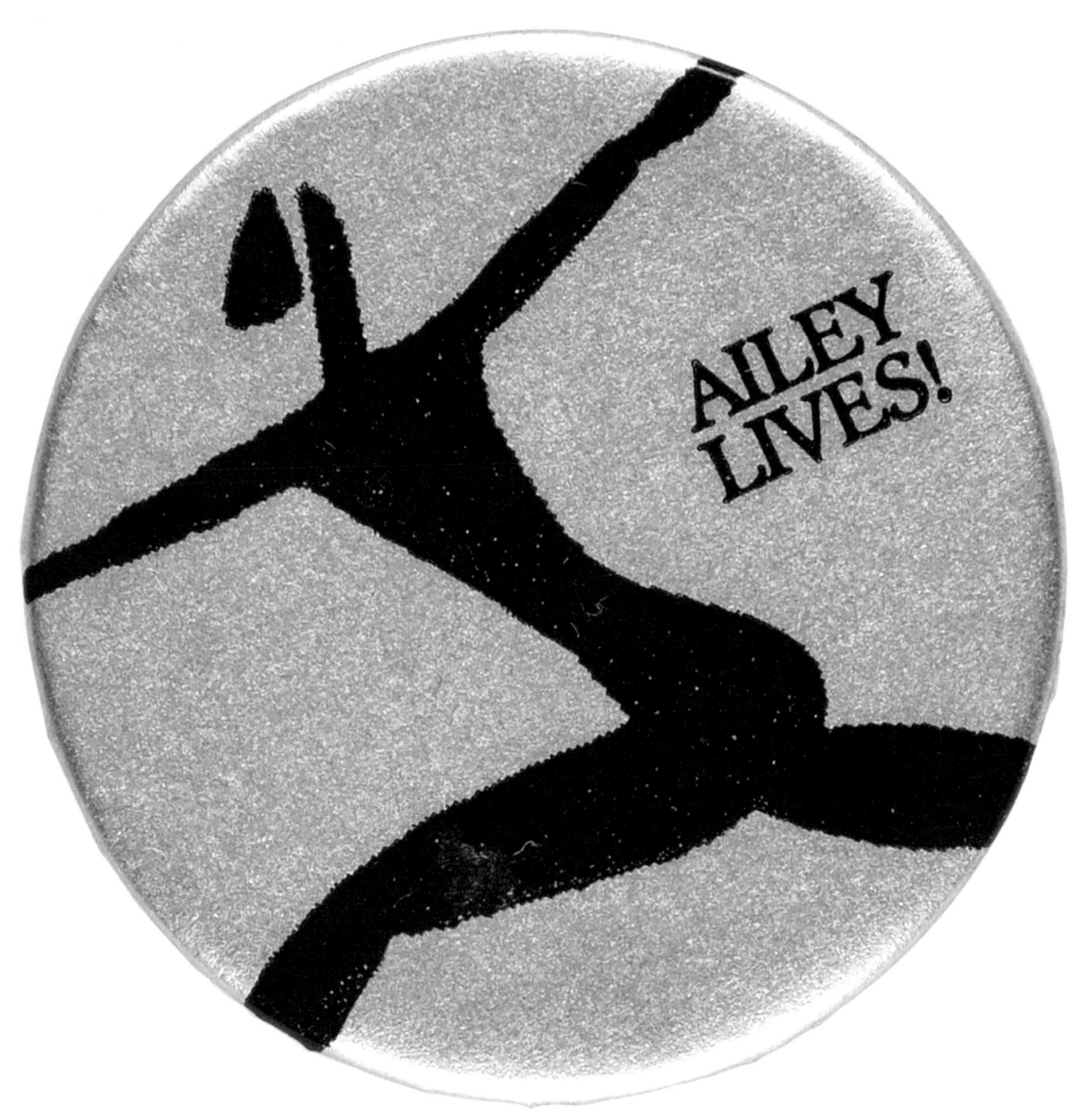

Kyle Abraham
Claire Bishop
Aimee Meredith Cox
Brenda Dixon-Gottschild
Adrienne Edwards
Jennifer Homans
Jamila Wignot
Jawole Willa Jo Zollar

After Ailey

A Conversation

Adrienne Edwards
When I started to think about this show in 2018, I went to see a lot of Ailey performances. At one of them, a woman behind me was absolutely ecstatic in response to what she was watching. What I overheard made me wonder about the phenomenon that is the "Ailey experience" and, more precisely, about each of your first experiences with Ailey, whether it was with the man himself or with the company.

Brenda Dixon-Gottschild
I first came upon Ailey in New York, where I grew up, when I was about twenty years old. This would have been in the early 1960s, at the beginning of the Ailey company. Their home base then was at the Clark Center, in the YWCA building at Eighth Avenue and Fifty-First Street, where I had been invited to present a dance I choreographed called "Lonely Woman," in one of the center's New Choreographers' Concerts. So, I was back and forth to the Clark Center quite a bit, and what an experience it was to encounter the Ailey company. At the time, Ailey, Carmen de Lavallade, the glorious Thelma Hill, and Minnie Marshall were all dancing, and it was unlike any other company I had ever seen before as a young Black dancer—or really as a young anything dancer—with its variety of body shapes and its groundedness, if you will. Back then, both Mr. Ailey and Thelma were performing with the ensemble, and in general, the dancing bodies of the 1960s were less streamlined, athletic, and balletic than they are now. The mere fact of the company's existence offered a justification for the fact that I dance and I exist, and that there is a concert stage for people like us.

    At that time, because there were no university dance departments, we were New York dance junkies, going from one studio to another, taking classes, trying things. When I was nineteen, I took classes with Dorene Richardson at the New Dance Group. There I met Donya Feuer, who offered me a full scholarship to dance at her studio, which she had cofounded with Paul Sanasardo. Loretta Abbott was a student there, and she suggested that I might be interested in going with her to Mary Anthony's studio. James Truitte, whom I knew as Jimmy, regularly took Mary's Saturday morning class because her teaching was great for long bodies, and Jimmy and I both had long, lyrical arms and legs. It was Jimmy and Mary who said to me, "Oh, you should be an Ailey dancer." I didn't think I had the quickness or rhythm for it; after all, I'd started dance late, at age fifteen. But Jimmy arranged

fig. 1

Ailey Lives! button, n.d.

a one-on-one rehearsal audition for me with Mr. Ailey, and so there we were, just Mr. Ailey and me, in a room on a Saturday afternoon; I don't even remember where it was. He taught me, I realized later, a piece from *Revelations*, "Rocka My Soul in the Bosom of Abraham." I was so nervous, and I was to learn the combination and perform it without music. It was a disaster. But I will always appreciate Jimmy for doing that for me.

Jawole Willa Jo Zollar

I grew up in Kansas City, Missouri, in a segregated, all-Black community. I was what would be the equivalent of a street dancer, performing in clubs and revues. It wasn't until I was a student at the University of Missouri at Kansas City in the early 1970s that I realized I could major in dance, something that I had loved to do all my life. That is when I started learning about concert dance and training in ballet and modern dance. I read *Dance Magazine*, and I joined Black Exodus, an all-Black dance company organized by fellow university student Milton Myers. Ailey was the buzz, and we read everything we could about his company. When they came to perform in Kansas City, in 1971 or 1972, I went to see them—Judith Jamison, John Parks, Sylvia Waters. I was blown away, but it was clear to me that I'd never be able to do what they were doing. I did not have the flexibility or the physicality or that kind of training.

So, I continued to learn and absorb as much as I could about Mr. Ailey and the Black dance community. I looked to where I might fit in, because I knew that no one was ever going to come see me lift my leg in the air. But they might come see me in the other forms that I grew up doing—working with strippers, exotic dancers, flash acts. When I saw some of the works of Mr. Ailey, such as *Blues Suite*, *Revelations*, and particularly *Masekela Langage*, they showed me the possibility of what I could do. They gave me a sense of story and activism and societal commentary. I later took a class at the Wolf Trap/American University Summer Program, and Loretta Abbott and Al Perryman were my teachers there. I fell in love with both the Ailey and the jazz aesthetic, but I knew my body didn't have the lines or physicality required to pursue those directions.

Jennifer Homans

I arrived in New York in the mid-1970s as a young dancer. I had trained mainly in ballet, and in New York I was so overwhelmed by and interested in everything I could do. I continued to study ballet, but I also studied Limón and Cunningham and Graham techniques, and I took classes with Joyce Trisler, Kazuko Hirabayashi, and others. We were all just whirling in this incredible moment in dance, and of course Ailey was a part of that.

As a young person, I wanted movement that would completely transport me, and I saw that in the Ailey company. I was also obsessed with Pearl Primus and started reading about Katherine Dunham. I wanted to figure out what made dance so powerful, and Ailey's dances seemed to pour out of the performers, which made me feel that dance was something worth doing. I never had an opportunity to study any of the Ailey repertory, but I was certainly an avid watcher of it. I left New York to dance professionally, but I returned when I stopped dancing and enrolled in Columbia University, where I ended up studying American social dance of the thirties, forties, and fifties. So, I was again drawn into a world that took me back to Ailey, among other artists, and I've been interested ever since.

Kyle Abraham

My first exposure to the company was watching the Ailey dancers perform Ulysses Dove's *Vespers* on the PBS special *Two by Dove*. Seeing that performance in my first year of dancing—like Brenda, I started dance late, during my senior year of high school—I was so empowered to think about the possibilities of making dance and the power of dance vocabulary in a way that extended beyond what I knew from my experience thus far.

When I think about Mr. Ailey and his legacy, I think about his generosity, which extended to the idea of repertory and bringing in artists such as Jawole. Generosity is also what led him to start a school, which is what gave me the most immersive connection to Ailey that I had in my early dancing years. The summer I turned nineteen, I attended the Ailey summer program; it was 1996, the same summer that Ulysses passed away. Being in the studio where *Two by Dove*, and *Vespers* in particular, was filmed was a very special and powerful experience for me.

Jamila Wignot

I first encountered the Ailey company through my college's Black student organization, which had gotten tickets for an Ailey performance on campus. I was familiar with the company by name, and that was about it; I hadn't really been exposed to any sort of dance forms. I walked into the theater with no expectations, except that it was going to be a night of concert dance. *Revelations* was the dance that stood with me; as Jennifer said, I felt something kind of flowing through the dancers. The experience of the saga unfolding before me was visceral and impactful.

When I started to dig into Ailey's own words and experience as part of my research for my film *Ailey*, I learned that he had gone to junior and senior high schools that exposed him to art, music, and dance. He was a teenager when he encountered Dunham, and she was something entirely new to him. The profound jolt he experienced in recognizing that what Dunham was presenting was something both different and familiar gave him a sense of possibility. Likewise, when I saw the Ailey performance in college, I felt as if something in the world had opened up. There was a diversity of dancing bodies on the stage, in terms of actual body types but also skin tones and hairstyles and hair textures. Something about possibility was represented on that stage. That night I became a super, fan of the company—although, interestingly, I don't think I was curious to know more about its founder at that point.

Aimee Meredith Cox

I grew up in Cincinnati in the eighties, and I was determined to become a world-renowned Black ballerina. It was very naive. I studied at a little storefront dance school where you took ballet for a half hour, then jazz, and then tap. I excelled in ballet, and I really loved the way ballet felt in my body, even though I had a sort of love-hate relationship with it. When I was about eleven or twelve years old, my dance teacher told me that she thought I had outgrown her training, and she recommended that I study at the University of Cincinnati's Conservatory of Music.

I enrolled in the school's pre-professional ballet program. After my first year, I was at the barre during class, and I saw the most elegant human being I've ever seen in my life. He was a tall, graceful man, and when he walked, he looked as though he were gliding on water. It was James Truitte, although at the time I had no idea who he was. My story is not a story of a Black community or a Black family in Cincinnati that knew Ailey. We knew the Dance Theatre of Harlem.

I thought Mr. Truitte was this otherworldly, mesmerizing figure who haunted the hallways of the university. We were terrified of him, because he never spoke to us. When I would peek into his classes, I didn't know what the Horton technique was. I had never danced barefoot. But I watched the dancers making these shapes, and there was percussion, and I thought, "Oh, my God, this is amazing." In the summer, I took a few classes with Mr. Truitte. He was difficult. He was hard. I thought he was cold. I didn't understand who he was. Now I look back and one of my biggest regrets is that I didn't develop a relationship with him.

Fast-forward, I took a year off from college, and I was dancing in New York on a scholarship at the Dance Theatre of Harlem. I was trying to make my body a ballet body. My body didn't want to do that, but my spirit did. At the end of the summer, Lowell Smith said to me, "Baby, this is not going to work for you. You need to go to Ailey." So, I auditioned for Ailey and was on scholarship there for a while, and then I was asked to join the second company. What I learned at Ailey was training in a different sense; it was this sort of ethnographic social training that was like an excavation of lineage. Dancing with Ailey disrupted the binary between the individual and the cultural, and it taught me what it means to be of a Black American lineage that has roots in the South but also has diasporic tentacles all over the globe. It made me really consider what we think of as innate—what we should know just by virtue of being Black and living in a Black body—and what we think of as something that we are trained into. All these things were kind of battling within me the whole time that I was dancing in the second company.

Claire Bishop

I have to confess, when I first saw the Ailey company perform, it was not love at first sight. I'm going to be upfront about this because learning to respect and understand Ailey's work has been a process for me, and gradually I've come to love it. Ailey was not a part of the air that I breathed growing up in the United Kingdom, so it was seeing Netta Yerushalmy's *Paramodernities* in 2017 that first brought me to Ailey. *Paramodernities* is a series that draws on the work of six modern choreographers: Ailey, George Balanchine, Merce Cunningham, Bob Fosse, Martha Graham, and Vaslav Nijinsky. The performance I attended, *Paramodernities #3 (A Response to Ailey)*, was held in the rotunda of the National Museum of the American Indian in New York. Five dancers performed a deconstructed and remixed *Revelations*, subtitled *The Afterlives of Slavery*, and Tommy DeFrantz gave a searing lecture performance. The whole thing was so powerful, and I wondered, "Why don't I know Ailey? Why have I never heard of *Revelations*? What vacuum in my education led to this?"

So, I took myself to see *Revelations* at City Center that Christmas, and I have to confess it struck me as corny—all the long skirts, the hats, the fans. It just didn't speak to me. At the same time, I saw that it was speaking to the audience, and I realized that I needed to learn more. In the spring of 2023, Adrienne and I taught a graduate seminar on Ailey at the Whitney and the CUNY Graduate Center, and as a result of this, I've since come through to the other side. Now I see that Ailey stands for an important counter to the Cunningham-Judson lineage, which is what we are force-fed as the dance history that matters for contemporary art. For me, Ailey has opened up a whole other vector of performance and a way of relating to popular music, the body, and Blackness that I think is really valuable.

Adrienne Edwards

I wanted to go back to what Aimee said about diasporic tentacles. It seems easy for us to see a line through Dunham, Primus, and de Lavallade, who brought Ailey to his first dance class. We know that Ailey danced with Lester Horton, and it is so interesting to look at Horton's archive and the nature of his dances. Modern dance of the twenties, thirties, and forties was profoundly influenced by Black, Indigenous, and other non-Western cultures, including those embedded in the West but not recognized by Western discourse as having an aesthetic influence.

When we look at Ailey, though, we don't necessarily point directly to some of these other influences. You can go to an Ailey show and enjoy it, and recognize it as beautiful and amazing in its virtuosity, but not know that he was, in fact, deeply influenced by a surprising range of artistic references. Take, for example, Merce Cunningham. The extent to which Cunningham is mentioned in Ailey's notebooks was really surprising to me, as was the relationship Ailey had with Ted Shawn. And Jack Cole and Martha Graham. All were touchstones for Ailey's choreography. Ailey also was very interested in literature—myths, novels, plays. I wonder what your thoughts or perspectives are on how we think about this truly motley group of references, influences, and people that Ailey was looking at and thinking about. Are there other people or influences whom you might pinpoint or cite in relationship to his work?

Jawole Willa Jo Zollar

When I first moved to New York in 1980, one of the places I frequented was the Nuyorican Poets Café. I love poetry, and I love the Nuyorican's intersection of visual artists, poets, dancers, and musicians. One night I was at the café and someone asked me if I knew who was up in the booth. I didn't know, and they told me it was Mr. Ailey. He was very good friends with the café's founder, Miguel Algarín, and the café was one of Ailey's places of solace, where he could be anonymous up in the booth and run the lights. I understood that it was his private place, so it wouldn't be right for me to interrupt him. But it told me more about him and his legacy and his interactions with the literary and visual art worlds. The artists who frequented the café were cutting edge and avant-garde.

Adrienne Edwards

I'm so glad you brought that in, Jawole, because it's a great story. The importance of nightlife and the club to Ailey cannot be overstated. When speaking about *Night Creature*, for example—and this is what I mean when I talk about the veneers of Ailey—he would say, "It's in reference to the Duke Ellington piece." But in Ailey's notebooks, it was clearly also about clubs—bars, queer clubs, gathering spots in the East Village. For him, these nightlife spaces were deeply important to his dances. And you might detect this or not, but if you know what you're seeing, the relationship is clear.

Brenda Dixon-Gottschild

Adrienne, you asked if there are other figures whose work can be seen in Ailey's dances. Ailey brought together Black vernacular and sacred dance, which is so fundamental not only to the African American aesthetic but also to the American aesthetic. I think in ways, Claire, that may be why Ailey's work felt so foreign to you. Both Black vernacular and sacred dance narrate and tell stories, but they also contain deeply abstracted and conceptual ways of seeing and experiencing dancing bodies. This is an American but also an African American way of understanding dancers and dancing bodies in concert dance culture. I was impressed by the fact that Balanchine and Lincoln Kirstein used to go up to Harlem and hang out in clubs. Whether you went to Harlem or it came to you, if you are in the American stew, you are taking home the "Ailey-est" part of America with you. All of us feed and draw on these things either consciously or unwittingly. American concert dance is one of the sites in which Africanist movement is abstracted. I think everyone here understands the idea of the "shout," for example, in that it is a trope that holds these very simply abstracted seeds as well as it being a story about a hallelujah moment.

Adrienne Edwards

What you've described is the big *M* word—Modernism. This is how we would characterize Ailey's work, right? We shouldn't be so surprised, but we just don't think about it in that way.

Jennifer Homans

Adrienne, it is so interesting to me that you mentioned what you found in Ailey's notebooks, because it is similar to what I found in researching Balanchine, who also admired Jack Cole and absorbed a lot from popular, social, and concert dance. I'm thinking about the myths of modernism that were created by their makers. Balanchine built a whole story around himself about being a simple man who didn't really read and had few other interests; he just made dances. Well, forget it! He was voracious. And as you and Brenda both said, Ailey was seeing, absorbing, taking in; you can see it in his work, and that was true of Balanchine too.

We know from the archives that Balanchine saw Ailey dances, but we don't know much about what he thought of them. But I agree with Brenda that there was a sort of soup that they were all in. When I was in New York in the 1970s, it all seemed very much opposed and different: Cunningham is this, Graham is that, Ailey is this, Balanchine is that. There was uptown, and there was downtown—and within each technique or style, there were fierce debates and sects. But as I look at it from a distance, they were all interested in many of the same questions, including the relationship between form and narrative or words, which is a fundamental problem in dance.

Brenda Dixon-Gottschild

Exactly—they were all in the modernist moment.

Jennifer Homans

And, Claire, to your comment, there have been times when I've seen *Revelations*, *Blues Suite*, or other Ailey performances, and thought, "Somehow I can't feel or enter this dance anymore." But there is also a question of how dances change over time, especially as they become iconic. *Revelations* is surely one of the most iconic dances we have, and for a while I was concerned that it was being ruined by its commercial appeal and repeated performance night after night. Yet there are still times when I am moved by it, which makes me wonder if repetition in this case has also produced something quite valuable. The dance starts to take on a ritual aspect, and it also educates dancers—dancers who are watching, dancers who are doing—generation after generation. It seems to me that this is one of Ailey's legacies. Although this legacy has not always been consistent or untroubled, he—and *Revelations*—established a tradition, a way of moving and thinking about dance that has been fertile. It has inspired new works but also strong departures, a tribute to Ailey's legacy. To me that seems important.

Kyle Abraham

I'd like to come back to the idea of Mr. Ailey's generosity, and more than that, the idea of curation. I think a lot of the things that we feel aren't obvious in Ailey's works are much more obvious in the work of, for example, Rudy Perez or Eleo Pomare. We see it also in the work of Talley Beatty. One of my favorite pieces is Beatty's *Stack-Up*, which is as camp and as queer as they come. I mean, there's a moment in it that to me very much represents a glory hole. It doesn't get any more explicit or queerer than that. Having a work such as that in the Ailey repertory is a testament to someone saying, "Even if this is not something that I would put out as my own work, I'm interested in it, and I think this is an important voice to be sharing on our stage as a way of representing our culture and our community."

Regarding what Jennifer mentioned about the repetition of a work such as *Revelations* and how a piece can shift over time, this is a conversation right now in dance, the idea of how dancers are taking ownership of choreography and living in the material, while also trying to make sure they stay in dialogue with the true intention of the work. For example, the height of the leg in "Fix Me, Jesus," which is such an iconic dance in *Revelations*, is an issue that is constantly debated. In the nineties in particular, the leg was getting higher and higher, but if you look at earlier representations of that dance, the leg was clearly positioned at a very certain point. It's about what the intention of that line is within the context of the dance, and maybe its meaning shifts over time. Who knows? It's not my work. But I think that questions such as this are part of a conversation that honors a work and its legacy.

Jawole Willa Jo Zollar

I keep thinking about what the avant-garde is and who decides that. Part of the reason I founded the Urban Bush Women Choreographic Center Initiative was because I was participating in a lot of panels and the Black women's work that I was seeing was not getting funded because it was seen as earnest or representative, or it was simply not understood. But I could see how these choreographers were breaking and cracking open form in different ways. When I watch Mr. Ailey's work, I find that as well, but because his works hit at deeply held stories and feelings, maybe they aren't seen as a part of the avant-garde. Years ago, while trying to figure out this conundrum, I came up with the theorem that European-influenced aesthetics diminish emotion to heighten structure and form, while Africanist work uses structure and form to heighten emotion and feeling. Now, I don't know if that is completely true, but it's a place for me to kind of work with in order to understand what's not seen as powerful art. When I saw Mr. Ailey's *Flowers*, which is about Janice Joplin, I wondered how it wasn't seen as avant-garde. The question of what we see and how it is defined intrigues me.

Jamila Wignot

With *Revelations*, what is so striking to me is that it really depends on the night you go or if you go to a matinee versus an evening performance. The dancers are in a different head space; I went with my seven-year-old daughter, and *I* was in a different head space. It's an interesting lightning strike that happens. For me, the coming together of community and the resolution at the end of *Revelations* sometimes translate and other times do not. What I find myself drawn to now are the architectural, structural pieces in the beginning, in the darker part of the dance. "Fix Me, Jesus" feels very structured. And the opening, everyone is so excited for it, and when the curtain comes up, there is already applause, right? In a way, the audience is trying to prompt how you should feel. That to me is very modern, but I also feel that it's embodying all these other things. It is intriguing because Ailey was very invested in reaching audiences. He was at the tail end of a certain kind of tradition, and the later schools, which are again in conversation, were kind of rejecting that tradition.

But Ailey is certainly a significant piece of the puzzle. With *Revelations*, it is a dance that offers multiple vignettes and ways in. You don't have to get to the big finale; you can focus on just one section. "I Wanna Be Ready," which was choreographed by Ailey and James Truitte, continues to be such an incredible moment of alienation, of soul searching. I very much see a queer lens in that space. By creating a repertory company, Ailey made space for not only Pomare but also Bill T. Jones, whom he commissioned to put on works. He was bringing the downtown to the uptown. Ailey was not going to make that dance, but he was invested in using his platform to support it.

What I think is difficult about Ailey is that there is so much encoded in his work. He had a whole life outside the institution that he was actively building, an institution that had to be built in certain, very formal ways, with State Department funding and all sorts of things. He's so complex. His was not a bifurcated life; it was prismatic. Adrienne, you and I have talked about *Night Creature*. At that point, people had seen Ailey out in the

Meatpacking District; people had spotted him in queer clubs. I watch *Night Creature* now, and I think about Ailey being in a queer club, dancing. But then I imagine him saying something such as, "Okay, I'll do it, but I'll set it to Ellington, and I'll include some social dance of that era." To me, though, I see disco and certain very modern movements in it. I'm mixing up terms, I'm sure, but I see movement and gestures in that dance that were contemporary to the social dances of the 1970s. You have to read Ailey, and then read him again, and then read him again. The more you know, the dances become much richer, about Ailey personally but also about where the company was at.

Aimee Meredith Cox

Jawole, I wanted to follow up on what you were saying. To me, a complicated critique of Ailey becomes also a complicated understanding and critique of Black life writ large. I think what you were getting at—the sentimental aspects, the idea that it's all right there and so legible and so clear—is a lack of study, a lack of Black study, if you will. There's an assumption that Black expression has to do so much work—it has to be historical, it has to educate, it has to fill the void that has been created by white supremacy.

There's all this work that Black expression and the Black artist has to do. I'm trying to think about the reception of Ailey in the past and into the future within the larger conversation of how we understand, first of all, Black life and Black aliveness—not Black death—and Black expression and Black art, and the binary ways that we are called to read and critique Black art against what might be called modern or white or European. I wonder about the layers that are missed when we assume that it is all legible and a clear representation of Black southern life or the Black church, especially without having the experiential, social, or political study needed to understand signification, to understand a nod and a wink, and to understand the layers that are beneath the surface.

An image that stays with me, maybe as a metaphor for better or for worse, is Mr. Ailey always having his notebook, and what is in that notebook. It's what he experienced as he walked down the street or was in a nightclub, and it's his relationships, his desires. He holds multitudes. His dances hold multitudes. I wonder, especially when I read reviews of Ailey's dances, how much work we're doing as audience members, as viewers, or as critics, and how much we're holding on to false assumptions. Modernity is built on Black life, period. How do we then understand that a critique of Ailey's work as simplistic or representational or feel good or sentimental misses the same things that are missed in the complicated understanding of what Black aliveness means as a praxis, as an art form, and as a political act?

Jamila, with *Revelations*, I feel the same way; after "Wade in the Water," I'm ready to sneak out. I danced these pieces, and I still feel them in my body. Repetition is a beautiful and a troubling thing, right? Repetition is ritual. It creates a groove that we can step into, and we can assume that we know what it is. Our bodies respond to it just as much as our hearts and our minds. There's a lot, a lot, a lot to unpack if we want to think about Ailey as an individual artist and the Ailey company as a corporation. We have to consider his aspirations as an artist who wanted to make universal, crowd-pleasing dances. But we also need to think about funding, and Ailey's relationship with Jones and the way they both thought about what it means to be a Black artist. It's hard not to bring into this conversation all these other ways of thinking about Blackness and Black life and about Ailey as a man and as an organization, as well as the critiques of Ailey in that larger conversation of Black.

Jamila Wignot

While researching *Masekela Langage* for my documentary, part of my endeavor was to show other dances that Ailey made around the same time as *Masekela*. Although I couldn't find a final, filmed performance of *Masekela* from the time, I found a filmed rehearsal of it, which I felt gave insight into Ailey's feelings in 1969. *Masekela Langage* is inspired by the death of Fred Hampton and what was happening in South Africa. It is set in a South African bar and has a very loose narrative to it, kind of akin to *Blues Suite*. It begins where it ends; people come in, they're listless, they experience this night that has a bit of drama—somebody dies in the middle of the dance—and at the end, they are stuck in the exact same place as where they began. So, it is a dance that goes nowhere. At the conclusion of the company's first performance of the piece, which was in 1969 at Connecticut College and featured George Faison, a recording of Ailey's voice could be heard saying, "Thank you. Thank you very much. Thank you. Thank you very much." At the end of this dance about an evening of drama, pain, violence, and death, where nothing changes politically, nothing moves forward, Ailey engaged the audience in this thank you, this interrogation: What have you just watched? What have you been a spectator to? Have you enjoyed it? It's a really interesting moment.

The piece no longer ends this way, and I'm not aware of any records suggesting why the recording was removed. Who can say, but was such an interrogation going to be something to showcase overseas as part of a State Department–sponsored tour? I don't know, but what it reveals is that a choice was made. I can't see how it could have been purely an aesthetic one in which Ailey decided, "Oh, never mind, this very interesting interrogation that I do, that's spectatorship. Let's just leave it out." It is an editorial choice that suggests how political he could be.

Brenda Dixon-Gottschild

Was it his choice?

Jamila Wignot

Exactly right. He had a board he had to answer to, and you all know what that is like.

Adrienne Edwards

I'm so glad that you circled back to *Masekela Langage*. I'd like to ask you all to reflect a bit on this dance, because it's the Ailey piece that everyone describes pretty readily as political. Yet I keep asking myself which of his other dances might be equally political, but this isn't obvious in some ways. It goes back to the questions of abstraction that Brenda contributed so wonderfully. What are the political limits and the possibilities that we find in Ailey's dances? When I read the reviews of his plotless dances, such as *Streams*, critics hated them. They were relentless in their critiques of what Ailey insisted upon calling ballets, which was his terminology for describing most of his dances.

Aimee Meredith Cox

I loved dancing *Streams*. It is one of my favorite ballets.

Adrienne Edwards

I want you to talk about that, because when I looked back at the Ailey repertory and the number of performances of each piece over the years, *Revelations* is number one, of course. I think number two is *Blues Suite*. Third is *Streams*, which is surprisingly tied with *Cry*. Despite receiving far less critical attention than these other dances, *Streams*, and his plotless dances in general, has been performed again and again and again, and I have a deep appreciation of the fact that Ailey insisted on showing it and other non-narrative ballets. I would welcome your thoughts on the question of the political in his work. I feel that it intersects in very meaningful ways with questions of queerness as much as it does with questions of Blackness and of bringing different scenes into the context of modern dance, whether those scenes are the church or the nightclub or Broadway or Hollywood. What are the stakes in making these dances?

Kyle Abraham

There are politics surrounding the ownership of who Ailey was and making sure that who he was is really seen in his work. With *Revelations*, and also well beyond it, its rootedness, its queerness, and its cultural connections to church make the dance experiential in a way that is reflective for so many people. And if it's not your experience, you feel either that you're invited or that it's a place you want to be or an experience that you want to be a part of in some way. There is something powerful and profound to that, in that it is not asking for acceptance from non-Black bodies, but it's saying, "This is who we are. This is how we are. We are celebrating who we are. We are celebrating us, and you are welcome to see us." This makes people more curious to know us, and hopefully there are levels of respect that go into the love of the culture that Mr. Ailey was sharing and bringing forth.

Brenda Dixon-Gottschild

The question about where are the politics—all of it is politics. Every time we are in the dominant caste world, we are an individual and collective body politic speaking ourselves, our truth. Even if you're on a dance stage, you are a body politic speaking yourself in a place where, as Jawole said, European art lessens emotions to heighten form and structure.

Rennie Harris spoke of that when hip-hop became mainstream. When studio dancers, white studio dancers, come to take hip-hop class, they have to learn to diminish their training that stressed the importance of structure and form in order to find their emotions. In a very simplistic way, the dominant caste and world cultures are in a sense at polar opposites. And, of course, here in America, and really all over the world, we are more and more playing with sometimes appropriating—and sometimes even worse—others' forms.

Jawole Willa Jo Zollar

My statement about European art and emotions is deliberately provocative and binary to open out our thinking. I consider all of Mr. Ailey to be political, including his audaciousness of putting these bodies on stage and telling these stories. In thinking about the first time I saw the opening of *Revelations*, and seeing Black dancers who were trained in and could do these European forms, I realized that it's not an either/or of training. When I saw the Ailey company perform *Lazarus*, the program opened with Wayne McGregor's *Chroma*, and I thought, "What company can go from *Chroma* to *Lazarus*? What company can do that, and with such integrity?" When you talk about Ailey the man, the individual, the person in society, the person inside a corporation, maybe he didn't give the same breadth to his creative expression that he might have if he had been an independent choreographer, but through his generosity, he wanted to have a place for people and to pay the dancers and to provide them with a structure.

For me, all that is political. At a time when most dance companies outside of ballet were those of single-vision choreographers, Ailey made this other kind of thing. There are individual works that strike me as political, but I would say the whole of Ailey was political.

Claire Bishop

I, again, might go against the grain a little bit. There are so many ways of trying to calibrate what is political in art and culture: it can be the formal language, the thematic content, how something reaches a public, who's performing it, how it's used by those in power. What is perplexing about Ailey is that by any of these conventional criteria, he is very tricky to position as explicitly political. He doesn't come out swinging, declaring, "I am a political artist." I wonder, then, about the usefulness of this term as a way of evaluating Ailey's work and significance.

For example, he was making conventional-length concert dances for a ticket-paying audience with music that is on the whole popular rather than experimental. He was a gay choreographer who came to prominence during McCarthyism, but in most of the works you can't tell he was gay (even while a handful of others, such as *Quintet*, are screamingly camp). He came of age during segregation, but his racial politics were not militant, especially when you compare his dances to something as explicit as Dunham's *Southland* or the work of the Black Arts Movement. He touched on racial division only infrequently and lightly. Historians want to find a political work, and this is why *Masekela Langage* becomes the central example; Ailey found a way to speak about racial politics via South Africa. *Masekela* gives us the "political" work that we want to see in 1969, but it is really the exception rather than the rule. In general, Ailey tends to work with (rather than to oppose) political power. He was sent to represent the US throughout the world by the State Department, and in the eighties, he received the Kennedy Center Honors, with a reception hosted by President Ronald Reagan.

There is nothing conventionally oppositional in this trajectory. So, maybe the question should be reframed—to something such as, what is the capacity of dance? What can a choreographer do? What else can a career produce? We need to rethink what renders something political outside the lens of oppositionality. When you frame Ailey's work as building worlds, generating opportunities, and creating legacies, it seems to open things up. What he accomplishes is not just great dance but the labor of institution building, education, commissioning, and sheer visibility. Being seen, this visibility—it's not just a different kind of politics but a different kind of modern.

It's a modern inflected with Blackness, and that means popularity and repetition and pleasure. I appreciate that every year at Christmas you can go see *Revelations* at City Center; it's the alternative *Nutcracker*. For Ailey to have become a presence in this way, to be one of the defining figures of American modernism, is huge. I think we should rethink the association between politicality and criticality. It can also be about what worlds the work generates.

Adrienne Edwards

One of the thoughts I've been sitting with is the idea of a kind of politics of sparkle. What does it mean? It isn't shine; it's something else, but it is akin to the notion of showing off. It also taps into what Aimee was saying about Black life. I've thought so much about pleasure in Ailey's work, more so after sitting with his notebooks. He was facing so many things, and I wonder what it means to run a company, what it means to try to be a creative in that context, what it means to have ambitions—to be in all these different spaces. These are the very things that exhausted him.

But for me, pleasure is really his utmost desire in some ways. Maybe that is what got him on the dance floor in the first place. I imagine this young man whom de Lavallade took to the Horton studio. He could barely contain himself, but he sat in the back for a long time and did not dance, until I think it was Horton who said to him, "Are you actually going to do something? You came here, but you're not doing anything." I wonder what ultimately compelled him to move and thereby come to move us. I feel like language fails us in a way. We can't articulate it, but it's something that can be felt.

Claire Bishop

Again, this is a different model of the modern: it's not about alienation and estrangement but about embracing and participating and sparkling.

Jawole Willa Jo Zollar

Regarding showing off, if I hadn't become a choreographer, I probably would have become a folklorist. I love the boasting traditions that are so much a part of African American culture: "I just did that, y'all. I just did that." You have to recognize what I just did. I feel as though Ailey captured this: "Here it is, y'all. Here it is."

Jennifer Homans

In a way, isn't that so human? I think there is something big about Ailey the man, even though at times he felt very small. He suffered and had incredibly difficult moments. But he was open in his curiosity and in his pulling in of different sources, from Horton and Charles Weidman to his own experiences, to almost everything that he saw. He was someone who took in things and used them to produce something of his own.

For Ailey, I think a broad version of political is maybe a useful one. Political then was not necessarily our vision of what is political today. When his dances came out, they were in conversation with what was happening in society around him. He went to the Soviet Union during the Cold War, for example, which brings up questions of Socialist Realism and the Soviet audience's reaction to a Black man coming via the US State Department to show them his "American" work. I think almost any dance is political. It's just a question of defining the terms, so I kind of agree, Claire, that perhaps "political" is not only being critical of power structures. It can be an engagement with form as much as content, and it is a way of putting a vision on stage.

Aimee Meredith Cox

One way that I like to define political is as something that is potentially transformative, that is about world-making and self-making together, that is about creating the possibility of something different from the world we know. We have come to understand that much of what Ailey was doing in terms of the realm of the political was not about the audience or the outcome or the product but about the process—his mapping out how he moved through the world, and how he created dance and what that meant for a dancer.

I really only understood *Revelations* after I learned *Streams*. To the point about form and function, the form of the movement serves the function of a more open and abstract story in *Streams*, which enabled me to narrate my own story through the choreography. However, in *Revelations* the story felt predetermined to me, and I always questioned whether I was accurately or adequately portraying the Black southern experience. But, at the level of the actual steps and movement, there are many of the same Horton- and Graham-based movements in both ballets. This commonality, once I really felt it in my body, allowed me to step into *Revelations* more fully as myself. What both ballets share narratively, from my perspective, is a story about connection, community, and relationships.

I wonder if it's useful to think about Ailey's process of embodying the movement. Especially in *Streams*, he was experimenting with relationships and how through contact and intimacy one can develop different understandings of what it means to be in relationship, to create community. Everybody talks about the ending of *Streams* and wonders why Ailey chose to end it in unison. It's so simple: he's saying something about the collective.

If we think about the power of the political statement of the collective moving together, of relationality, and of process, we see that there was a reason why the Ailey Extension program was so important to Mr. Ailey. It is the educational piece. In the second company, we toured across the country, and we spent more time performing lecture demonstrations at nursing homes or run-down schools than we did rehearsing. We would teach the audience dances from *Revelations*—for example, "I Been 'Buked"—because the process is not just showing a community the work but getting individuals to feel the movement in their own bodies. There is something powerfully political in the process of embodiment, and I think Mr. Ailey was very interested in this. That is why to this day the educational and outreach components of the organization remain so important. It's not about just watching a work. It's about what it feels like in the space of your own body. Whether you're a professional dancer or not, the embodiment of the movement is such a key part of the political project.

Jawole Willa Jo Zollar

I just want to thank you all. Sometimes in the world of dance that I live in, I miss these kinds of conversations. Part of what took me to the Nuyorican was that the poets and artists there would stay up all night, talking art, aesthetics, and various things. These conversations are important.

Online conversation held January 15, 2024

CHRONOLOGY

CJ Salapare

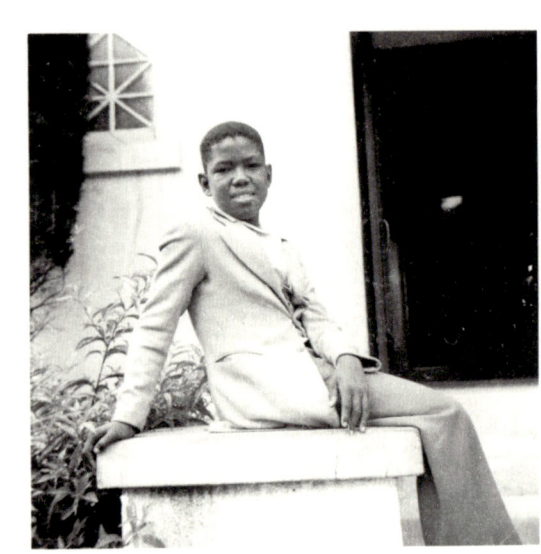
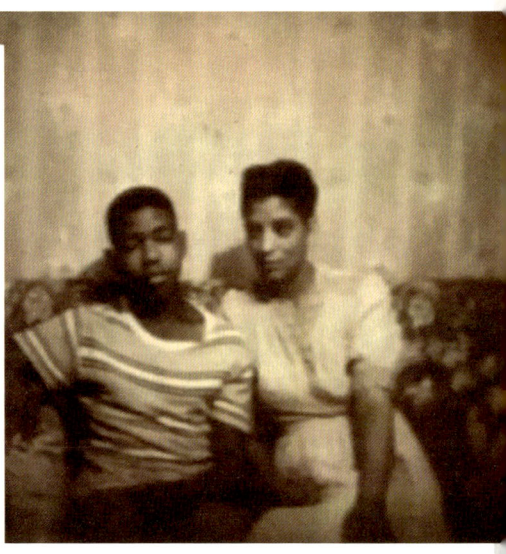

Ailey, ca. 1944

Ailey and his mother, Lula Cooper, ca. 1945

1931

January 5: Alvin Ailey Jr. is born in Rogers, Texas—a rural and largely segregated small town—to Alvin Ailey Sr. and Lula Elizabeth Cliff. Cotton was first planted in the area in 1825 by the enslaved, supporting an agricultural economy that would endure for generations to come, from slavery to sharecropping, with both of Ailey's parents descending from this lineage.

When Ailey is three months old, the family of three moves into a home of their own, a cabin on white-owned property outside Rogers, in exchange for working on the farm—a common economic dynamic for many Black workers in the region. Three months later, Ailey Sr. abandons the family, and Lula decides to remain in the house and raise Ailey on her own.

ca. 1933

A late-night doctor's visit for a distended stomach proves fateful for Ailey and his mother. After driving Lula and Ailey home and seeing their living conditions, E. L. Etter—a white doctor who treated Black patients—offers them residence in his servants' quarters in exchange for domestic work.

1935

May: Ailey Sr. returns to the family, marking an unwelcome reunion.

Early September: With her young son in tow, Lula leaves the Etters and her estranged husband, taking the midnight train to Wharton, Texas—the farthest place she could afford tickets to with her available funds, eight dollars in total. Maggie Earl, a fellow Black passenger on the train, takes Ailey and his mother under her wing, temporarily housing them and employing Lula.

Following their stay with Earl, the pair finds a home of their own in a deserted wood-frame shack, a short-lived stay due to the snakes and insects that Ailey, to his mother's horror, turned into his companions.

Lula and Ailey move back to Rogers, where Dorothy Ball, a white woman in town, offers them a cabin in exchange for work. Ailey's childhood in Rogers is anchored by a number of formative memories: playing roadside games, watching trucks and trains go by, and attending four-hour Sunday services at the Mount Olive Baptist Church. The church, with its tight-knit community, its rousing musical and spiritual traditions, and its rites—particularly that of baptism—would leave a profound imprint on the young boy. Ailey would later vividly recall the voice of Sister Hattie Taplin singing "I Been 'Buked and I Been Scorned" during his own baptism.

Lula is violently raped one day after work, prompting her to move with Ailey three times in rapid succession: first living with Nettie Corouthers, Ailey's paternal aunt; then with Inez Douglas, Lula's sister; and later returning to stay with Corouthers.

1936

Summer: Ailey and his mother leave Rogers and move to Navasota, Texas—beginning a period that Ailey would later "remember as one of the happiest of his life."[1]

Navasota was much larger and more cosmopolitan than the places Ailey had previously lived. Sited at a railway crossroads, the city was a pit stop for traveling stock companies and entertainers, and Ailey would attend performances by blues singers and minstrel shows. He also occasionally visits the local Dew Drop Inn, a tavern establishment often found in small southern towns. During the day, people of all walks of life would come to the inn for meals, and on weekend nights, the space became a dance floor and juke joint. Although Ailey was too young to attend the latter, he would peek in on the action.

Fall: Ailey enrolls in an elementary school located in a white section of the city.

Outside of school, he is preoccupied with scribbling and doodling in his ruled notepads, which he carries with him everywhere. He has a few close friends during this time. One is an older boy named Chancey, with whom Ailey experiences his queer sexual awakening, after Chancey rescued Ailey from nearly drowning in the local water tank. Years later, recalling this moment, as well as the two friends' wrestling sessions, Ailey described the encounter as "not just as an instance of youthful sexual exploration but as an experience of haunting purity and loss."[2]

Lula is courted by Amos Alexander, a successful Black businessman fifteen years her senior. After she and Ailey move into his home, Alexander attempts to assume the role of provider and father figure, although neither Ailey nor his mother fully buys into this proposition. Lula considers Alexander a boyfriend but has no intent to marry him.

1937

Following an emergency appendectomy and eye operation, Lula starts working at the local hospital, sterilizing surgical instruments and assisting elderly patients.

1941

Fall: Lula follows friends to Los Angeles in search of job prospects, moving there permanently in January 1942. Los Angeles in the 1940s is buttressed by

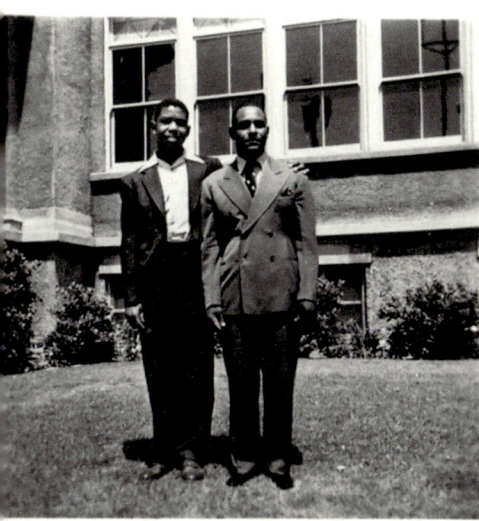

Ailey and his stepfather, Fred Cooper, 1945

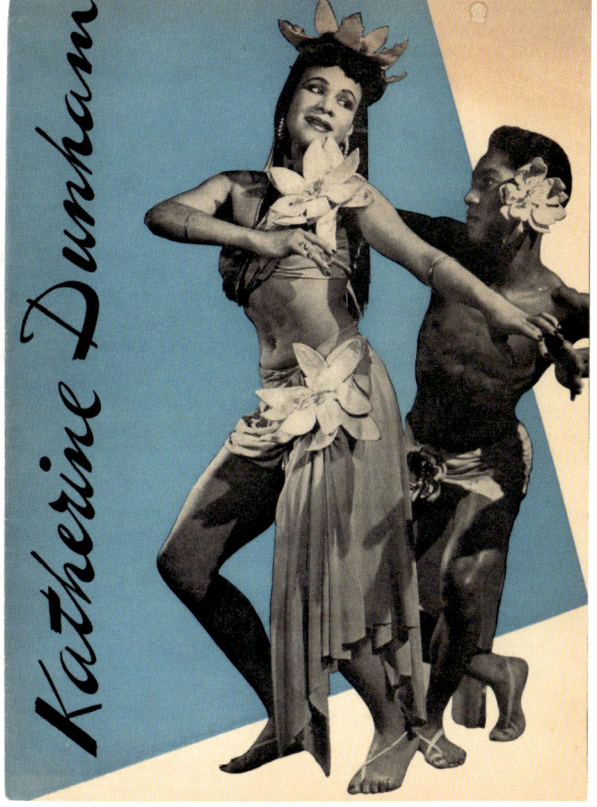

Cover of program for Katherine Dunham's *Tropical Revue*, ca. 1943–45

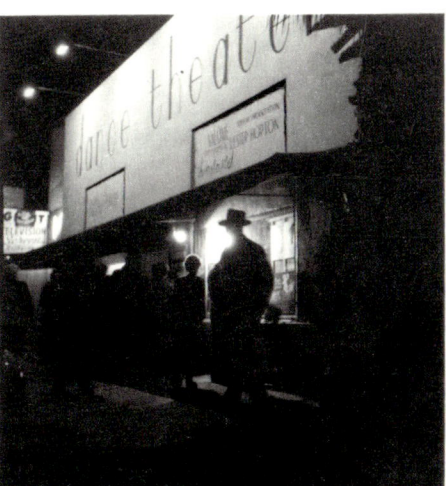

Lester Horton Dance Theater, Melrose Avenue, Los Angeles, California, n.d.

three industries—agriculture, wartime production, and Hollywood—that offer educational and economic incentives for Black workers and families to move westward, part of a larger twentieth-century movement known as the Great Migration. Ailey remains in Texas with Alexander to finish the school year.

1942

Upon securing employment and housing, Lula invites Ailey to join her in Los Angeles, and he travels alone from Texas to California. Such long-distance journeys were common for Black children during this period of intense migration.

In Los Angeles, Ailey struggles to adjust to the white neighborhood public school. As a result, Lula moves them to an apartment at 912½ East Forty-Third Place, which allows Ailey to enroll in the more diverse George Washington Carver Junior High School. Lula secures better-paying employment at Lockheed Martin.

At Carver, Ailey's academic strengths, interests, and dislikes emerge: an aptitude for languages, an aversion to mathematics, a reticence toward competitive sports, a short-lived stint with tap dance, and a burgeoning interest in poetry and writing. The school sought to expose students to cultural opportunities, often partly subsidized by teachers. Through these efforts, Ailey meets actor and singer Lena Horne, a soon to be a fixture of his cultural upbringing, and sees a production of the comic opera *The Mikado*.

During this time, the theaters, restaurants, and nightclubs of Los Angeles's Central Avenue are a vital hub for Black social life, and the area becomes Ailey's stomping ground and site of inspiration. He spends many weekends in its movie houses and theaters, including the Florence Mills Theatre and the Lincoln Theater, where he would see for the first time Black vaudeville acts; the entertainers Pearl Bailey, Billie Holiday, and Dewey "Pigmeat" Markham; and films featuring Fred Astaire, Gene Kelly, the Nicholas brothers, and Bill Robinson.

1945–48

1945: Lula marries Fred Cooper, and they would bear a son, Calvin, a few years later. Such family additions and newfound subjects of his mother's attention leave Ailey feeling devastated and frustrated in equal measure.

Fall 1945: Ailey enrolls at Thomas Jefferson High School, located at Hooper Avenue and East Forty-First Street in South Central Los Angeles. Like Carver, Jefferson offered programs and opportunities that exposed its students to the city's cultural scene. Ailey first experiences downtown Los Angeles and concert dance through a Saturday matinee performance by the Ballet Russe de Monte Carlo, notably featuring Maria Tallchief (Osage) and Yvonne Chouteau (Shawnee). Karel Shook, a company dancer, would become one of Ailey's ballet teachers in New York a decade later.

This exposure yields a pattern of entertainment seeking for Ailey, who splits his weekends between the venues of Central Avenue and downtown theaters. At the Los Angeles Civic Light Opera, he sees Jack Cole's theatrical movement styles for the first time in *Magdalena: A Musical Adventure*; at the Orpheum, he first hears Duke Ellington and his band play live; and at the Biltmore, he sees Katherine Dunham's *Tropical Revue*, featuring all-Black dancers, which would be a formative experience for the teenaged Ailey. He is enchanted by Dunham's sensuous and dynamic approach to rhythm, social dance, theatricality, and Afro-Caribbean rituals and movement styles. He would venture backstage to get her autograph and return to her performances multiple times throughout her company's time in Los Angeles.

In school, Ailey is known as a curious and quiet yet confident student, with a penchant for languages and a budding interest in dance, the latter spurred by and nurtured through his friendships with Ted Crum and Carmen de Lavallade. The former enrolls in Dunham classes with Ailey, who attends only one class, and introduces him to the idea of studying with Lester Horton. Ailey's admiration for de Lavallade, whose dancing in school assemblies and during impromptu lunch breaks left him spellbound, would ultimately be what prompts him to visit the Horton studio on Melrose Avenue during his last year of high school. Ailey is stunned by the experience, and he enrolls in beginner classes after this first encounter.

Horton's studio occupied a unique position in the pre-modern dance landscape. Blurred boundaries between background, genre, discipline, and influence informed his approach to choreography and company building. His racially integrated company was radical during this time of intense segregation, being the first of its kind in the United States, and was equally progressive in its openness to sexuality and political engagement. Horton's admiration for and propensity to borrow from popular culture and non-Western forms and aesthetics—a lingering tendency from influences such as Isadora Duncan, Ruth St. Denis, and Ted Shawn—became a cornerstone of his technique and informed his sense of theatricality. Dancers were expected to be well-versed in body, mind, and community: together, they would learn about the history of art, music, and design in tandem with rehearsals and practical workshops in lighting and stage management. This all-encompassing approach would become a critical model of education for Ailey, who stayed with

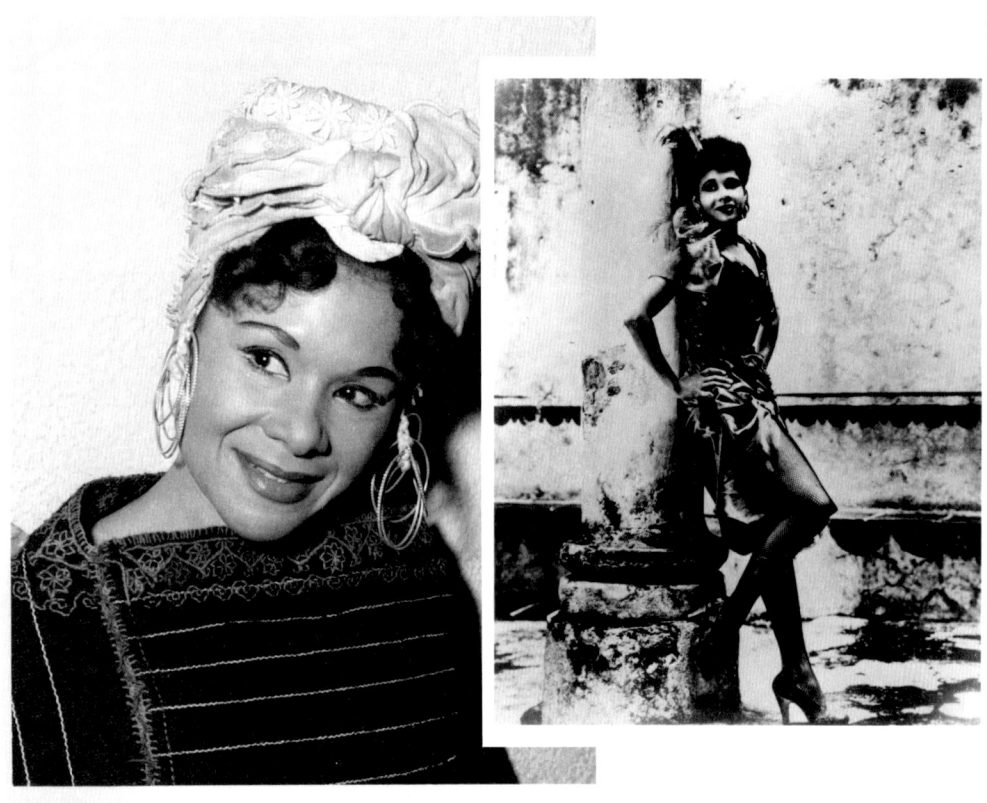
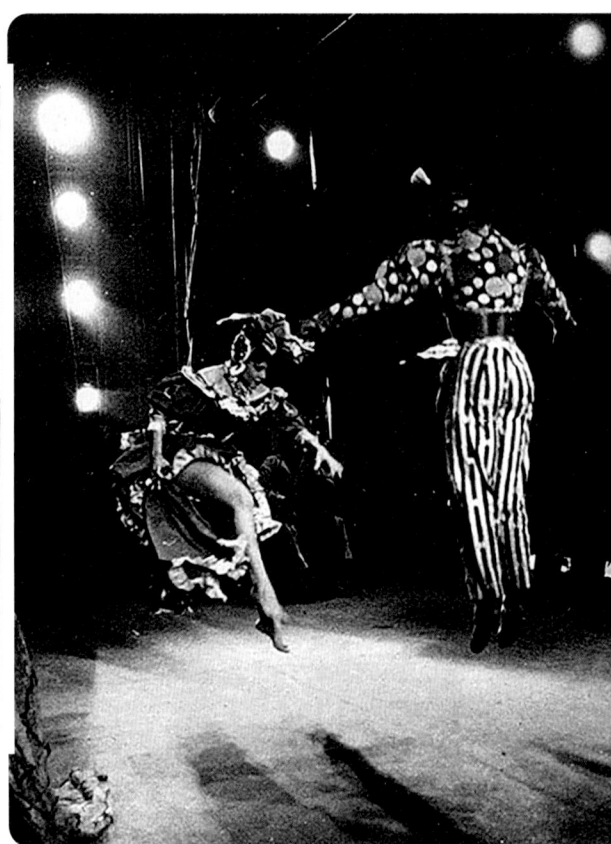

Dunham, 1956

Dunham, ca. 1950s

Dunham in *Le Jazz Hot: From Haiti to Harlem*, ca. 1939

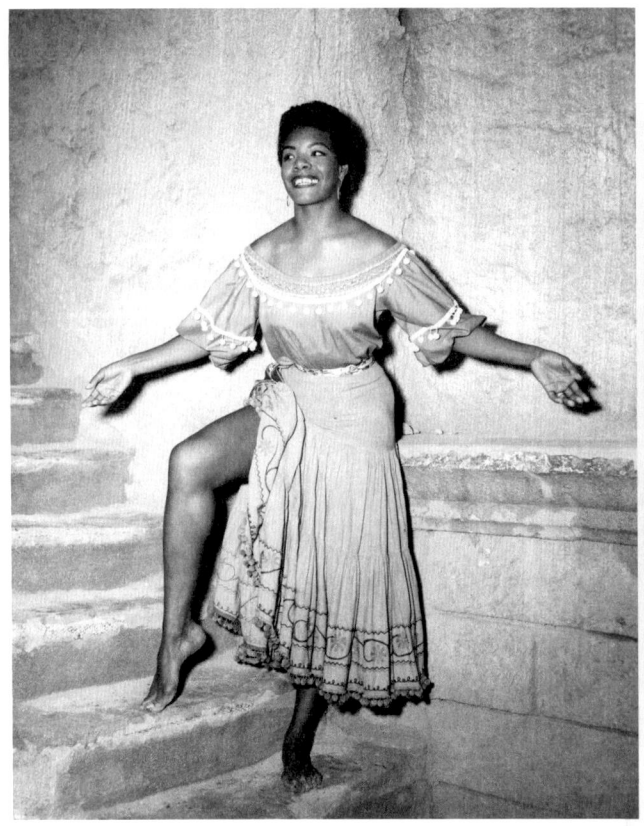
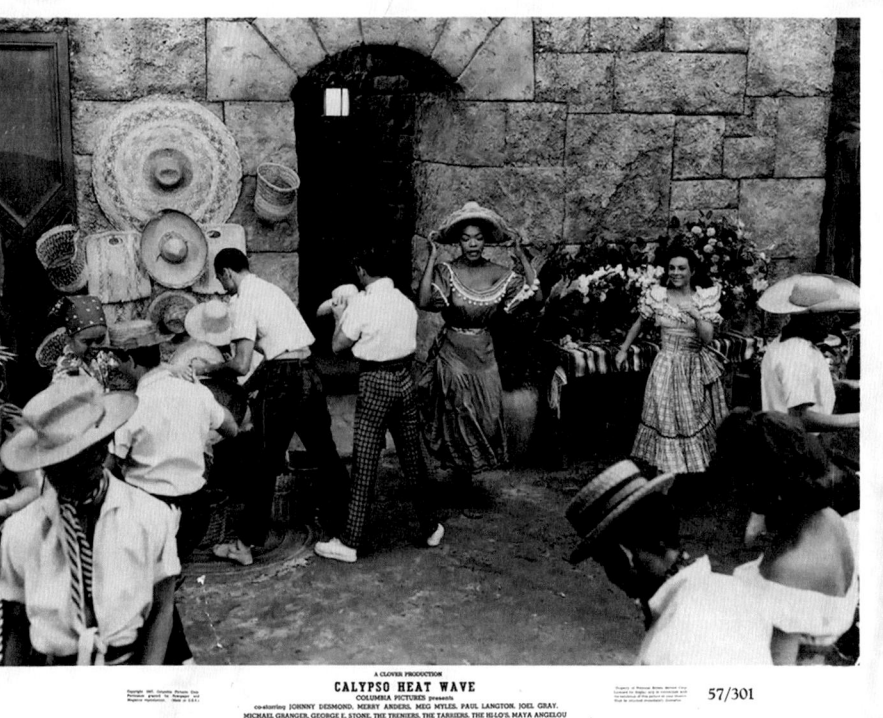

Maya Angelou in a press photograph for the film *Calypso Heat Wave*, 1957

Poster for *Calypso Heat Wave*, with Angelou at center, ca. 1957

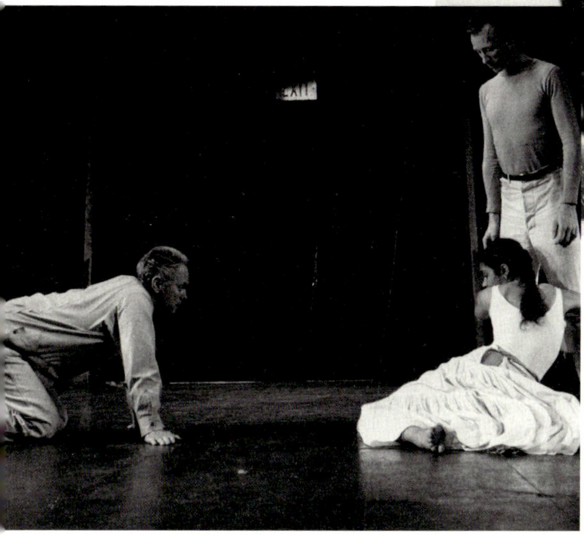

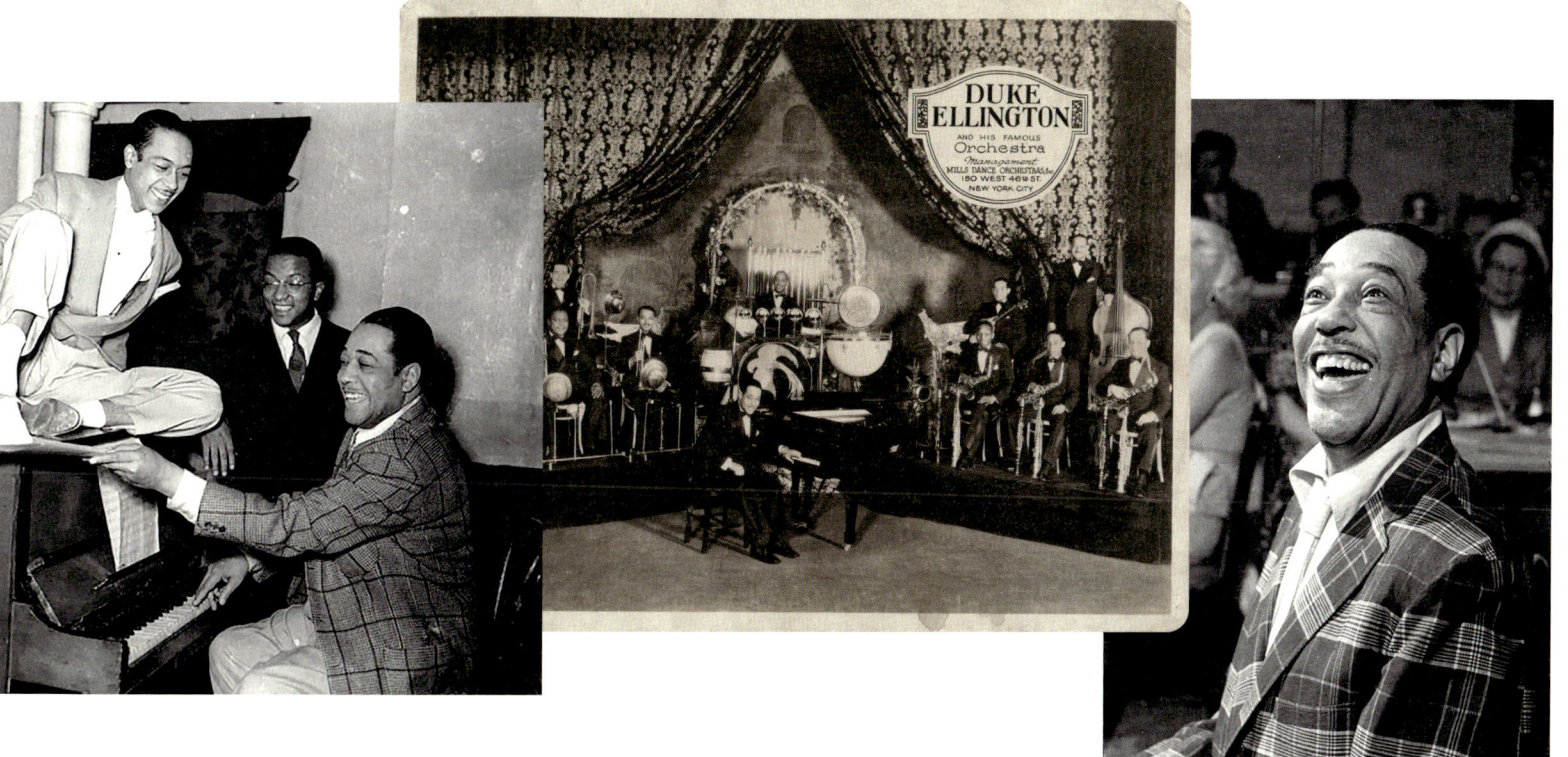

Horton and company dancers in rehearsal, n.d.

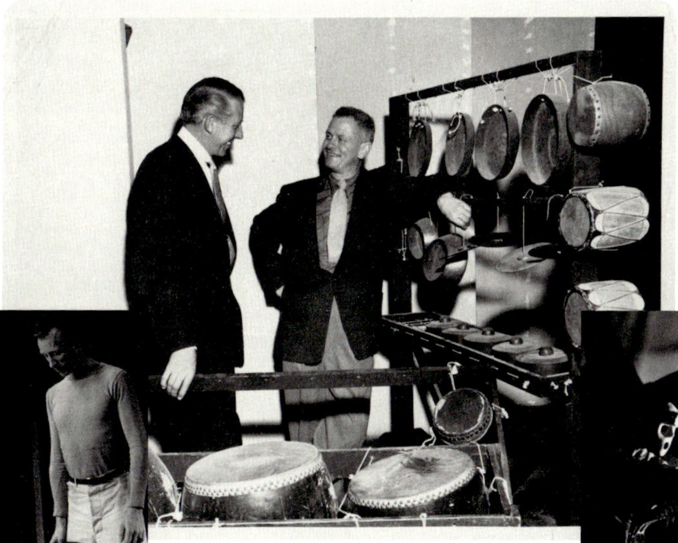

Stan Kenton and Horton on set for *Another Touch of Klee*, ca. 1951

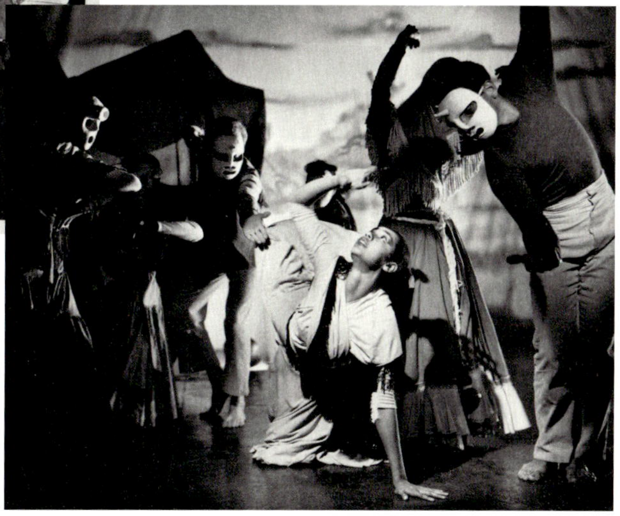

Horton company dancers, n.d.

Ellington at piano, with Billy Strayhorn and possibly dancer Ralph Brown on top, backstage at the Stanley Theatre, Pittsburgh, ca. 1942–43

Ellington and his orchestra, 1930

Ellington, 1957

Chronology

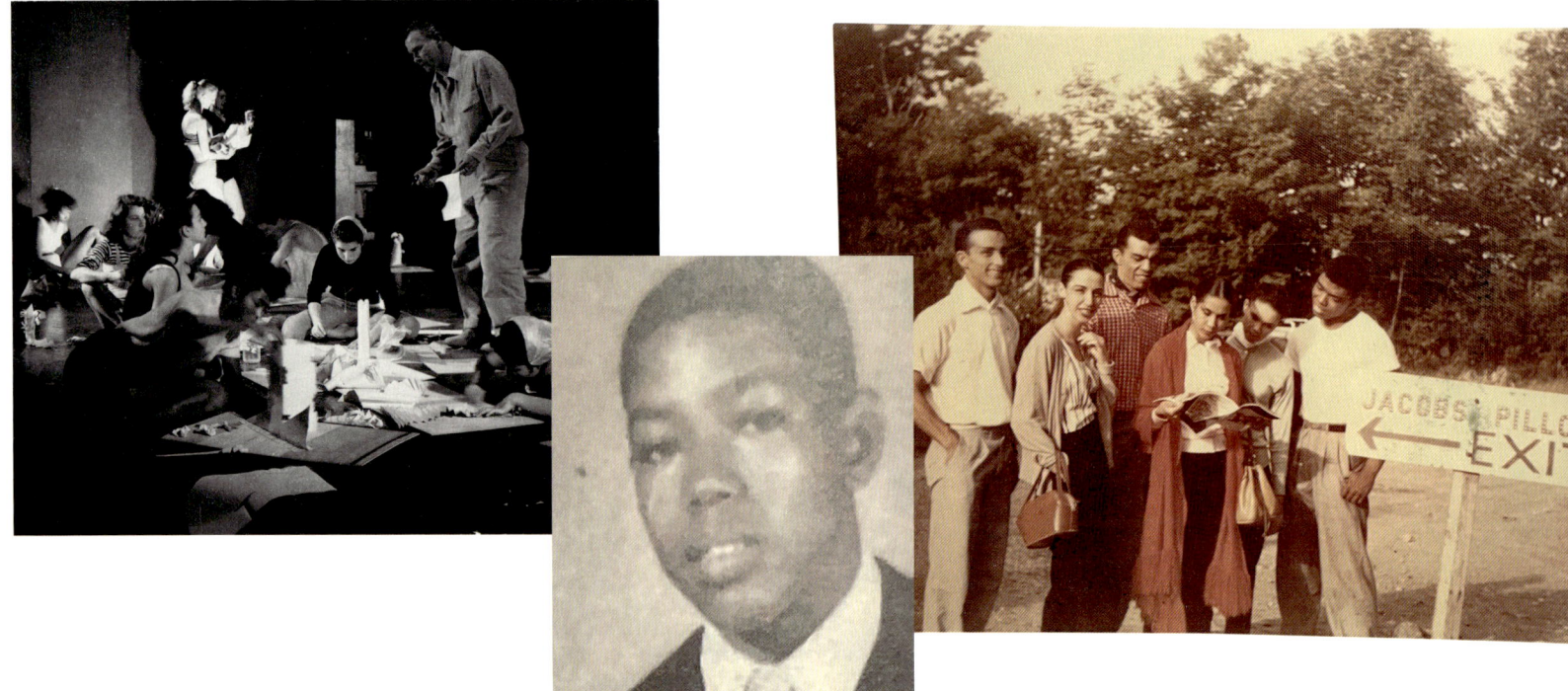

Horton (right) and company dancers making stage props, ca. 1940s–50s

Ailey's senior yearbook photograph for Thomas Jefferson High School, Los Angeles, 1948

Ailey (far right) with (from left) an unidentified person and dancers likely Lelia Goldoni, James Truitte, Carmen de Lavallade, and likely Joyce Trisler, Jacob's Pillow, Becket, Massachusetts, 1953

the Horton company for five years. During this time, he would build lifelong friendships with figures such as de Lavallade, Lelia Goldoni, Bella Lewitzky, Joyce Trisler, and James Truitte.

June 1948: Ailey graduates from high school and starts working full-time as an office clerk at the Atomic Energy Commission (AEC).

1949

January: Ailey leaves his job at the AEC and begins coursework at the University of California, Los Angeles (UCLA), balancing his studies with part-time employment.

Horton offers Ailey, in whom he sees potential, a scholarship to take classes with him on Saturdays, in exchange for Ailey's help around the studio. During this period, Lewitzky—who was responsible for codifying Horton's teachings into technique—leaves the company, and Frank Eng slowly enters the picture as the company's general director and Horton's lover.

Commuting to and taking classes at both UCLA and the Horton studio prove taxing for Ailey, who struggles to balance study, employment, and lodging. His interactions with Horton, the company dancers, and fellow UCLA student David McReynolds help Ailey grapple with his queer identity.

1950–51

Spring 1950: After a difficult first semester at UCLA, Ailey transfers to Los Angeles City College.

Horton offers Ailey additional responsibilities, including as a stagehand and the manager of the children's summer workshop performances. Ailey finds the rigors and expressivity of Horton technique to be challenging and sources of motivation and self-doubt. He reaches a breaking point before one of his first performances with the company, and he flees the premises.

Late summer 1951: Having moved back in with his mother and stepfather, and growing uncomfortable with his living situation, Ailey leaves Los Angeles and moves to San Francisco. He finds work as a filing clerk and then as a baggage handler and occasional translator to make ends meet.

1952

Ailey enrolls in San Francisco State College as a language major but withdraws after one semester due to being hospitalized and having his kidney removed.

He slowly returns to dance. At the studio of Waelland Lathrop and Anna Halprin, Ailey befriends Maya Angelou and together they form an occasional nightclub act called "Al and Rita."

Hollywood choreographer Jack Cole selects Ailey and de Lavallade to dance in the film *Lydia Bailey*, to be released in the spring. Cole ends up dancing with de Lavallade instead of Ailey, who pulls out due to illness and is recast as a fowl carrier.

1953

Spring: After a fortuitous encounter with dancer and choreographer Lon Fontaine, who was in need of male dancers for one of his nightclub acts, Ailey starts working as a waiter and dancer at the New Orleans Champagne Supper Club, the largest Black-owned nightclub in San Francisco.

Fontaine's act moves to Los Angeles and Ailey follows. He returns to the Horton company, taking several classes daily and starting to learn dances as part of the choreographer's workshop group—an apprenticeship of sorts.

For a Horton workshop, Ailey creates his first formal concert dance, *Afternoon Blues*, set to music by Leonard Bernstein from the Broadway musical *On the Town* and inspired by Vaslav Nijinsky's ballet *Afternoon of a Faun*.

While Ailey shuttles between Los Angeles and San Francisco, the Horton company is asked to perform at key events and venues—including the Bal Caribe Masquerade in Los Angeles, the 92nd Street YM-YWHA in New York, and the Jacob's Pillow dance festival in Becket, Massachusetts—although some plans are curtailed due to poor publicity and financial strains.

November 2: Horton dies suddenly of a heart attack.

Ailey, in San Francisco at the time of Horton's death, returns to Los Angeles amid Eng's calls for new choreography beyond the Horton repertory. Ailey brings ideas for eight dances to the company's next meeting.

1954

June: Two of Ailey's ideas become his first major works: *According to St. Francis*, a dance inspired by the life of Saint Francis of Assisi performed by Truitte and Misaye Kawasumi; and *Morning Mourning*, a dance for three influenced by Tennessee Williams's atmospheric writings about the American South. Both debut in June at the Wilshire Ebell Theatre in Los Angeles, where Horton had shown his last premieres. Although the

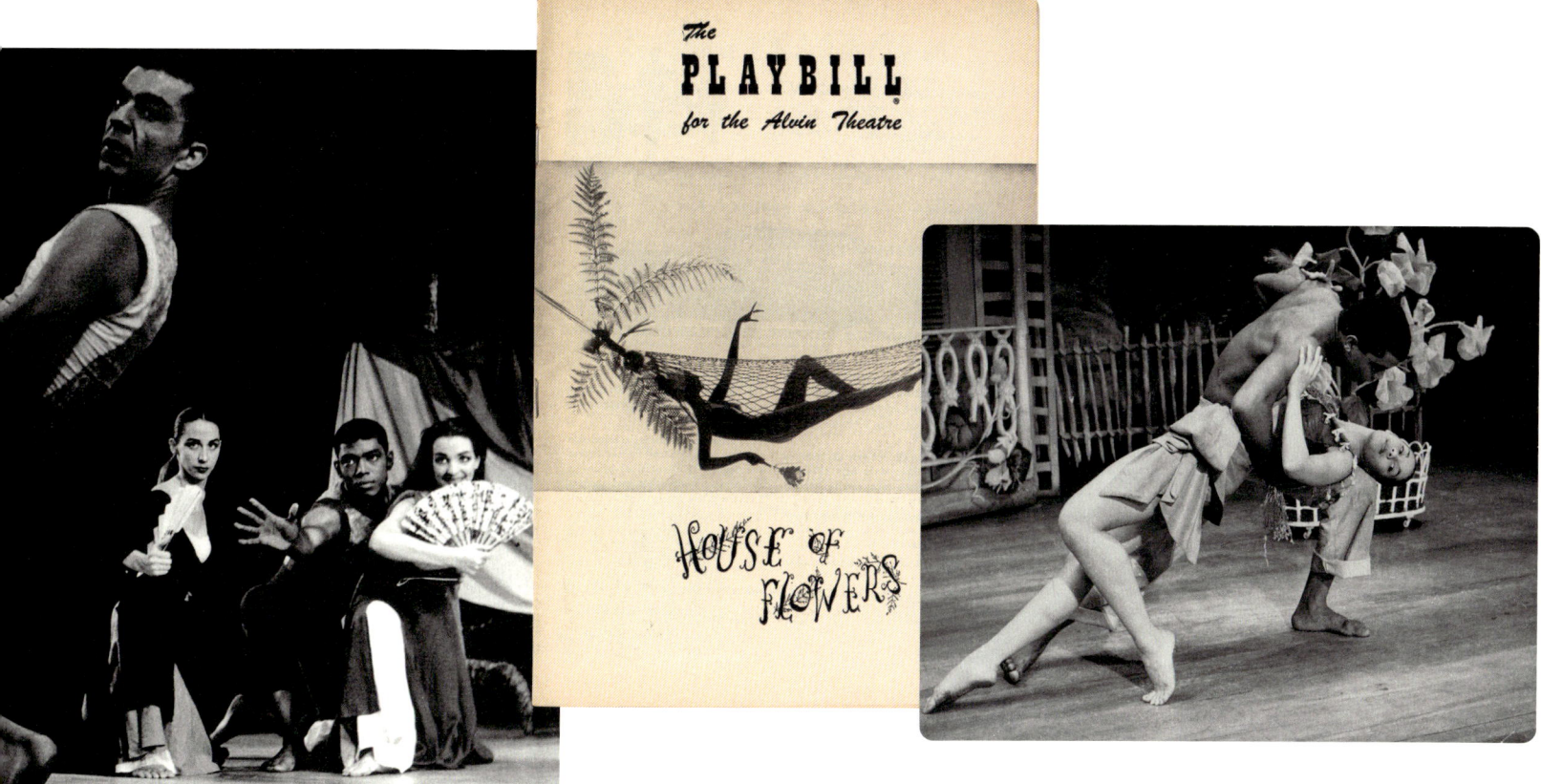

From left: Truitte, Trisler, Ailey, and Goldoni performing at Jacob's Pillow as part of the Lester Horton Dance Theater, 1954

Cover of playbill for *House of Flowers*, Alvin Theatre, New York, 1954

Ailey and de Lavallade in *House of Flowers*, ca. 1954

works are met with mixed reception, many critics see promise in Ailey's choreographic skills.

Around this time, the Horton company members agree that Ailey choreograph a commissioned piece set to Darius Milhaud's *La Création du Monde* for the San Diego Symphony, which premieres on July 13, 1954. Ailey subsequently takes over the company's creative direction, becoming a key choreographer of the Horton repertory.

As the de facto Horton choreographer, Ailey cultivates traits that would become mainstays of his choreographic process: copious note-taking; a curiosity for mining the histories of modern dance, literature, and music; abundant and evolving storytelling; and a desire to create from the specificity of his own experiences.

Week of July 22: The Horton company, under Ailey's creative direction, makes its second appearance at Jacob's Pillow. The works they perform are panned by festival founder Ted Shawn and dance critic Walter Terry, a humiliating blow for Ailey, Eng, and the company.

At promoter Monty King's invitation, the Horton company dancers audition for television work in New York. Arnold Saint-Subber, a producer present at the auditions, was casting for *House of Flowers*, a Broadway musical adaptation by Truman Capote of his short stories, to be directed by Peter Brook and choreographed by George Balanchine. Saint, as Saint-Subber was known, was keen on hiring Ailey and de Lavallade, both of whom initially decline. Difficulties with Eng, along with Balanchine being fired from the show and replaced by Herbert Ross, prompt the pair to reconsider.

December: Ailey and de Lavallade leave Los Angeles for Philadelphia, making their way to New York for *House of Flowers* rehearsals. With rehearsals and touring already well underway, they work intensively to catch up before the show's December Broadway premiere. *House of Flowers* brought together a legion of Black artists working in ballet, modern dance, and entertainment, and Ailey and de Lavallade find themselves in the company of Pearl Bailey, Diahann Carroll, Geoffrey Holder, Louis Johnson, Cristyne Lawson, Arthur Mitchell, and Albert Popwell. The show's largely Black cast, fusion of blues and calypso, and lush tropical stage setting would become a key driver of the "calypso craze" of the mid- to late 1950s.

December 30: *House of Flowers* opens on Broadway to mixed reviews.

Ailey and de Lavallade perform as uncredited dancers in the film *Carmen Jones*.

1955

Now twenty-four years old, Ailey finds himself immersed in the bustle, glamour, and vibrant energy of postwar New York. His demanding Broadway schedule does not stop him from enjoying the city, especially its rich cultural and nightlife offerings, and he keeps abreast of developments in film, literature, poetry, music, and especially theater. After their nightly performances, he and fellow *House of Flowers* cast members often go out dancing at nearby bars and clubs. Being involved with the show gives Ailey the opportunity to meet an array of luminaries, including Capote, Marlene Dietrich, Langston Hughes, Carson McCullers, and Carl Van Vechten.

Dance was flourishing in New York: the New York City Ballet was in full swing; pioneering choreographers such as Merce Cunningham and Martha Graham were actively at work; and classes of varying styles and teachers were abundant—although most opportunities were still racially segregated. Despite these barriers, Ailey enrolls in classes taught by Dunham, Graham, Hanya Holm, and Doris Humphrey, among others.

Fellow *House of Flowers* cast member and dancer Louis Johnson takes Ailey to classes taught by Karel Shook, who would cofound the Dance Theatre of Harlem with Arthur Mitchell. Ailey frequents Shook and Mitchell's home on West Twenty-Third Street, partaking in communal meals and conversations about art and culture. He also attends classes at the New Dance Group, a Depression-era center for modern dance built upon leftist populist principles, on West Forty-Seventh Street. Classes there are inexpensive, informative of a range of dance techniques and histories, and accessible to nonwhite dancers. The organization would become a lifeline for Black dancers in the mid-1950s, as its classes often provided artists such as Ailey with connections and potential work opportunities.

May 21: *House of Flowers* closes.

Ailey has difficulty finding work. He briefly returns to Los Angeles to film a television pilot for the *Amos 'n' Andy Music Hall* at the invitation of Holder, the show's choreographer. He also plays a Chinese bandit in the Broadway play *The Carefree Tree* at the Eden Theatre. To make ends meet, Ailey teaches modern dance classes at several venues, working regularly at Michael's, a Manhattan studio offering inexpensive rehearsal space, and he gains a reputation for being an effective teacher.

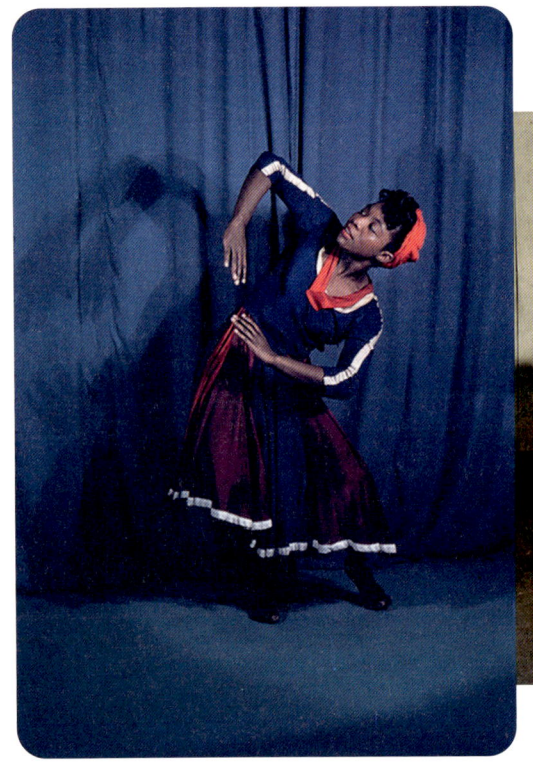

Carl Van Vechten, Pearl Primus performing *Hard Time Blues*, 1943

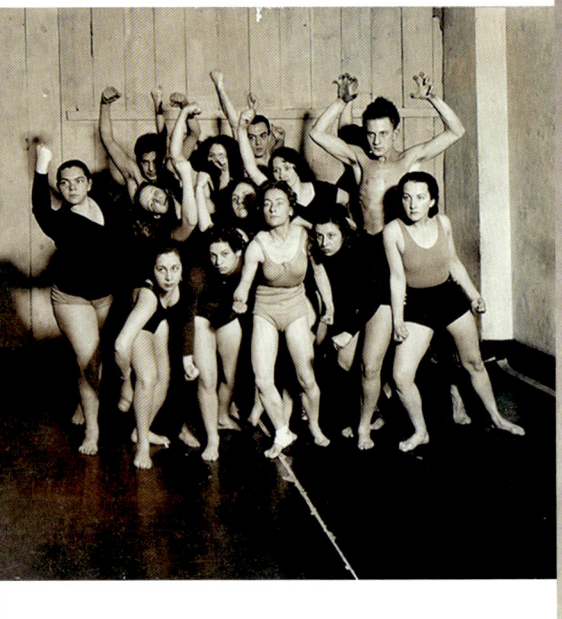

Members of the New Dance Group in *Improvisation*, 1932

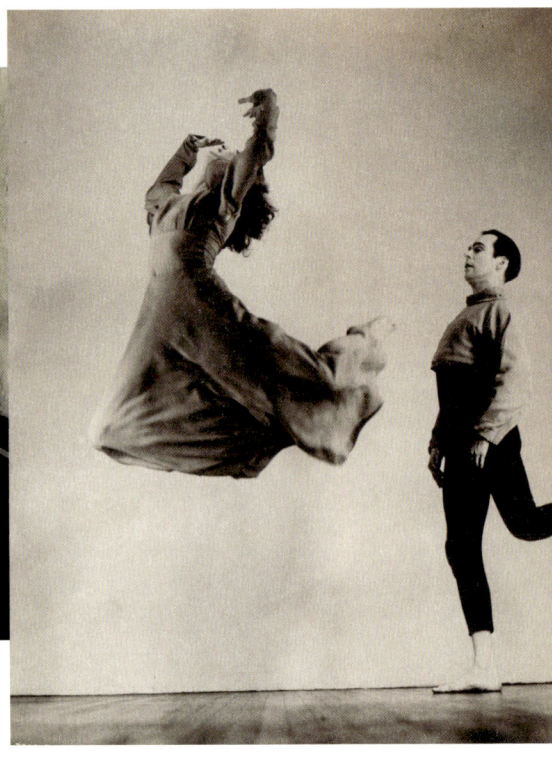

Doris Humphrey and Charles Weidman, ca. 1928–30

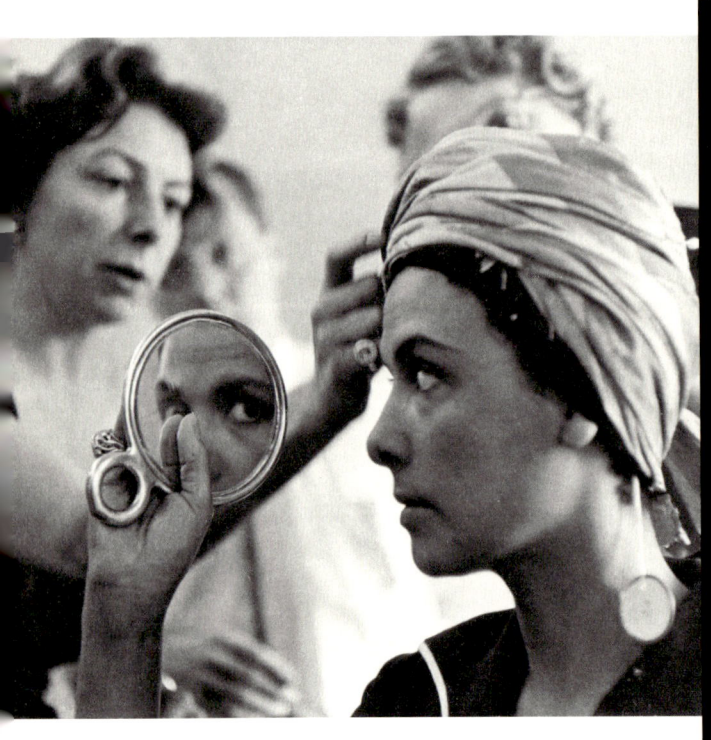

Lena Horne at a costume fitting for the Broadway musical *Jamaica*, 1957

Carl Van Vechten, *Langston Hughes*, 1942

Jack Cole, ca. 1930s

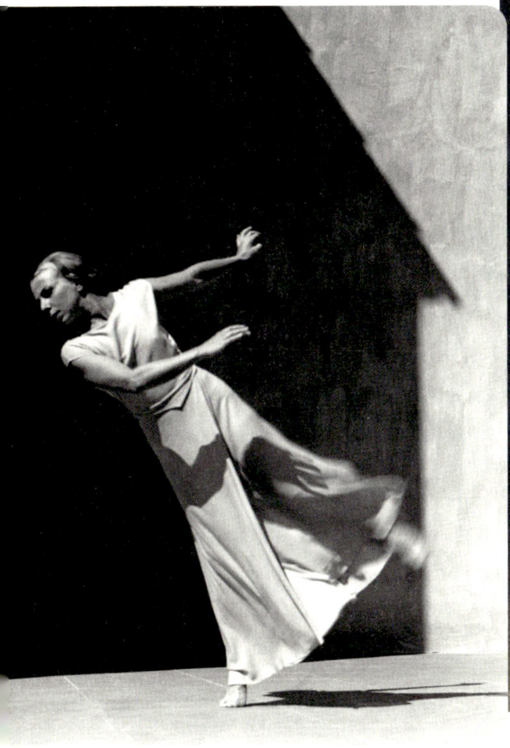

Hanya Holm performing at Mills College, Oakland, California, 1936

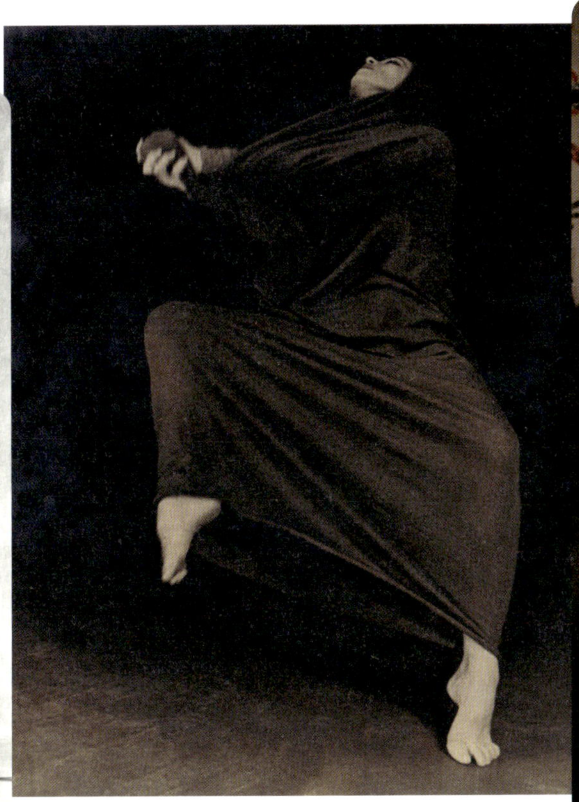

Martha Graham performing *Lamentation* at Bennington College, Vermont, ca. 1939

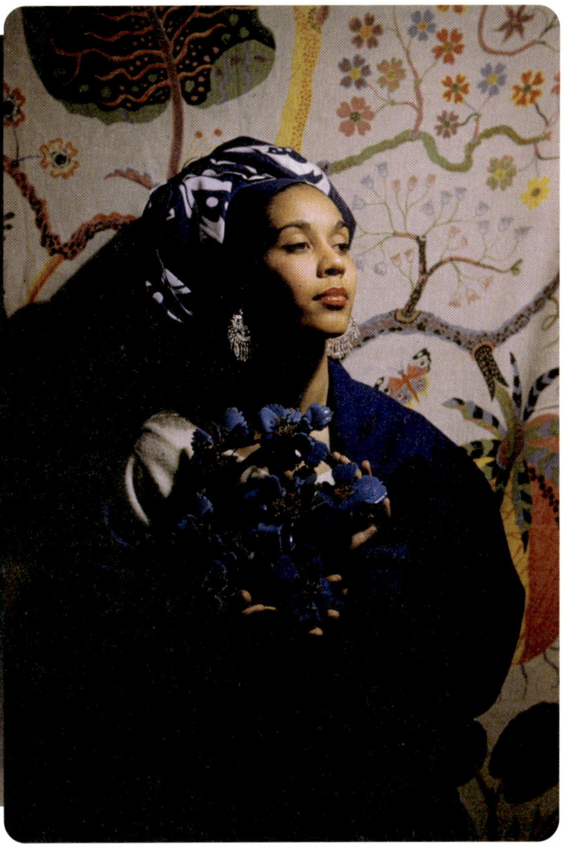

Carl Van Vechten, *Carmen de Lavallade*, 1955

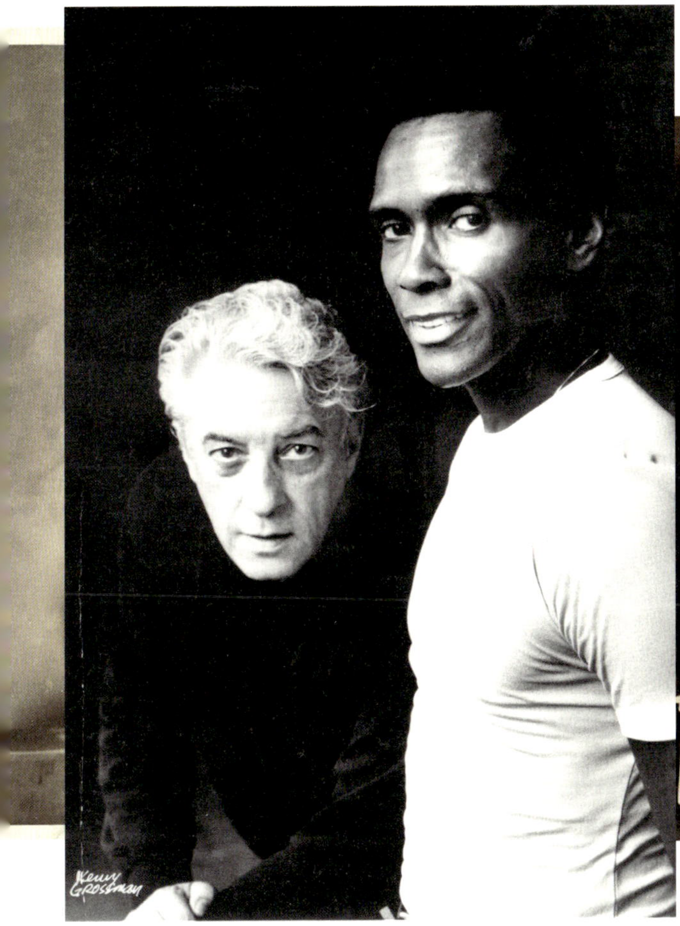

Karel Shook and Arthur Mitchell, cofounders of the Dance Theatre of Harlem, 1971

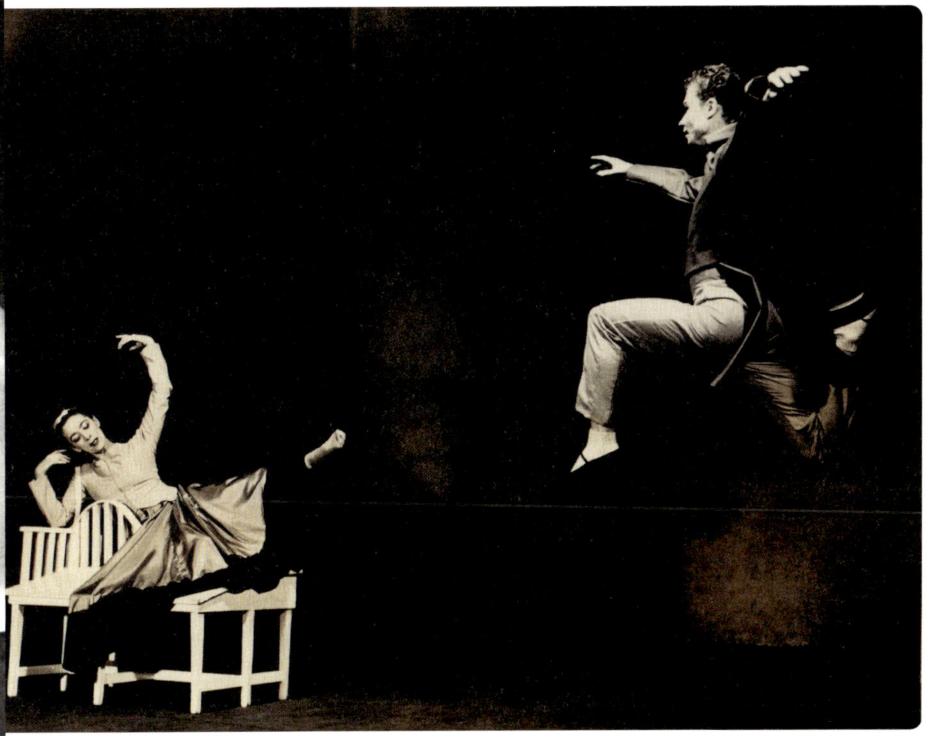

Graham and Merce Cunningham in *Letter to the World*, n.d.

Chronology

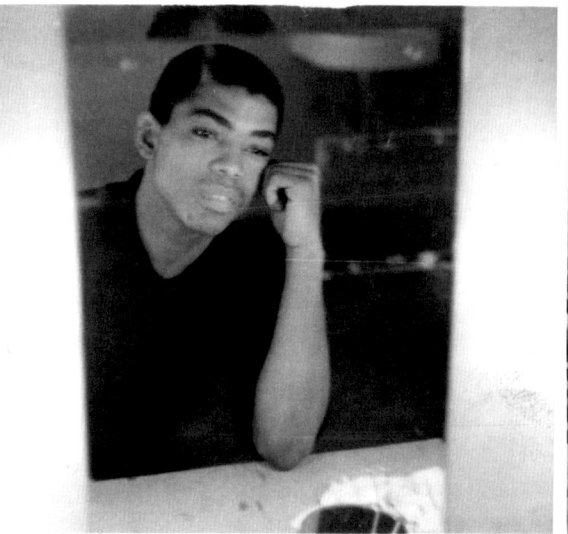

Ailey, n.d.

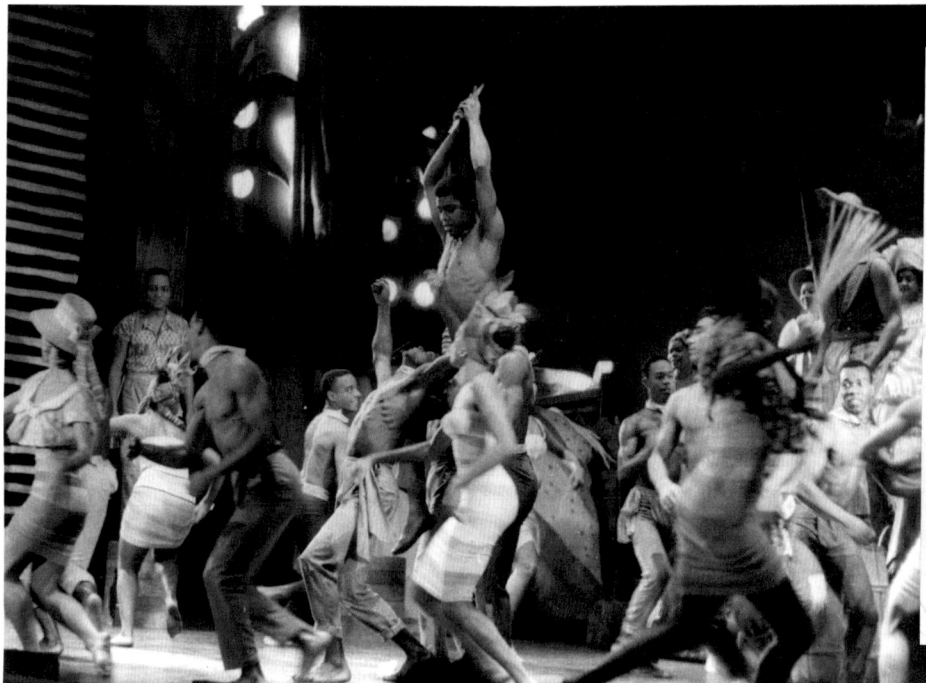

Ailey (top center) in the Broadway production of *Jamaica*, 1957–59

Ailey moves to 109 East Ninth Street, at the edge of Greenwich Village, and soon meets Marilyn "Mickey" Bord, a widow in her twenties who takes Ailey's classes at the Broadway Congregational Church. Enamored with Ailey, Bord helps support his Broadway performances and assists with his classes.

Ailey occasionally attends meetings hosted by the Committee for the Negro in the Arts, founded by Harlem-based writers and performers to break down racial barriers in culture, especially in the fields of ballet, modern dance, and Broadway theater. These scenes in particular are highly segregated, offering scant opportunities and often relying on stereotyped roles for Black dancers. Ailey's contemporaries during this time—such as Talley Beatty, de Lavallade, Holder, Johnson, Lawson, Donald McKayle, and Pearl Primus, among many others—resisted and subverted these barriers through their active presence.

1956

For money, Ailey joins two touring productions: *Sing, Man, Sing* (a roadshow with Harry Belafonte as its lead) and *Caribbean Calypso Carnival* (a Holder-directed revue starring Angelou and McKayle). McKayle hires Ailey as a chorus dancer and assistant choreographer for a summer production of *Show Boat* at Jones Beach in Nassau County, New York.

1957

Ailey auditions for *Jamaica*, an all-Black Broadway musical that would further catalyze the calypso craze. For the audition, he creates a duet with Lawson, with whom he had danced in *House of Flowers*, with costumes designed by McKayle. Cole, the show's choreographer, casts the pair and rehearsals—technically demanding and physically grueling—begin in August.

October 31: Starring Lena Horne and Ricardo Montalbán, *Jamaica* opens at the Imperial Theatre and runs until April 11, 1959. Horne is a firm advocate for racially integrated productions on all fronts, from performers and musicians to back of the house, which is reflected in her casting decisions and social openness. The show's welcoming atmosphere and, more generally, Broadway's restless hustle and vibrant rhythms provide a formative sense of community for Ailey and other dancers.

During the run of *Jamaica*, Ailey devotes considerable time and energy to developing a new project. Horne suggests that the show's dancers use the theater's stage for their own purposes when it is otherwise not in use. Ailey begins to focus on teaching choreographic ideas versus pedagogical steps, and makes concerted efforts to see other choreographers' work in New York, particularly at the 92nd Street Y.

Ailey and Ernest Parham, a dancer then performing in the Broadway musical *Bells Are Ringing*, pay the one-hundred-dollar rental fee to host a performance at the Y. They decide to split the program, and they invite Beatty to be a guest artist. The date and time of the performance are set for March 30, 1958, at 2:40 p.m., and Ailey and Parham proceed to recruit Black dancers around New York for rehearsals.

Ailey begins rehearsals with thirteen dancers, all of whom share backgrounds in Broadway and modern dance. They practice for three hours daily, three to four days a week in the six-month lead-up to the show. These sessions are generally structured with a modern dance class as warm-up, followed by combinations of step, gesture, and movement, with Ailey creating and changing choreography in real time, partly from prepared notes and partly improvised. As dancer Dorene Richardson recalled, Ailey "sort of maneuvered everybody like a painting. Sketched everything in, more or less, without anything finalized or set, sometimes until the day of performance."[3]

For the performance, Ailey choreographs three pieces incorporating Horton technique: *Redonda* (later reworked as *Cinco Latinos*); *Ode and Homage*, a solo created as a tribute to Horton; and *Blues Suite*, a piece set in a barrelhouse with archetypal Depression-era characters—a world informed by Ailey's cultural roots, childhood memories of the Dew Drop Inn, and long-standing love for blues music. A production of this scale required collaboration from a number of people in Ailey's network of dancers and choreographers. Paquita Anderson and José Ricci are brought in to play live music; Normand Maxon makes the costumes for *Redonda* and *Ode and Homage*; and Holder makes the costumes for *Blues Suite*.

1958

March 30: Ailey and company perform at the 92nd Street Y, marking the dance theater's founding. Altogether, twenty-eight Black dancers, along with various musicians, perform in Ailey's and Parham's programs. Beatty stars as Icarus in Parham's *Trajectories*, while Ailey dances solo in *Ode and Homage*. The thirteen Ailey dancers are split among *Redonda*'s five dances. *Blues Suite*, the concert's closing piece, is met with great acclaim, and the debut of Ailey's company garners mostly positive reviews.

Ailey wants his company, unlike others at the time, to be "a living repository of its classics and curiosities,"[4] a vision that would guide his creation of an unparalleled

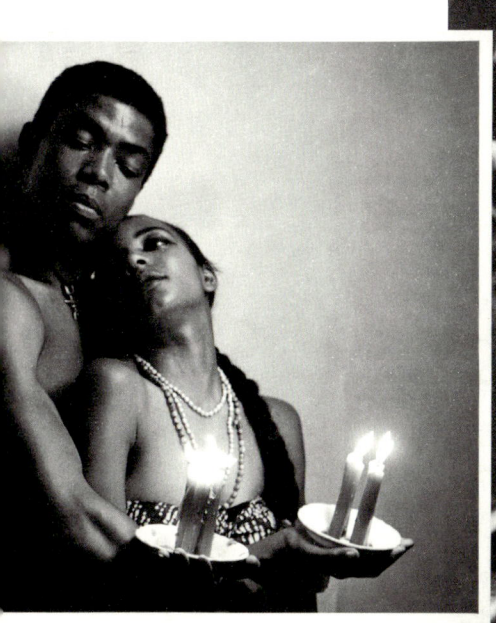
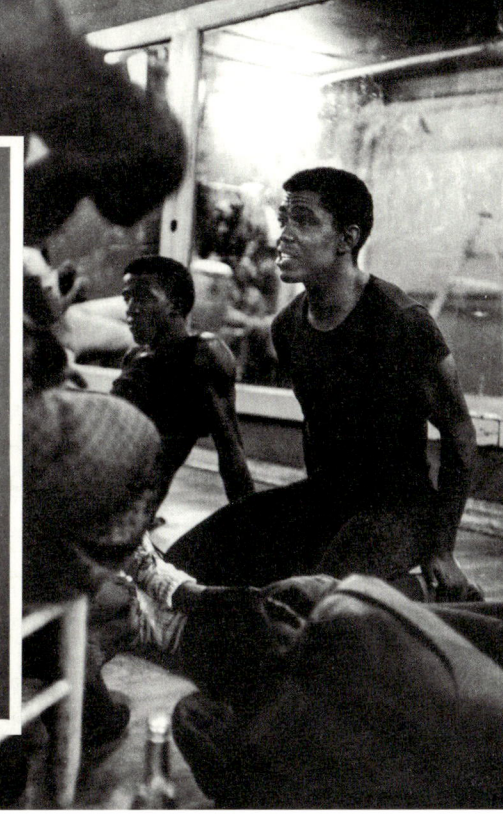
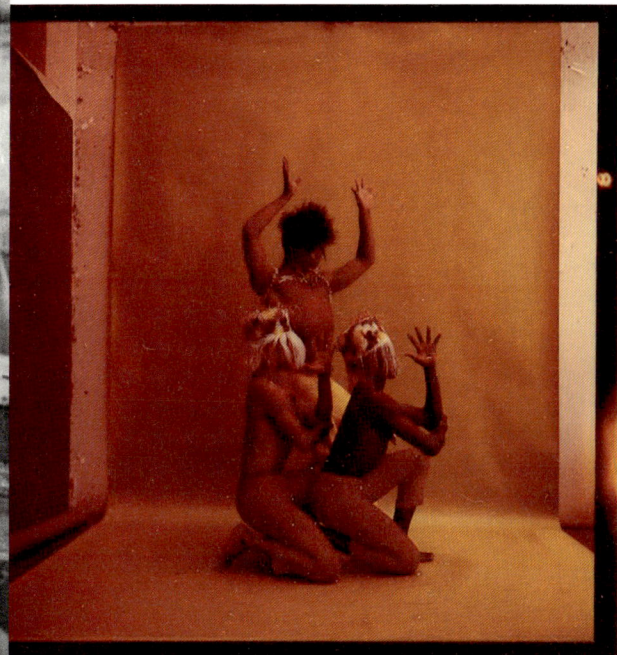

Ailey and Cristyne Lawson, 1957

From left: Harold Pierson and Ailey, 1958

Ailey (standing) with company dancers in *Cinco Latinos*, 1958

platform for modern dance. To this end, Ailey endorses bringing works of other choreographers into his repertory's fold, while also inviting emerging choreographers to create dances for his company. Inspired by Horton, Ailey's collaboration with and generous support of outside choreographers become a hallmark of his company.

To build on the momentum of the company's first performance, Ailey schedules a subsequent concert for December. In the intervening months, the company goes on what Ailey dubs "the station wagon tours,"[5] in a vehicle driven by Bord. During this early period, Ailey frequently enlists Ves Harper and Maxon to design costumes and scenery and Nicholas Cernovitch for stage lighting.

December 21: The Ailey company's second performance at the Y takes place, with Ellington and other celebrities among the sold-out audience. The program includes selections from *Cinco Latinos*; *Ariette Oubliée*, a new work danced by Ailey, de Lavallade, and Don Price, and set to music by Claude Debussy; and *Blues Suite*, which Ailey had reworked since its premiere in March. Ailey and the company, having received increased recognition and acclaim, are offered more opportunities to dance and choreograph performances.

1959–60

Shirley Broughton commissions Ailey to choreograph for her modern dance group. The result is *Mistress and Manservant*, a riff on August Strindberg's play *Miss Julie* and set to Maurice Ravel's *String Quartet*. Ailey directs and choreographs a production of *African Holiday* at the Apollo Theater in Harlem, and summer touring productions of *Jamaica* and *Carmen Jones*. He enters *Sonera*, a new work comprising a suite of three plotless dances informed by Cuban dance styles, into a competition judged by Balanchine and Lincoln Kirstein, but it is not among the winning entries.

June–July 1959: Ailey and the company are invited to Jacob's Pillow, where they perform *Rite*, *El Cigaro* (comprising two of the five dances in *Cinco Latinos*), and *Blues Suite*, presented alongside pieces by St. Denis and choreographer and former Graham dancer Pearl Lang.

August 1959: Representing the United States, the company performs in the World Dance Festival in New York's Central Park.

This string of opportunities adds to the growing reputation of Ailey and his dancers as a force in the dance landscape, with the potential to grow into an established company. Susan Pimsleur, head of a concert management firm that represents the companies of José Limón and Jean-Léon Destiné, wants to add the Ailey dancers to her roster, under the name Alvin Ailey American Dance Theater, although the company does not adopt this name until years later.

Late 1959–early 1960: Ailey prepares for his third performance at the 92nd Street Y, slated for late January 1960. Charles Blackwell, Ailey's friend and stage manager, finds rehearsal space at the Capital Hotel, which was being converted into a YWCA. Blackwell has a fortuitous conversation with Edele Holtz, the YWCA's director of activities, who agrees to offer Ailey rehearsal space for fifteen dollars a month, a deal and lifeline compared to the two-dollar hourly rate for renting studios at Michael's.

The company's composition had changed since its first performance in March 1958, as many dancers had moved on to better economic opportunities on Broadway or in teaching. New company dancers include sisters Merle and Joan Derby, Nat Horne, and Dudley Williams. Ailey invites Matt Turney, a leading Graham dancer, to be a guest performer in *Creation of the World* (formerly *La Création du Monde*, which Ailey had since reworked into a duet).

Ailey intends for his January concert to pay homage to Black culture through rich musical traditions, ranging from the blues and spirituals to Kansas City jazz and contemporary music. However, he abandons this idea for a more manageable program, including *Sonera*; reworked versions of *Creation of the World*, *Blues Suite*, and *Canto al Diablo* (formerly *Rite*); and a new work, *Revelations*. Initially comprising sixteen sections with a total run time of one hour, *Revelations* was, according to the show's program, inspired by the "motivations and emotions of Negro religious music which, like its heir the Blues, takes many forms—'true spirituals' with their sustained melodies, ring-shouts, song-sermons, gospel songs, and holy blues—songs of trouble, of Love[,] of deliverance."[6] The dance is deeply informed by Ailey's childhood memories of Black churches, including praying with his mother and the congregation and Sister Hattie Taplin singing at his baptism, and by his choreographic influences, including Cole, Dunham, Graham, and Horton.

January 31, 1960: Ailey's third concert takes place. At the conclusion of *Revelations*, the dancers are first met with silence followed by a rapt standing ovation. This reaction causes confusion among the performers, but it is quelled by William Kolodney, head of dance programming at the Y, who informs the audience that the company would return for a repeat performance the following month, on February 28.

May 1960: Ailey choreographs the play *Dark of the Moon* for the Equity Library Theatre at the Lenox

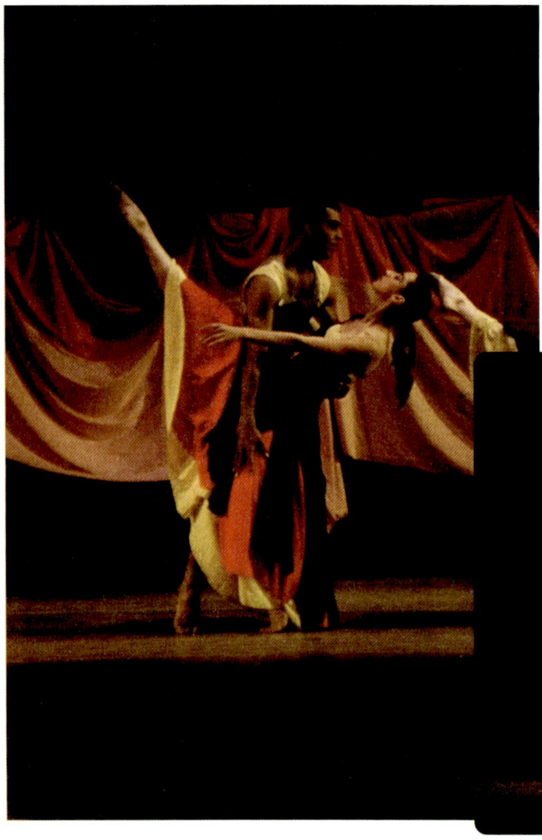

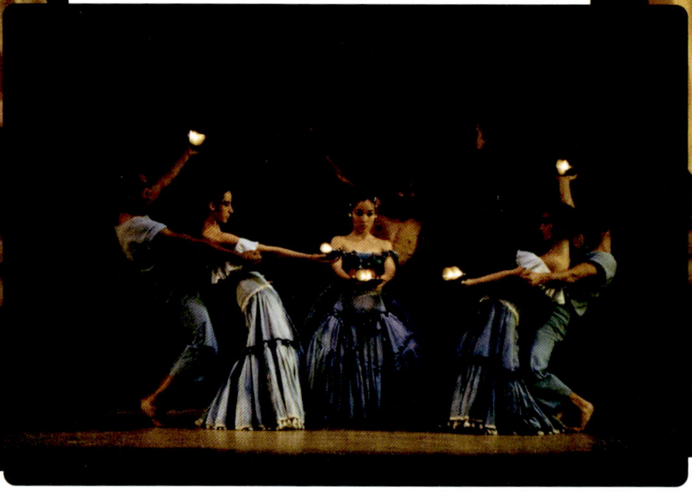

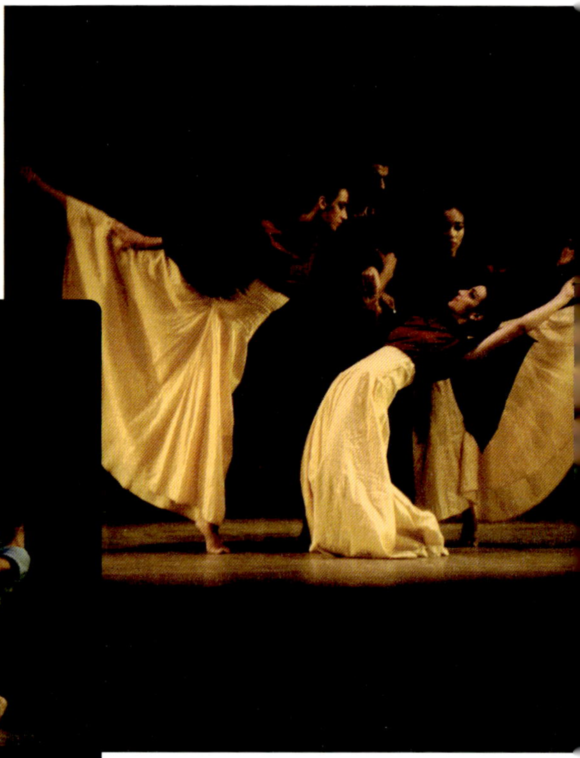

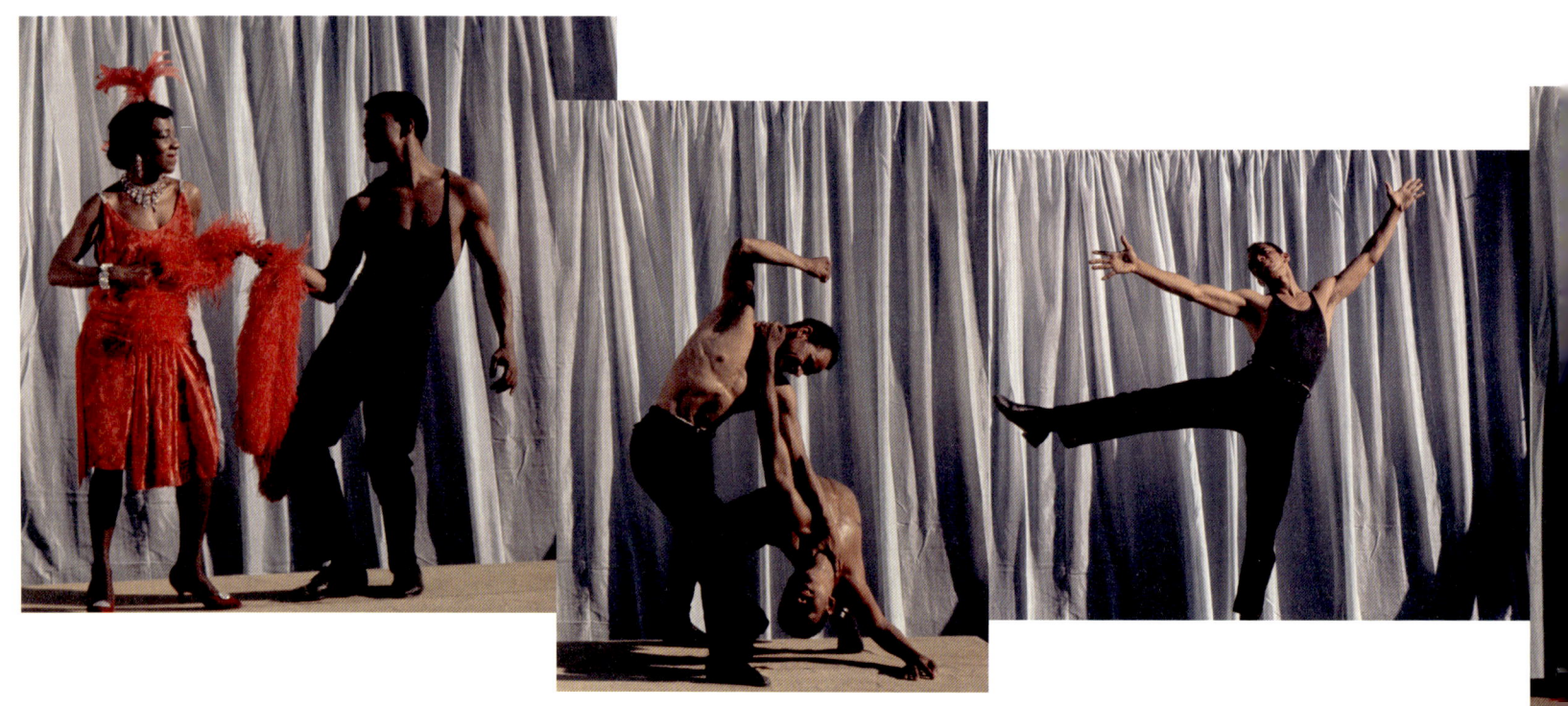

Truitte performing at Jacob's Pillow as part of the Lester Horton Dance Theater, 1954

Ailey (back center) performing in *Bal Caribe* at Jacob's Pillow as part of the Lester Horton Dance Theater, 1954

Lester Horton Dance Theater company members performing at Jacob's Pillow, 1954

Ailey and company dancers at Jacob's Pillow, 1959

CJ Salapare

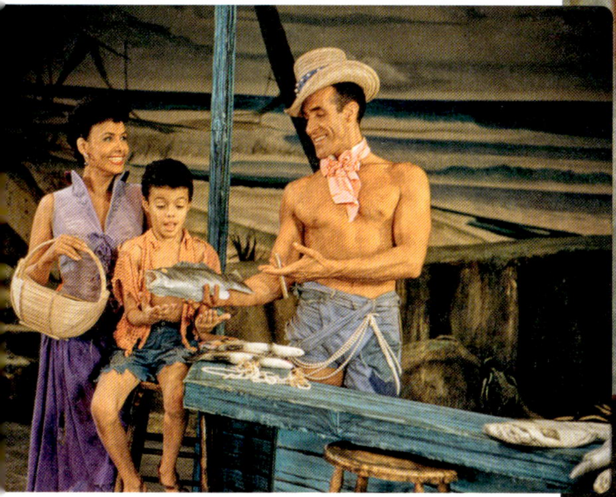

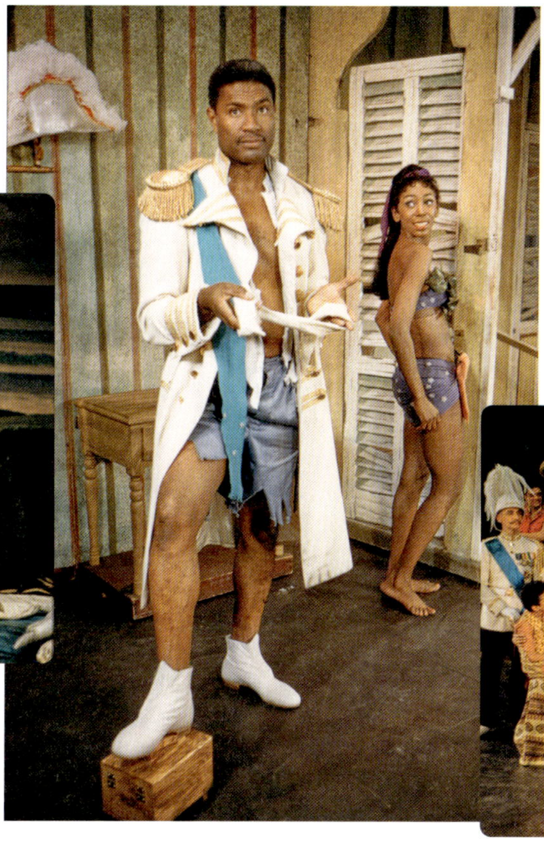

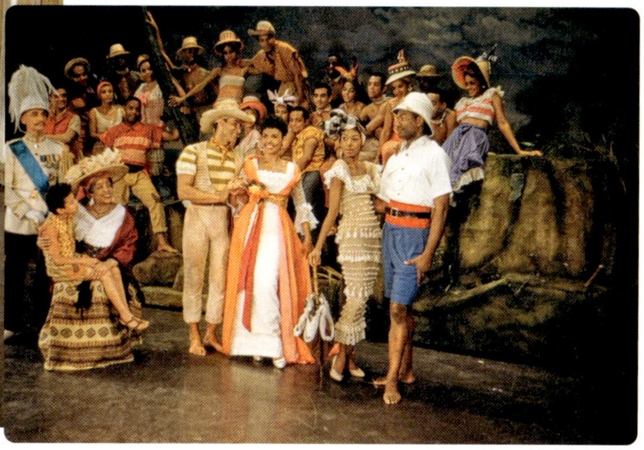

Lena Horne, Augustine "Augie" Rios, and Ricardo Montalbán in the stage production of *Jamaica*, 1957

Ossie Davis and Josephine Premice in *Jamaica*, 1957

Lena Horne and Ricardo Montalbán (center) with the cast of *Jamaica*, 1957

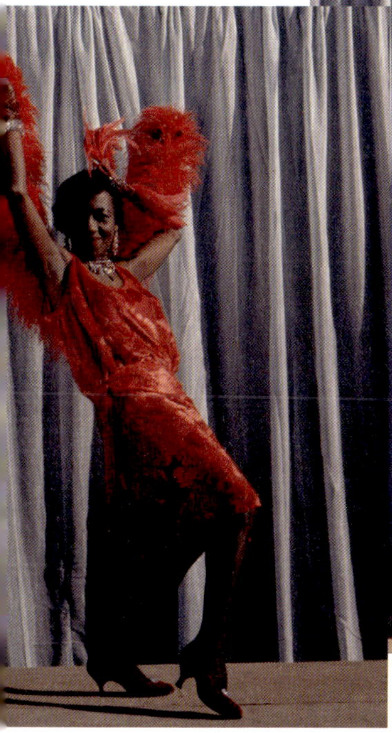

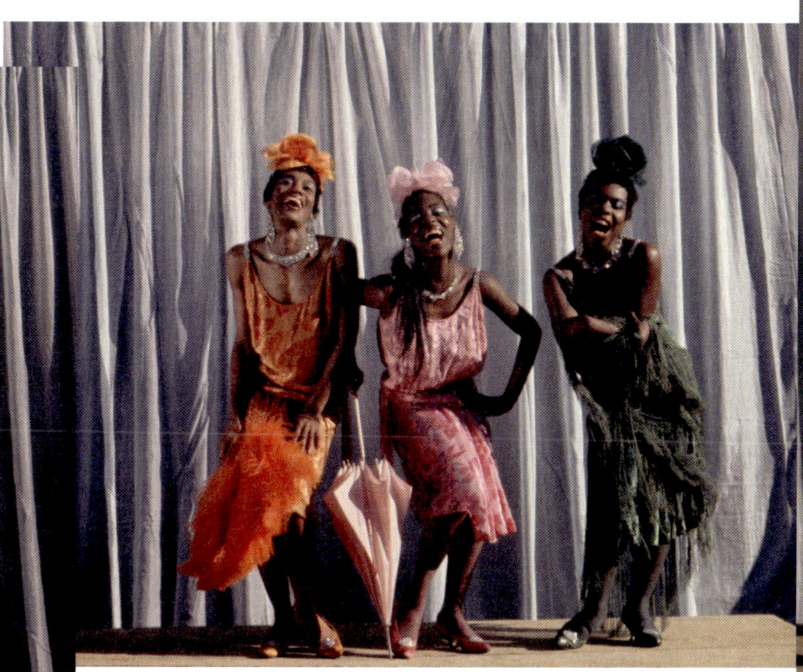

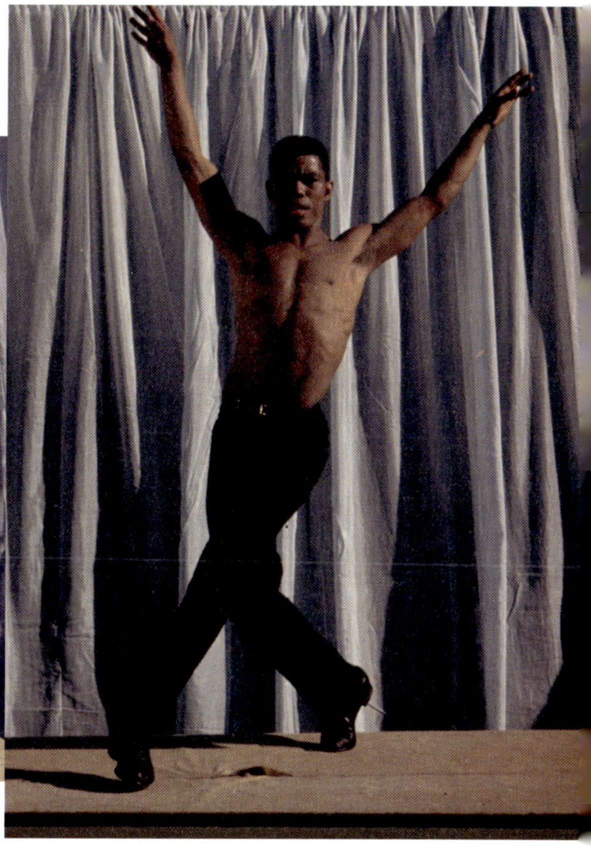

Chronology

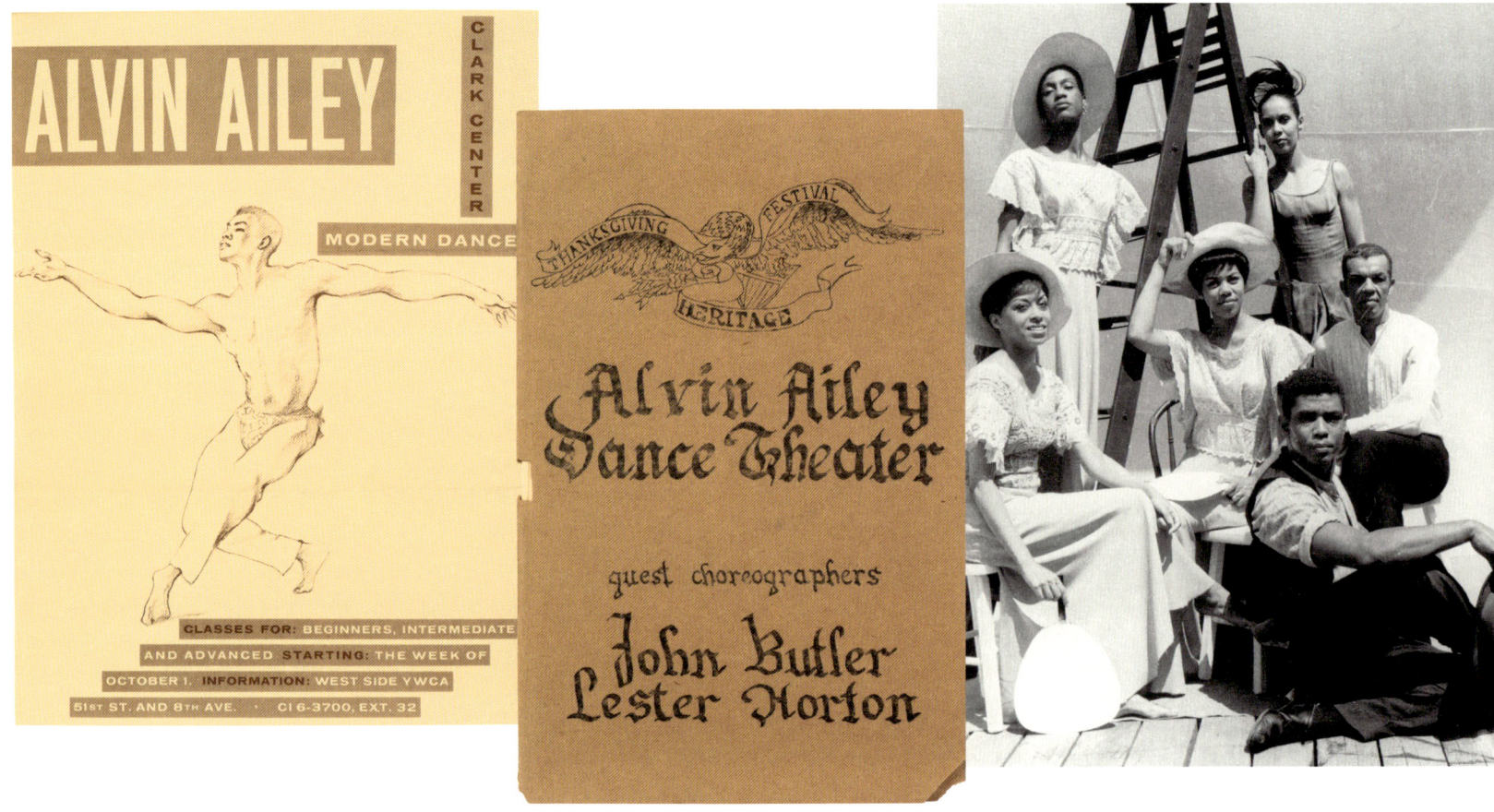

Advertisement for Ailey dance classes at the Clark Center at the West Side YWCA, New York, n.d.

Cover of program for an Ailey company performance at the Clark Center, featuring choreography by John Butler and Horton, 1960

Ailey (lower right) with company dancers (clockwise from lower left) Ella Thompson, Minnie Marshall, de Lavallade, Truitte, and Myrna White at Jacob's Pillow, 1961

Hill Playhouse, marking his first collaboration with Langston Hughes.

October 1960: The Clark Center for the Performing Arts at the West Side YWCA, founded under Ailey's guidance with the help of Holtz, opens to the public. The company, which rehearsed in the center's modest spaces during the building's renovation, had played an active role in remodeling the facilities.

November 27, 1960: Ailey dancers perform at the Clark Center for the first time. Although some works in the program are lauded, Ailey's newest pieces—*Three for Now*, a plotless jazz dance, and *Knoxville: Summer of 1915*, an abstraction of James Agee's autobiographical novel *A Death in the Family* and Ailey's childhood memories—are panned.

The Clark Center would become a pillar of the community, offering dance, drama, opera, and musical performances; a variety of classes and workshops; and a space for people to gather. Ailey is central to the development of the center's robust programming and in the creation of a forum for emerging choreographers, an unprecedented concept at the time.

Late 1960: Casting director Michael Shurtleff invites Ailey to audition for a lead role in *Call Me by My Rightful Name*, an off-Broadway play featuring two unknowns at the time—Robert Duvall and Joan Hackett. Ailey lands the part of Paul, a Black college student at Columbia University who finds himself in the crosshairs of an interracial friendship and romance. Rehearsals begin at the Clark Center in November. Through this opportunity, Ailey befriends Dustin Hoffman, then a relatively unknown actor.

1961

January 30: *Call Me by My Rightful Name* premieres and is met with largely positive reviews, with Ailey's performance praised. The play runs for five months.

June: Having been invited to present jazz dance at the Tenth Annual Boston Arts Festival for its retrospective of American dance since the dawn of the twentieth century, Ailey and the company premiere *Roots of the Blues*, set to music by Brother John Sellers, who performs live during the program in Boston Common.

Ailey premieres *Gillespiana*, a concatenation of Dizzy Gillespie's rhythms of modern dance and jazz.

June–July: The Ailey company performs *Roots of the Blues* at Lewisohn Stadium at the City College of New York and then at Jacob's Pillow, where they also dance a pared-down version of *Revelations*.

Throughout the year, many job opportunities come Ailey's way, including a summer stock production of *Ding Dong Bell* and an NBC broadcast of *Porgy and Bess*, where he takes part in a pas de deux with de Lavallade. Following their collaboration on *Dark of the Moon*, Hughes asks Ailey to choreograph a ballet inspired by his twelve-part poem *Ask Your Mama*; Ailey was also slated to choreograph and act in Hughes's production of *Black Nativity* (formerly *Wasn't That a Mighty Day!*), which opens at the Forty-First Street Theatre in Midtown in mid-December 1961. Neither project pans out for Ailey, and he and de Lavallade—cast as Joseph and Mary, respectively, in the latter— leave the show due to differences in belief regarding racial integration.

In addition to dance classes and rehearsals, Ailey takes acting classes with Stella Adler and Milton Katselas.

Fall: Following the company's performances that summer in Boston and at Jacob's Pillow, US government officials approach Ailey with the prospect of his company touring in Australia and Asia the following year. The thirteen-week tour, sponsored by President John F. Kennedy administration's Special International Program for Cultural Presentations, would begin in Sydney and make stops in Burma (Myanmar), South Vietnam, Malaya (Malaysia), Indonesia, the Philippines, Hong Kong, Taiwan, and Japan before closing in Seoul, South Korea. Under the umbrella of the de Lavallade–Ailey American Dance Company, Ailey accepts the invitation and identifies eight dancers to join him and de Lavallade on the tour, including Georgia Collins, Connie Greco, Thelma Hill, Minnie Marshall, Don Martin, Charles Moore, Ella Thompson, and Truitte. Also traveling with them are percussionist Horacee Arnold, bass player Leslie Grinage, guitarist Bruce Langhorne, and Brother John Sellers.

October 22: The off-Broadway play *Two by Saroyan*, consisting of two one-act plays by William Saroyan, opens at the East End Theatre, with Ailey in the role of Blackstone Boulevard.

December: Ailey premieres *Hermit Songs*.

1962

Prior to departing for their first international tour, the company films a performance of *Revelations* for the CBS television series *Lamp unto My Feet*. The episode, which is nominated for an Emmy award, airs on March 4.

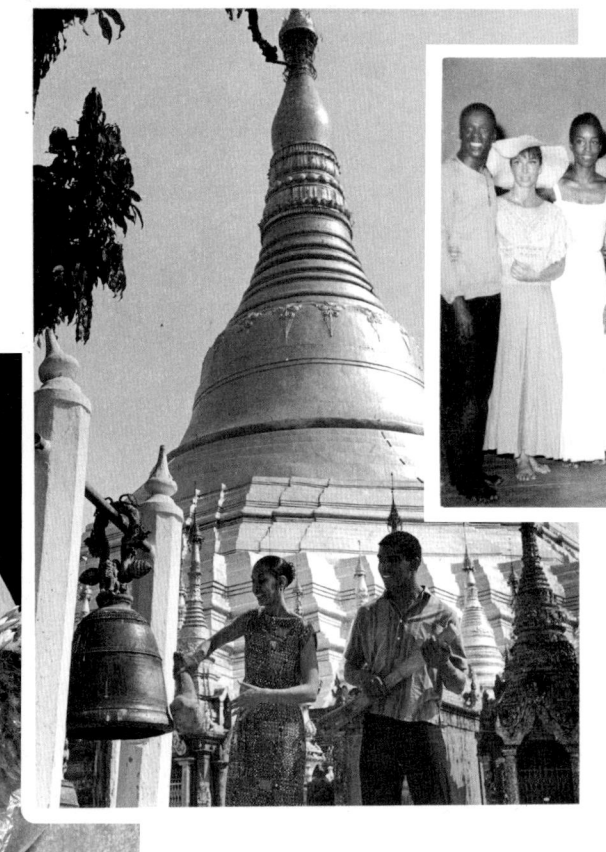

De Lavallade and Ailey with an unidentified person, Saigon (Ho Chi Minh City), Vietnam, 1962

De Lavallade and Ailey in front of the Shwedagon Pagoda, Rangoon, Burma (Yangon, Myanmar), 1962

Ailey (fourth from left) with company dancers including Georgia Collins, de Lavallade, Connie Greco, Thelma Hill, Marshall, Don Martin, Charles Moore, Thompson, and Truitte; musician Brother John Sellers; and others, during the Ailey company's Southeast Asian tour, 1962

January 30: Ailey and the company leave for Los Angeles, the first of several pit stops en route to Sydney, and while there, Ailey reunites briefly with his family. He and his dancers then make stops in Hawai'i and Fiji.

February 3: The tour opens with a weeklong set of performances at the Palace Theatre in Sydney, and includes the premiere of *Been Here and Gone*. The first show has an audience of roughly twenty-five in the eleven-hundred-seat venue; the remaining shows are sold-out.

Between performances, Ailey and the company explore the city's cultural sites, and meet with locals and learn about their traditions. Such experiences become mainstays of the company's tours.

February 11: The company performs at the Princess Theatre in Melbourne, Australia.

Their next show, in Rangoon (Yangon), Burma, nearly coincides with the deposition of the Burmese government in a coup d'état.

They then travel to Bangkok, Thailand; Phnom Penh, Cambodia; and Saigon (Ho Chi Minh City), Vietnam. The latter has a portentous military atmosphere (US troops had been stationed there since 1961), and the company performs at an old movie house because the original venue had been bombed.

In Malaya, the company has shows in Kuala Lumpur, Seremban, Ipoh, and Penang. Conflicts among the dancers come to a head during this leg of the tour, with various members, including Moore and Thompson, at odds with de Lavallade's poor treatment of them.

They then perform in Djakarta (Jakarta), Indonesia, amid postrevolutionary turmoil. The dancers arrive at their show ninety minutes late, to jeers and demands for an apology, which the company provides.

In the Philippines, they perform in several remote rural locations, including Cotabato. After an incident at a performance in which the audience laughed during Glen Tetley's *Mountain Way Chant*, Ailey decides to cut *Roots of the Blues* from the program, as he is concerned about how to make his works appealing to audiences who are not familiar with the relevant cultural context.

April 9: The group, by now exhausted, travels to Hong Kong.

In an interview with the *South China Post Herald*, Ailey claims that modern dance and theater originated in Asia, stating that "[he] learned the real basis of theatre, including songs, dance, lighting, costumes—everything that makes for the total theatre effect—from the East."[7]

The company departs for its penultimate leg: Tokyo and other stops in Japan, where the group is well received by audiences.

Finally, they travel to their last stop, Seoul, leaving the city on May 12. The international tour is lauded by the press as a success and is estimated to have reached 146,791 people through sixty performances.[8]

Upon returning to New York, the company faces changes in its composition, with the departures of Moore and Thompson and with de Lavallade drifting from Ailey, though not completely.

July 21: The company performs at the American Dance Festival, held annually at Connecticut College in New London, to great acclaim.[9] The festival is known for hosting premieres by the greats of modern dance.

While there, Ailey becomes involved professionally with choreographer Robert Joffrey and heiress Rebekah Harkness. Harkness invites Ailey to come stay at Holiday House, her home in Watch Hill, Rhode Island, marking the start of a number of collaborations between the two of them.

Ailey choreographs *Feast of Ashes*, a dance adaptation of Federico García Lorca's *House of Bernarda Alba*, for the Joffrey Ballet. Harkness continues supporting Ailey and his company by inviting them to perform at her dance festival in Central Park. As recompense for their participation, she funds live accompaniment and new costumes, along with a restaging of *Creation of the World*.

Ailey is recruited by theater director Joshua Logan for a Peter Feibleman play called *Tiger Tiger Burning Bright*, which is slated to open on December 18. The stress and pressure of the production cause Ailey to have a nervous breakdown mid-rehearsal. The play receives positive reviews but closes shortly after its premiere, marking the end of Ailey's forays into acting.

1963

Over the course of the year, the company experiences many changes to its membership, including the additions of Benjamin Jones, who arranges logistics and acts as an impresario for them, and dancer Kelvin Rotardier.

Chronology

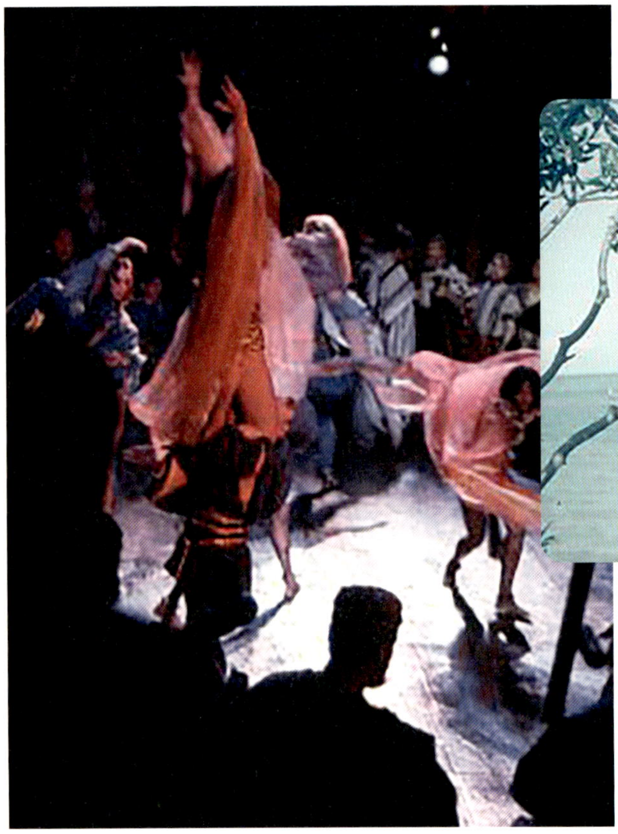

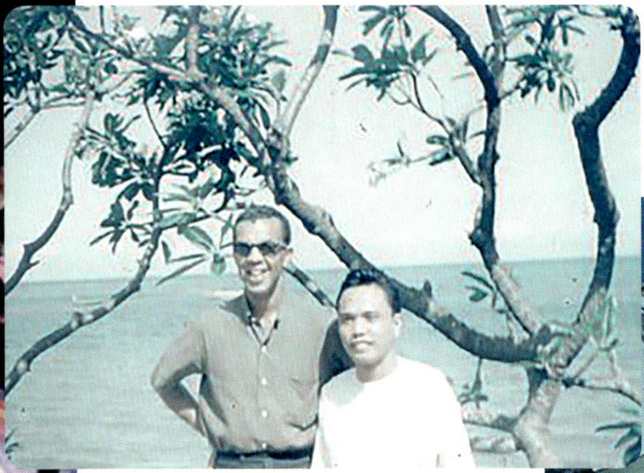

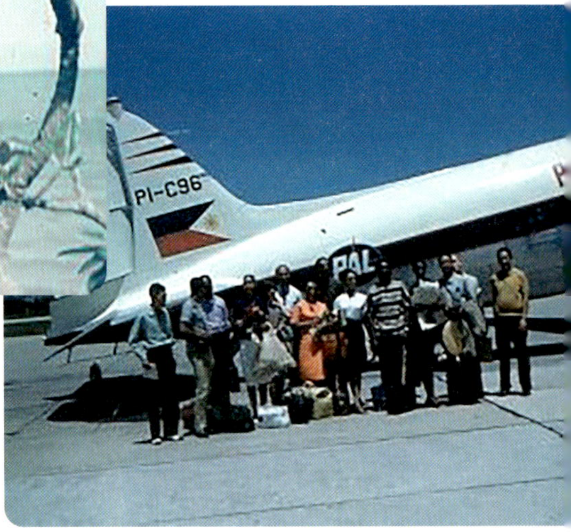

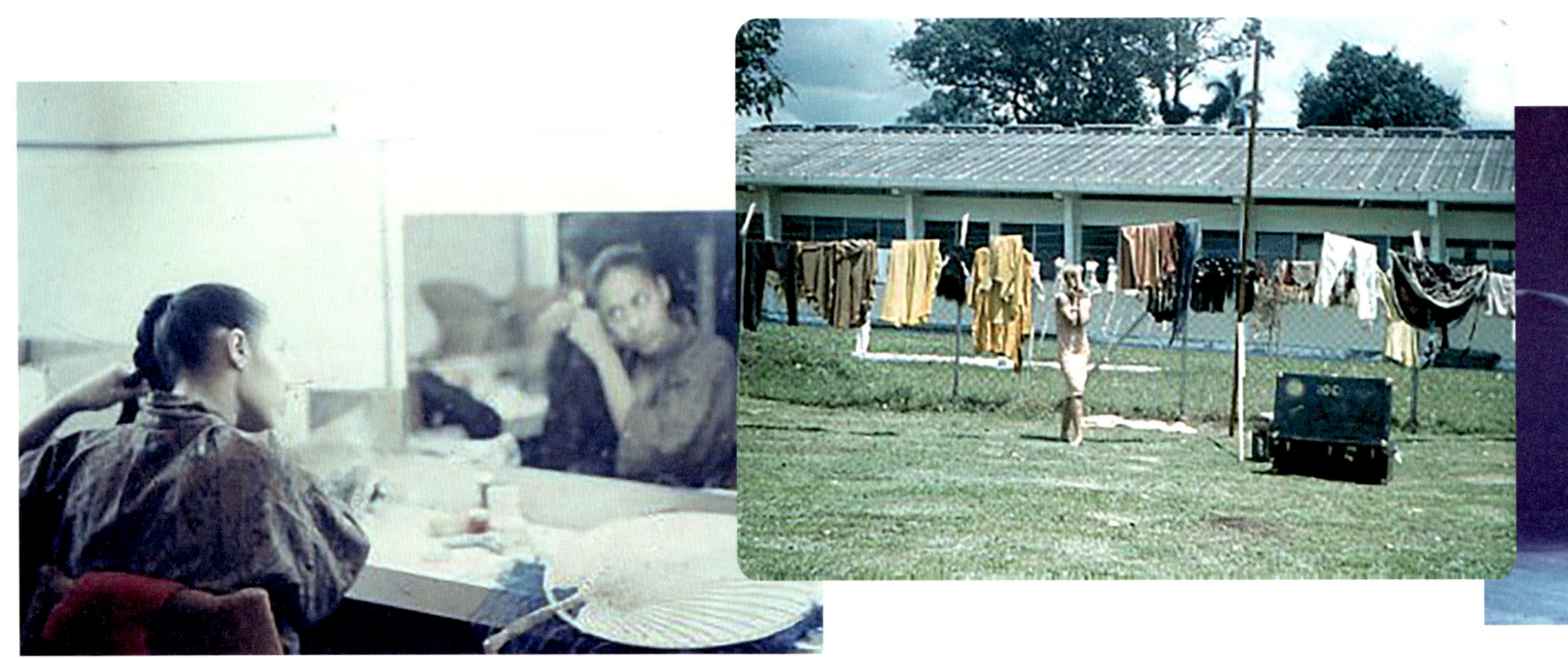

Ailey, de Lavallade, and company dancers performing during the Southeast Asian tour, 1962

Truitte with an unidentified person during the Southeast Asian tour, 1962

Ailey and others standing in front of a Philippine Airlines plane during the Southeast Asian tour, 1962

De Lavallade in a dressing room during the Southeast Asian tour, 1962

Revelations costumes drying on clotheslines during the Southeast Asian tour, 1962

CJ Salapare

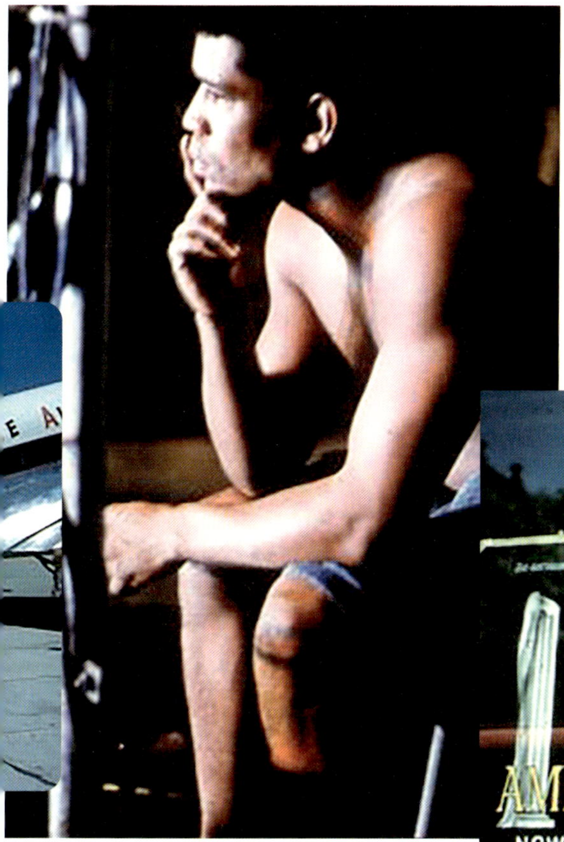

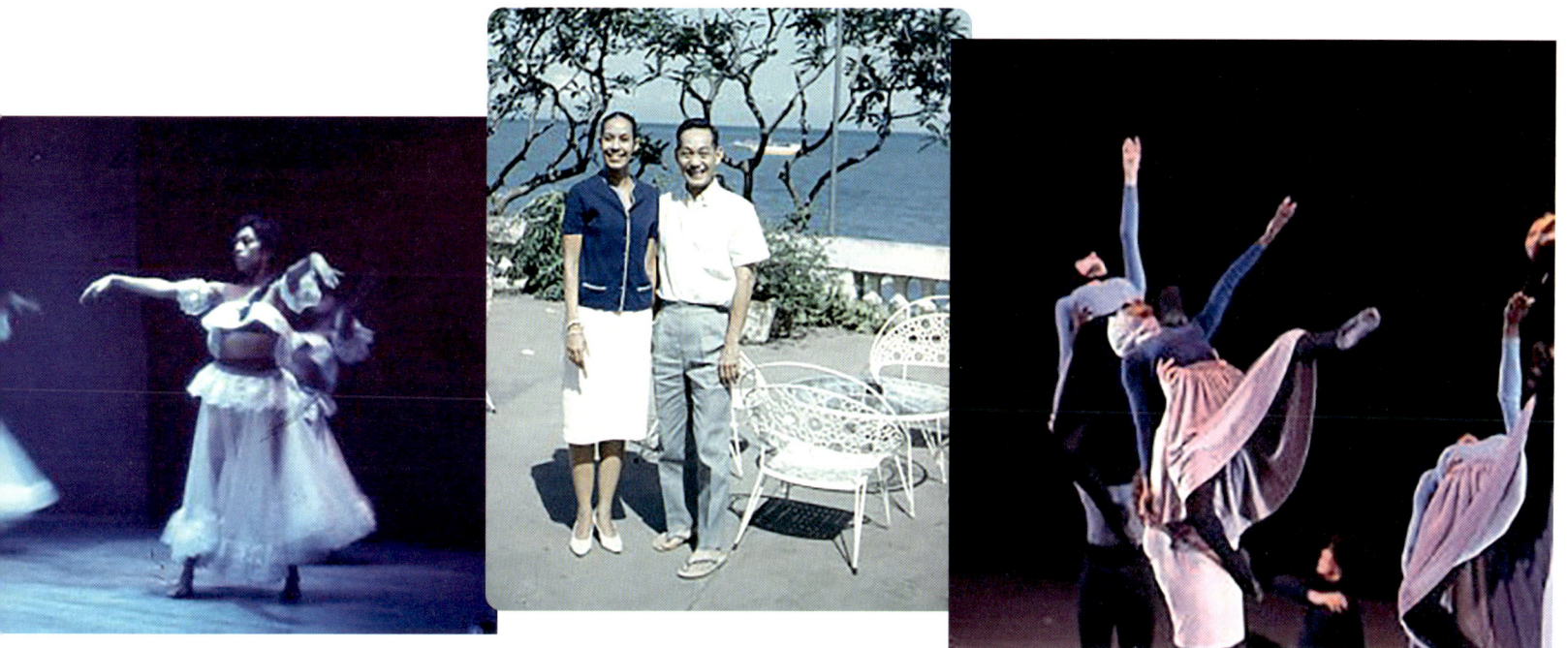

Ailey during the Southeast Asian tour, 1962

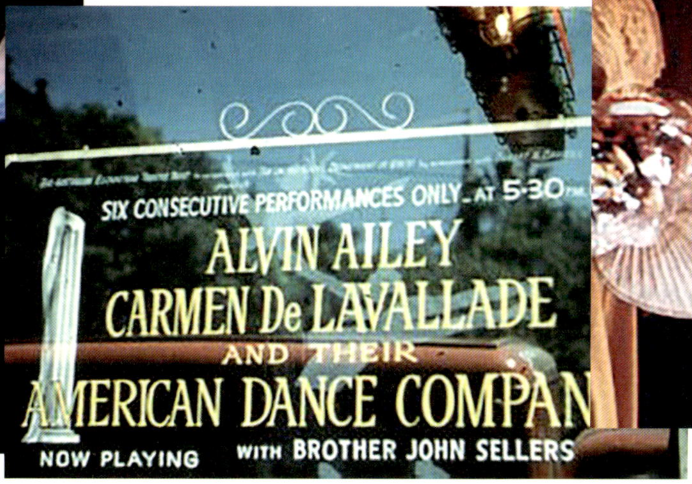

Sign advertising performances by "Alvin Ailey, Carmen de Lavallade, and their American Dance Company with Brother John Sellers," during the Southeast Asian tour, 1962

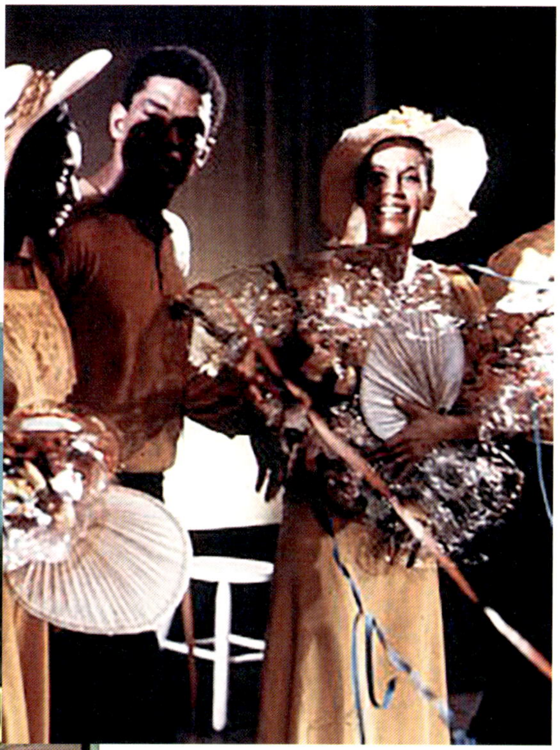

Ailey and de Lavallade during the Southeast Asian tour, 1962

Ailey company dancers performing during the Southeast Asian tour, 1962

De Lavallade with an unidentified person during the Southeast Asian tour, 1962

Ailey lifting de Lavallade (front) during a performance on the Southeast Asian tour, 1962

Chronology

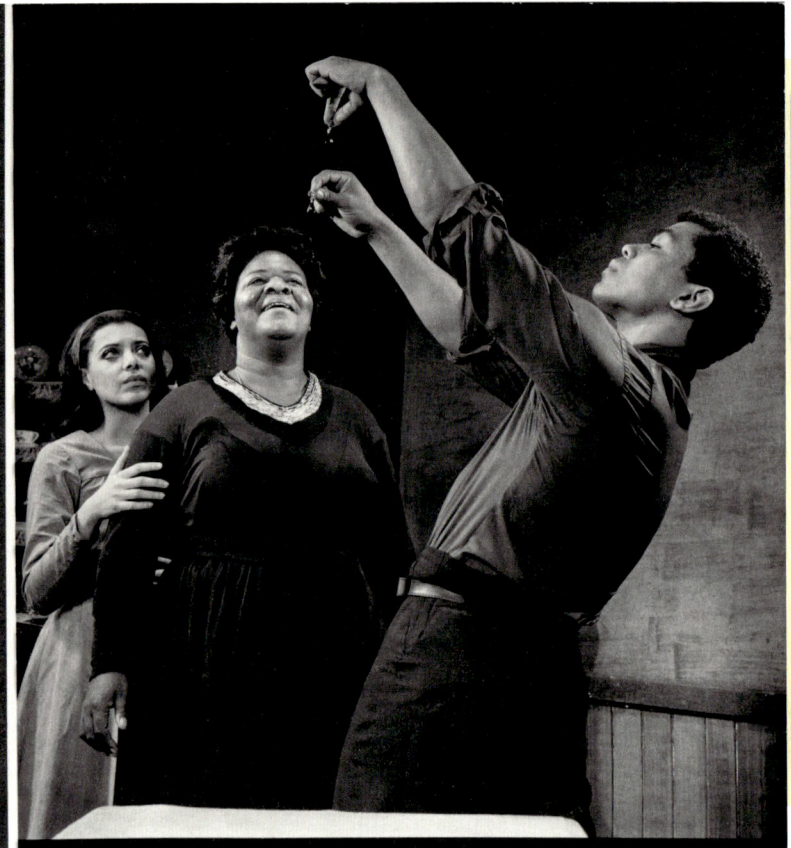
From left: Ellen Holly, Claudia McNeil, and Ailey in the stage production of *Tiger Tiger Burning Bright*, 1962

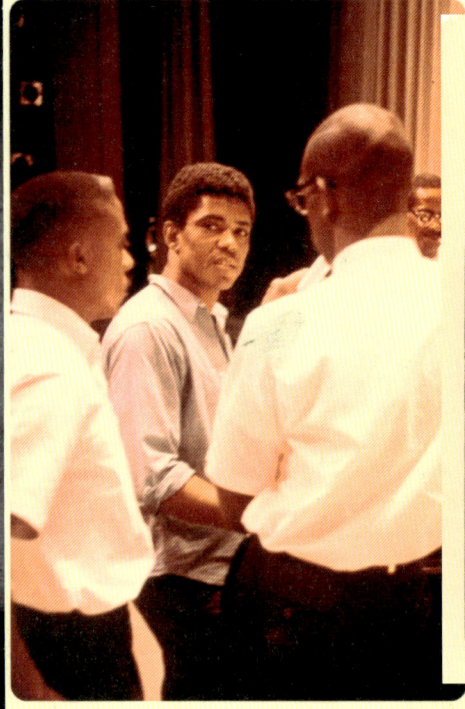
Ailey, ca. 1960s

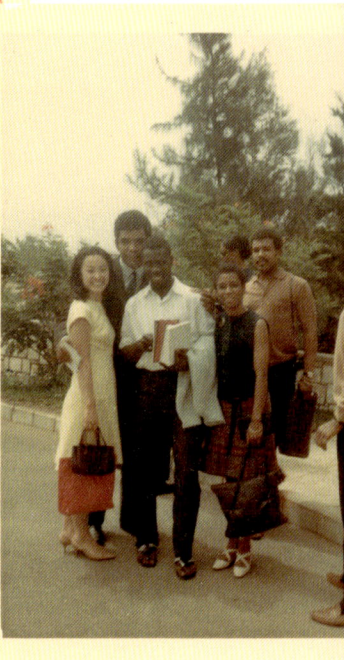
Ailey (second from left) with company dancers and guide, Dakar, Senegal, 1966

April: Ailey and the company—with only three members remaining from the Australian and Southeast Asian tour—perform in a benefit concert at the Brooklyn Academy of Music, where they premiere *Reflections in D*, a solo danced to Ellington's titular piano piece; and *Labyrinth*, a short-lived piece that creatively interpreted the legend of Theseus and the Minotaur.

June 2: The company performs in a benefit concert at the Clark Center, which raises funds for Martin Luther King Jr.'s civil rights efforts in Birmingham, Alabama.

They tour extensively throughout the summer, performing at Jacob's Pillow, various colleges, and other venues.

August 16–September 2: *My People: First Negro Centennial*, an ambitious stage work chronicling Black musical history, produced by Ellington in collaboration with Ailey and Beatty, premieres at the four-thousand seat Arie Crown Theater in Chicago, on the occasion of the Century of Negro Progress Exposition. The production is presented daily over the course of the eighteen-day exposition commemorating the centennial of the Emancipation Proclamation. The process of producing the show opened up creative differences and conflicts in sensibility among the three collaborators.

September: Following Chicago, the Ailey company performs at the International Music Festival in Rio de Janeiro, where they premiere *Rivers, Streams, Doors*. They are beset with problems throughout the performance—namely, an accompanying musician losing rhythm mid-show and, due partly to a lack of advance publicity, an audience expecting a more classical ballet presentation. The company's subsequent time in São Paulo is better received, but Ailey, still upset by what occurred in Rio, takes a week off in Bahia in northeastern Brazil to decompress and do research for *Macumba*, a new Harkness commission.

November: The Ailey company embarks on their first national tour, a six-week event that takes them for the first time to the American South, where they perform in variable conditions and become involved with civil rights activist organizations, such as the Student Nonviolent Coordinating Committee. Southern Black audiences are among the most receptive to the company's performances, and in Jackson, Mississippi, the company meets Gilbert Moses, then director of the underground Free Southern Theater.

1964

January 12: Hughes's musical *Jerico-Jim Crow*, co-directed by Ailey and William Hairston, opens at the Greenwich Mews Theatre on West Thirteenth Street in New York. The production, taking its themes from the Civil Rights Movement and its soundtrack from gospel traditions, has a successful run until its closing at the end of April.

February: Michael Dorfman, who had been responsible for presenting Hughes's *Black Nativity* in Europe, invites the Ailey company to do a three-month European tour, opening in Paris, in the fall.

Former Horton dancer Joyce Trisler is brought into the company. For the year's upcoming tours, Ailey aims to enact his "idea of turning his company into a library for the dances by other choreographers that he loved and thought deserved attention."[10] As such, he brings a variety of works into his repertory, including Horton's *To José Clemente Orozco*, Johnson's *Lament*, Paul Sanasardo's *Metallics*, Anna Sokolow's *Rooms*, Trisler's *Journey*, and Truitte's *Variegations*.

In the months before their departure for Europe, the company performs at a Horton tribute in Los Angeles, on April 12, and in a YWCA benefit at the Clark Center. At the Jacob's Pillow festival in August, de Lavallade and Truitte perform in the premiere of Ailey's *Twelve Gates*.

After many revisions and reworkings, *Revelations* is finalized by Ailey in preparation for the second Harkness Foundation Dance Festival, which opens on August 31 at the Delacorte Theater in Central Park. Ailey drops five dances from the work and cuts some musical interludes, reincorporating others elsewhere. Only five of the work's dances remain largely untouched.

September 4: The company departs for their European tour, performing three days later in Paris at the Théâtre des Champs-Élysées, where they are enthusiastically received.

They next perform in London at the Shaftesbury Theatre as part of a six-week residency, with seven shows a week—a schedule that confirms their widespread popularity.

During this year, Ailey begins to dance less, which allows other dancers—particularly Williams—to come into their own. He invites Hope Clark and William Louther to join the company.

1964–65

Ailey enters a relationship with a white schoolteacher named Christopher (last name unknown), who is younger than him.

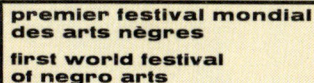

Poster for the Ailey company's performance at the First World Festival of Negro Arts, Dakar, Senegal, 1966

Ailey (lower left) and others, Dakar, Senegal, 1966

Attendees at a reception for Dunham (seated center), Dakar, Senegal, 1966

Touring has become a cornerstone of and a financial lifeline for the Ailey company. However, the mounting pressures and responsibilities of running a company—from dealing with individual personalities to addressing structural mismanagement by Benjamin Jones and Pimsleur—are taxing for Ailey. Pimsleur accuses Ailey of thousands of dollars in unpaid fees, a situation that culminates in her being fired from the company.

Edele Holtz and her husband, Alwin, become more involved with establishing the company's business operations. Ailey asks Edele, who left her position at the Clark Center and had been helping Ailey on weekends, to lay the groundwork for a publicity campaign for the company, which includes creating two brochures and an advertisement for *Dance Magazine*, liaising with government foundations and entities, and researching colleges in New York and New England as possible tour locations.

1965

January: After returning to New York from Europe, the company soon embarks on their next tour, to Australia. It begins at the Tivoli Theatre in Sydney, where Ailey presents two different programs—one devoted to blues and jazz and another that is more melancholic and austere.

February: They next travel to Melbourne, and despite a rough start, their tour is extended by two weeks. Harkness, however, calls Ailey back to France to finish his commissioned piece *Ariadne*.

March 12: Ailey's second creative interpretation of Theseus and the Minotaur, *Ariadne* premieres as part of the Harkness Ballet's debut season at the Opéra Comique in Paris. Created in collaboration with composer André Jolivet and set designer Ming Cho Lee, the work marks Ailey's first large commission for a major dance company.

After the debut of *Ariadne*, Ailey returns to Melbourne, two days before the end of the company's Australian tour.

March–April: The company embarks on a second European tour, performing at festivals and for one-night events in Belgium, Italy, Denmark, Sweden, Finland, Switzerland, Yugoslavia, Germany, and France. Ailey is especially fond of Copenhagen, and the company receives great acclaim in Germany.

May: The group represents the United States at the Festival of Nations held at the Théâtre des Nations in Paris.

Interpersonal tensions among company members come to a head, which Ailey attributes to dancers' inflated egos. At an inflection point, Ailey decides to dissolve the company, choosing instead to focus on his own choreography upon returning to New York that September. This plan, however, does not materialize due to a previously booked college tour slated for June through December. Ailey hires new dancers, including Miguel Godreau, Judith Jamison, and Clive Thompson.

During this year, Ailey stops dancing to focus on choreography and running his company.

1966

February: Another European tour commences, opening in Münster, Germany, with stops in Italy (Milan and Rome), Germany (Berlin and Cologne), and the Netherlands (Amsterdam). The dancers tour by bus and earn extra revenue through televised performances.

The pay dispute between Ailey and Pimsleur is decided in her favor, and she is owed nearly $8,000 in unpaid fees.

Consuelo Atlas joins the company.

The company is effectively stranded in Milan after several canceled tour gigs (due to the prior unpopular reception of a Black performance troupe headed by Dorfman), but they are presented with an opportunity to perform at the First World Festival of Negro Arts in Dakar, Senegal, in April. Choreographer and organizer Arthur Mitchell lacked the funds to fly his dancers in the US to Africa, so he instead opted for the less-expensive option of flying the Ailey dancers, already in Europe, to Senegal. Ailey accepts the offer in the hopes of traveling to Spain after the festival to ask Harkness, whose company would be performing in Barcelona, for her continued support.

April: The brainchild of Senegalese president Léopold Senghor, the First World Festival of Negro Arts brings together more than two thousand artists, musicians, and writers from across the African continent and diasporas in celebration of Black culture. The Ailey dancers are a rousing success at the festival, despite many backstage troubles, illnesses, and last-minute replacements.

Late April–July: Ailey travels to Barcelona, where he reunites with Harkness. The trip proves tumultuous, however, with dancers leaving his company and Ailey having to work with Harkness on the choreography for two premieres: *Macumba*, which debuts in Barcelona in May, and *El Amor Brujo*, which premieres in Paris at the Festival du Marais (June 7–July 8).

Once again, Ailey considers disbanding his company. Amid these deliberations, he is commissioned

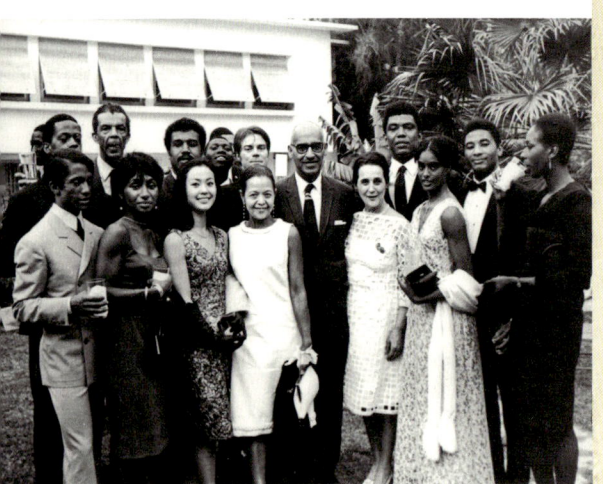
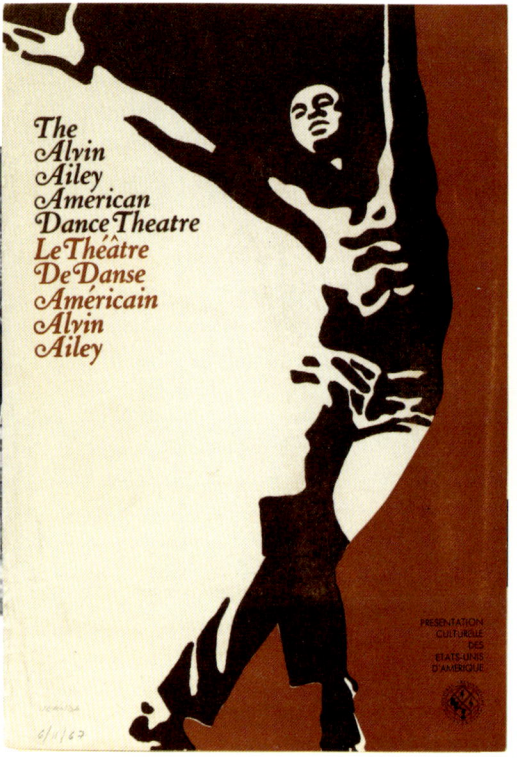
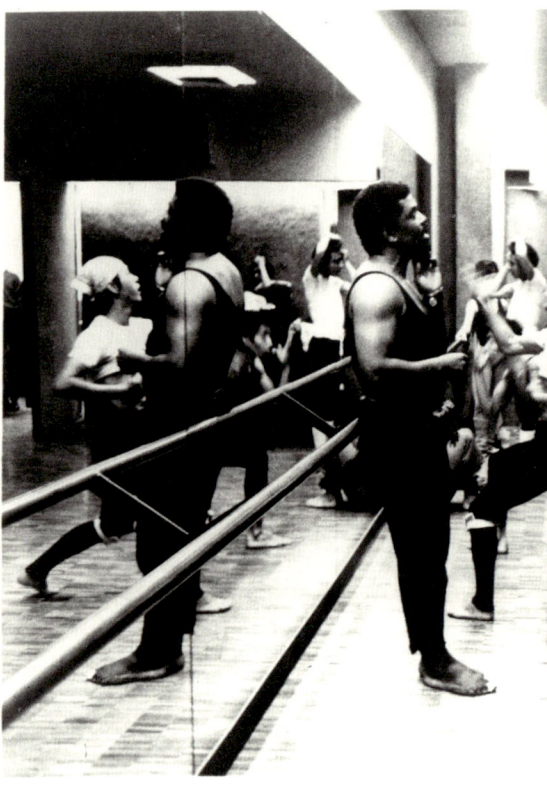

Ailey (back row, third from right) with company dancers including Loretta Abbott, Takako Asakawa, Consuelo Atlas, Miguel Godreau, Judith Jamison, Kelvin Rotardier, Truitte, and Morton Winston, and others, n.d.

Cover of a souvenir program from the Ailey company's North African tour, 1967

Ailey in rehearsal with dancers (likely from the Ballet Folklórico de México), Mexico City, 1968

to choreograph *Antony and Cleopatra*, an opera directed by Franco Zeffirelli and set to music by Samuel Barber, for the opening of the Metropolitan Opera House in New York in September. Ailey is also offered additional work with the Harkness Ballet.

Before undertaking these projects, he meets up with the Holtzes in Paris, and this interaction alleviates Ailey's doubts about the future of his company. The disorganized planning for *Antony and Cleopatra*, however, proves frustrating and tiresome for Ailey, who is further discouraged by the unsuccessful merger of his company with the Harkness Ballet.

Ailey receives an inaugural choreographer's fellowship from the National Endowment for the Arts, along with Cunningham, Graham, Limón, Alwin Nikolais, Sokolow, and Paul Taylor.

1967

Late April: Although the pressures of running a growing company are wearing on him, Ailey perseveres, and planning begins for the incorporation of his company as a nonprofit foundation. A possible location for the foundation is in the New York neighborhood of Yorkville, near the Harkness School, but the plan is scrapped.

Ailey's association with Harkness begins to fizzle after Ailey walks out on the second day of rehearsals for a restaging of *Ariadne*. The relationship between Ailey and Christopher ends, and Ailey vacations in Morocco, where he finds many lovers and where he would return twice.

Ailey and Alwin Holtz locate a ground-floor apartment at 28 West Sixty-Fifth Street, where they set up an office and Ailey's living quarters.

Ailey begins regularly meeting with Dr. Carl Goldman, a gay psychotherapist who helps Ailey process his ongoing issues with himself, his relationships, and his parents.

Late May: The company leaves for a tour in Israel and eight countries in Europe. In Sweden, Ailey creates the ballet *Riedaiglia*, which premieres on television there in the fall. Its title is a portmanteau of the work's three collaborators: Swedish composer Georg Riedel, Ailey, and producer Lars Egler. The piece is praised by Swedish critics, and Ailey is given the Grand Prix Italia, the most prestigious television award in Europe.

Summer: As he is walking home from dinner in New York, Ailey is wrongfully arrested by the police, who misidentify him for a man who had murdered four police officers in Cincinnati. With his passport, Ailey is able to verify his identity, but he is charged with pushing an officer and spends the night in jail before being freed by a lawyer hired by the Holtzes.

September: The company goes on a two-and-a-half-month tour of Africa for the US State Department, becoming the first American modern dance company to tour the continent. They perform in Côte d'Ivoire, Ethiopia, Ghana, Kenya, Madagascar, Senegal, Tanzania, Uganda, and Zaire (Democratic Republic of the Congo). The experience is successful and eye-opening for the dancers, who find themselves, in every country and city, in sites of cross-pollinating cultures and peoples.

1968

Buttressed by grants and support from major foundations, the company is back in New York for their first season in four years, followed by an extensive domestic tour.

Ailey meets with representatives from the Solomon R. Guggenheim and the Rockefeller Foundations, signaling a concerted effort to seek funding for his company and to begin the process of starting a school.

April 4: The company receives word of Martin Luther King Jr.'s assassination. Ailey travels to Atlanta to mourn and attend Dr. King's funeral.

Ailey faces many challenges in laying the groundwork for a financially viable company and school. He has difficulty finding the right locations, recruiting new board members, and raising $100,000 to help fund new repertory pieces and music as well as touring expenses.

However, the company receives several grants that allow for a degree of creative freedom hitherto unknown to them: $12,000 from the Guggenheim Foundation; $10,000 from the National Endowment for the Arts; and $5,000 from the Rockefeller Foundation. As such, Ailey begins to choreograph new dances, and he commissions Beatty and Lucas Hoving to create pieces. Unfortunately, Ailey overspends the grants, putting the company into financial trouble.

Sylvia Waters joins the company.

May: Truitte breaks ties temporarily with Ailey and the company after learning that his contract had not been renewed. Two years later, he and Ailey would reunite and collaborate again, with Truitte dancing as a company member for one more year before becoming a distinguished teacher of the Horton technique.

Summer: The company goes on their fifth European tour, performing throughout the Netherlands, Scotland, and Yugoslavia. They premiere Beatty's

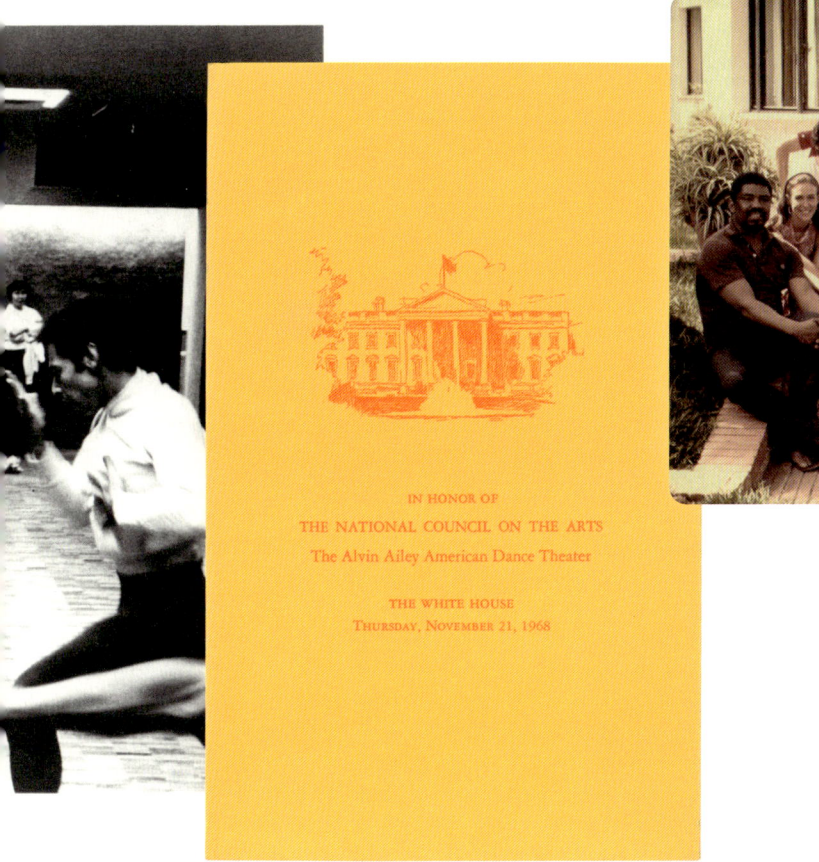

Cover of program for the Ailey company's performance at the White House, Washington, DC, 1968

Ailey (far left) with company dancers including Atlas, Alfonso Figueroa, Godreau, Avind Harum, Jamison, Mari Kajiwara, Linda Kent, Michele Murray, Leland Schwantes, and Sylvia Waters; costume designer Edwin Huntington Parker; and Department of State personnel, outside the US General Consulate, Casablanca, Morocco, July 4, 1970

Ailey, 1970

Black Belt, a revival of *Knoxville Summer of 1915*, and Ailey's new work *Quintet*, winning awards for best choreographer and best company at that year's Edinburgh International Festival.

Unable to afford to travel to Jerusalem for the Israel Festival, a monthlong celebration of music and dance, Ailey and the company return to New York at the conclusion of the European leg of the tour.

August/September: The Holtzes announce that they are moving to New Orleans, leaving Ailey stricken and feeling isolated in running the company.

October: With Ailey's permission, the Ballet Folklórico de México performs *Revelations* at the opening ceremonies of the 1968 summer Olympics in Mexico City, marking the only time Ailey allows the dance to be performed by a company not his own.

Late fall: Ailey meets and begins to collaborate with Ivy Clarke, who becomes integral to supporting the company's affairs.

November 21: The company performs at an event at the White House for President Lyndon B. Johnson, in honor of the National Council on the Arts.

1969

Late January: The company opens a weeklong engagement on Broadway at the Billy Rose Theatre.

The company moves its headquarters from the Clark Center to the Brooklyn Academy of Music, joining the Merce Cunningham Dance Company and Eliot Feld's American Ballet Company as dancers in residence. The Ailey company finds its temporary quarters at the academy insufficient for its growing needs.

The Alvin Ailey American Dance Center (now the Ailey School) is established, with classes in ethnic, jazz, and modern dance held at the Hanson Place Central United Methodist Church.

July 14: Ailey premieres *Diversion No. 1* at the Greek Theatre in Los Angeles, a program shared with the singing group the 5th Dimension.

August 16: *Masekela Langage* premieres at the American Dance Festival at Connecticut College. The dance draws parallels between apartheid in South Africa and race relations in Chicago, and is set to the jazz compositions of Hugh Masekela.

The company rounds out the year with televised performances in Hollywood, another national tour, and concerts in Latin America. Ailey is commissioned to choreograph the Broadway musical *La Strada*, based on the 1954 film by Federico Fellini.

December 4: Fred Hampton, chairman of the Illinois chapter of the Black Panther Party, is assassinated in Chicago, an event that deeply affects Ailey.

1970

Ailey is asked to create three pieces for the Brooklyn Academy of Music, one of which is a ballet set to an Ellington jazz score for the American Ballet Theatre's summer engagement at Lincoln Center.

April: *Streams* and *Gymnopedies* premiere to success, but Ailey again announces that he is dissolving the company because of financial pressures and touring conditions.

As recompense for canceling a planned Soviet tour for the Ailey company, the US Department of State offers to sponsor a five-week tour of North Africa in July and to fund two weeks of rehearsal. Ailey accepts the proposal.

June 25: *The River*, choreographed by Ailey for the American Ballet Theatre, debuts to rousing success. Four days later, Ailey and the company depart for their tour throughout Algeria, Morocco, and Tunisia.

July: Officially breaking ties with the Brooklyn Academy of Music, Ailey and Clarke decide to take up Charles Reinhart's invitation to perform at the Clark Center for the upcoming fall season.

A few months later, Clarke hears from Pearl Lang about a potentially usable space at 229 East Fifty-Ninth Street in Manhattan. It would become the company's rehearsal space after the Rockefeller Foundation provides the company with $37,000 to renovate the building.

September 24–November 1: After returning from North Africa in August, the company begins a six-week tour of the Soviet Union, becoming the first modern dance company to visit the country since Isadora Duncan's group performed there in the 1920s. Opening in the Ukrainian city of Zaporozhe (Zaporizhzhya), the tour travels to several cities including Moscow, where the performances are sold-out, and ends in Leningrad (Saint Petersburg), where the dancers receive a twenty-three-minute ovation. The company becomes the first American attraction to appear on Moscow television, reaching twenty-two million viewers.

The dancers next go on tour in Paris and London, sponsored by the Soviet Union. In Paris, Ailey is awarded the Étoile d'Or for best modern dance group and choreographer.

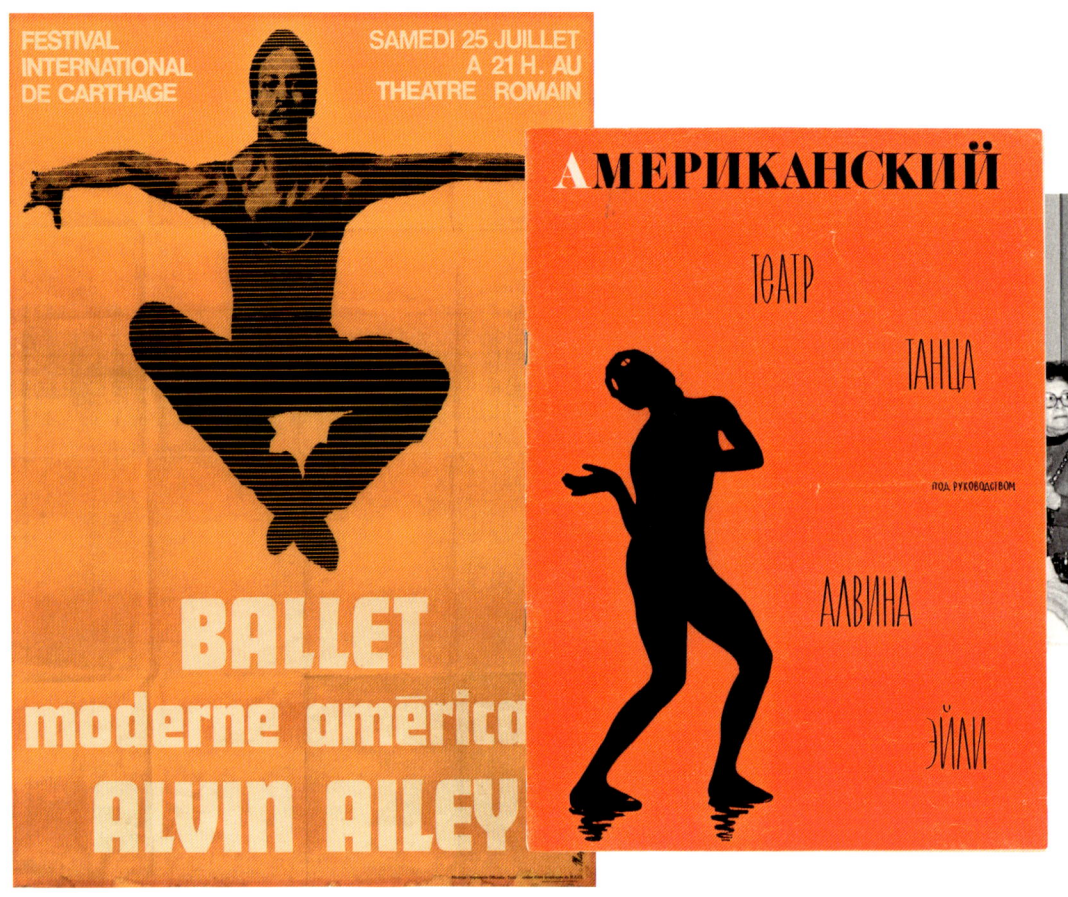

Poster for the Ailey company's performance at the Festival International de Carthage, Morocco, 1970

Cover of program for an Ailey company performance in the Soviet Union, 1970

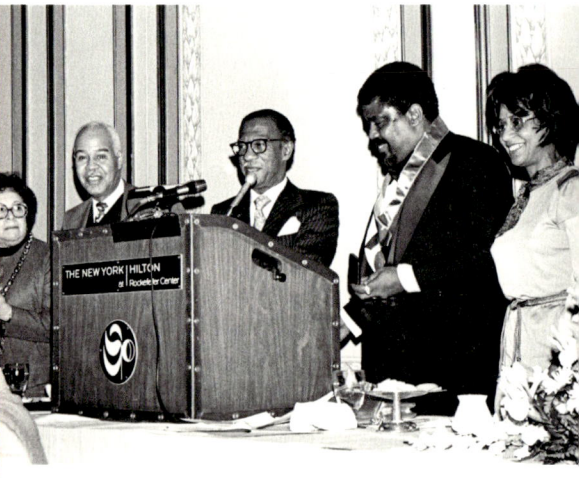

Ailey (second from right) receiving the National Association for the Advancement of Colored People's Spingarn Medal, 1976

1971

January 18: The company opens the New York City Center American Dance Season at the ANTA Theatre in Midtown, where they perform for the first two weeks of the two-month-long program. This engagement includes the opening-night premiere of *Archipelago*, which, like *Streams*, is another of Ailey's plotless "water" dances and is set to music by André Boucourechliev. *Flowers*, a dance inspired by Janis Joplin's life and the deleterious effects of fame, premieres one week later.

Following the engagement, the company embarks on a national tour for two months, followed by City Center's spring season (April 27–May 9), another national tour, and performances in Bermuda.

Premieres during City Center's spring season include *Choral Dances*, comprising six dances set to choral music from Benjamin Britten's opera *Gloriana*, on April 28; and *Cry*, a three-part solo honoring Black women, on May 4. *Cry*, which Ailey created as a birthday gift for his mother and choreographed specifically for Jamison, is met with glowing reviews in the *New York Times*.[11]

That spring, the company officially moves into the American Dance Center on East Fifty-Ninth Street, sharing the premises with Pearl Lang's company.

The company establishes a schedule of biannual seasons, each two weeks' long, as part of the City Center American Dance Season, a commitment that proves taxing for Ailey and his dancers in terms of premiering new pieces and balancing personal lives.

Ailey begins requiring his company members to take ballet training classes with two former dancers from the Harkness Ballet.

Summer: At the urging of his mother, Ailey's half-brother, Calvin, comes to stay with him in New York for a month.

September 8: As part of the opening gala for the John F. Kennedy Center for the Performing Arts in Washington, DC, the company performs in Leonard Bernstein's *Mass: A Theatre Piece for Singers, Players, and Dancers*, a musical genre-bending take on the Catholic mass, with choreography by Ailey.

October 13: Composed of five dances and four vaudeville episodes set to music by Charles Mingus, *The Mingus Dances*, choreographed by Ailey for the Joffrey Ballet, premieres at City Center.

December 9: *Mary Lou's Mass*, a piece set to music by pioneering jazz musician and composer Mary Lou Williams, premieres during the company's season at City Center. Six days later, *Myth* premieres there, danced to Igor Stravinsky's *Symphonies of Wind Instruments*.

1972

The company still faces a financial shortfall but continues to gain momentum and strives to become solvent as an organization.

Two company premieres materialize this year, and both debut at City Center: *The Lark Ascending*, a lyrical and balletic dance set to Ralph Vaughan Williams's *Romance for Violin and Orchestra*, on April 25; and *Love Songs*, a duet of yearning set to music by Donny Hathaway and Nina Simone, on November 18.

Ailey also choreographs *Shaken Angels*, a duet for Dennis Wayne and Bonnie Mathis, which debuts in September at the Tenth New York Dance Festival at the Delacorte Theater; and *Sea Change* for the American Ballet Theatre, which premieres in October in Washington, DC.

Cedar Crest College and Princeton University bestow Ailey with honorary degrees.

Masazumi Chaya joins the company.

August: The company officially joins the City Center program, rebranding itself temporarily as the Alvin Ailey City Center Dance Theater.

September 19: The Metropolitan Opera's production of *Carmen*, with choreography by Ailey, opens.

Fall: Ailey moves into an apartment at 467 Central Park West. He envisions bringing back dances by Horton, Humphrey, Sophie Maslow, and St. Denis, along with other unrealized proposals. He ultimately revives two dances: Shawn's *Kinetic Molpai* and Dunham's *Choros* for the company's repertory, with their premieres taking place on November 16 and 25, respectively.

Ailey is plagued by problems with the company and its administration, specifically Clarke, although his therapist, Dr. Goldman, suggests that the benefits outweigh the consequences of having her on staff.

1973

February: Ailey choreographs the Metropolitan Opera's mini-production of Virgil Thomson's *Four Saints in Three Acts*, which premieres at the Vivian Beaumont Theater in New York.

May 17: His only new dance for the year, *Hidden Rites*, an abstraction of African rituals, premieres at City Center.

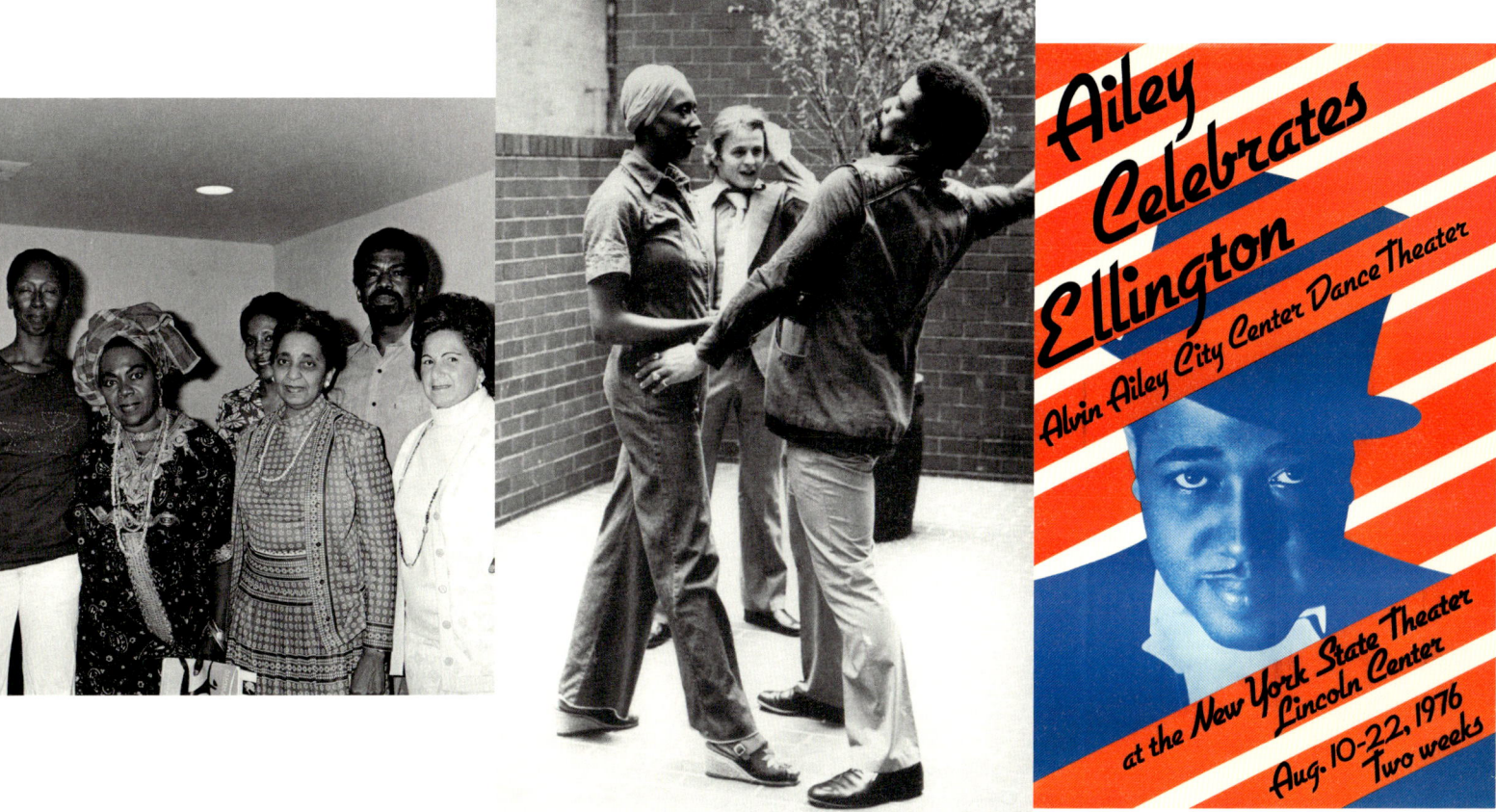

Jamison and Primus (first and second from left) with Ailey (back right) and others, 1974

Jamison, Mikhail Baryshnikov, and Ailey at the press conference for *Pas de Duke*, 1976

Poster for the Ailey Celebrates Ellington festival, New York State Theater, Lincoln Center, 1976

June: The company embarks on another international tour, beginning with a two-week-long stint in London before traveling to Tehran, Iran, and Baalbek, Lebanon.

August 31: Jacqueline Latham, a doctoral student at Texas Woman's University, completes the first dissertation on Ailey, titled "A Biographical Study of the Lives and Contributions of Two Selected Contemporary Black Male Dance Artists—Arthur Mitchell and Alvin Ailey—in the Idioms of Ballet and Modern Dance, Respectively."

1974

Attorneys Stanley Plesent and Howard Squadron spearhead efforts to establish an executive board for the Ailey company. For the spring City Center season, Ailey asks Janet Collins and Primus to choreograph pieces.

May 6: Ailey and the company are featured in the television special *Alvin Ailey: Memories and Visions*, produced by Ellis Haizlip.

May 11: Ailey's father dies at age sixty-two in a nursing home in Wichita Falls, Texas. He and his son had only recently begun speaking again, after nearly four decades of no communication.

June–July: The company goes on a European tour, notably performing in locations in Eastern Europe, including Hungary, Romania, and Yugoslavia.

Ailey establishes the Alvin Ailey Repertory Ensemble (now Ailey II), a junior troupe that prepares dancers for joining the first company, and selects Sylvia Waters to head the program. A third group, the Alvin Ailey Student Workshop, formed under the stewardship of Kelvin Rotardier, offers students performance and training opportunities.

November 28: *Ailey Celebrates Ellington*, a television special produced by Herman Krawitz in honor of the eponymous musician, who died in May, premieres on CBS with six new pieces by Ailey. Two of the dances become part of the company's repertory in April 1975—*The Mooche* and *Night Creature*.

1975

April 28: Ailey receives the prestigious *Dance Magazine* award in recognition of his contributions to the field of dance.

The tension between Ailey and Clarke comes to a head, and Ailey fires her.

1976

Ailey is awarded the Spingarn Medal of the National Association for the Advancement of Colored People.

August 10: The Ailey Celebrates Ellington festival opens at the New York State Theater at Lincoln Center, in commemoration of the bicentennial of the United States. The two-week event includes *The River* and new Ailey repertory, including the company premiere of *Pas de Duke*, a reworking of the classical pas de deux set to music by Ellington and created for Mikhail Baryshnikov and Jamison, and *Black, Brown and Beige*, a historical survey of Black life spanning slavery, emancipation, and the political milestones leading up to the present moment. Revivals and commissions by other choreographers are also featured in the program, including Beatty's *Road of the Phoebe Snow* and Horton's *Liberian Suite* as well as pieces by Louis Falco, Cristyne Lawson, and Milton Myers. Prior to the festival's opening, Ailey was faced with various managerial matters, ranging from dissension among the company's dancers to raising the funds necessary for the project.

Ailey choreographs *Three Black Kings*, a dance set to Ellington's last score, left unfinished at his death and completed by his son, Mercer. The piece follows the arcs of three historical figures: King Balthazar, King Solomon, and Martin Luther King Jr.

1977

January 19: The company dances at the Kennedy Center for President Jimmy Carter's inaugural gala. Their performance of excerpts from *Revelations* receives a standing ovation.

March 3: Ailey is one of twenty-one inaugural recipients of the Award of Honor in Arts and Culture, established by New York City Mayor Abraham Beame. Other recipients include Robert Joffrey and Lincoln Kirstein.

April 26: The Ailey II company performs at Studio 54 for the club's opening night.

May: Guest choreographer Dianne McIntyre premieres *Ancestral Voices*, with scenery and costumes designed by Romare Bearden, marking the beginning of the artist's collaborations with Ailey.

June–July: Ailey cancels a two-week engagement at the New York State Theater, instead going on an international tour that travels to France, Egypt, Hong Kong, India, Japan, the Philippines, Taiwan, Thailand, and Turkey.

Ailey is awarded honorary degrees from Adelphi University and Bard College.

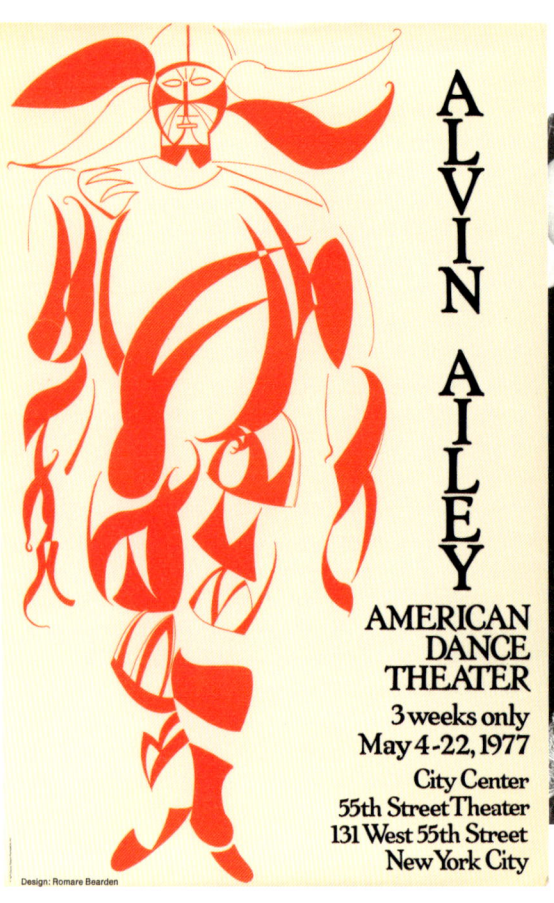

Poster for the Ailey company's spring season at City Center, New York, 1977. Design by Romare Bearden

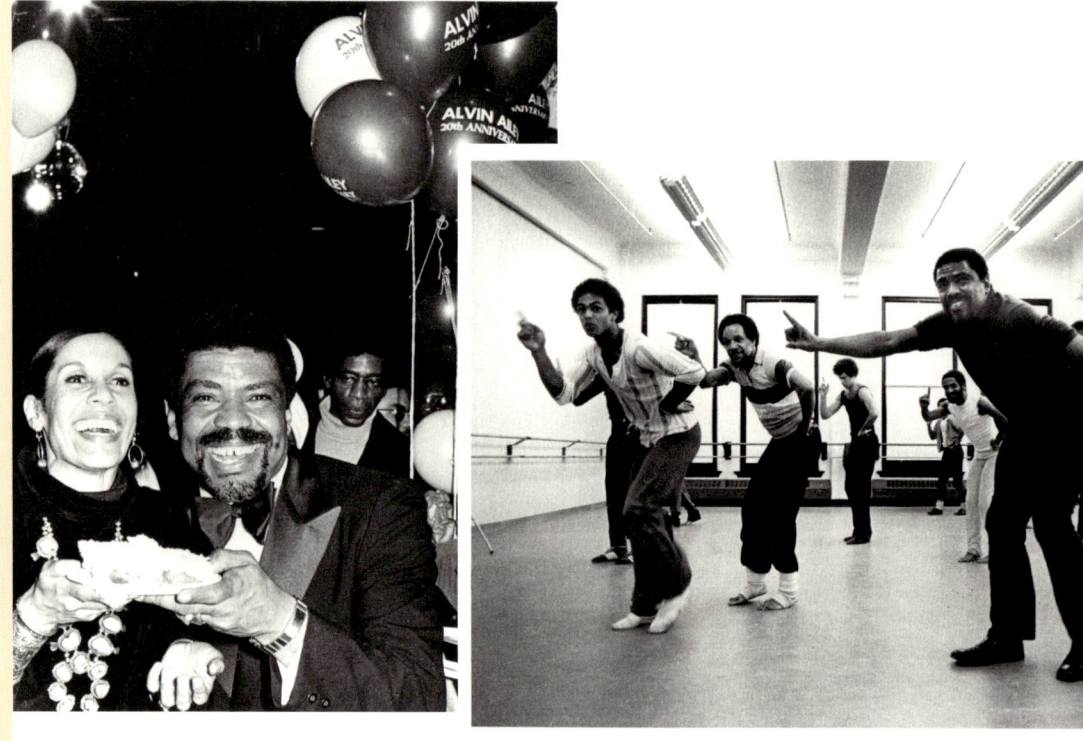

De Lavallade and Ailey at a meet and greet for the company's twentieth annual gala at City Center, New York, November 29, 1978

Ailey (right) leading rehearsal, 1978

1978

The company, celebrating its twentieth year, has twenty-nine dancers on its roster and an annual budget of $3 million, marking a new phase for the now established organization. Key former dancers, including de Lavallade and Godreau, return to the Ailey stage for various anniversary reunions and celebrations.

Administrative tasks prevent Ailey from choreographing regularly. He starts distancing himself from friends and exhibits behavior that is concerning to those around him.

Ailey begins scouting locations for new company and school headquarters, but possible opportunities in southern Harlem and Midtown do not materialize.

May 3: *Passage*, an homage to vodou queen Marie Laveau, premieres at City Center. Created as a solo for Jamison upon her return to the company, the dance is set to music by Hale Smith and features set design by Bearden.

May–July: The Ailey company tours in Central and South America, performing in Brazil, Chile, Mexico, Peru, and Uruguay.

July 1: *The Alvin Ailey American Dance Theater*, the first book-length publication about the company, is released. It features commentary by *Dance Magazine* editor Joseph H. Mazo and photography by Susan Cook.

August 17: Ailey premieres *Shigaon! Children of the Diaspora*, a disco-inflected ballet, created for the Israeli ballet company Bat-Dor.

November 15: The company gives a special performance for President Carter at the White House.

December 31: At the invitation of Moroccan King Hassan II, who had seen the Ailey company perform at the White House, the troupe performs for the king's New Year festivities in Rabat, Morocco.

1979

Performances this year include shows in Canada in January, two seasons at City Center, and a two-month, eleven-city tour of Europe during the summer.

Spring: Ailey receives the Capezio Dance Award for his contributions to dance. Choreographer George Faison and singer Roberta Flack present the award to him in a private ceremony at the New York Public Library for the Performing Arts.

May 2: *Solo for Mingus*, an homage to the jazz bassist and bandleader, premieres. It is set to the musician's "Myself When I Am Real," a 1963 improvisation that Ailey also used in *The Mingus Dances* (1971), which he choreographed for the Joffrey Ballet.

Bearden creates the *Bayou Fever* series of collages for an Ailey-choreographed ballet that would go unrealized. These twenty-one collages, vignettes of the Louisiana Bayou, fuse the imagery and traditions of the American South with a larger southern imaginary.

October 13: Trisler, Ailey's friend and colleague, is found dead of a heart attack in her Manhattan home. Ailey choreographs *Memoria* in her honor, and the work premieres on November 29 at City Center.

Following Trisler's death, Ailey is acting more recklessly, and he becomes romantically involved with Abdullah (last name unknown), a young man whom he had met while on tour in Paris. He begins frequenting the Nuyorican Poets Café on the Lower East Side and befriends its cofounder Miguel Algarín. One evening, Ailey spontaneously choreographs the ending of *Nuyorican Nights*, a play created by Algarín and Miguel Piñero.

October 18: After the demolition of the American Dance Center on East Fifty-Ninth Street, a ribbon-cutting ceremony is held for the company's new three-story, theater-district headquarters in the Minskoff Building on Broadway, between Forty-Fourth and Forty-Fifth Streets.

Issues relating to greater pay and roles among Ailey dancers arise with increased frequency as the company grows in size and stature.

1980

March 7: Ailey is arrested for trespassing and harassment at International House, a graduate residence of Columbia University, where he had gone in search of Abdullah. Ailey is taken to Bellevue Hospital and undergoes psychiatric testing. Although he is released a week later and the charges are later dropped, his reputation is tarnished. He returns to work as if nothing happened, troubling his close colleagues and friends.

April 15: Jamison is announced as the lead role in the new Broadway musical *Sophisticated Ladies*, based on Ellington's music. Ailey marks her departure from the company by choreographing *Spell*, a duet that Jamison and former Bolshoi Ballet dancer Alexander Godunov would perform as guest dancers at the Ailey company's opening night gala

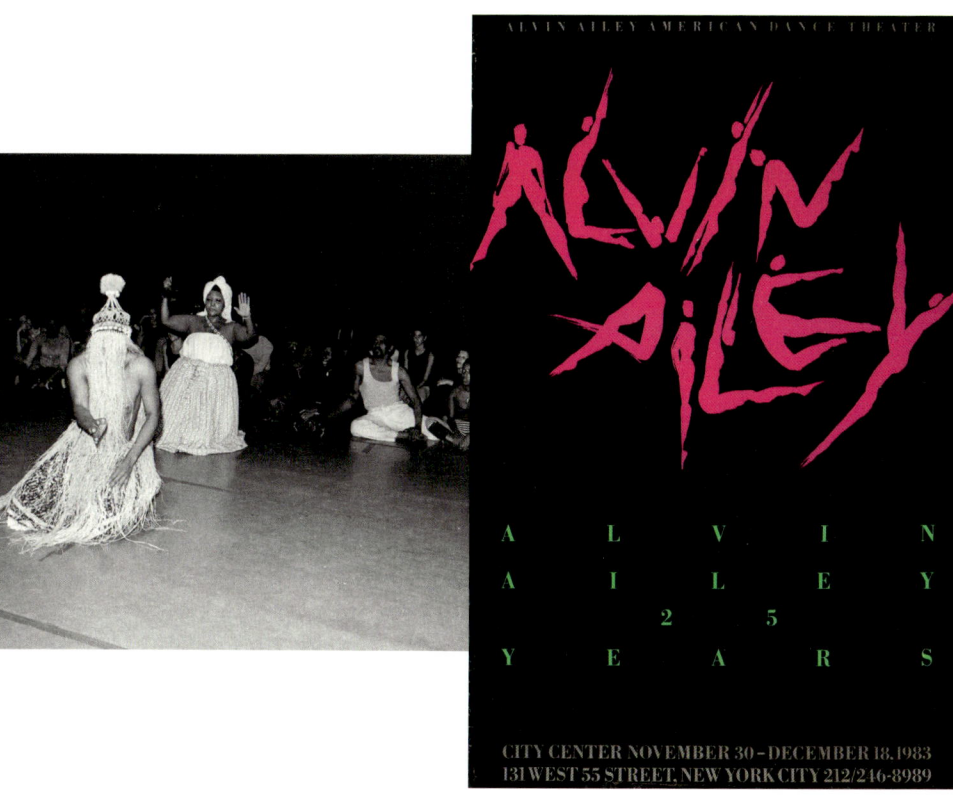
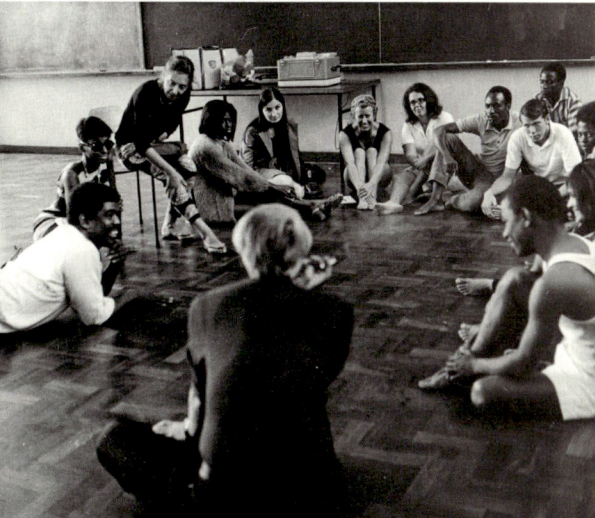

Samba demonstration during the company's tour in Brazil, 1978

Poster for the Ailey company's winter season at City Center, marking the company's twenty-fifth anniversary, 1983

Ailey leading a class for visually impaired students, ca. 1980s

at City Center the following year, on December 3, 1981.

April 30: Ailey is arrested again, after yelling "Fire!" in his apartment building's hallway and forcing his way into another resident's unit. He is taken to St. Luke's Hospital for a psychiatric examination and then spends the night in jail on burglary and assault charges.

In court, an agreement is reached that the charges against Ailey would be dropped if he committed himself to the New York Hospital/Cornell Medical Center in White Plains, New York. There, Ailey undergoes psychiatric treatment and is diagnosed as manic-depressive (bipolar) and prescribed lithium. He returns to New York City at the end of June. The company, kept afloat due to the efforts of Jamison and company members Chaya and Williams, again finds itself in dire financial straits.

September: Ailey travels with the company for their performances in Canada.

Ailey moves out of his Central Park West apartment into a place on 301 West Fifty-Third Street.

December 5: Inspired by African American jazz musicians Donald Byrd, Max Roach, and Pharoah Sanders, Ailey's *Phases* premieres at City Center to critical acclaim, with the *New York Times* describing it as "wildly exciting" and "an artistic success and a hit of the season."[12]

1981

June–July: The company embarks on international tours spanning Argentina, Brazil, Canada, Colombia, Denmark, and Mexico.

December 11: *Landscape*, a piece Ailey created for company dancer Mari Kajiwara and set to a Béla Bartók piano concerto, debuts at City Center.

1982

Summer: The company begins touring in China and Japan, followed by stops in France, Greece, Israel, and Italy.

November 29: Ailey initiates Arts for the Handicapped, a pilot program for blind and visually impaired dancers at the Ailey School.

December: Ailey premieres *Satyriade*, a restaging of mythological dynamics between nymphs and satyrs set to Ravel's *Introduction and Allegro for Harp, Flute, Clarinet and String Quartet*.

Ailey receives the United Nations Peace Medal, and the Ailey School receives accreditation from the National Association of Schools of Dance.

1983

April: Ailey premieres *Au Bord du Précipice* in Paris with the Opera Ballet. Inspired by rock musician Jim Morrison and French ballet dancer Patrick Dupond, the work marks Ailey's most recent exploration of the theme of being "on the edge." This collaboration gives Ailey a sense of what it is like to work with a better-funded institution than those in the US.

May 10: *Fever Swamp*, commissioned by Ailey from emerging postmodernist choreographer Bill T. Jones, debuts in New York.

Summer: Ailey works on a new piece, *Escapades*, in Italy, commissioned by the Aterballetto of Reggio Emilia and set to jazz music by Max Roach.

October 22: The company performs with singer-songwriter Lionel Richie for a televised program celebrating the Metropolitan Opera's centennial anniversary.

November 30: The Ailey company's twenty-fifth anniversary gala, a three-and-a-half-hour-long celebration at City Center, is a great success and is star-studded with guest appearances, including many Ailey alumni and *House of Flowers* star Diahann Carroll. The festivities include the debut of *Can't Slow Down*, a pièce d'occasion set to the titular song by Lionel Richie, and continue throughout the weekend with the premiere of Ailey's *Isba*.

1984

Early spring: Ailey asks Allan Gray—a Kansas City, Missouri, resident whom Ailey had befriended previously—if Kansas City would be interested in being the second home of the Ailey company. In the process of deliberations, the nonprofit organization Kansas City Friends of Alvin Ailey is founded.

June 17: The Christian A. Johnson Endeavor Foundation establishes a $90,000 scholarship endowment for the Ailey School.

July 9: The company, which did not return for a spring season at City Center, is invited to open a two-week engagement at the Metropolitan Opera House. The experience provides the company with crucial support and infrastructure as well as a reunion with former member Ulysses Dove.

September 28: The company continues to travel intensely and arrives in Kansas City for a two-week residency, which entails six performances, including master classes and lectures.

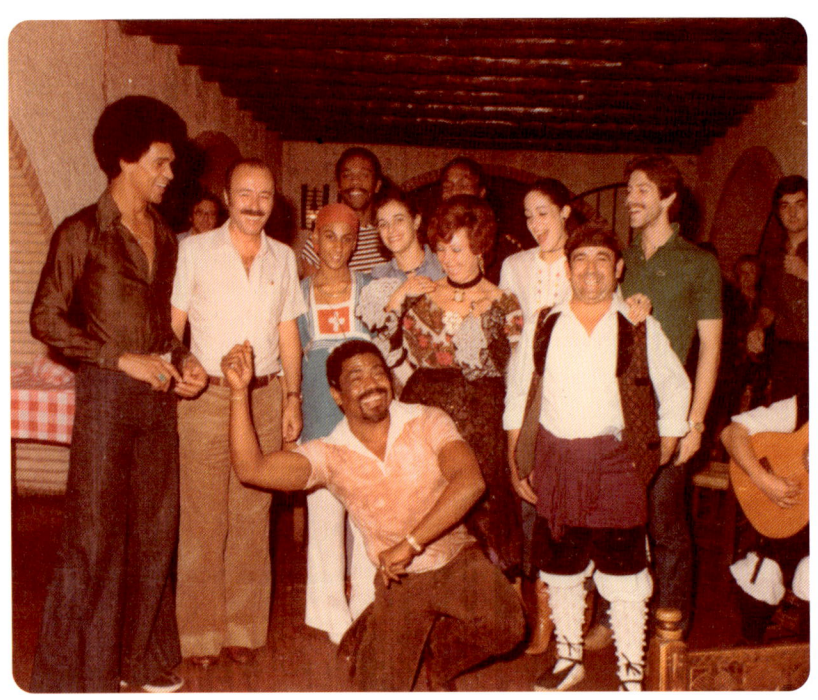

Ailey (kneeling at center) with company members and others, Madrid, 1976

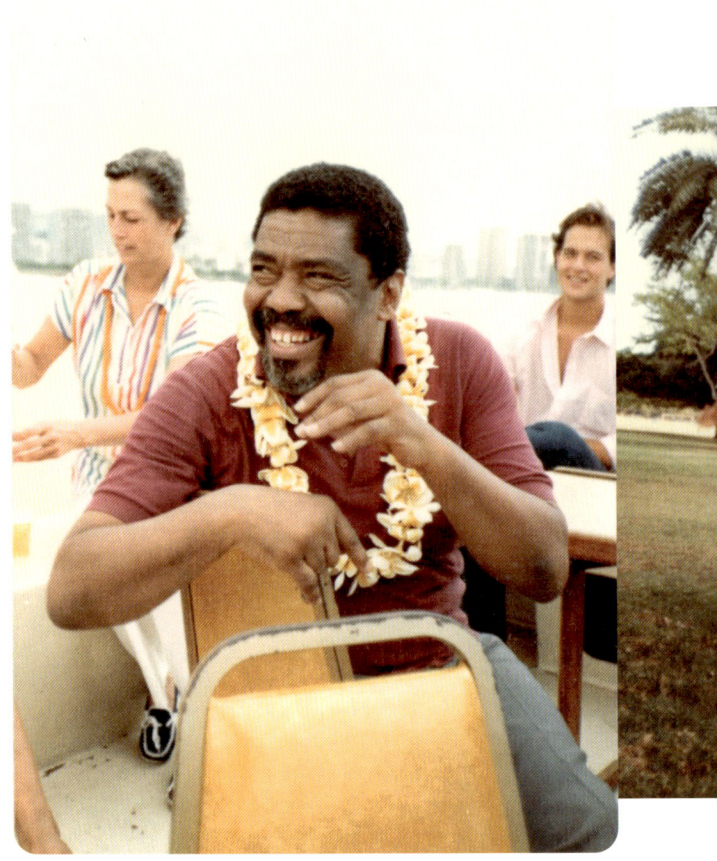

Ailey on a boat in Hawai'i, 1982

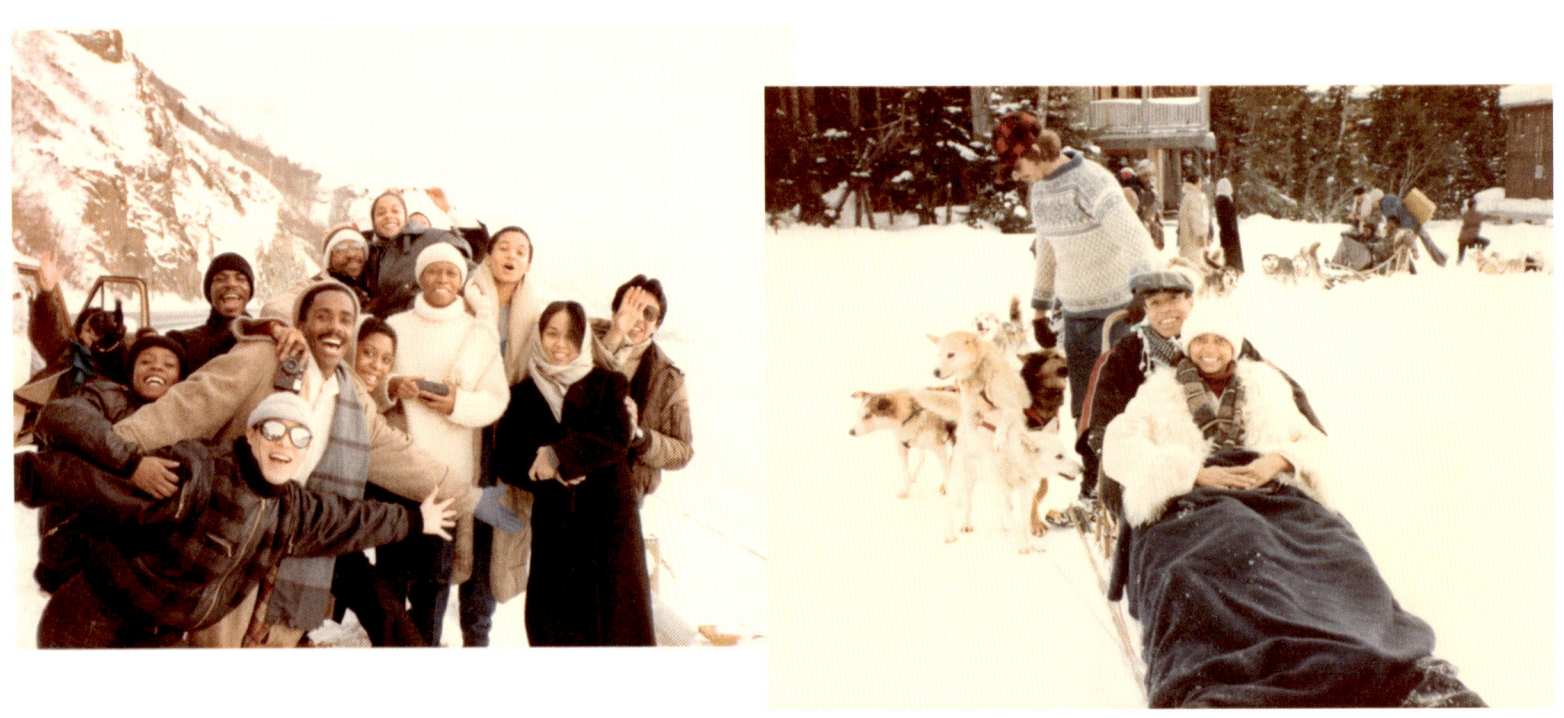

Ailey company dancers in Alaska, 1984

Donna Wood and Keith McDaniel on a dogsled, Alaska, 1984

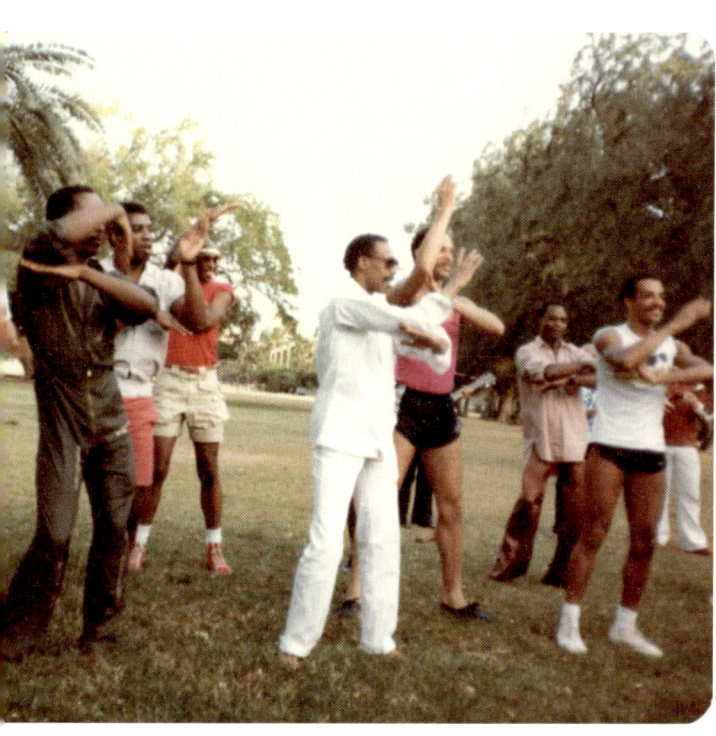

Ailey company dancers learning traditional Hawaiian dance, Hawai'i, 1982

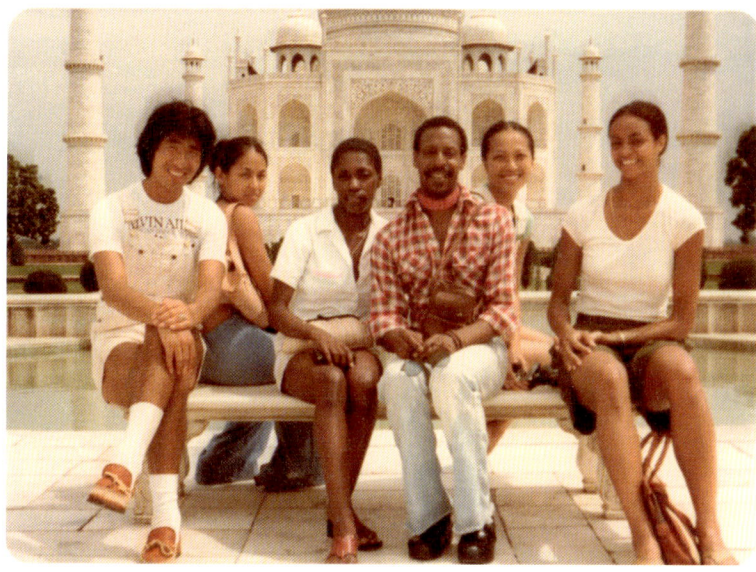

Ailey company dancers (from left) Michihiko Oka, Mari Kajiwara, Estelle Spurlock, Dudley Williams, Tina Yuan, and Donna Wood at the Taj Mahal, Agra, India, 1977

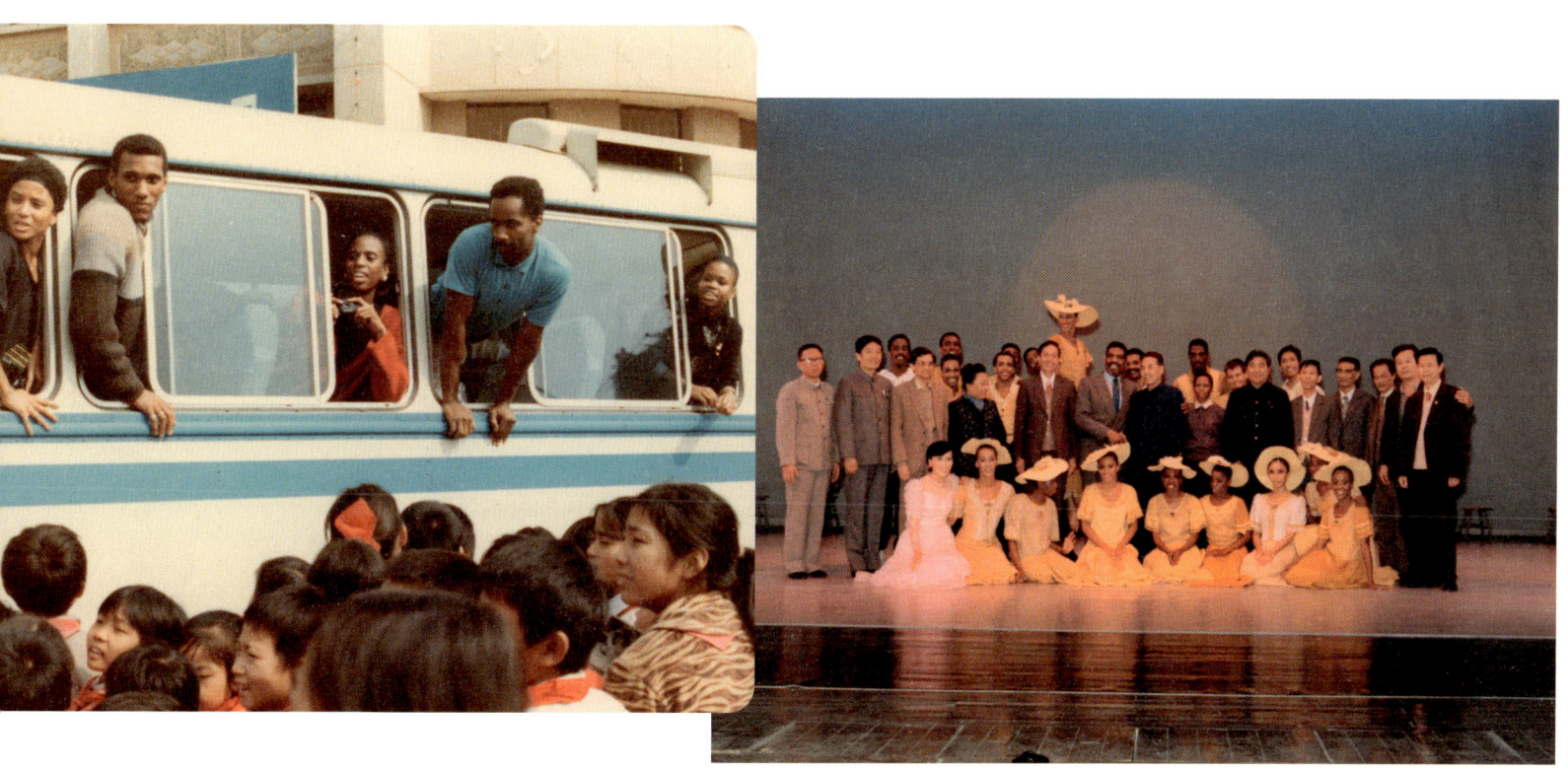

Ailey company dancers on a tour bus, China, 1985

Ailey (standing at center) with company dancers and others, following a performance of *Revelations* in China, 1985

Chronology

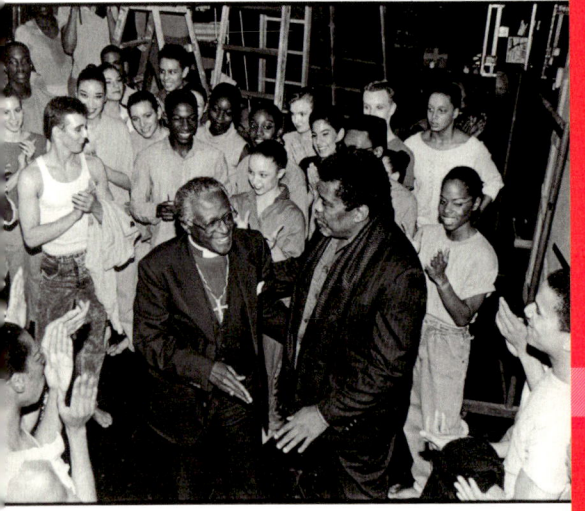
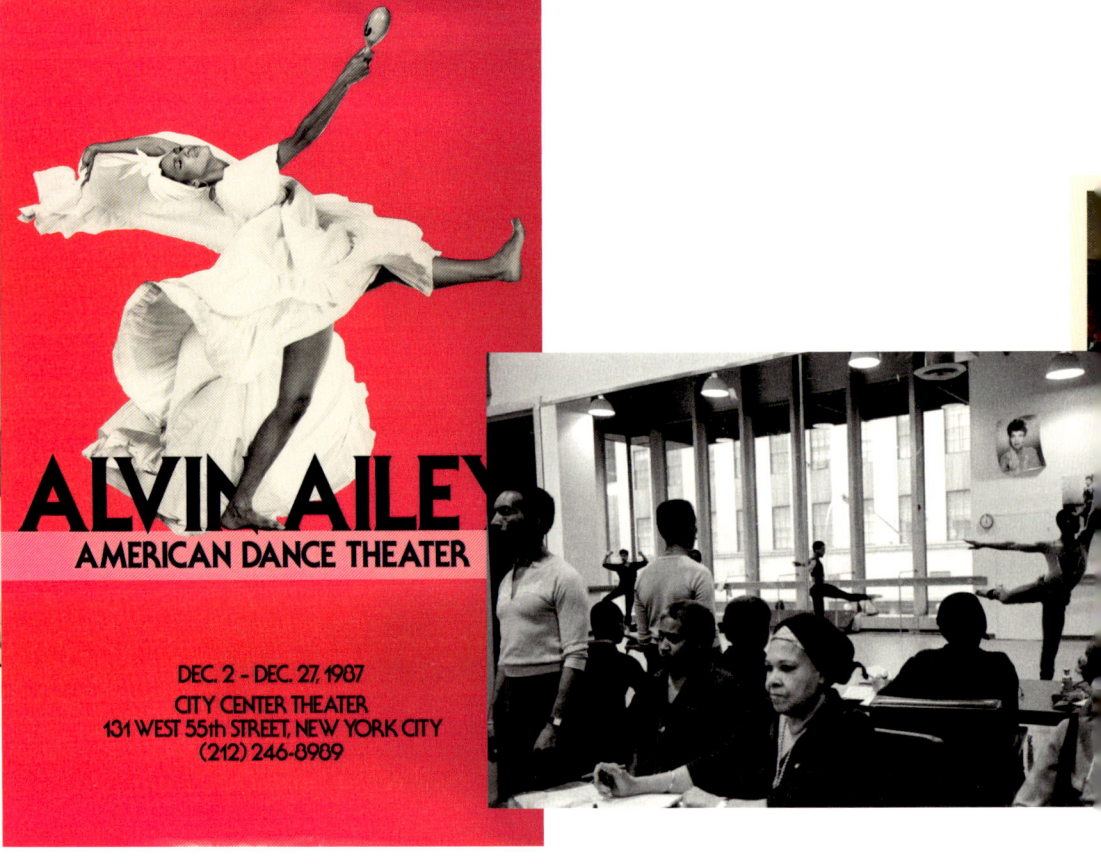

Desmond Tutu and Ailey with Ailey company dancers and students backstage at City Center, New York, ca. 1985

Poster with company dancer April Berry advertising the Ailey company's winter season at City Center, featuring *The Magic of Katherine Dunham*, 1987

Dunham (front center) at a rehearsal for *The Magic of Katherine Dunham*, 1987

With Gray's encouragement, Ailey choreographs his next major piece, *For 'Bird'—With Love*, a tribute to the late jazz maestro Charlie "Bird" Parker. Created in honor of the Kansas City Friends of Alvin Ailey and made for Ailey company member Gary DeLoatch, the dance premieres at the Folly Theater in Kansas City.

1985

August: The company tours throughout Australia.

September: Ailey becomes the first choreographer to be awarded a distinguished professorship at City University of New York, where he is tasked with developing a dance major and a high-school dance program at the Borough of Manhattan Community College.

October 18: Ailey's *Blues Suite* is featured alongside Bill T. Jones's *Fever Swamp* and McKayle's *Rainbow Round My Shoulder* in the PBS television special *Three by Three*, part of the network's *Dance in America* series.

November: The company is the first modern dance troupe to embark on a government-sponsored tour of China, with the support of the United States Information Agency. They perform in ten cities and teach classes at the Beijing Dance Academy.

The Philip Morris company offers the Ailey company a $300,000 grant, which underwrites their national and international touring for the next two years.

1986

January: Ailey travels to Copenhagen to work with the Royal Danish Ballet, for whom he restages his piece *The River* and choreographs *Caverna Magica*, a commissioned group dance. While in Denmark, he also creates *Witness*, a solo for senior ballerina Mette Hønningen. The work has its US premiere in Kansas City later in the year.

Ailey is acting temperamentally, in part because he is not taking his prescribed medication for bipolar disorder. The company is dealing with internal tensions due to infighting and the unclear delegation of roles.

Spring: The company goes on a three-week tour of Hong Kong and Japan.

November–December: The company withdraws from its fundraising efforts to convert 890 Broadway, their shared headquarters with the Feld Ballet and the American Ballet Theatre, into a nonprofit dance space.

November 13: Ailey premieres *Survivors*, a tribute to Nelson and Winnie Mandela that he co-choreographed with Mary Barnett, in Kansas City. The dance debuts in New York a month later.

December 4: The annual Ailey gala, chaired this year by Harry Belafonte and his wife, Julie, marks the start of the company's City Center engagement.

1987

Ailey co-produces and introduces the video series *Conversations on Black Dance: Black Choreographers in Film, Video, Broadway*.

Ailey starts practicing Buddhism.

May 17: Ailey receives an honorary degree from the C. W. Post Campus of Long Island University.

June 7: Ailey is given the Samuel H. Scripps American Dance Festival Award at the American Dance Festival in Durham, North Carolina, which includes a $25,000 prize. As the recipient of modern dance's greatest honor, Ailey recognizes that he has entered the pantheon of American modern dance.

Fall: Ailey reunites with many former Horton dancers in Los Angeles.

December 2: Although preparations for the program proved difficult and tense, the Ailey company produces *The Magic of Katherine Dunham*, a tribute to the eponymous choreographer. Premiering at the company's opening night gala at City Center, the program is composed of Dunham's dances between 1937 and 1950, including her hallmark works *Barrelhouse*, *Choros*, *L'Ag'Ya*, and *Shango*—all influential works for Ailey.

1988

Ailey begins a series of interviews with journalist A. Peter Bailey, that will later serve as the basis for his posthumous autobiography, *Revelations* (1995).

March 29: Ailey premieres *La Dea della Acqua* for La Scala Opera Ballet in Milan.

Early August: Ailey is announced as one of five artists to receive the year's Kennedy Center Honors. The gala, held on December 4, includes a reception at the White House hosted by President Ronald Reagan.

December 9: The Ailey company, in its thirtieth year, debuts Ailey's last work, *Opus McShann*, set to music by the American jazz artist Jay McShann.

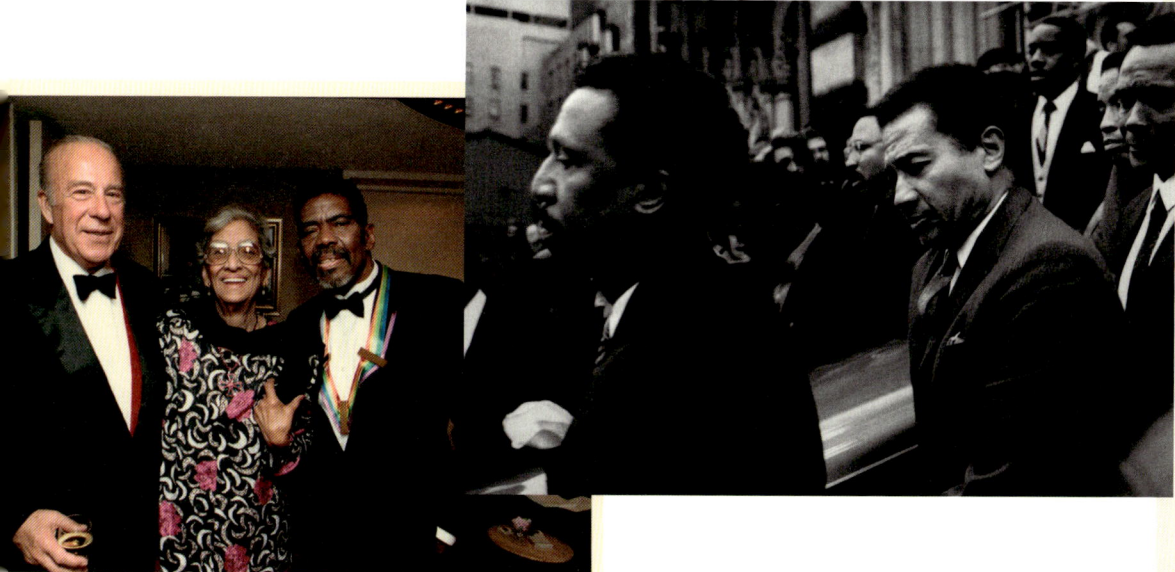

From left: US Secretary of State George Shultz, Lula Cooper, and Ailey at the Kennedy Center Honors, Washington, DC, December 4, 1988

Ming Smith, *Farewell to Alvin Ailey*, New York, 1989

Cover of program for Ailey's funeral service at the First Baptist Church of Artesia, 1989

December 13: Ailey, who is becoming increasingly ill, is awarded the Handel Medallion, New York City's highest cultural honor.

December 17: Ailey is admitted to Lenox Hill Hospital, where it is confirmed that he is HIV positive. While Ailey is hospitalized, the company makes temporary changes in leadership and to its schedule.

1989

February 3: Ailey is released from the hospital and takes a partial leave of absence from the company, appearing in Paris for *La danse en Révolution*, a program in honor of the French Revolution, in July.

June: Ailey travels to Port-au-Prince, Haiti, for a birthday party for Dunham.

The Kansas City Friends of Alvin Ailey initiate AileyCamp, which provides children in need with guidance and opportunities to explore their creativity. Ailey travels to Kansas City and makes a surprise appearance at the last performance of the camp session, much to the enthusiasm of the audience.

August 31: Ailey resigns as distinguished professor at the Borough of Manhattan Community College.

September: Ailey is readmitted to Lenox Hill. His mother comes to take care of him, and visitors are gradually welcomed.

November: Ailey's condition deteriorates, and he slips into a coma.

The company moves into its new, eighteen-thousand-square-foot headquarters at 211 West Sixty-First Street.

December 1: Ailey dies, with his mother, Chaya, Jamison, Waters, physician Albert Knapp, and nurse Anne McKnight by his side.

At the press conference announcing the death, Dr. Knapp states that Ailey died of terminal blood dyscrasia, following Ailey's wishes that AIDS not be mentioned. At television producer Ellis Haizlip's request, Waters plans Ailey's memorial service at the Cathedral of Saint John the Divine in Manhattan.

December 8: More than forty-five-hundred people attend Ailey's memorial service in New York. Ailey's body is then flown to Los Angeles for a service at the First Baptist Church of Artesia.

December 13: Ailey is buried at Rose Hills Memorial Park in Whittier, California.

1996

New York Times dance critic Jennifer Dunning publishes the biography *Alvin Ailey: A Life in Dance*.

1997

Thomas DeFrantz completes his dissertation "'Revelations'": The Choreographies of Alvin Ailey" for New York University's performance studies program. He would rework and expand upon his thesis, publishing *Dancing Revelations: Alvin Ailey's Embodiment of African American Culture*, the first scholarly book on Ailey, in 2006.

2001

The Ailey company, under the artistic direction of Jamison, is awarded the National Medal of Arts, becoming the first dance company to receive it.

2008

July 15: In commemoration of the Ailey company's fiftieth anniversary, the US Congress passes House Resolution 1088, recognizing the Alvin Ailey American Dance Theater as a "vital American cultural ambassador to the world."[13]

2014

November 24: President Barack Obama posthumously awards Ailey with the Presidential Medal of Freedom.

NOTES

The information in this chronology is largely drawn from Jennifer Dunning's *Alvin Ailey: A Life in Dance* (1996) and Thomas F. DeFrantz's *Dancing Revelations: Alvin Ailey's Embodiment of African American Culture* (2004) as well as newspapers and periodicals published during Ailey's lifetime.

1. Jennifer Dunning, *Alvin Ailey: A Life in Dance* (Reading, MA: Addison-Wesley, 1996), 11.
2. Dunning, 19.
3. Dorene Richardson, quoted in Dunning, 101.
4. Dunning, 128.
5. Alvin Ailey, quoted in "1958," History, Alvin Ailey American Dance Theater (website), accessed March 5, 2024, https://www.alvinailey.org/history/history-1958.
6. The program is illustrated at "1960," History, Alvin Ailey American Dance Theater (website), accessed March 5, 2024, https://www.alvinailey.org/about/history?page=1.
7. Ailey, quoted in the *South China Post Herald*, March 1962; cited in Dunning, *Alvin Ailey*, 161–62.
8. Dunning, *Alvin Ailey*, 165.
9. Ernestine Stodelle, "Paul Draper, Alvin Ailey Score at School of Dance," *The Day* (New London, CT), July 23, 1962.
10. Dunning, *Alvin Ailey*, 179.
11. Clive Barnes, "The Dance: Judith Jamison's Triumph," *New York Times*, May 5, 1971.
12. Anna Kisselgoff, "Dance: Ailey 'Phases' Set to Jazz Music," *New York Times*, December 7, 1980.
13. Recognizing and Commending the Alvin Ailey American Dance Theater for Fifty Years of Service as a Vital American Cultural Ambassador to the World, H.R. 1088, 110th Cong. (2008).

CHOREOGRAPHY

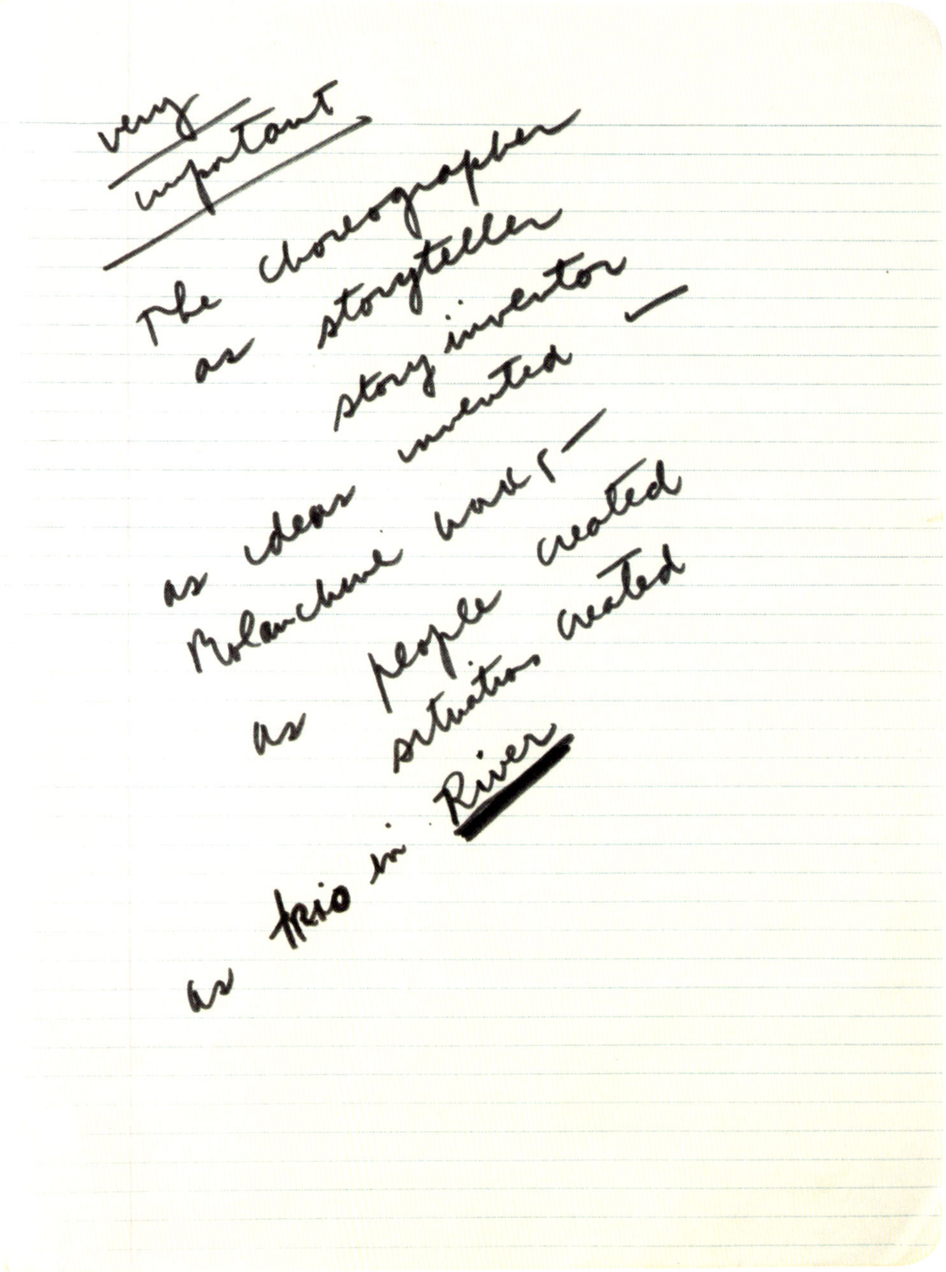

very important

The choreographer
as storyteller
   story inventor
as ideas invented —
   Balanchine ballets —
as people created
   situations created
as trio in **River**

Alvin Ailey once said, "I have always just done choreography out of my feelings, out of a reaction to music, out of a life situation, out of some need." His process of making dances was often intuitive, improvisational, and individualized as a result, never adhering to a single formula, subject, or structure. As Ailey's notebooks, rehearsals, and other dancers' stories disclose, dancing was not solely about finessing pose or perfecting gesture. Of equal importance to him was revealing the person behind the performer, with movement as their very means of illumination. If choreography was a matter of expression and a medium of experience, Ailey cast its conditions through the specificities of Black life, the virtuosic rigors of technique, and the evocation of history, myth, memory, and feeling. This understanding forms a key context for the sheer number of dances that Ailey made and their plurality of style, narrative, and technique. While many people are familiar with *Blues Suite, Cry, Revelations*, and other classics of the Alvin Ailey American Dance Theater (AAADT), a broader view of Ailey's choreography reveals a surprising range, an explorative and experimental spirit, and a sustained record of risk-taking. Although Ailey created the majority of his works for his own company, he also choreographed dances for other companies, including those of Rebekah Harkness, Lester Horton, and Robert Joffrey; for theater and opera productions; and for television networks in the United States and abroad.

   This section, a dynamic sequence of dance photography, illustrates the works that Ailey choreographed for the AAADT repertory and for other companies and collaborations during his lifetime (1931–1989). Only works that officially premiered have been included. The works are listed in chronological order by premiere date, with pieces that debuted on the same date arranged alphabetically by title. Premiere dates denote those agreed upon as AAADT company premieres, rather than first appearances or world (or New York) premieres. If a piece premiered outside the company and then entered the AAADT repertory during Ailey's lifetime, both the first and company premieres are noted. If a work is a non-dance piece, the type of work (e.g., opera or play) is indicated in parentheses after the title on the listing on the following pages. Ailey often reworked his dances many times over, and he would occasionally rename them. The evolutions of his dances are not tracked in this section, but name changes are denoted when known (e.g., *La Création du Monde/Creation of the World* and *Cinco Latinos/Redonda*). Those transformations—that is, whether a reworked dance is considered a new creation or a subsequent version—have been left to the discretion of the AAADT.

   The dance works are illustrated when possible; those with no photographic documentation are denoted by an em dash (—) on the listing on the following page. Because all of Ailey's lifetime choreographic contributions are included, some images feature performances by dancers from outside the AAADT. More detailed information, including venues (with names appearing as they were at the time of performances), locations (if known), and a full roster of AAADT dancers during Ailey's lifetime, can be found in the appendix in this volume. If a premiere was not a company premiere, the performing company or dancers are noted in parentheses in the appendix when known.

   This information was gathered from a range of sources, chiefly among them the AAADT, Jennifer Dunning's biography *Alvin Ailey: A Life in Dance* (1996), and Thomas DeFrantz's *Dancing Revelations: Alvin Ailey's Embodiment of African American Culture* (2006). It has been edited and fact-checked with guidance from Dominique Singer and Sylvia Waters.

Works with no available photo documentation are indicated by an em dash (—).

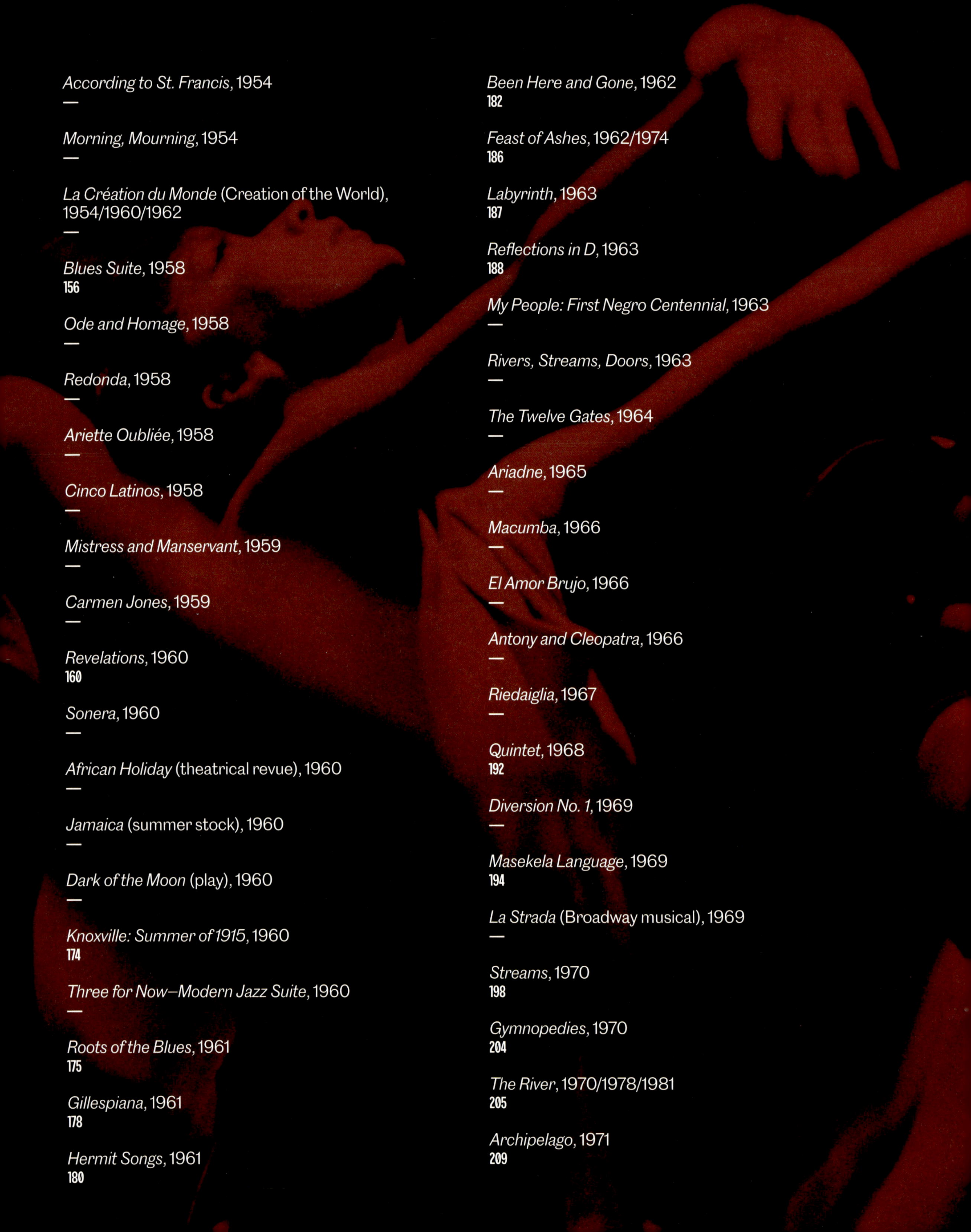

According to St. Francis, 1954
—

Morning, Mourning, 1954
—

La Création du Monde (Creation of the World), 1954/1960/1962
—

Blues Suite, 1958
156

Ode and Homage, 1958
—

Redonda, 1958
—

Ariette Oubliée, 1958
—

Cinco Latinos, 1958
—

Mistress and Manservant, 1959
—

Carmen Jones, 1959
—

Revelations, 1960
160

Sonera, 1960
—

African Holiday (theatrical revue), 1960
—

Jamaica (summer stock), 1960
—

Dark of the Moon (play), 1960
—

Knoxville: Summer of 1915, 1960
174

Three for Now—Modern Jazz Suite, 1960
—

Roots of the Blues, 1961
175

Gillespiana, 1961
178

Hermit Songs, 1961
180

Been Here and Gone, 1962
182

Feast of Ashes, 1962/1974
186

Labyrinth, 1963
187

Reflections in D, 1963
188

My People: First Negro Centennial, 1963
—

Rivers, Streams, Doors, 1963
—

The Twelve Gates, 1964
—

Ariadne, 1965
—

Macumba, 1966
—

El Amor Brujo, 1966
—

Antony and Cleopatra, 1966
—

Riedaiglia, 1967
—

Quintet, 1968
192

Diversion No. 1, 1969
—

Masekela Language, 1969
194

La Strada (Broadway musical), 1969
—

Streams, 1970
198

Gymnopedies, 1970
204

The River, 1970/1978/1981
205

Archipelago, 1971
209

Flowers, 1971
210

Choral Dances, 1971
215

Cry, 1971
216

Mass, 1971
222

The Mingus Dances, 1971
—

Mary Lou's Mass, 1971
224

Myth, 1971
226

Lord Byron (opera), 1972
—

The Lark Ascending, 1972
228

Shaken Angels, 1972
—

Carmen (opera), 1972
—

Sea Change, 1972
—

Love Songs, 1972
231

Four Saints in Three Acts (opera), 1973
232

Hidden Rites, 1973
234

The Blues Ain't (television broadcast), 1974
—

Night Creature (television broadcast), 1974
236

The Mooche (television broadcast), 1974
240

Praise God and Dance (Sacred Concert) (television broadcast), 1974
—

Sonnet for Caesar (television broadcast), 1974
—

Such Sweet Thunder (television broadcast), 1974
—

Night Creature, 1975
—

The Mooche, 1975
—

Black, Brown and Beige, 1976
243

Pas de Duke, 1976
244

Three Black Kings, 1976
246

Passage, 1978
252

Shigaon! Children of the Diaspora, 1978
—

Solo for Mingus, 1979
—

Memoria, 1979
255

Phases, 1980
256

Spell, 1981
258

Landscape, 1981
259

Satyriade, 1982
261

Au Bord du Précipice (Precipice), 1983/1984
262

Escapades, 1983
—

Isba, 1983
264

Can't Slow Down, 1983
—

For 'Bird'—With Love, 1984
266

Caverna Magica, 1986
267

Witness, 1986
270

Survivors, 1986
271

La Dea della Acqua, 1988
—

Opus McShann, 1988
272

Premiere, Kaufmann Concert Hall, 92nd Street Y, New York | **Blues Suite** | 1958

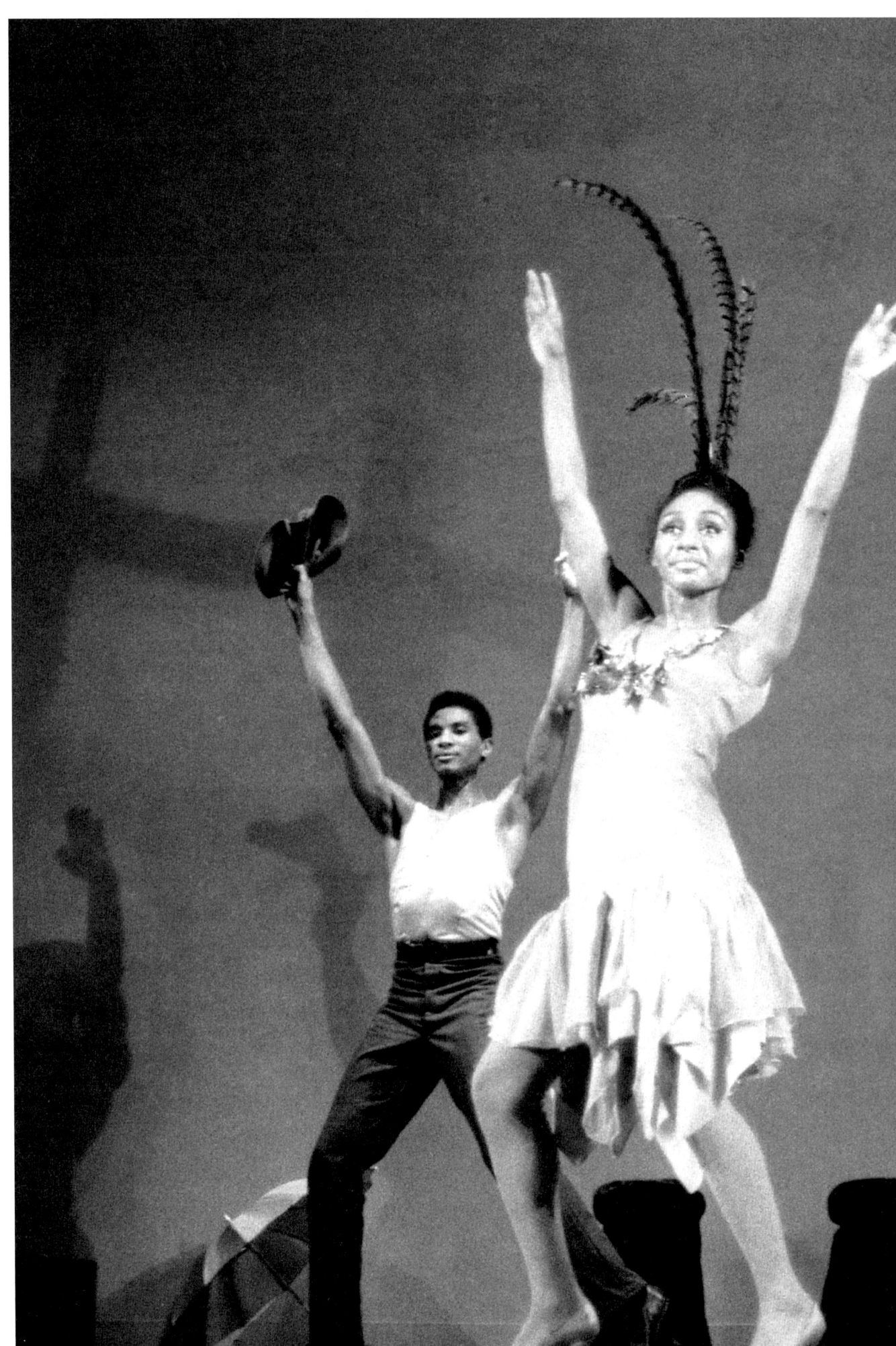

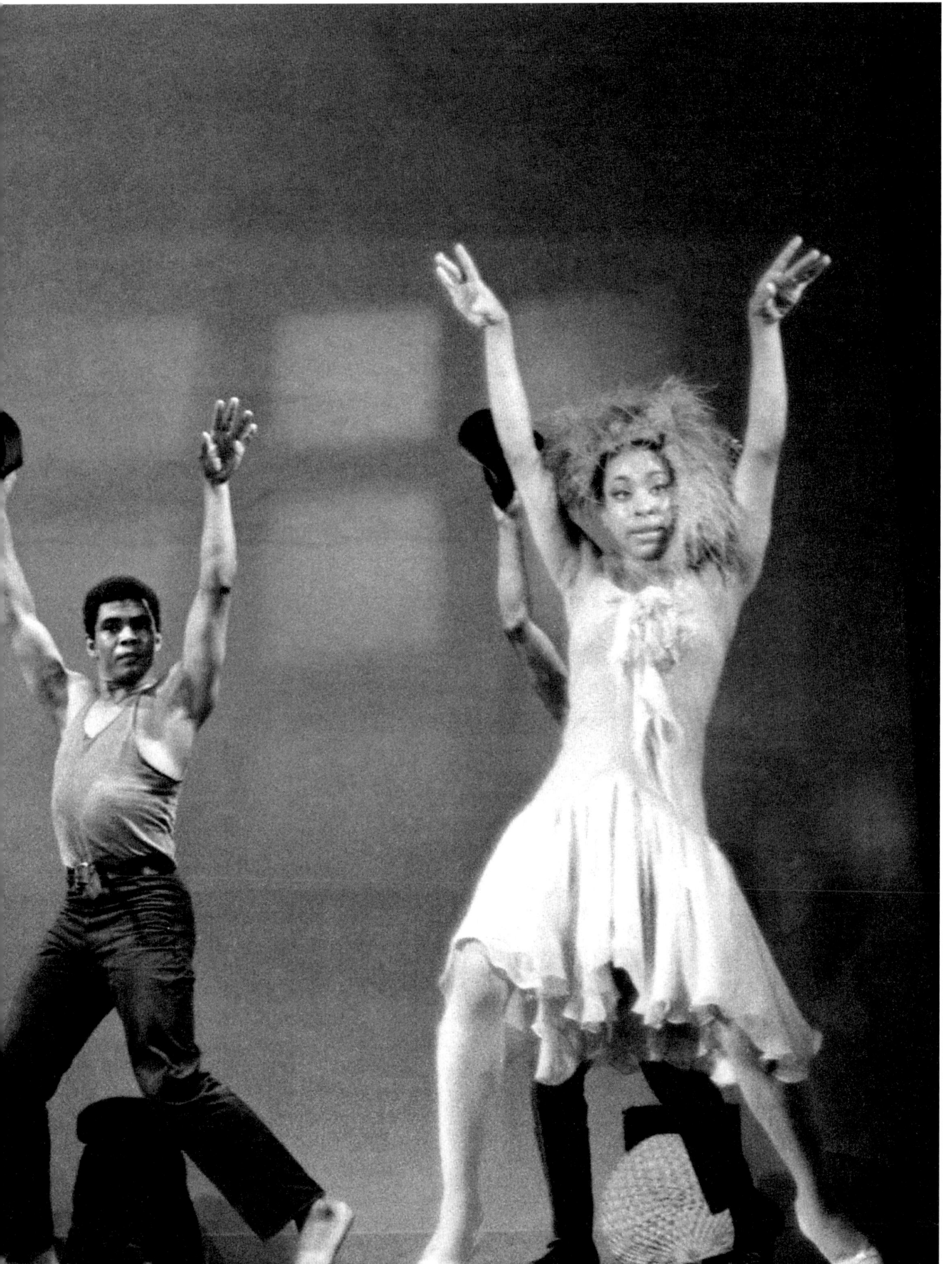

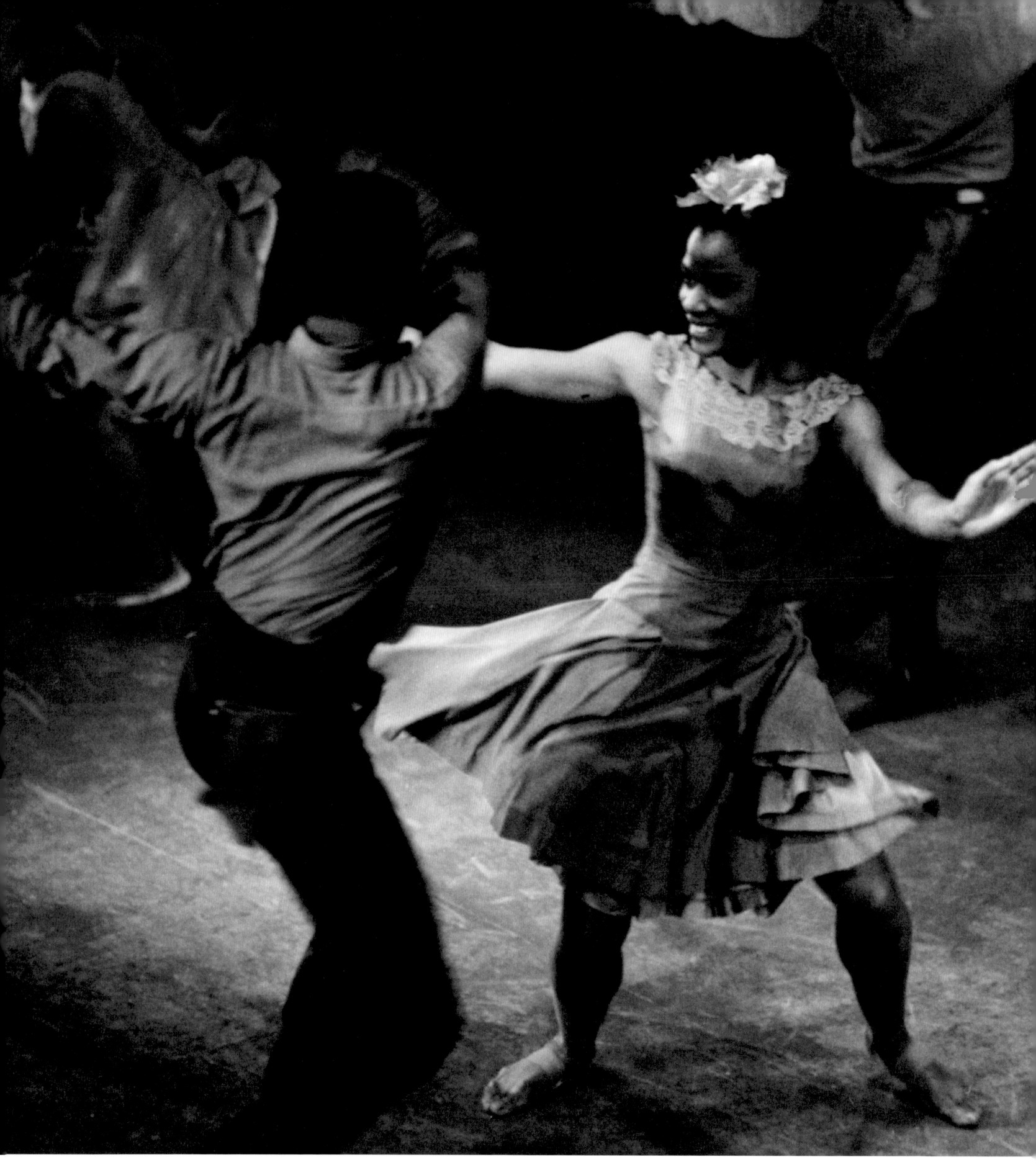
Blues Suite

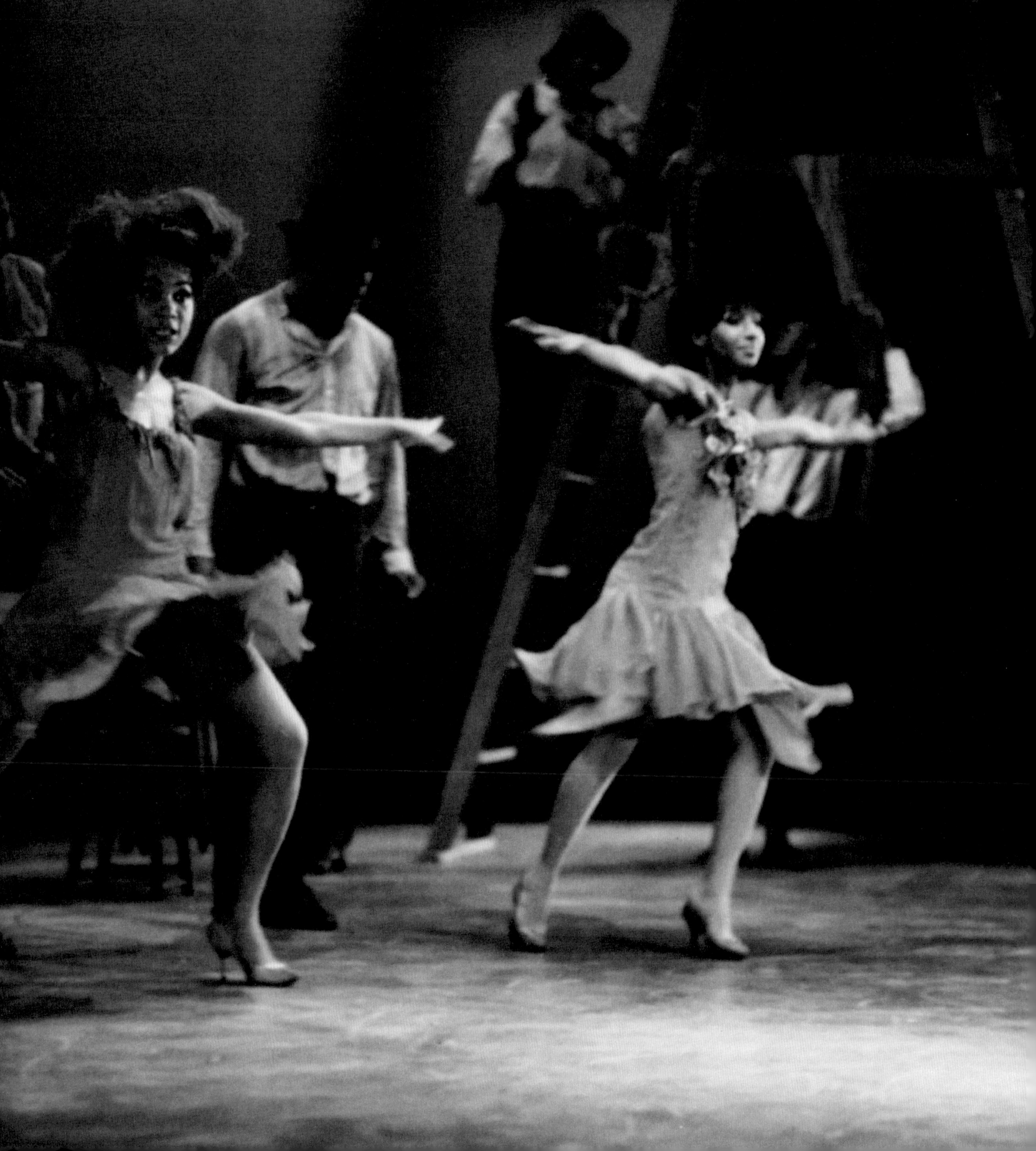

Premiere, Kaufman Concert Hall, 92nd Street Y, New York | **Revelations** | 1960

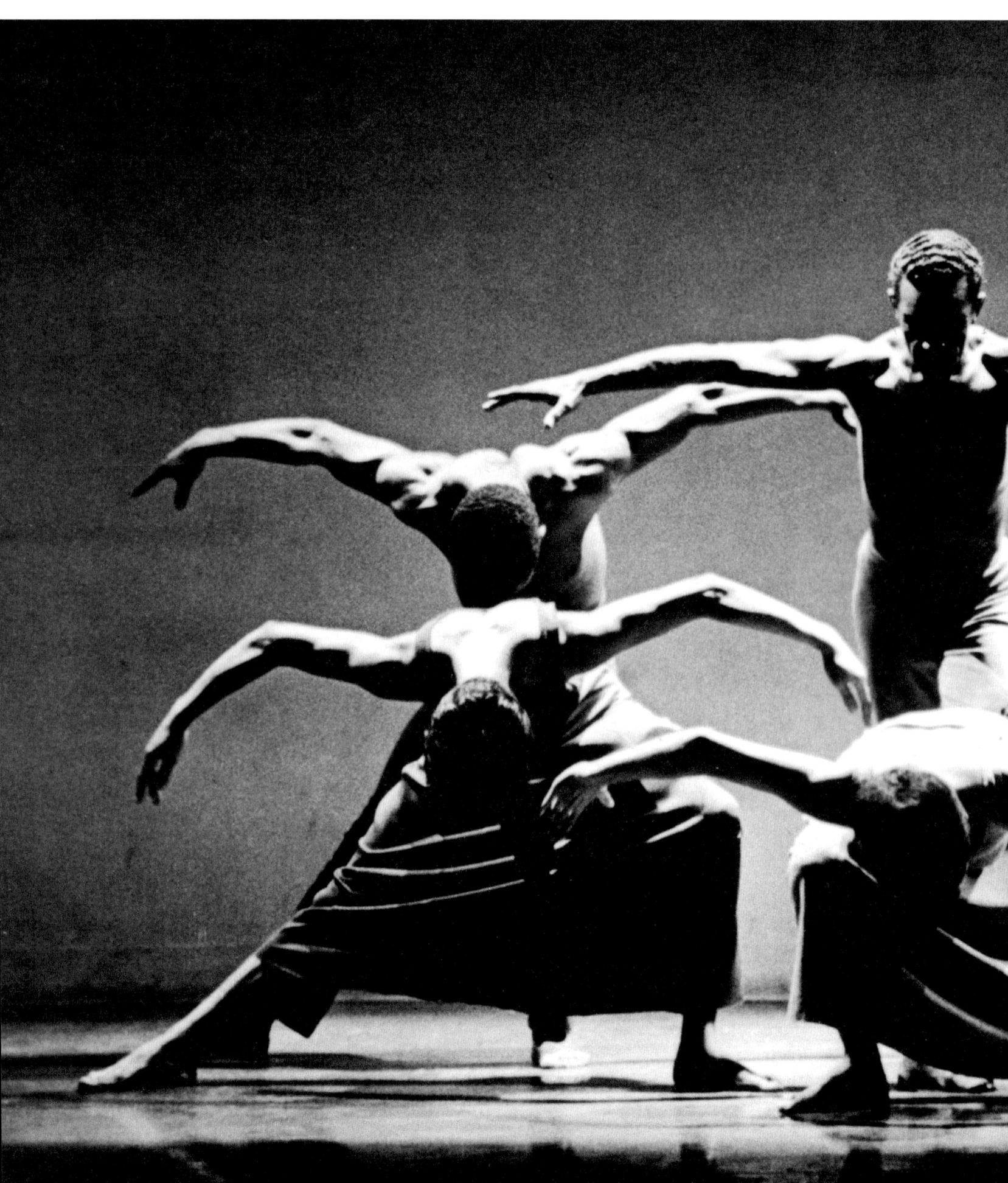

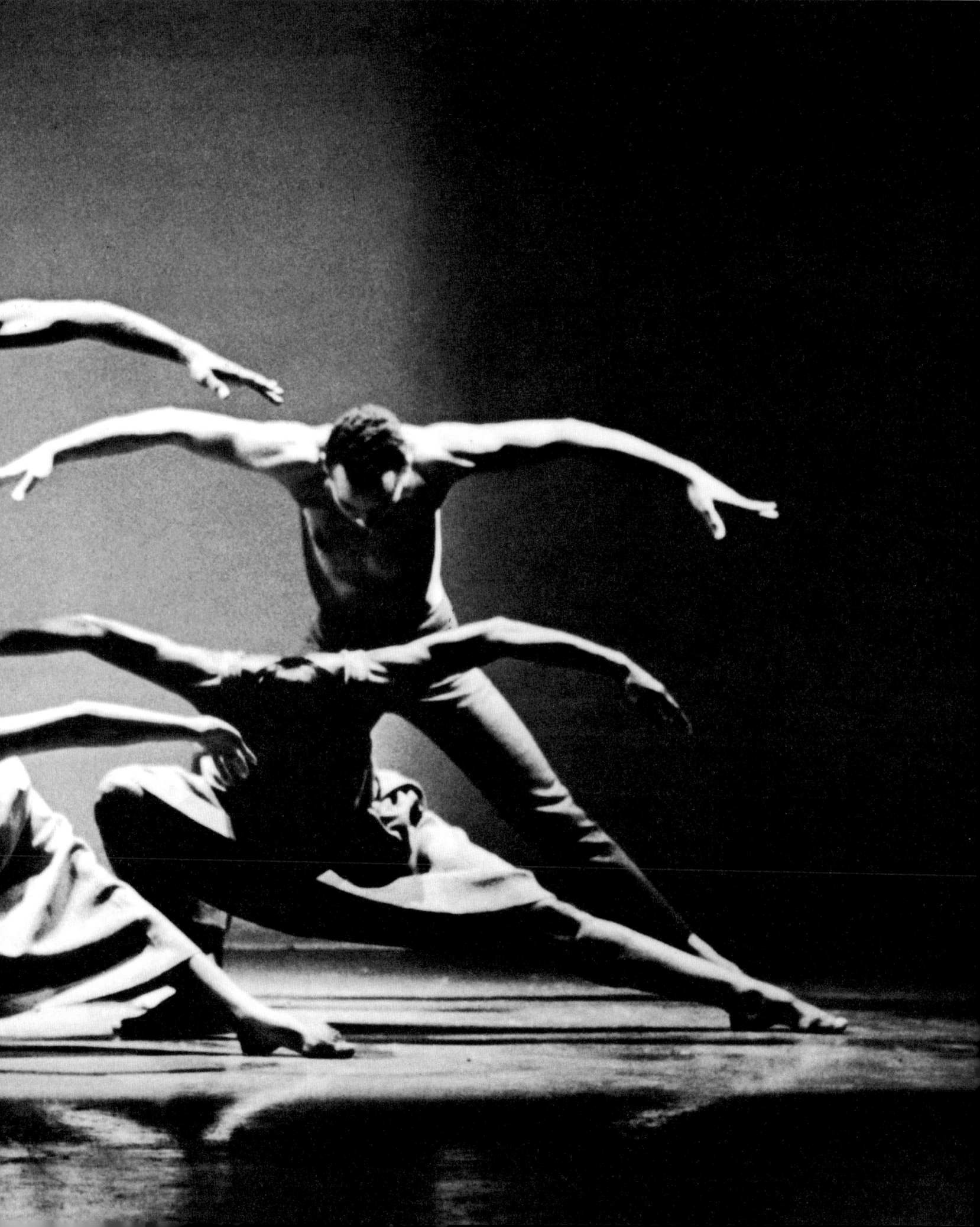

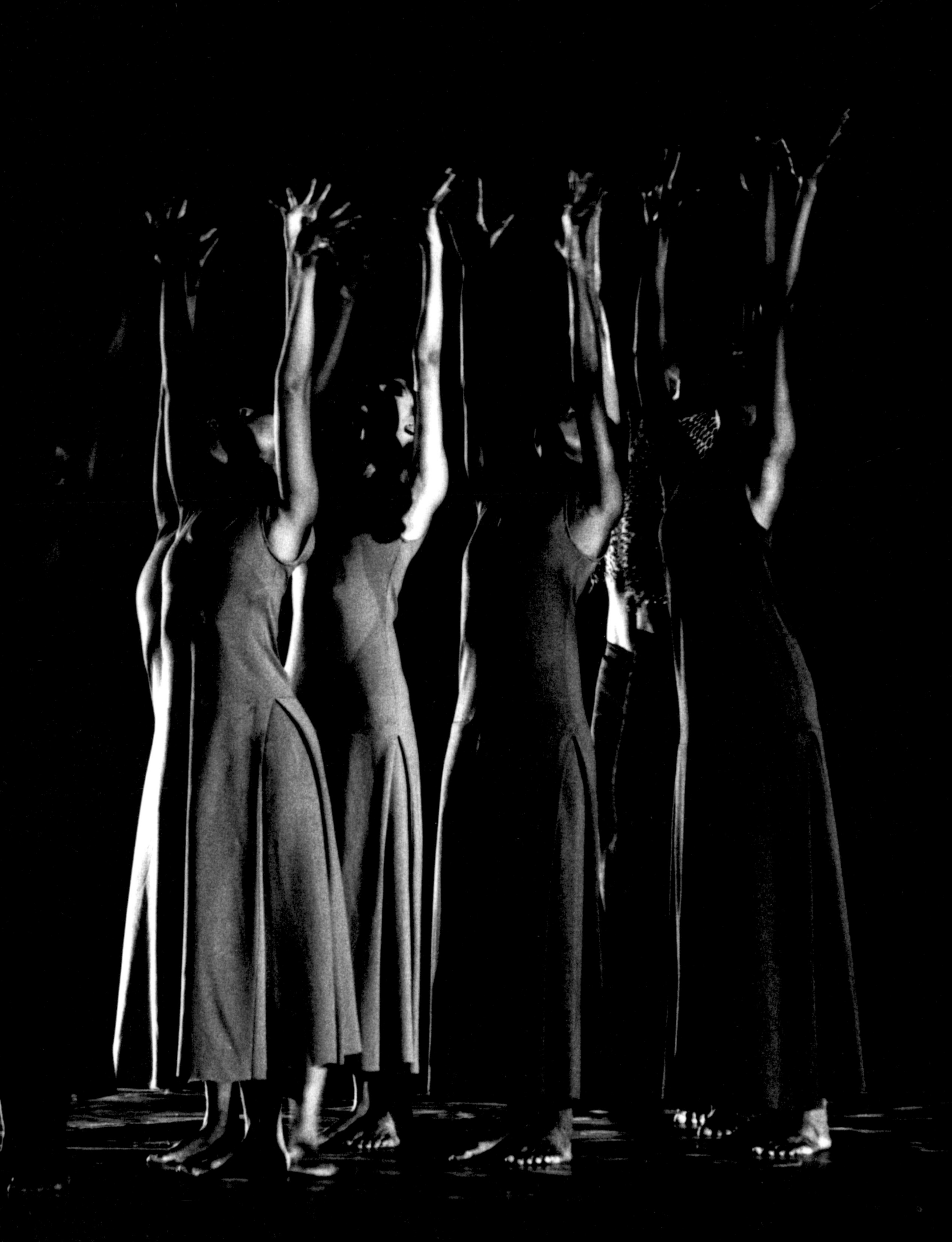

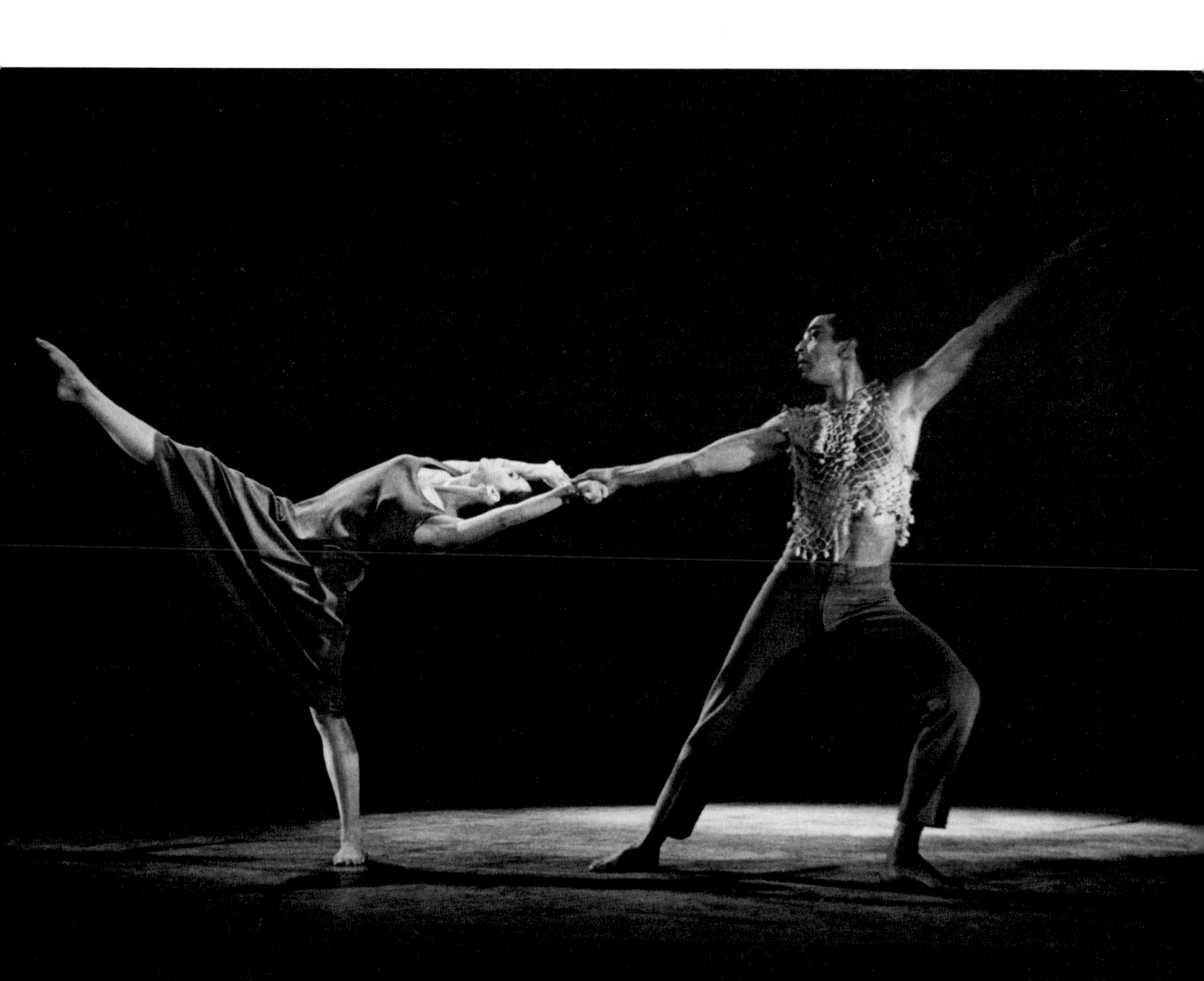

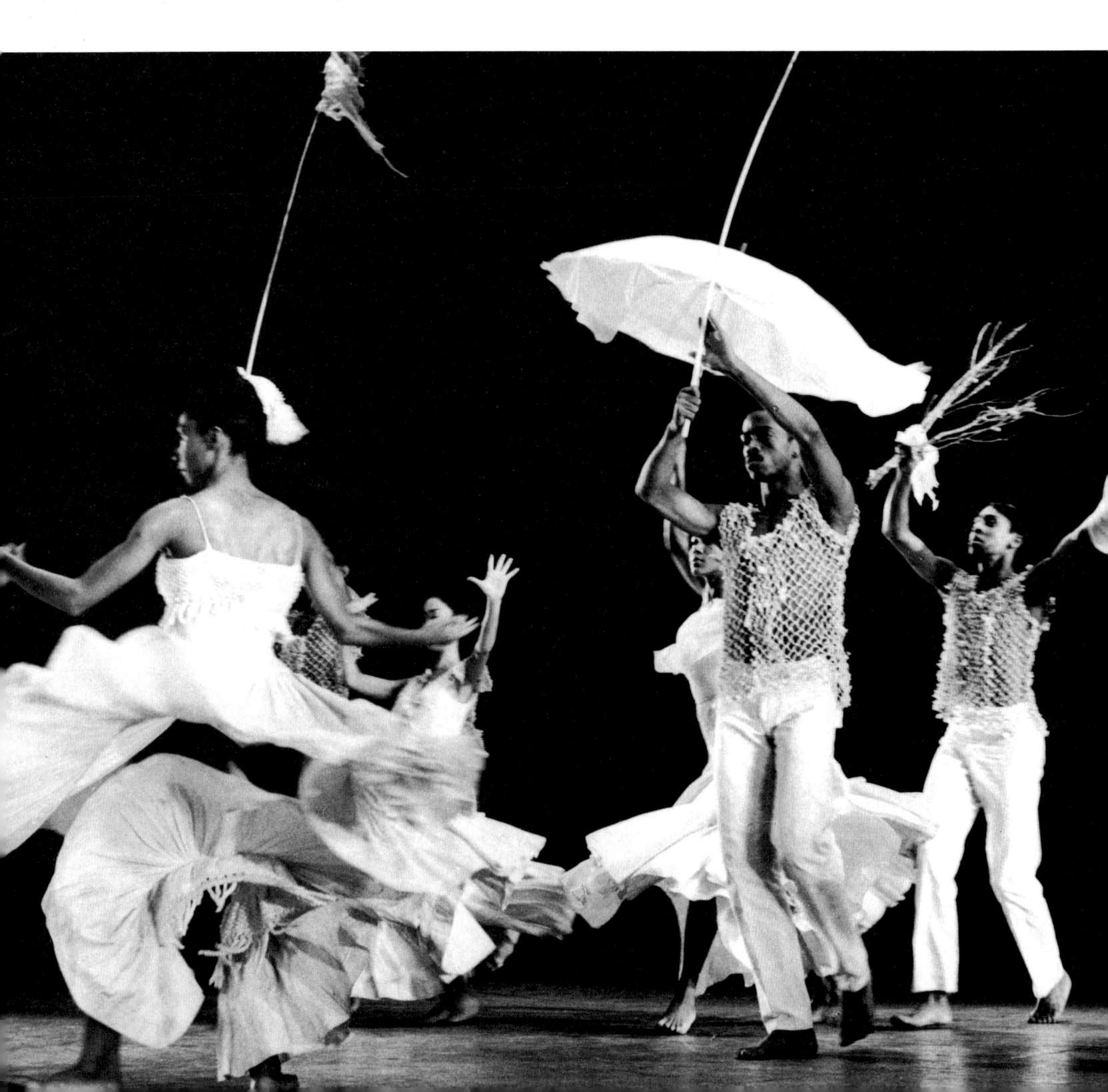

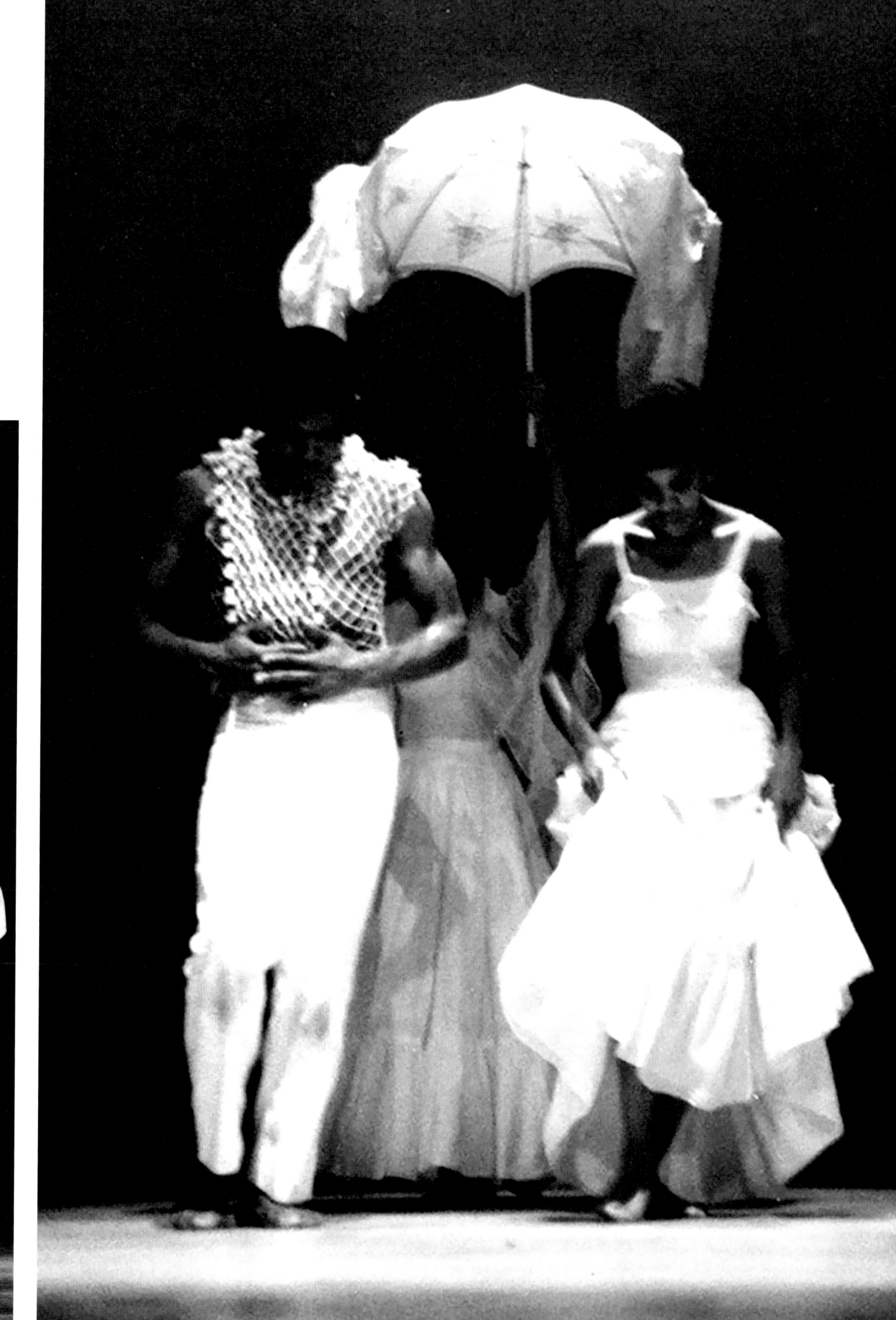

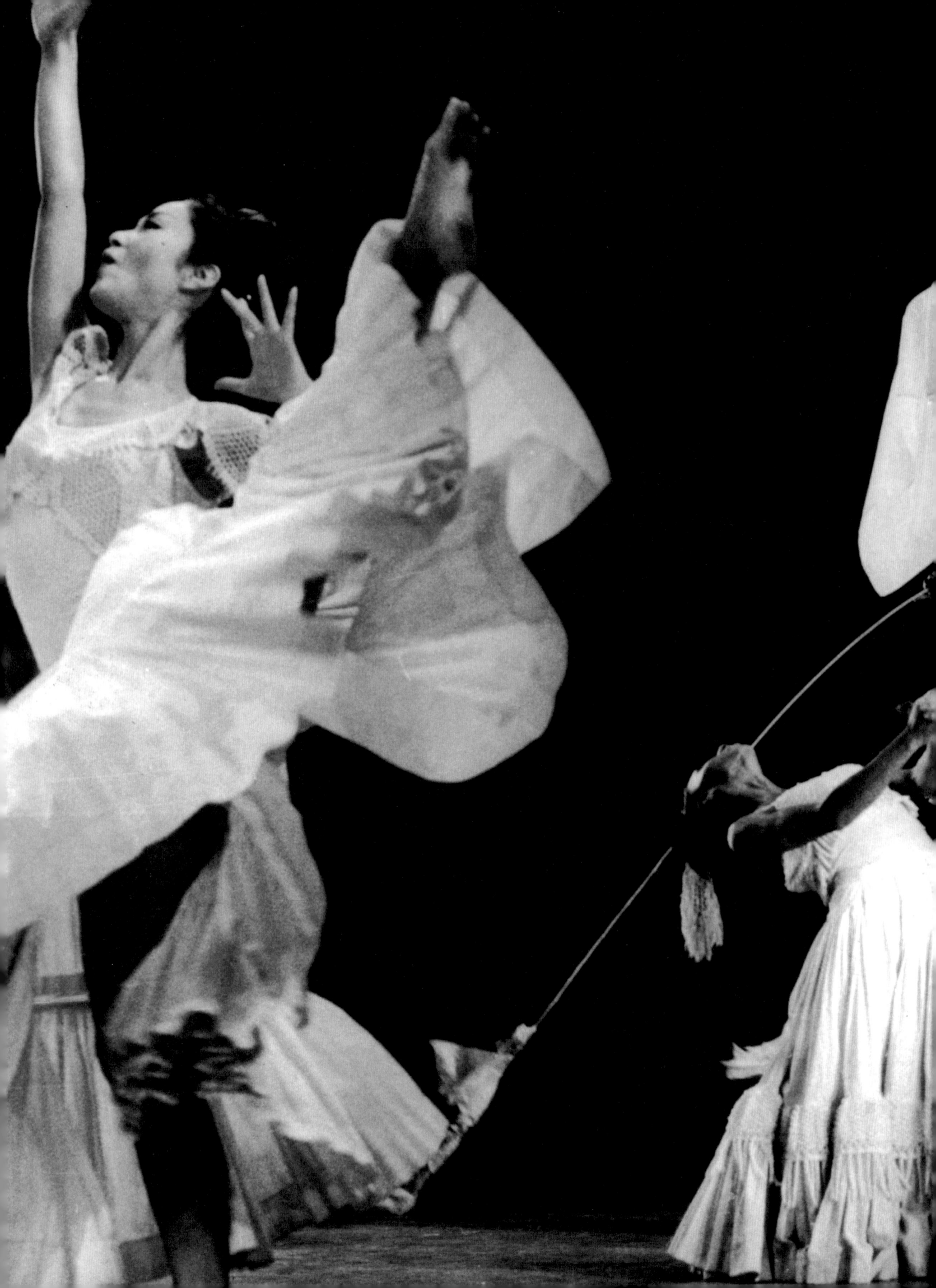

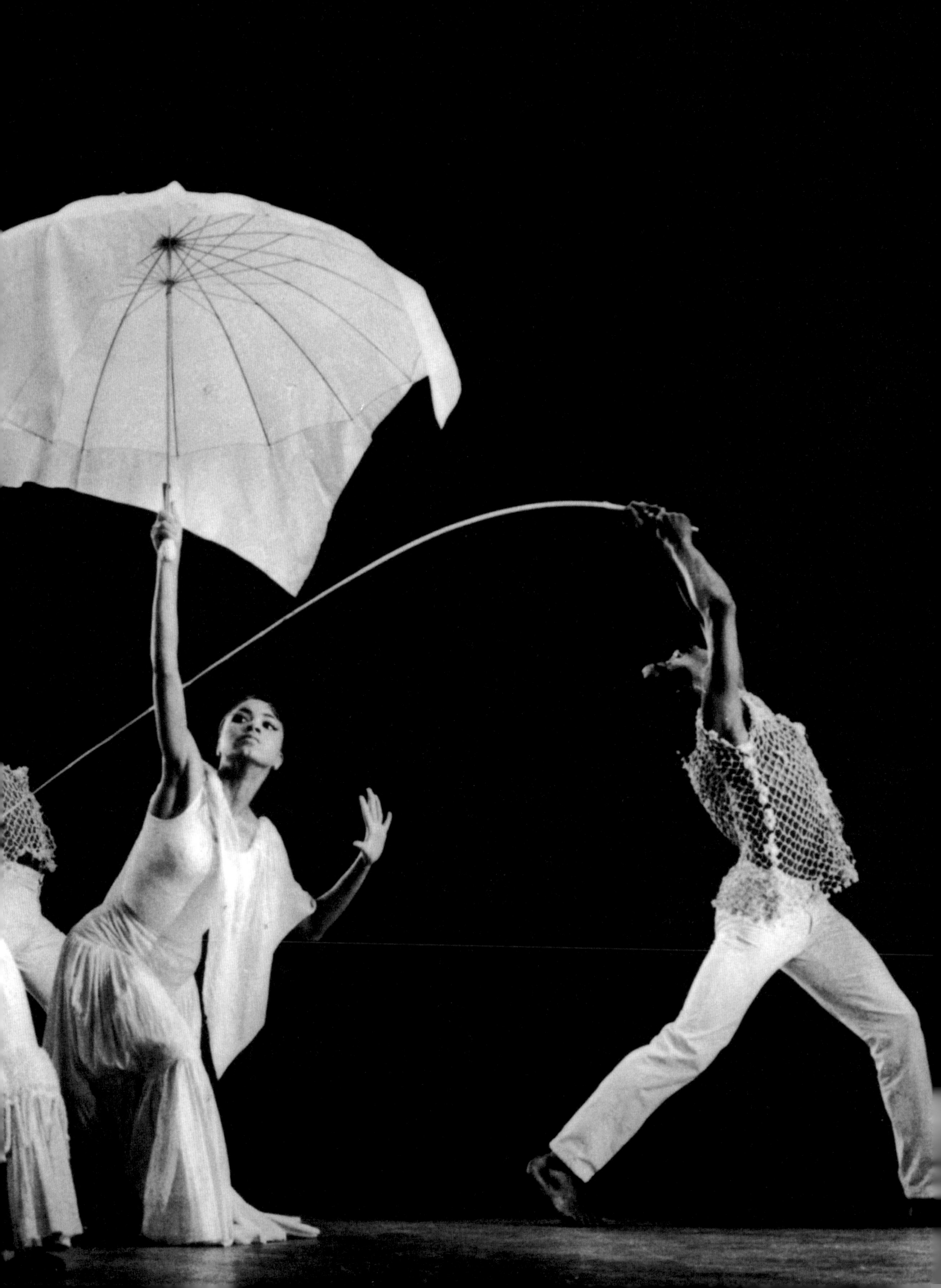

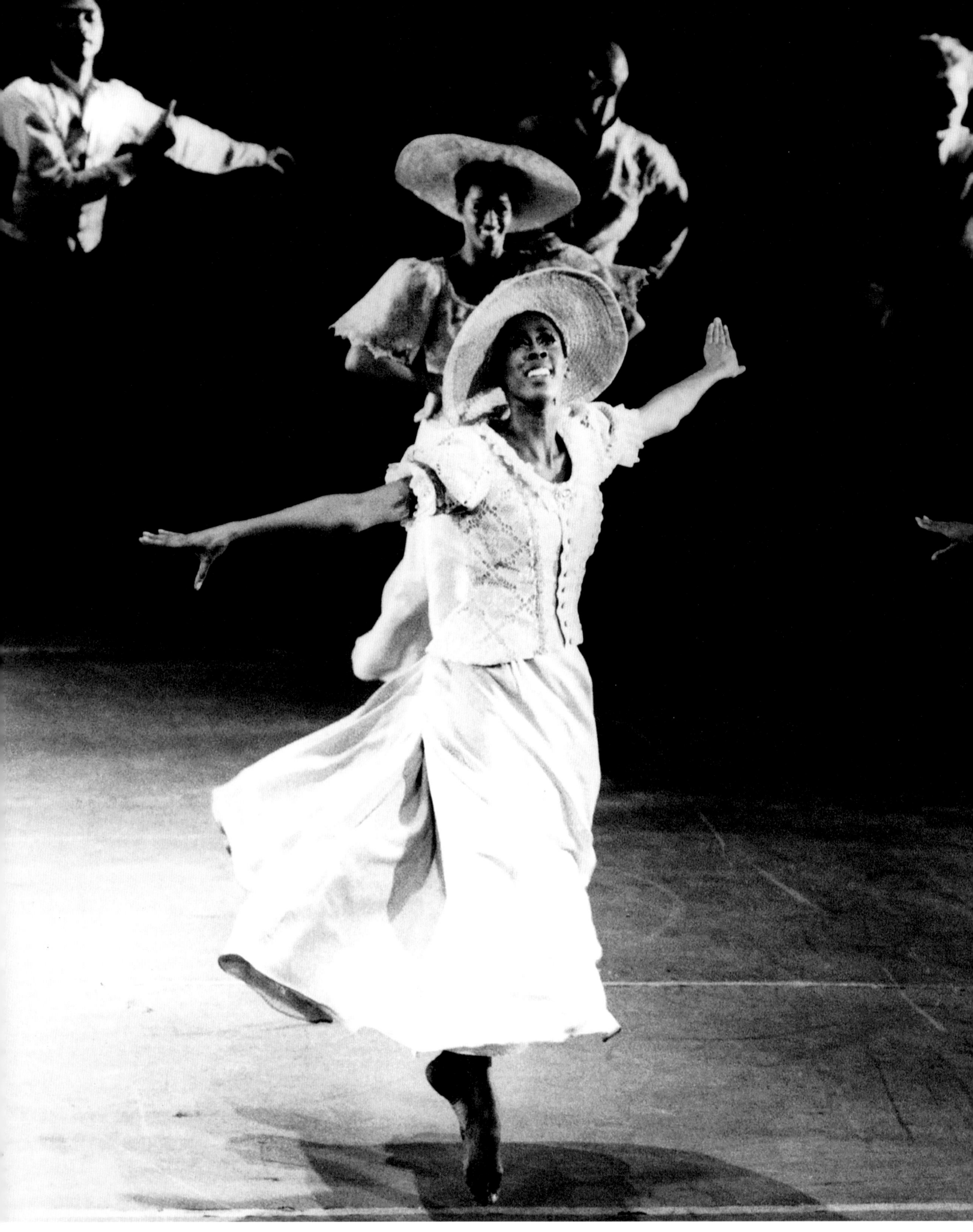

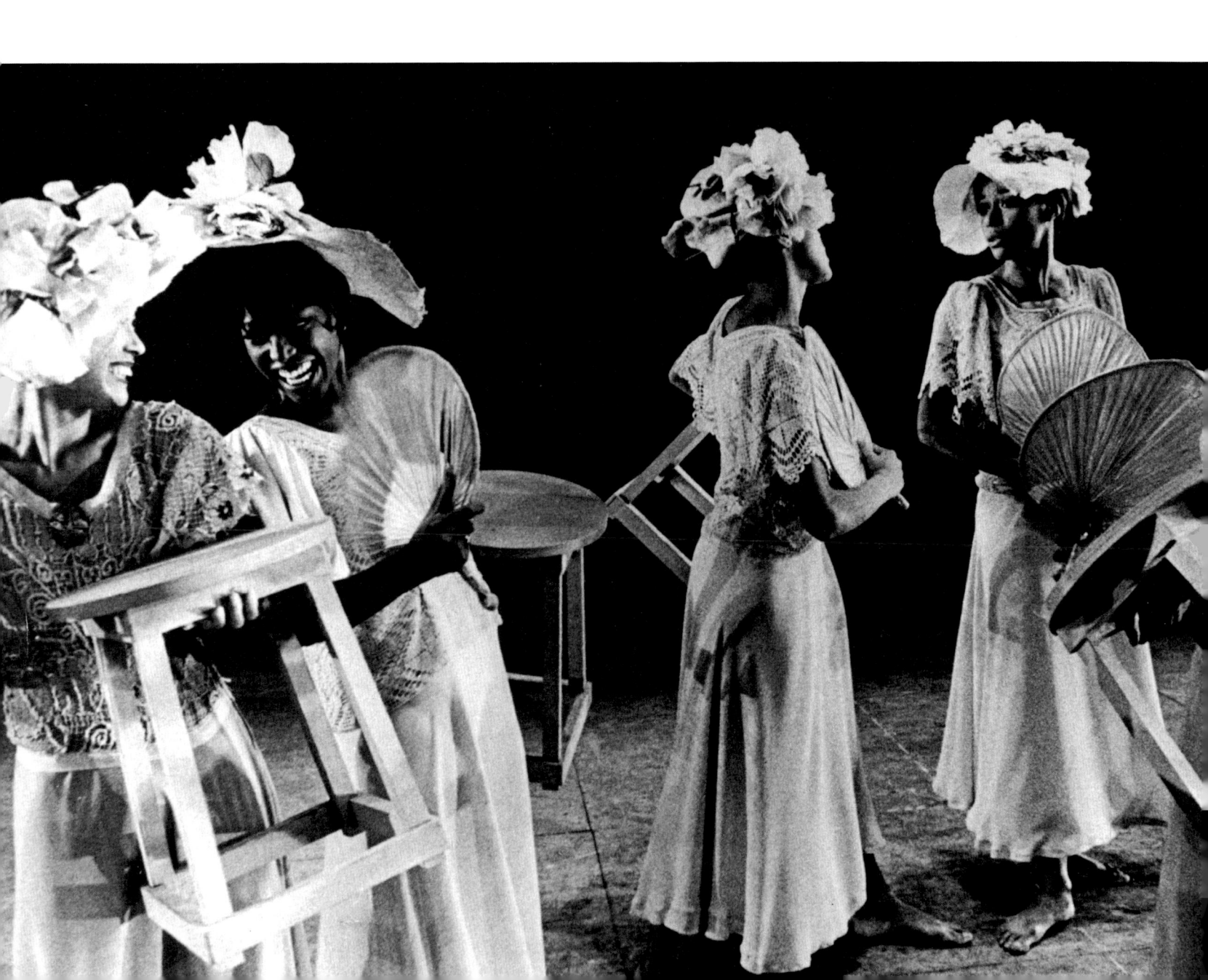

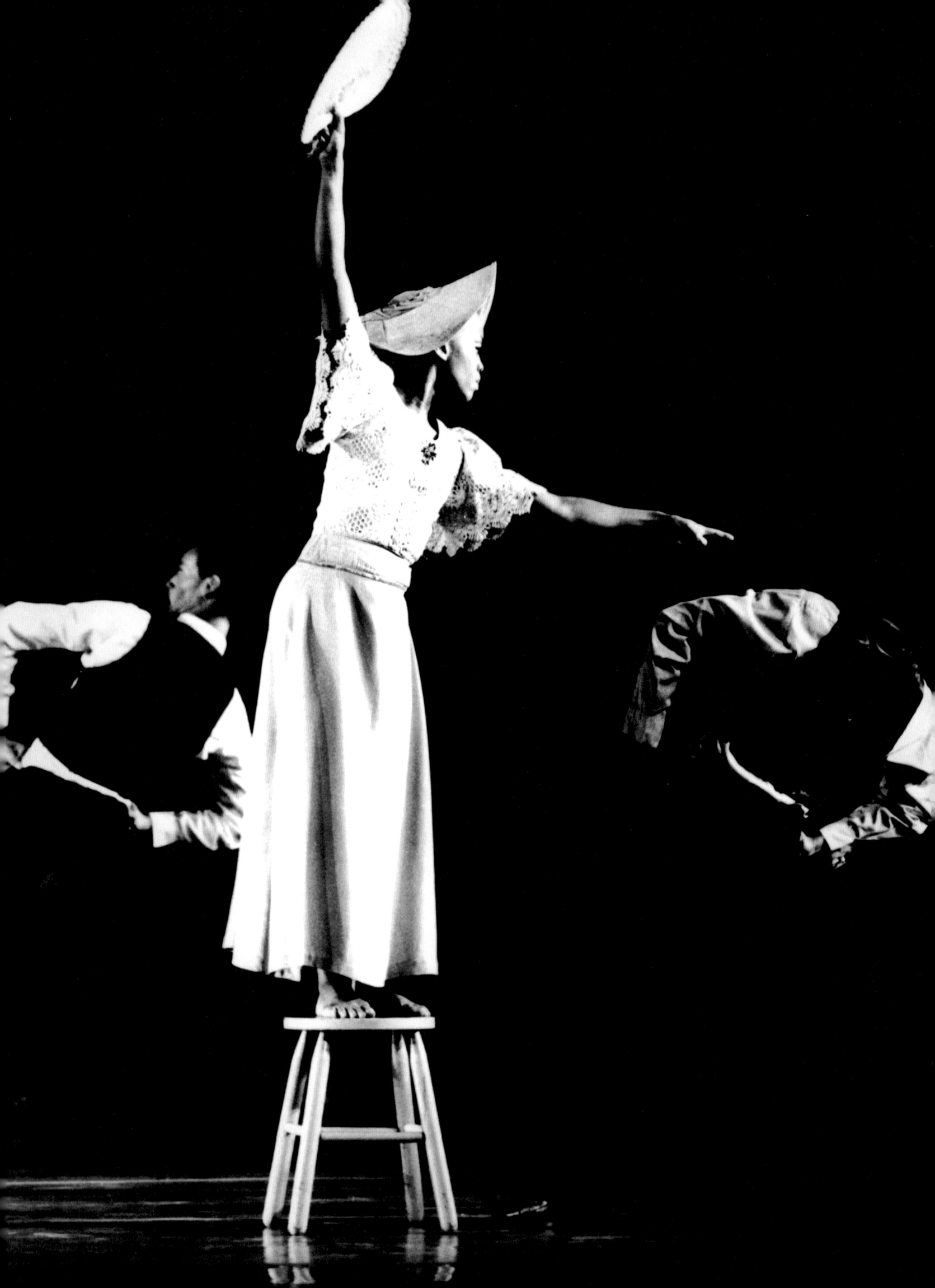

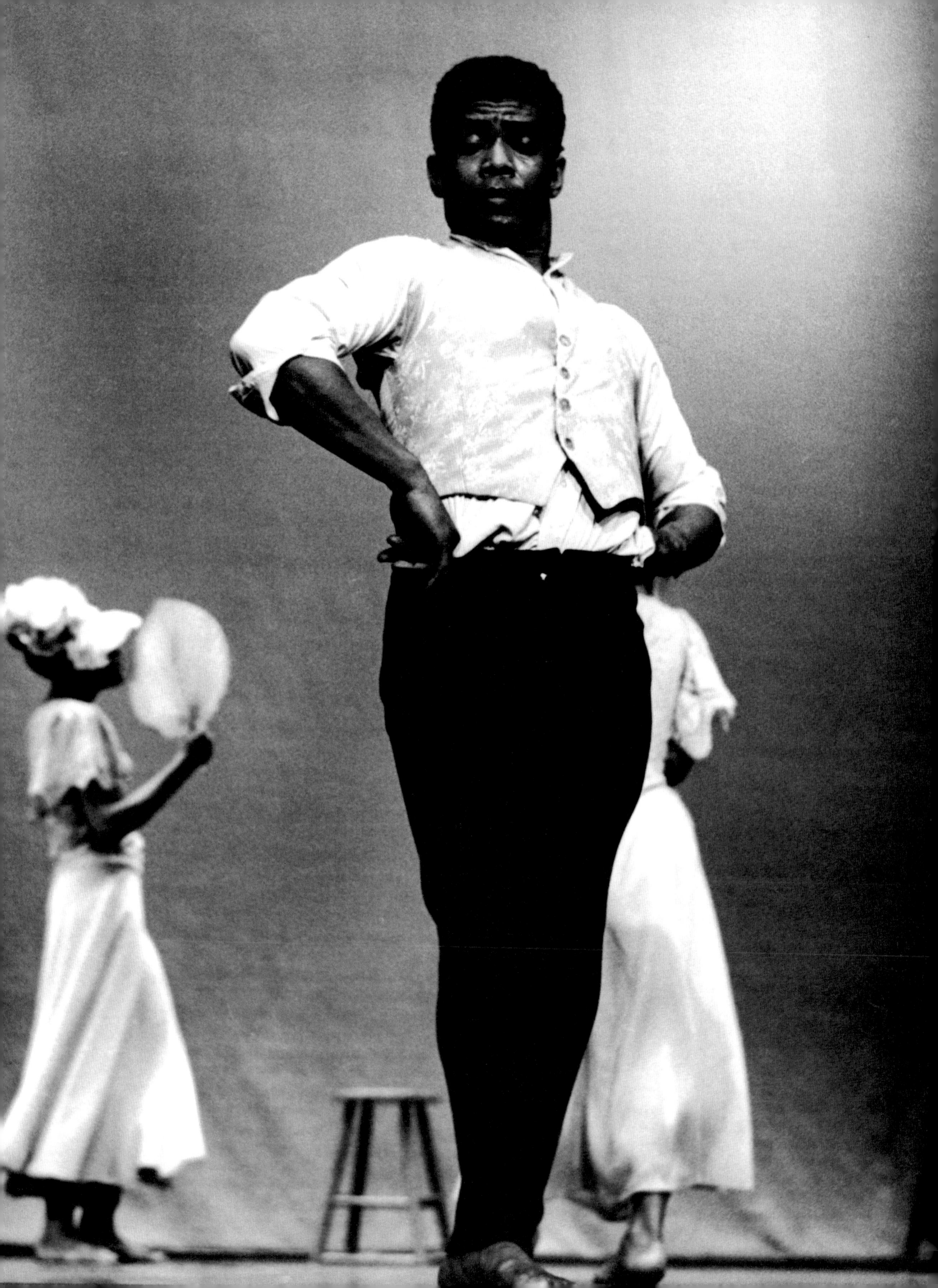

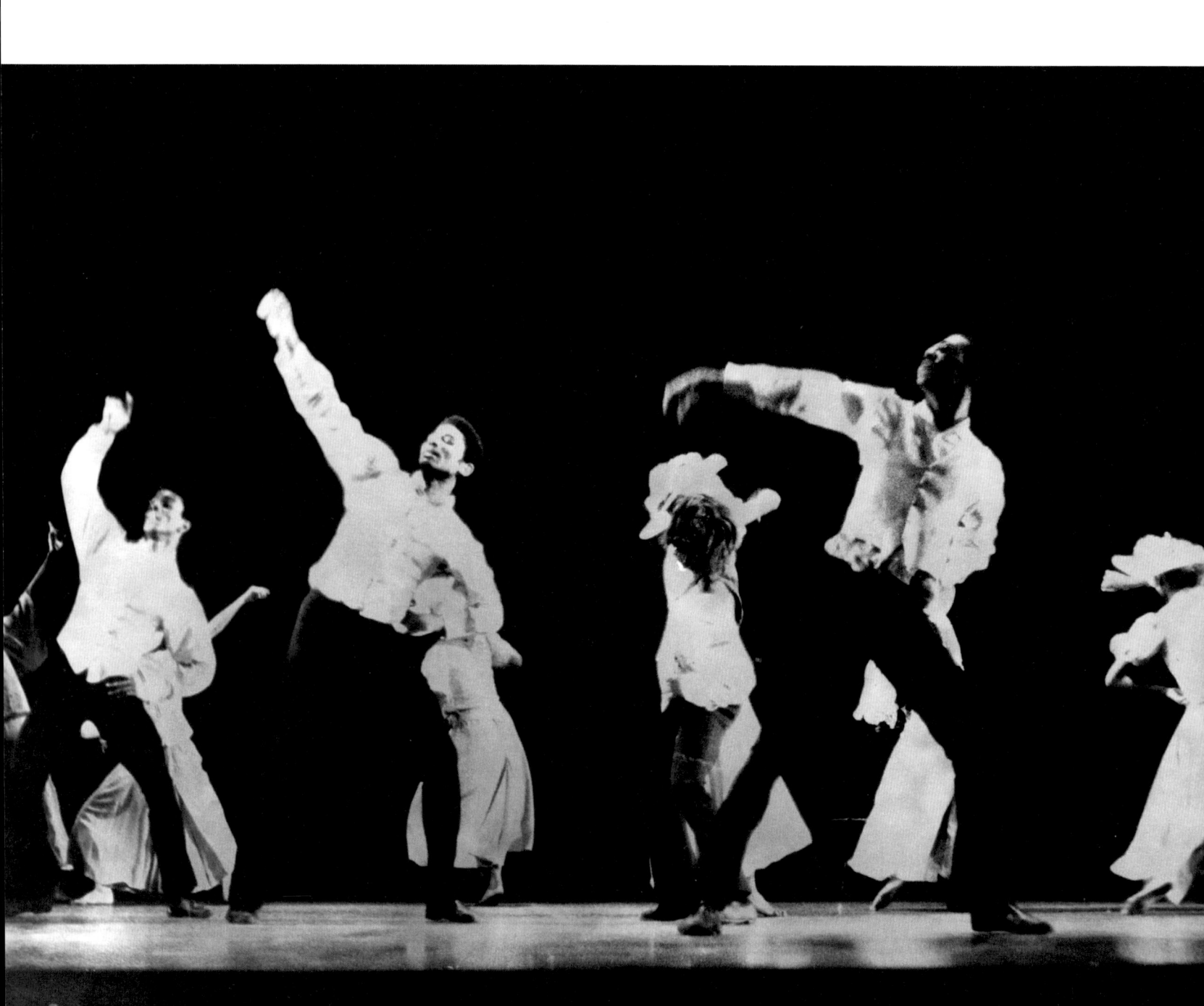

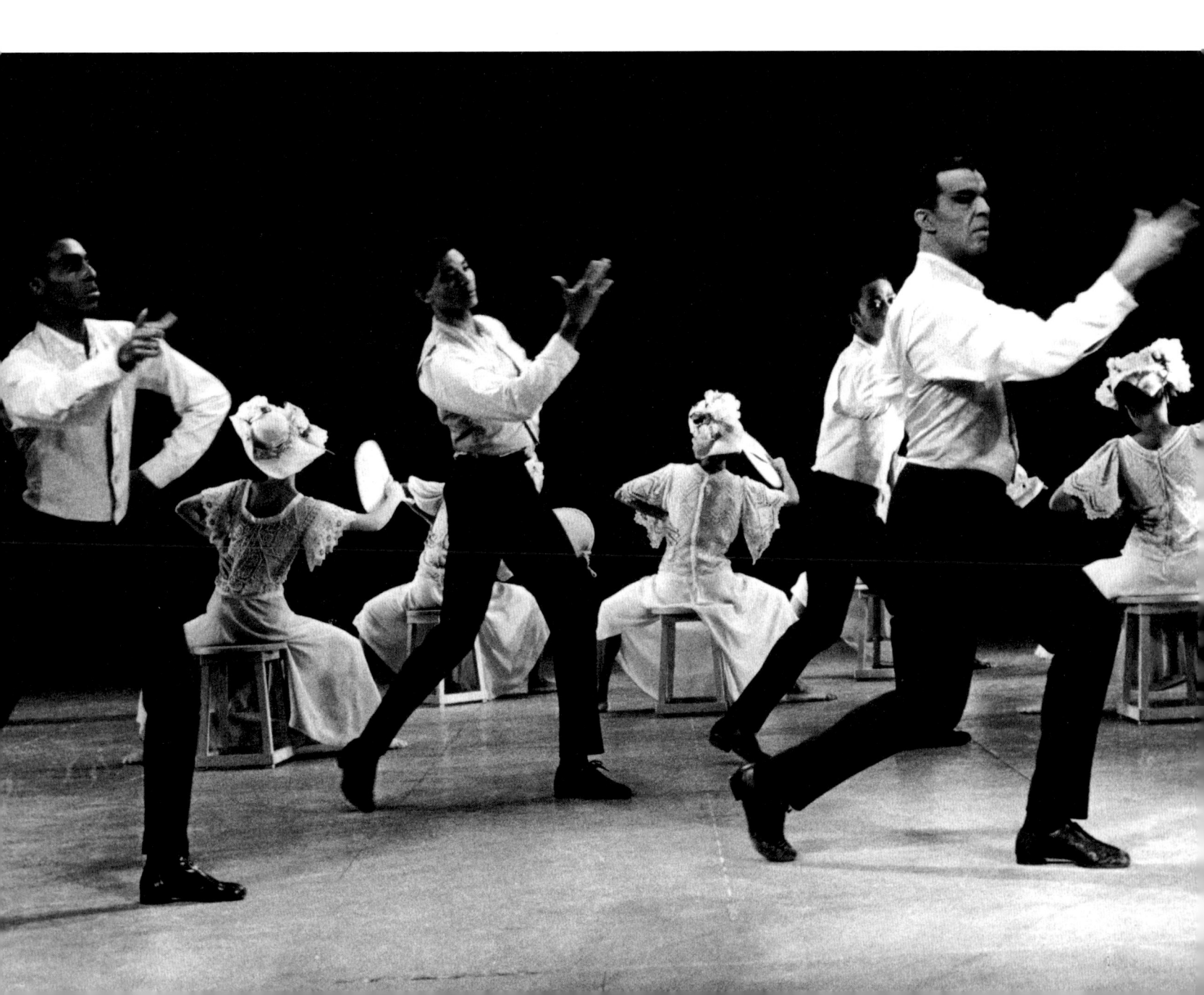

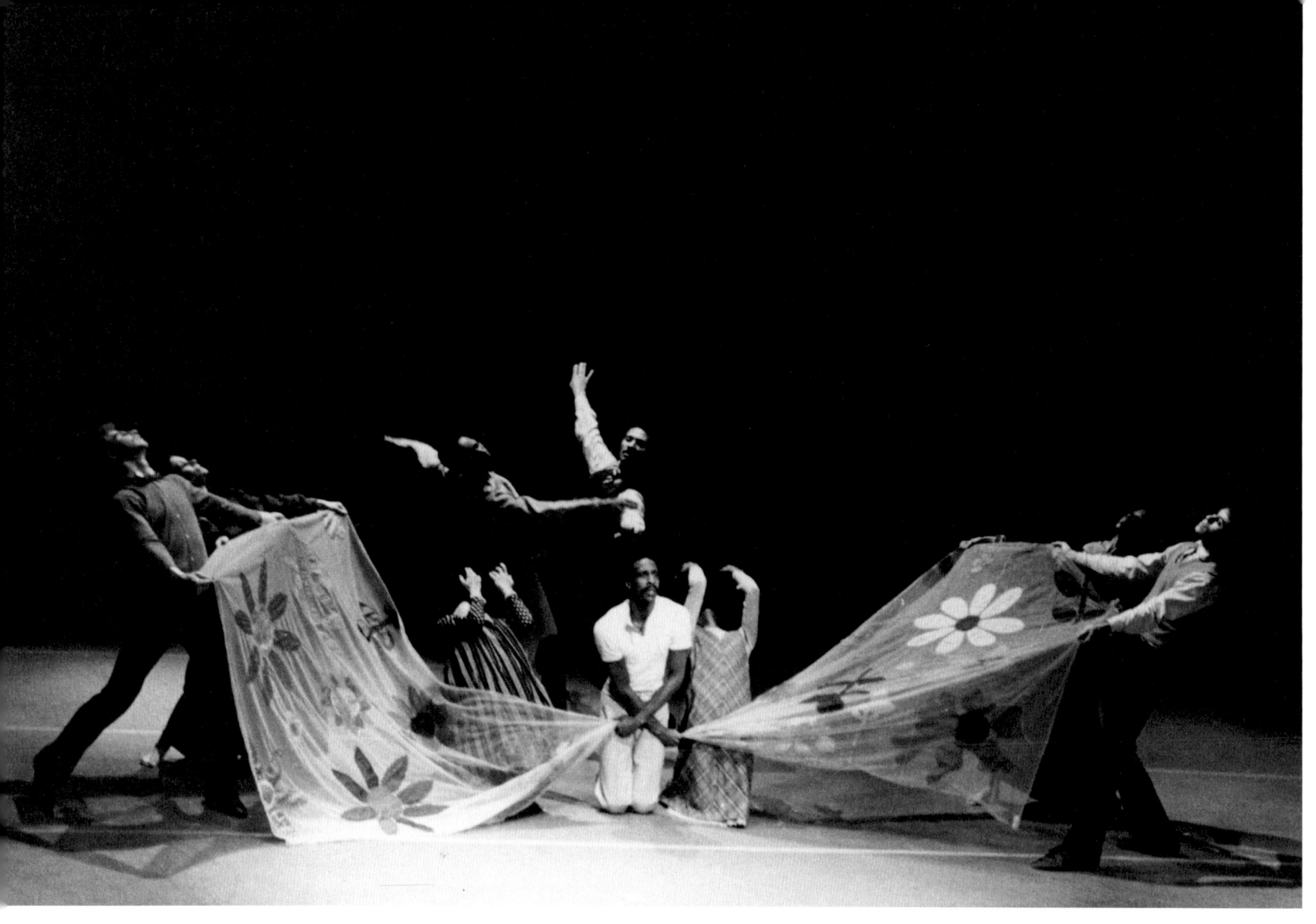

Premiere, Clark Center for the Performing Arts, West Side YWCA, New York

Knoxville: Summer of 1915　　　1960

Premiere, Tenth Annual Boston Arts Festival — Roots of the Blues — 1961

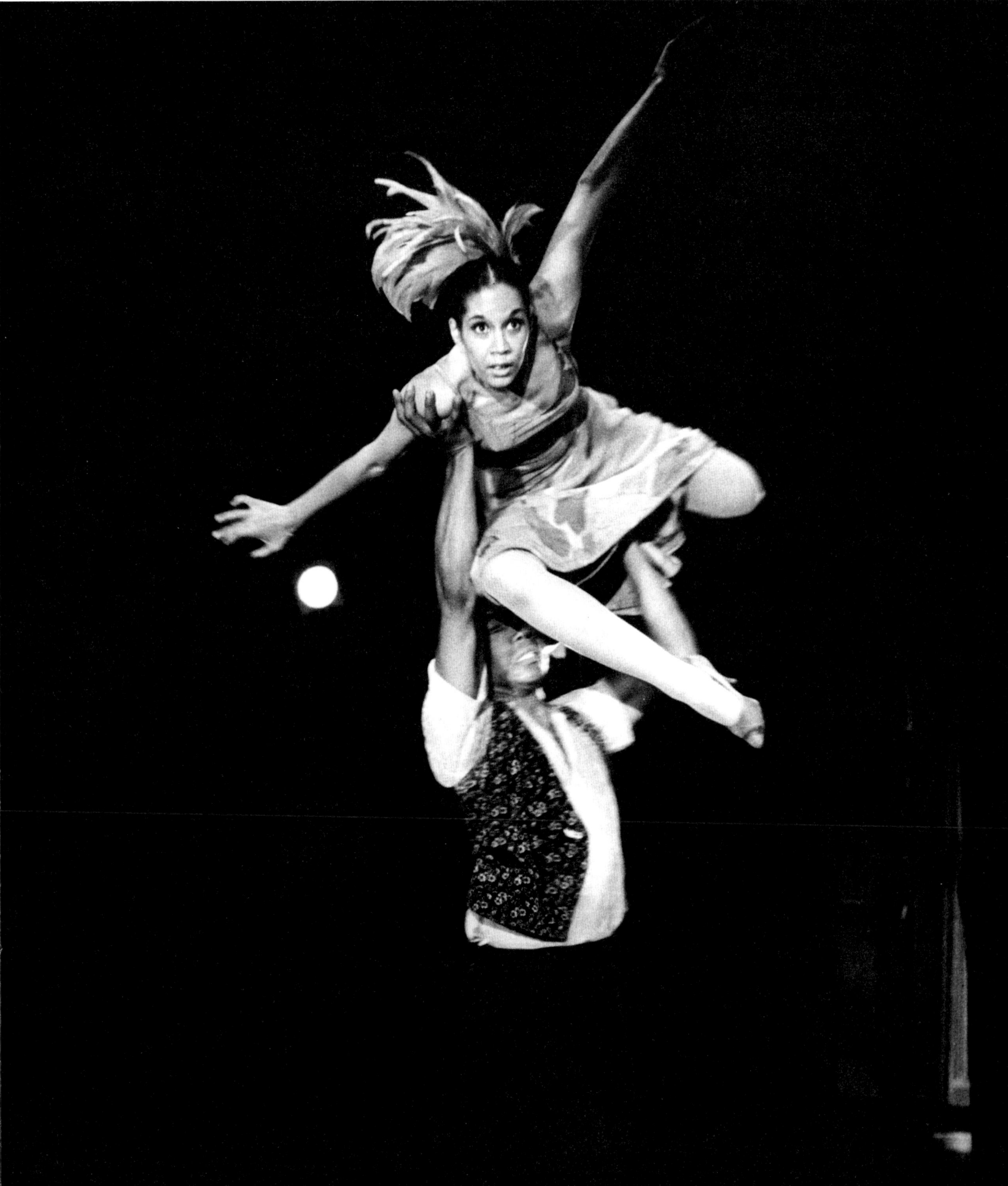

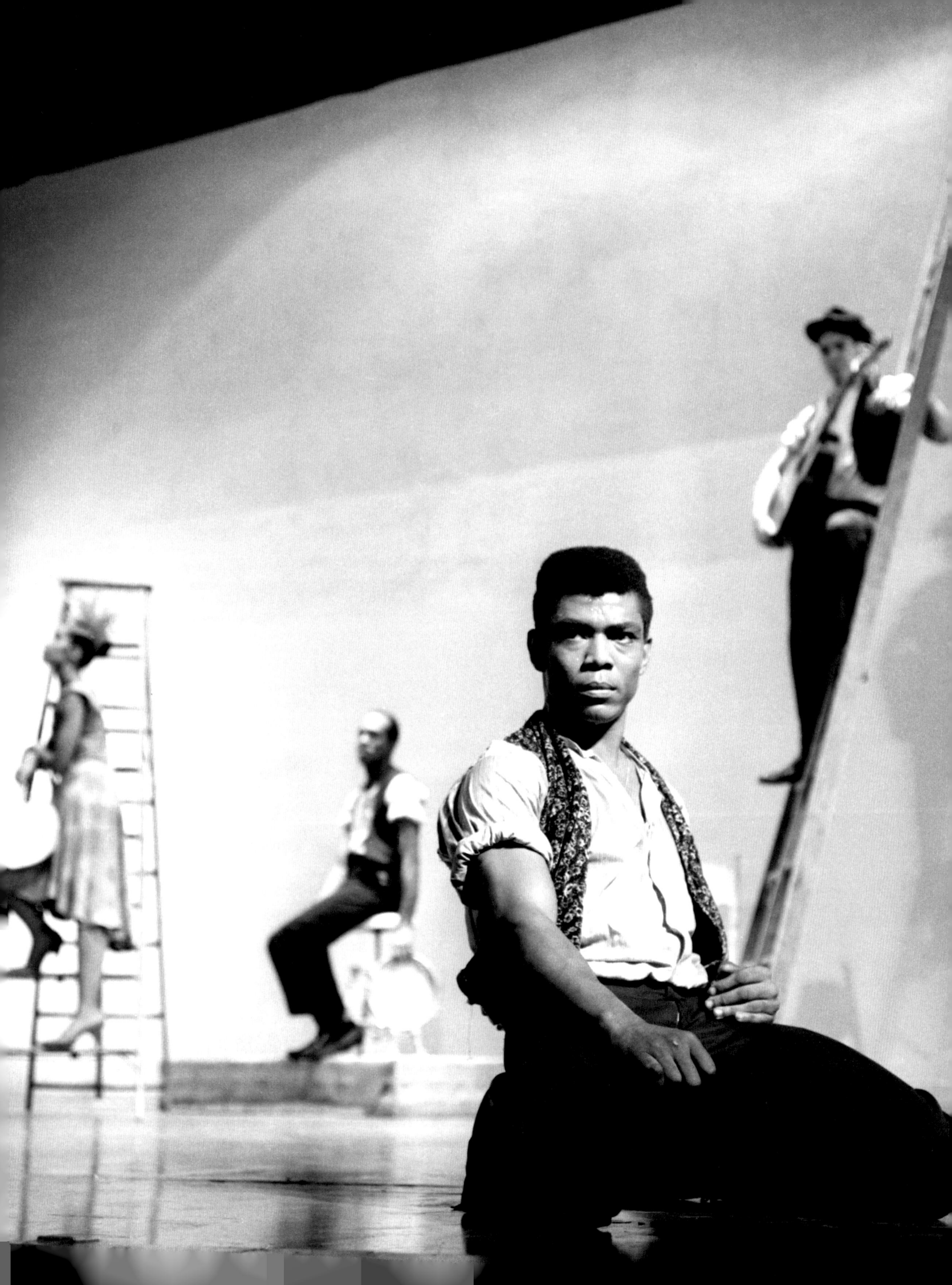

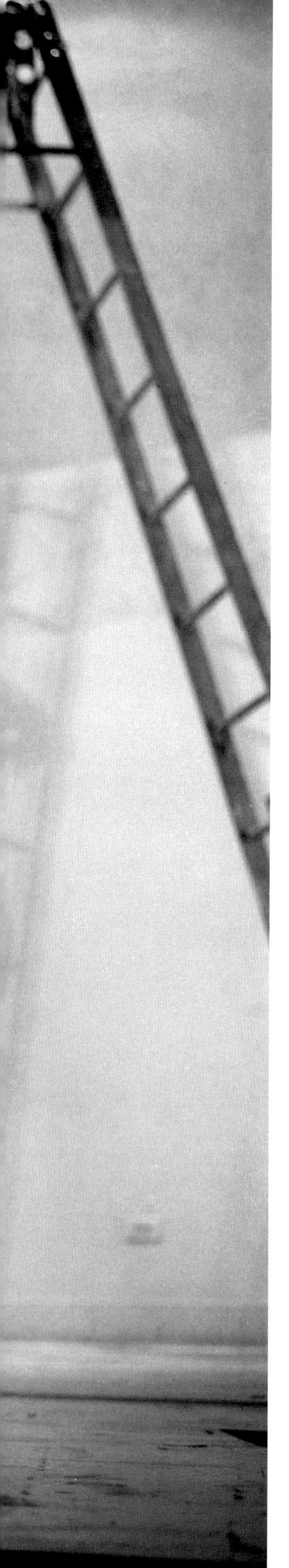
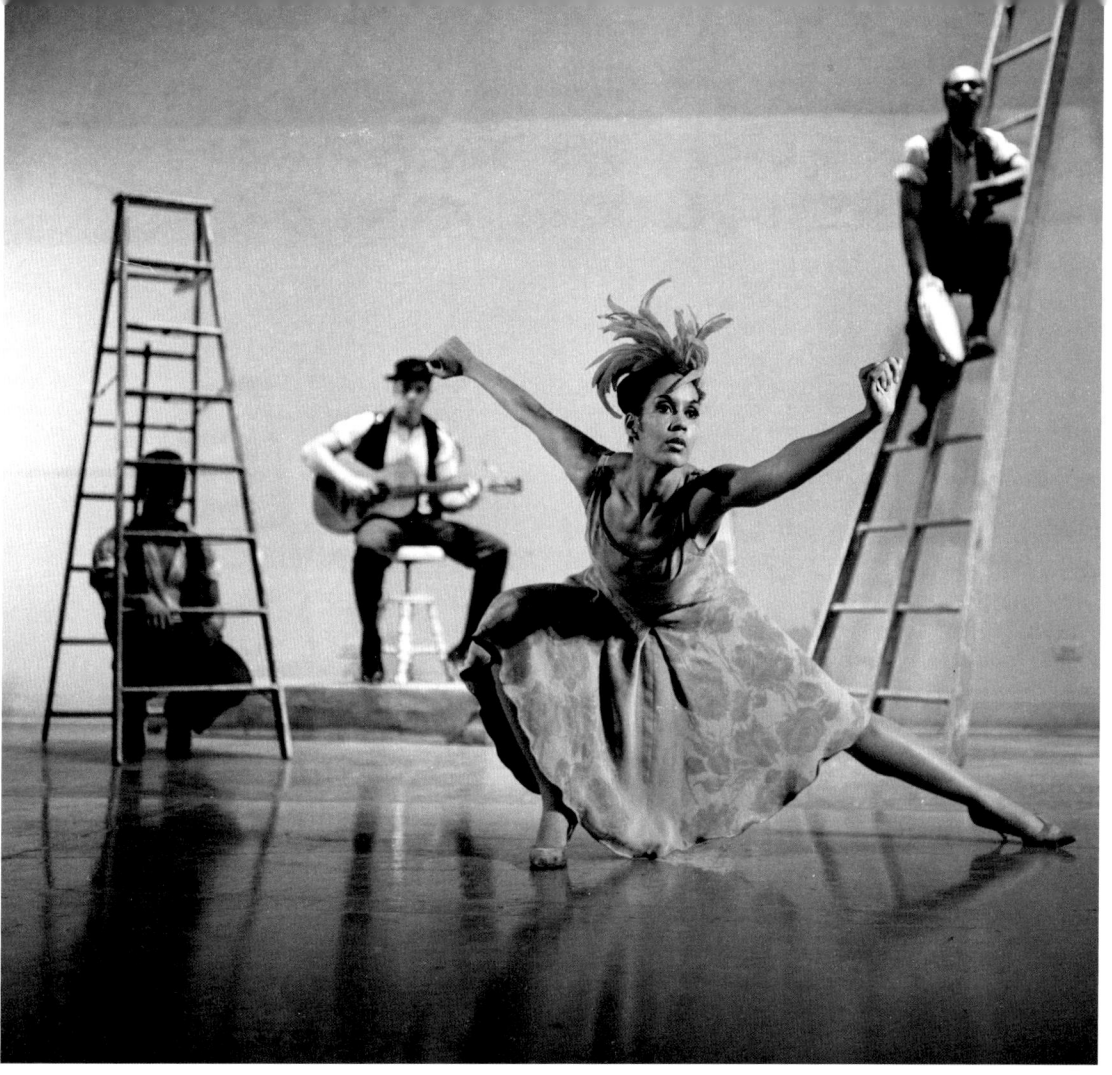
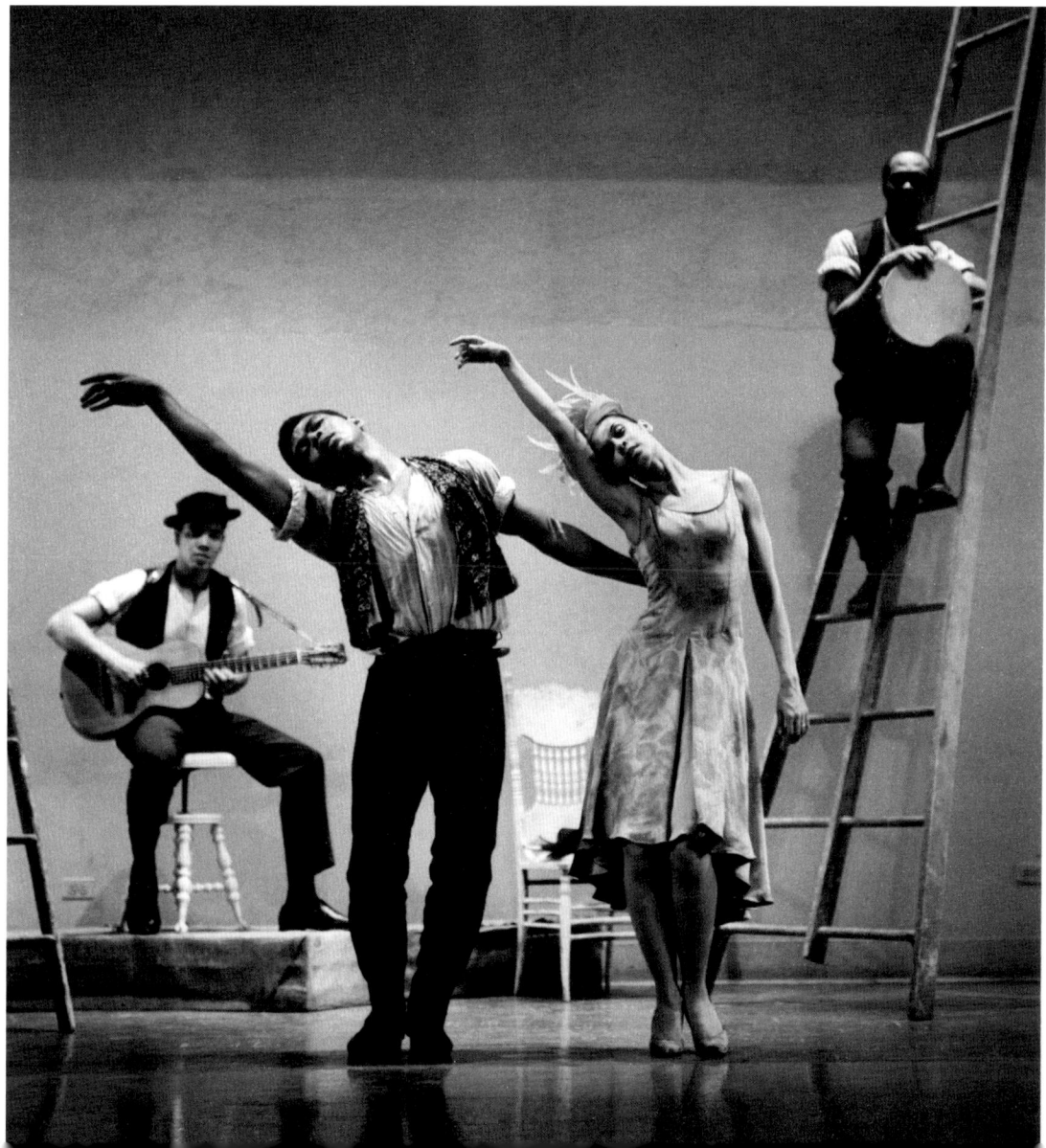

Premiere, location unknown | **Gillespiana** | 1961

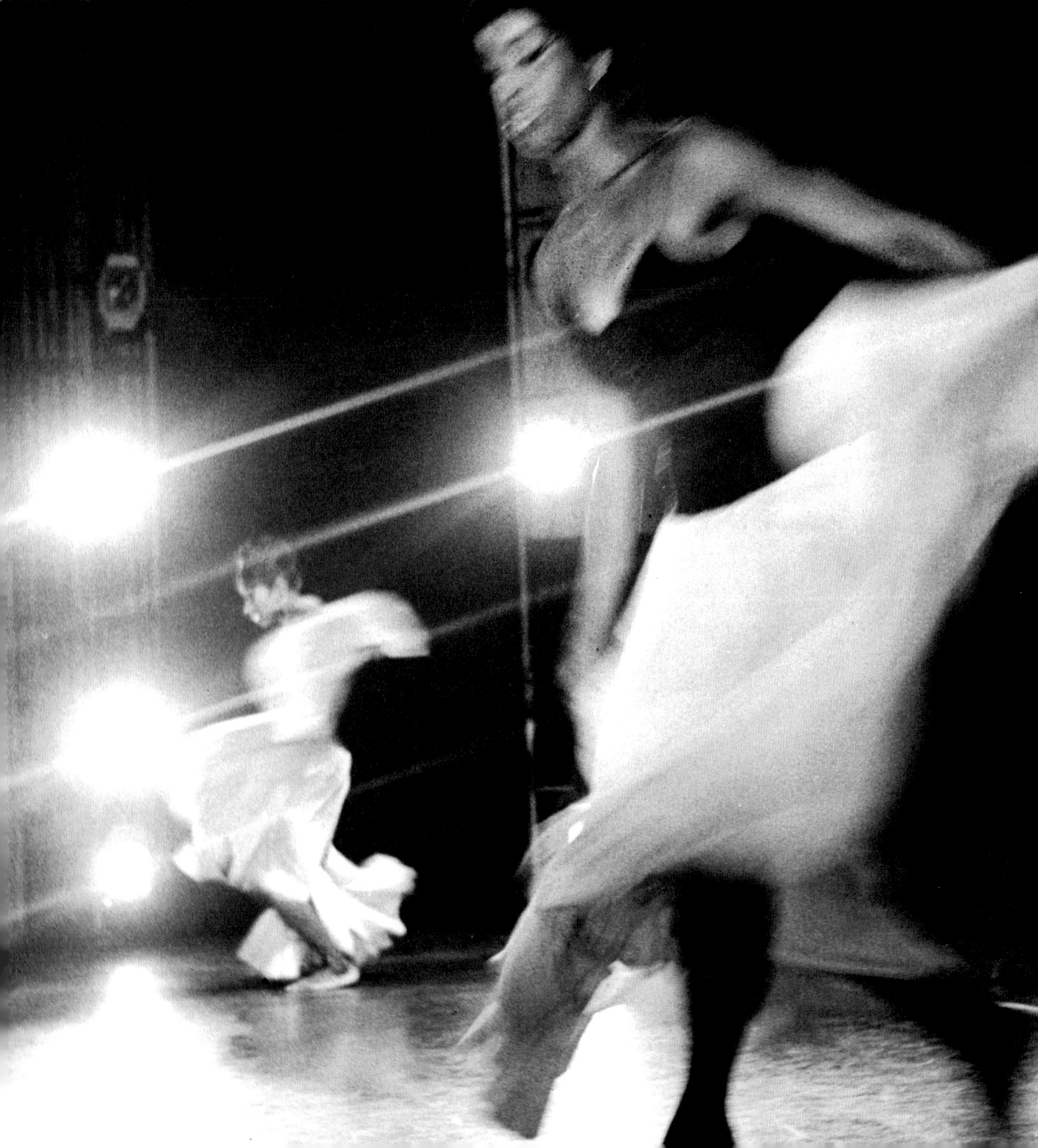

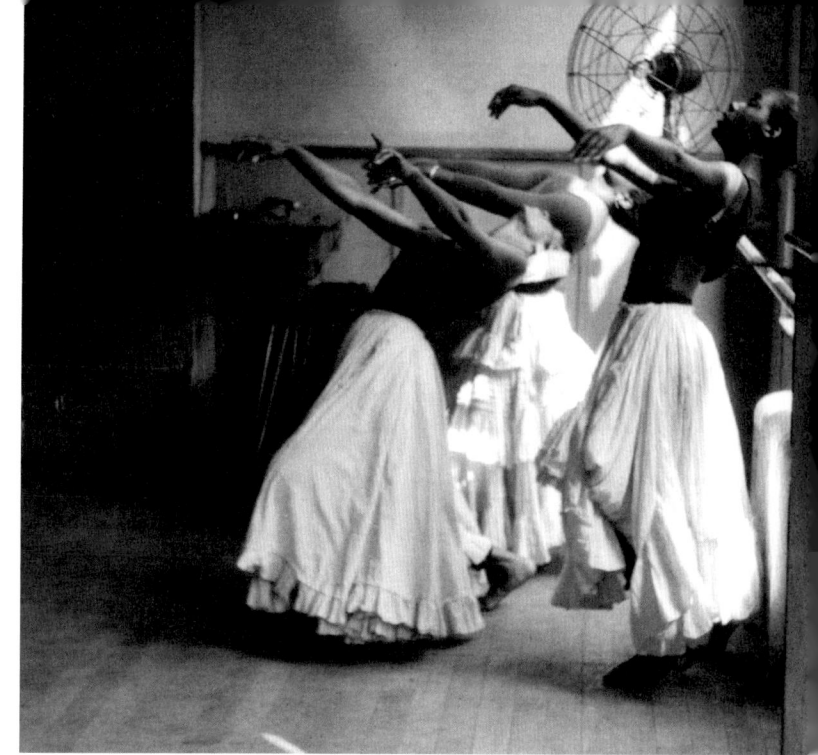
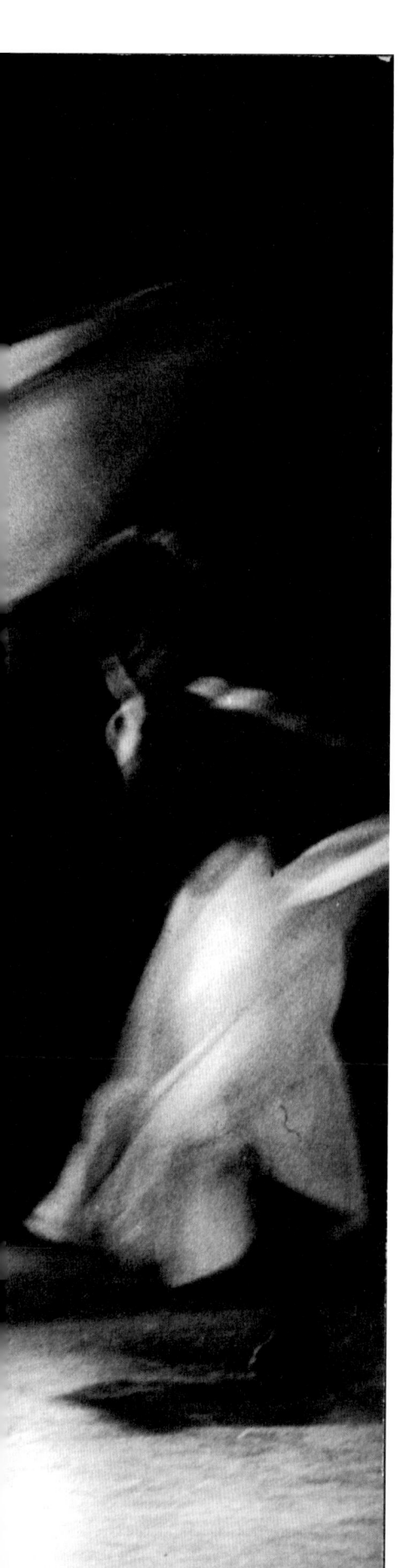
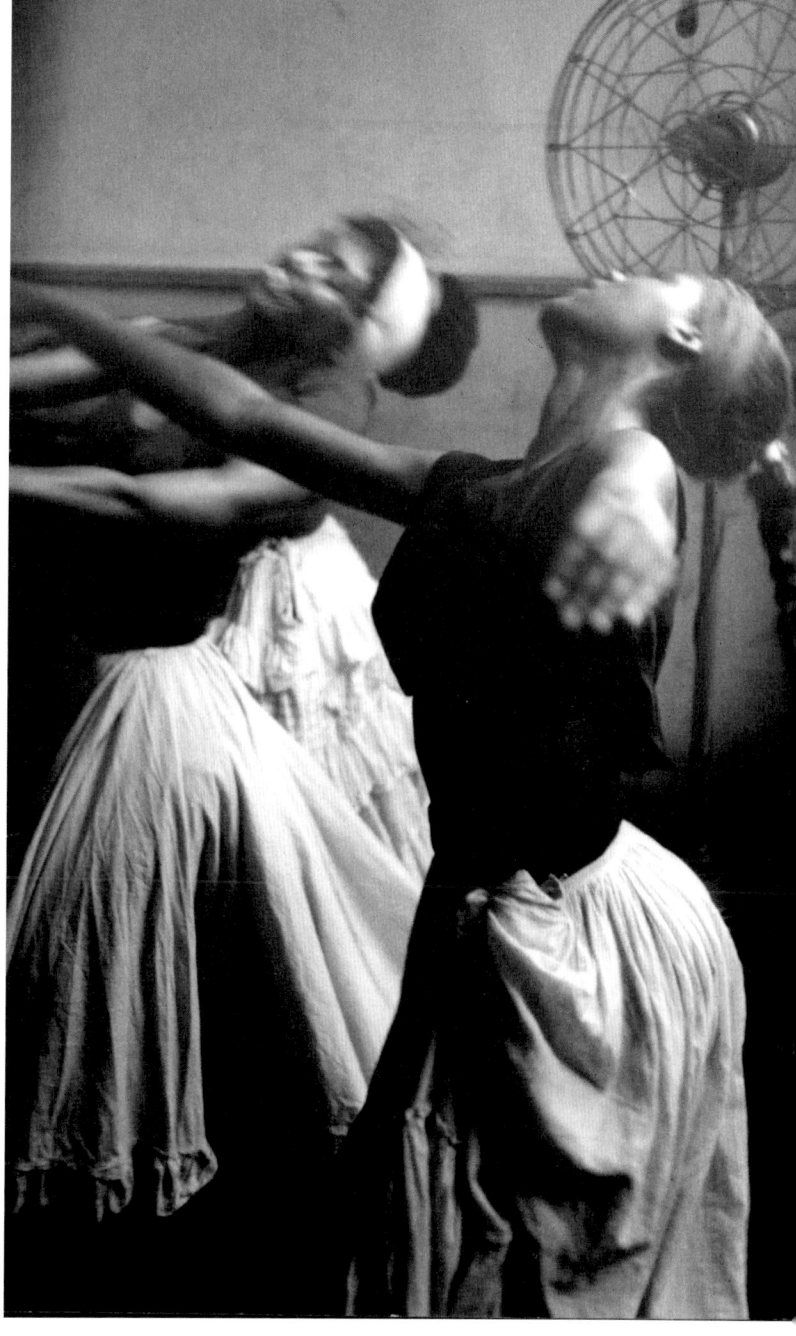

Premiere, location unknown | **Hermit Songs** | 1961

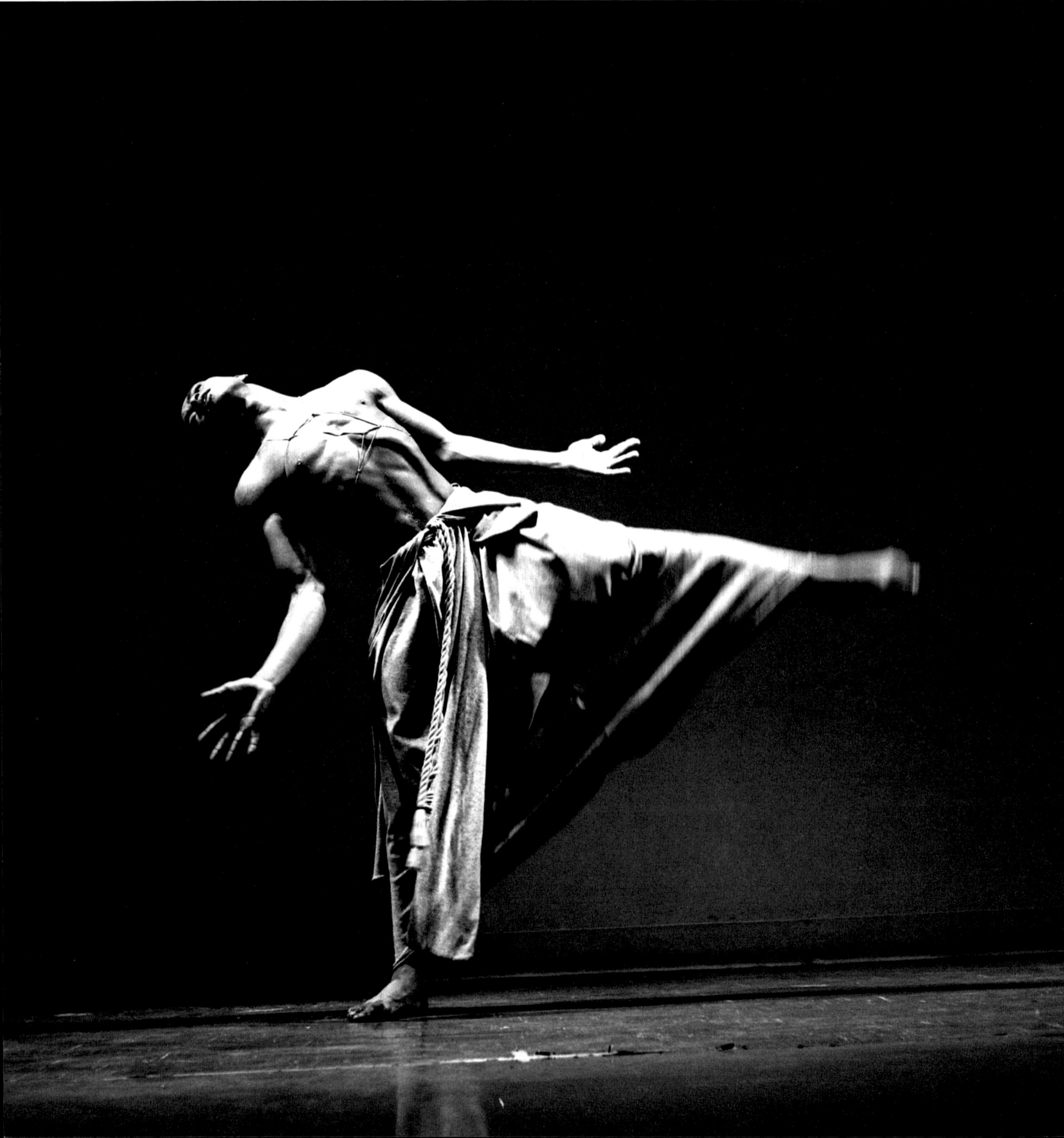

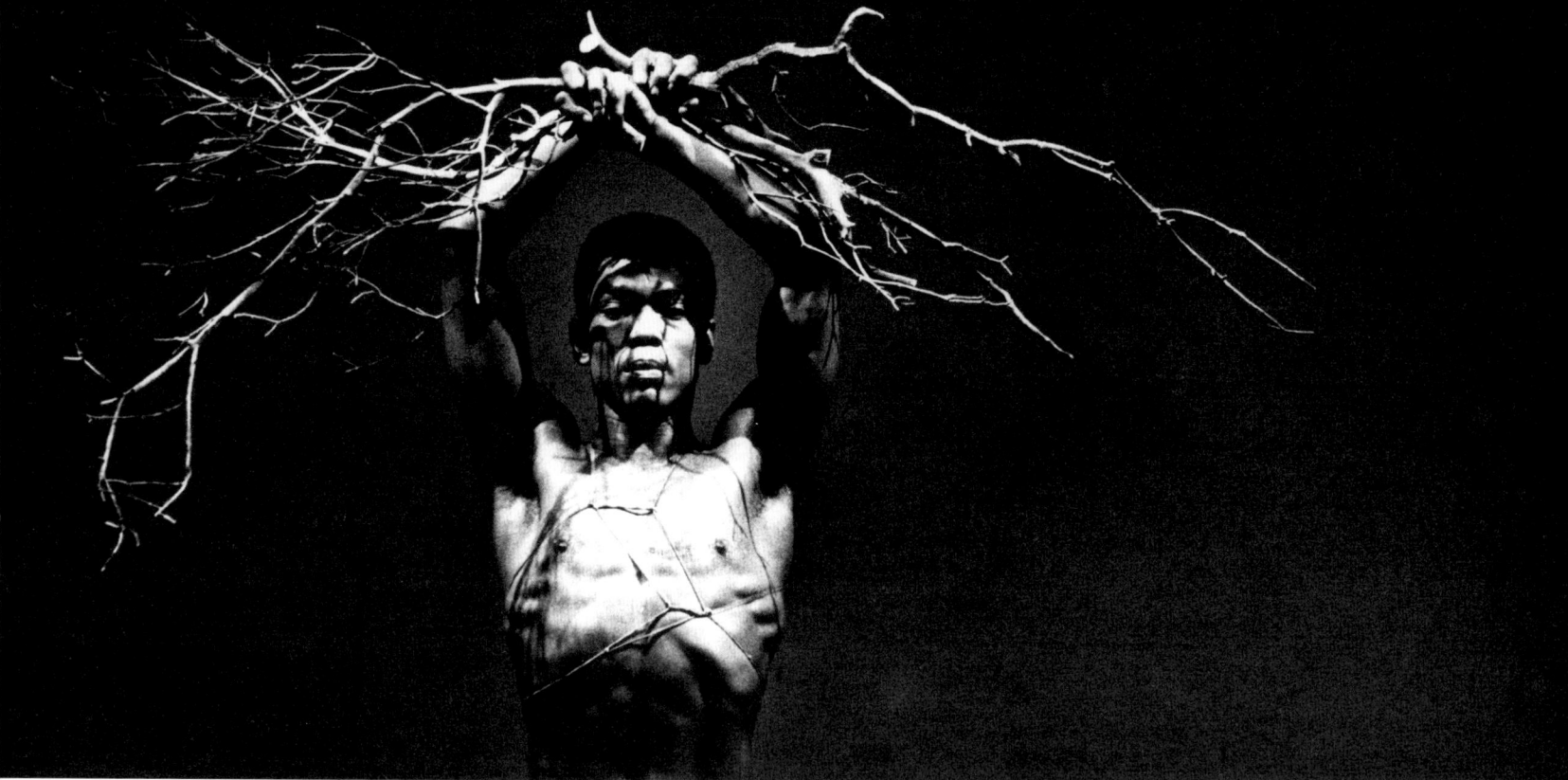

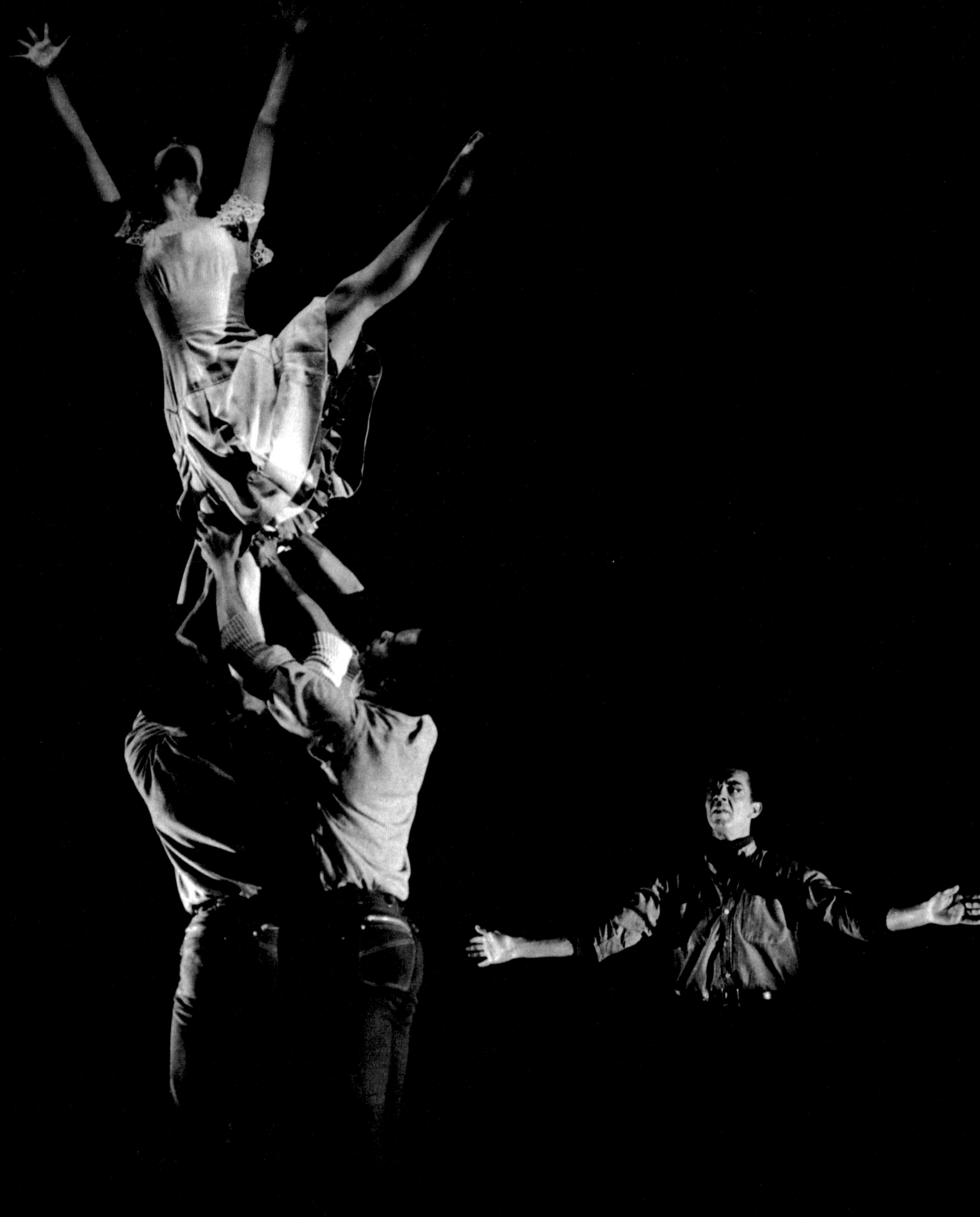

Premiere, Southeast Asia tour | **Been Here and Gone** | 1962

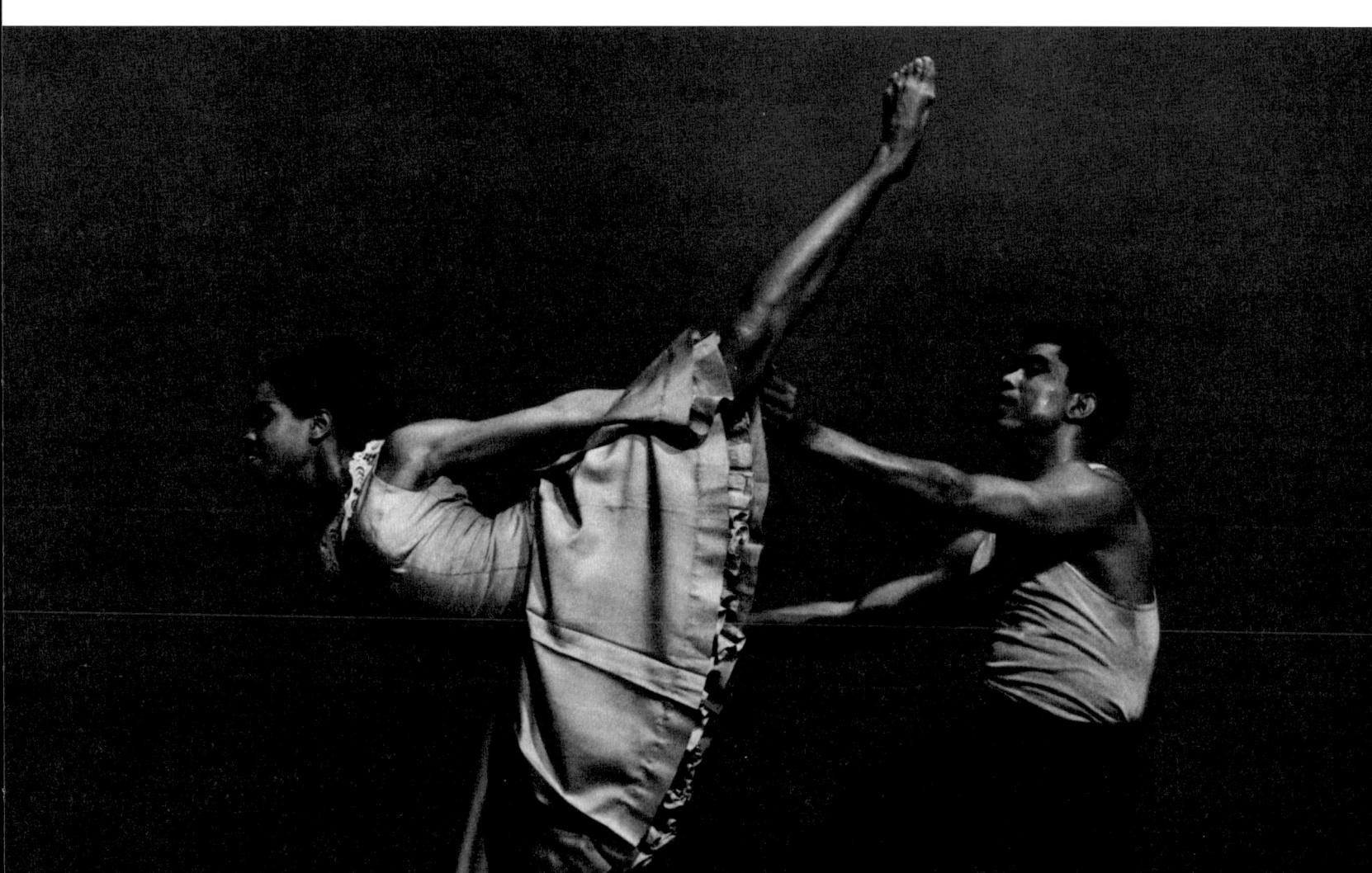

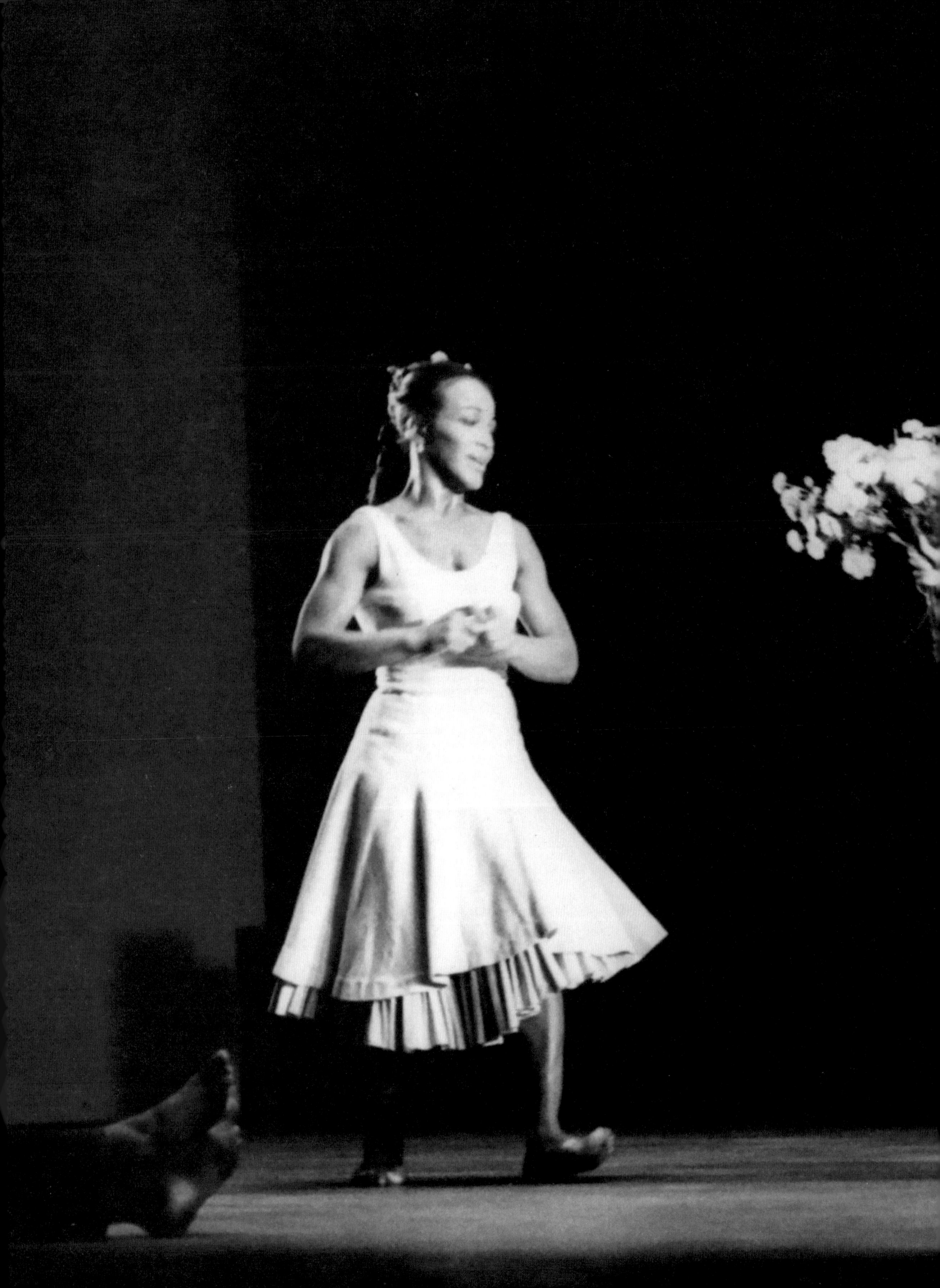

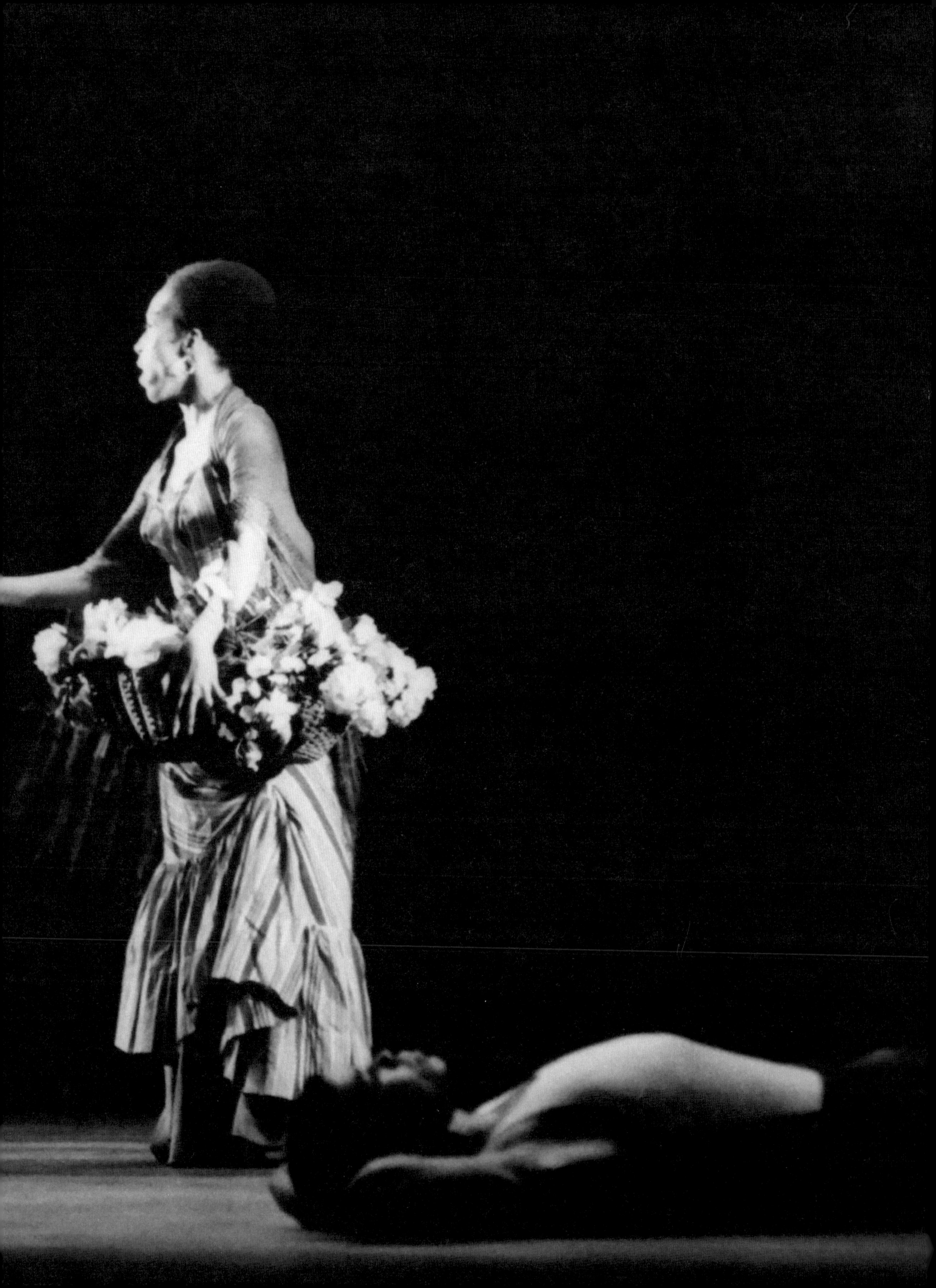

Premiere, Teatro Nacional de São Carlos,
Lisbon, Portugal

Feast of Ashes

1962/1974

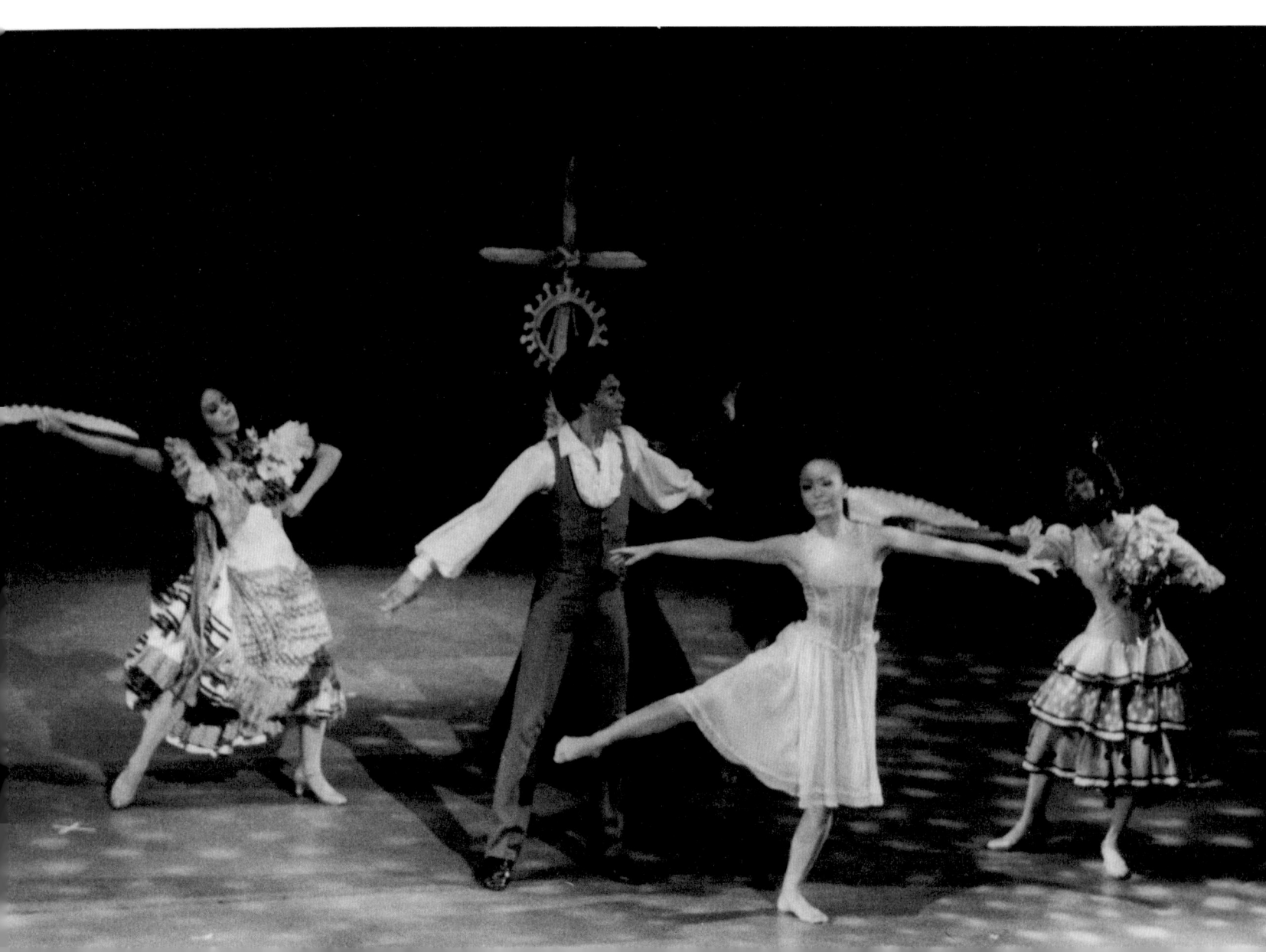

Premiere, Brooklyn Academy of Music | **Labyrinth** | 1963

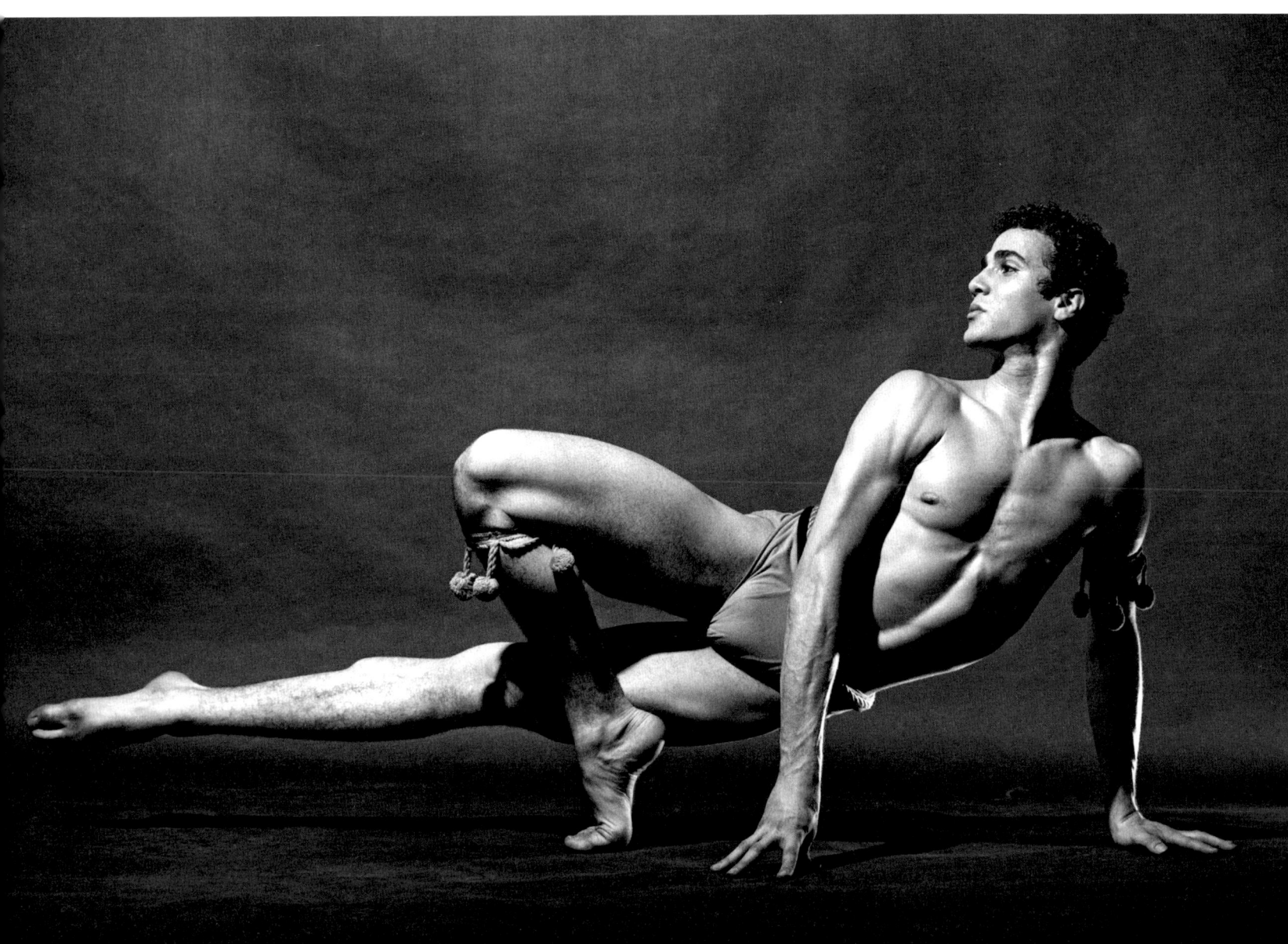

Premiere, Brooklyn Academy of Music | **Reflections in D** | 1963

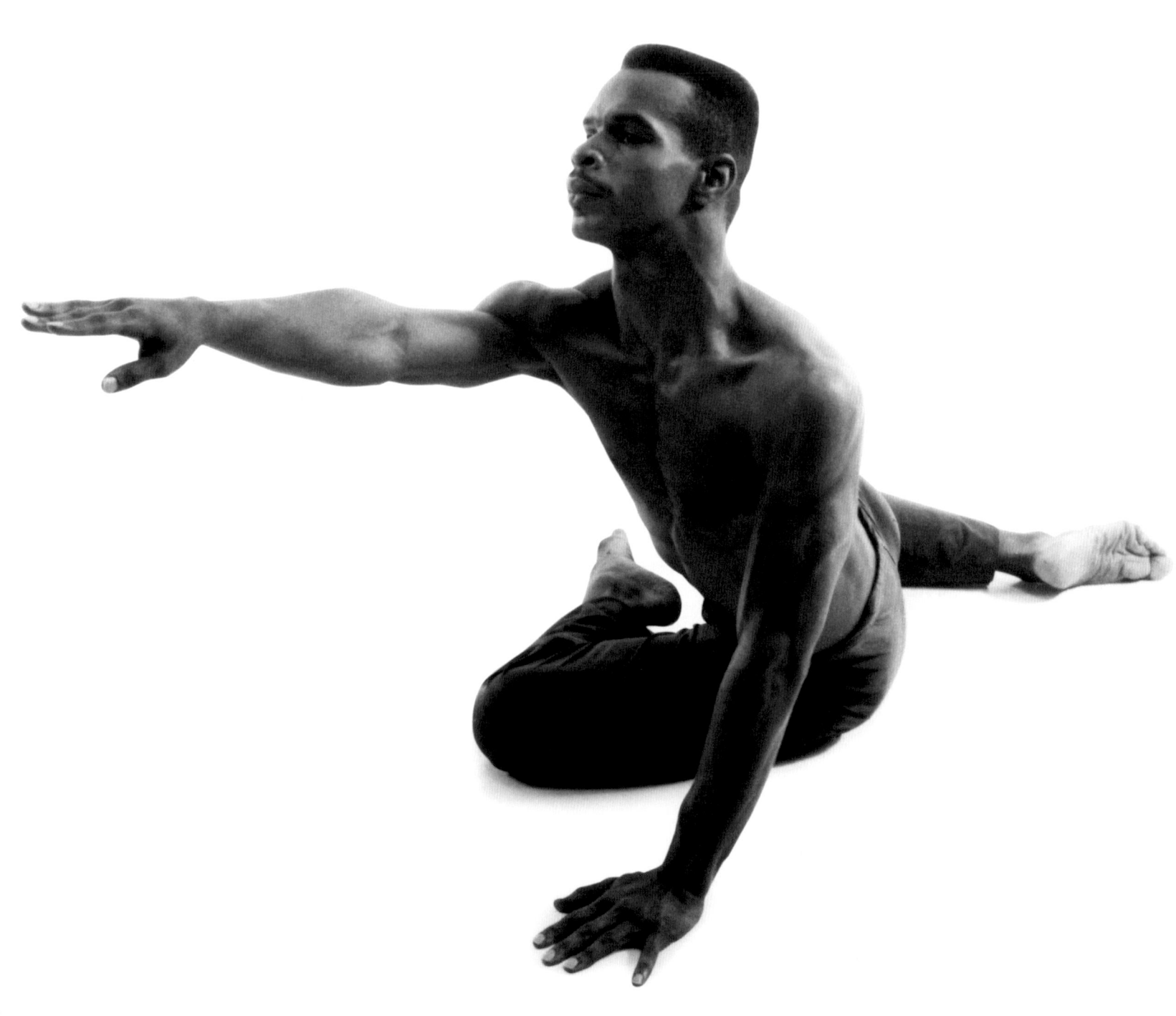

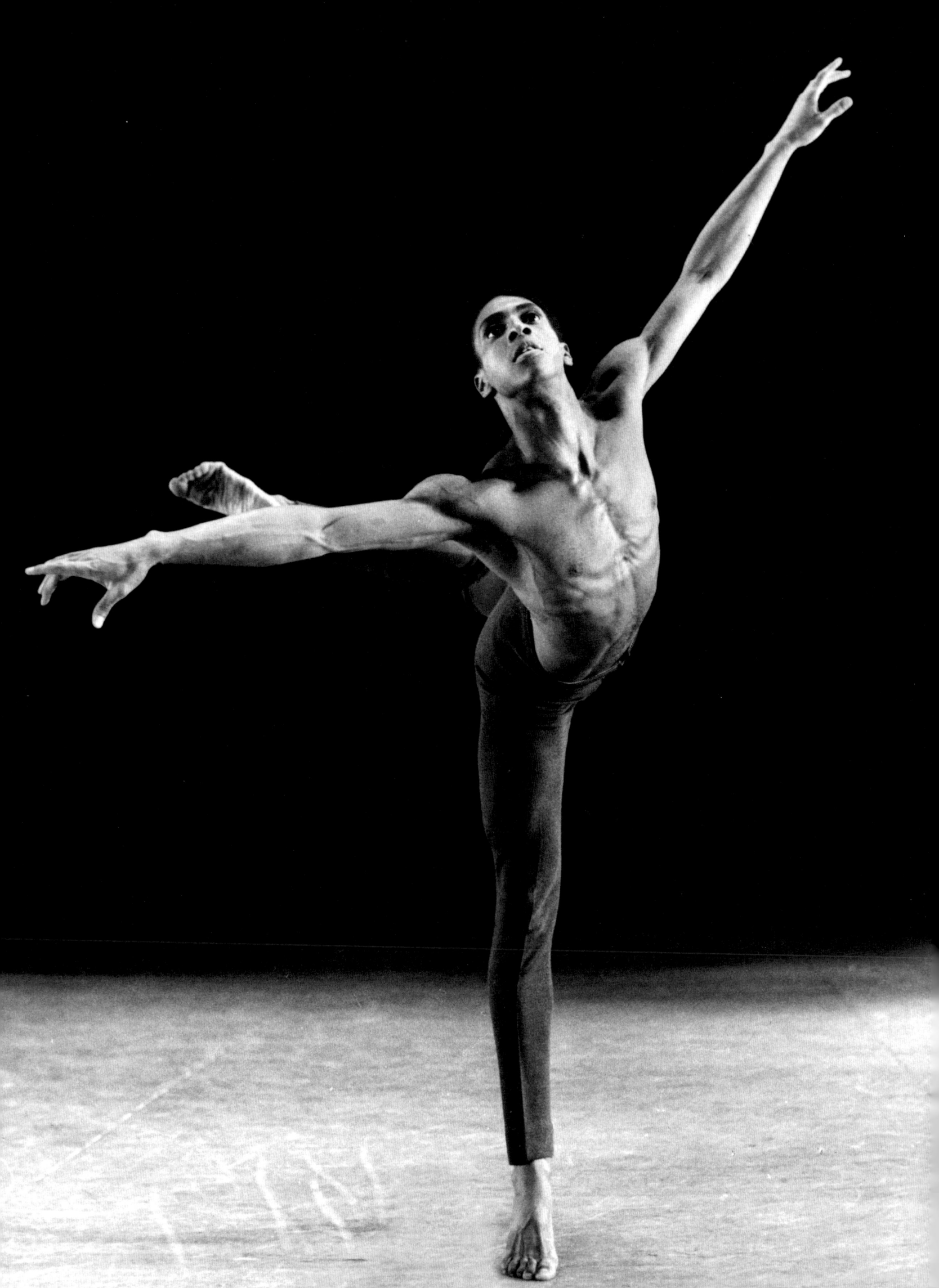

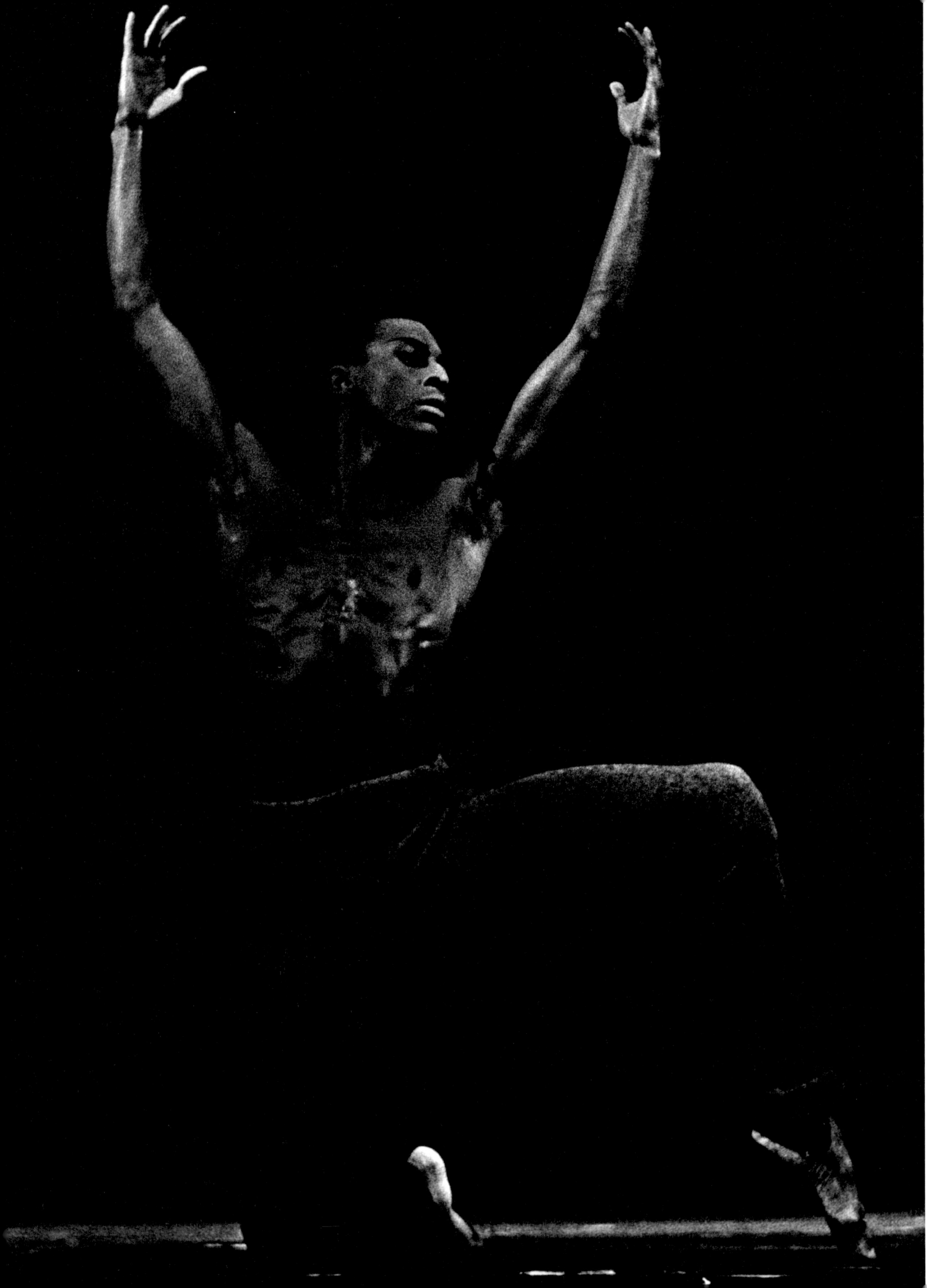

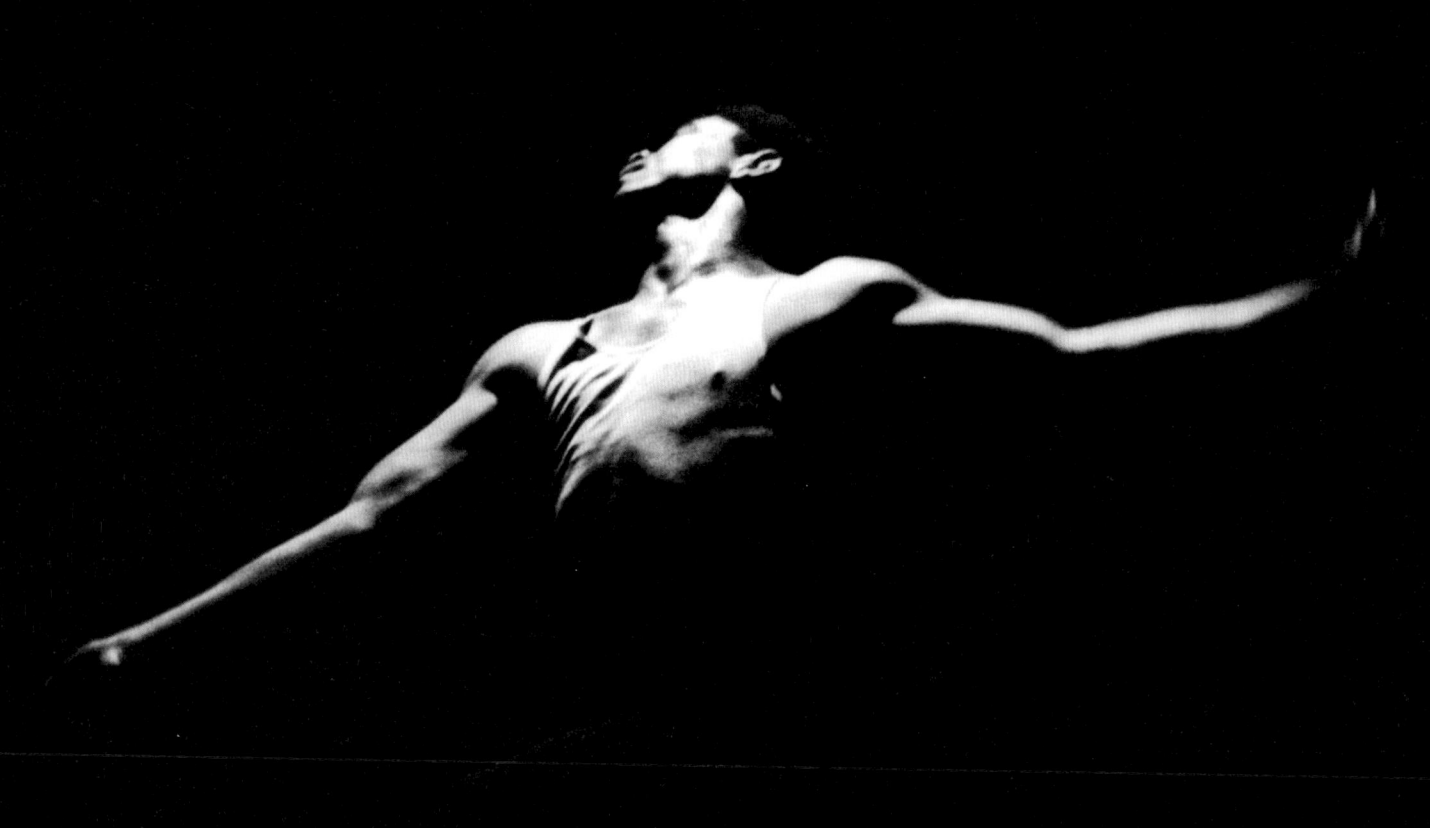

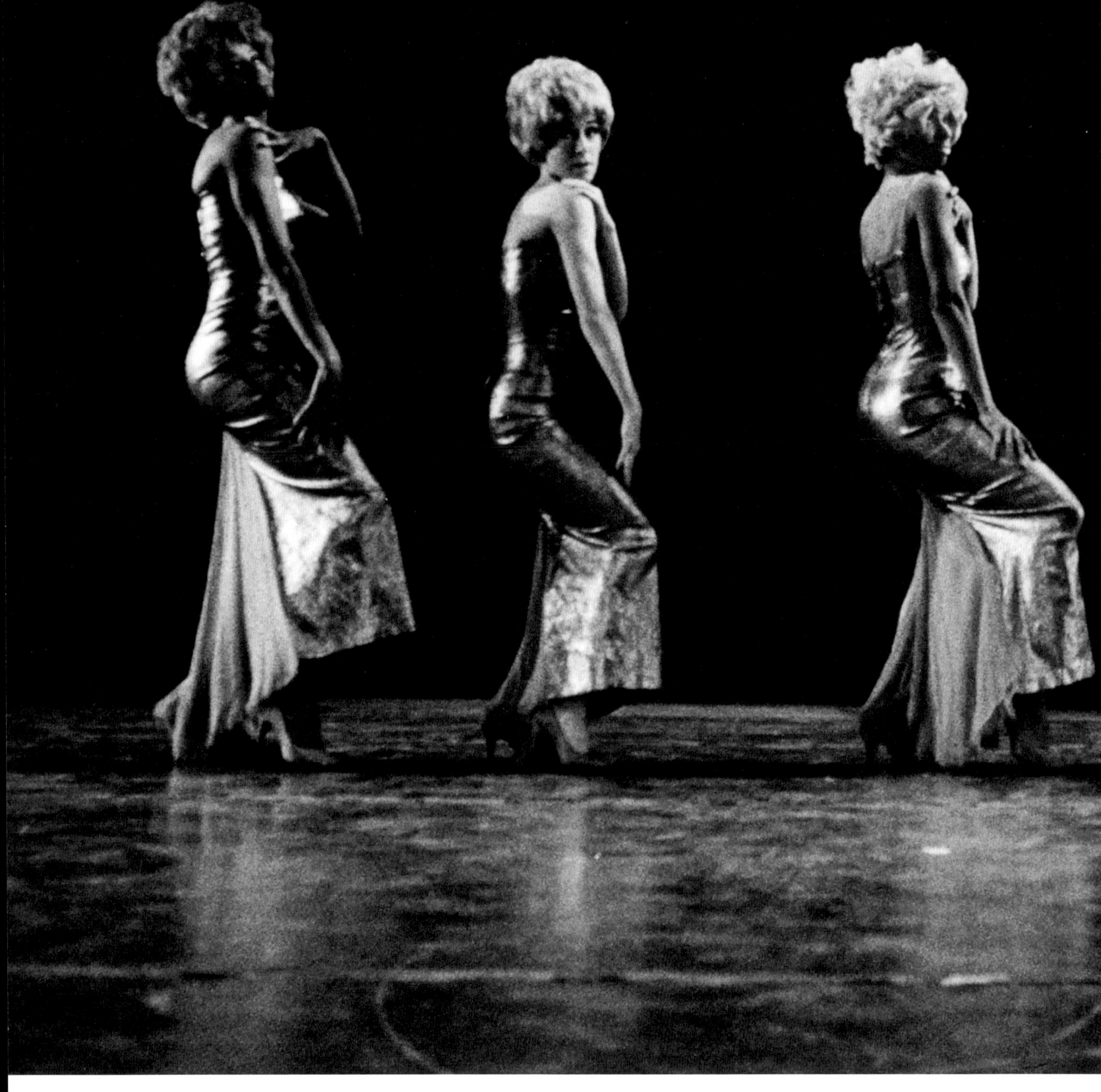

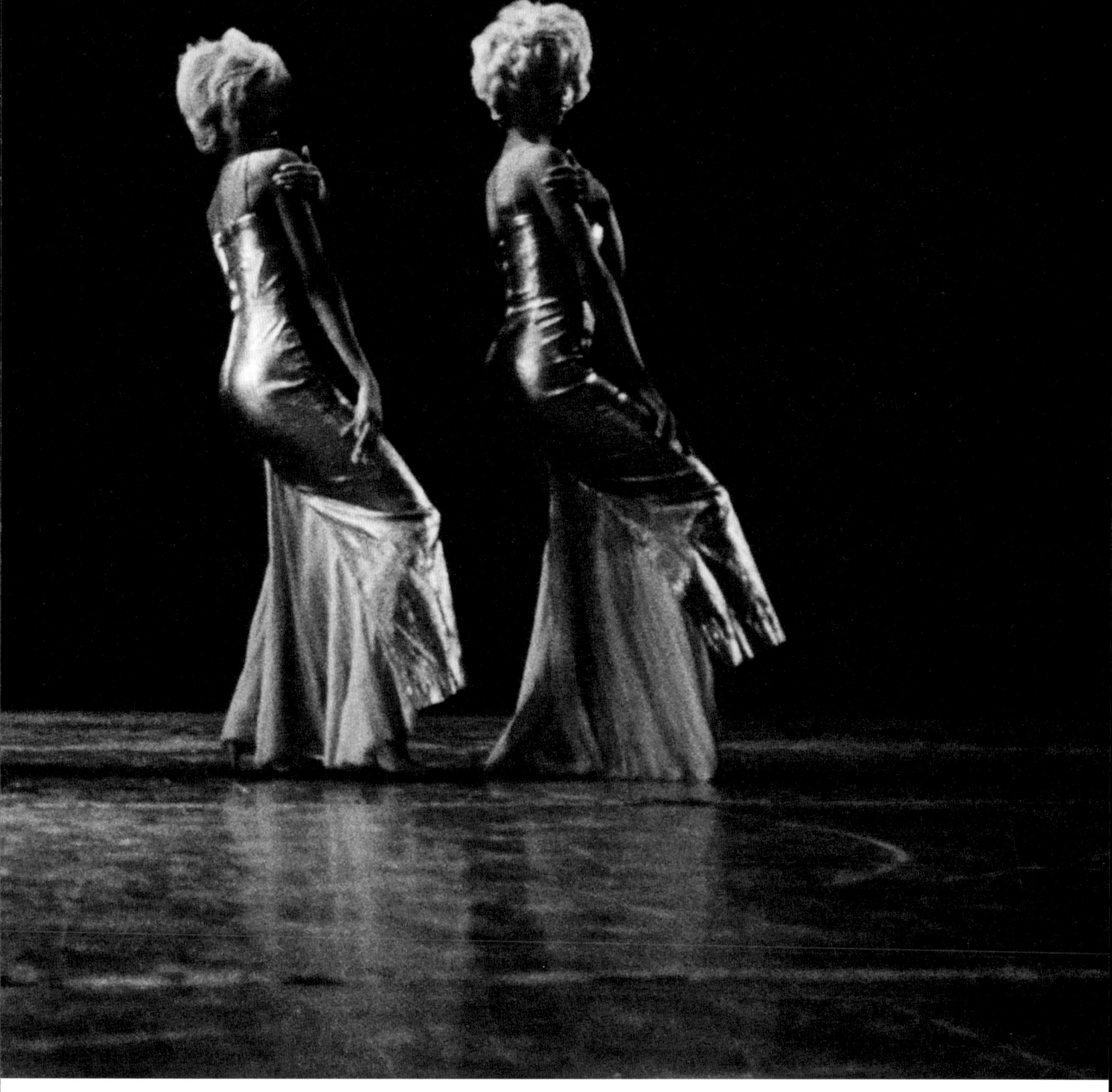

Premiere, Edinburgh International Festival, Scotland   **Quintet**   1968

Premiere, Connecticut College, New London   **Masekela Langage**   1969

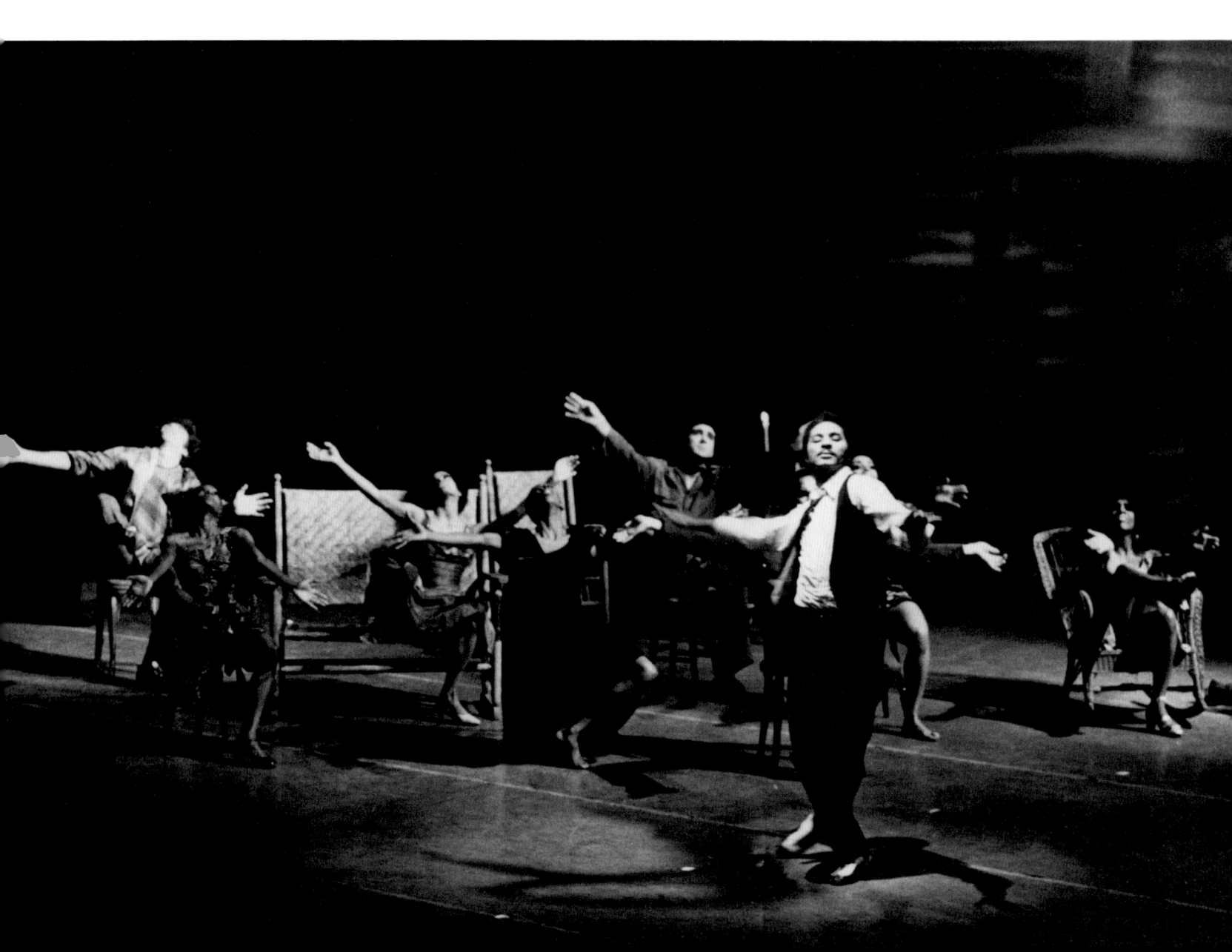

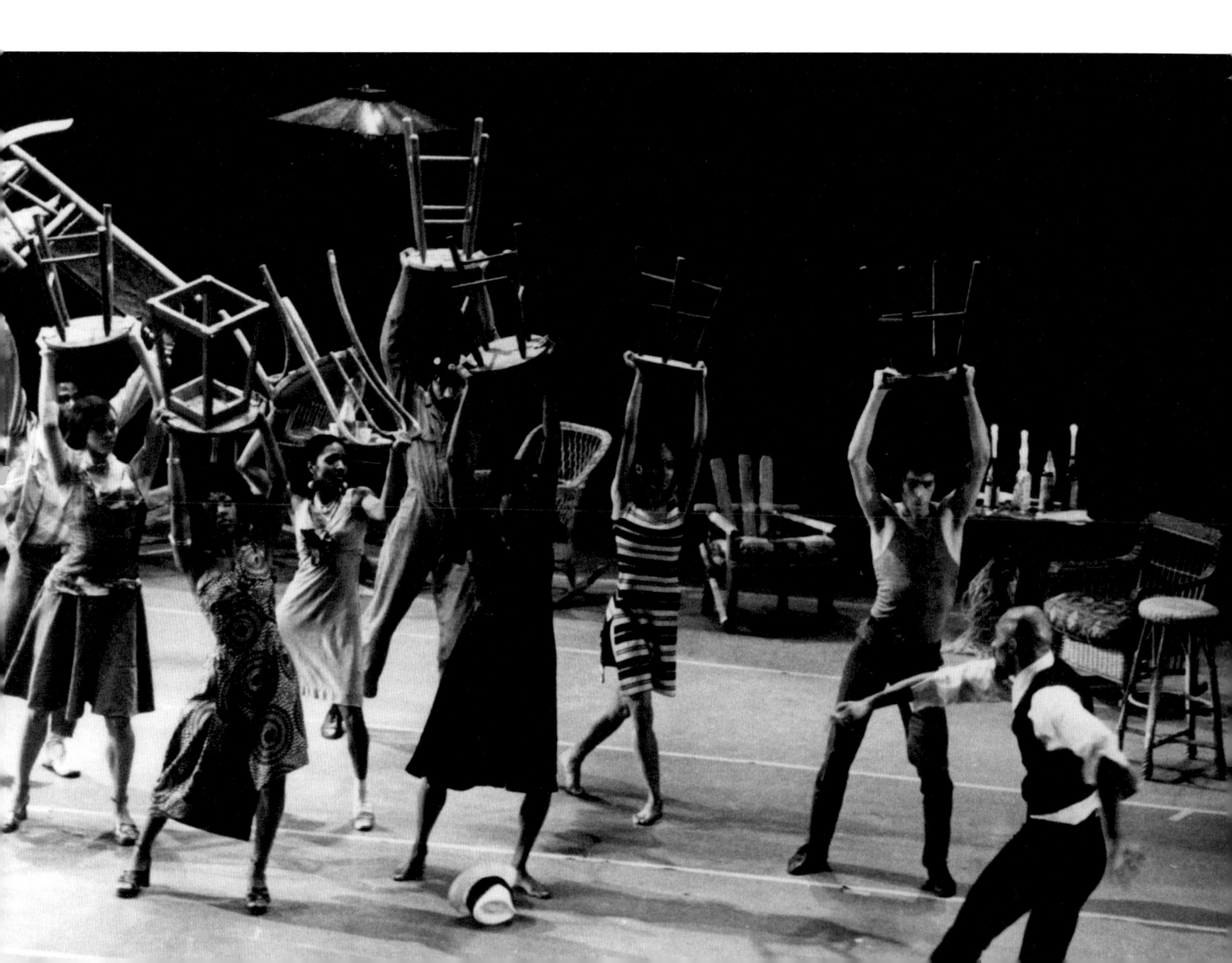

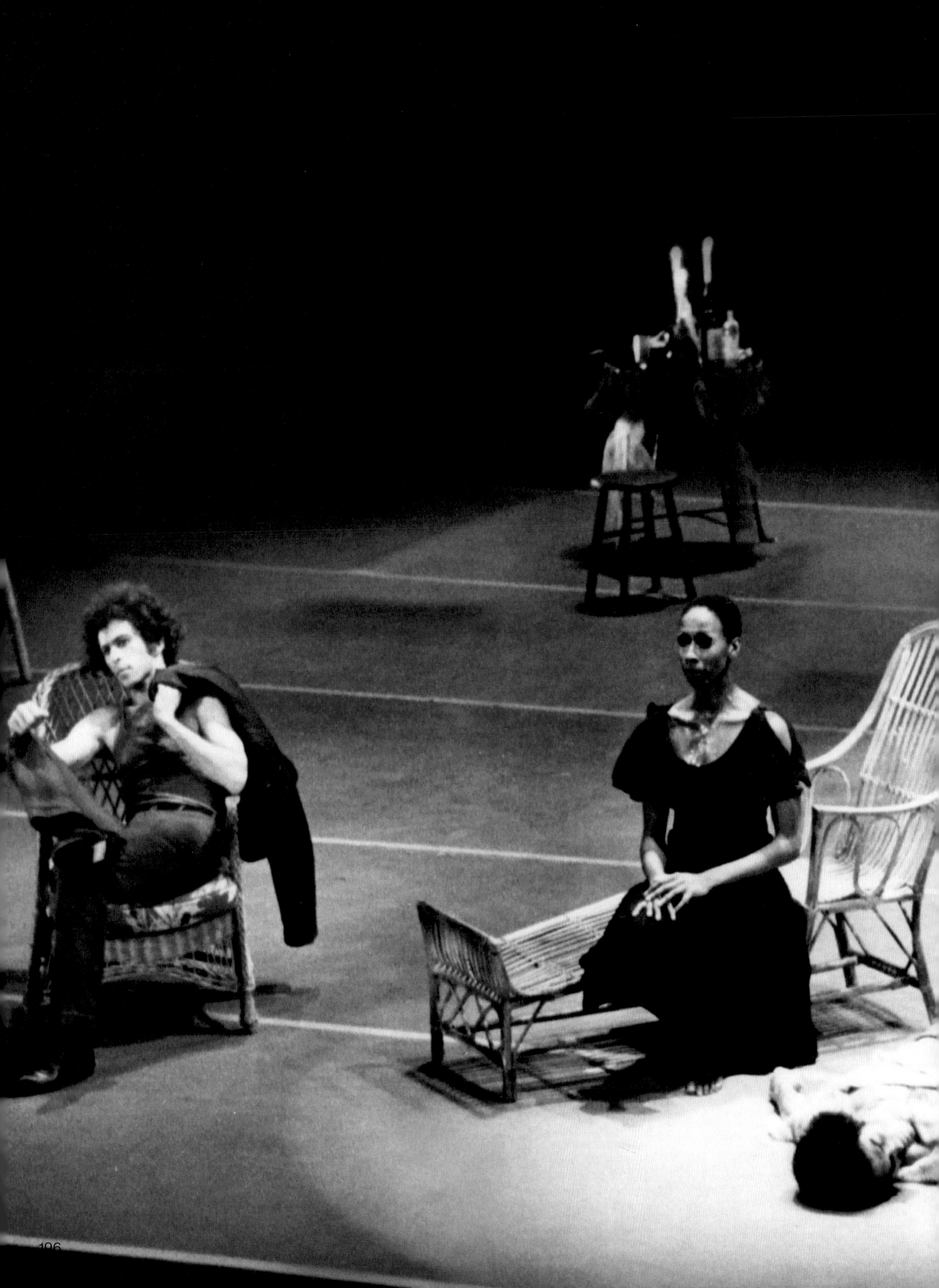

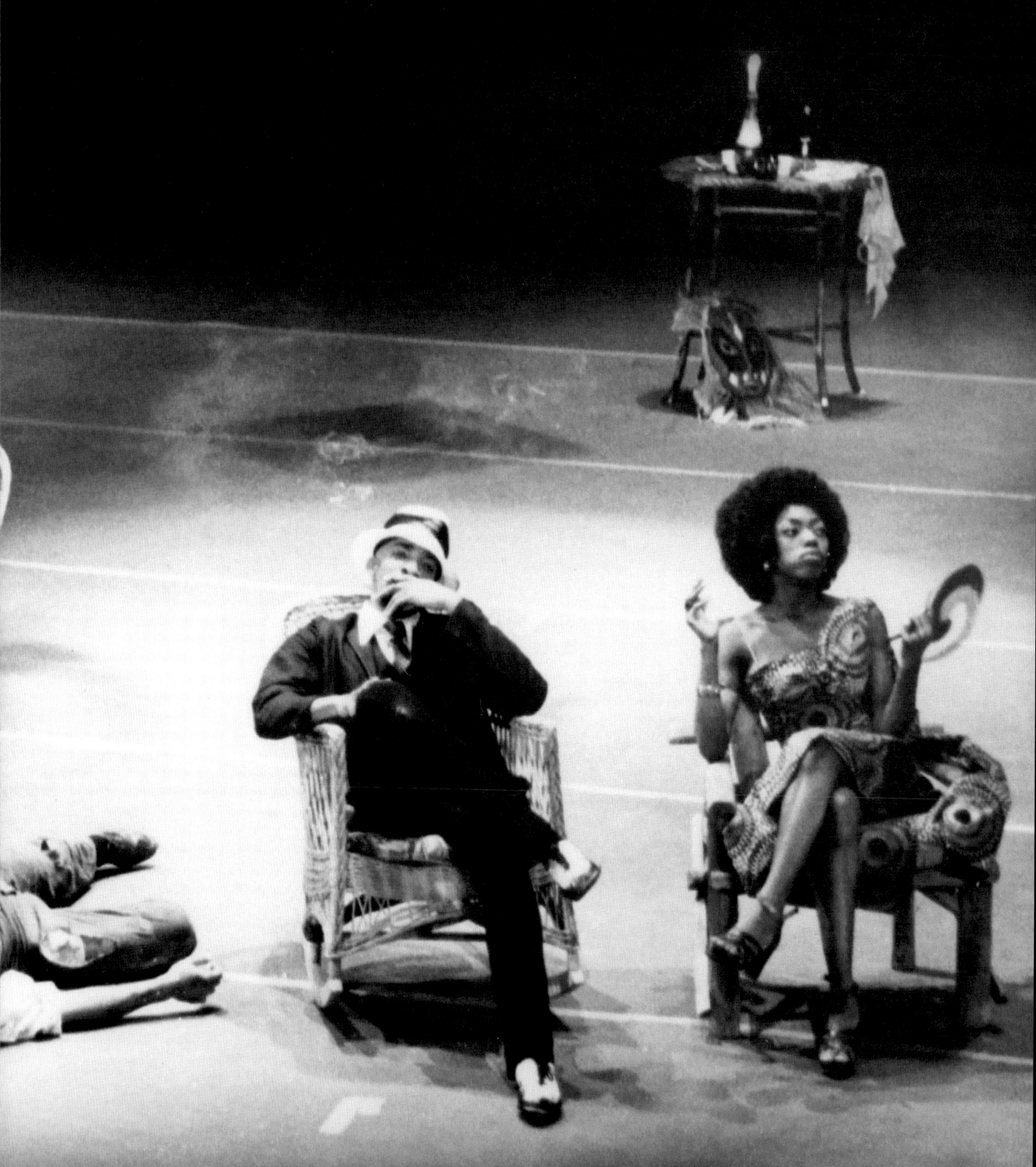

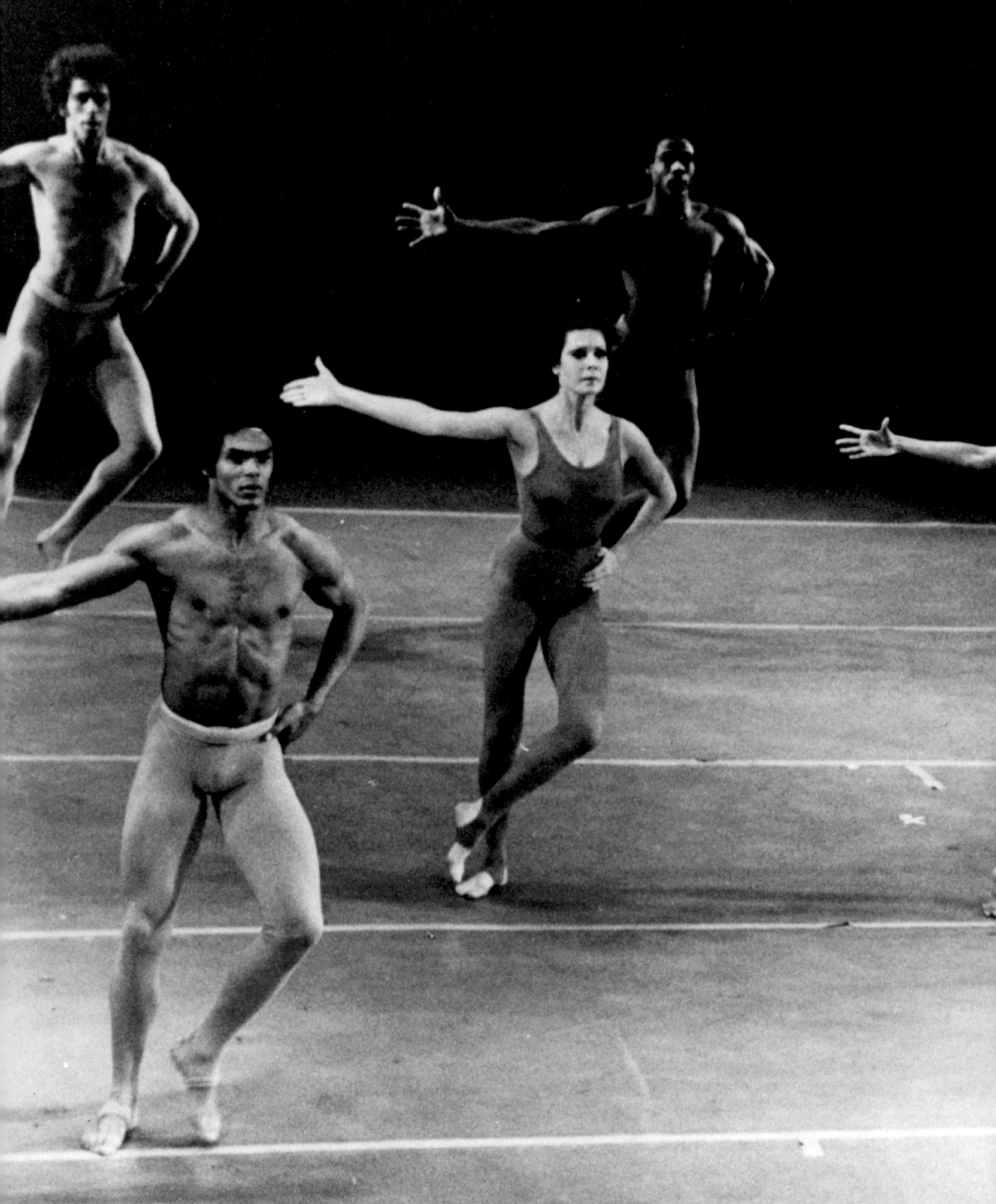

Premiere, Brooklyn Academy of Music | **Streams** | 1970

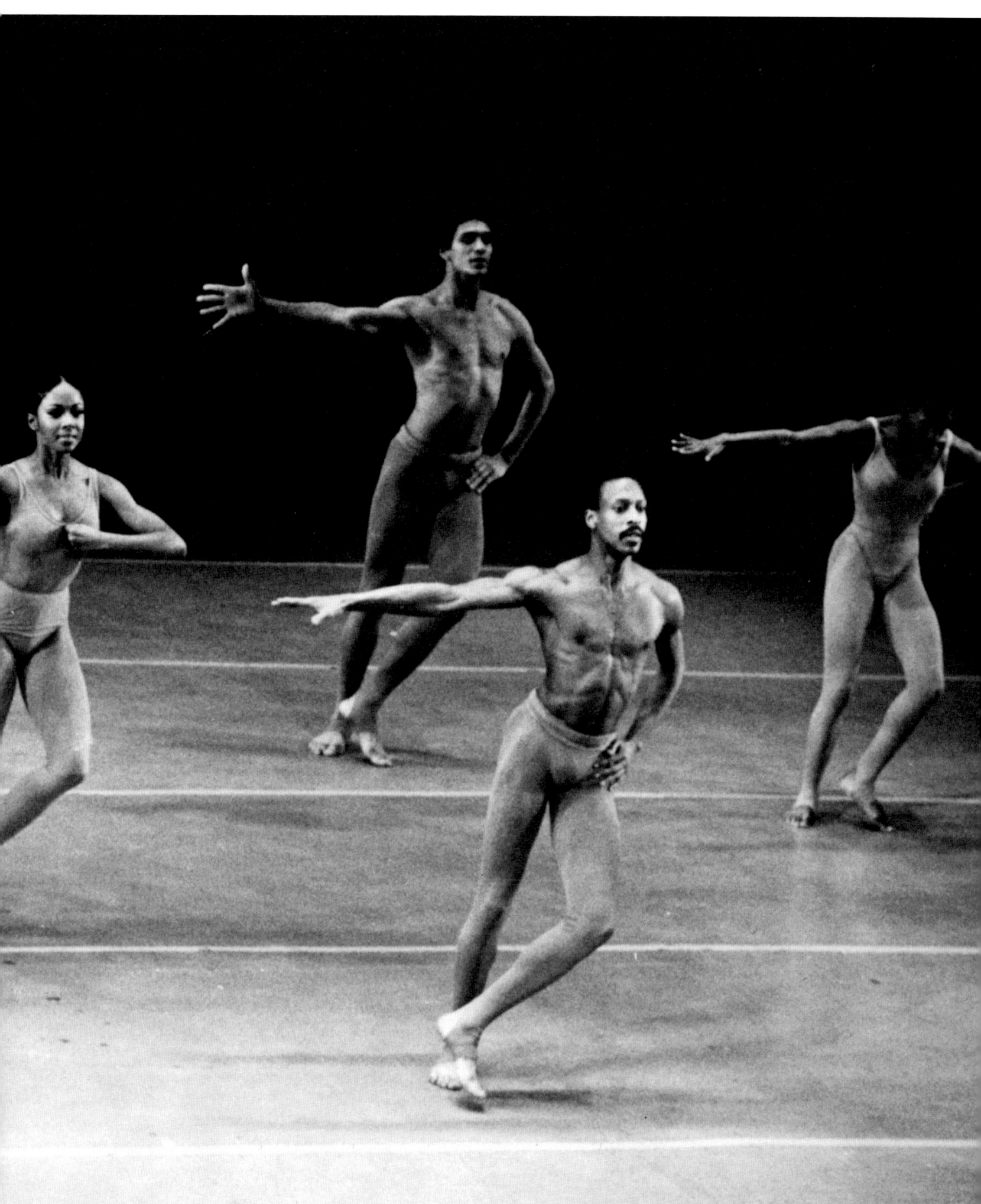

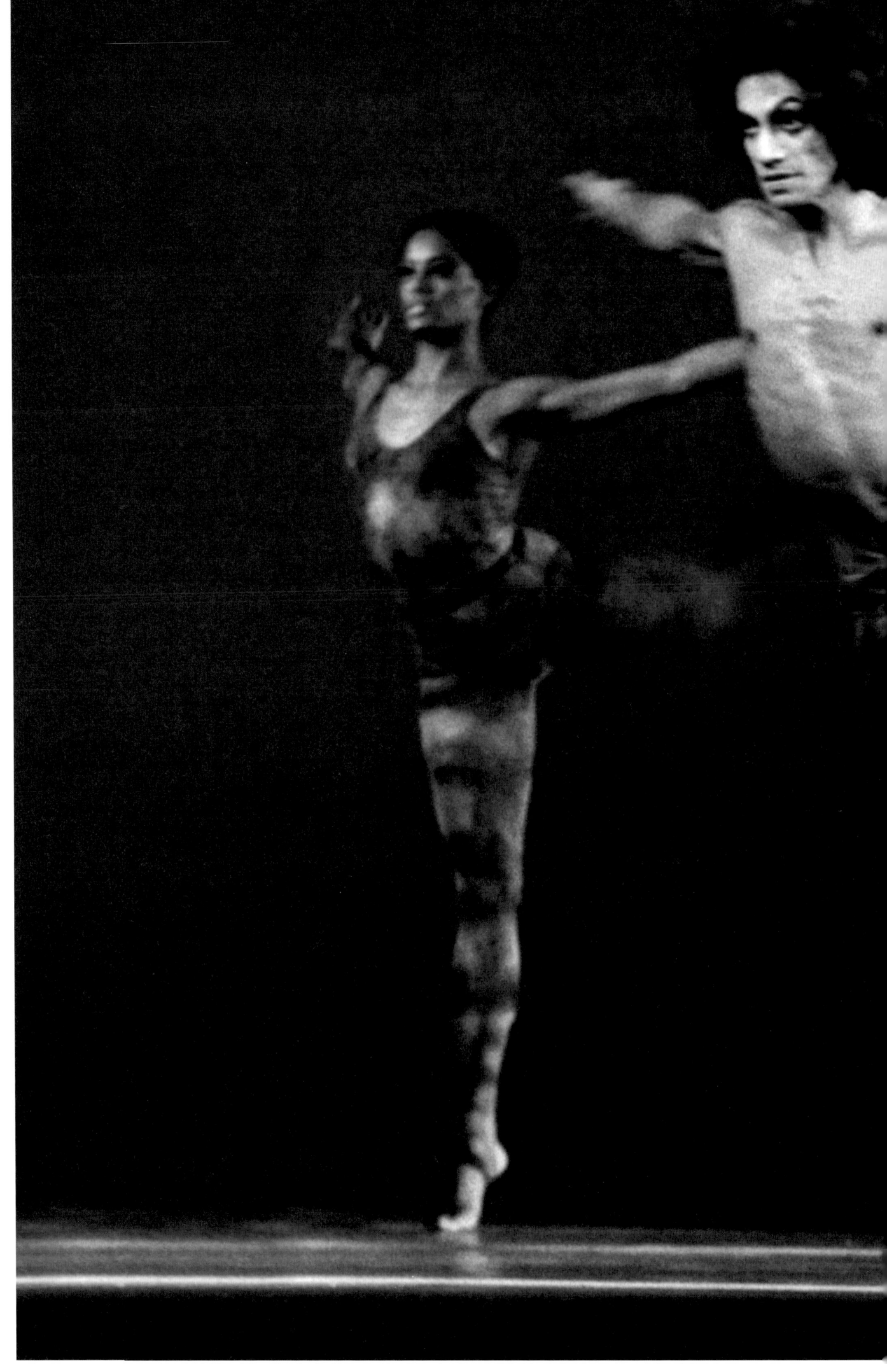

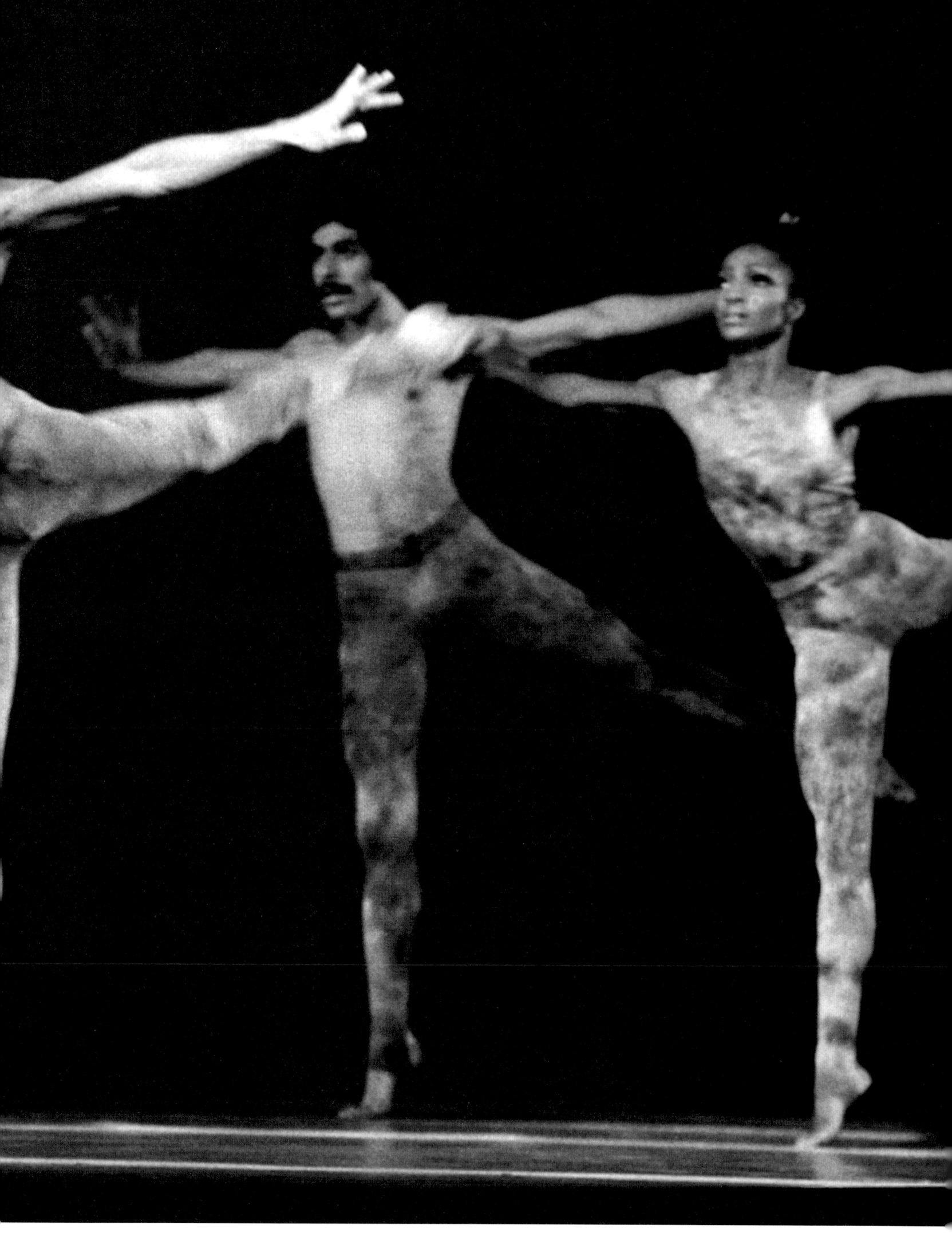
Streams

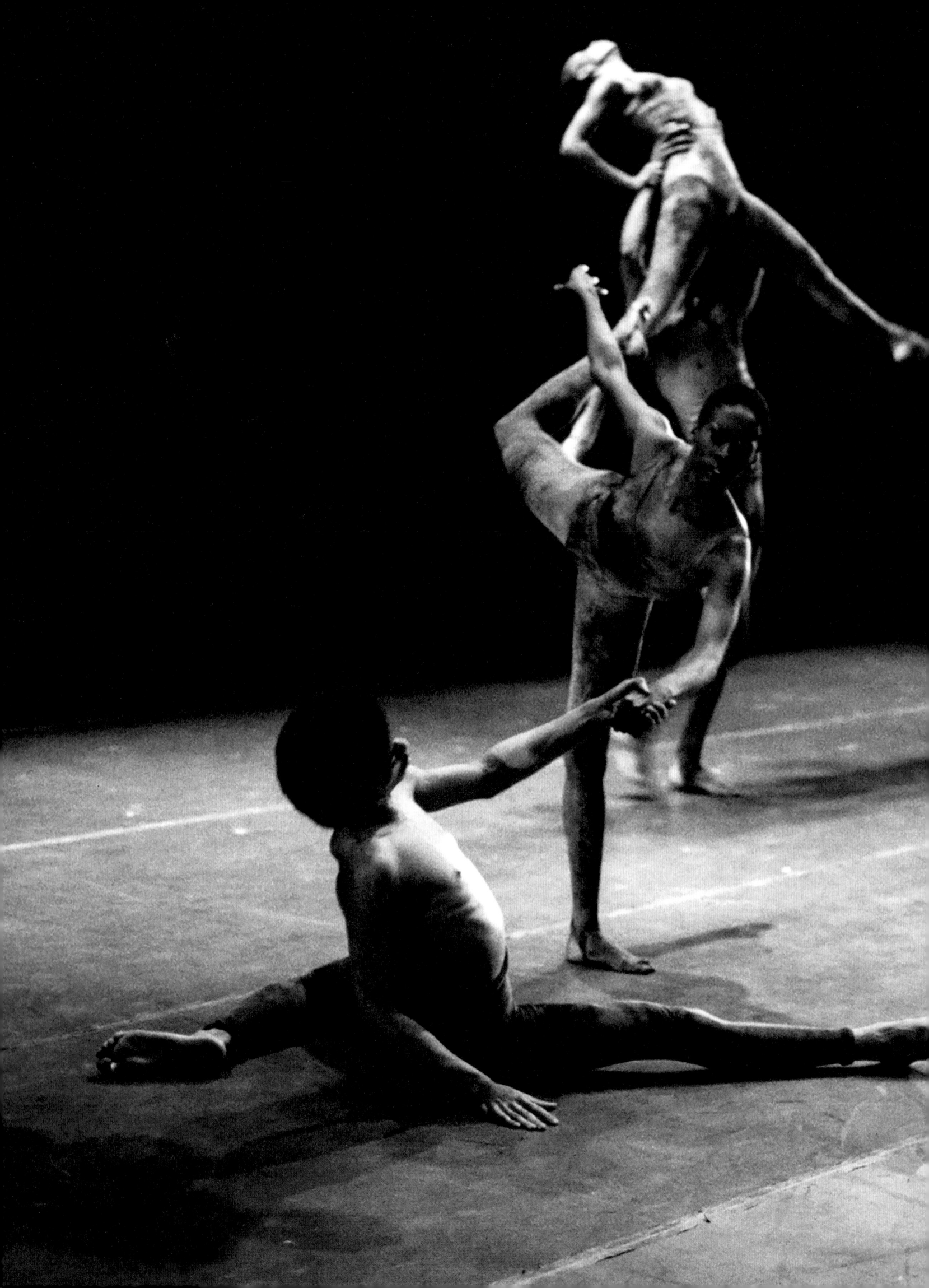

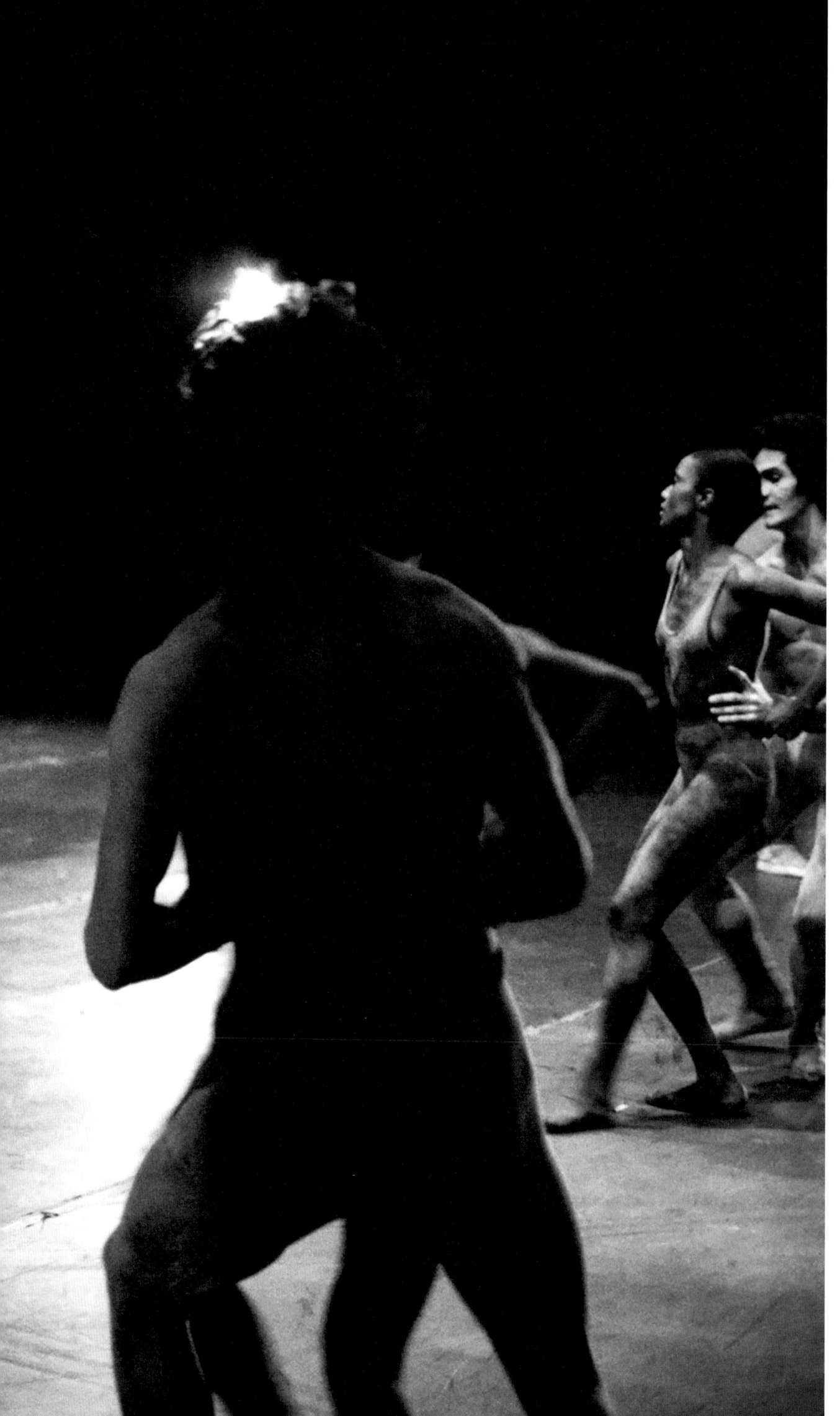

Premiere, Brooklyn Academy of Music **Gymnopedies** 1970

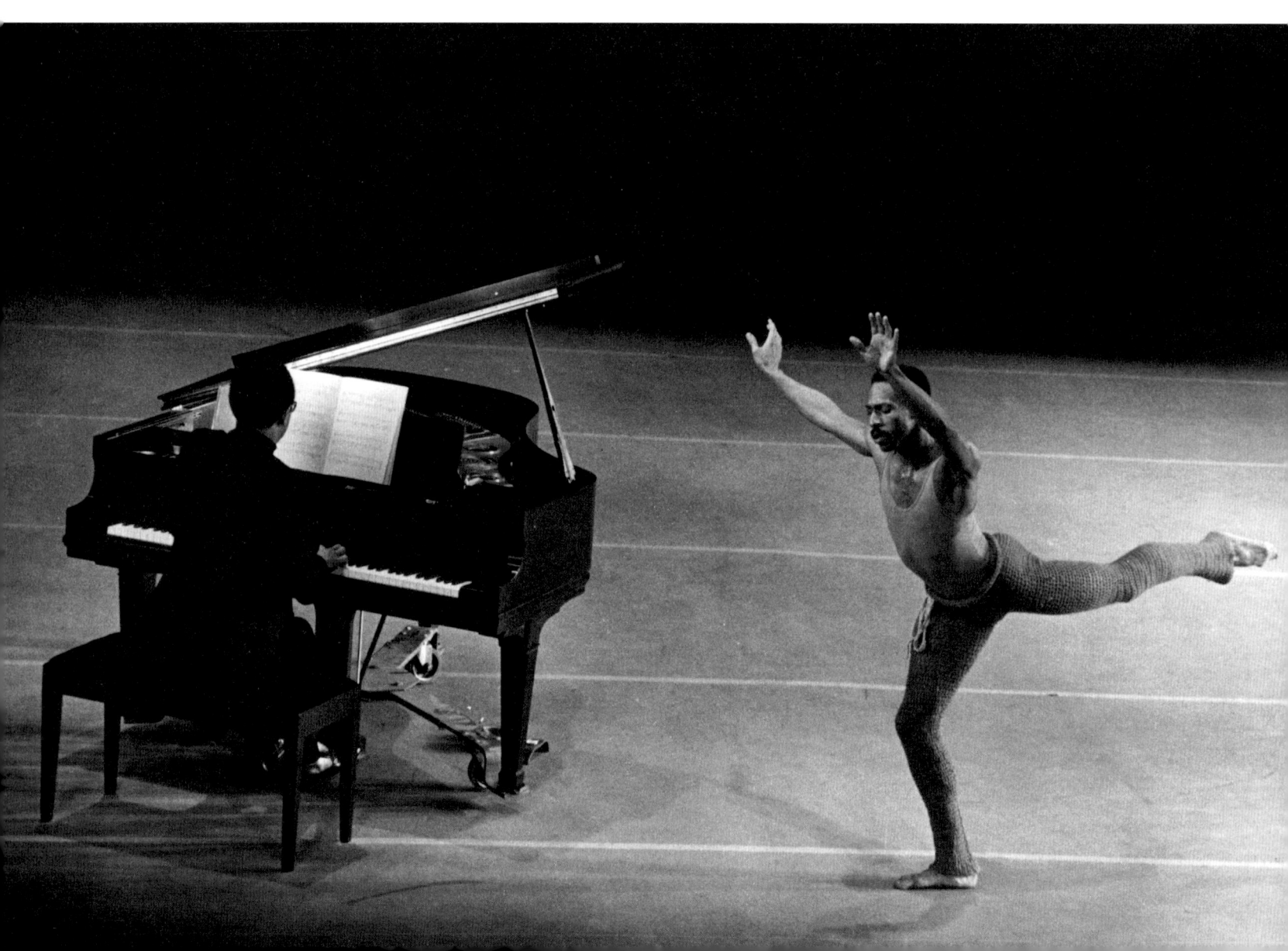

Premiere, New York State Theater, Lincoln Center — The River — 1970/1978/1981

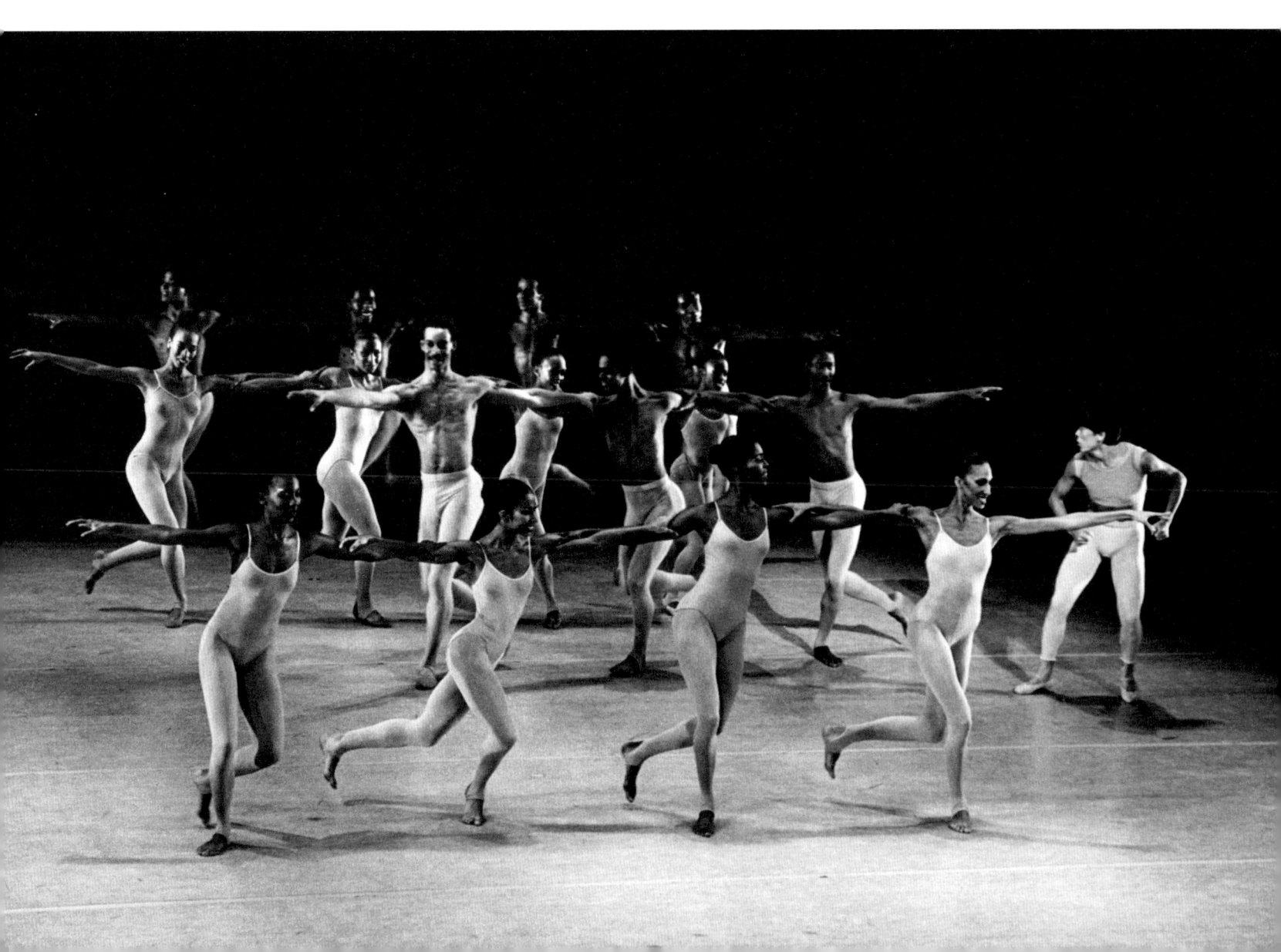

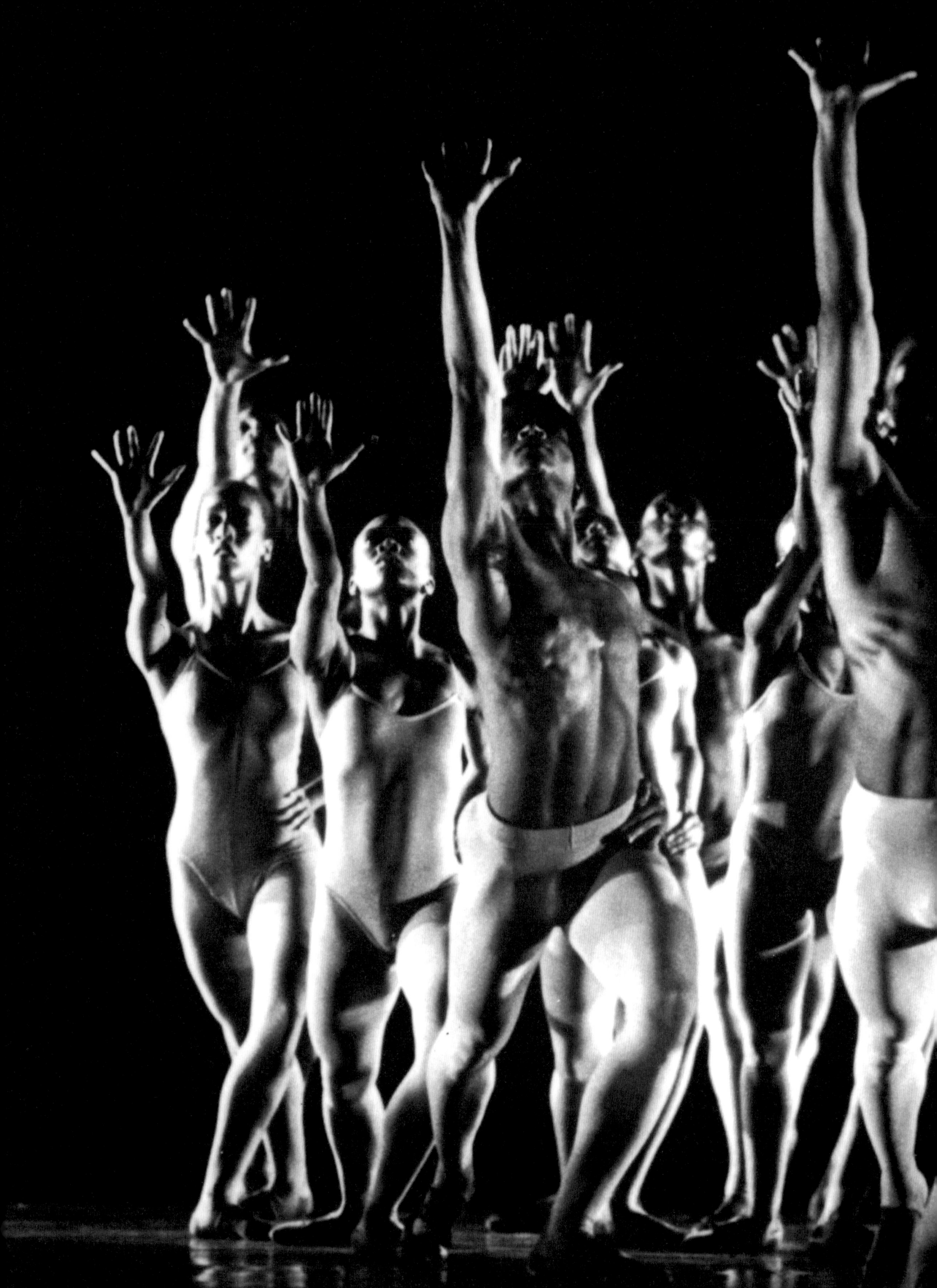

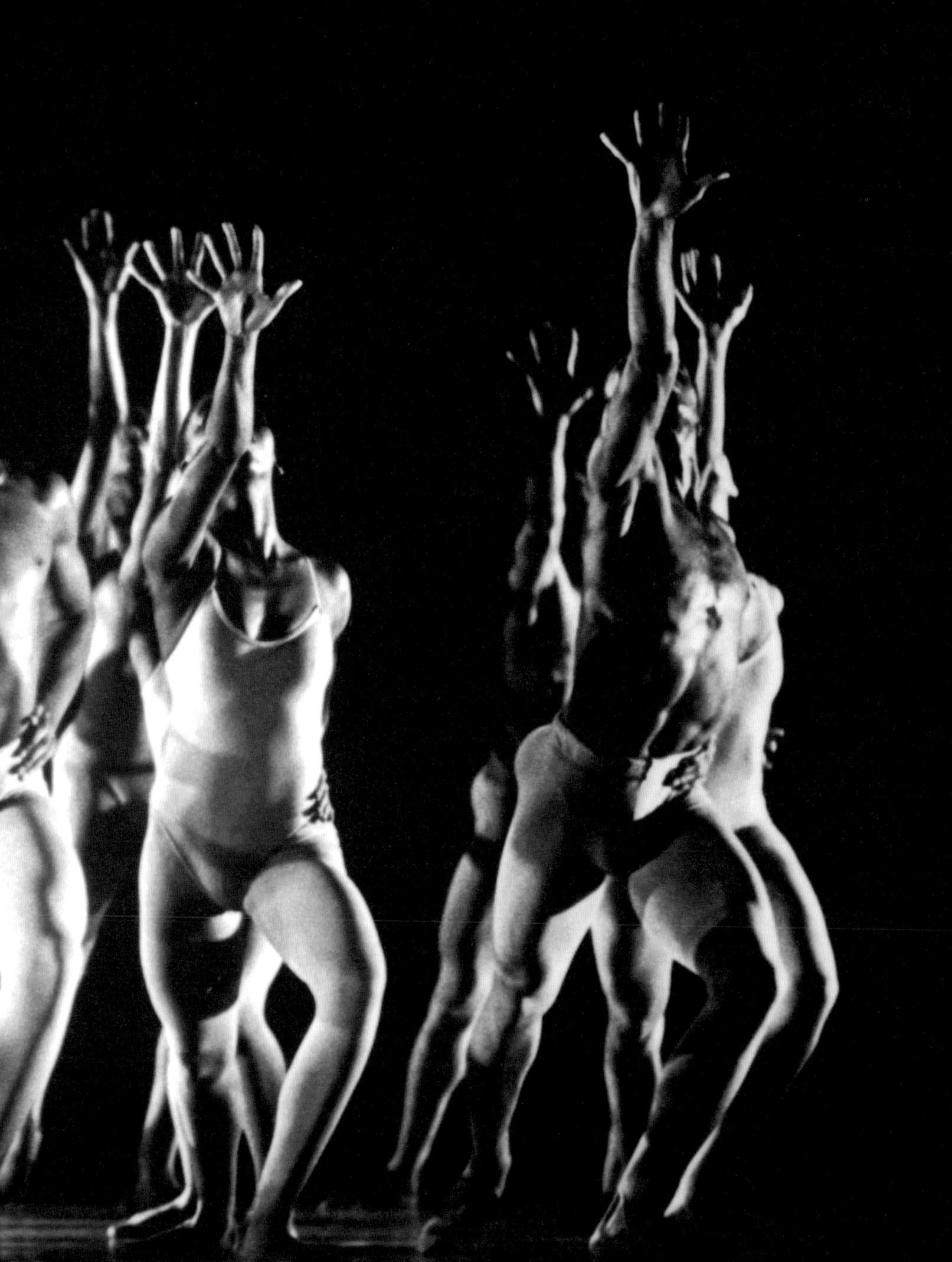

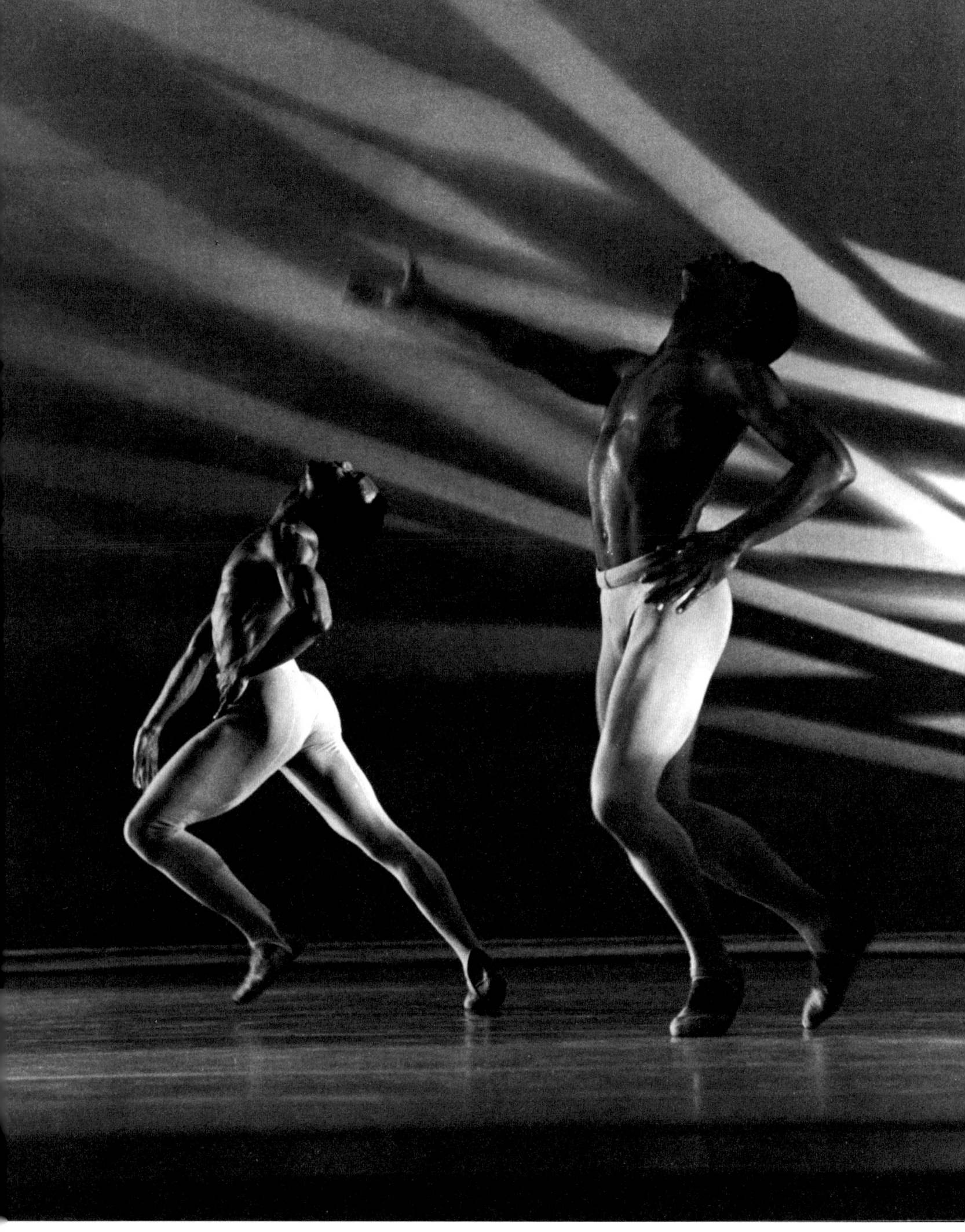

Premiere, ANTA Theatre, New York **Archipelago** 1971

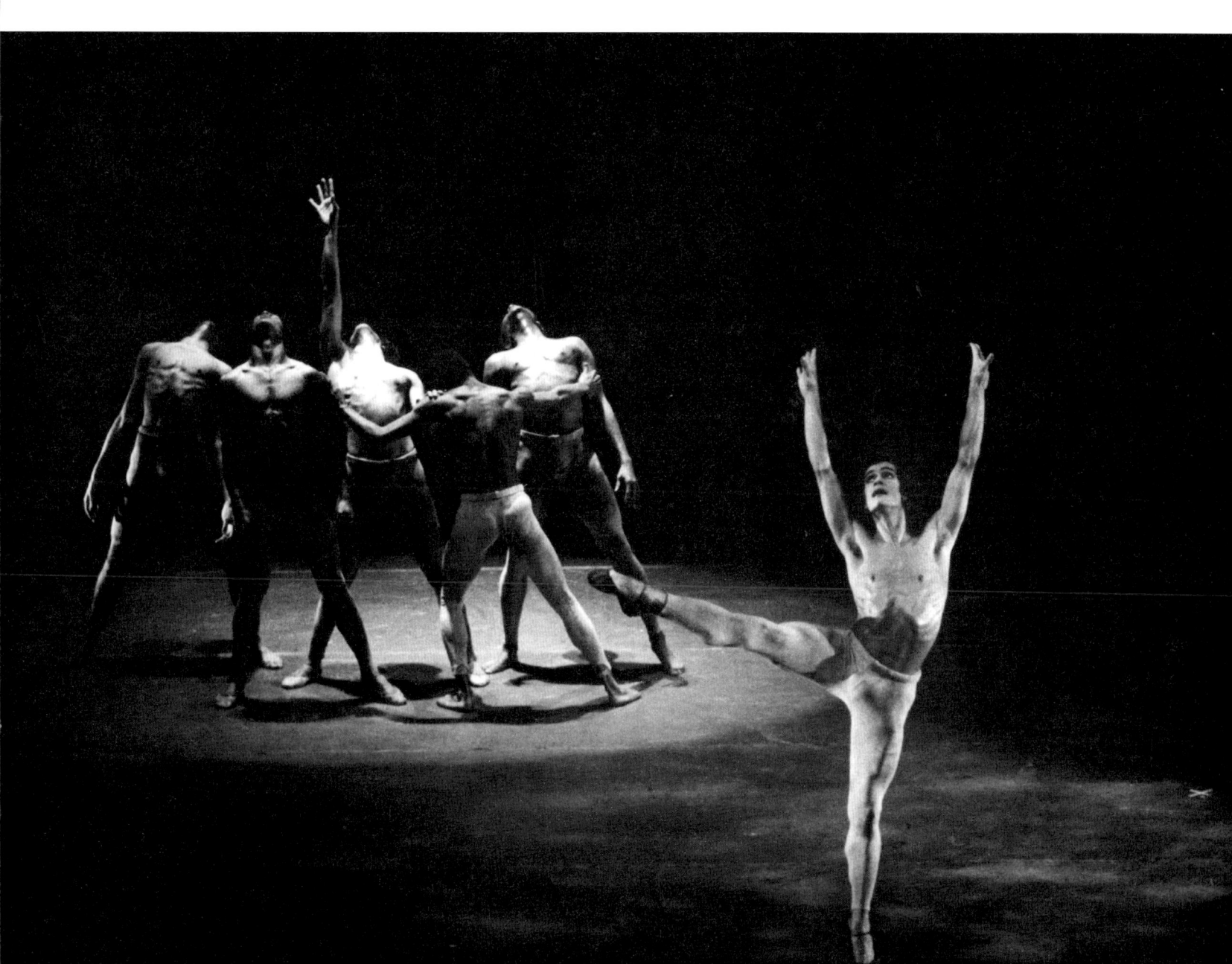

Premiere, ANTA Theatre, New York | **Flowers** | 1971

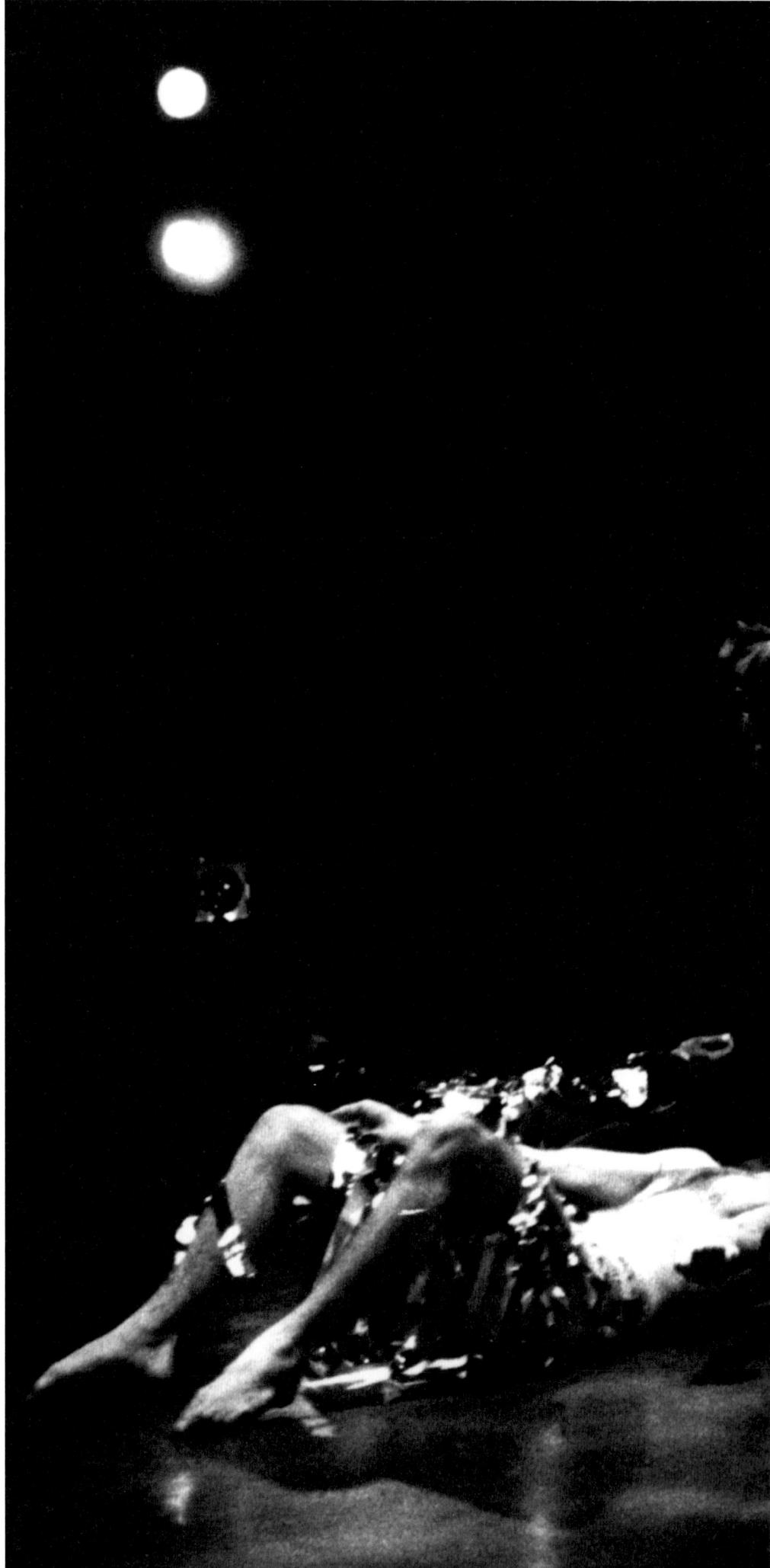

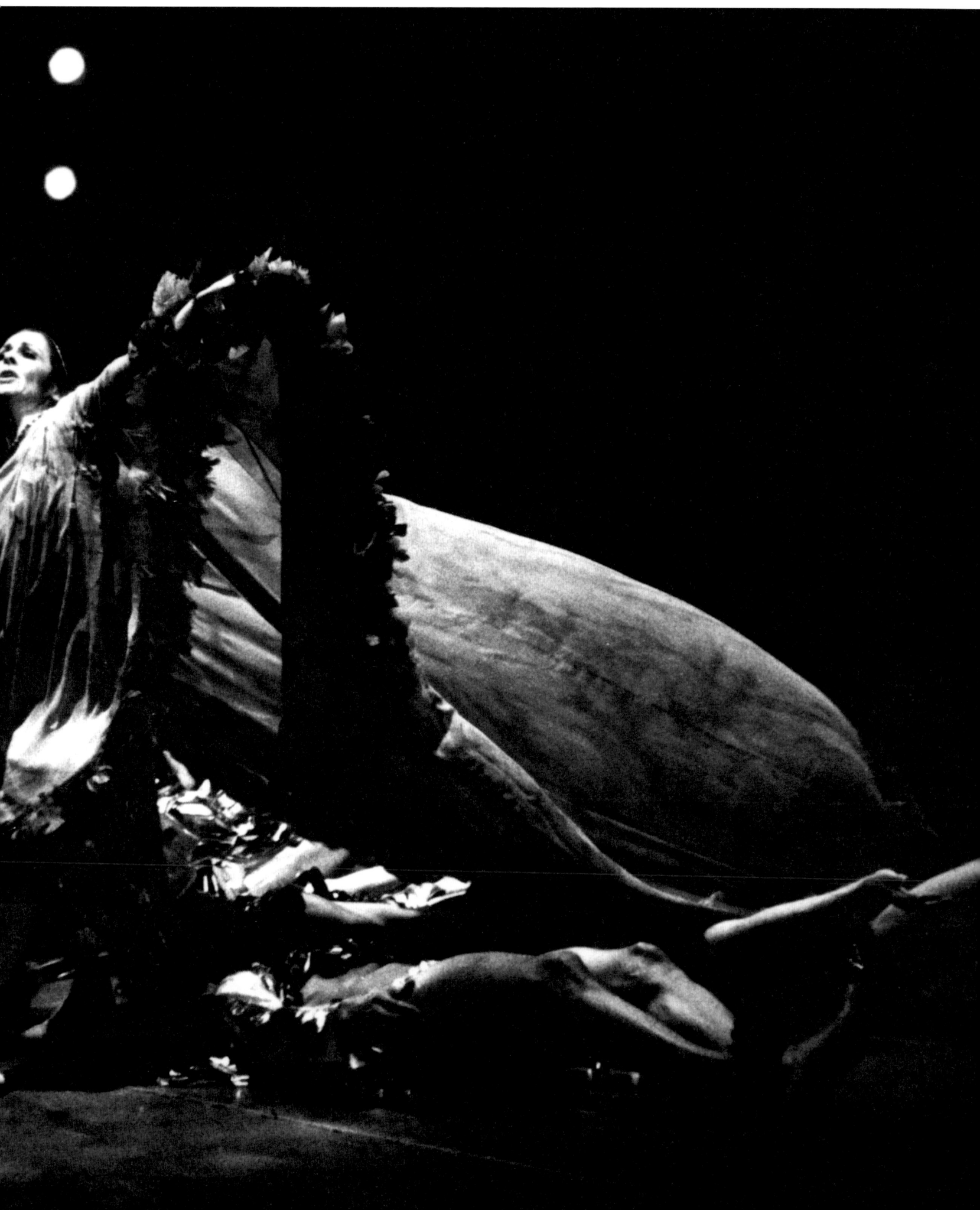

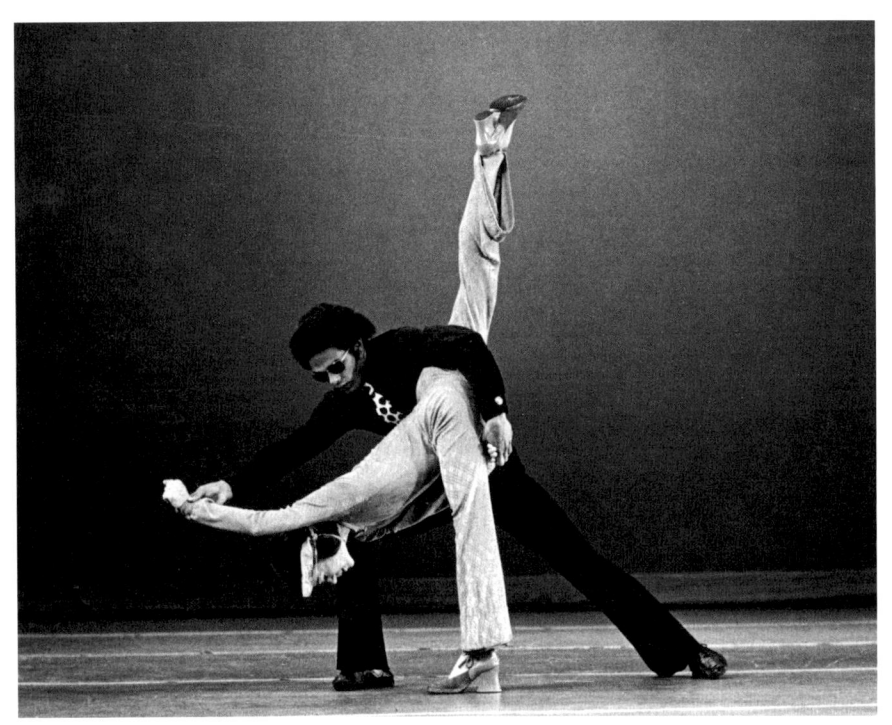

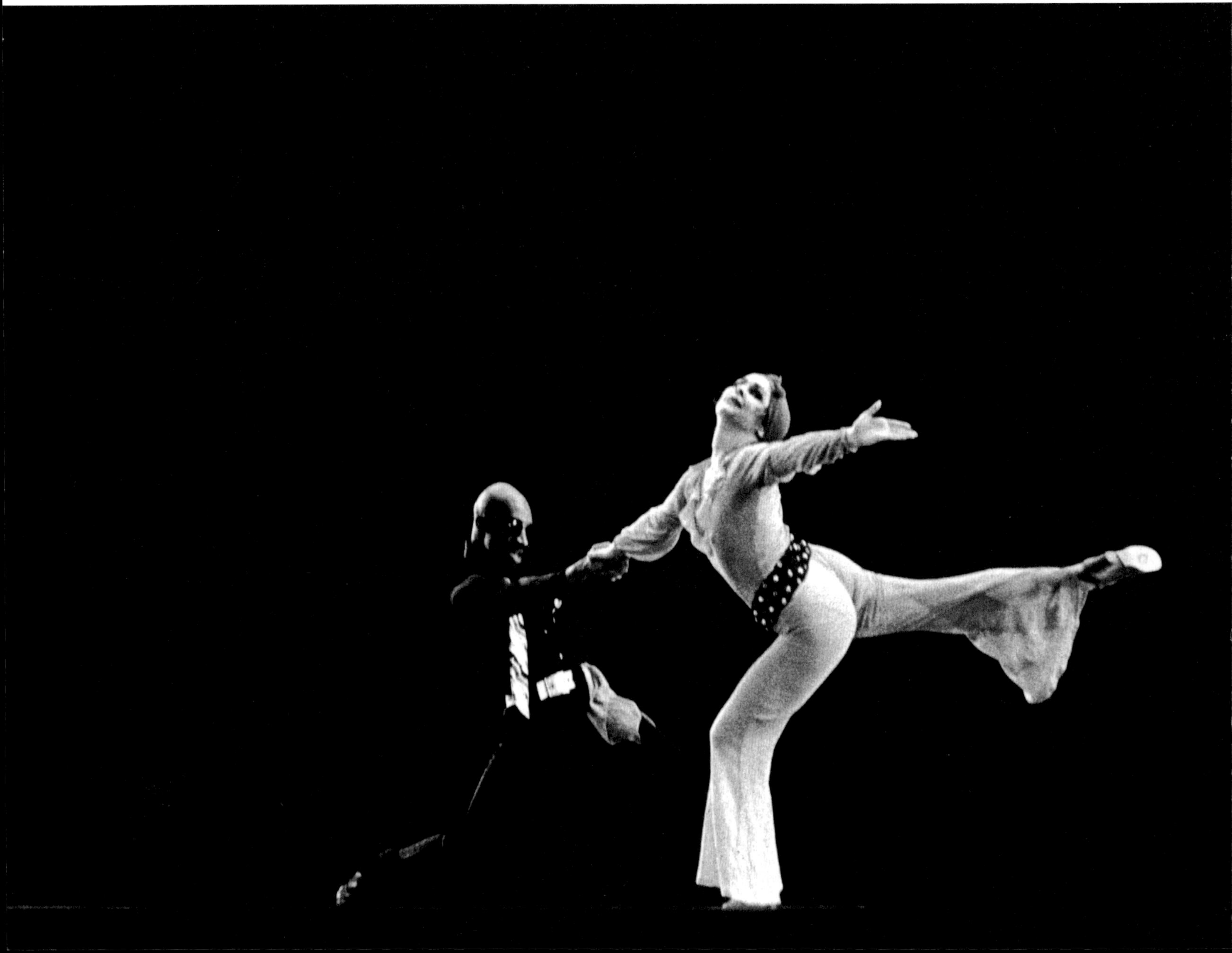

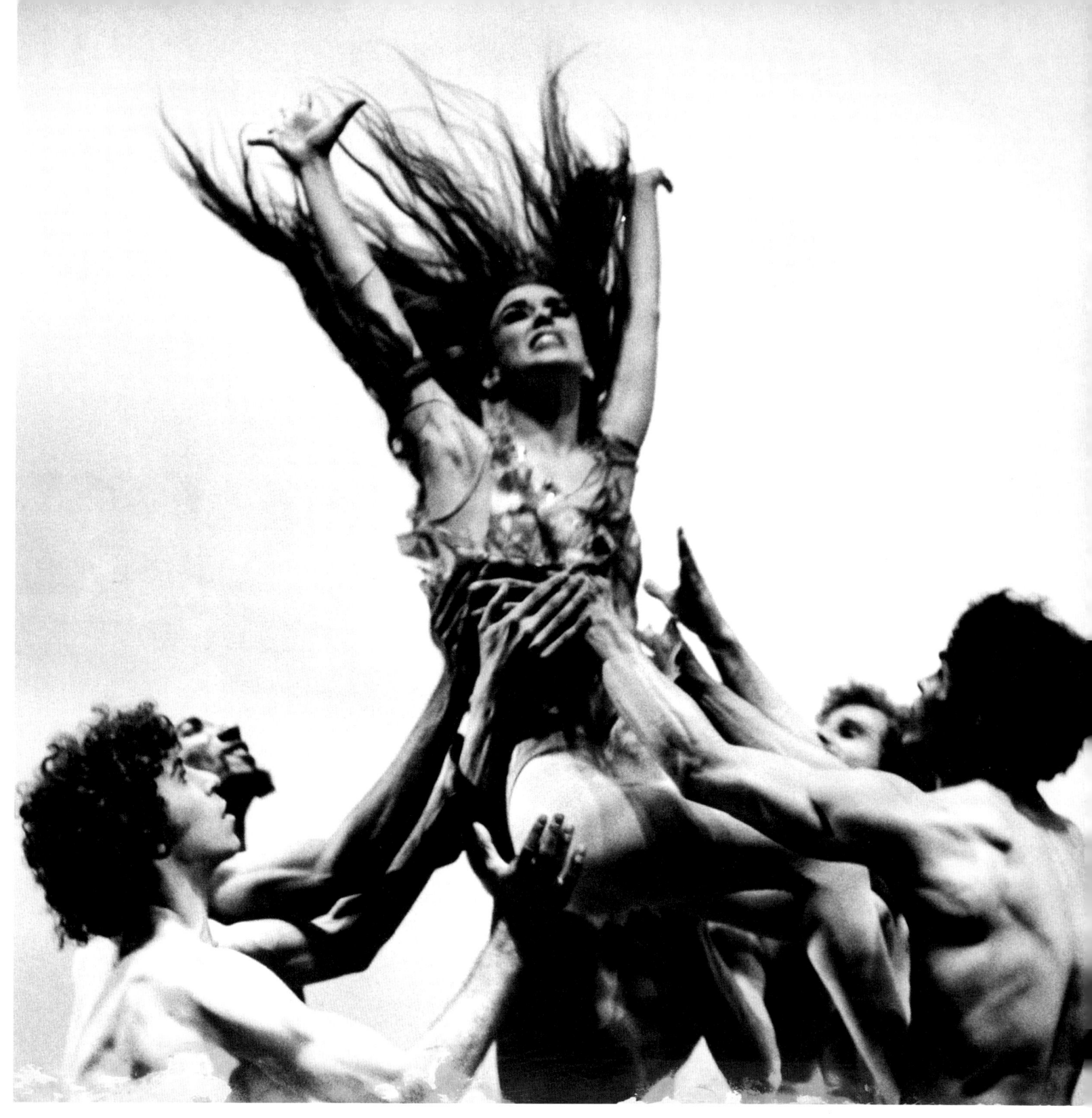

Flowers

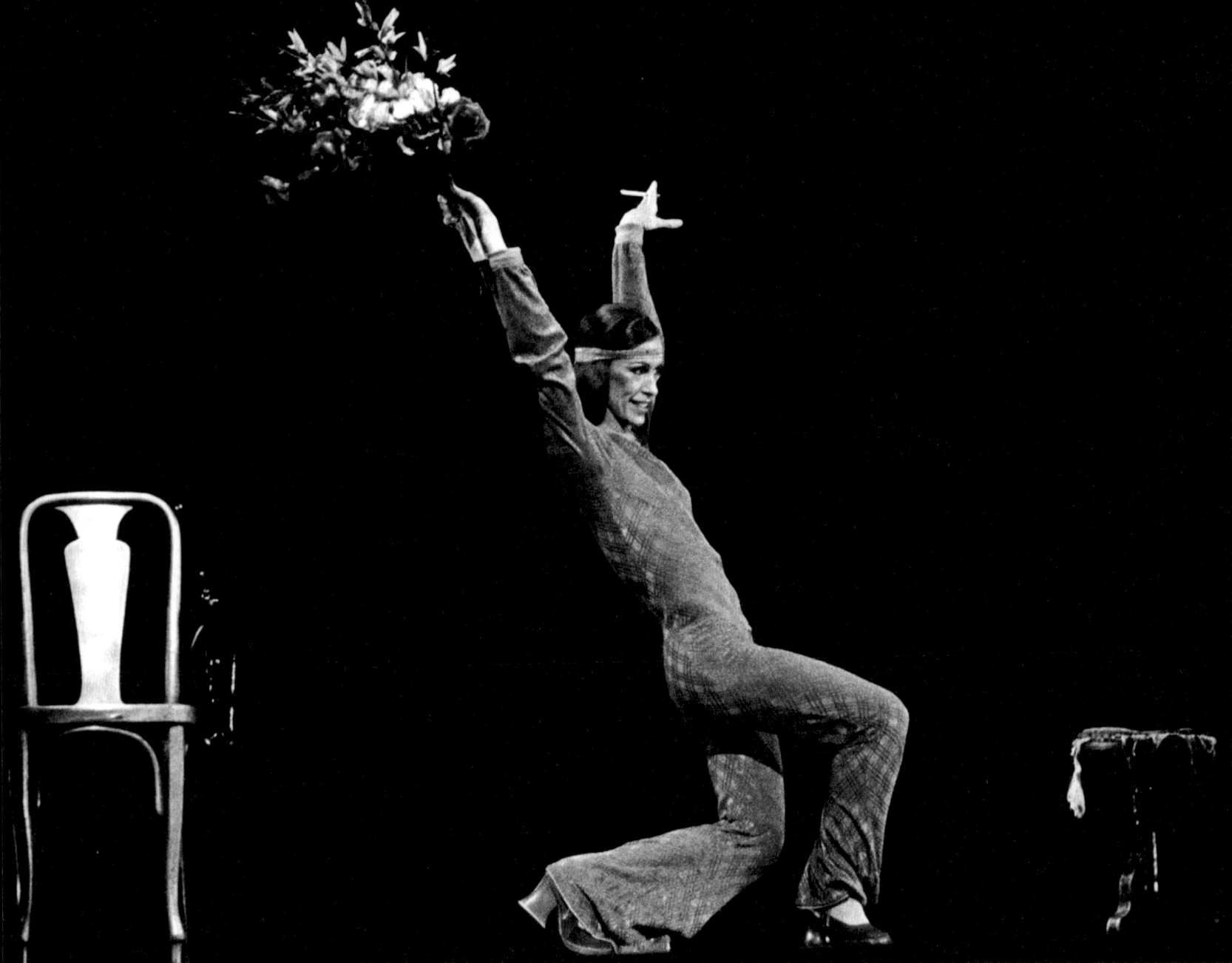

214 Flowers

Premiere, New York City Center | **Choral Dances** | 1971

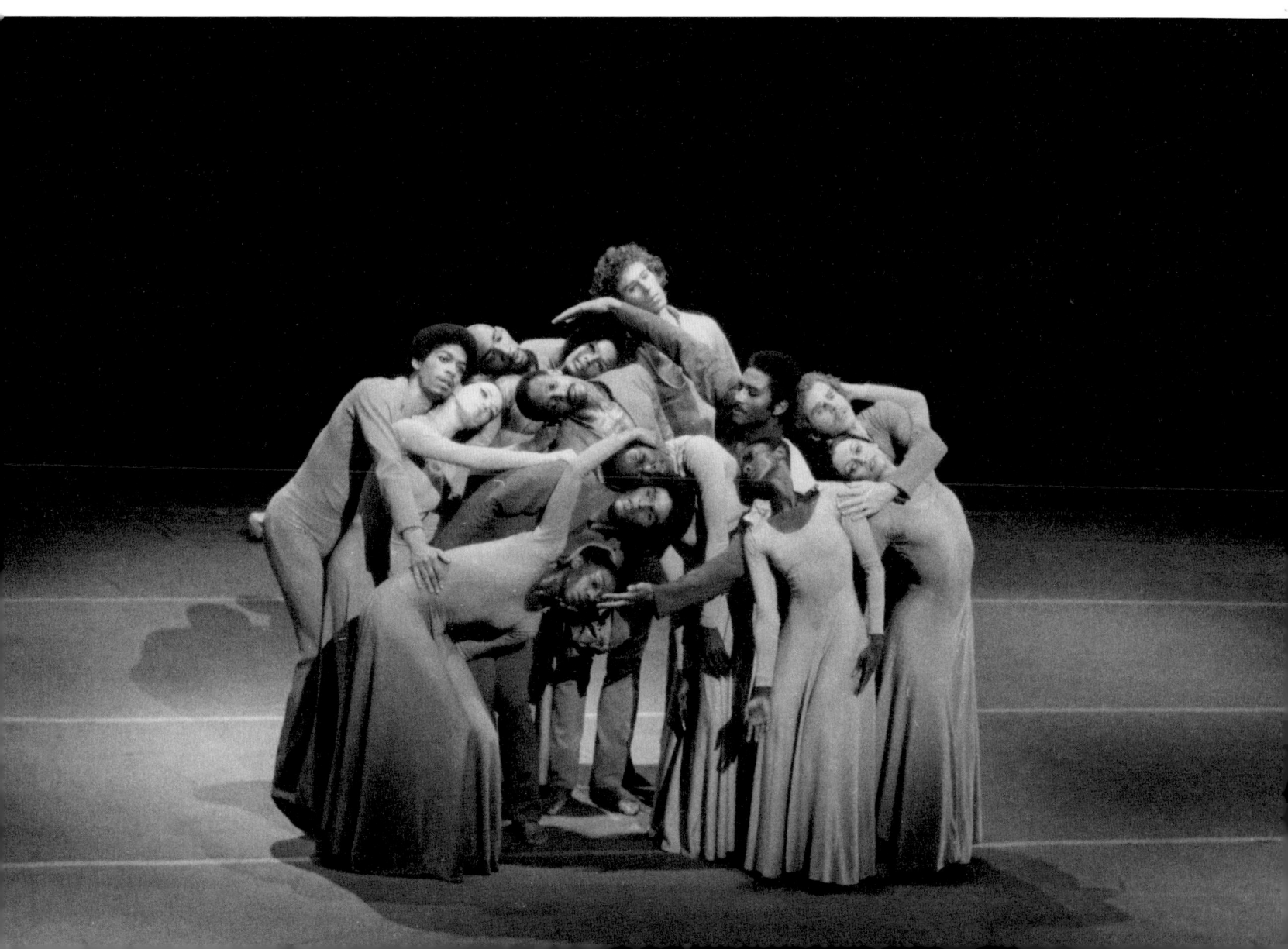

Premiere, New York City Center — **Cry** — 1971

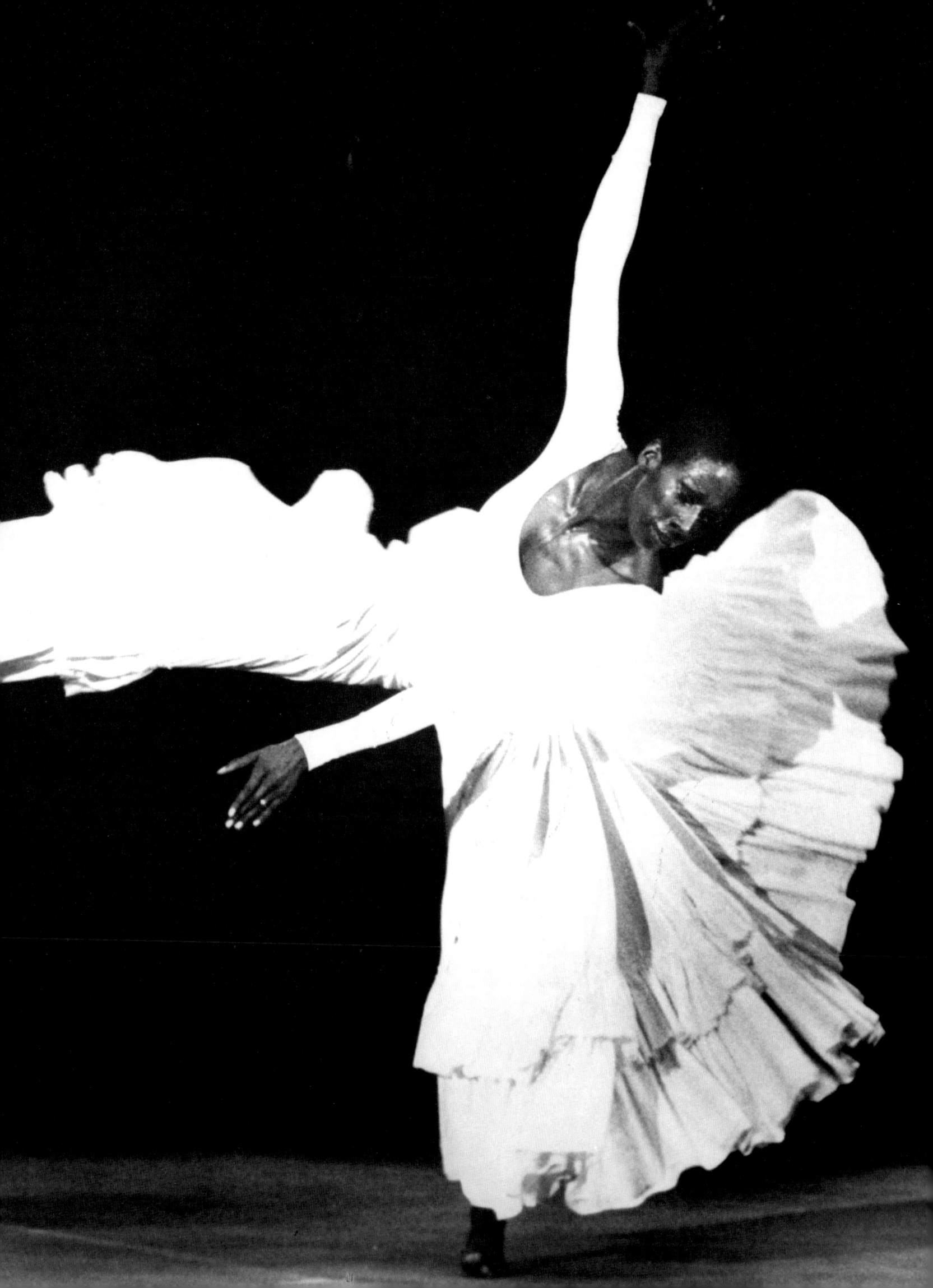

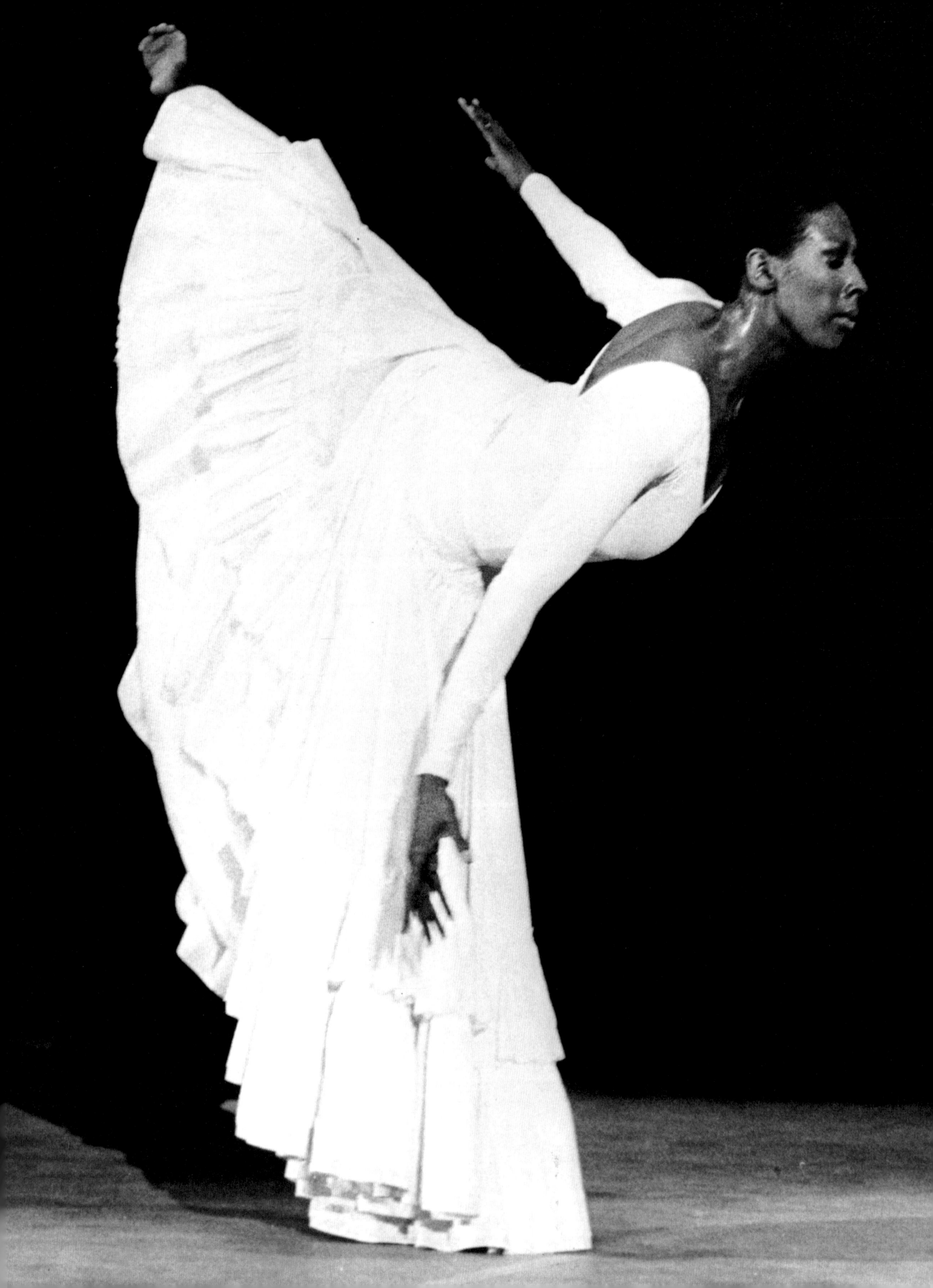

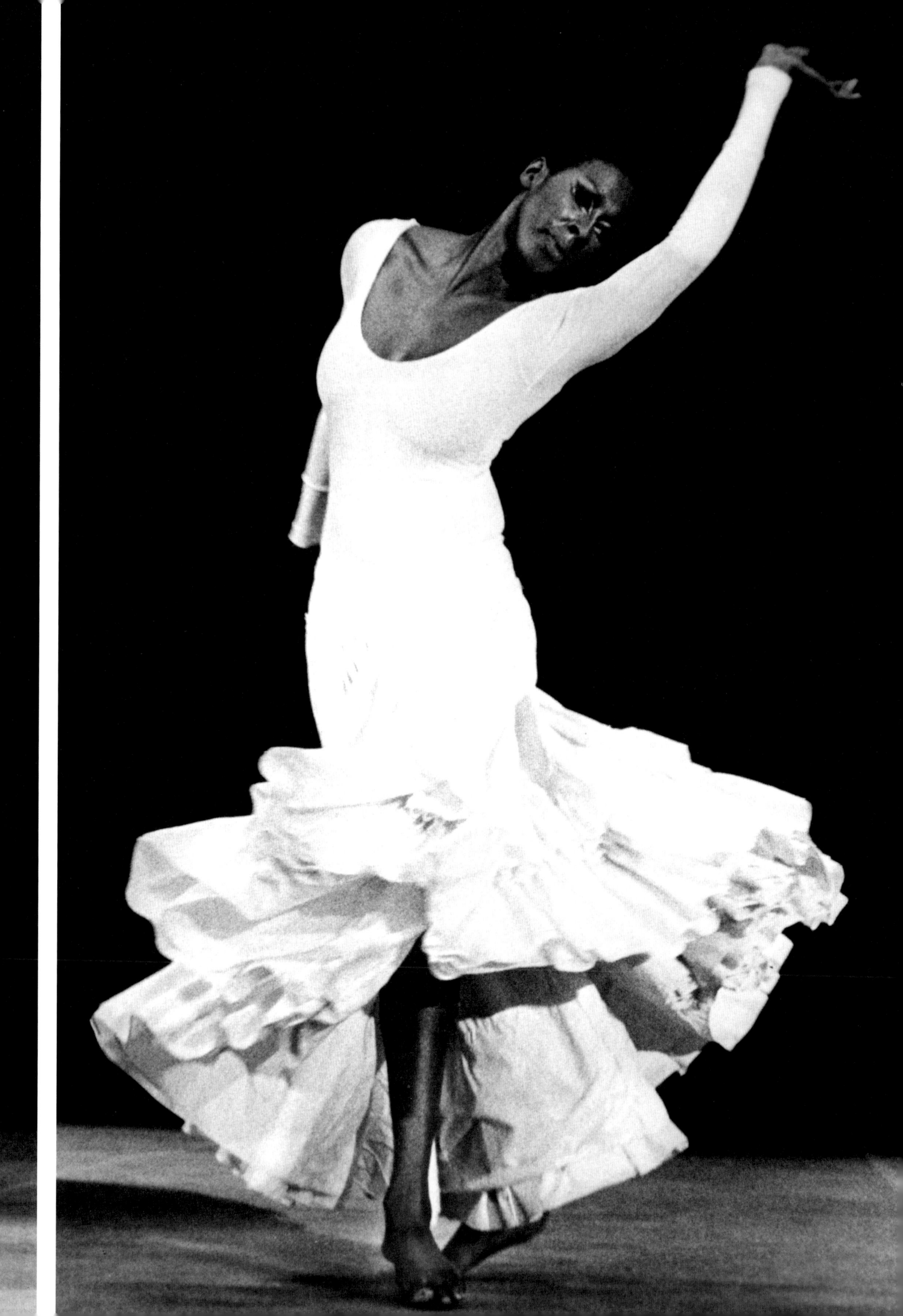

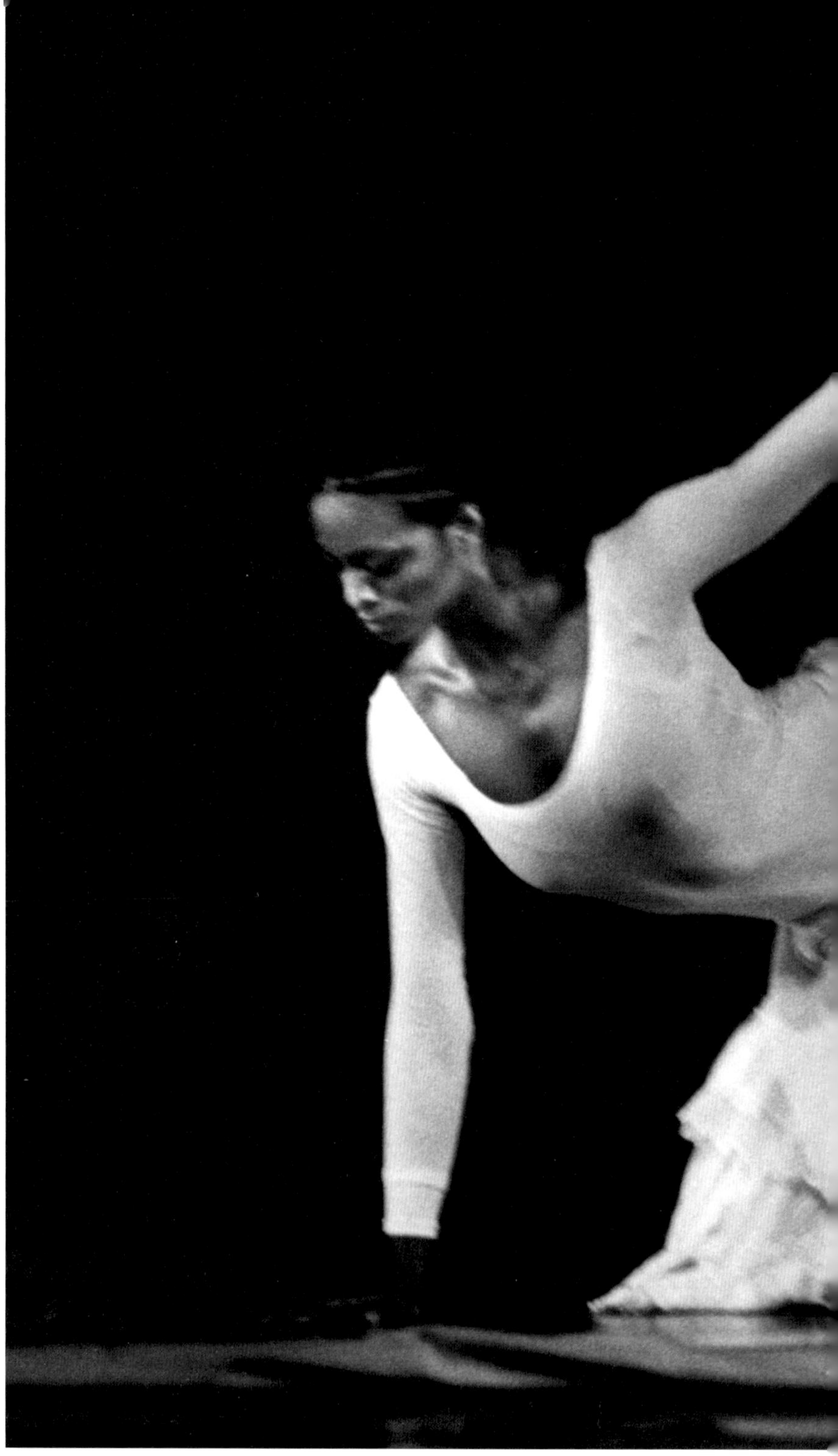

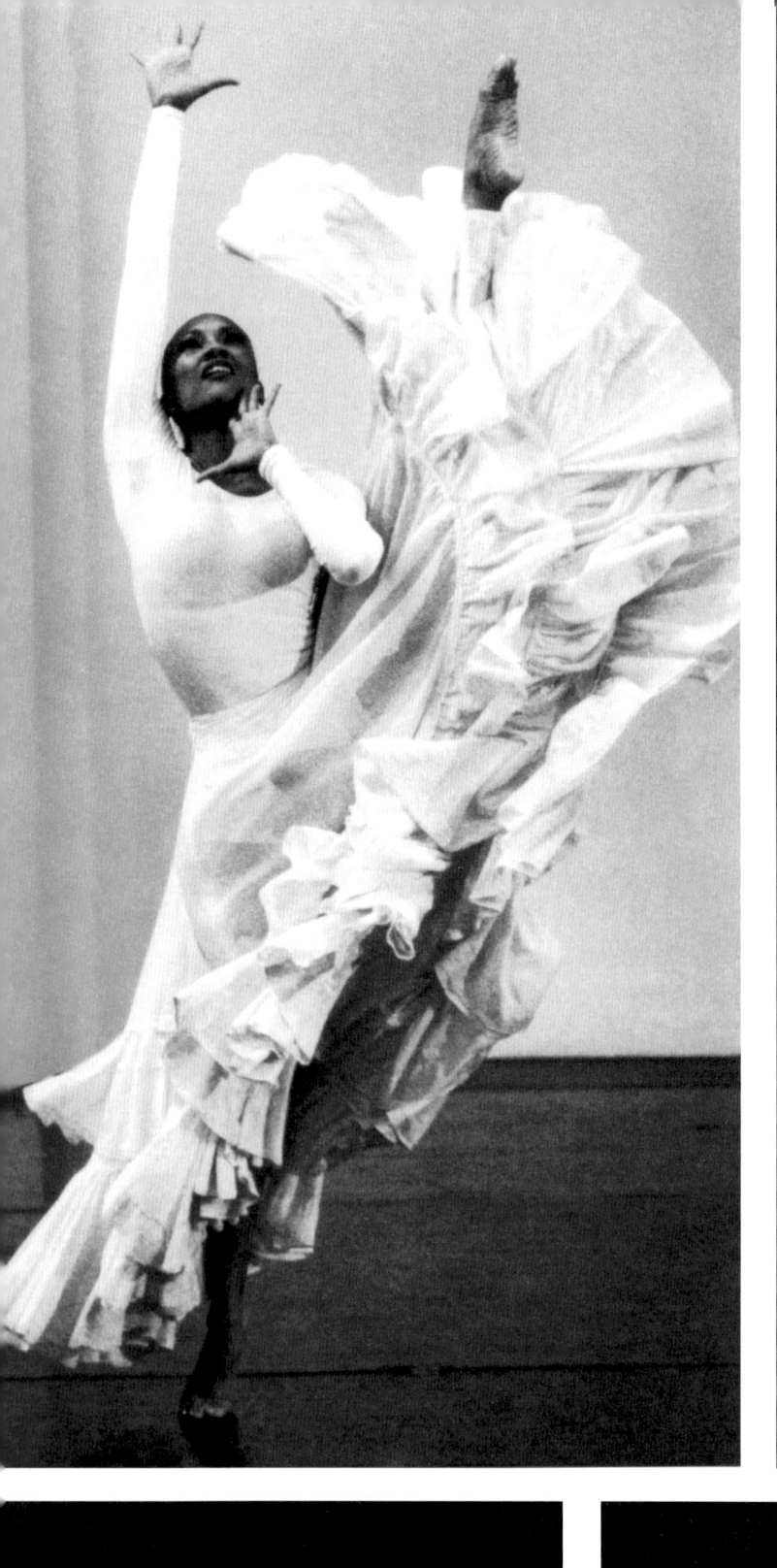
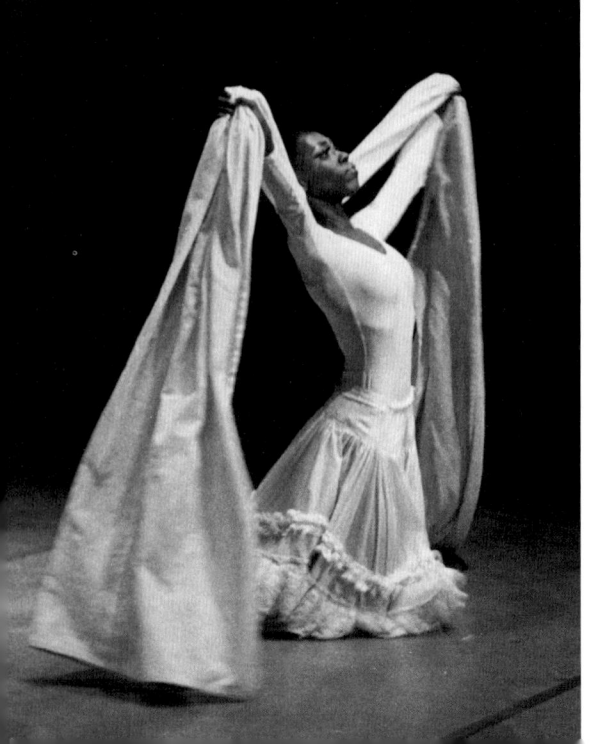
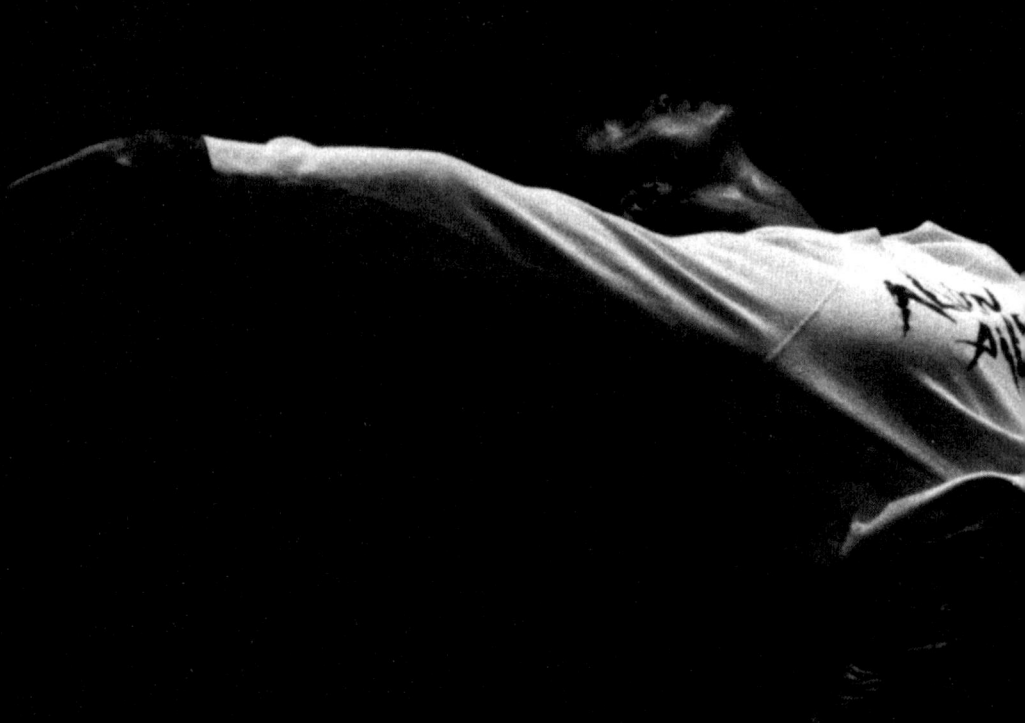

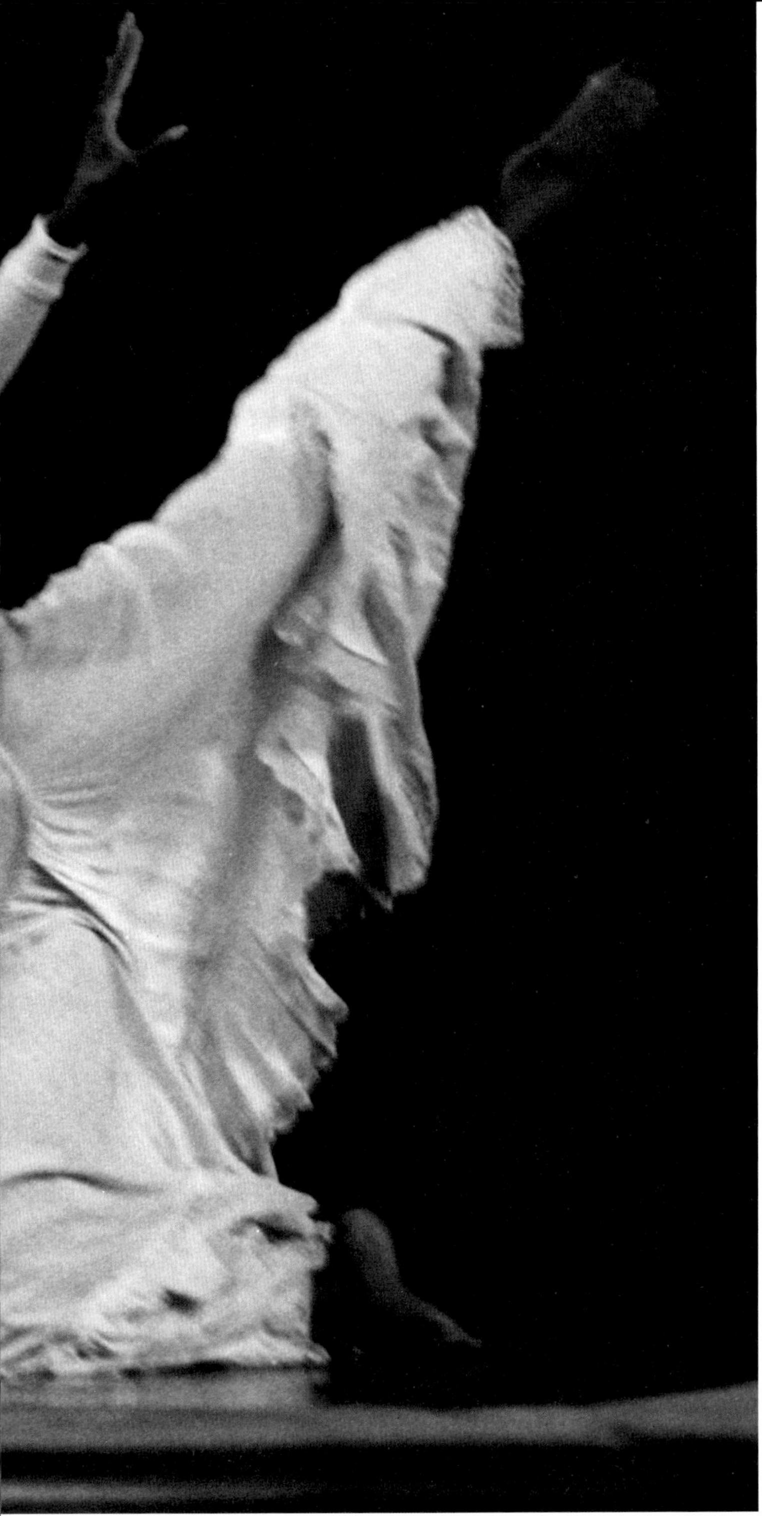

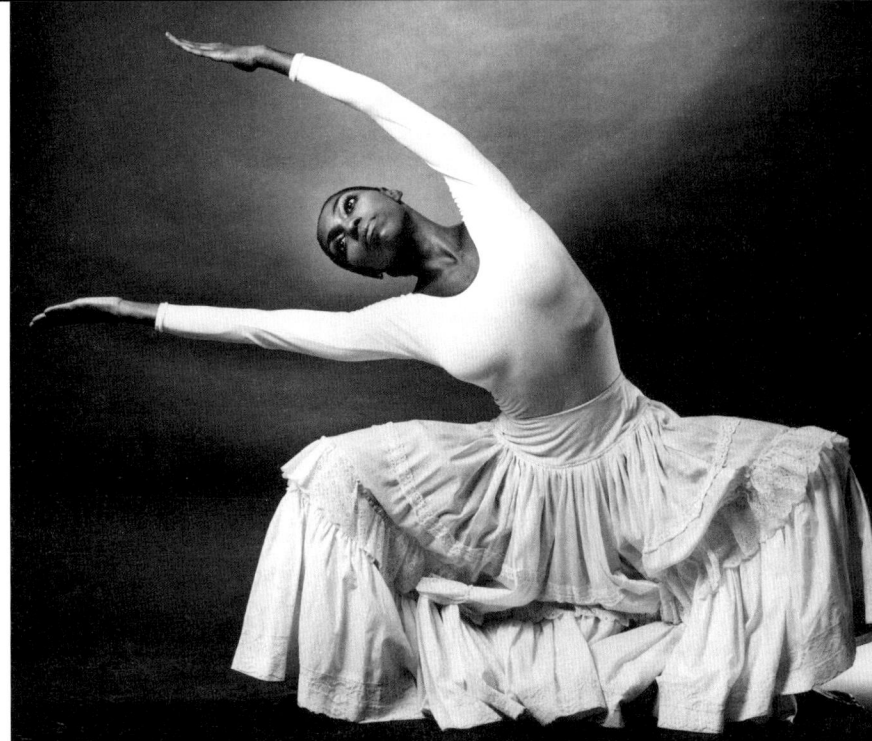
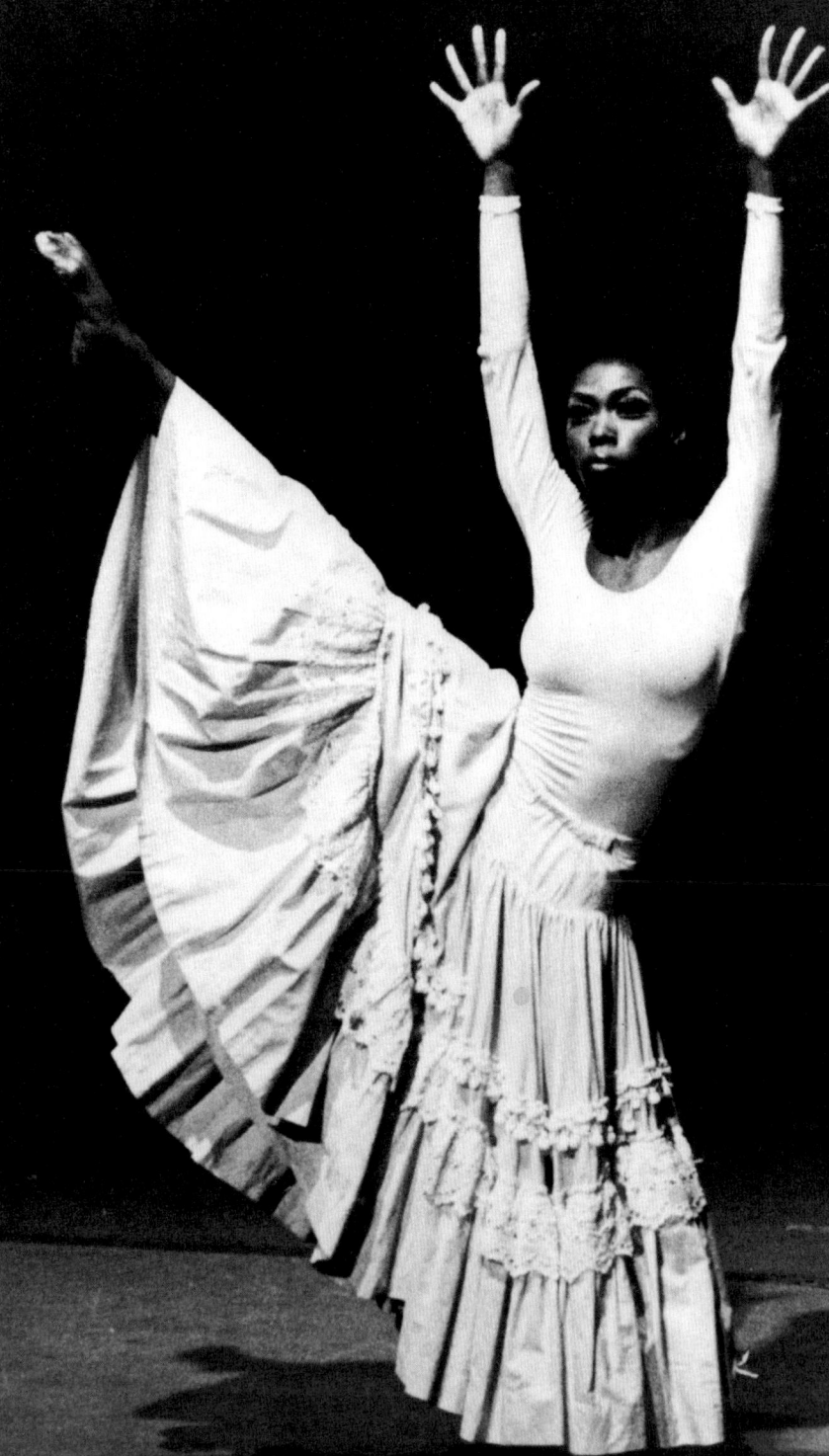
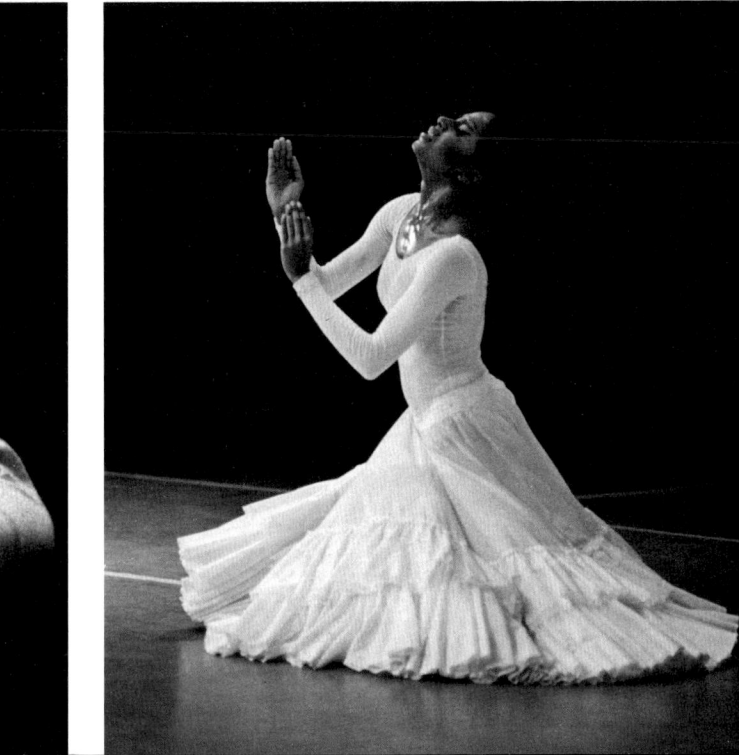

Premiere, John F. Kennedy Center for the
Performing Arts, Washington, DC

Mass

1971

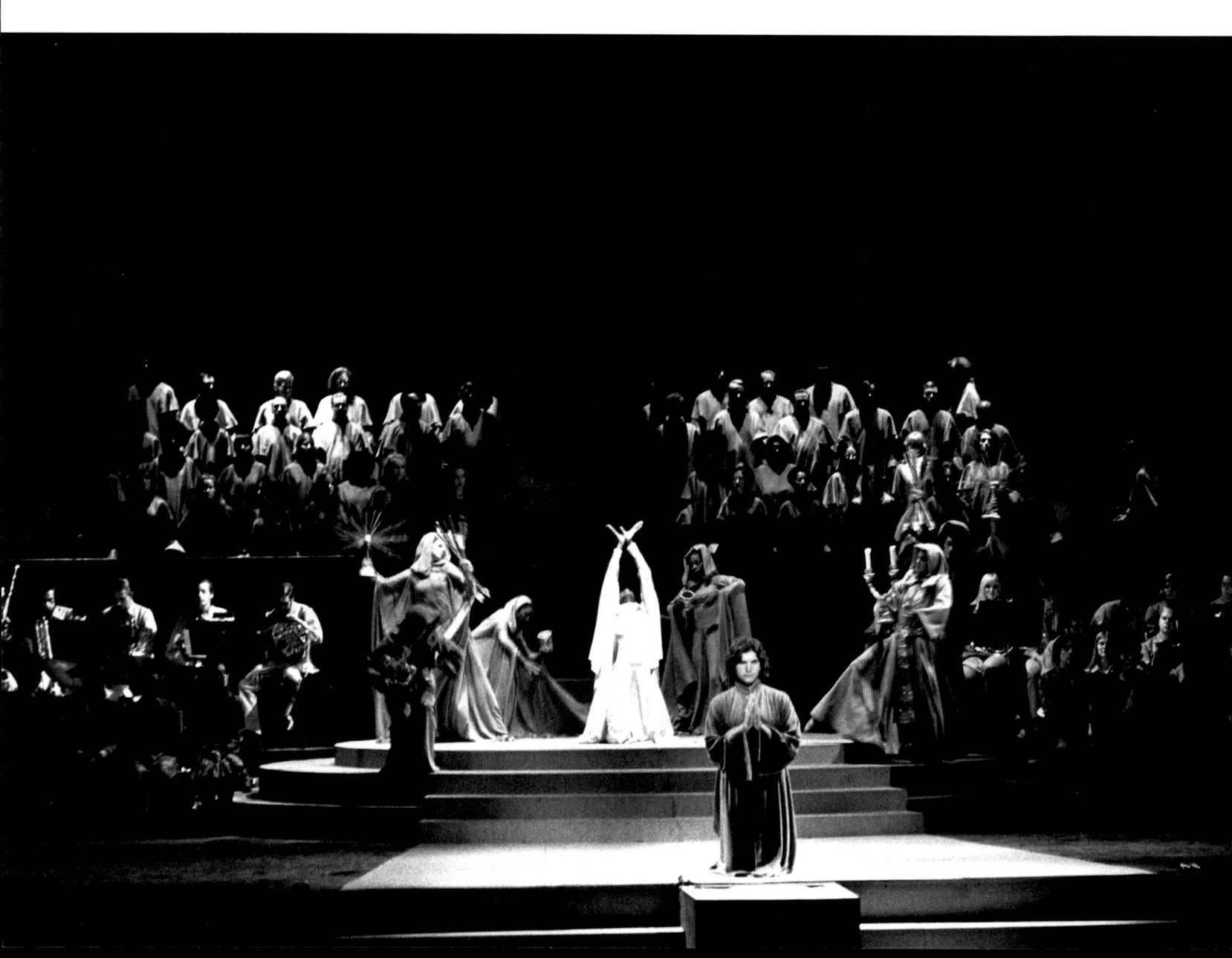

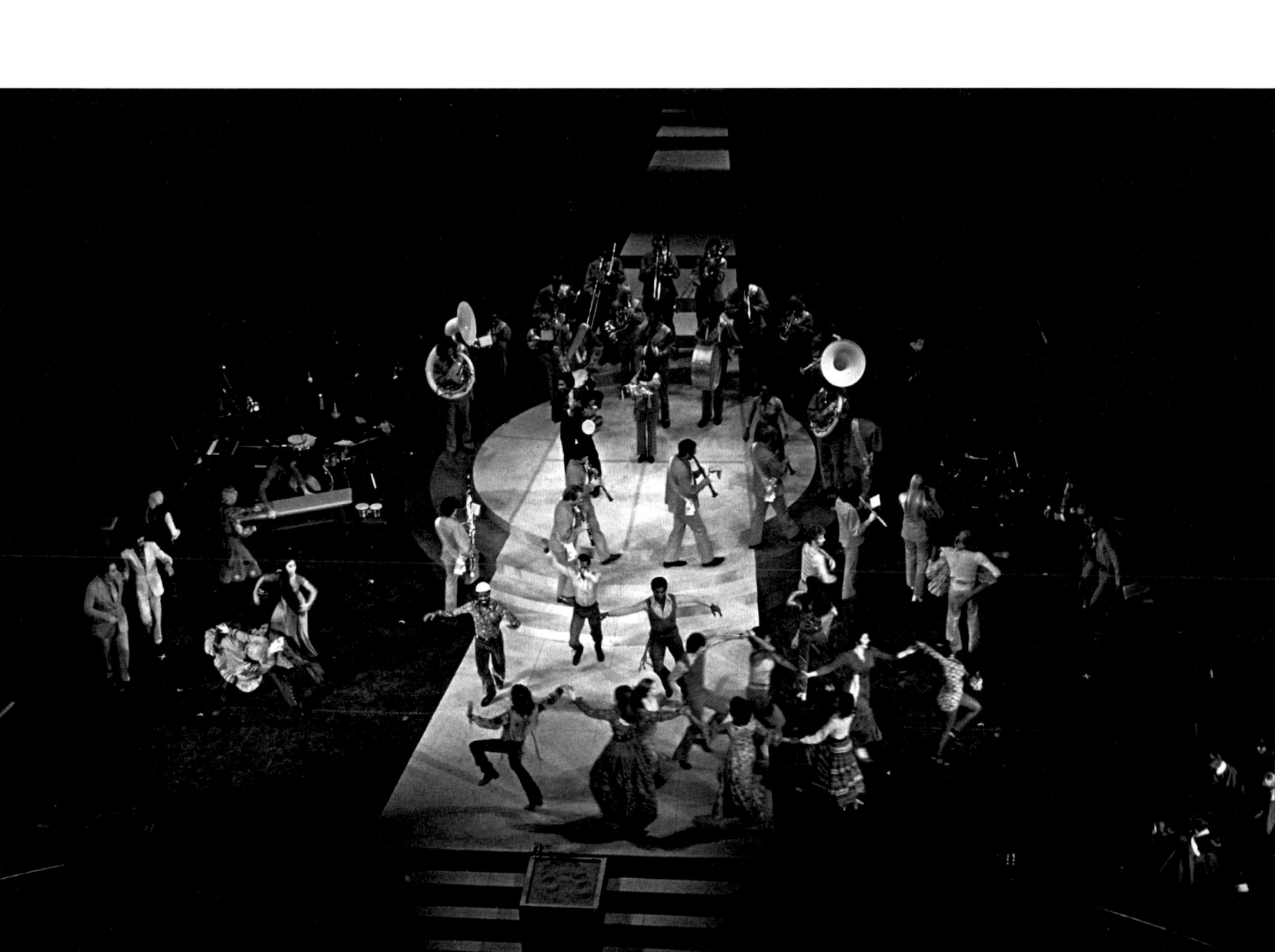

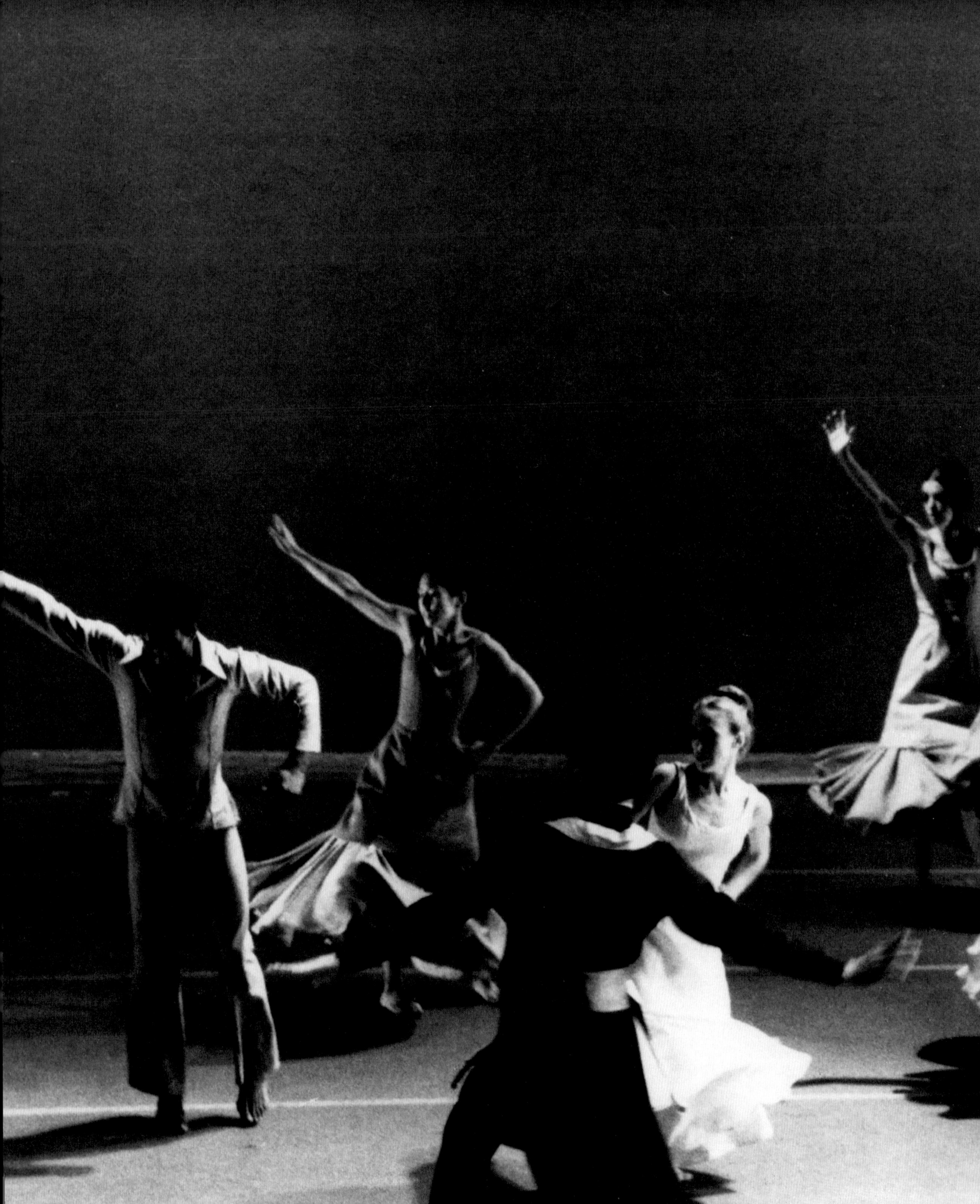

Premiere, New York City Center | **Mary Lou's Mass** | 1971

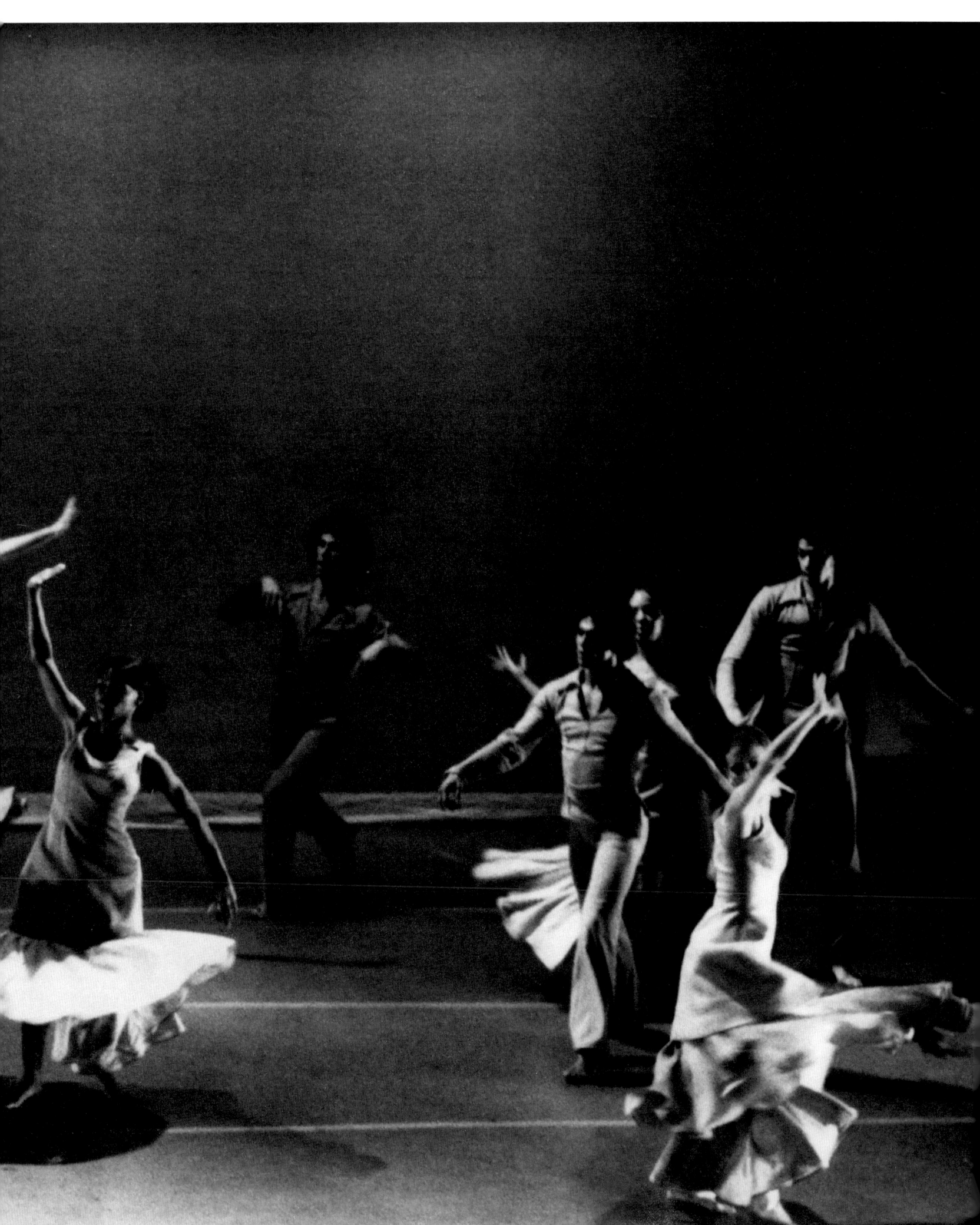

Premiere, New York City Center — **Myth** — 1971

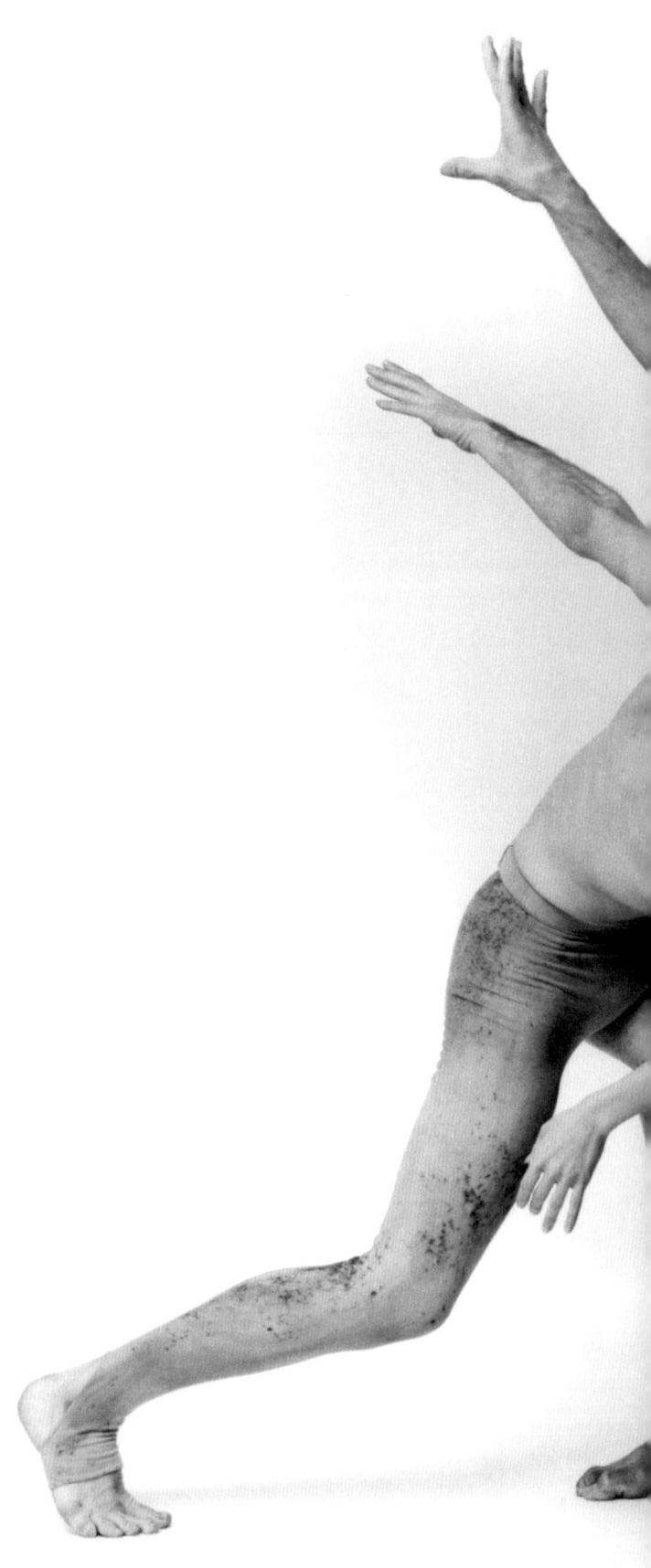

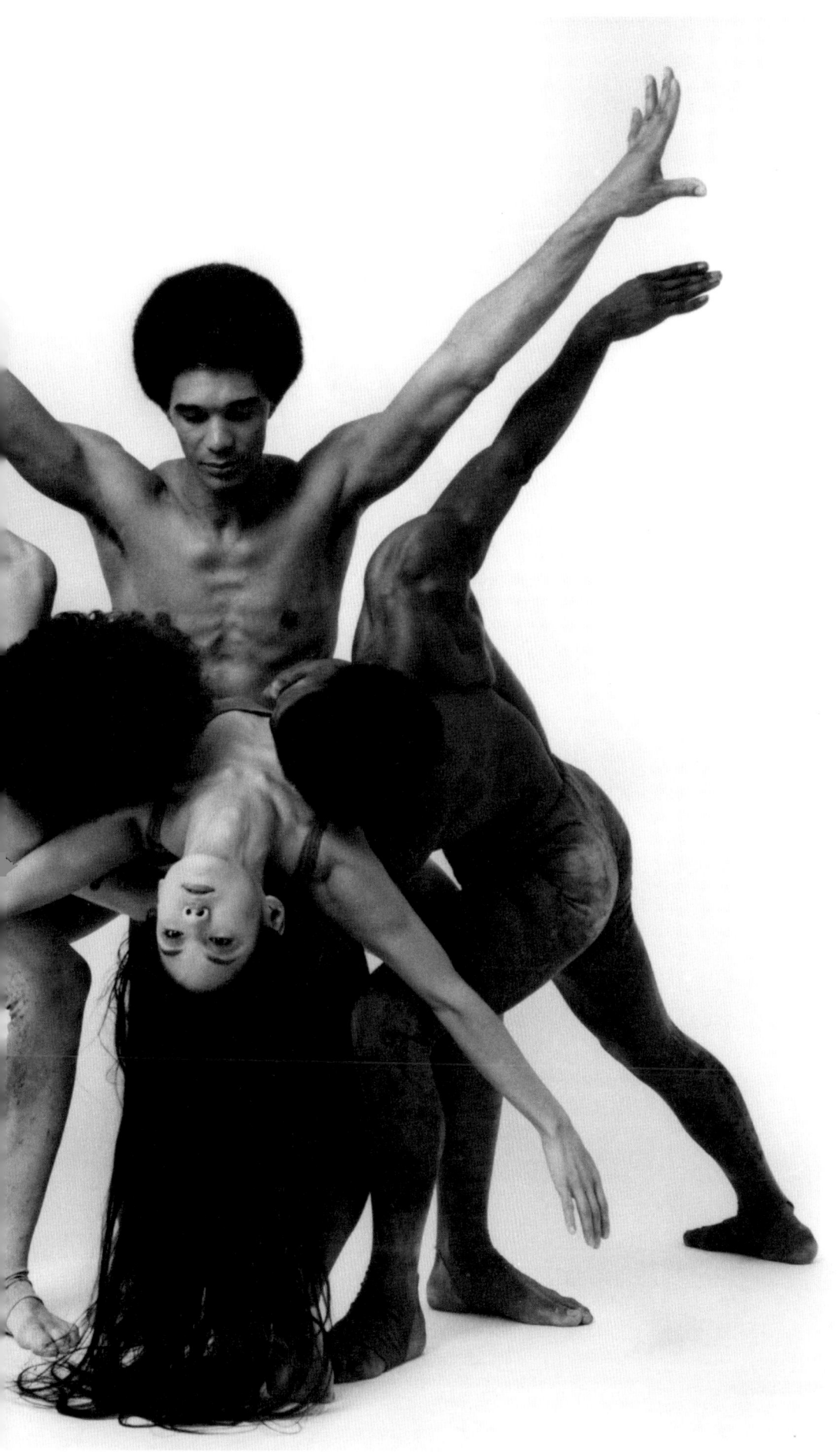

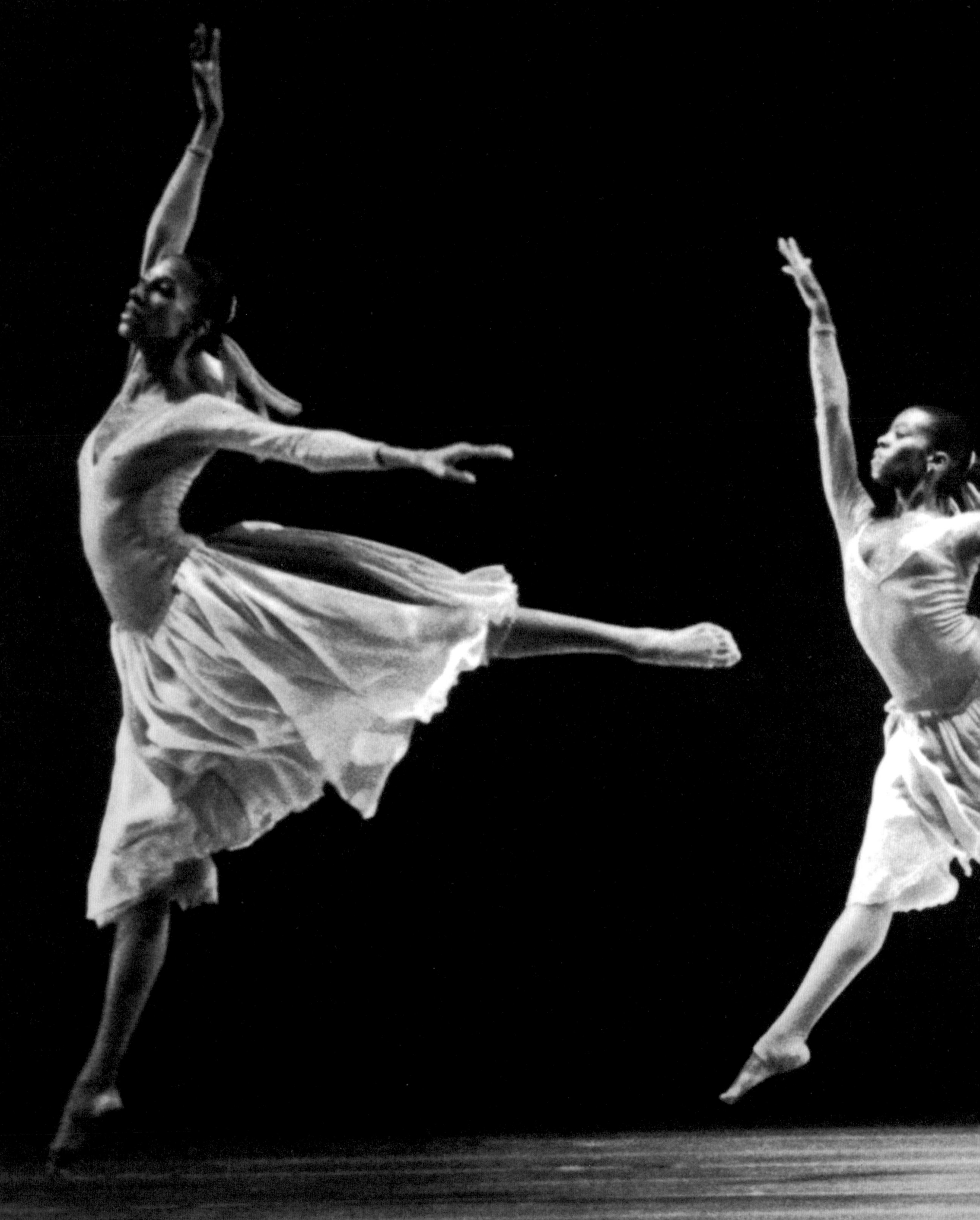

Premiere, New York City Center — The Lark Ascending — 1972

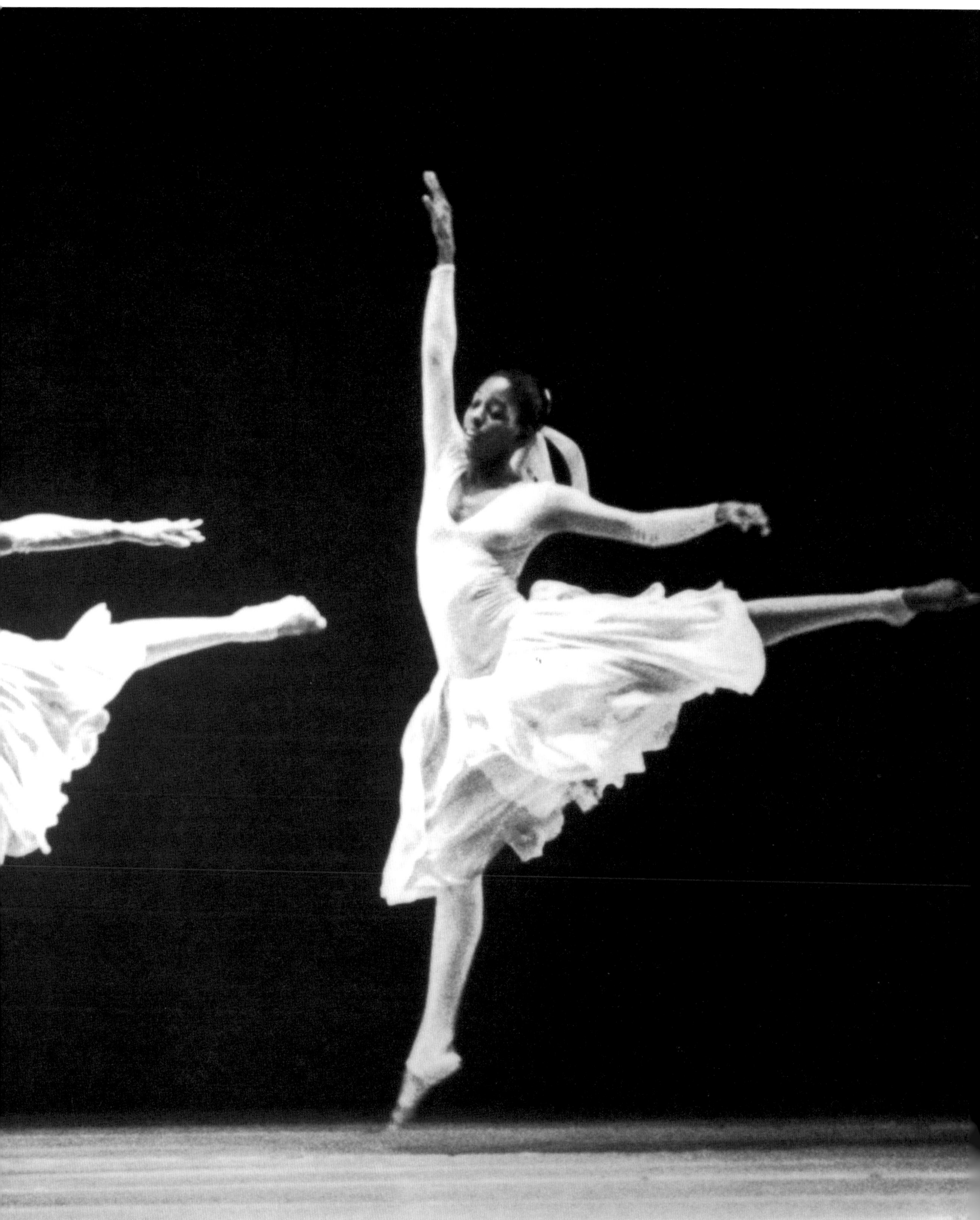

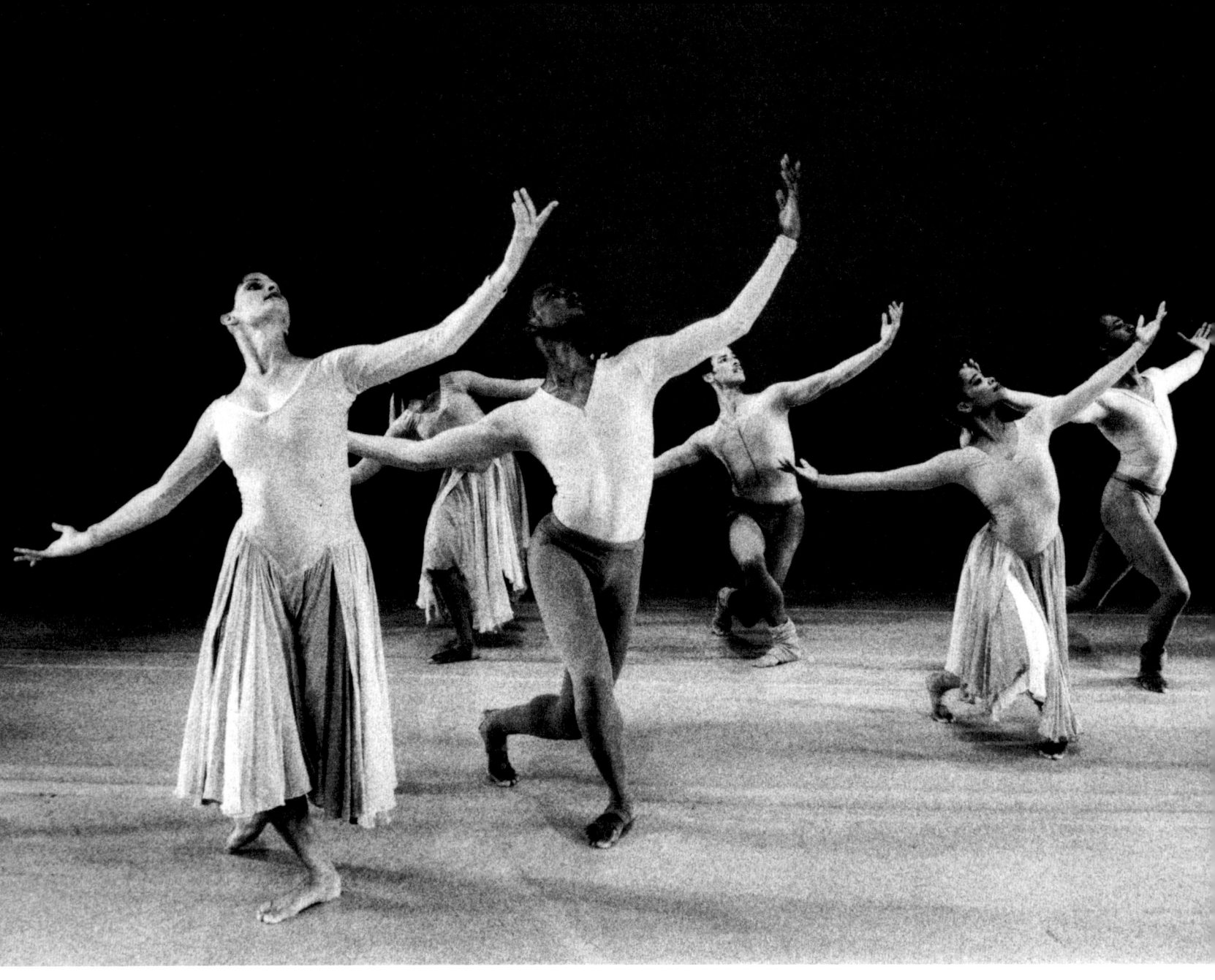

Premiere, New York City Center — **Love Songs** — 1972

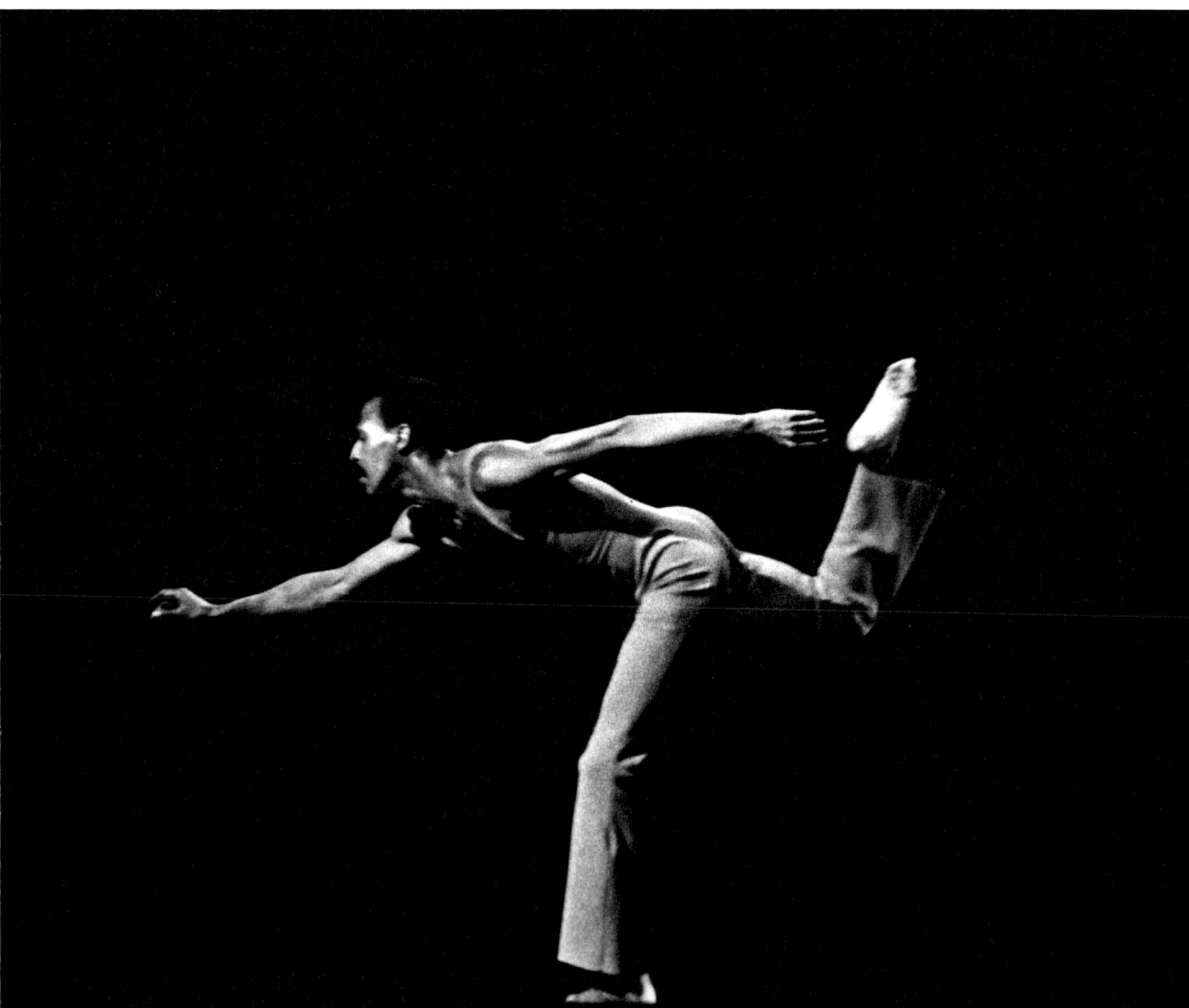

Opera, Vivian Beaumont Theater, Lincoln Center, New York

Four Saints in Three Acts

1973

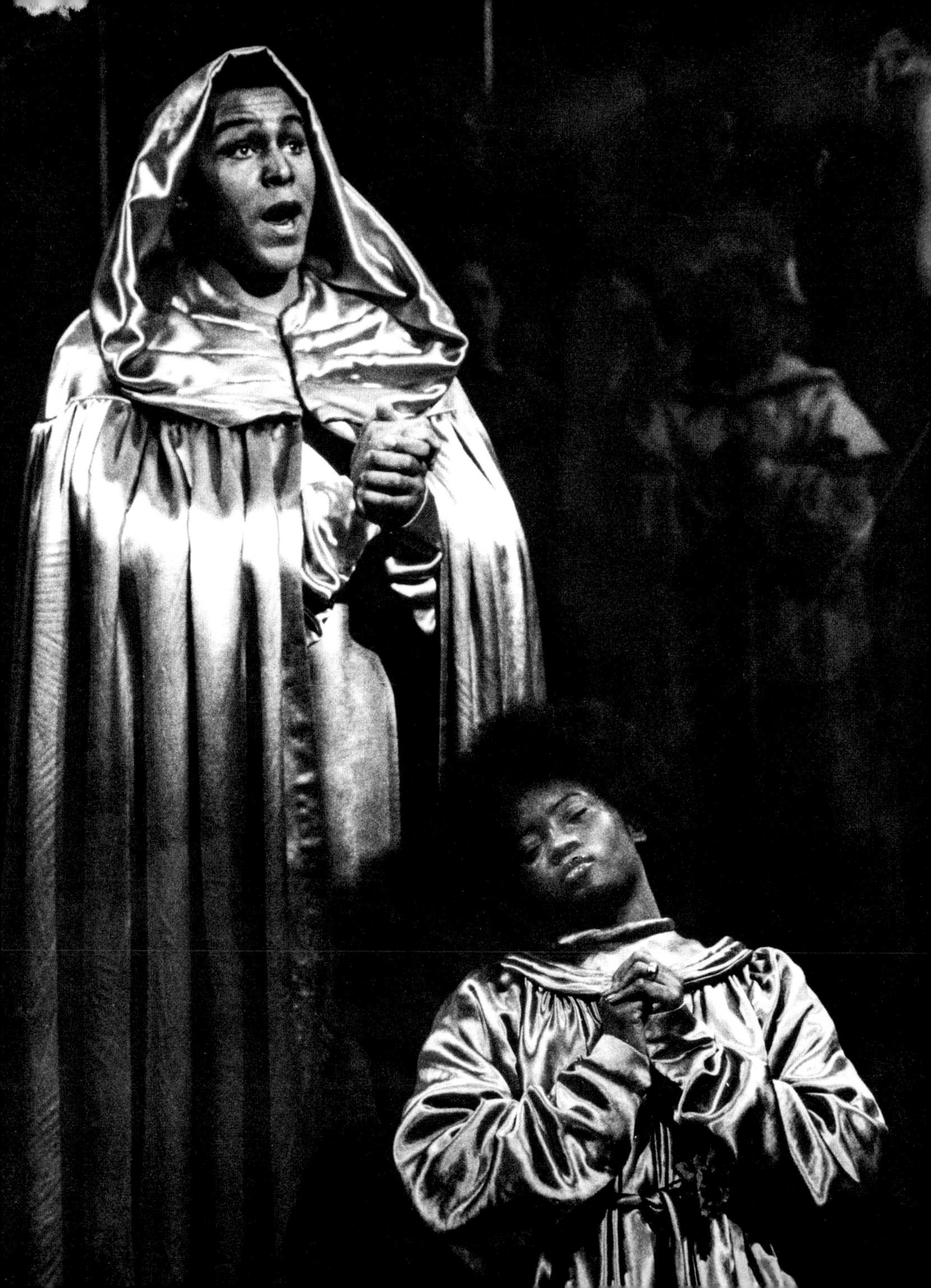

Premiere, New York City Center — Hidden Rites — 1973

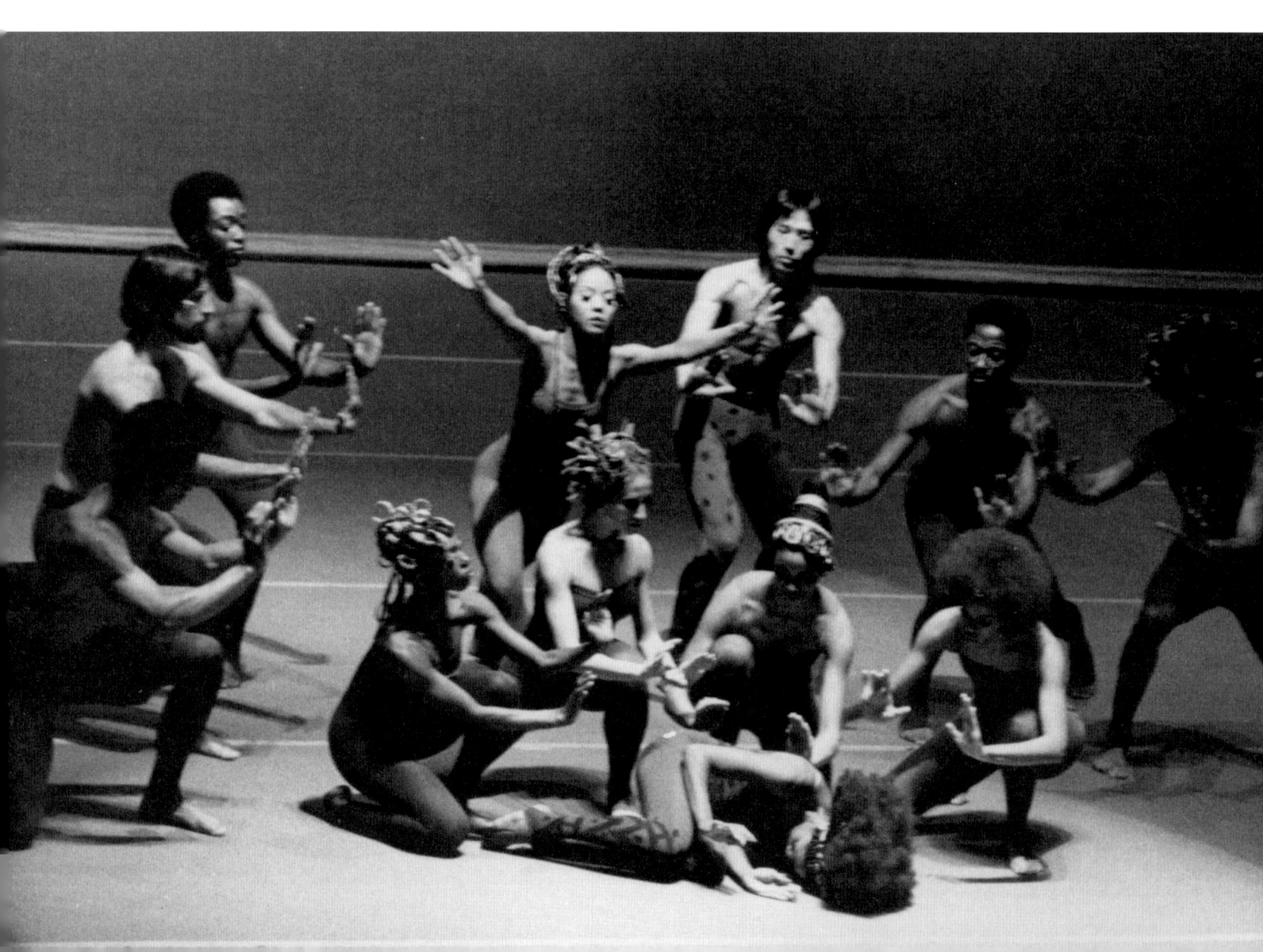

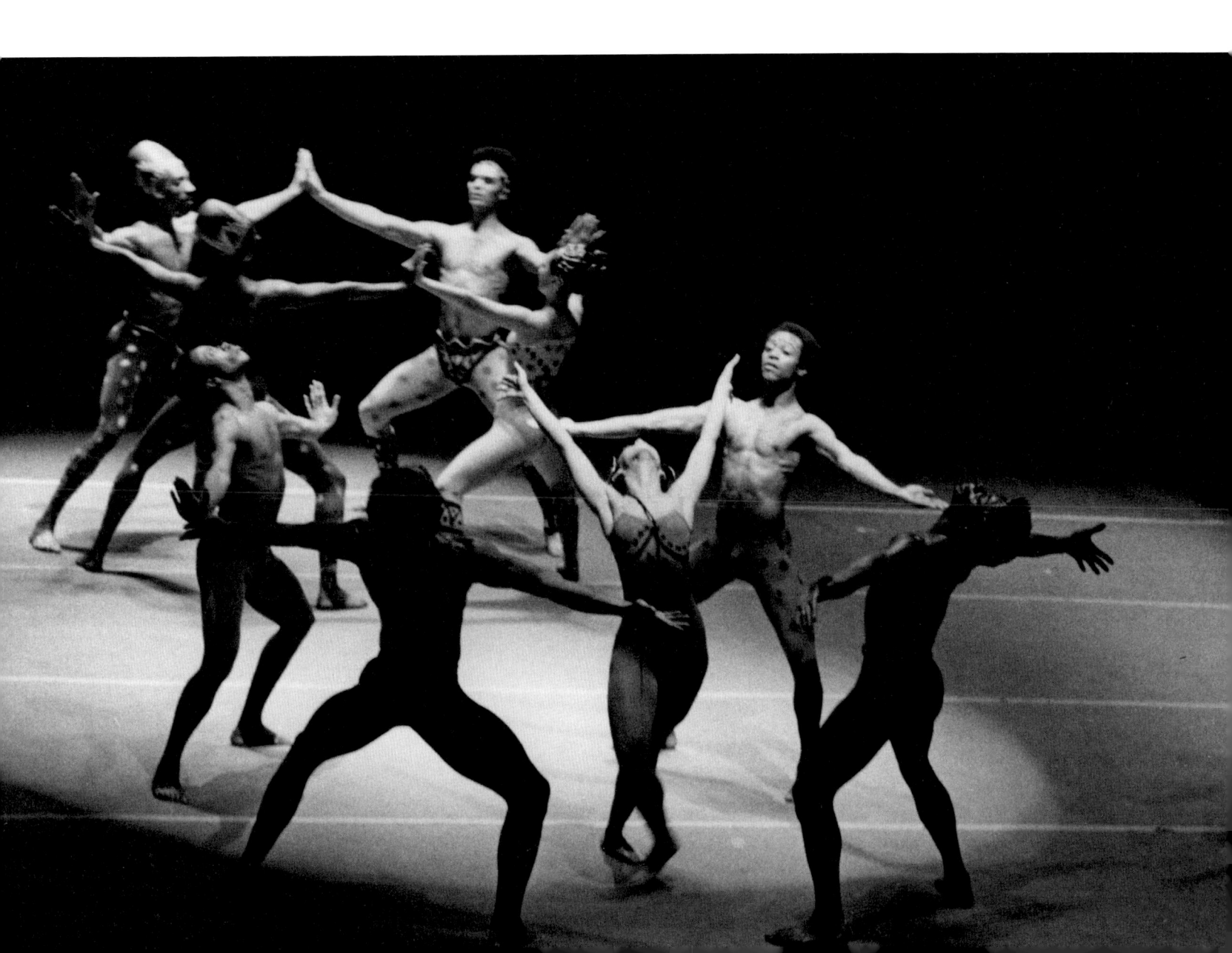

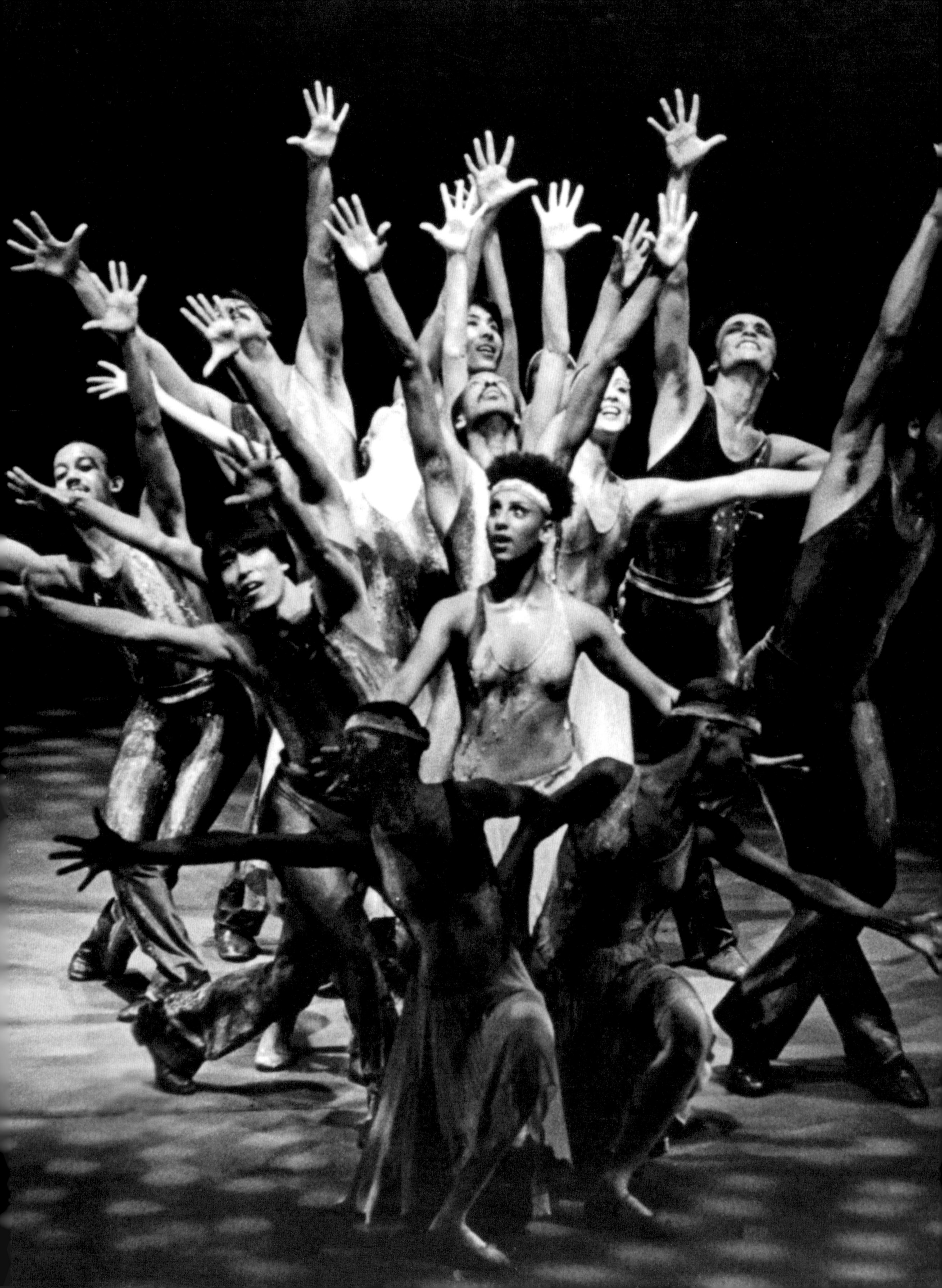

CBS television broadcast **Night Creature** 1974/1975

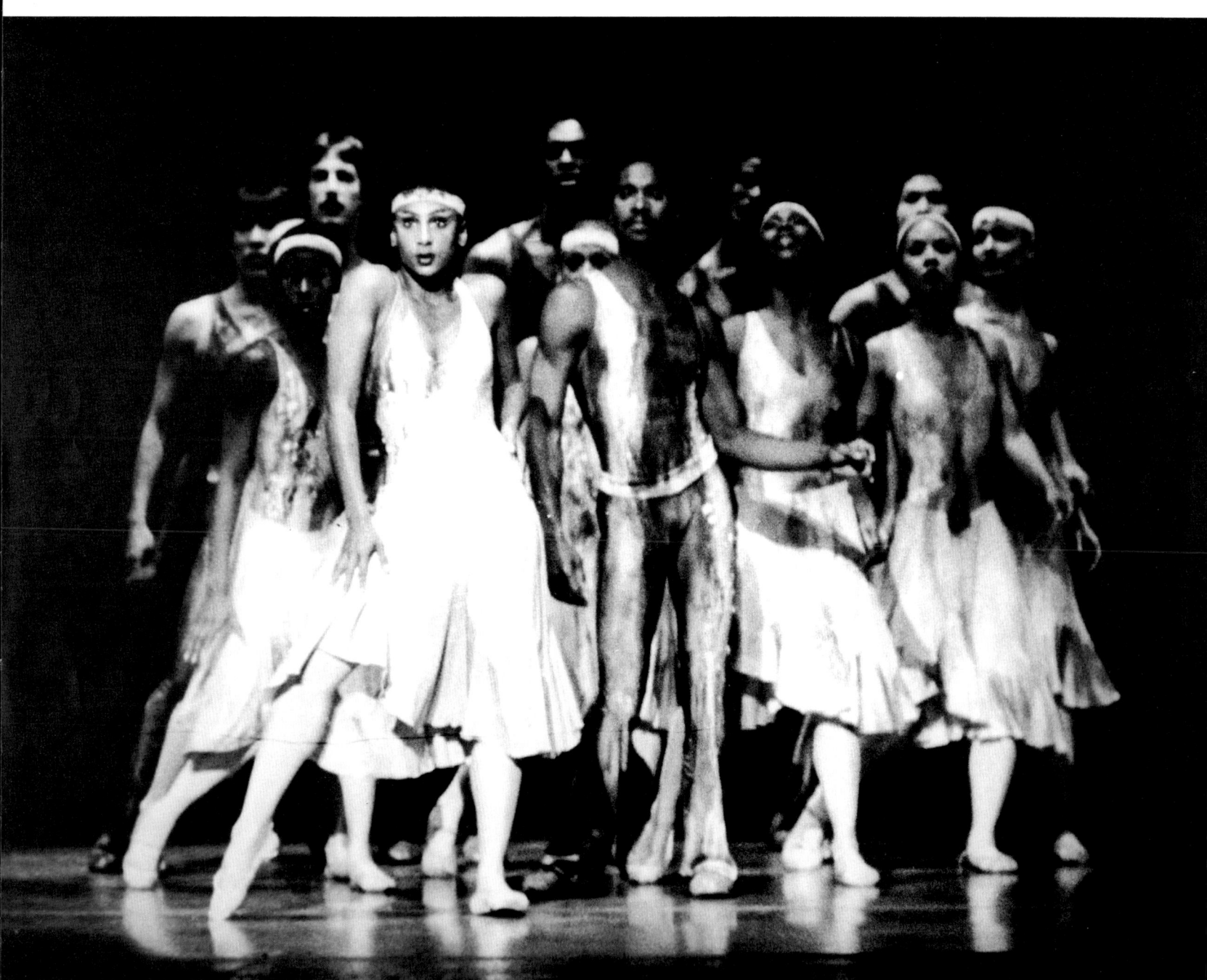

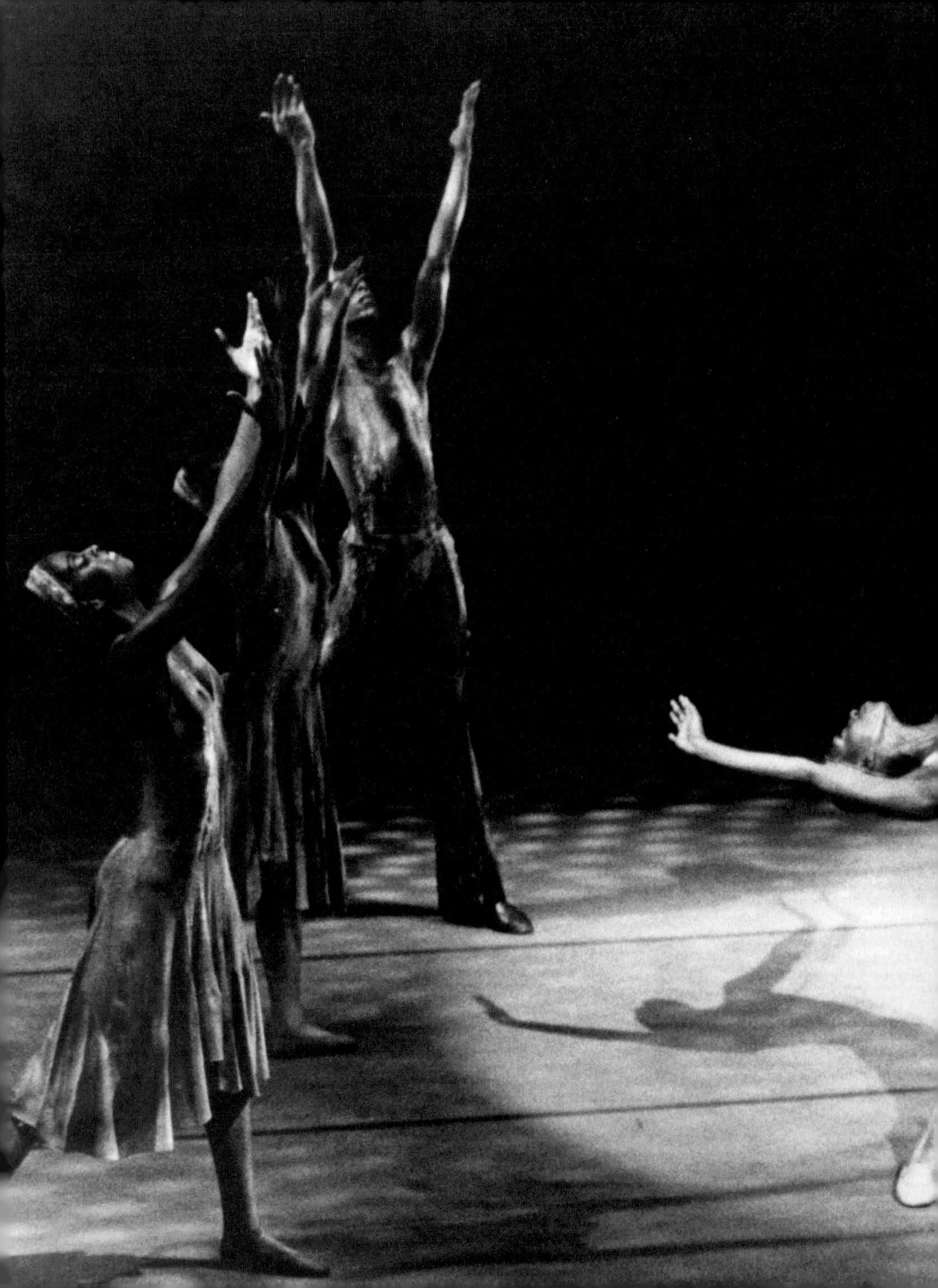

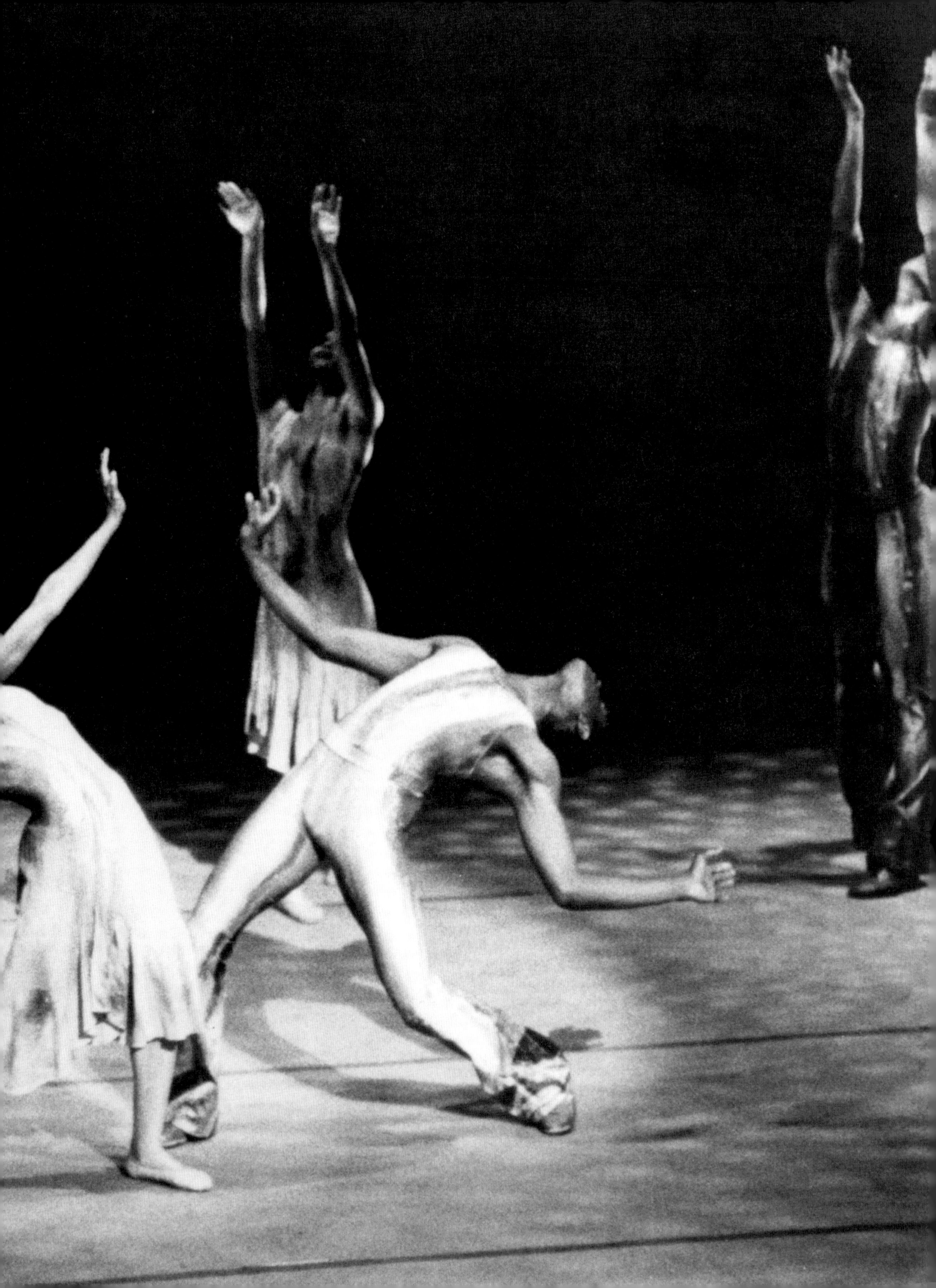

CBS television broadcast The Mooche 1974

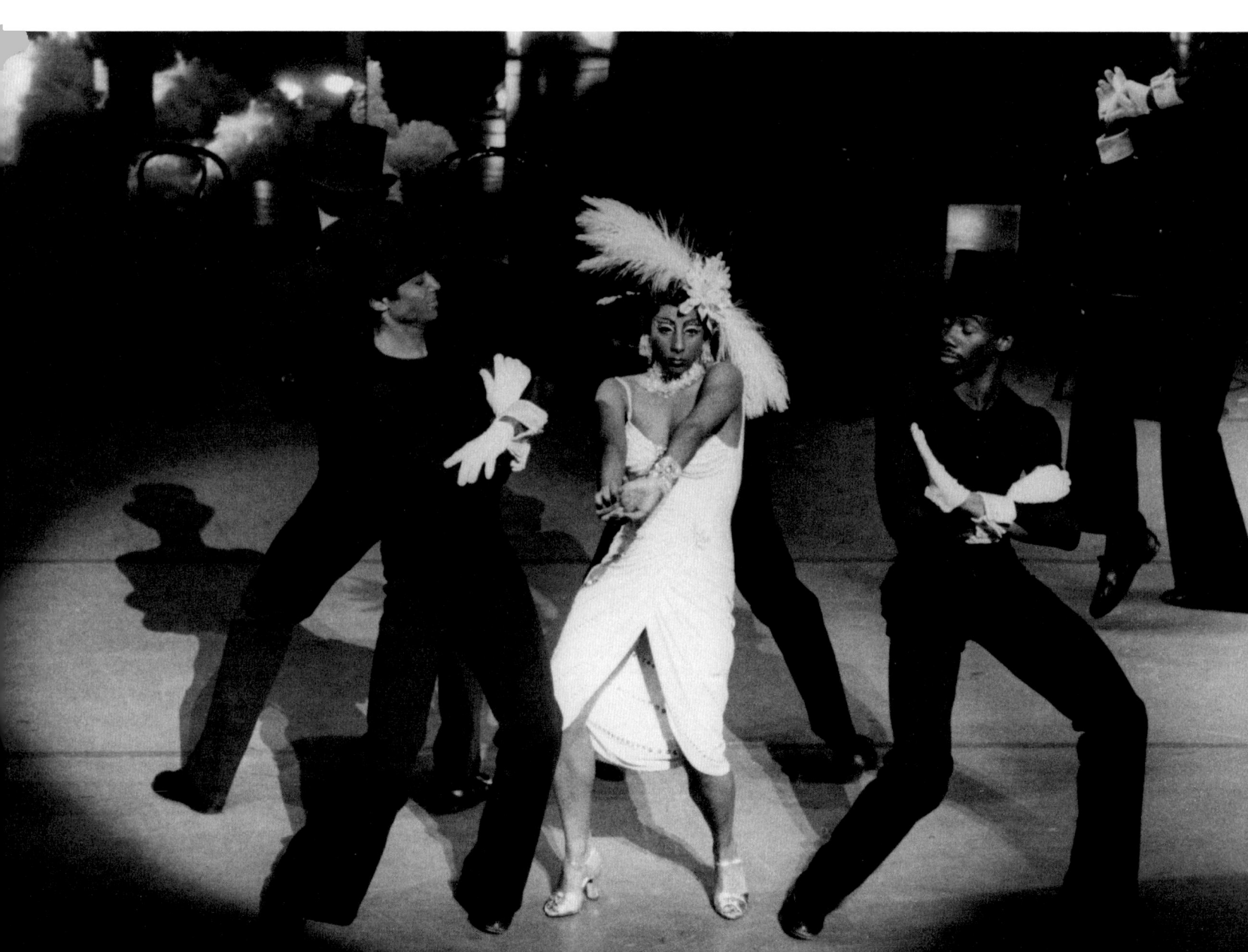

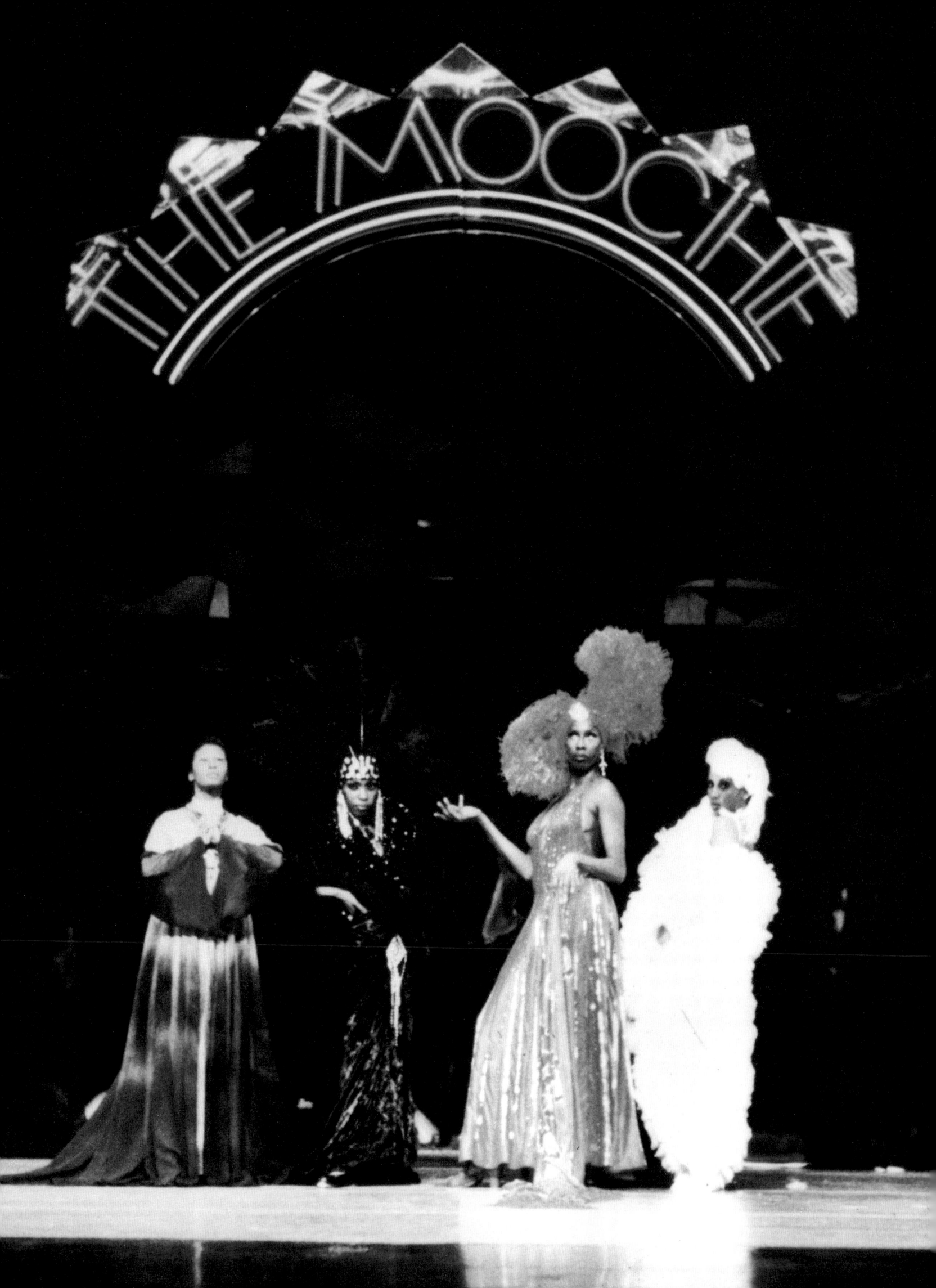

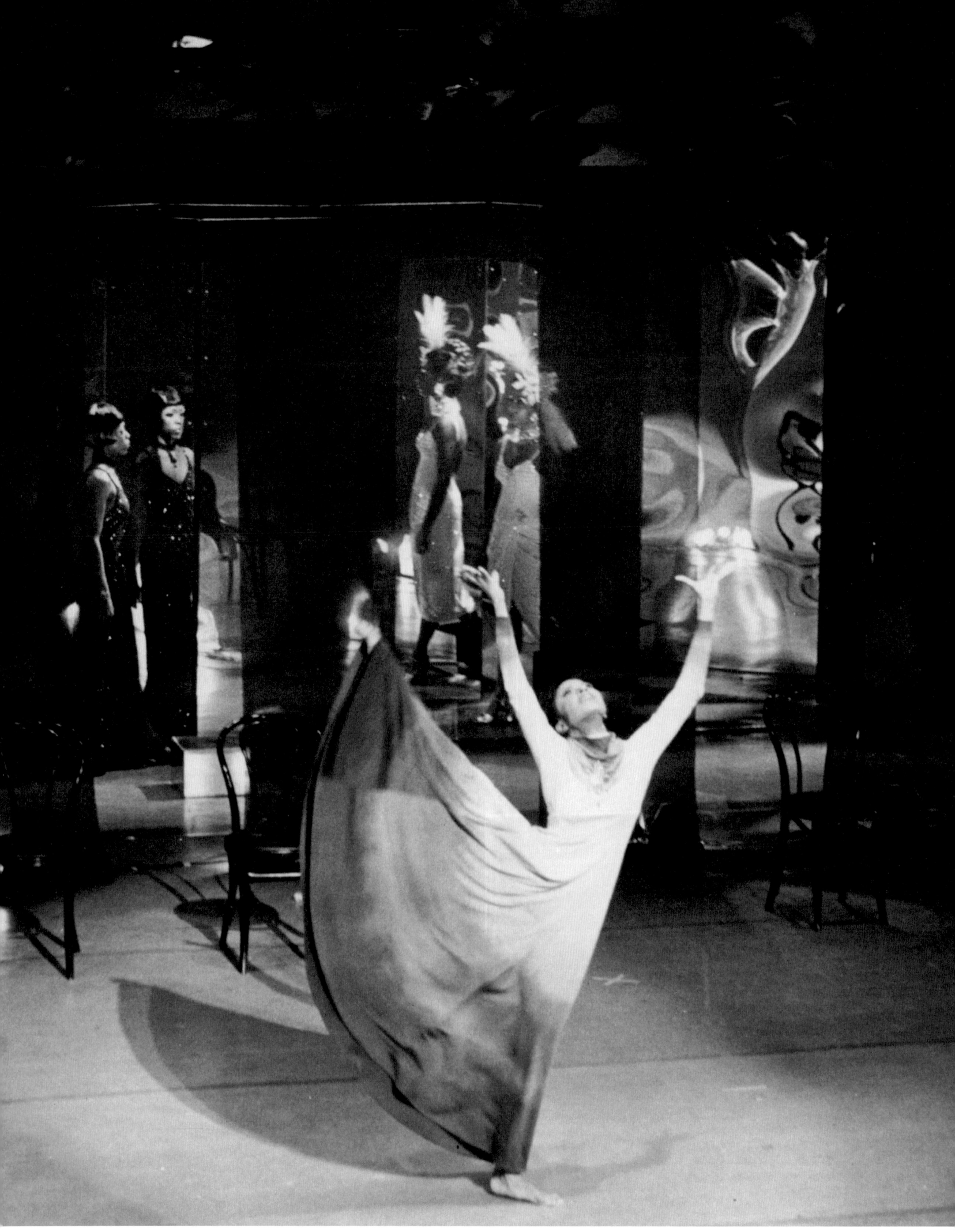
The Mooche

Premiere, New York City Center — **Black, Brown and Beige** — 1976

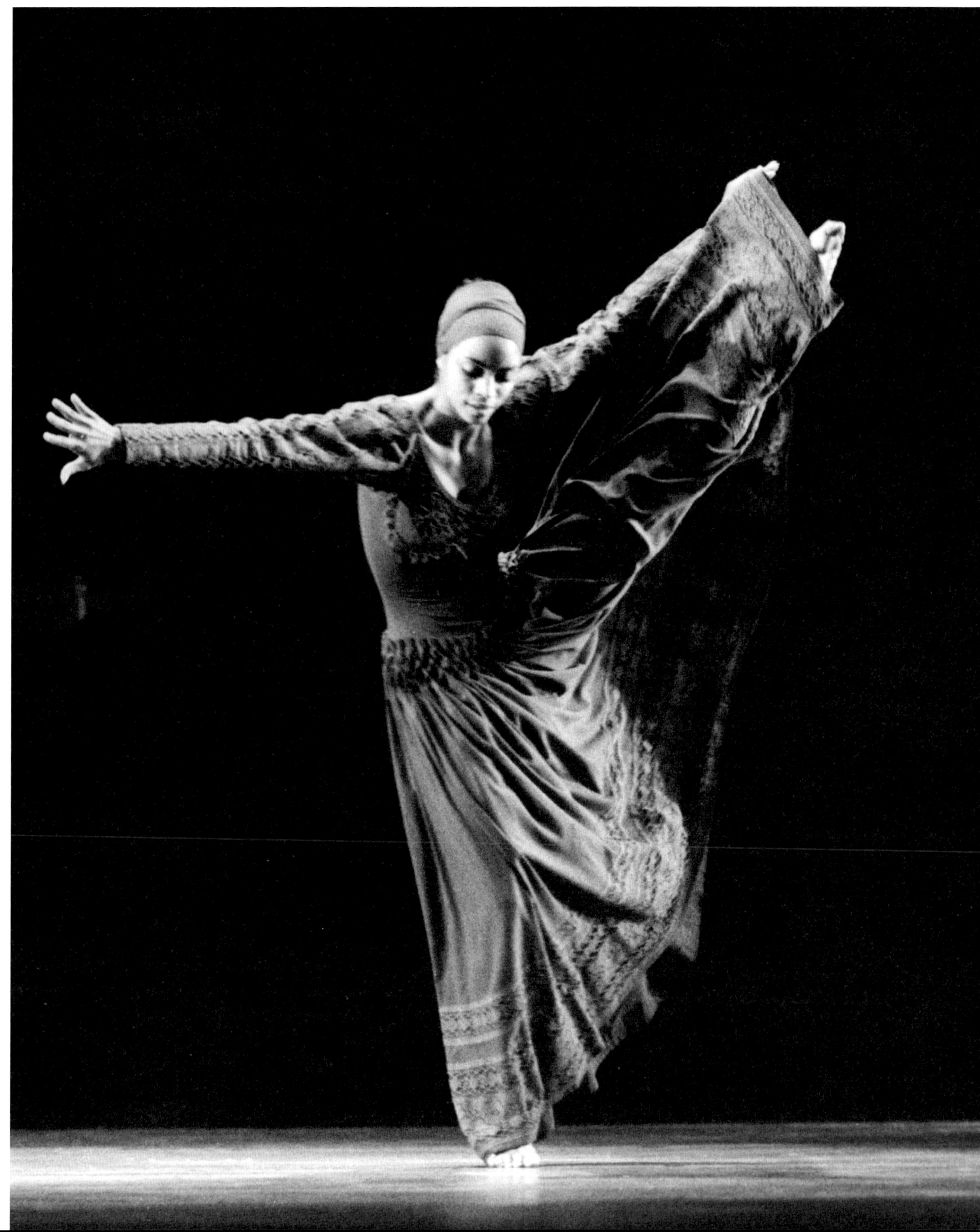

Premiere, New York City Center — **Pas de Duke** — 1976

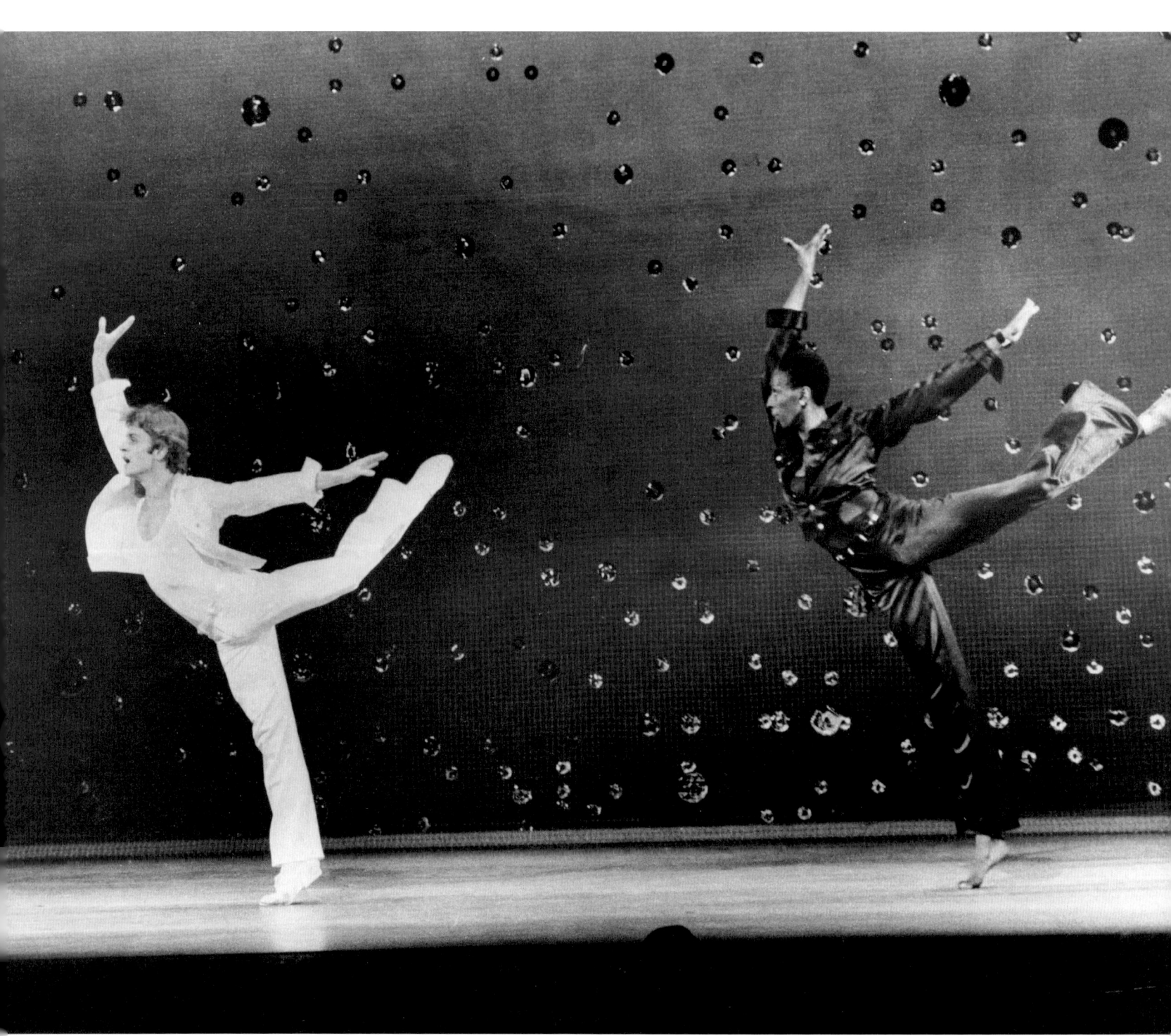

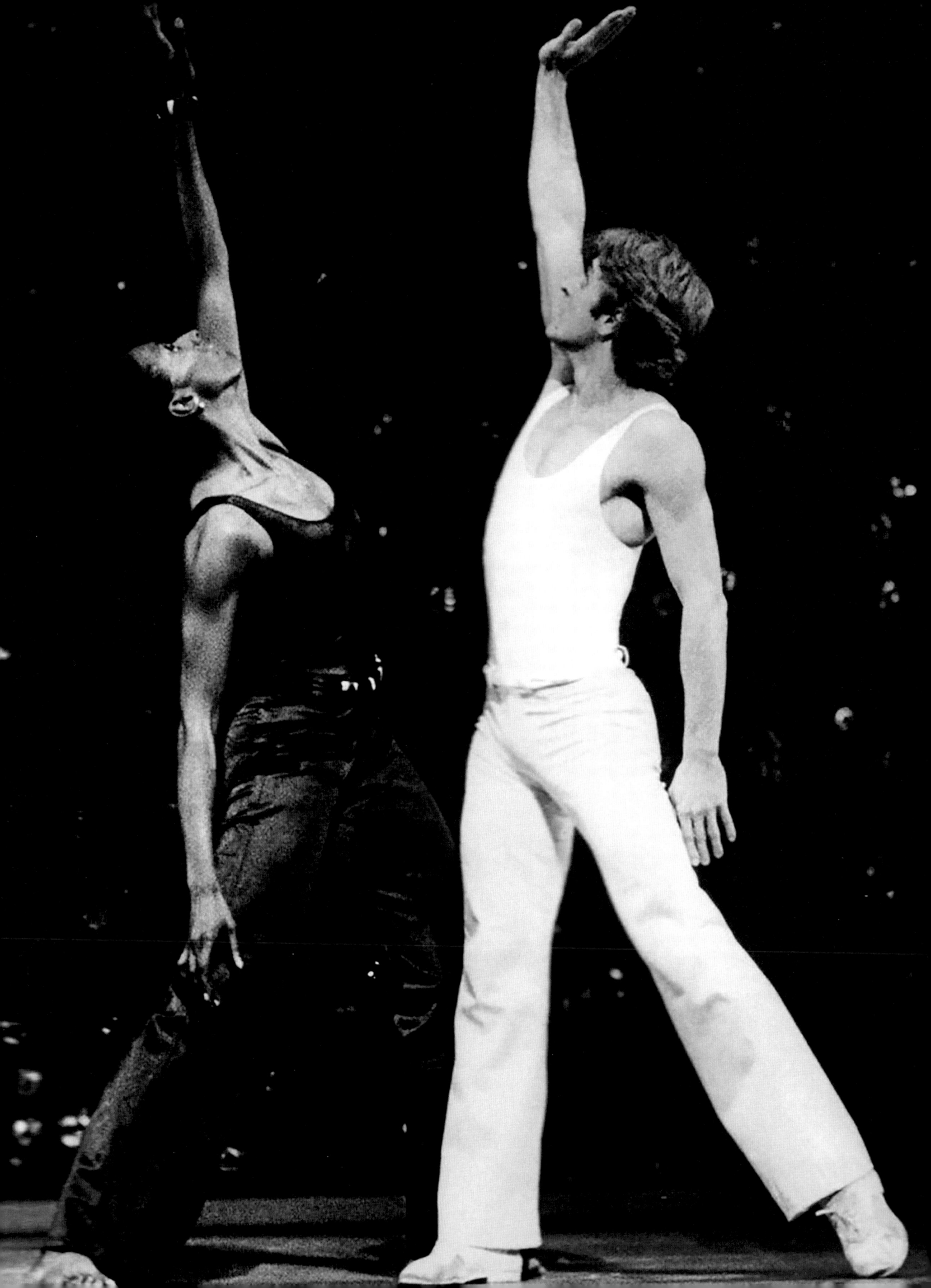

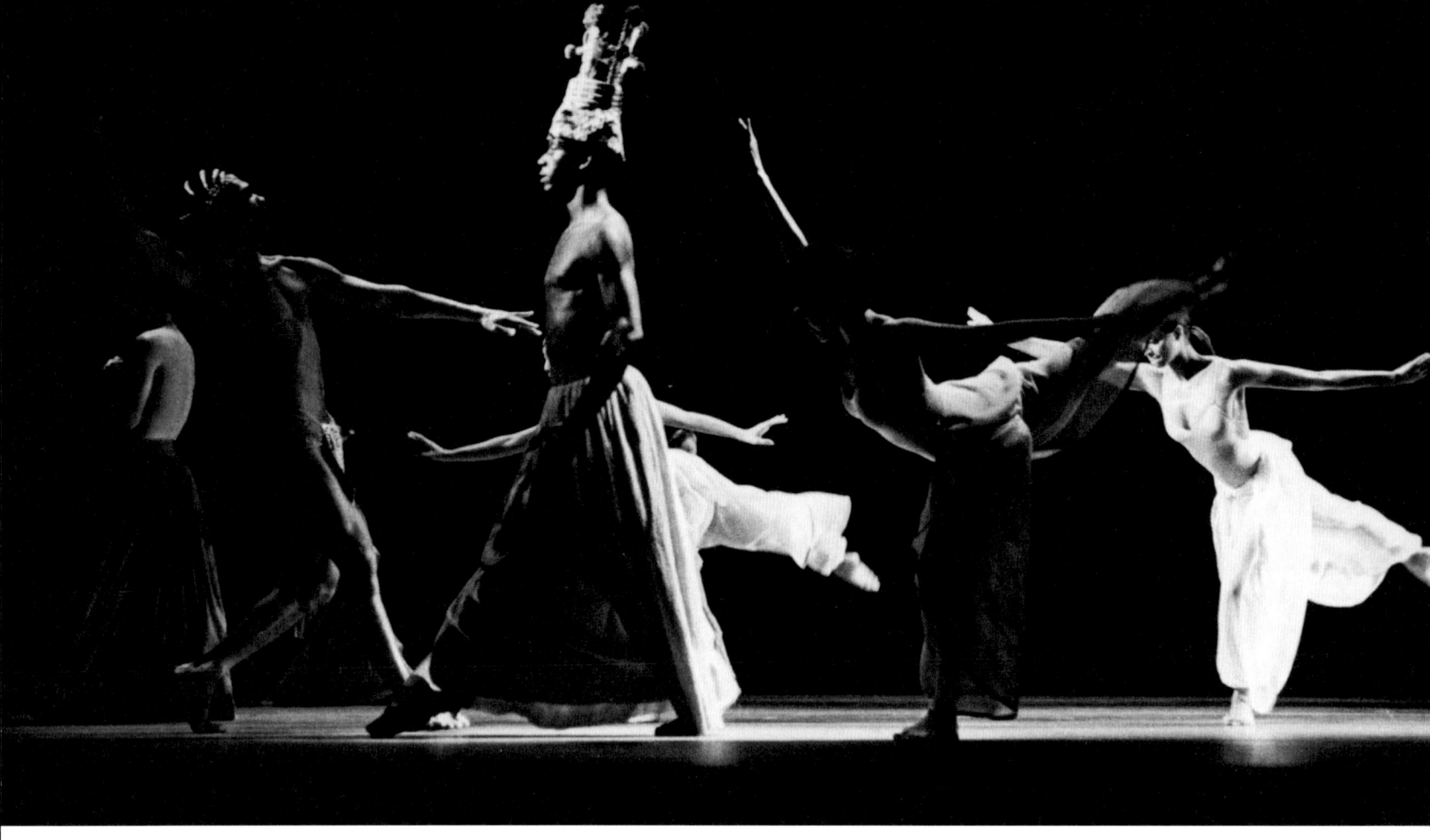

Premiere, Artpark, Lewiston, New York **Three Black Kings** 1976

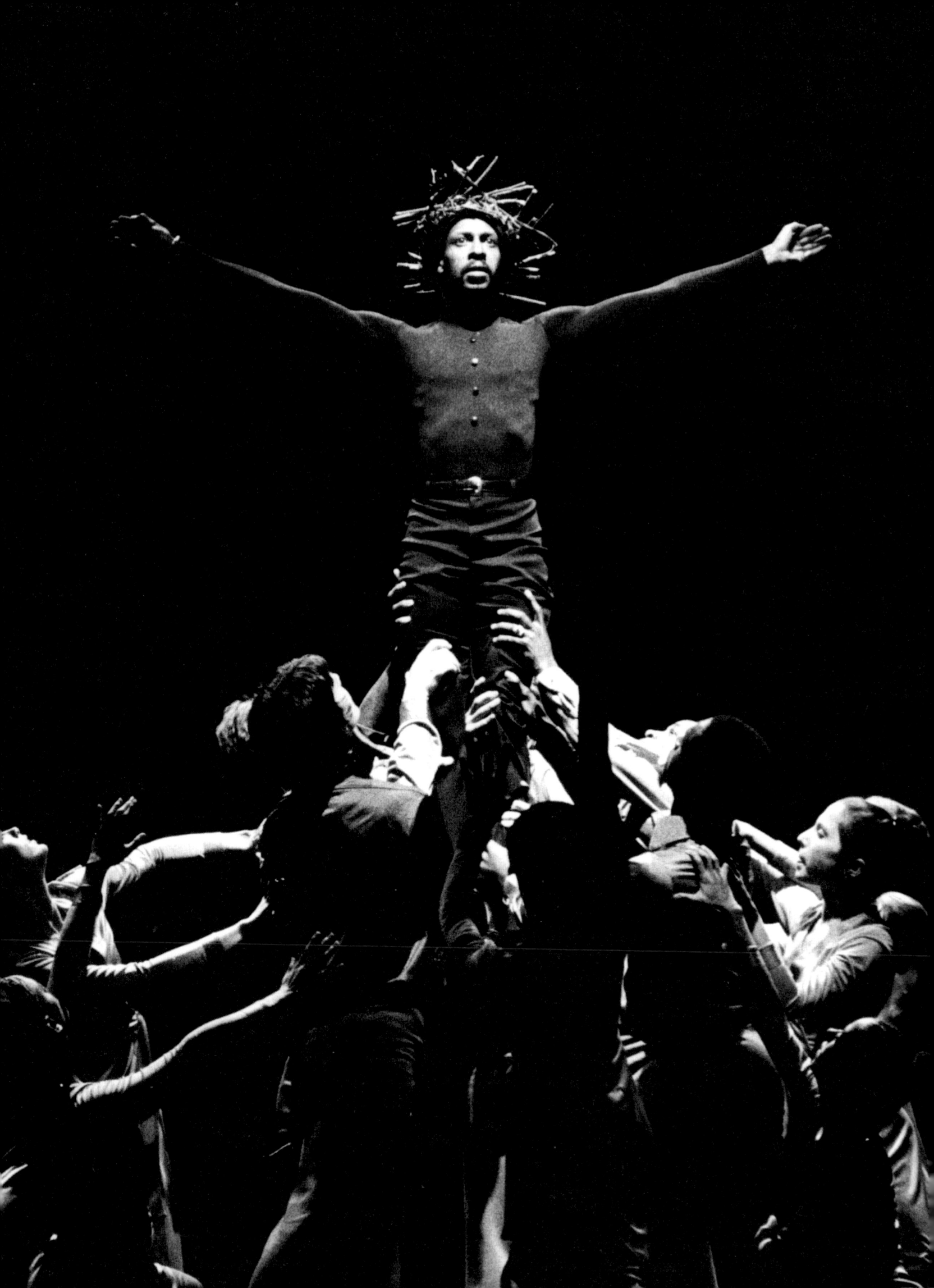

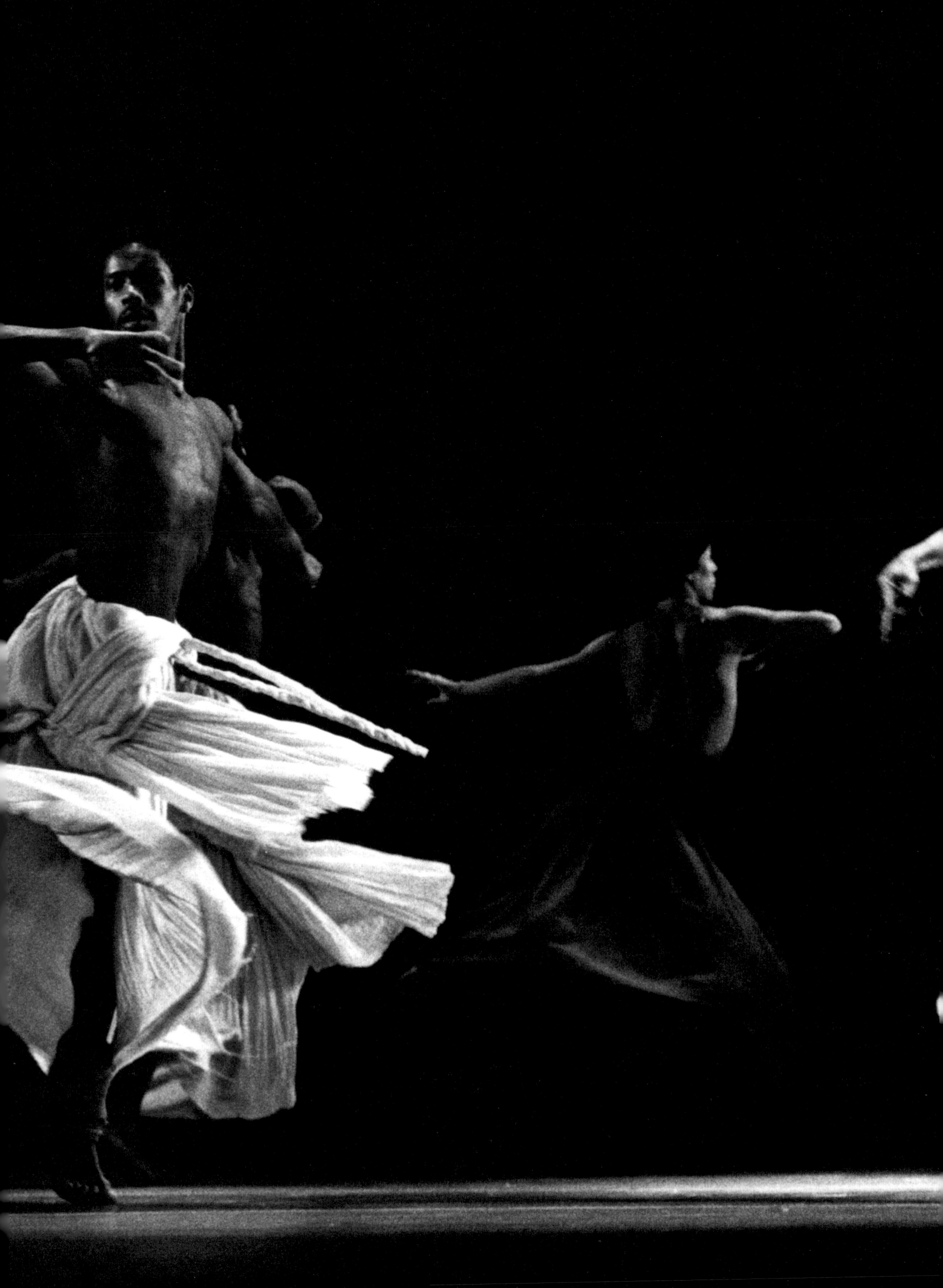

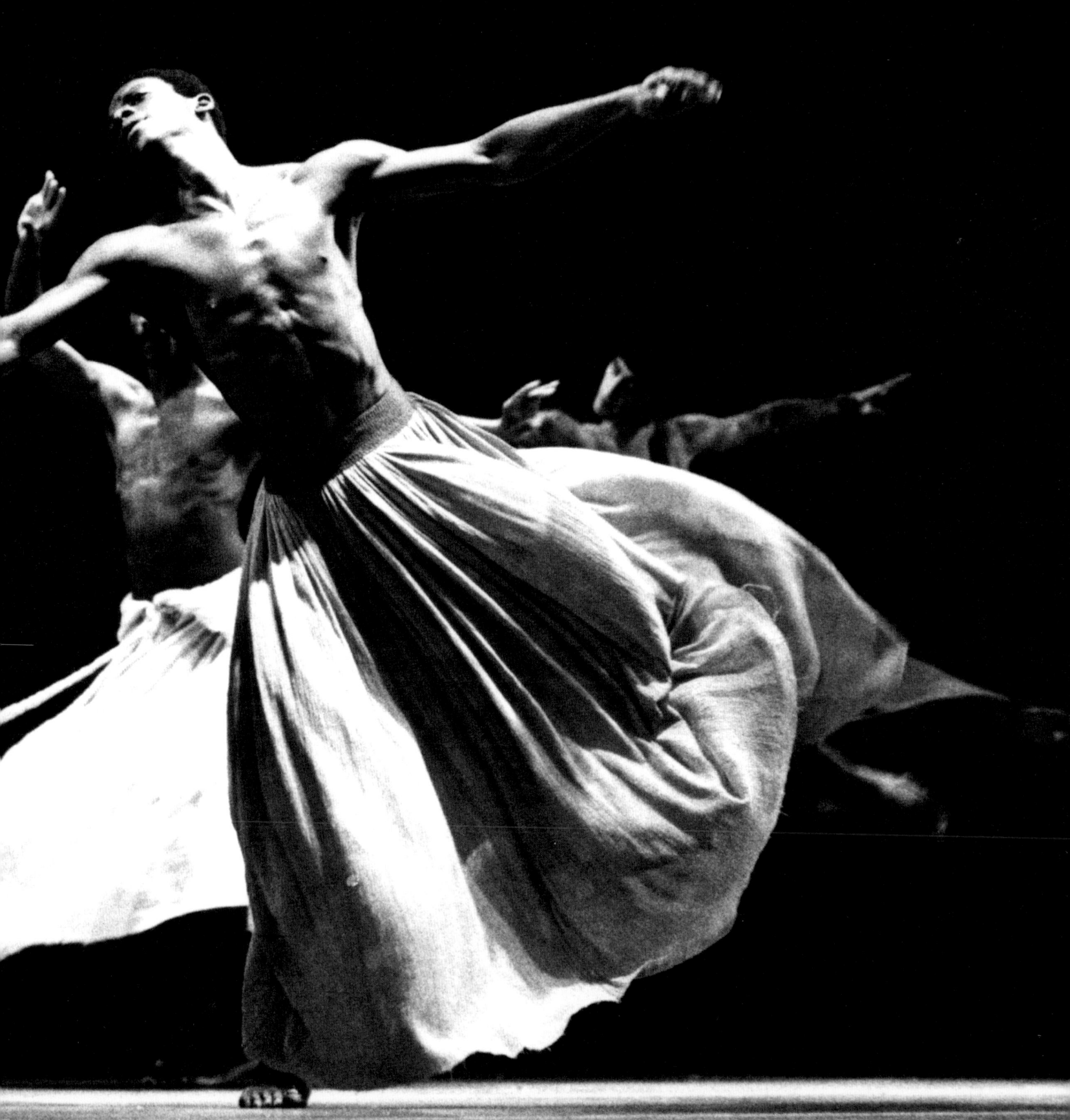

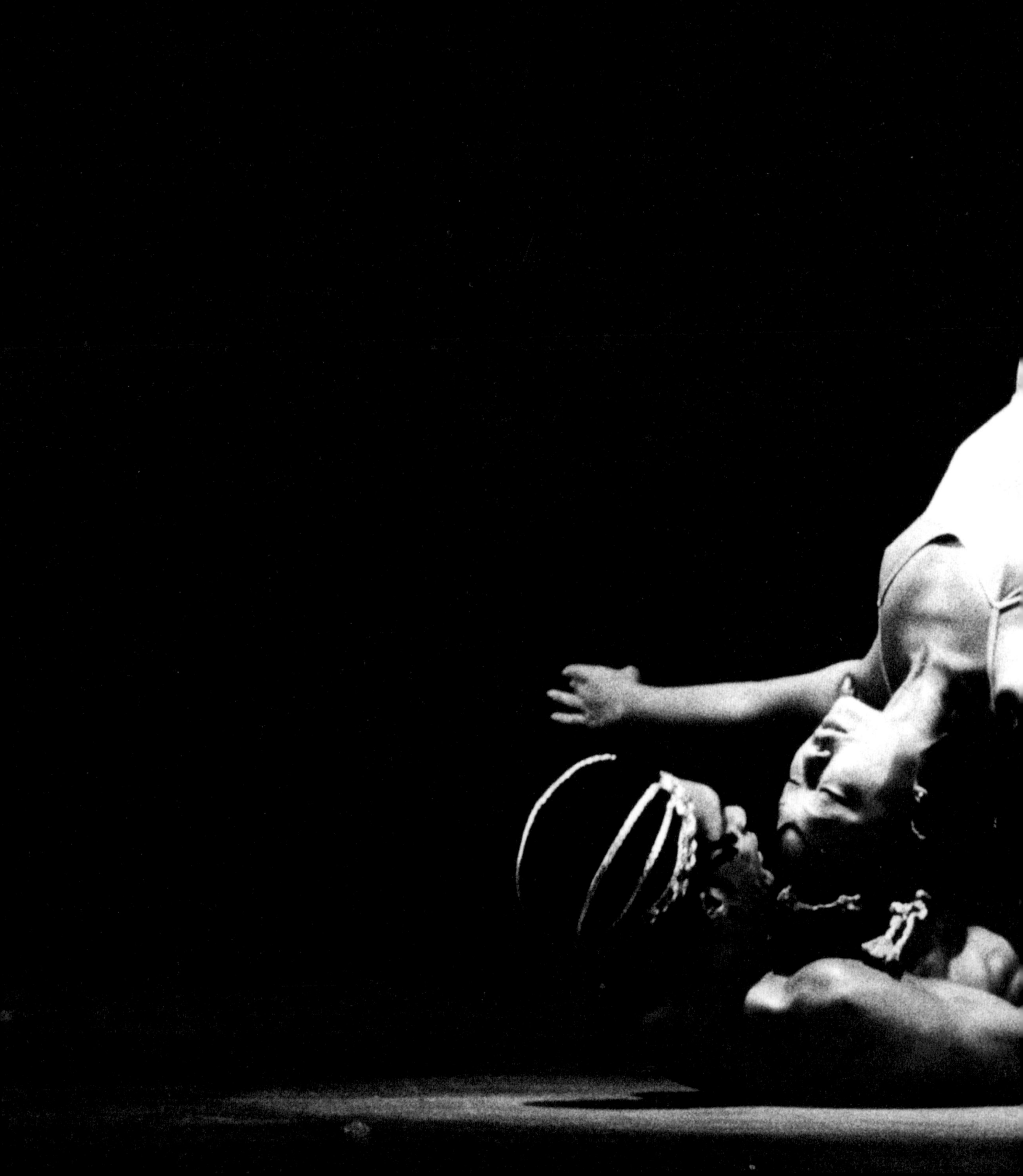

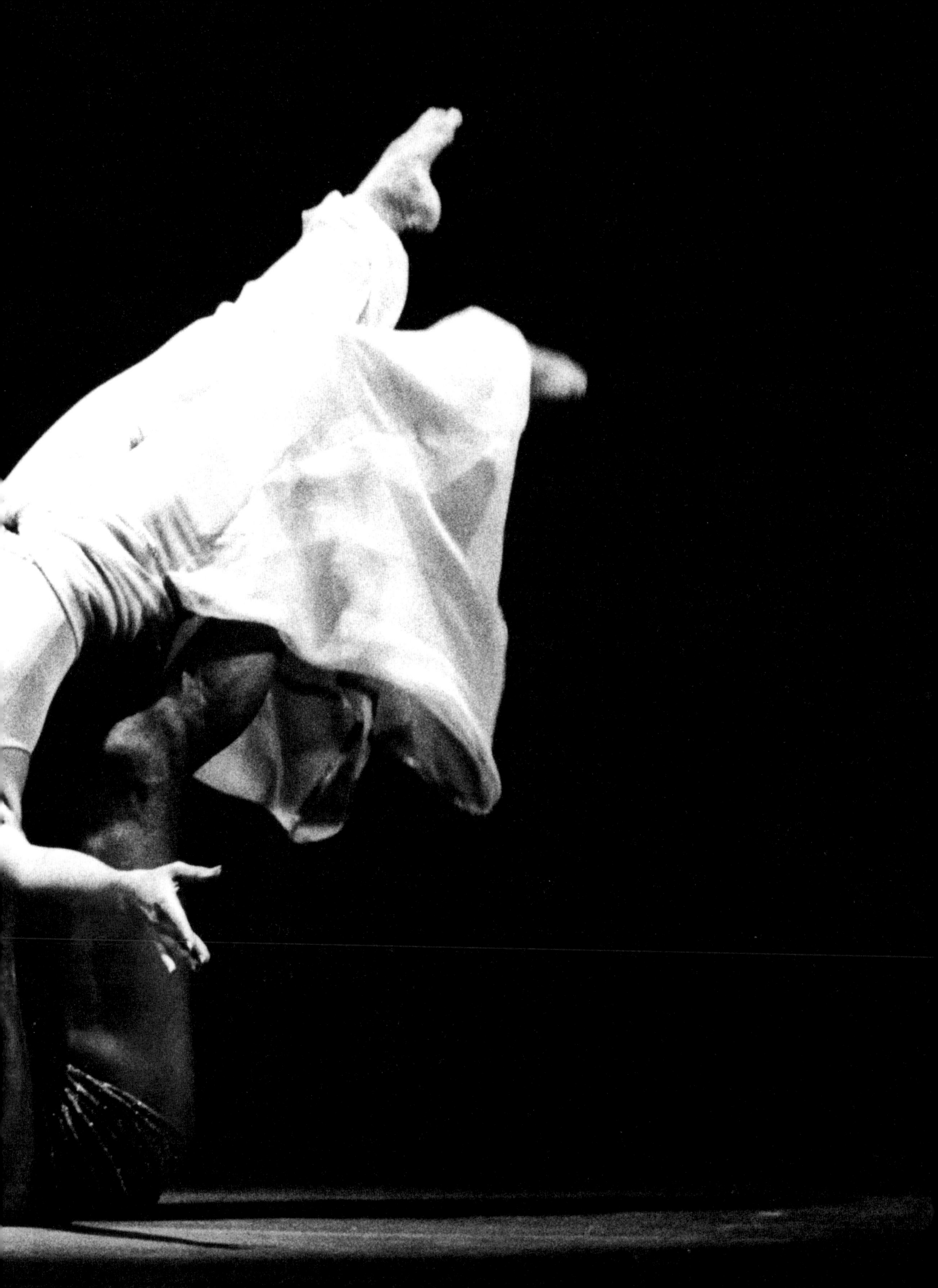

Premiere, New York City Center — **Passage** — 1978

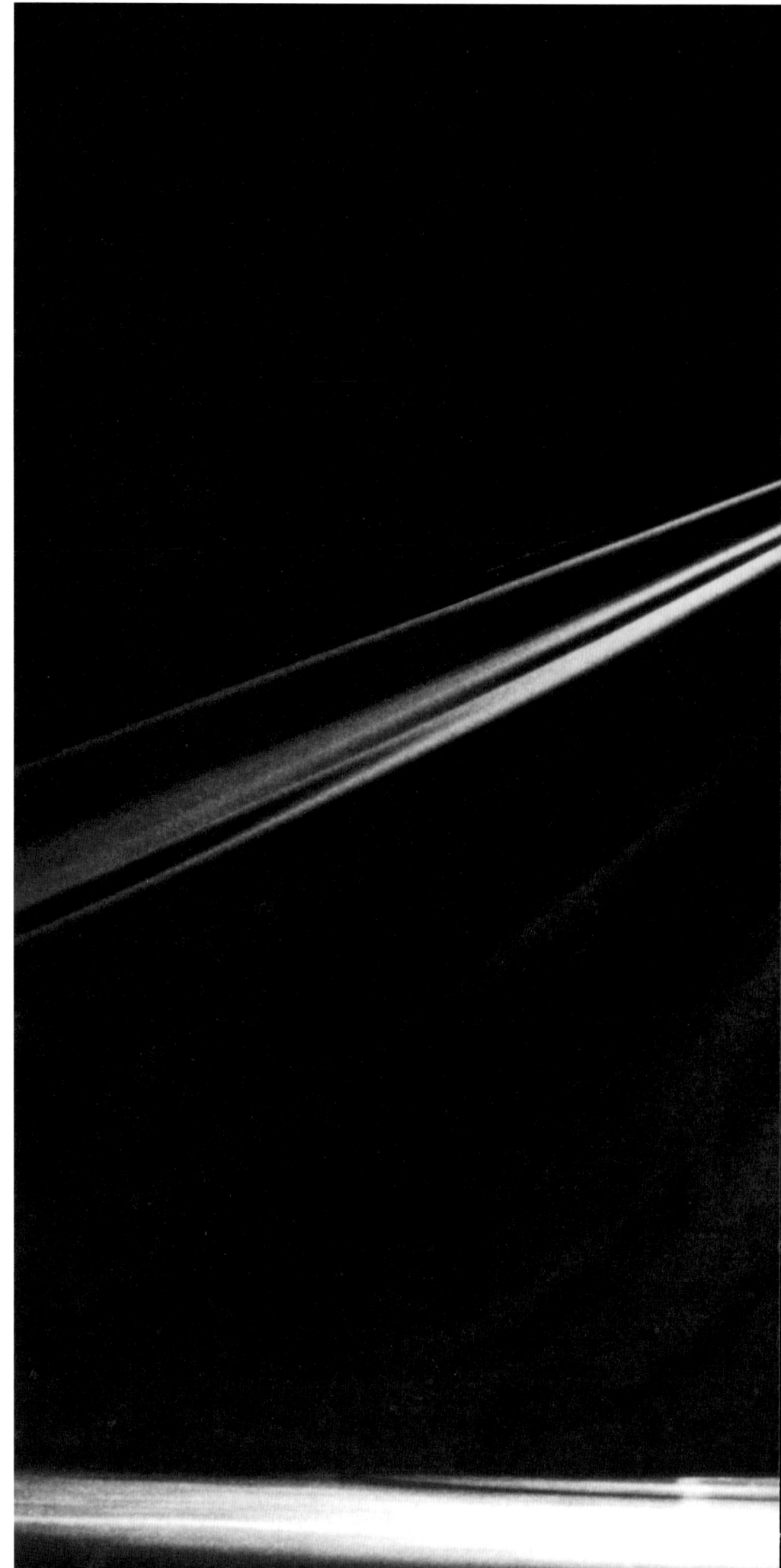

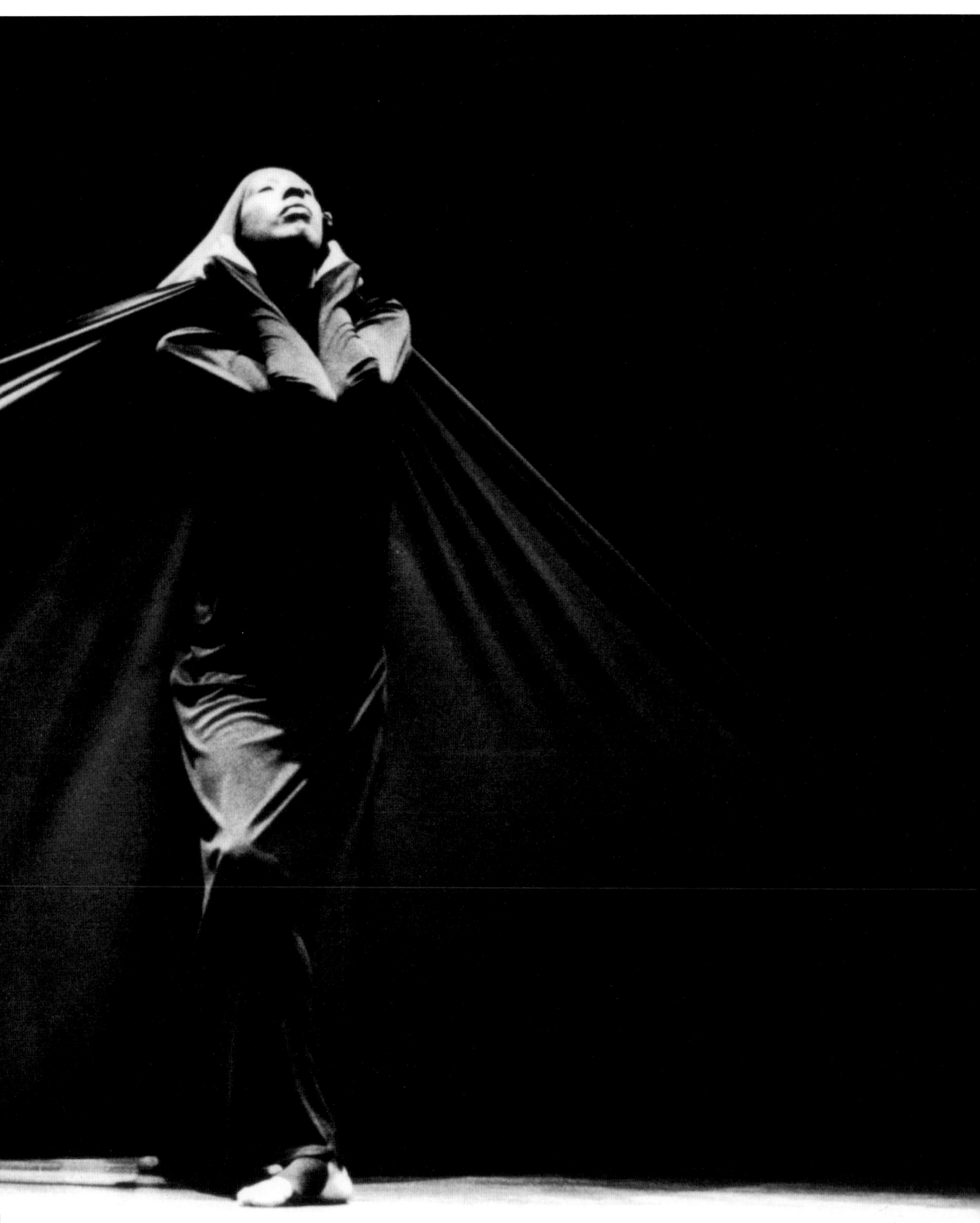

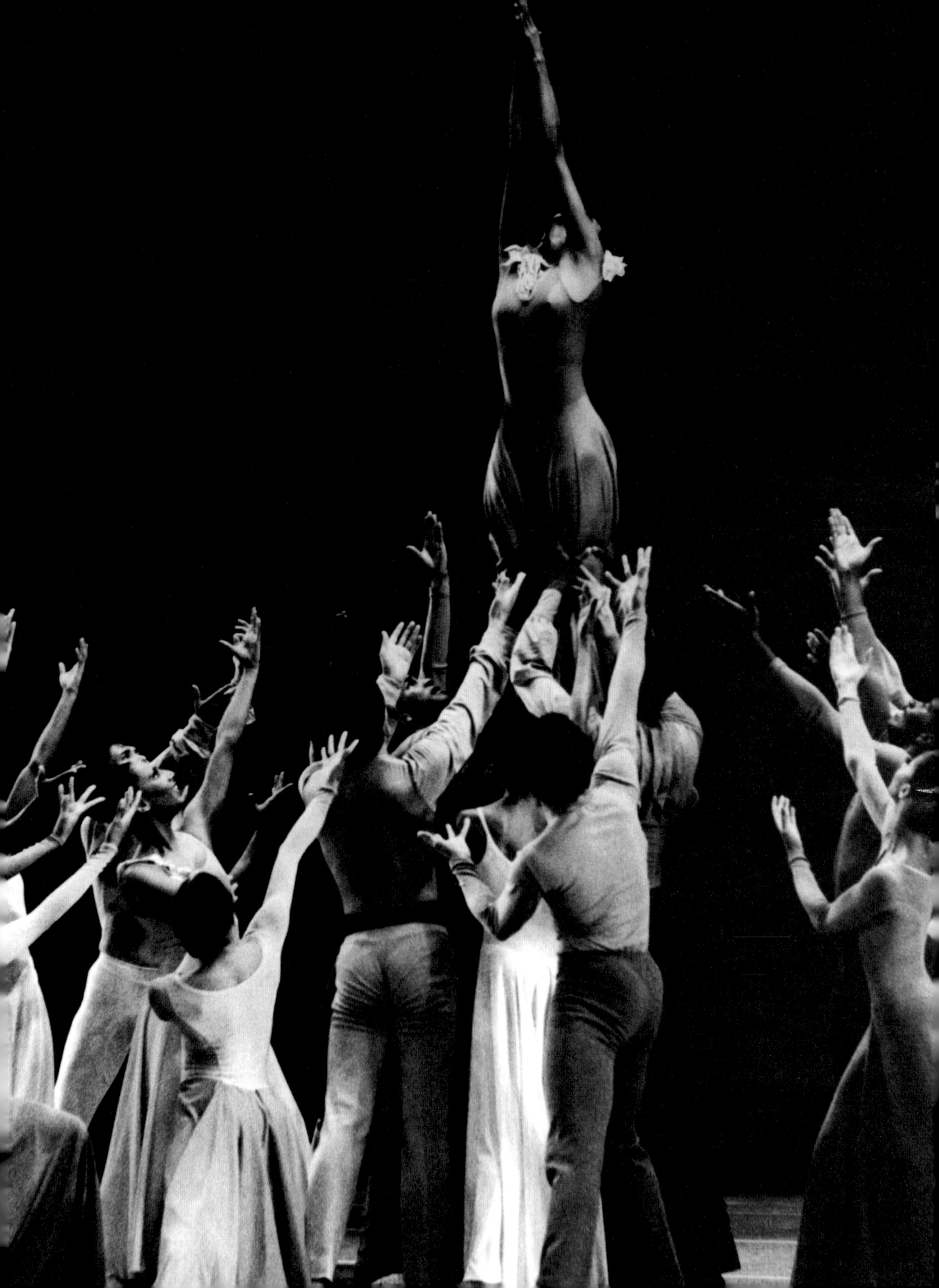

Premiere, New York City Center **Memoria** 1979

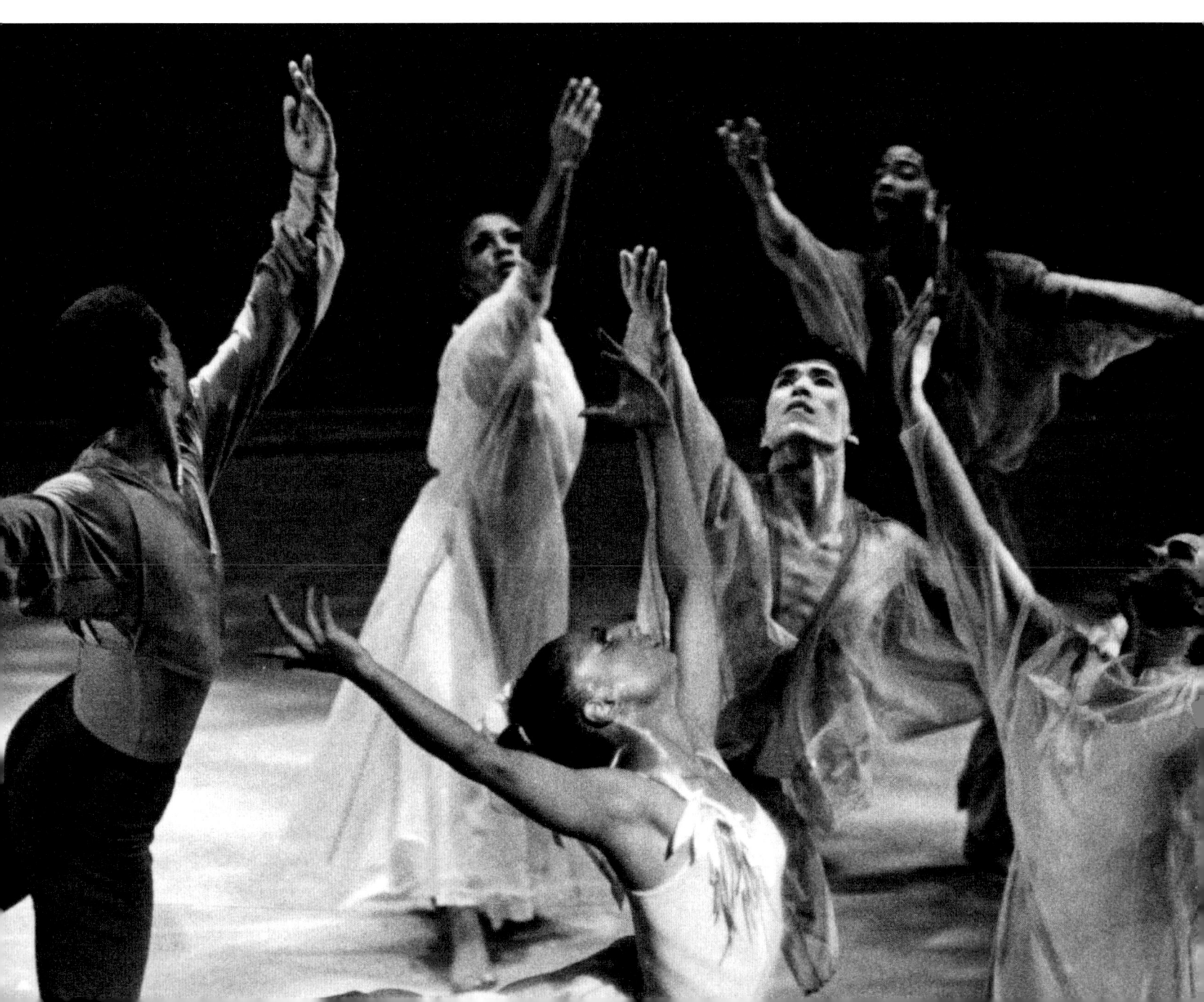

Premiere, New York City Center — **Phases** — 1980

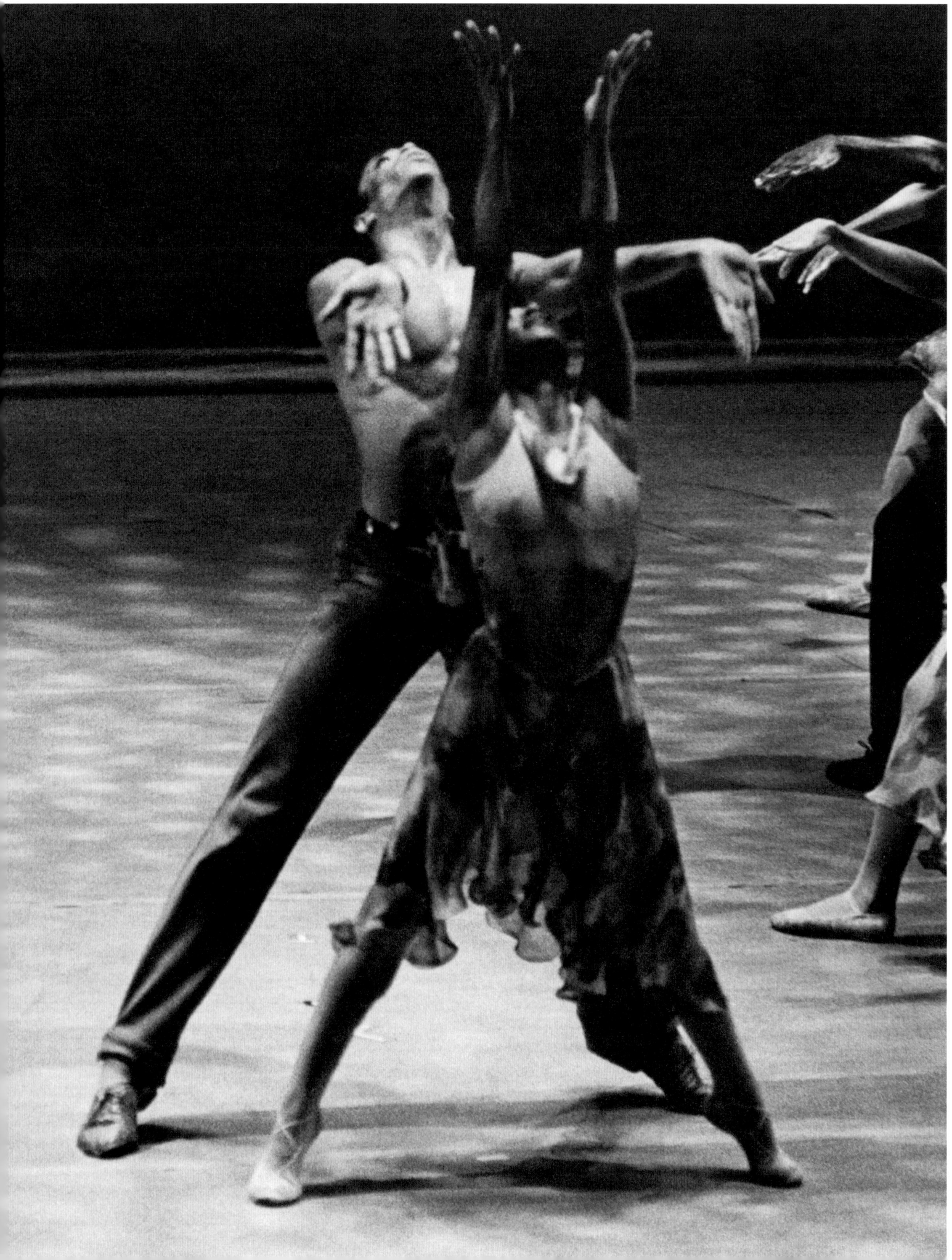

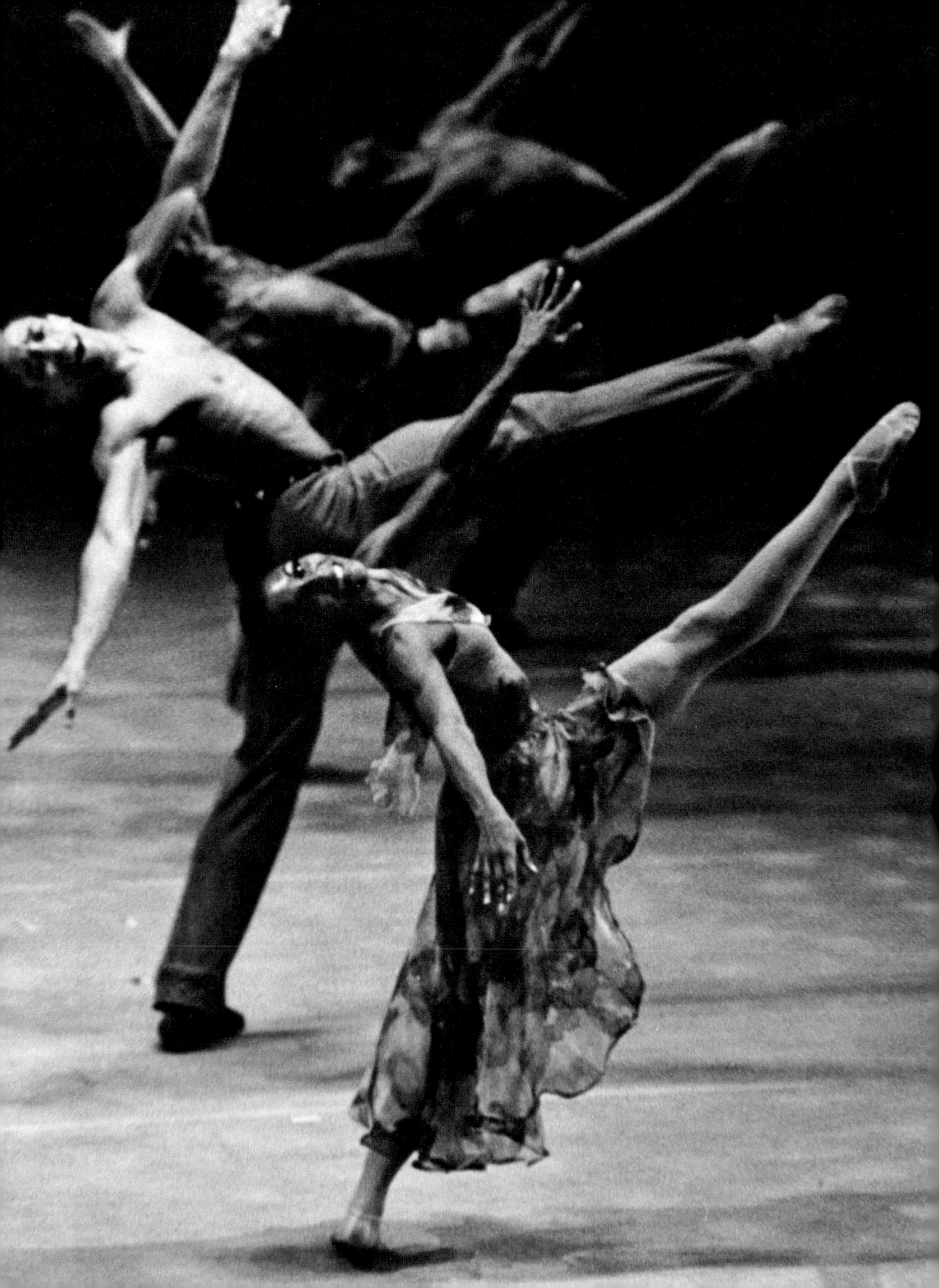

Premiere, New York City Center | **Spell** | 1981

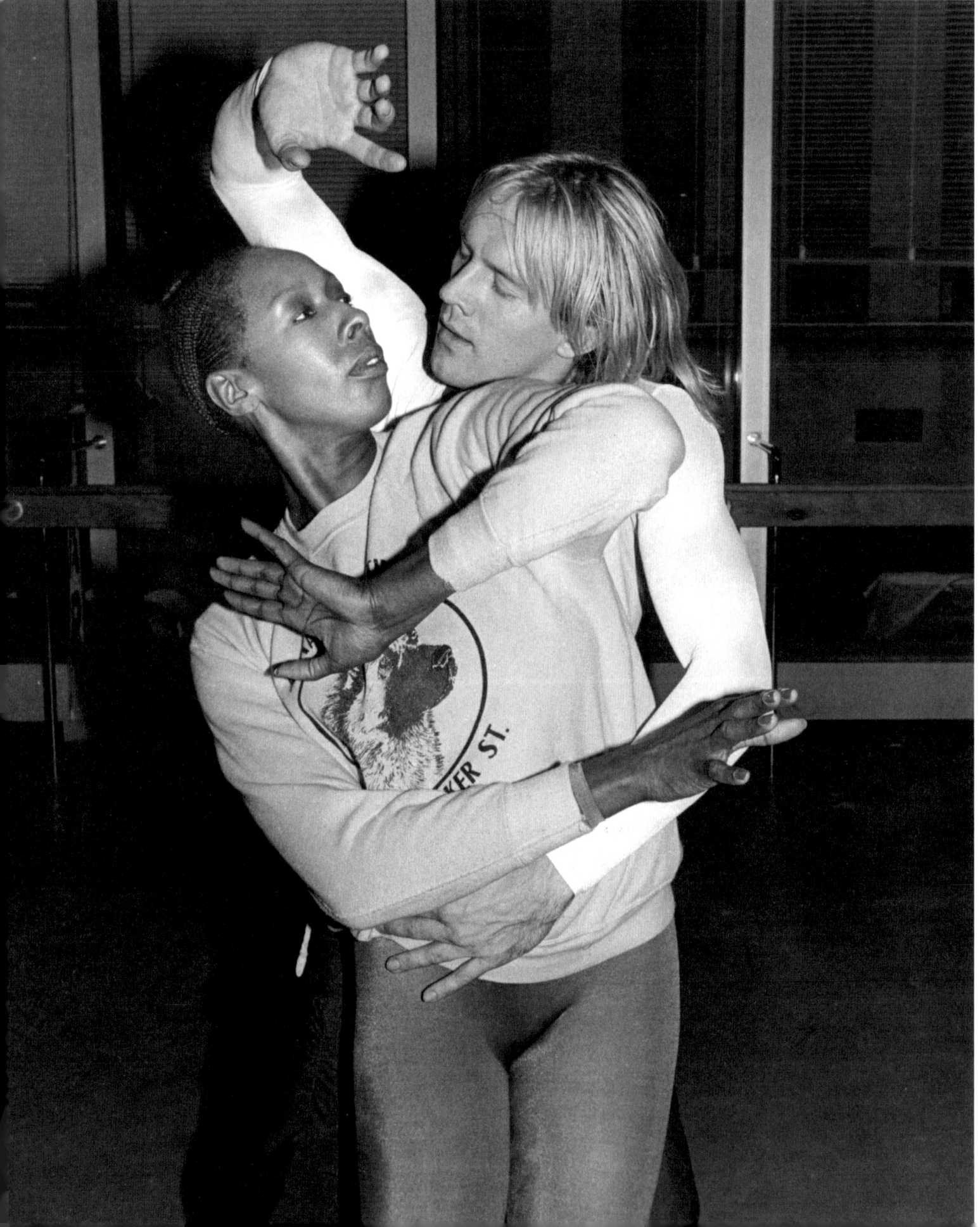

Premiere, New York City Center — Landscape — 1981

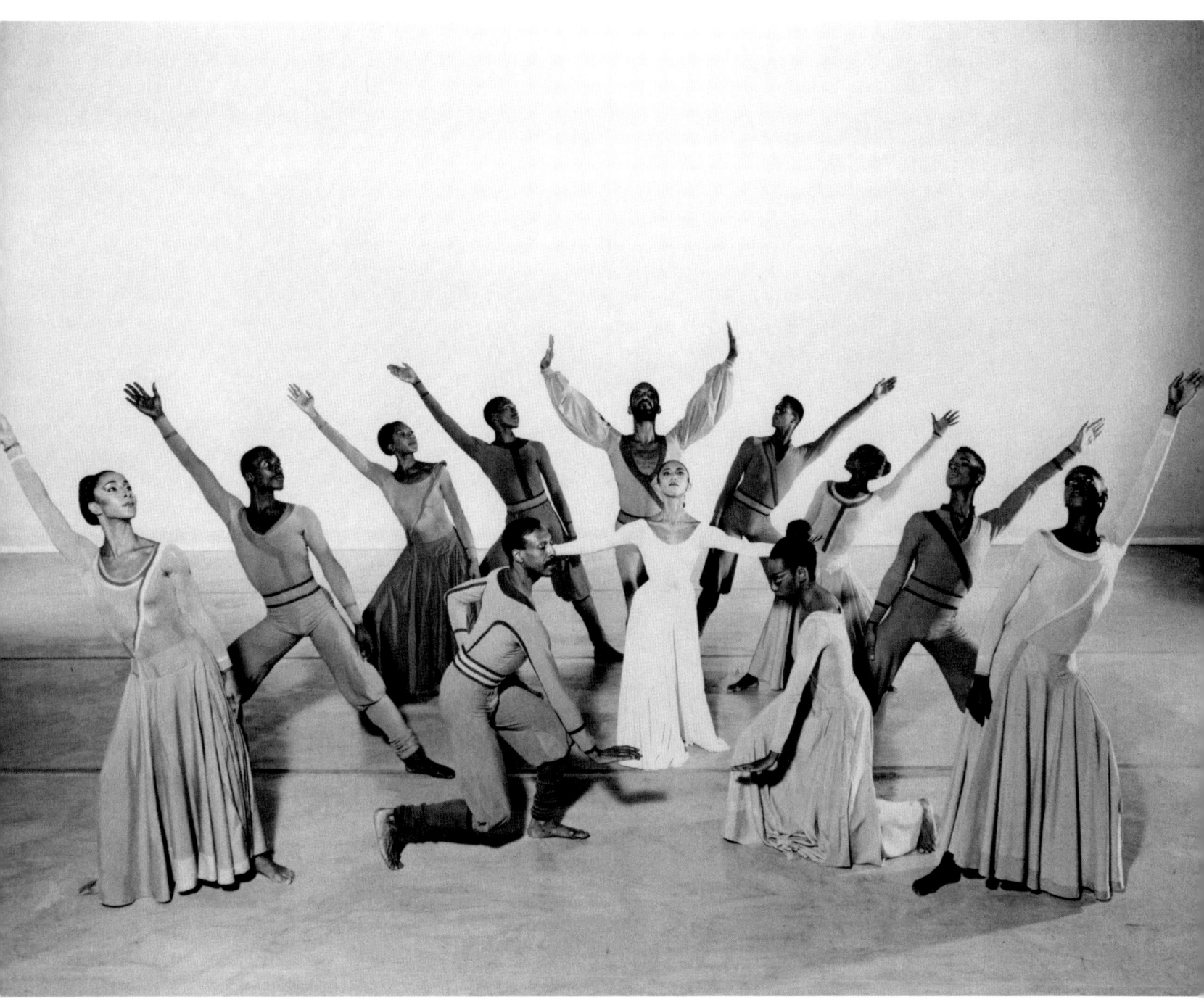

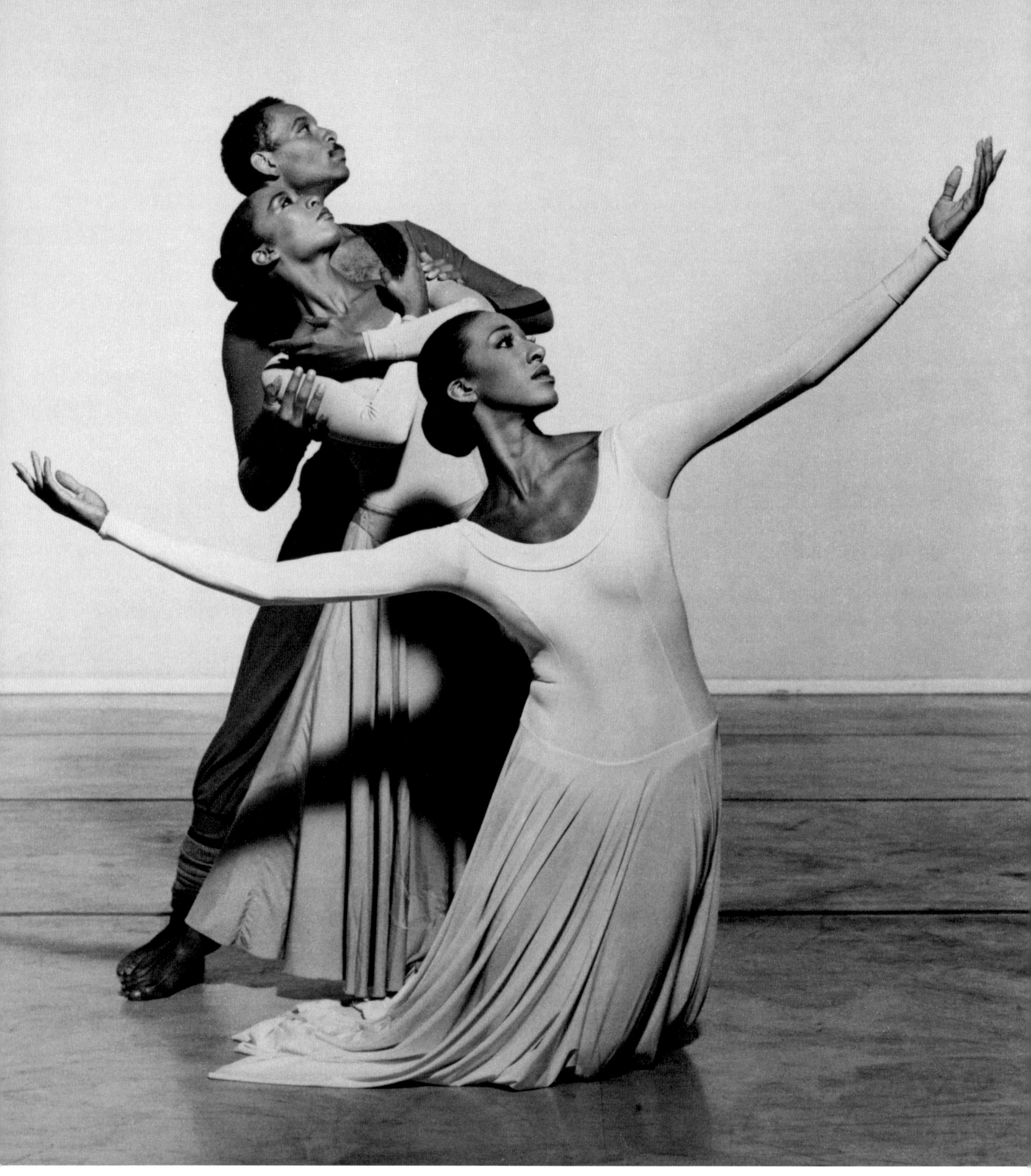

Landscape

Premiere, New York City Center — **Satyriade** — 1982

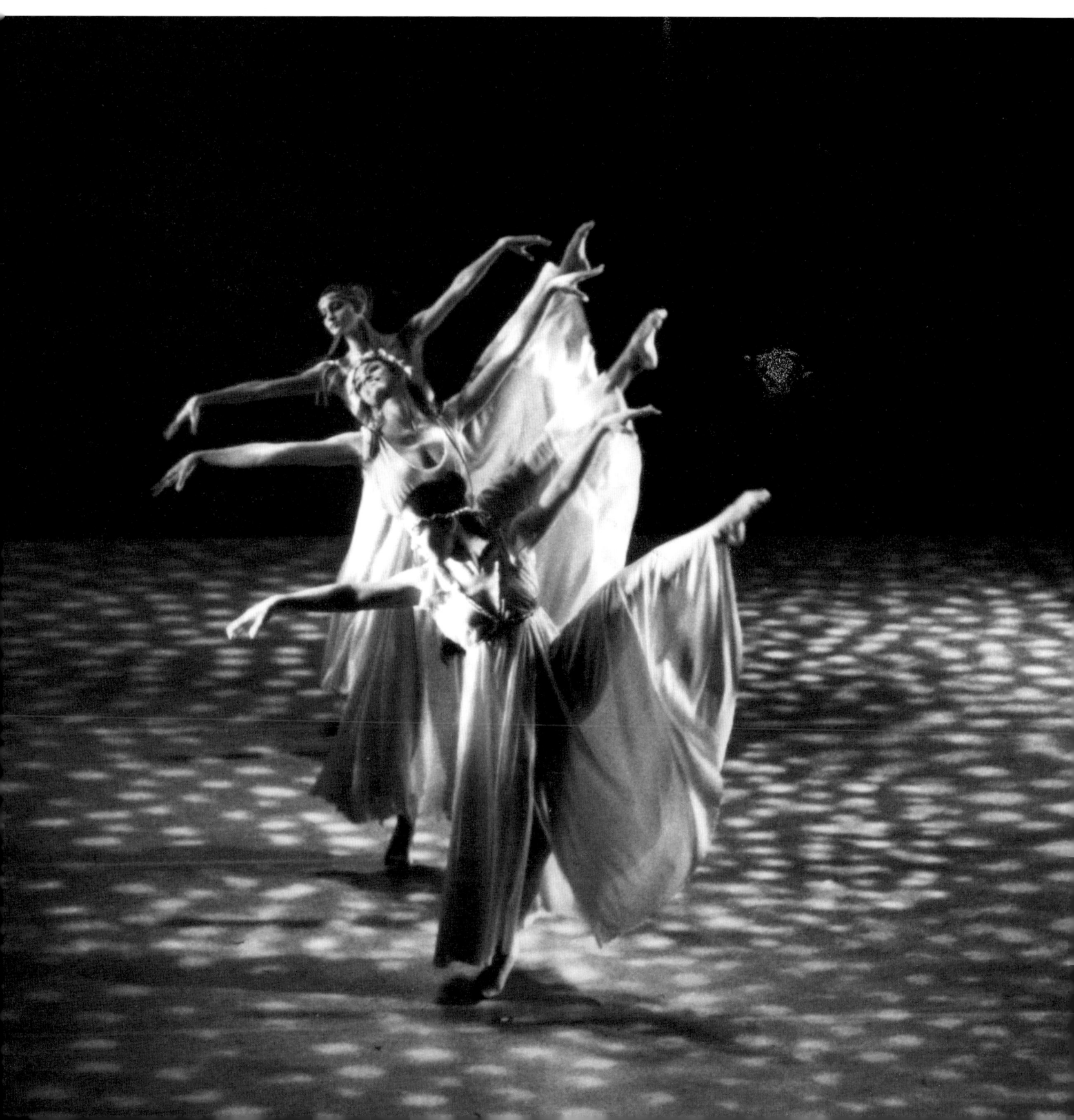

Premiere, Palais Garnier, Paris   Au Bord du Précipice (Precipice)   1983/1984

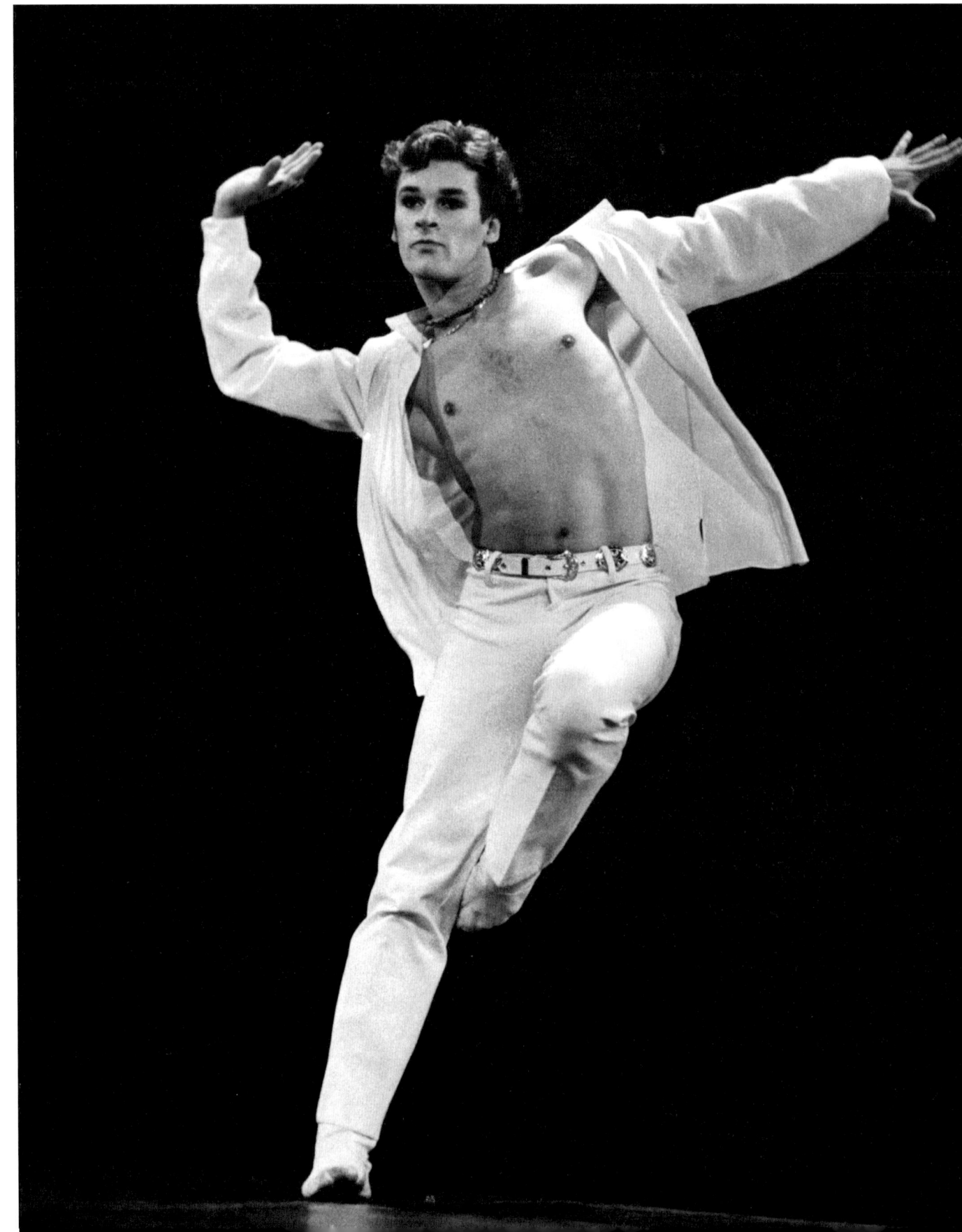

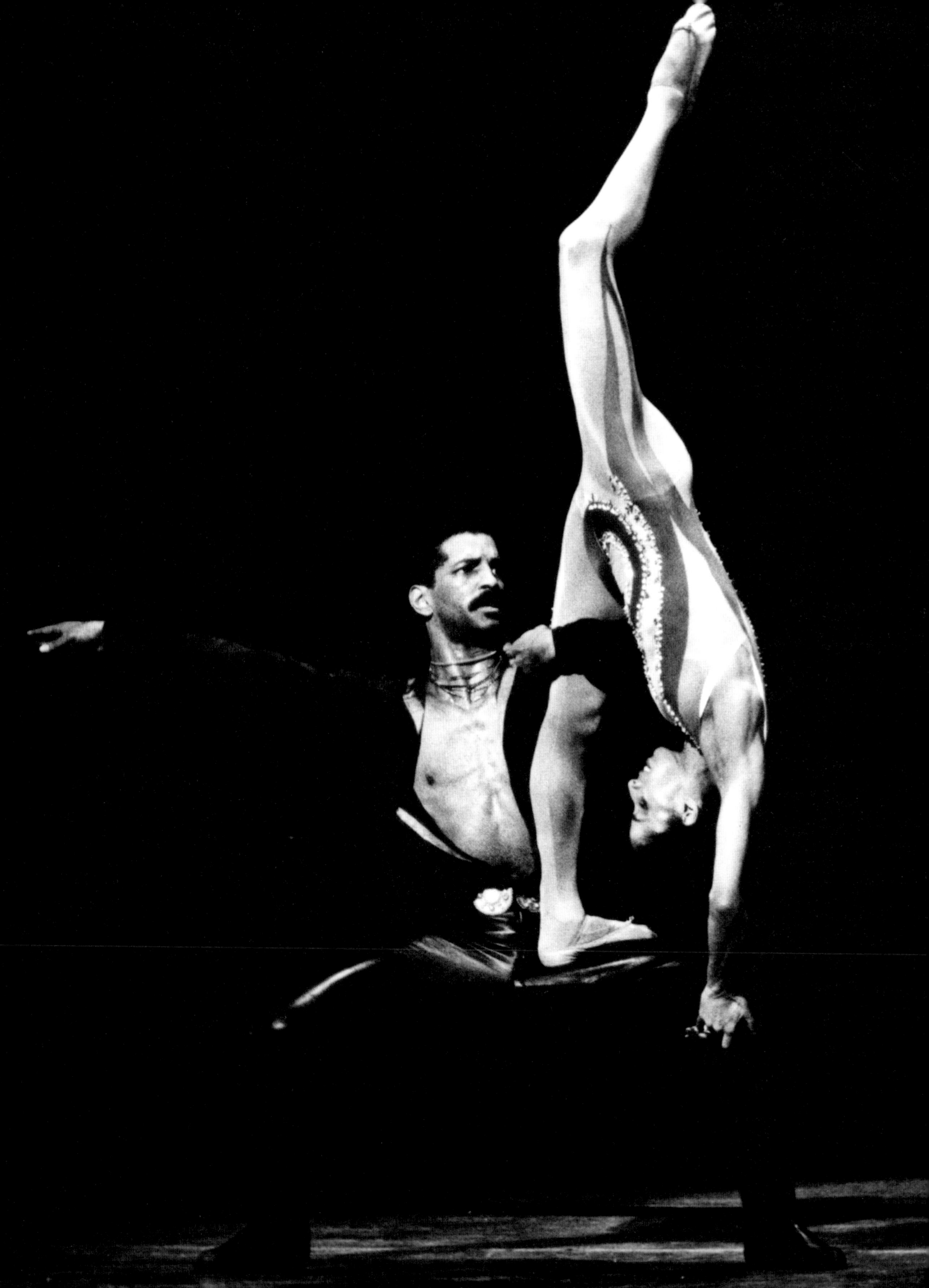

Premiere, New York City Center — **Isba** — 1983

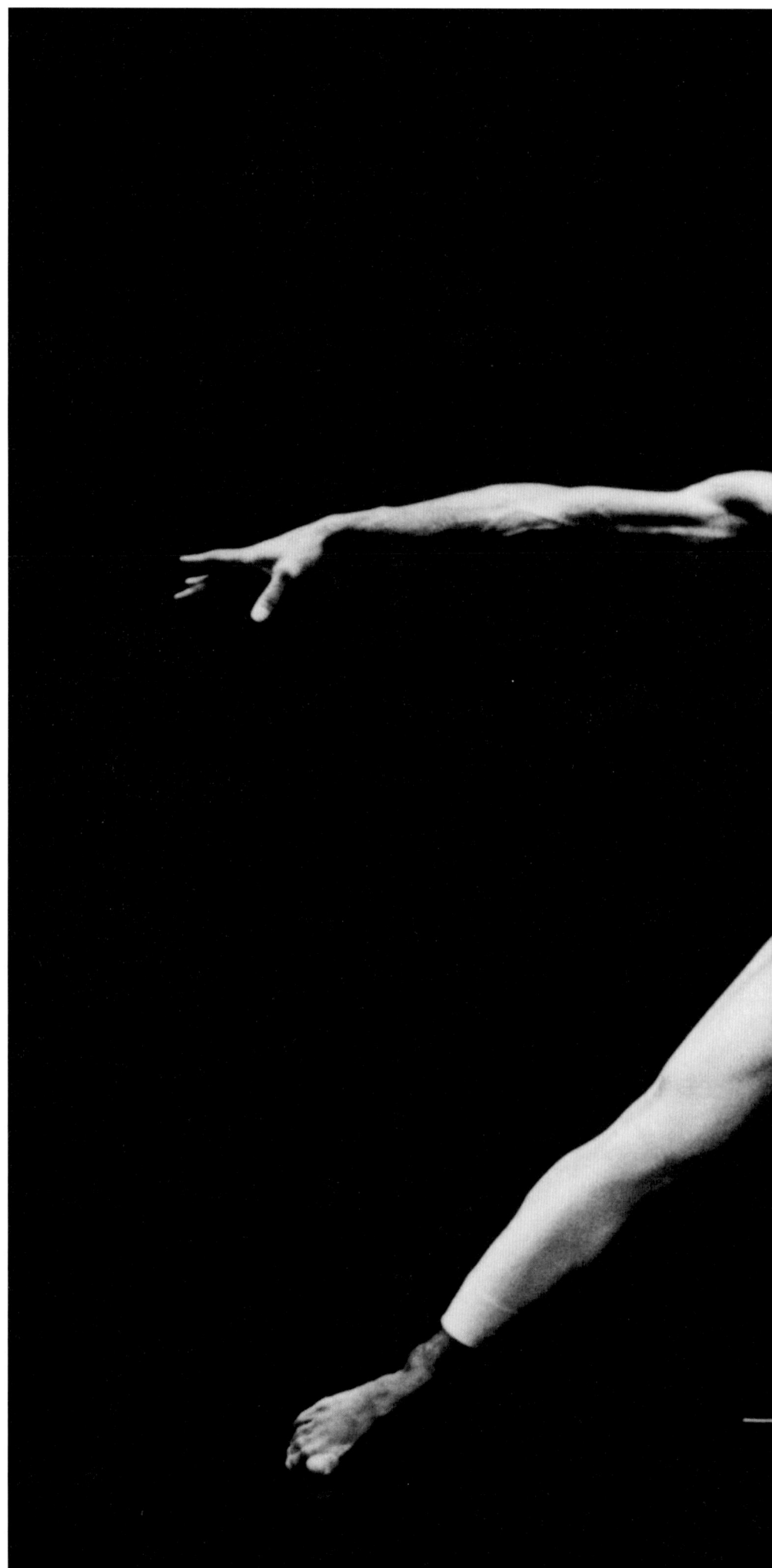

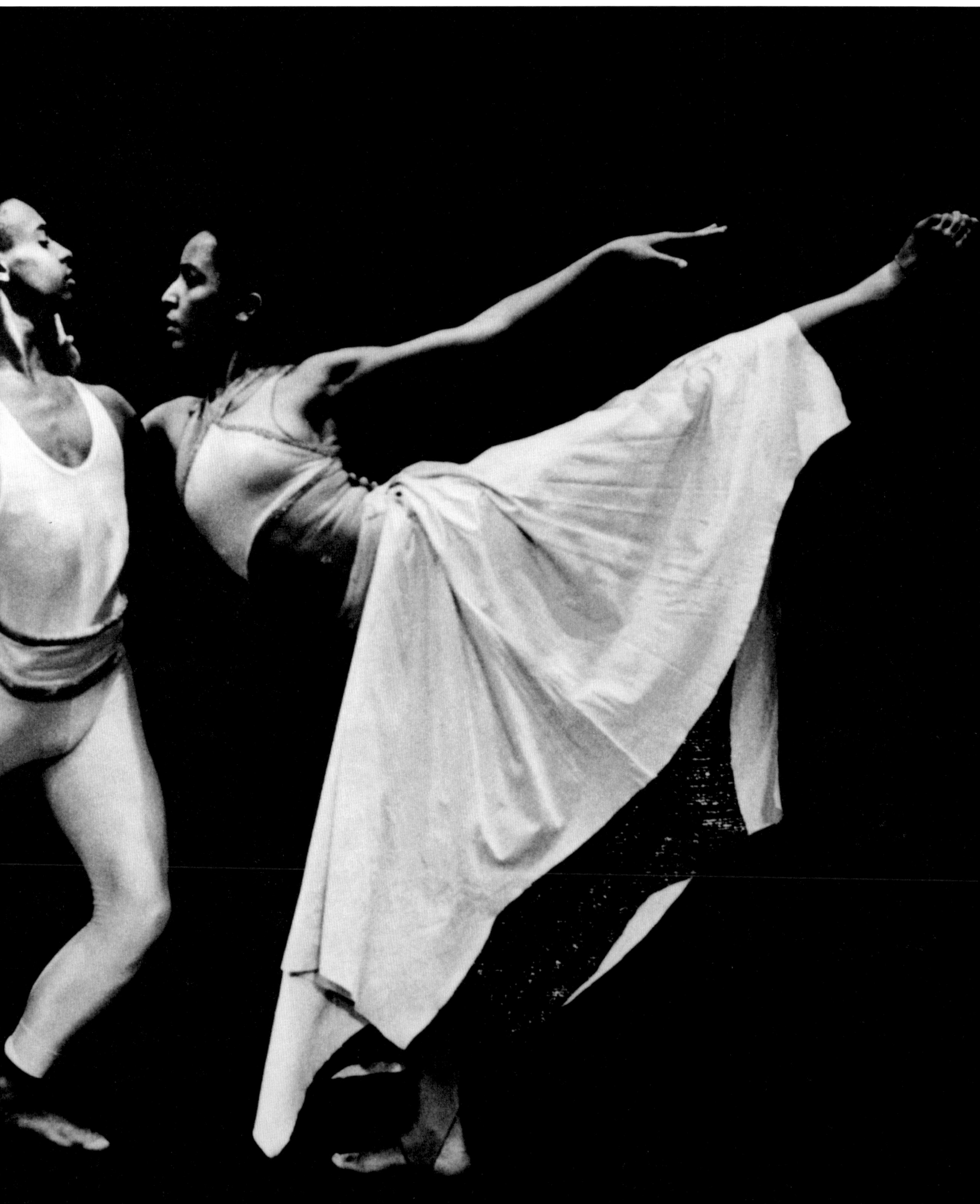

Premiere, Folly Theater, Kansas City, Missouri — For 'Bird'—With Love — 1984

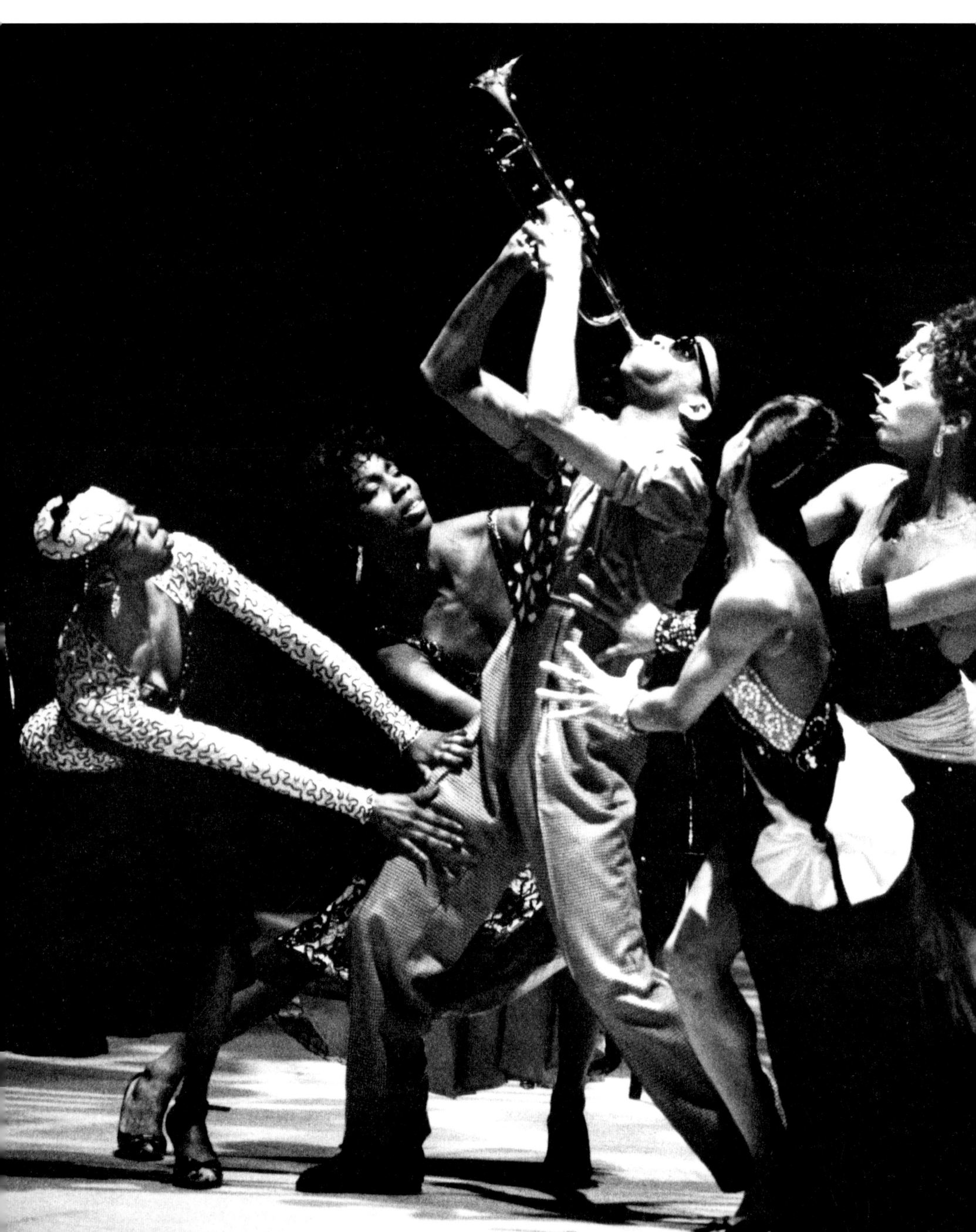

Premiere, Royal Theatre, Copenhagen, Denmark | **Caverna Magica** | 1986

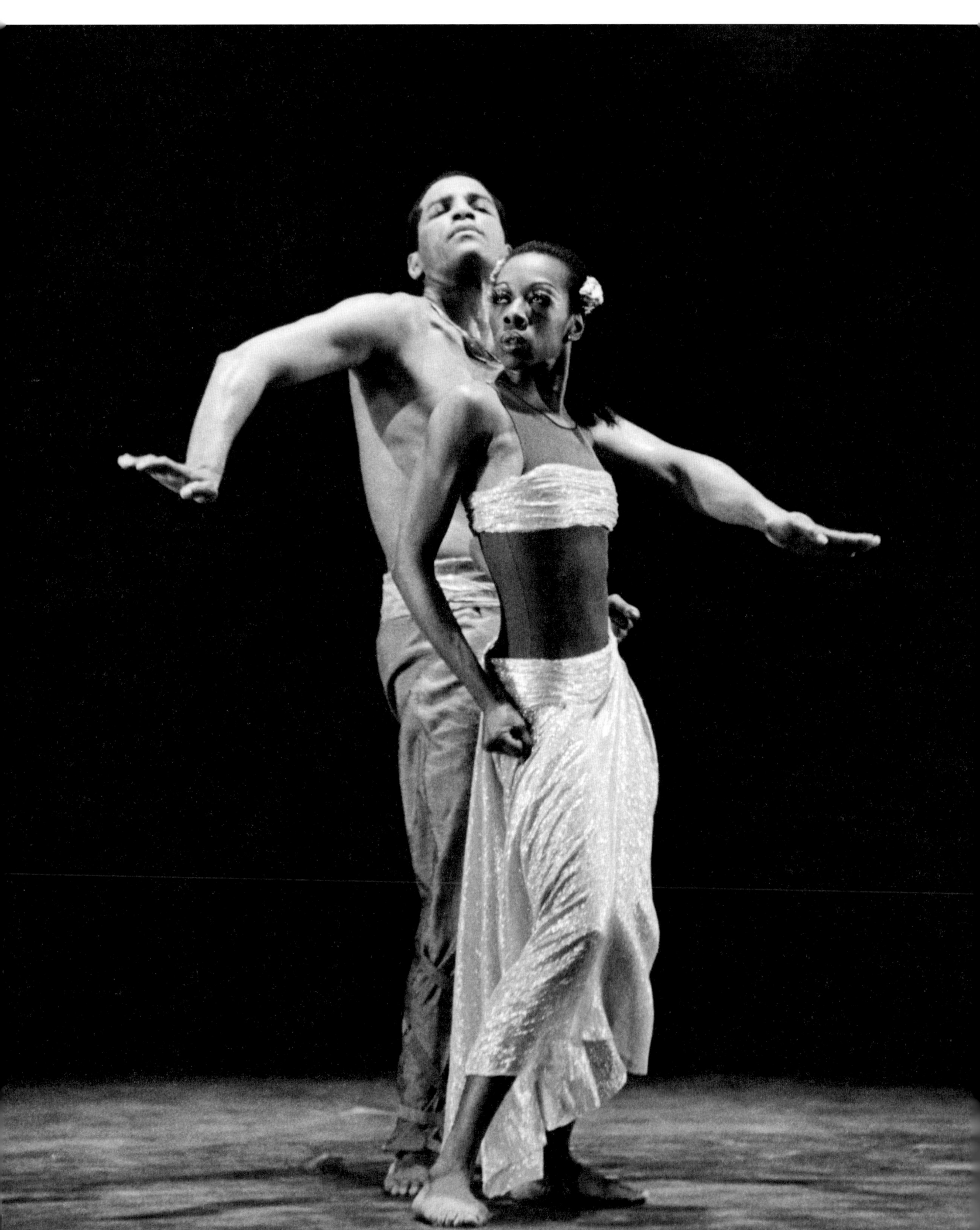

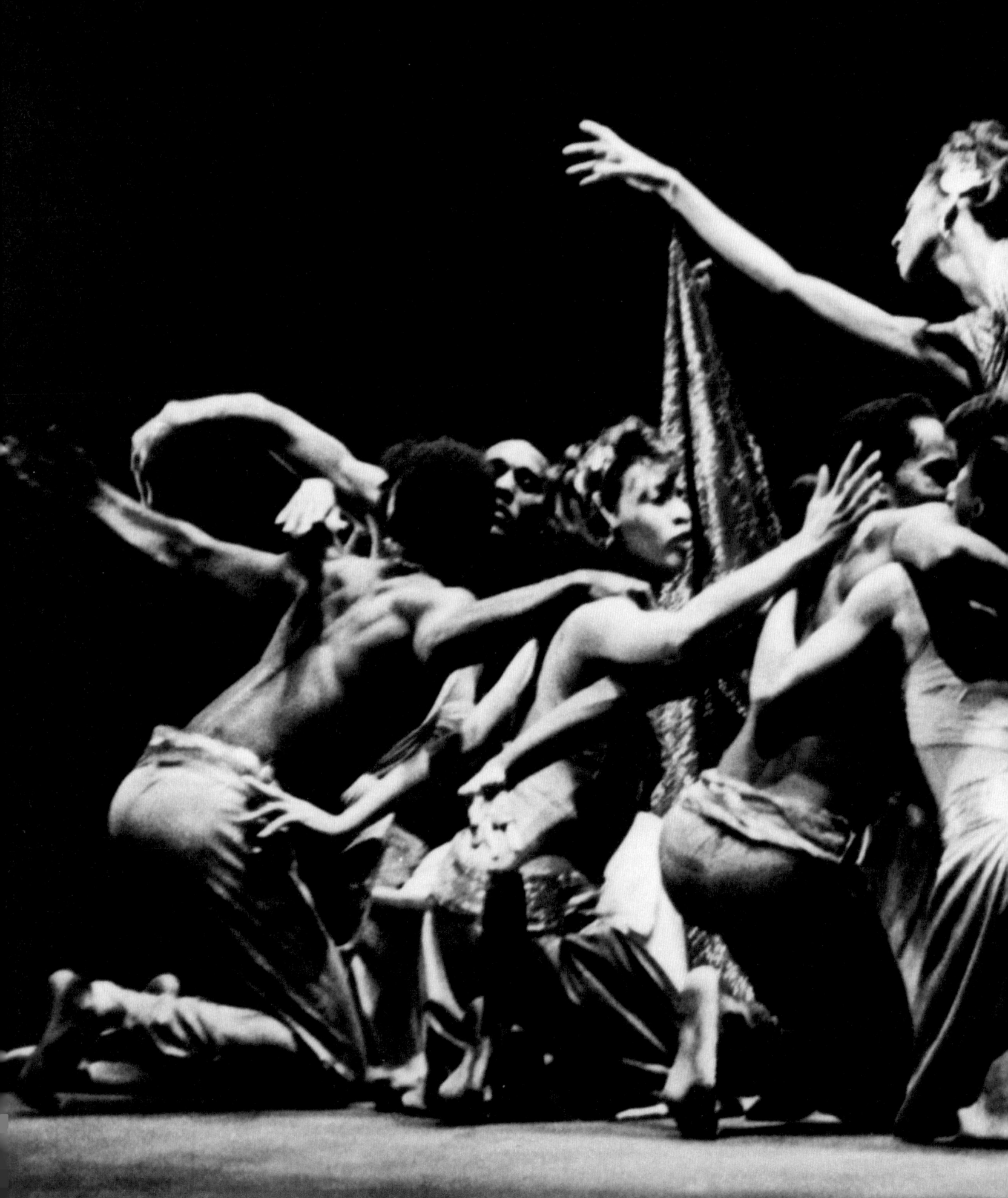

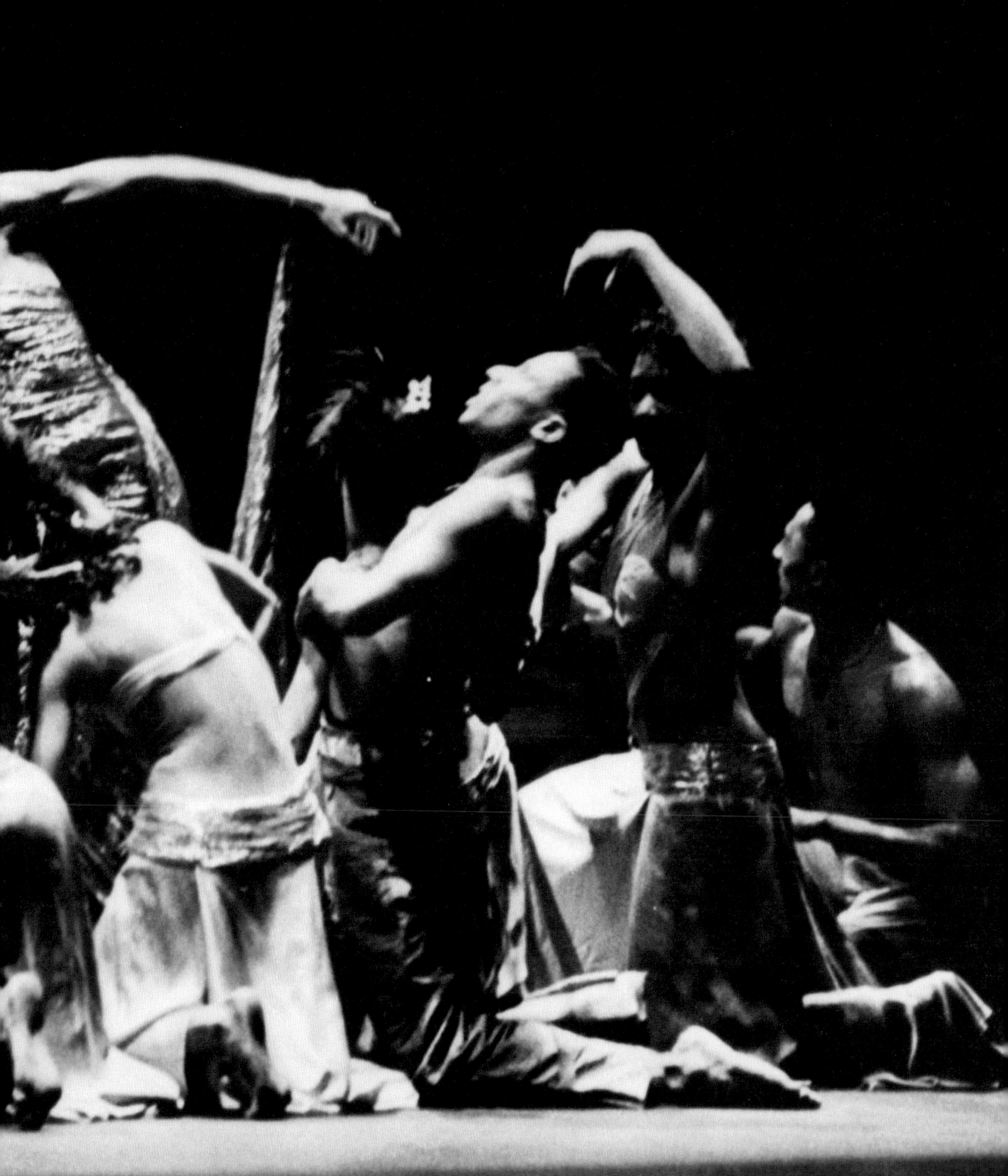

Premiere, Royal Theatre, Copenhagen, Denmark — **Witness** — 1986

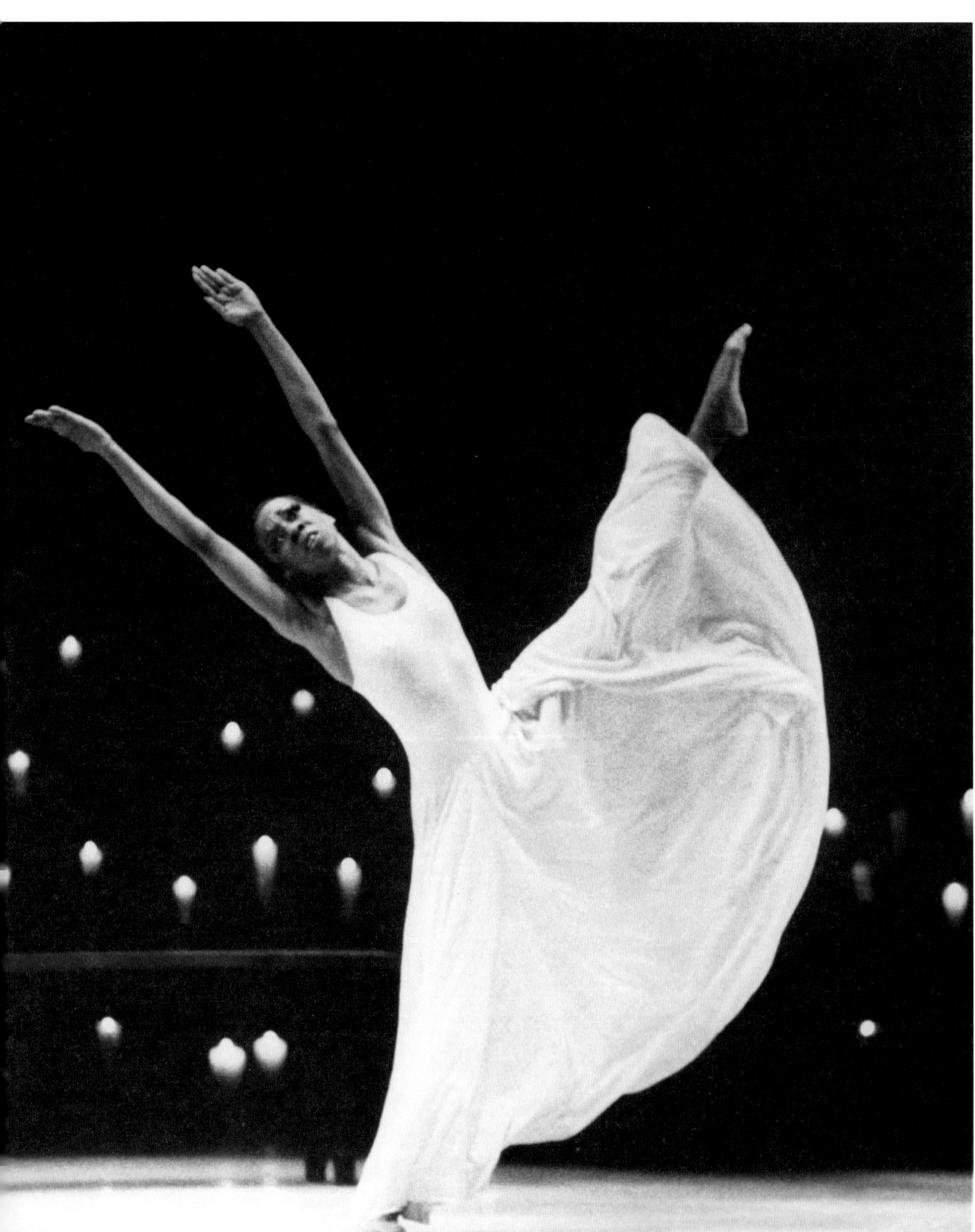

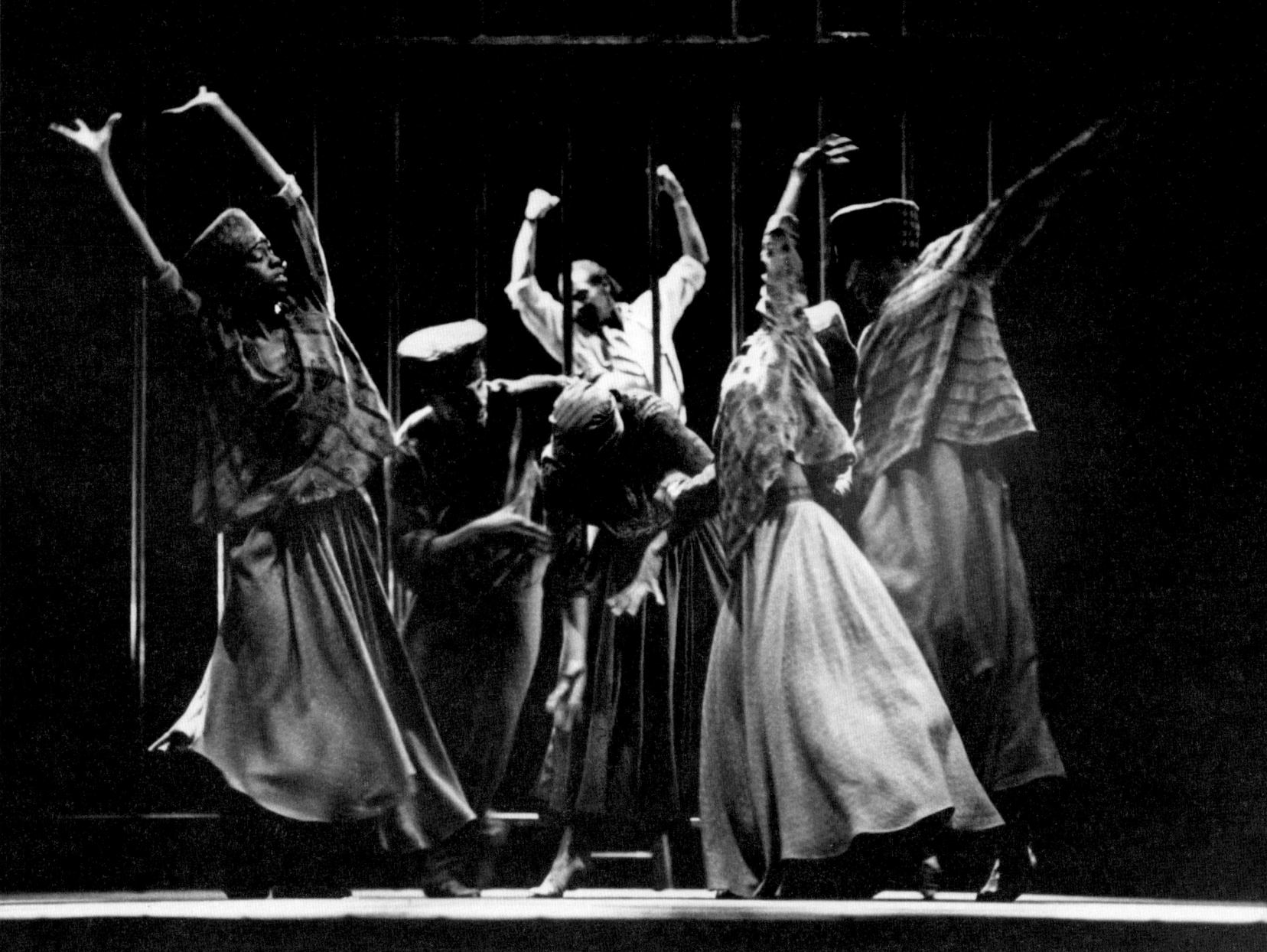

Premiere, Lyric Theater, Kansas City, Missouri   **Survivors**   1986

Premiere, Folly Theater, Kansas City, Missouri

Opus McShann

1988

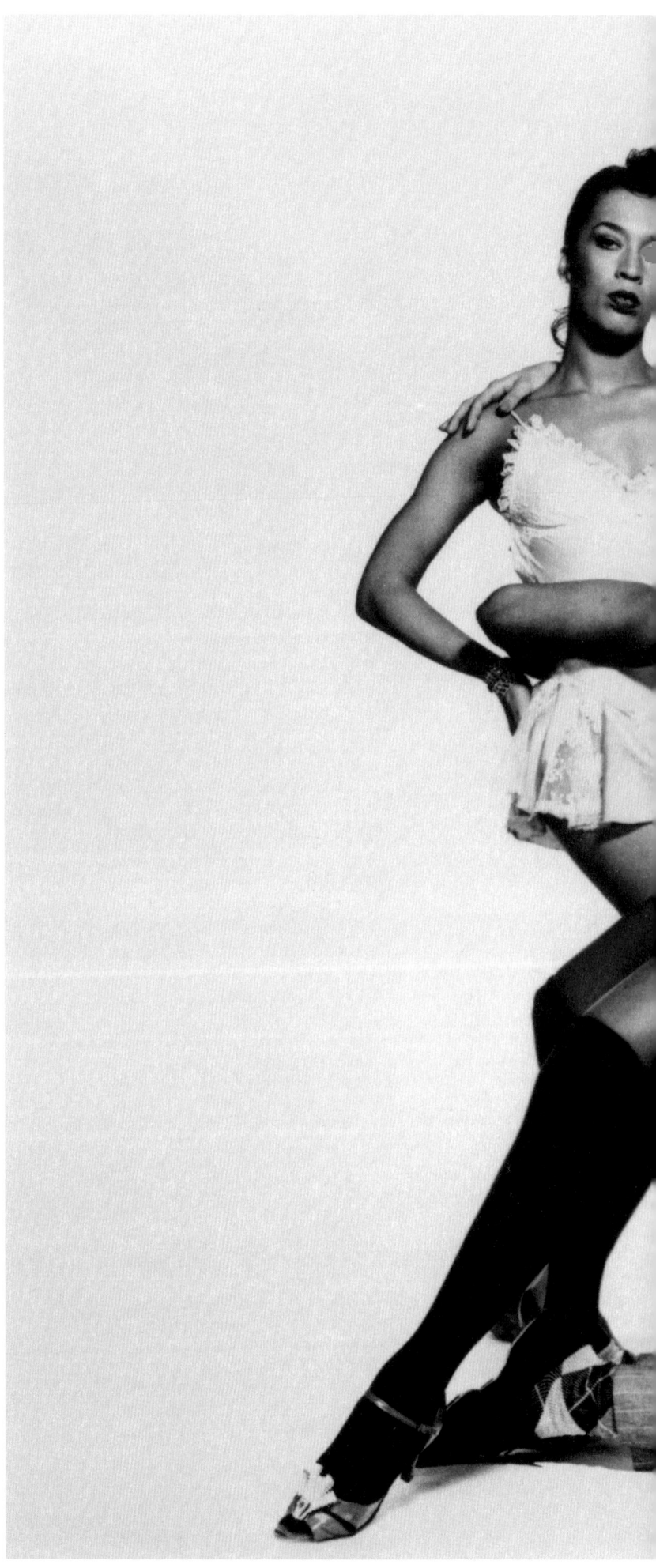

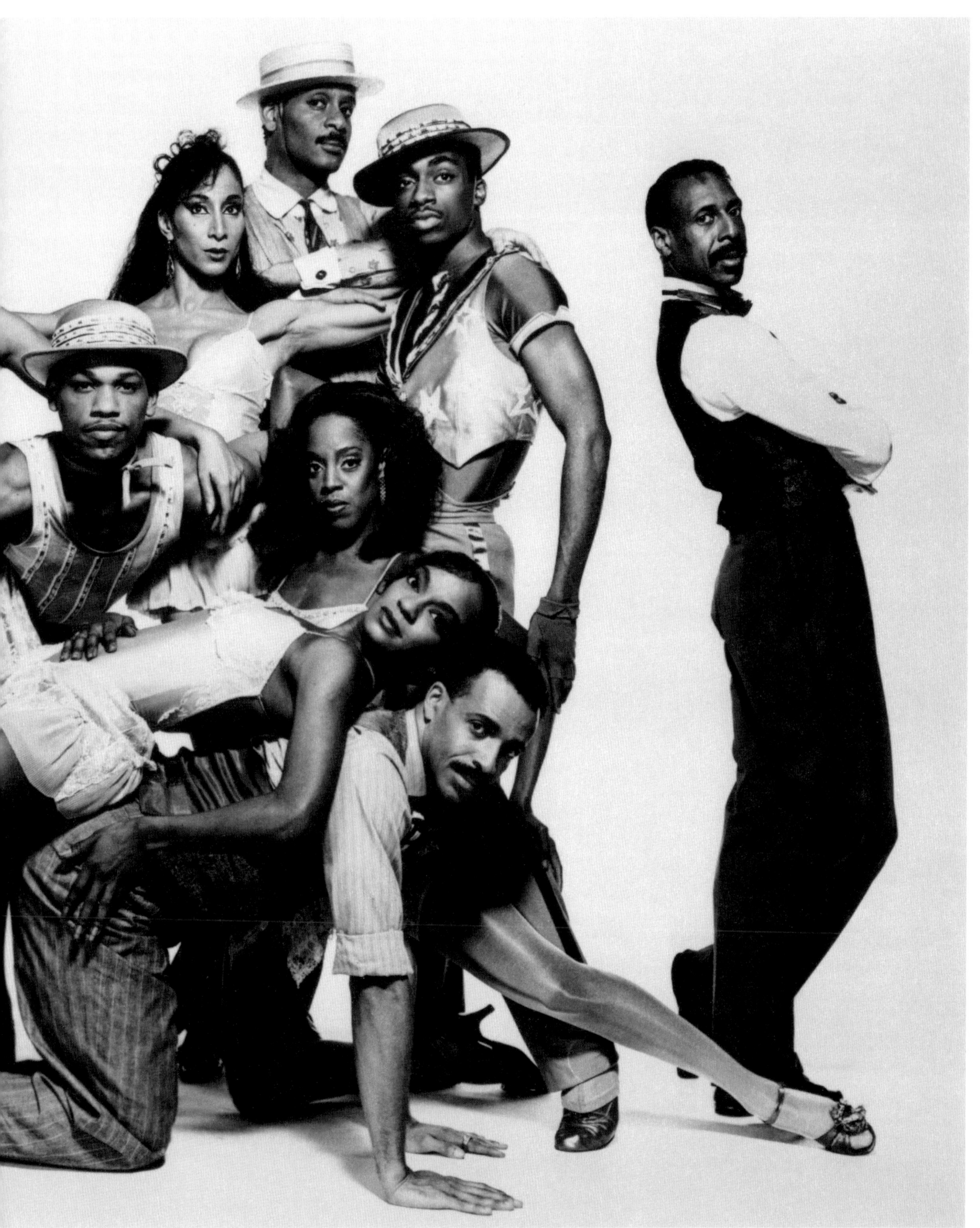

ARCHIVES

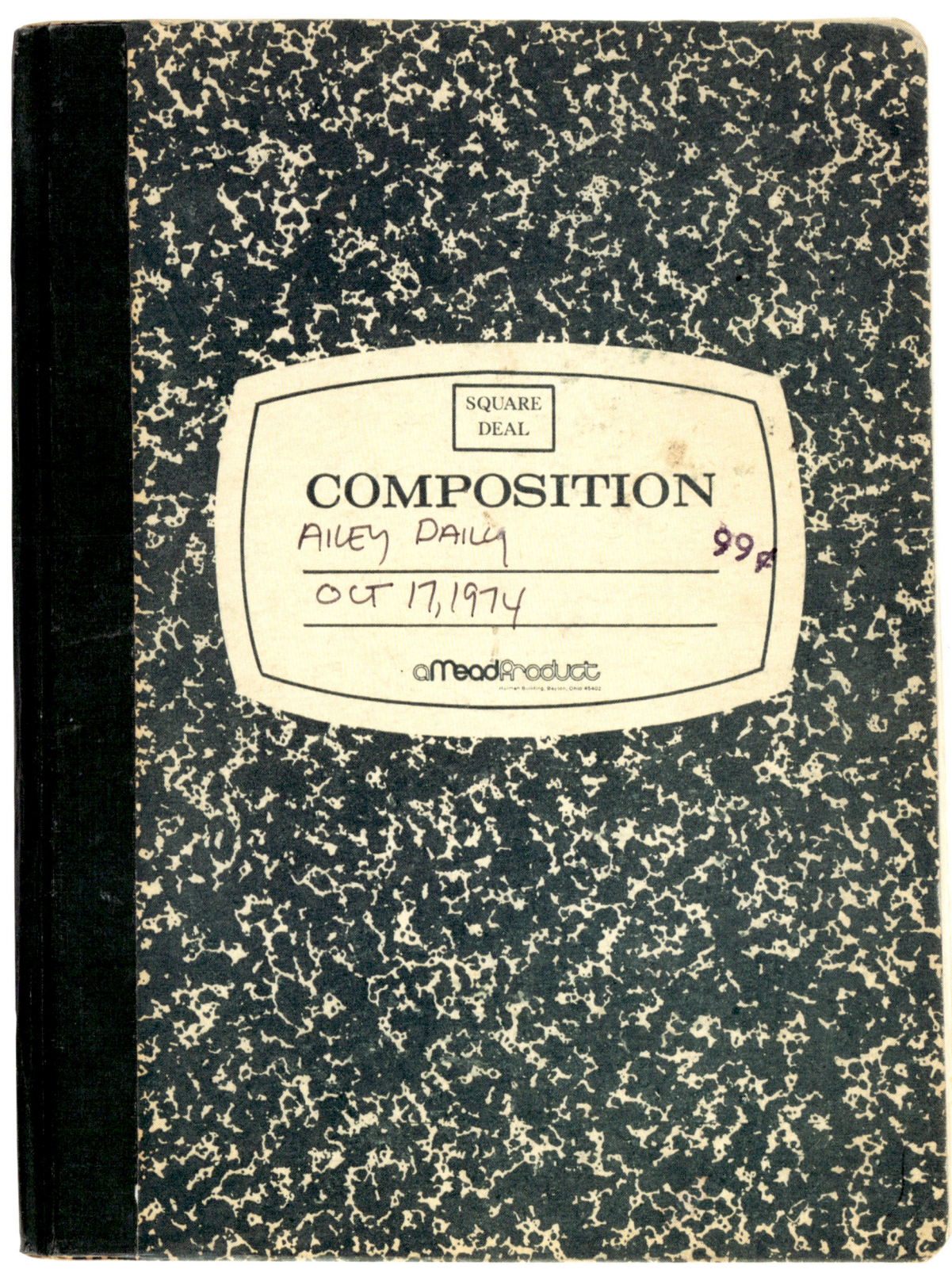

Edges of Ailey is the culmination of six years of research in over ten libraries and archives across the United States. This section is drawn from a selection of those findings, culled and digitized from the holdings of the Allan Gray Family Personal Papers of Alvin Ailey at the Black Archives of Mid-America in Kansas City, Missouri, and the Alvin Ailey Dance Foundation Collection at the Library of Congress, Washington, DC. The following dossier offers insight into the expansive output and prodigious scope of Ailey's thinking and interests, which are more fully represented in the exhibition. This sequence of documents is connective and constellatory, rather than strictly chronological, in keeping with his own associative nature and given that dates for these materials are often unknown. Ideation, for Ailey, took on many forms: lists, observations, missives, musings, drawings, short stories, and personal and professional rules—all vehicles for his curiosity and choreography. What unfolds is a surprising and revelatory intersection of concerns—at turns creative, practical, introspective, and historical—that reveals a mind and body, life and art, and Black dance and modern dance as fundamentally, inextricably intertwined.

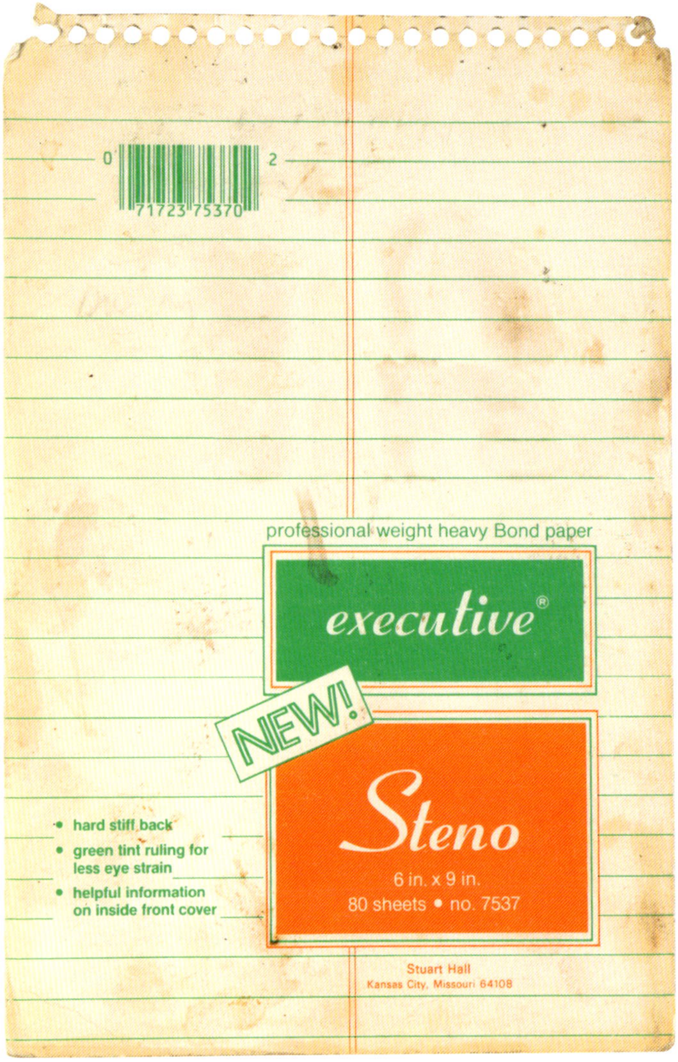

[Notebook cover: executive Steno, 6 in. x 9 in., 80 sheets, no. 7537, Stuart Hall, Kansas City, Missouri 64108]

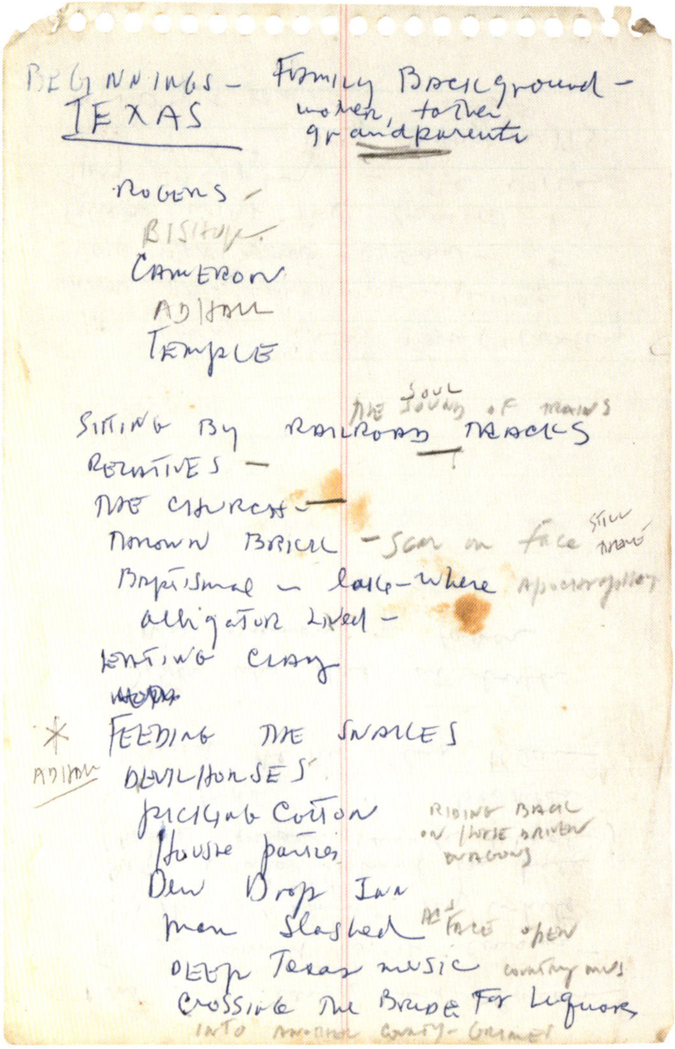

BEGINNINGS — Family Background —
TEXAS   mother, father
               grandparents

    ROGERS
    BISHOP
    CAMERON
    ADKINS
    TEMPLE

SITTING BY RAILROAD TRACKS — THE SOUL SOUND OF TRAINS
RELATIVES —
THE CHURCHES —
THROWN BRICK — SCAR ON FACE STILL THERE
BAPTISMAL IN LAKE — WHERE Apocryphally
    ALLIGATOR LIVED —
EATING CLAY

* FEEDING THE SNAKES
ADKINS DEVIL HORSES
    PICKING COTTON   RIDING BACK
    HOUSE PARTIES   ON MULE DRIVEN
    DEW DROP INN   WAGONS
    MAN SLASHED AT FACE OPEN
    DEEP TEXAS MUSIC   country music
    CROSSING THE BRIDGE FOR LIQUOR
        INTO ANOTHER COUNTY — GRIMES

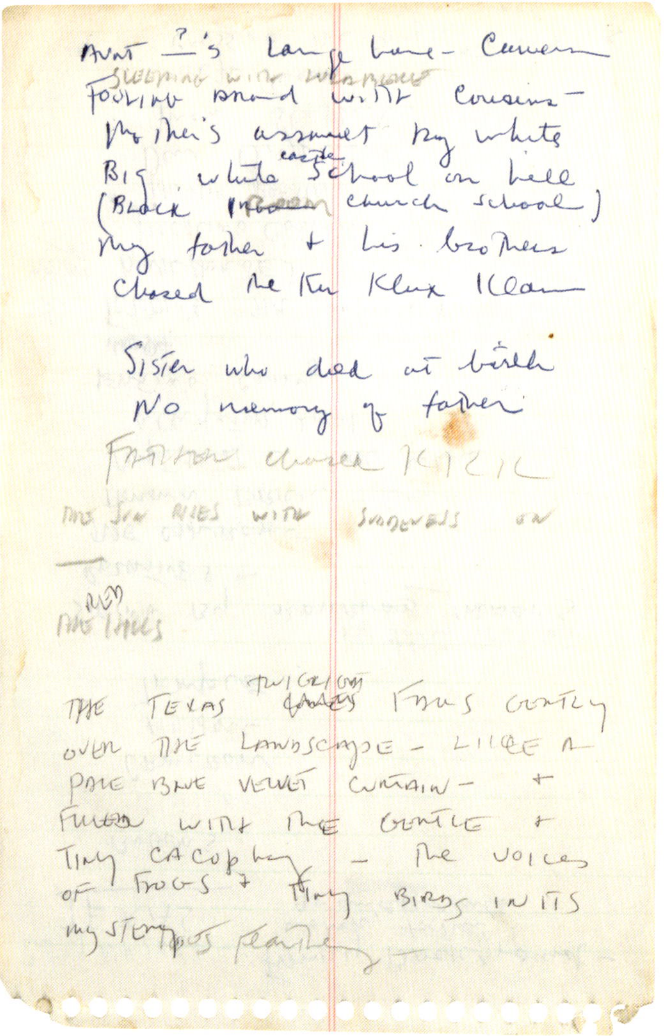

AUNT ?'s LARGE HOUSE — CAMERON
SLEEPING WITH RELATIVES
FOOLING AROUND WITH COUSINS —
Mother's assault by white
BIG white CASTLE SCHOOL ON HILL
(BLACK WOODEN church school)
My father + his brothers
chased the Ku Klux Klan

Sister who died at birth
No memory of father
Father chased KKK

THE TRAIN RIDES WITH SHOVELS ON
    TRACKS

RED
ANT HILLS

THE TEXAS TWILIGHT JAMES FALLS GENTLY
OVER THE LANDSCAPE — LIKE A
PALE BLUE VELVET CURTAIN — +
FILLED WITH THE GENTLE +
TINY CACOPHONY — THE VOICES
OF FROGS + TINY BIRDS IN ITS
MYSTERIOUS FEATHERY

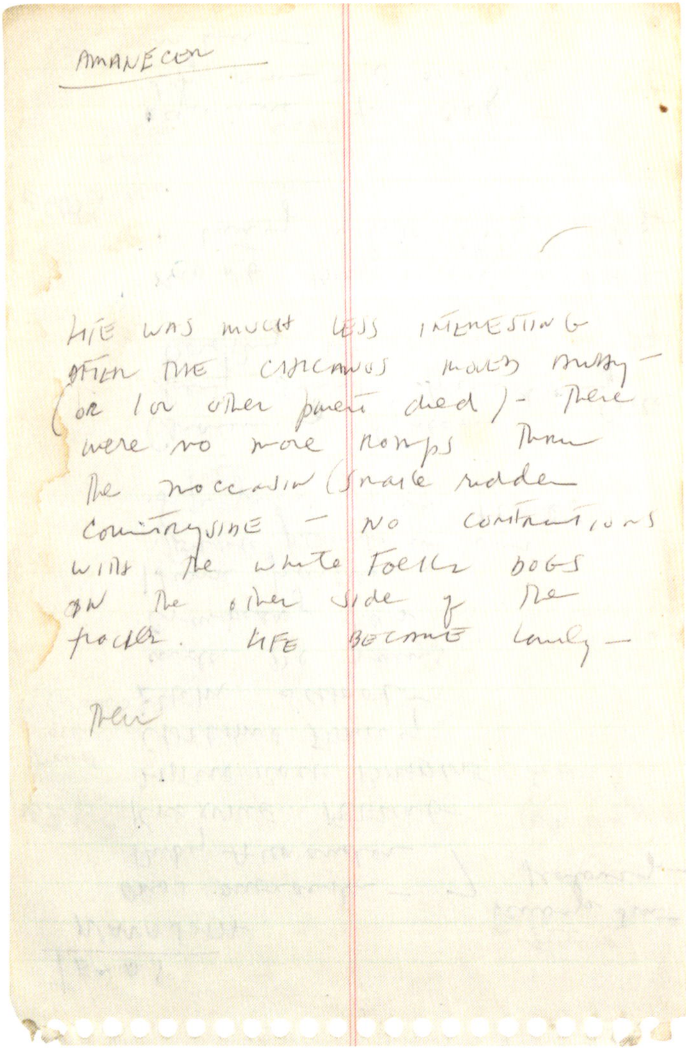

AMANECER

LIFE WAS MUCH LESS INTERESTING
AFTER THE CIRCUMSTANCES MADE MISSY
(OR ONE OTHER PARENT DIED) — THERE
WERE NO MORE ROMPS THROUGH
THE MOCCASIN (SNAKE RIDDEN
COUNTRYSIDE — NO CONFRONTATIONS
WITH THE WHITE FOLKS DOGS
ON THE OTHER SIDE OF THE
TRACKS. LIFE BECAME lonely —

Then

7-14-72

Hello there:

Know you are feeling better sence you got some rest. We are all well. You will feel better after you louse wight. That a funny thing. I knew you were lathes in Husb. are not feeling good are something. Cant fool the ald coon smile I told Fred. he said. Stop thanking like that. Calvin warsing hofter be on Job at 6:30, Am cntil 3:Pm. he Seems to like it. dont know yet. it very hat here. No rain in sight wich we need so bad Fred is still busy pittling around the house. I am sure all of you tests will come out ok. here is the writeup that was in times paper. You take cear of your self. and dont forget to pray--

Hello to all. Fred and Calvin Send hello
    all my good well wishes
    and love
      Mom

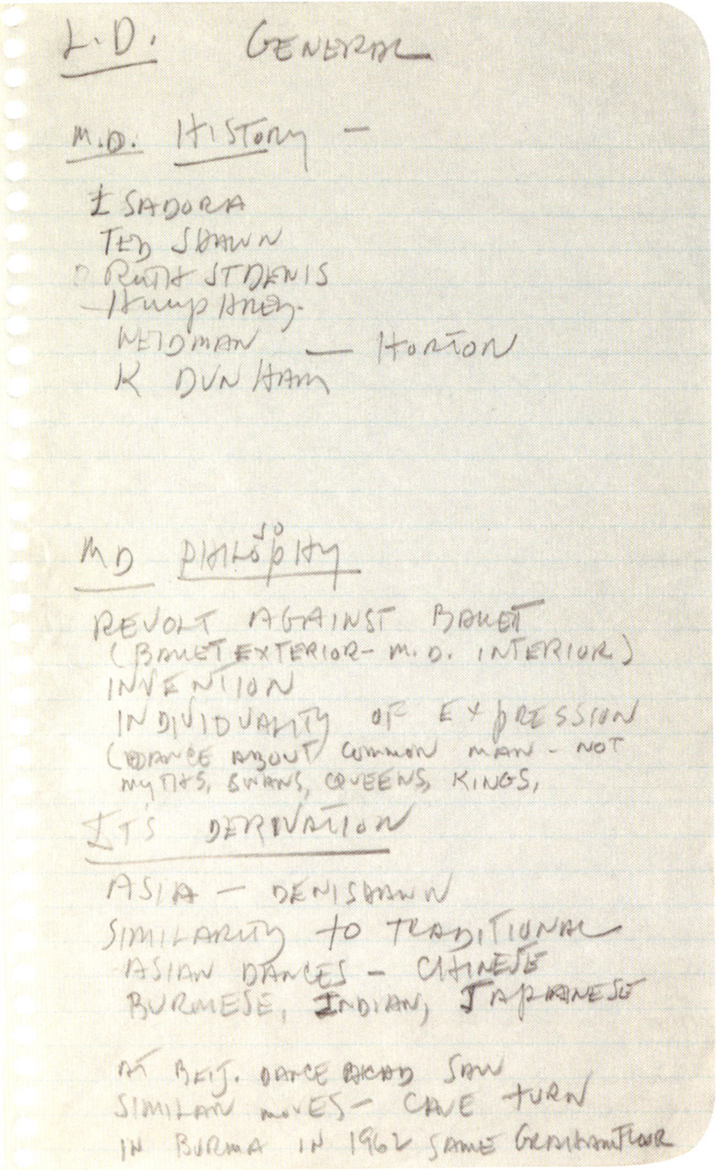

L.D. GENERAL

M.D. HISTORY —

Isadora
Ted Shawn
Ruth St Denis
Humphrey
Weidman — Horton
K Dunham

M.D. PHILOSOPHY

Revolt against ballet
(Ballet exterior — M.D. interior)
Invention
Individuality of expression
(Dance about common man — not myths, swans, queens, kings)

ITS DERIVATION

Asia — Denishawn
Similarity to traditional
Asian dances — Chinese
Burmese, Indian, Japanese

At Beij. Dance Acad saw
similar moves — cave turn
in Burma in 1962 same grandmother

GENERAL BEFORE START-UP

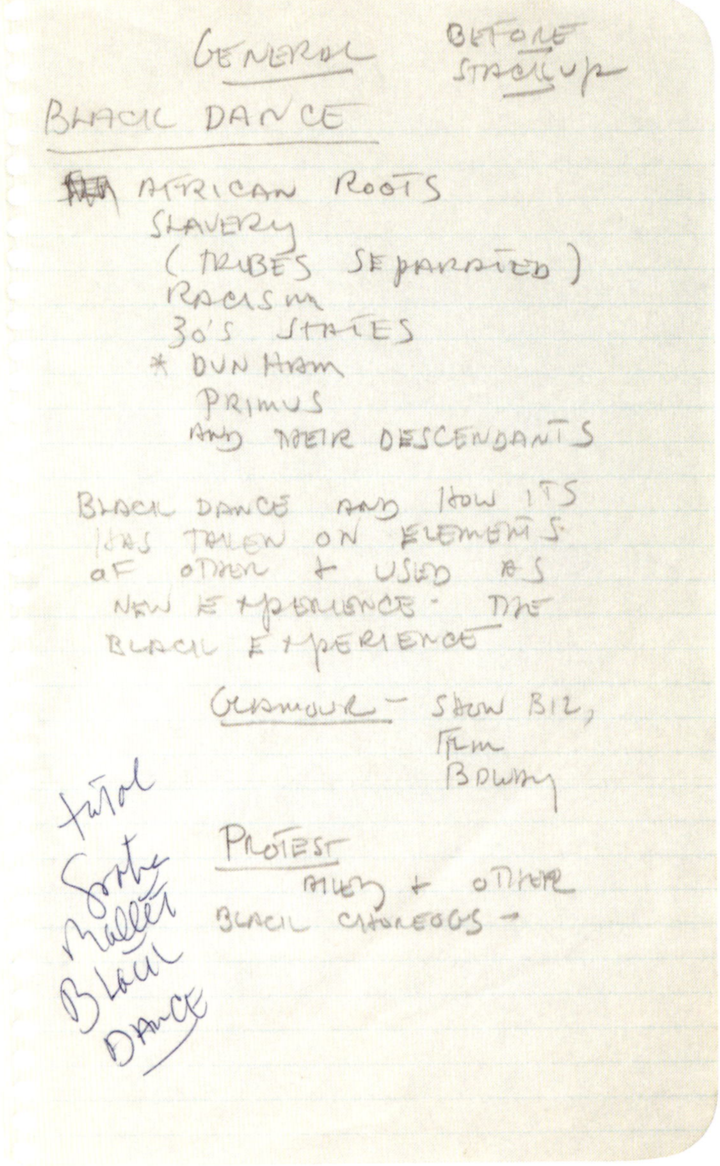

BLACK DANCE

African roots
Slavery
(Tribes separated)
Racism
30's States
* Dunham
Primus
and their descendants

Black dance and how it
has taken on elements
of other + used as
new experience — the
Black experience

Glamour — show biz,
film
B'way

Tutol
Sophie
Mullet
Black
Dance

PROTEST
Ailey + other
Black choreogs —

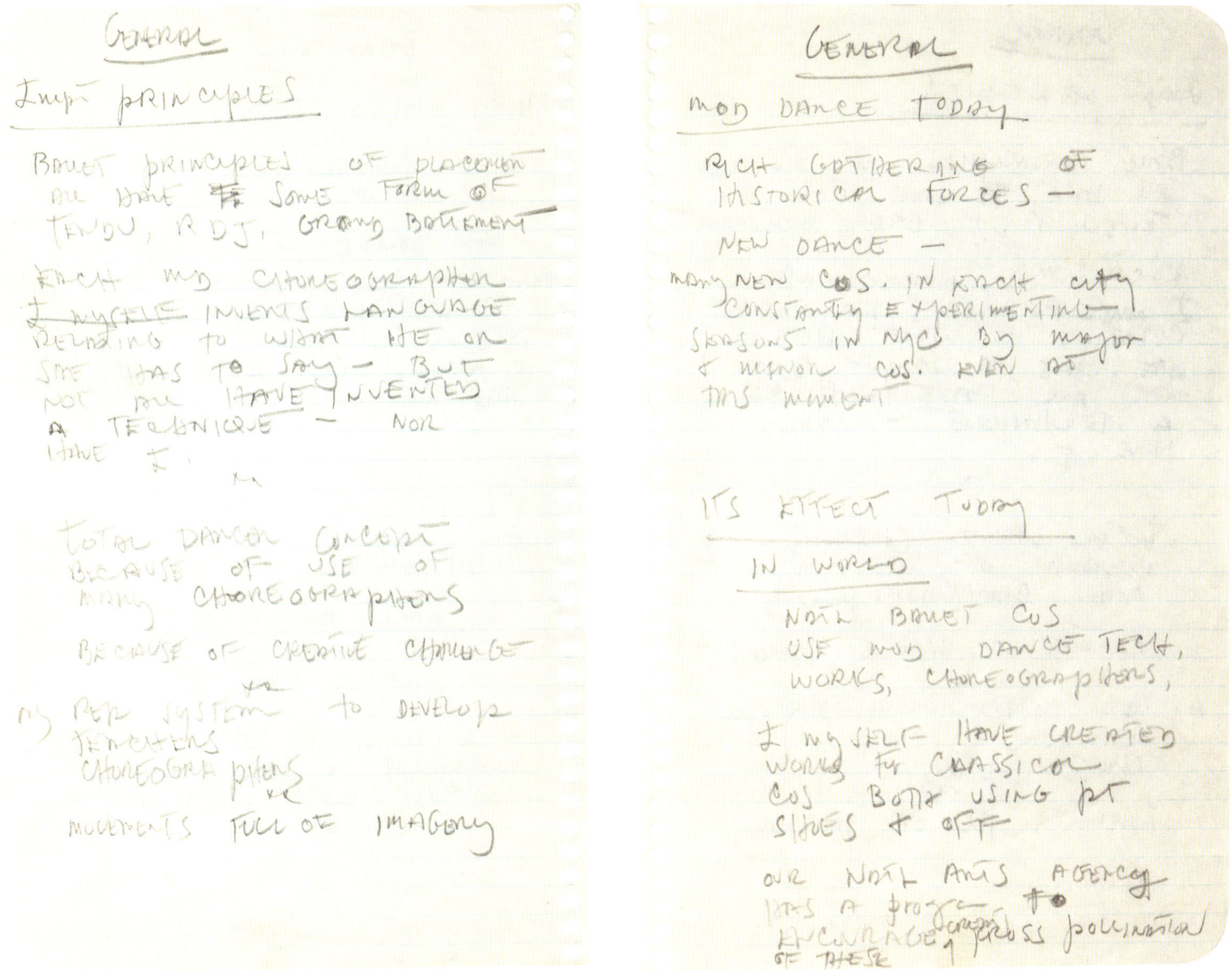

GENERAL

Impt Principles

Ballet principles of placement all have some form of tendu, R d j, grand battement

Each mod choreographer ~~myself~~ invents language relating to what he or she has to say — but not all have invented a technique — nor have I.

Total dancer concept because of use of many choreographers

Because of creative challenge

My Rep System to develop dancers teachers choreographers etc

Movements full of imagery

GENERAL

Mod Dance Today

Rich gathering of historical forces —

New Dance —

Many new cos. in each city constantly experimenting. Seasons in NYC by major & minor cos. Even at this moment

Its Effect Today

In World

Nat'l Ballet cos use mod dance tech, works, choreographers,

I myself have created works for classical cos both using pt shoes & off

Our Nat'l Arts Agency has a program to encourage cross pollination of these

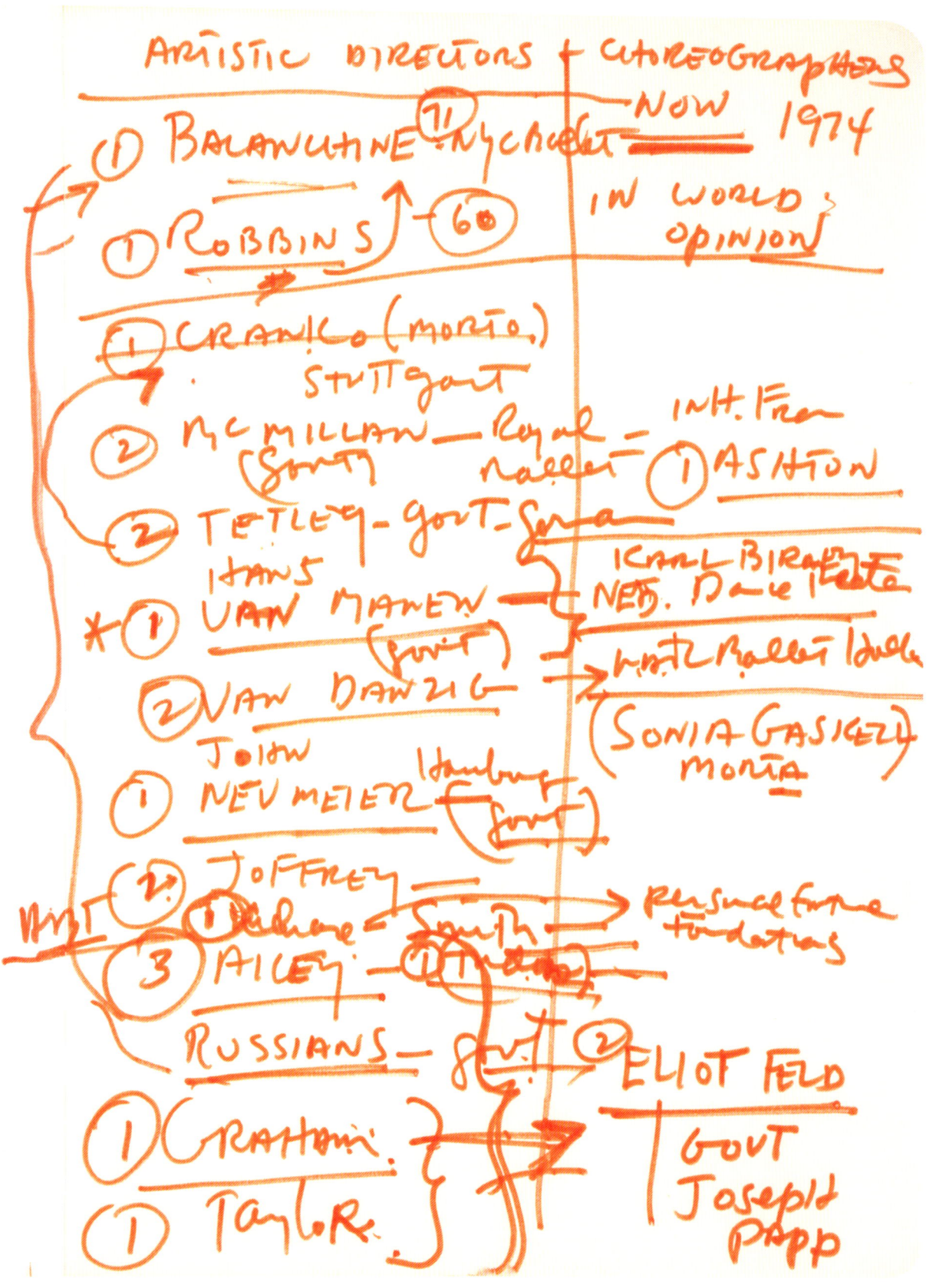

SUN Feb
~~8/13/4225~~

DO NOT TAKE ANY
~~More~~ COKE —

DO NOT TAKE ANY [smoke] MORE

IT CAUSES CHEST CANCER
THROAT CANCER — ~~YOU WILL~~
[plan] YOUR FUNERAL — DO WILL —
IF YOU CONTINUE SMOKING
C'EST PAS POSSIBLE !!

USE TEA FOR
DRUG NEEDS

BREAKFAST IS OVER
CALL AB KARIM
TELL AB TO [come] HELP —
AFTER INAUG. IS
STRAIGHTENED OUT —

THIS IS DISCIPLINE &
THERAPY FOR ME
USE HELP SITTING
PUT ON PRY. TOP.

SEX

8220717
678 4556

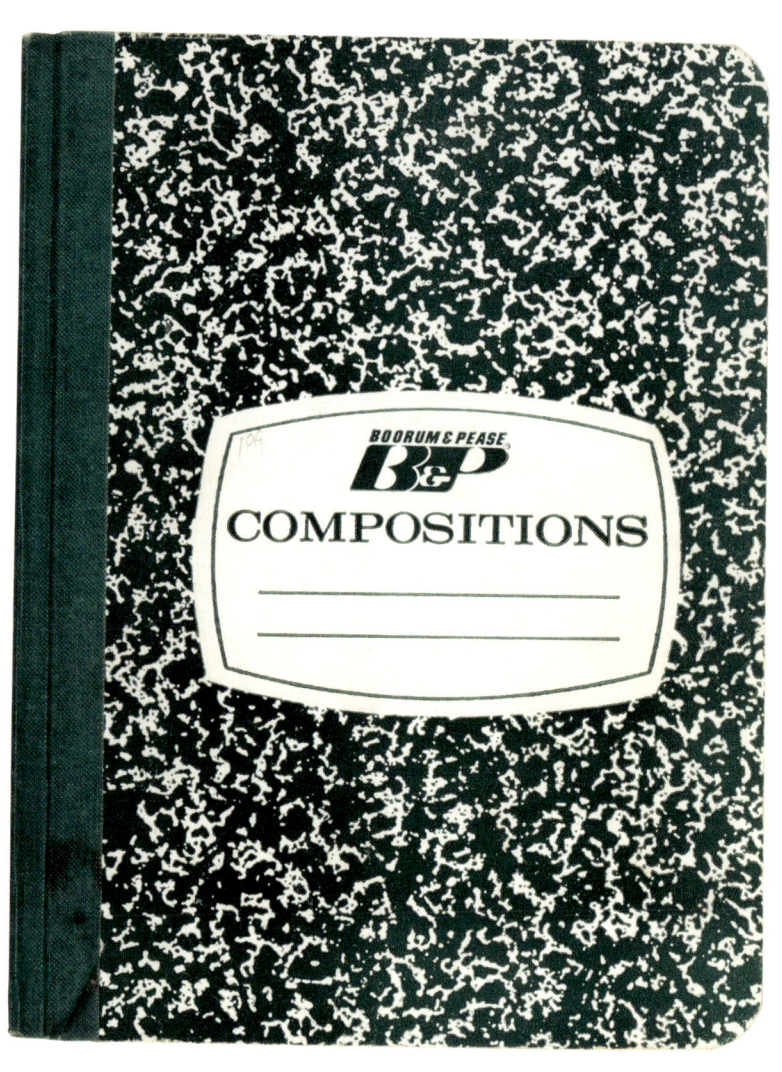

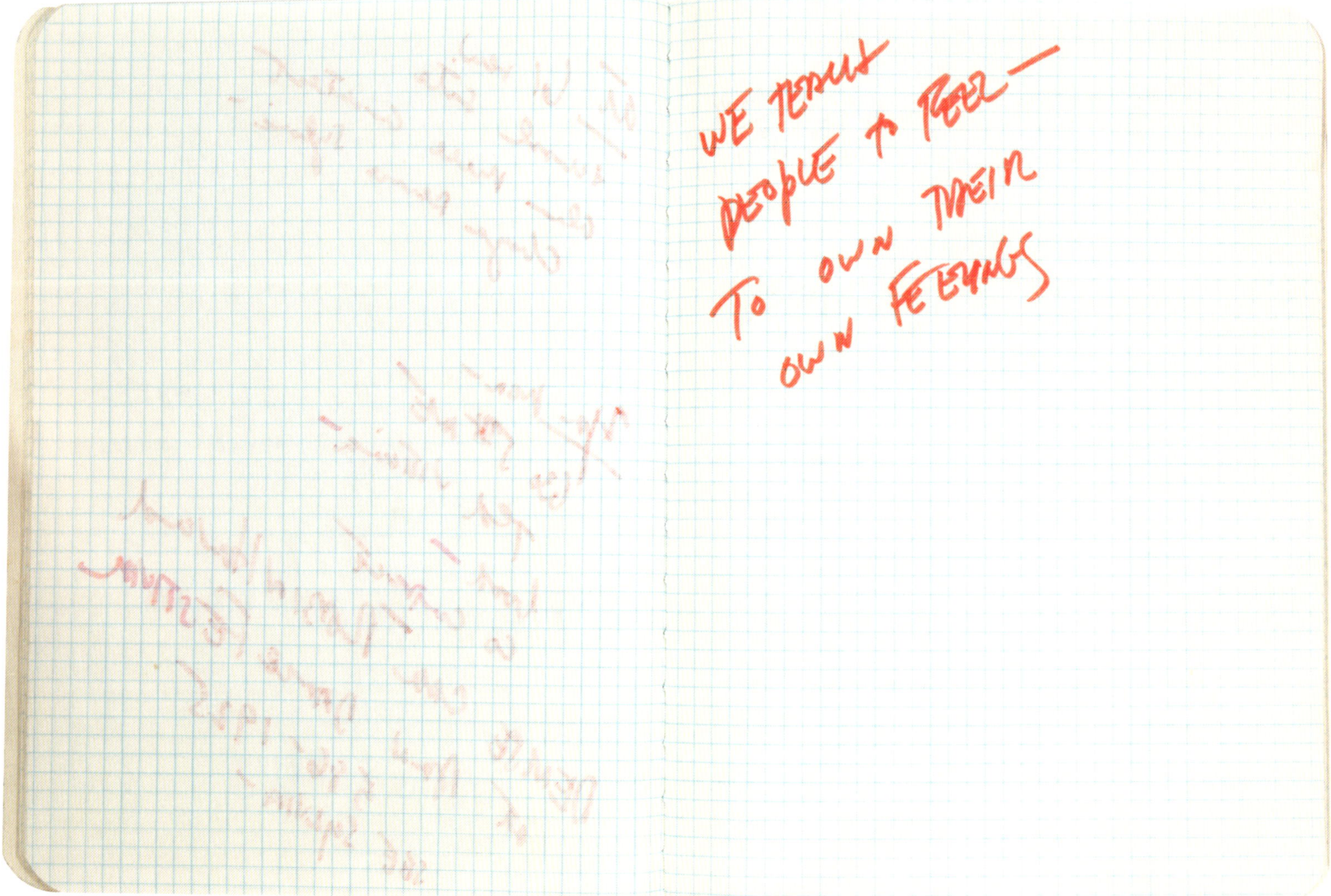

WE TEACH
PEOPLE TO FEEL —
TO OWN THEIR
OWN FEELINGS

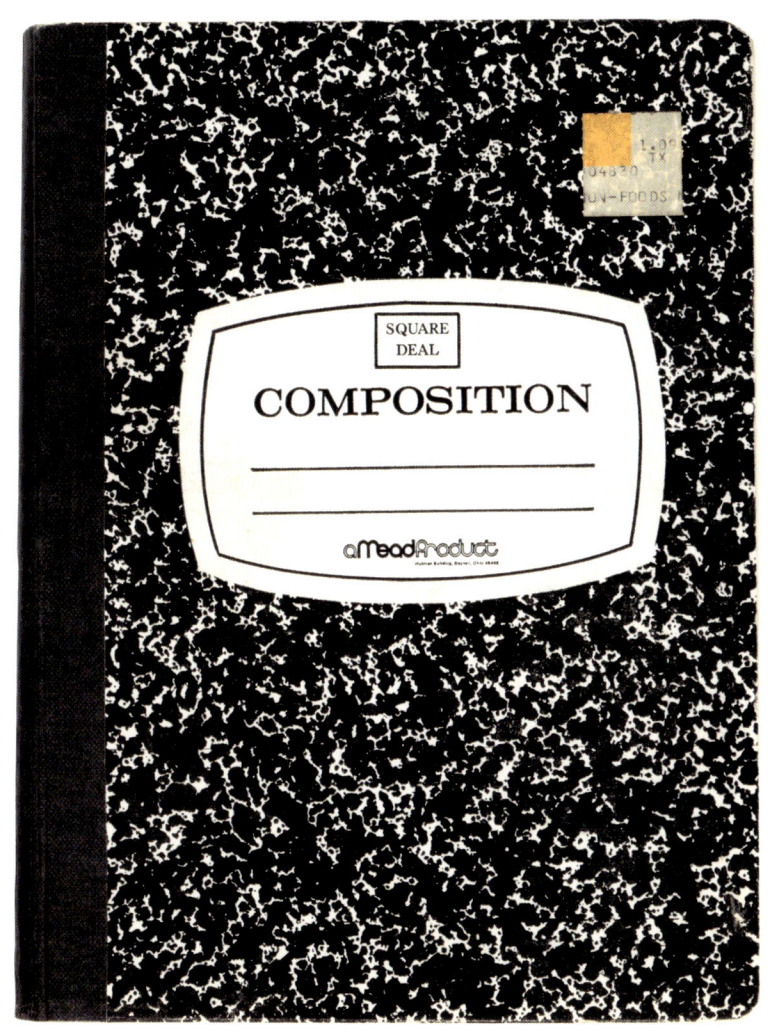

THE SCHOOL RULES — Scholarship Students

STUDENTS OF THE SCHOOL MUST NOT SMOKE, CIGARETTES, MARIJUANA, POT, HASHISH, ANGEL DUST MARLBORO KENT ETC

SCHOLARSHIP STUDENTS — NO BOONE'S FARM
(NO COLT 45
 NO BEER / ANGEL DUST / HASHISH
 NO MARIJUANA
 NO HEROIN / CIGARETTES ON SCHOOL PREMISES

WILL CALL FOR IMMEDIATE DISMISSAL —

NO LEG WARMERS
NO COVERING OF BODY parts
NO SWEATERS

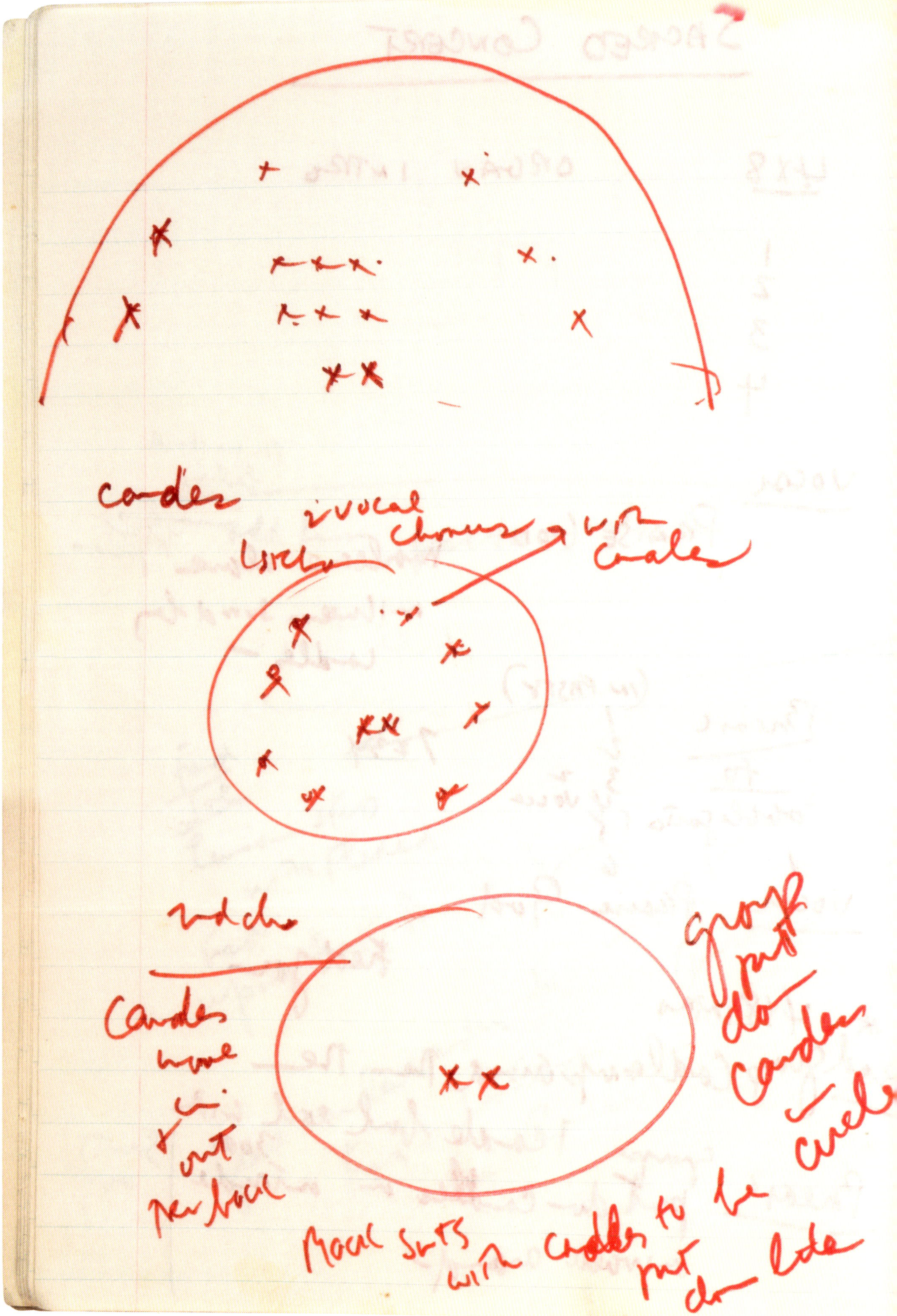

STAGED CONCERT

(large arc with x marks representing performers on stage)

candles

ivocal
Lstch   chorus g/vr
                candles
(circle with x marks inside)

vdchs

Candles
move
in
& out
per louse

(circle with xx marks)

group
put
do
candles
in
circle

Move slts with candles to be circle
put do lds

                                                        4
                                                    Boys + Fred

4×4   Trumpet   COLE CONTRACT STEP
___
 1
 2   Fred Marlene
 3   Leslie
 4   Tch marlene
                                        1st

12×4   TRUMPET   COLE
___   ___   some?
 1 5 9   Fred   Leslie   join?
 2 6 10   Marlene 3 girls?
 3 7 11   1st
 4 8 12
8×4   chop steps
___   CLARINETS HIGH   _____
 1   Boys alone
 2   +
 3   Fred
 4
 5   DANCE   six people
     1   join
 6   from
 7   PRAISE GOD + DANCE
 8   ~~spklrs~~
                                        boys leave

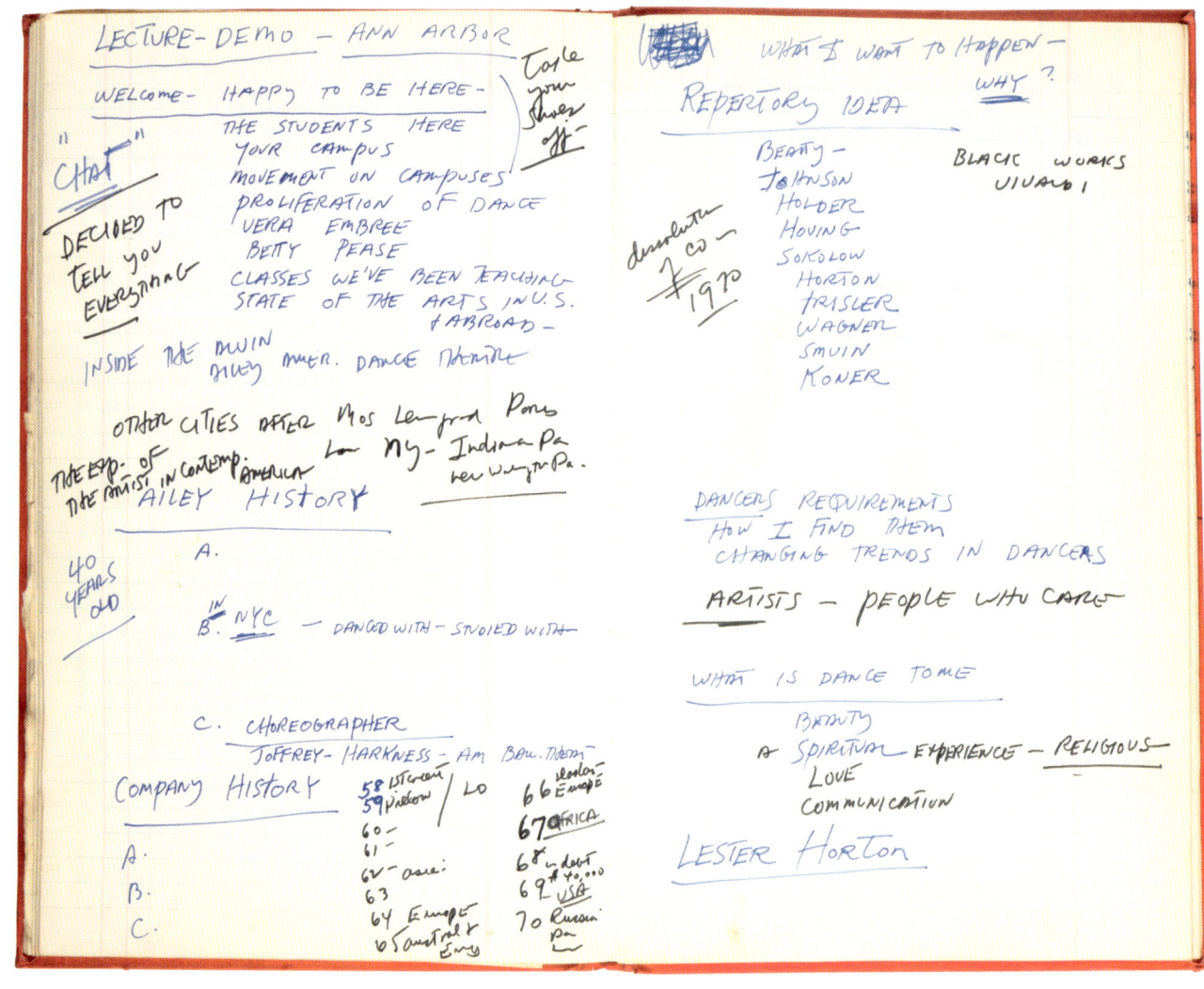

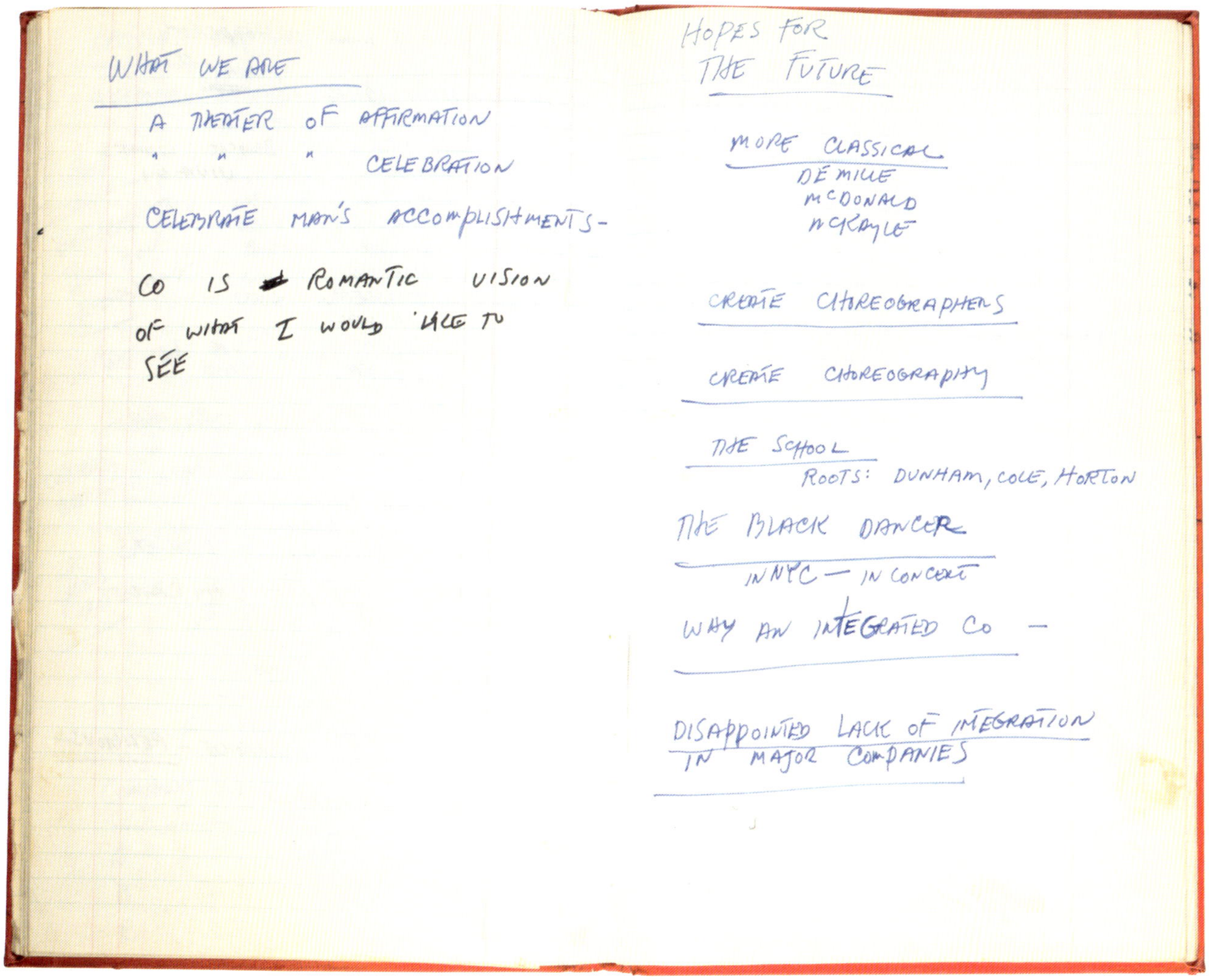

WHAT WE ARE

A THEATER OF AFFIRMATION
" " " CELEBRATION

CELEBRATE MAN'S ACCOMPLISHMENTS —

CO IS ROMANTIC VISION OF WHAT I WOULD LIKE TO SEE

HOPES FOR THE FUTURE

MORE CLASSICAL
   DEMILLE
   McDONALD
   McKAYLE

CREATE CHOREOGRAPHERS

CREATE CHOREOGRAPHY

THE SCHOOL
   ROOTS: DUNHAM, COLE, HORTON

THE BLACK DANCER
   IN NYC — IN CONCERT

WHY AN INTEGRATED CO —

DISAPPOINTED LACK OF INTEGRATION IN MAJOR COMPANIES

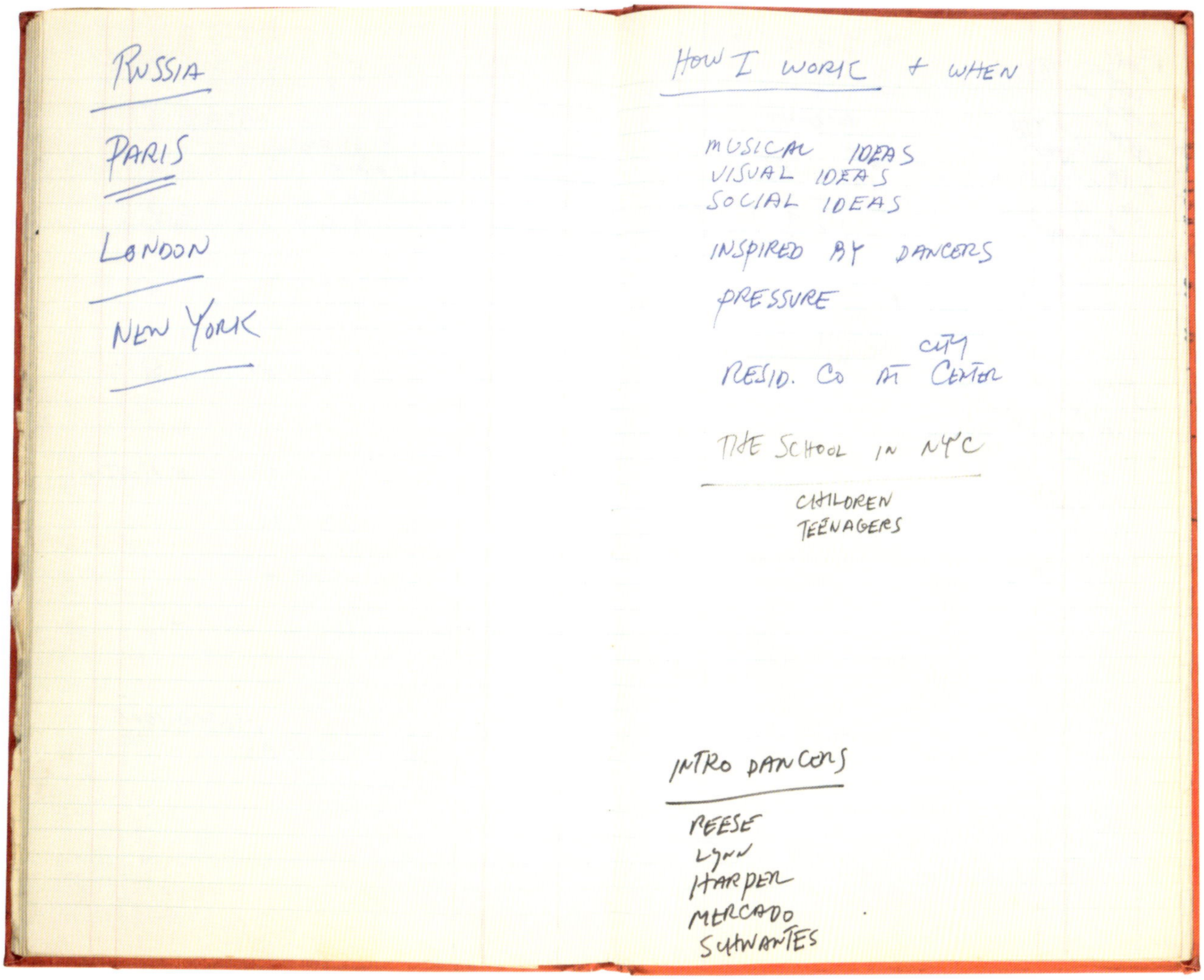

RUSSIA

PARIS

LONDON

NEW YORK

HOW I WORK + WHEN

MUSICAL IDEAS
VISUAL IDEAS
SOCIAL IDEAS

INSPIRED BY DANCERS

PRESSURE

RESID. CO AT CITY CENTER

THE SCHOOL IN NYC
   CHILDREN
   TEENAGERS

INTRO DANCERS
   REESE
   LYNN
   HARPER
   MERCADO
   SCHWANTES

SLAVES   pg 72 — Eyewitness

PROCESSIONAL OF HUDDLED MASSES

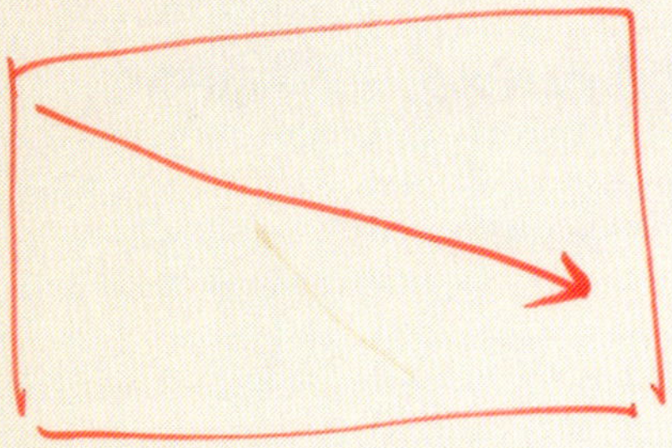

HISTORIC PANORAMA   Set / Ropes

SLAVES —

IMAGE OF TRIBAL BREAKUP —
Huddled Group center moves slowly to all directions in ever-increasing circle

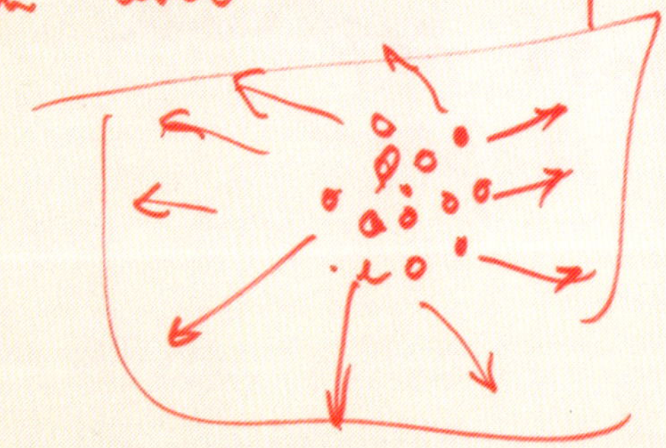

BB+B

use Kenya, Christopher, Jason
2nd co as supers, extras
Sch ship students as
mass of slaves

SOLDIERS + WARS —

BLACK HEROES
   ADAMS
   DOVE
   JONES
   WATSON

) REV WAR
  CIVIL WAR
  Span Am WAR

Canvas
TENT AS SET

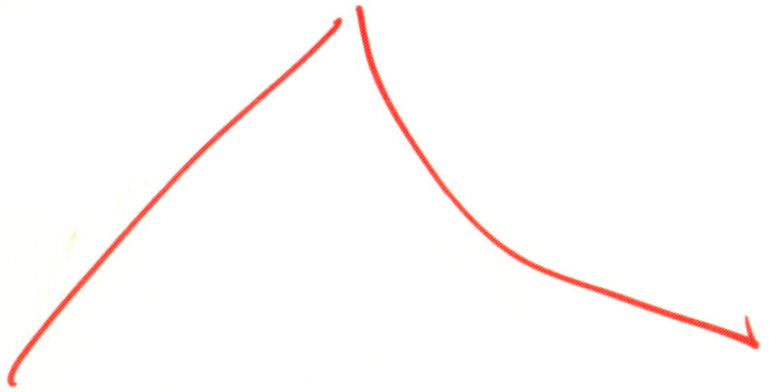

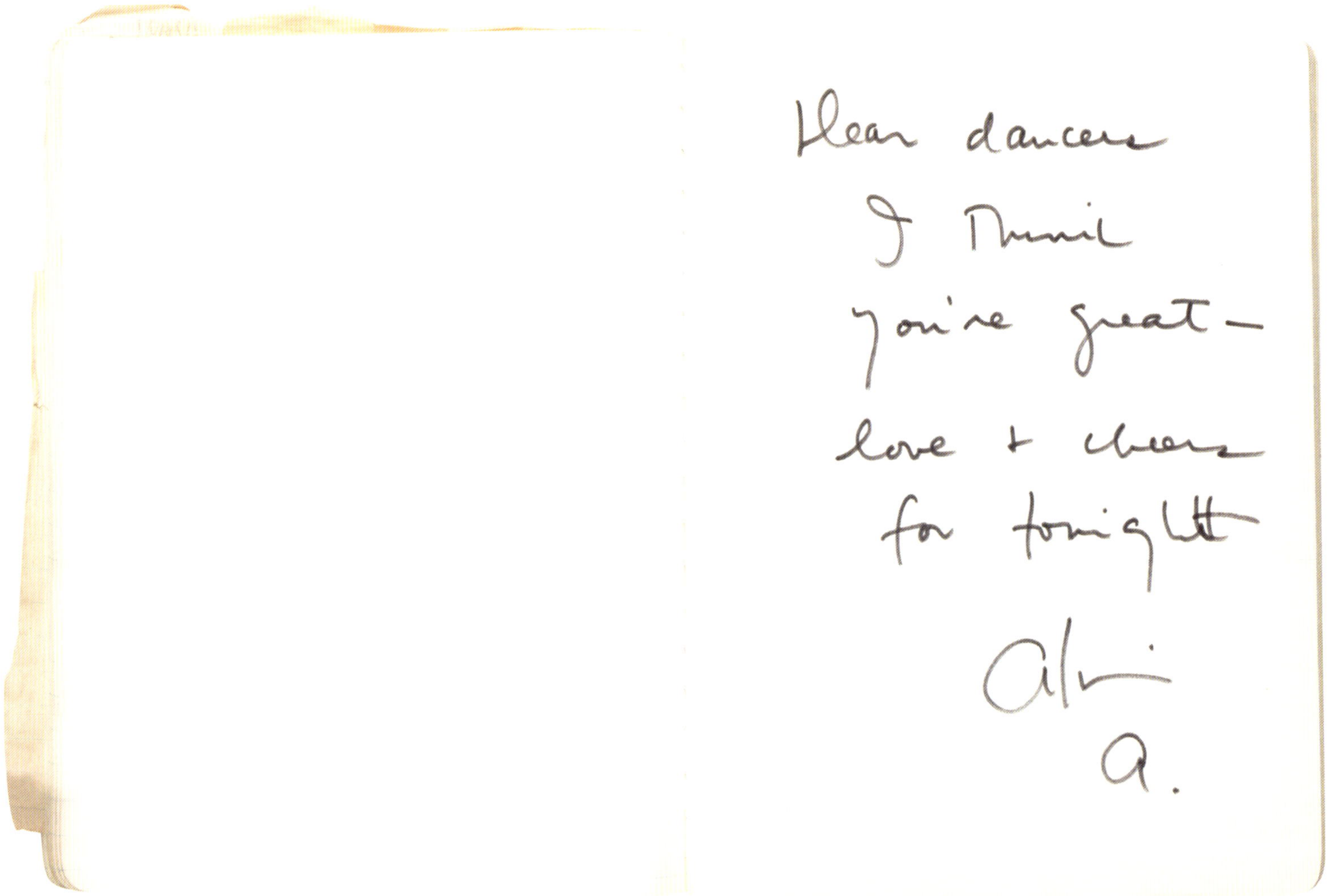

Dear dancers
I think
you're great —
love + cheers
for tonight

Alvin
A.

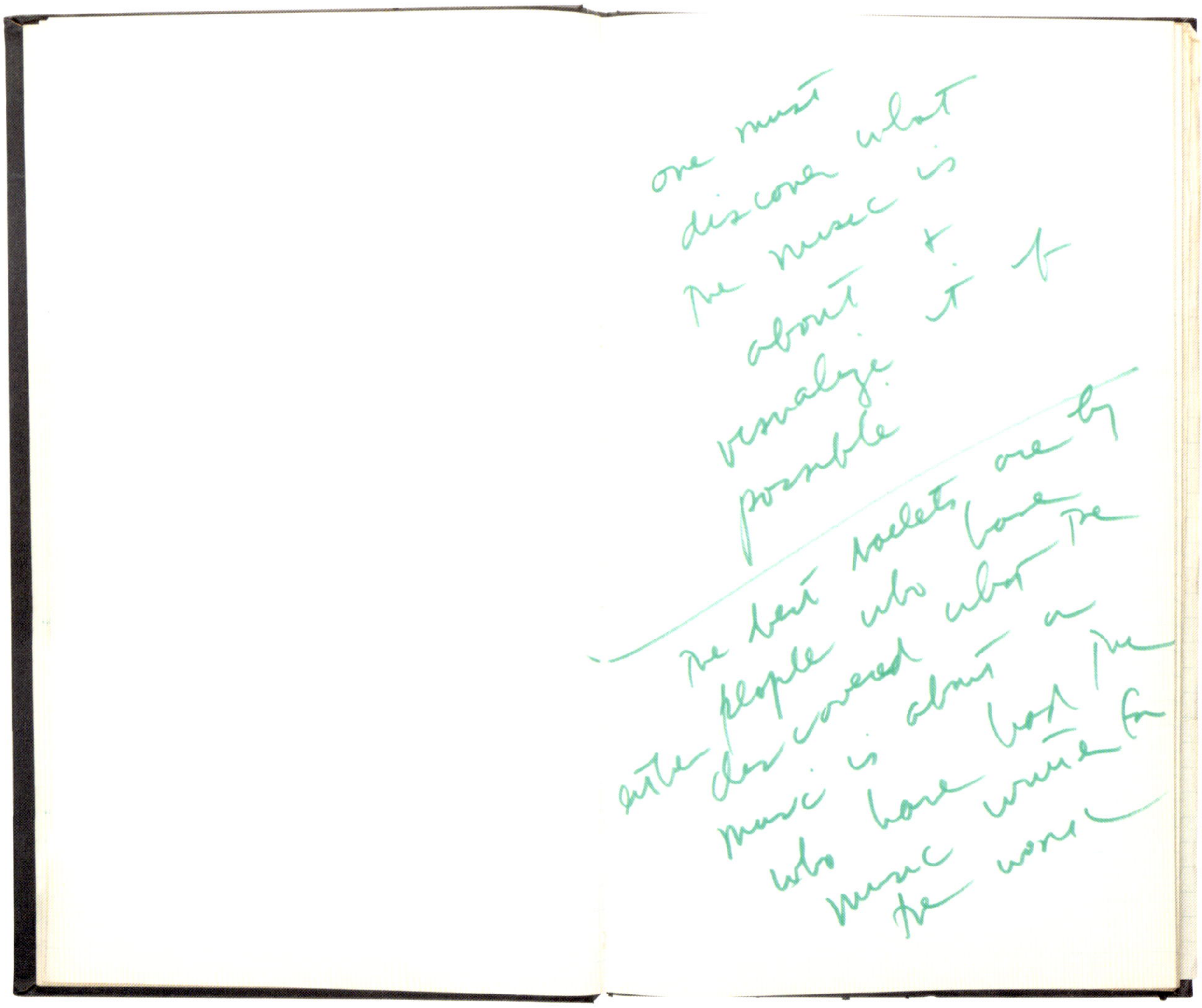

one must
discover what
the music is
about + to
visualize it if
possible

The best ballets are by
people who have
discovered what the
music is about. The
music is best
who have visual for
the music work
for

"There is not a single emotion that jazz cannot encompass. Not only joy and depression, but indignation, anger, and scores of specific emotion.

                        Marc Blitzstein

Jazz <u>is</u> specific. It is what each musician feels as he plays; and that concatenation of emotions comes from specific experiences in each players life. There is no one "philosophy" of jazz. Each player is his own prophet, and the messages range from picaresque defiance to comfortable acceptance of whatever values are peripheral at the moment.

<u>POSITIVE</u>
Good sense of humor
Basically honest
Strong sense of pride
Extremely sensitive
Bright
Considerate
Strong willed

<u>NEGATIVE</u>
Bad temper
Stubborn
Lack of self-control
Lack of common sense
Irresponsible

Panel should — what is our record-prestige?
no para- for proposal Carl Rothenberg

PRISON PROGRAMS

performances & exhibits in prisons—

perfs. by prisoners of their materials & other materials

Black ballet

Africa ballet

Trad plays

exhibits of Prisoners' arts
poetry music drama, sculpture

Provide materials to work with—

Commission prisoners to do works: dance drama music

Alaskan
Puerto Rican   representation
Hawaiian

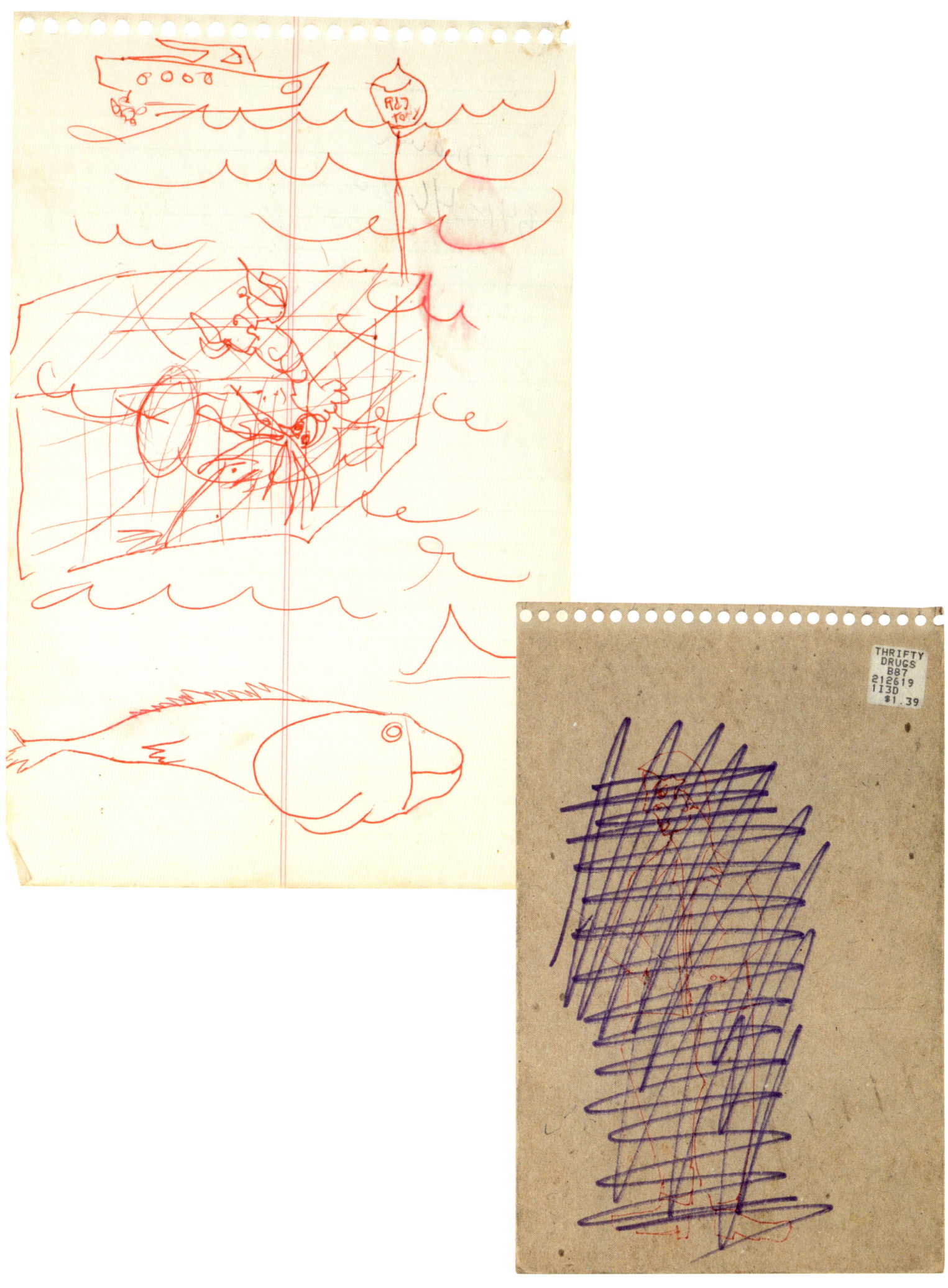

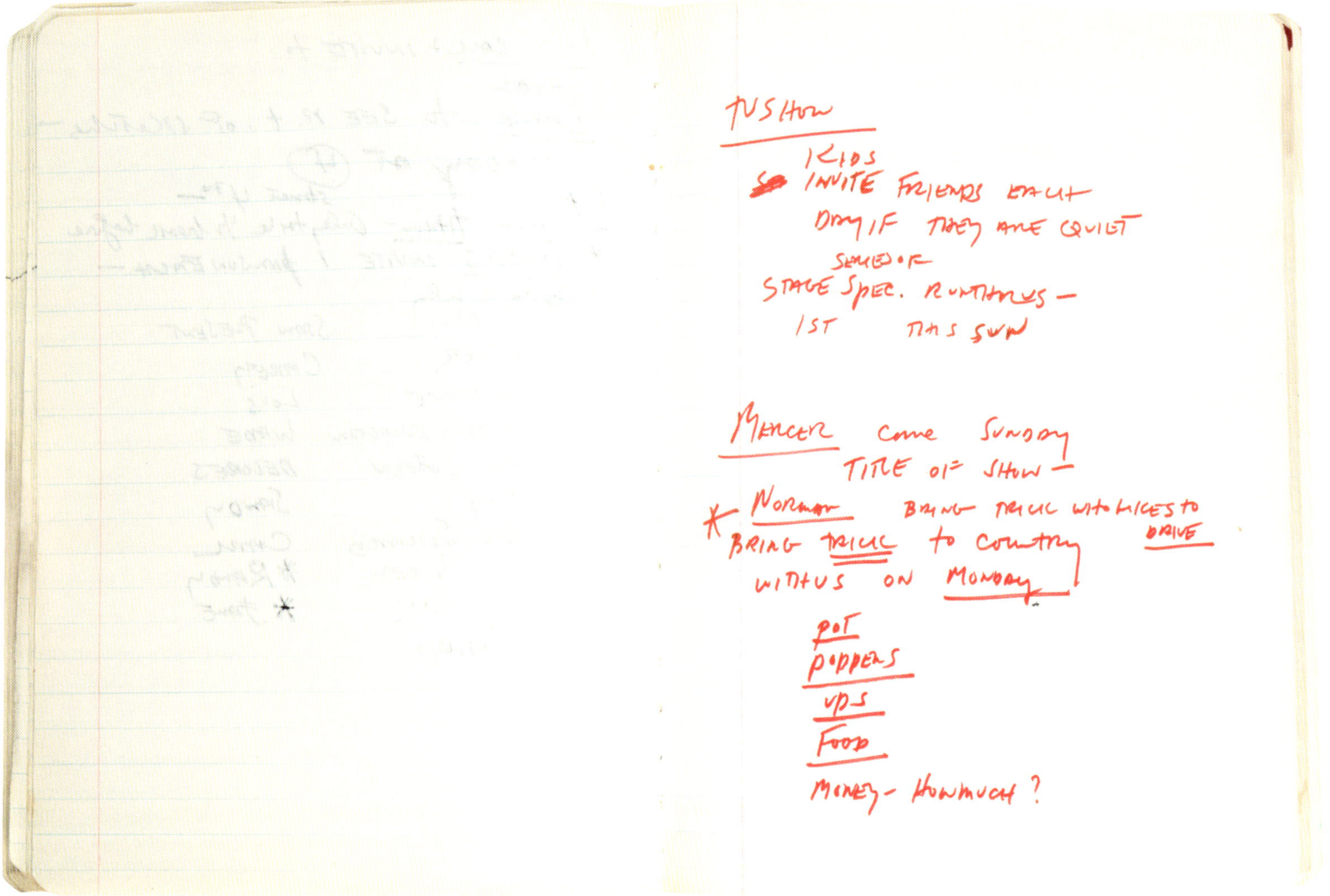

TV SHOW
- KIDS
- ~~So~~ INVITE FRIENDS EACH DAY IF THEY ARE QUIET
- STAGE SPEC. RUNTHRUS — SEMI OR
- 1ST TAPS SUN

MERCER COME SUNDAY
TITLE OF SHOW —
★ NORMAN BRING TRICIA WHO LIKES TO
BRING TRICIA to COUNTRY DRIVE
WITH US ON MONDAY

- POT
- POPPERS
- UPS
- FOOD

MONEY — HOW MUCH?

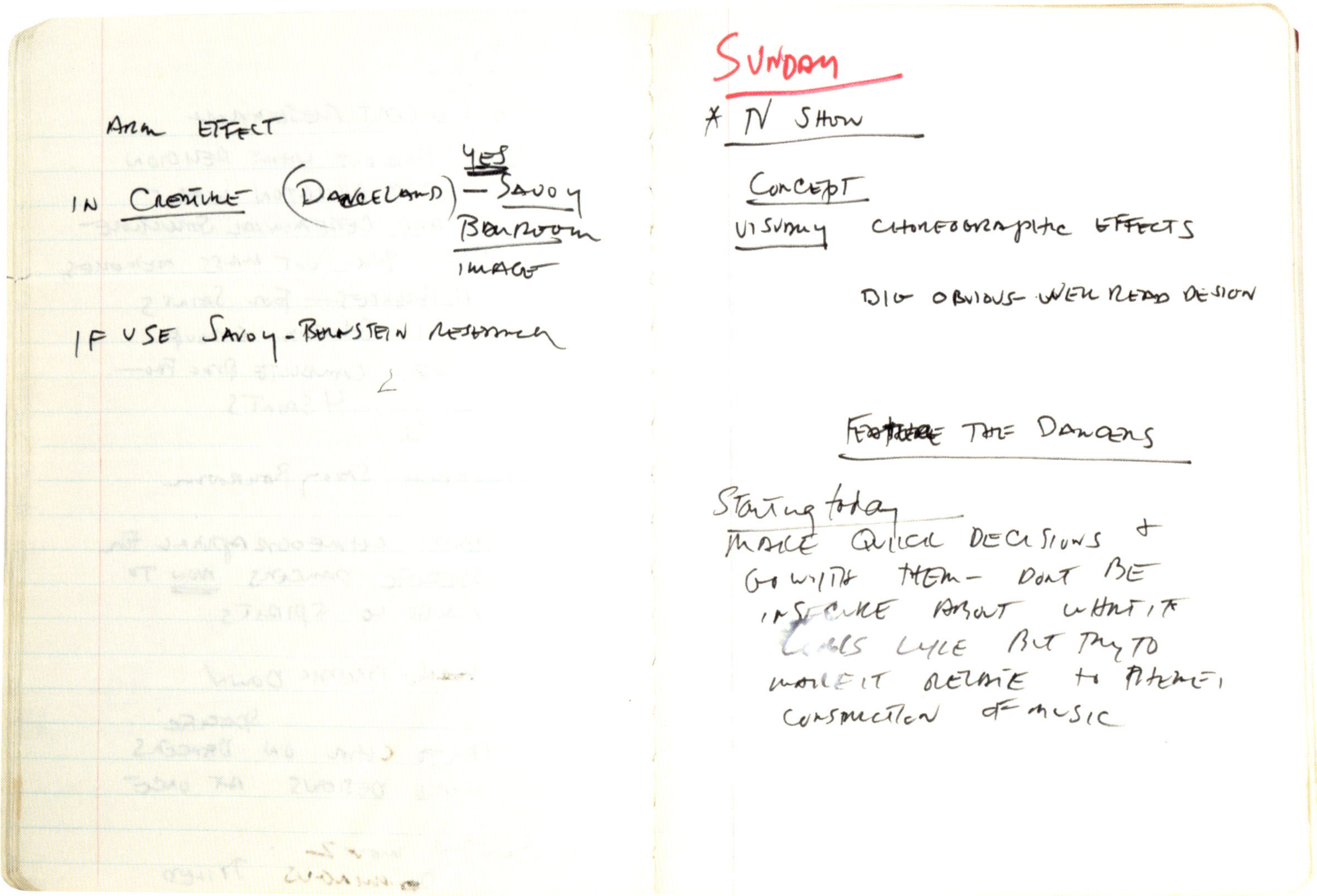

ARM EFFECT
IN CREATIVE (~~DANCELAND~~) — SAVOY YES
BALLROOM
IMAGE

IF USE SAVOY — BERNSTEIN RESEARCH

SUNDAY
★ TV SHOW

CONCEPT
VISUAL CHOREOGRAPHIC EFFECTS

DIG OBVIOUS WELL READ DESIGN

~~FEATURE~~ THE DANCERS

Starting today
MAKE QUICK DECISIONS & GO WITH THEM — DON'T BE INSECURE ABOUT WHAT IT LOOKS LYKE BUT TRY TO MAKE IT RELATE TO PRESENT CONSTRUCTION OF MUSIC

PUBLICITY

NEW
Quote for posters or flyers

Alvin Ailey and his dancers enhance
the theater with the exuberance of jazz,
the ecstasy of spirituals, and the dark
rapture of the blues

NEW pix

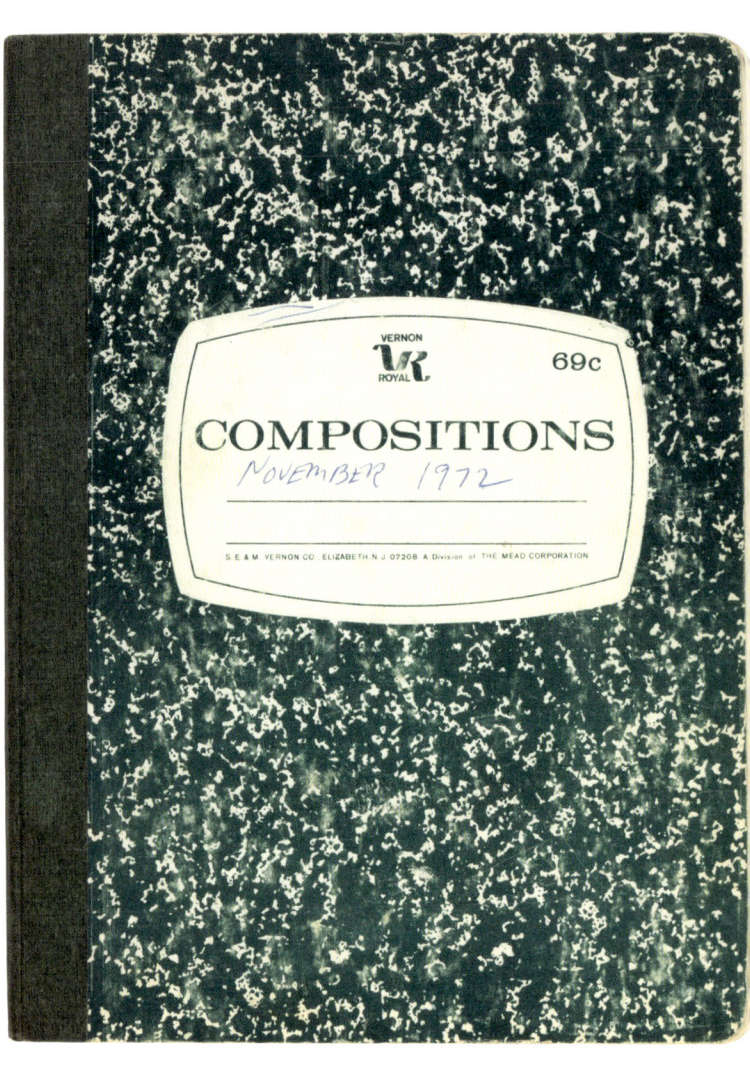

Four Saints
American Ballet Theater
The Company
The Apartment
Finances Personal
The Board
Judy Jamison 982 1434 Have lunch
Agnes de Mille GR 33024
Chas Reinhart PL 98931
ABT - get reh shed for December - get reviews of wash from Florence
Apt - Schedule couch + rug delivery
Apt - super re windows
Apt - alarm system
4 Saints - discuss timing with Al + Ivy - call Ree Mals -
call Carmen re sgrs wee
call -
4 Saints - get tape from Schirmer
4 Saints - Ree Mals - theater

4 saints – designer – cost. decor designer – call Bill Mies
4 saints – put out general call for young black singers
4 saints – call Schuyler Chapin re problems
Co – Find music for Hudley's solo –
Call mother re birthday
Schedule Xmas presents to close people – Al, Ivy, Carl, Mickey, Glen, Judy, Hudley, other Co. principals –
See John's ballet
Xmas presents to family – Edele – Bro John –
Buy basic new wardrobe –
Apt – get Bloomingdale's a/c from Steve & turn over to,
Al – give Al Sternberger's a/c – weekly –
Al – make budget for apt, food, clothing – care of animals

Apt – schedule clearing up records & books
Apt – get extra keys from H. Ward brought to office
Co – analyze reh. sheet for Hudley
Co – call Hudley re no music – ask him for suggestions –
Apt – Have basic keys made for Ivy & Al, Steve
Board – call Squadron re my board construction participation –
Harry Kraut re J. Kennedy
Board – sched time to call Goheen,
Squadron – Call Goldman to board
Carl – How worked out Glen financial & work problem, etc.
Apt – buy basic cleaning equipt – get cleaning lady – see Ivy – get keys for cleaning lady

Apt – stash basic keys outside apt in park –
Apt – alarm system – Harvey?
Co – City Center program – stuff Auta programs with CC brochures –
Co – sched next season's concept & things – call Cobb –
Co – at Apt make arrangt with
Office – clear up office & categorize
Co – tell Al how much I appreciate his work then – tell Ivy the same
Co – give Ivy flowers – have them sent to her office daily for 1 week with note – sign of appreciation – have Suzy do this from our office & call wet pets – note: just to remind you how much I

appreciate you & your work for me & Co –
Same to – Carl Goldman –
send Mr. G. big pot of flowers from our florist – have delivered today – Nov 1 – because he is not feeling well – have Suzy call florist & deliver today –

Dr G. – discuss overcommitment & my of personal organization – How to cope with too much to do – am I setting myself up for failure –
Pers – call Dr Goessel re, weight loss & plan see her now –
Pers – see dentist
Dr. G. – discuss Judy –
4 saints – Hough get tape for Schuman – get tape loc. to apt for Hudley & save

Group 2
ROCK SEC
GAY BAR IMAGE
MEN WITH MEN
WOMEN WITH WOMEN

1980
Nervous Breakdown
7 wks in Hosp —

LAST NIGHT

Lady & DOG

Off to Marin Hospital

Bi Centennial Ideas — Re-naming
Theaters   Airports   Rivers

Rename streets, malls, parks, new sites after great American esp. Black creative + performing artists: in Black communities but not solely

Billie Holiday Ave.
Ellington Ave. BLVD
The Ives River
Roger Sessions Park
Stravinsky Blvd.
The Martha Graham Dance Theater
Katherine Dunham Hill
Louis Armstrong Ave
Florence Mills

St. Denis St.
Shawn Blvd.
Isadora

In every Amn city — pop. over certain population rename a major thorofare after a american creative artist —
Eugene O'Neil Blvd.

Duke Ellington Airport

Railroad Stations

American Indian greats or perf.
Mex. American greats

Duke Ellington Drive
Bigard Street

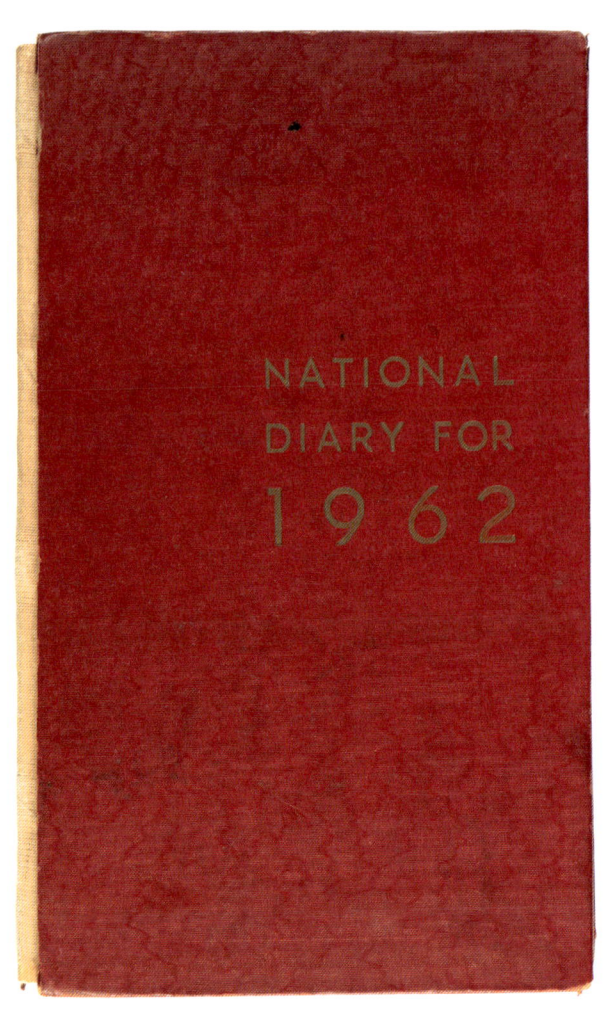

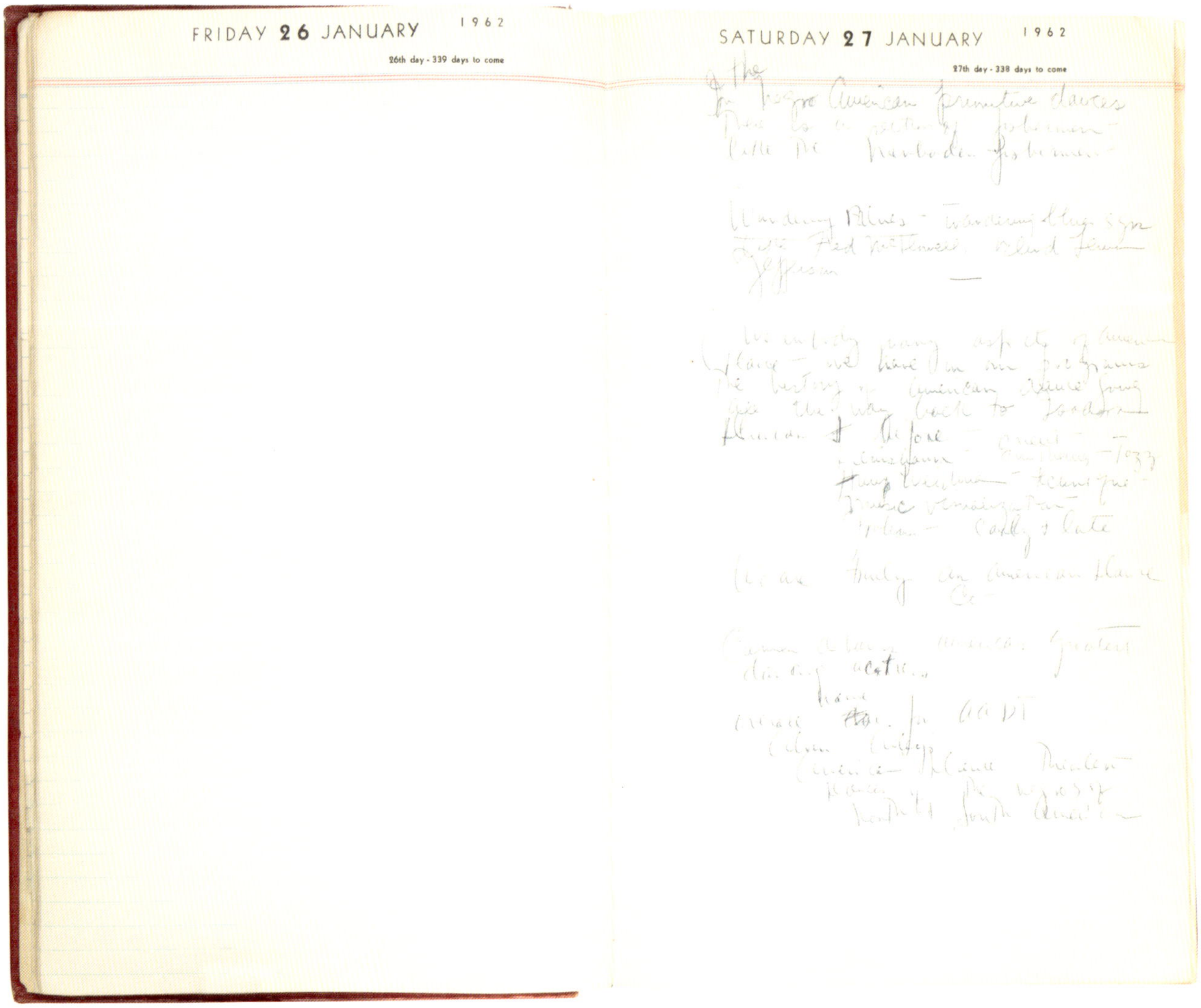

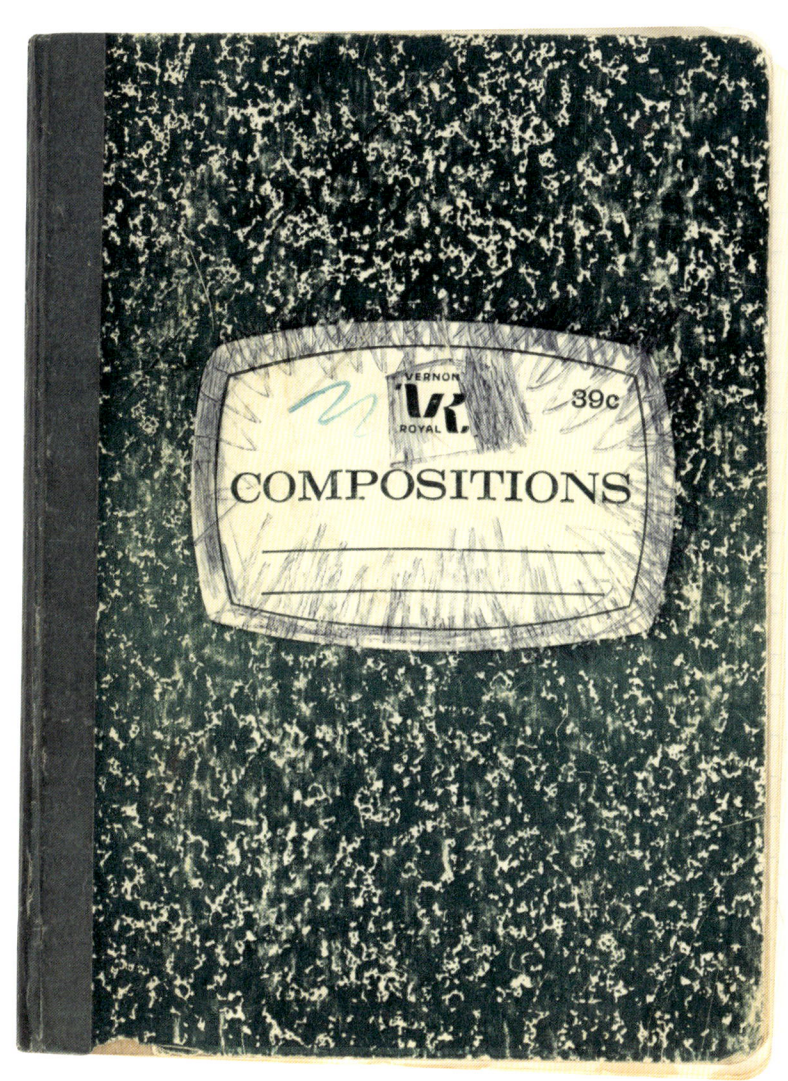

Hum—Umm!

Freedom for your mama— Freedom for your daddy Freedom for your brothers and sisters but no freedom for me

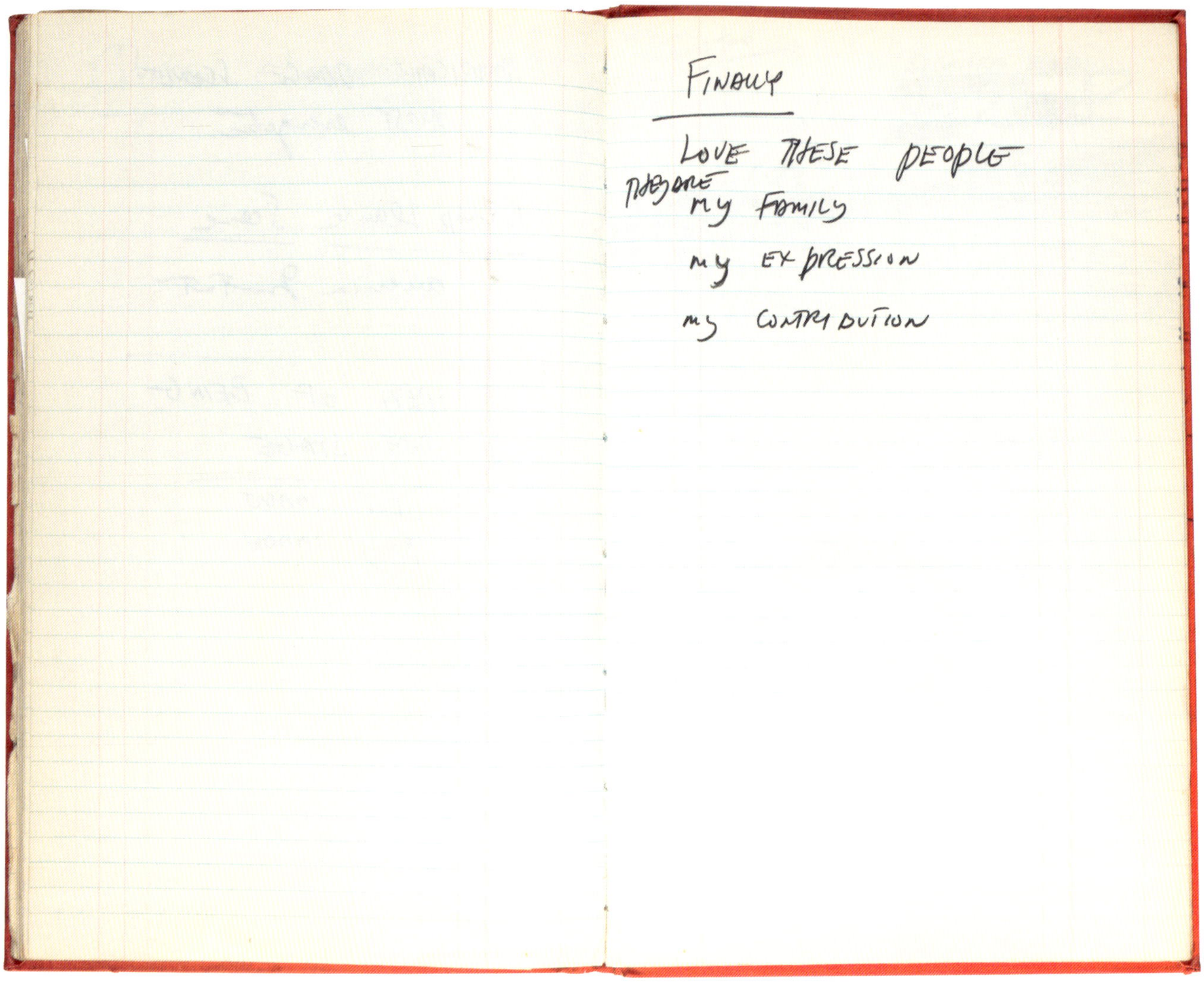

FINALLY

LOVE THESE PEOPLE
THEY ARE MY FAMILY
MY EXPRESSION
MY CONTRIBUTION

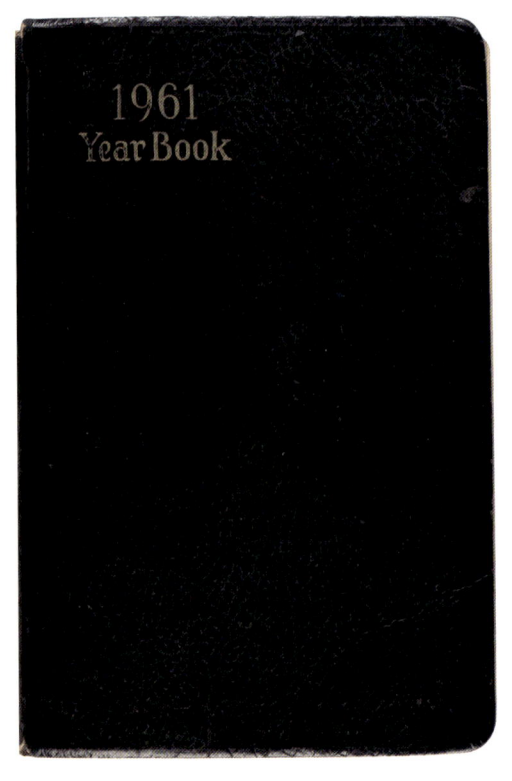

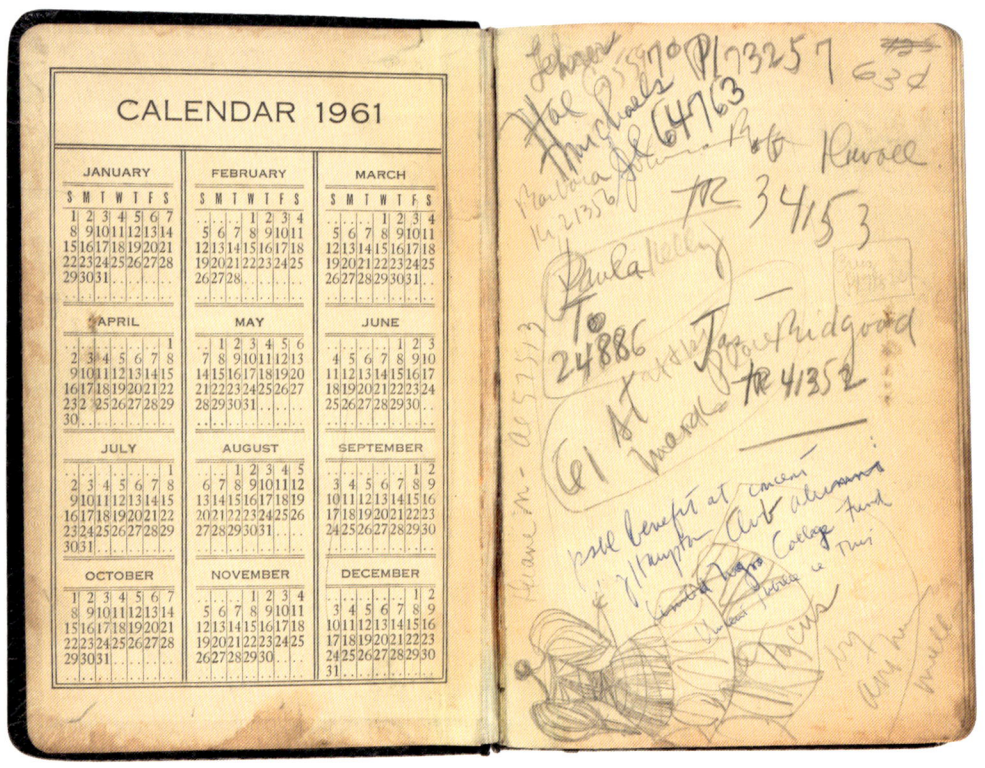

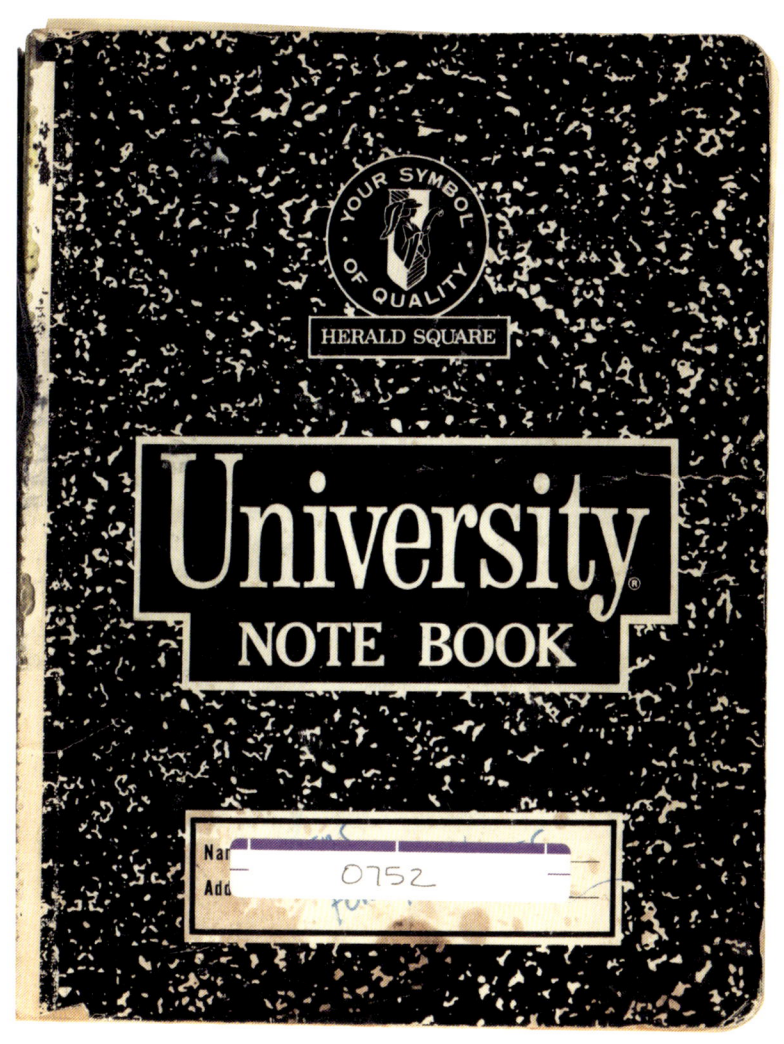

OF LOVE
LOVE DANCES
LOVE SONGS
SONGS OF LOVE
    DONNY HATHAWAY

DIFFERENT KINDS OF LOVE +
LOVE RELATIONSHIPS

1. Sexual love of man for woman
(singular) duet

2. Sexual love of man for man

3. of woman for woman

4. of men for women
group dance — orgy
    slow moving

5.

OF LOVE

5. Paternal
love of parent for child
(protective, instructive)

6. of man for man
(helpful - brotherly) aiding
    + abetting
(He Ain't Heavy)
men's dance

7. very
deep love of man for woman
male solo to woman

8. OF LOVE FOR SELF

Don Shirley

Being a female is a biological ~~fact~~
xx

But being a woman is a strategy
**

Lieder Solo for Donna for Germany
xx

Contemplations
on VIOLENCE
KUNG FU
DRAG QUEENS
WORLD THREE

SOUL
OPENING ROCK DANCE
FOR [Jamie?]
ELLINGTON Solo for Sarah
Florence Mills

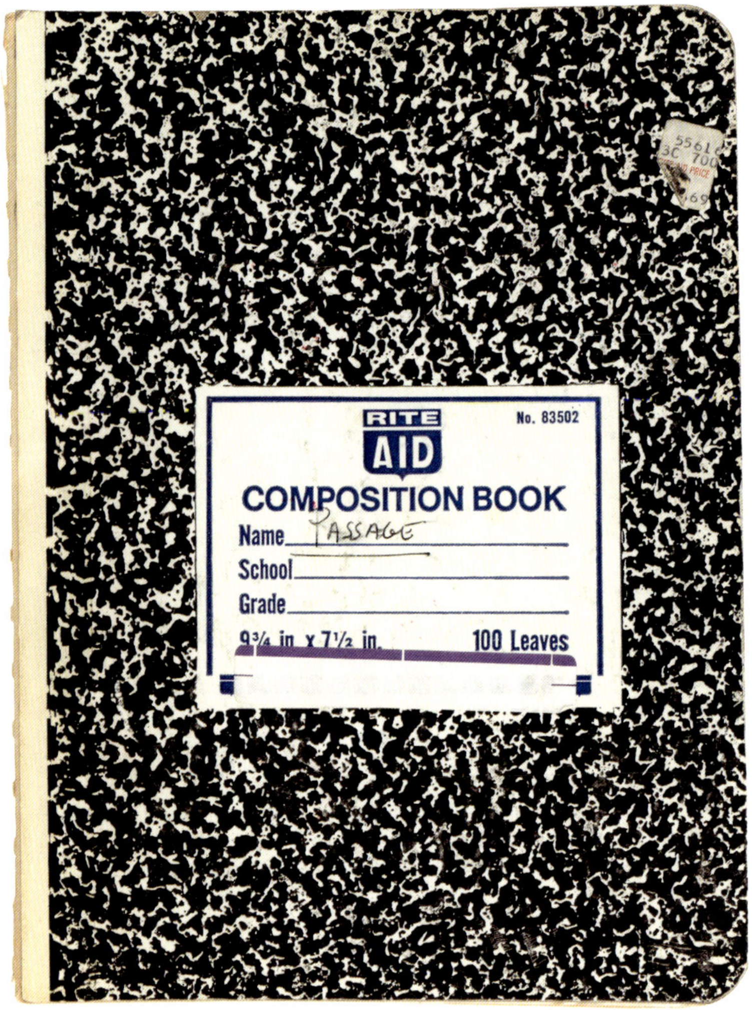

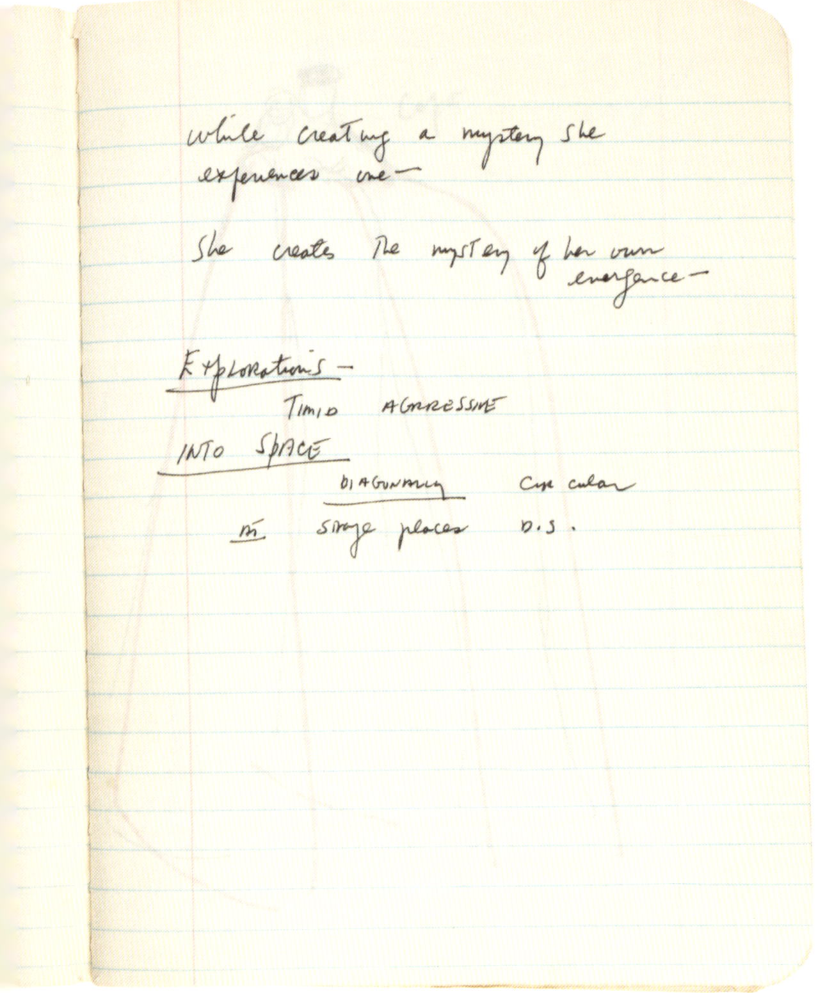

COMPOSITION BOOK
Name: PASSAGE

---

while creating a mystery she
experiences one —

She creates the mystery of her own
emergence —

Explorations —
    TIMID   AGGRESSIVE
INTO SPACE
        DIAGONALLY   Circular
  in strange places D.S.

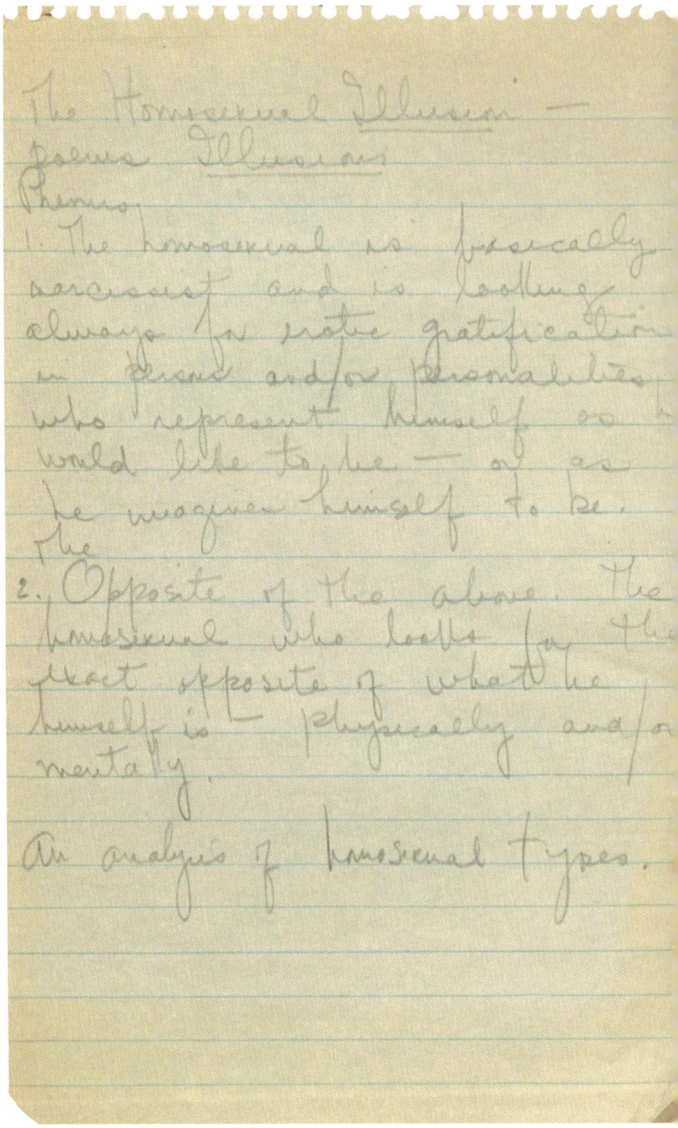

The Homosexual Illusion —
poems Illusions
Phemus
1. The homosexual is basically narcissist and is looking always for erotic gratification in persons and/or personalities who represent himself as he would like to be — or as he imagines himself to be. The
2. Opposite of the above. The homosexual who looks for the exact opposite of what he himself is — physically and/or mentally.

An analysis of homosexual types.

SEVERAL HARD-HIPPED HUSTLERS
AND MORE I AM I WILL ALWAYS
BE QUEERS GAZING
AT THE CROTCHES OF
SMALL TRAGIC-THIGHED
MAGAZINES —
SIGHING
"OH" —

MORMONS — MARRIED VERY LATE TO SOMEBODY ALREADY DECEASED
BAPTIST
PRESBYTERIAN
EPISCOPALIANS   SOUTHERN CHRISTIAN
UNITARIANS   LEADERSHIP CONFERENCE
CATHOLIC
JEWISH
MOSLEM
HINDUISM
ISLAM
AMISH —
SHAKERS
ROSICRUCIANS
CHRISTIAN SCIENTISTS —
(TIM HOWELL'S)
AM. ASSOC. FOR THE ADV. OF ATHEISM — P 8116

CONRAD
GOD IS FOR MEN + RELIGION FOR WOMEN

SCORNED
PROPHETS —

* STREET PROPHETS — "STREET PREACHERS" AS ON
42 ST
SIGNS CARRIED — TRACTS PASSED

* THEME?
 CON
ARTISTS, RACKETEERS, CONFIDENCE MEN — GLIB PSYCHOTICS
USING RELIGION TO MAKE MONEY —

* BILLY GRAHAM — UNCLE B.O. ?
 THE EVANGELISTS

* MRS. ID.
ONE CAW BELOWE

Episodes of the waiting strangers
short sketches about people
whose habit patterns make them
meet strangers + connect themselves
intimately with these people
× ×

~~11:30~~
~~11 — poses turn up on bed~~
~~12~~
~~12:30 — Jim Carmen Bolero~~

~~Sh—— This~~
~~B— to 2 hr~~
~~Rhu——~~
~~Pete~~
~~Cortijo~~
~~Nero~~

cuba libre

Eroticism ~~[sketch]~~ FABLE

A sensory ~~(vision)~~.

I saw you standing between two cypress trees, naked— white like a marble statue. And the moss from the trees cast lacy shadows on your whiteness and spiders moved in + out of your mouth to their nest in the roof of your mouth. And your eyes were like slime from the river bottom, your arms long, milky.

I lay there in the tall grass, trying to hide myself. + I pressed my body down into the mud and curled around a dead branch from the tree. It was wet and ~~felt~~ good to my body. And I watched you. watched you standing there, not moving.

Then the moon came ~~out~~ thru the trees and fell on you and your naked roundness and I pressed my body deeper into the mud, until i was completely covered, watching you. You were breathing and the black widows kept moving in+out + down across your body.

then when the trees pushed the moon away I moved slowly, toward you, breathing, curling, feeling the mud slushing around me.

through the grass, moving toward

Seascapes – San Fr.

Ocean Beach – Evening

~~and~~ the multitudinous noises of
evening settling into ~~its~~ then wonderplace, ~~and~~
~~then~~ the fourteen gulls circling above
the pale cacophony of the fog
the flight patterned in the air, and
to the trenchant wave sound
losing itself now in the ~~mysteries~~ grey
~~mysteries~~ of nightfall.....

~~and~~ this above everything: the wildcrazy
~~//////~~ wave song eating holes
in the air, which now, as trombones ~~and~~ dissolving in the
~~trombones, or woman-wild-land~~ sand where the
summer ~~showed~~ ~~its feet over the~~ ~~to-day have~~ feet shrouded the
face of the sand. ~~As~~ the wave sound
becomes music, dissolves, ~~then~~ into the death bright air
                                                    of summer
and facade of smoke ~~declares~~ throttles the wind with certain fingers
           ~~the fourteen gulls, silent now,~~
           ~~superimpose upon the dining~~
           ~~perspective of the evening's wonderment....~~

"... So what is there left? ~~////~~ This only: the
sound of the sea, muted ~~////~~ now and far
far away like ~~///~~ echoes of the voices
                the
of drowned ~~/////~~ the evening dissolves
into itself and ~~xxxxx~~ becomes morning

and the song,
which was the wave song
and their song
and our song
and a love song
and finally a
sleep ~~that~~ ~~may well~~
        all be ended —
        as the evening becomes
        morning

SEASCAPE for a small room

A lone figure on horseback against the roaring of the ocean. A horse with a wild shock of a tail standing out in the breeze. Standing against the sound of the sea. (&saying the sea-sound by onomotopaeic use of "o"). darkgrey Seagulls hanging on the sea-air. Débris. And a lonely, shy boy breathing grass blades between glances at a sleeping figure in a bathing suit. The figure stirs and notices the boy is watching. The boy sits down, affecting nonchalance. The figure turns over on its stomach revealing a pale white, muscular back. Then turns back as suddenly as the mid section touches the other side. The boy gazes. The head of the figure opens now and smoke pours from its mouth & nostrils. The boy fishes in his pockets for a cigarette. Finds one. Lights it. Smoke from his mouth only. (Lament to a red spider of smallness.) Their eyes meet. Turn away. Meet again and hold. The **bathing suit stretches.**

1

INSTRUCTIONS:

① How to Play Drums

Be born in Africa
(seven centuries ago)
Run free on the white sand of
the beach —
Laugh! Throw your black body
against the white sand —
Pick up a tiny stone —
Throw it out toward an island —
(A world you know is there
but cannot see —)
Wait and see if the waves
bring it back — (they do not)
Splash in the water like a
black fish — walk slowly
home thru the green leaves
becoming emerald with nite —
Then —

Try to run away when they
come for you with whips +
guns + nets —

Feel anguish & terror as they
lash you together with others of
your kind in a dark ships hold —

POEMS FOR XANGO

Xango came this way last night —
quickly mounted a filha de santo
and rode off with her —
bearing her into the fierce
ecstacy of the night —
took her hands — placed them on
her back
thrust back her head
closed her eyes — placed his
rustled her   sword in her
red   hand
satin
skirt
and
    said "dance!

Perhaps you'd like to know
how the dawn comes to Salvador —
Well I'm going to tell you —
It is all dove's wings
and the sea's sighing
and a small hand cold then warm
— and it is a waiting — a hush — a held breath
more than anything else —
It is a waiting dance of waves — a romance of nature
It is the waiting dance of the fishermen's boat —
The sad song dancewise of Oxun's drums — still in the night-warm bodies
of the celebrants —

To a Nearer Phantom

He is a god whom nobody knows —
a frieze of eyes;
a waste — far away and
suspended above everywhere;
a clot of memory-blood;
a fog of silver sound;
a cello-theme over rooftops.
    Subtle,
      off key.

He is a foreign dream of specious clouds,
a jewel lost in a
      tomb
        a womb unopened;
          a shang of flesh
then a veil of wonder — and a
tiny star whom everyone finds
        everywhere
         everytime —

Je le connais — but
He is a god whom nobody knows —
a frieze of eyes...

PERFORMANCES

PERFORMANCE ART
MASTER PIECE

BILL T JONES
WITH OBJECTS

Throughout the presentation of *Edges of Ailey*, a robust performance program in the Whitney Museum of American Art's theater unfolds alongside the multimedia exhibition presented in the fifth-floor galleries—inspired, motivated, and organized by Alvin Ailey's belief in building a platform for Black and modern dancers and choreographers. The company's repertory—its embodied archive—doubles as a vital, ongoing repository for revivals, canonical dances, and new commissions alike. This series of performances operates in this same vein, assembling for the first time the Ailey company in concert with a suite of leading choreographers: Kyle Abraham/A.I.M by Kyle Abraham; Ronald K. Brown/EVIDENCE, A Dance Company; Trajal Harrell; Bill T. Jones; Ralph Lemon and Kevin Beasley; Sarah Michelson; Okwui Okpokwasili and Peter Born/Sweat Variant; Will Rawls; Matthew Rushing; Yusha-Marie Sorzano; and Jawole Willa Jo Zollar.

    The Alvin Ailey American Dance Theater is in residence monthly at the museum, each occasion a weeklong period to showcase the company's breadth of offerings, including performances of classic and contemporary works by the first company and Ailey II, its junior counterpart; workshops led by the Ailey School, a key training ground for dance since 1969; and educational initiatives, such as the Ailey Extension program, which offers classes to the public for all ages.

    The Dance Advisory Committee, comprising members of the Ailey company's artistic leadership and Adrienne Edwards, curator of *Edges of Ailey*, selected the eleven aforementioned choreographers as participants in the performance program for their plurality of styles and approaches. They have been commissioned to create new or restage existing works inspired by Ailey's life, influences, or themes. Together, this program at once attests to and affirms Ailey's undeniable presence—whether as influence, imprint, or shadow—for contemporary dancers.

ALVIN AILEY

Alvin Ailey American Dance Theater

Founded by Alvin Ailey in 1958 and forged during a pivotal moment in the Civil Rights Movement, the Alvin Ailey American Dance Theater uplifts the African American experience while transcending boundaries of race, faith, and nationality with its universal humanity. Recognized as a "vital American cultural ambassador to the world," it is one of the most acclaimed dance companies worldwide. Having performed in more than seventy countries on six continents, the Alvin Ailey American Dance Theater continues to bring joy to audiences everywhere while upholding Ailey's legacy for future generations.

September 25–29, 2024; January 22–26, 2025

Ailey II

Ailey II is a world-renowned repertory company—the junior company of the Alvin Ailey American Dance Theater—presenting new and classic works performed by the brightest young dancing talent. Founded in 1974 as the Alvin Ailey Repertory Ensemble, Ailey II has advanced Alvin Ailey's vision by giving early-career dancers the vital experience of transitioning from training as a student to becoming a professional dancer and by forging a new path for modern dance—one that is inclusive, experimental, and transformative.

September 25–29, 2024; November 20–24, 2024; December 18–22, 2024; January 22–26, 2025

The Ailey School

The Ailey School offers students ages three through twenty-five a comprehensive dance education in an inclusive and nurturing environment. Founded in 1969 in Brooklyn, New York, the school has grown into a world-class educational institution housed in the bright studios of the Joan Weill Center for Dance, the largest center for dance in New York City. In addition to multidisciplinary training, the school encourages students to explore their own creative voices, preparing them for fulfilling careers in dance and beyond.

January 22–26, 2025

Ailey Extension

Ailey Extension offers dance classes and workshops to members of the public of all ages, backgrounds, and experience levels. Since 2005, Ailey Extension has welcomed everyone to take part in the energy and connective spirit of dance through classes and workshops in ballet, Afro-Cuban, modern, hip-hop, West African, NY-style mambo, and many other dance forms.

October 15–20, 2024; November 20–24, 2024; December 18–22, 2024

Ailey Arts In Education and Community Programs

Ailey Arts In Education and Community Programs build on Alvin Ailey's guiding principle: that dance came from the people and should be returned to the people. In 1989, Ailey founded AileyCamp, a free summer day camp offering dance and arts classes for children. The last initiative he spearheaded before his death, it is one of the clearest expressions of his outreach philosophy. Ailey Arts In Education furthers Ailey's vision with programs that use dance, music, and art to build community, instill pride and self-confidence in children, enrich the lives of seniors, and forge stronger connections across social barriers.

October 15–20, 2024; November 20–24, 2024; December 18–22, 2024

COMMISSIONED CHOREOGRAPHERS

Kyle Abraham
A.I.M by Kyle Abraham

Kyle Abraham is an acclaimed choreographer whose singular style is a "postmodern gumbo" of movement exploration—drawing on traditional and vernacular dance as well as exploring issues of identity, sexual orientation, history, and geography, both universal and personal. "As an artist born in the late 1970s," he has said, "I've experienced a change in society that brings me hope. My choreography is a reflection of that hope, but also lives in the reality of my experiences and the cultural work that still needs to be done." In addition to performing and developing new works for his company, A.I.M by Kyle Abraham, Abraham has created commissioned works for many of the world's leading dance companies, including the Alvin Ailey American Dance Theater, the New York City Ballet, and the Royal Ballet.

The mission of the New York–based company A.I.M by Kyle Abraham is to create a body of dance-based work that is galvanized by Black culture and history and features the rich tapestry of Black and queer stories. The work, informed by and made in conjunction with artists across a range of disciplines, entwines a sensual and provocative vocabulary with a strong emphasis on music, text, video, and visual art. While grounded in Abraham's artistic vision, A.I.M draws inspiration from a multitude of sources and movement styles.

January 3–5, 2025

Ronald K. Brown
EVIDENCE, A Dance Company

Widely recognized for his fusion of African, Afro-Cuban, contemporary, and social dance styles, Ronald K. Brown's work illustrates and reinforces the importance of community, history, and spirituality in African American culture. An advocate for the growth of the African American dance community, he has been instrumental in encouraging young dancers to choreograph and develop careers in dance. The recipient of numerous awards and fellowships, Brown's first commission for the Alvin Ailey American Dance Theater (AAADT), *Grace* (1999), is an audience favorite in both the Ailey and EVIDENCE repertories. In all, he has choreographed seven works for the AAADT, including *Serving Nia* (2001), *Ife: My Heart* (2005), *Dancing Spirit* (2009), *Four Corners* (2013), *Open Door* (2015), and *The Call* (2018). "I hope that when people see the work, their spirits are lifted," Brown has said. "I am interested in sharing perspectives through modern dance, theater, and kinetic storytelling. I want my work to be evidence of these perspectives."

Inspired in part by a performance of the AAADT, Brown founded EVIDENCE, A Dance Company in Brooklyn, New York, in 1985. The company features a core of eight to ten dancers trained in Brown's signature integration of dance styles. Through its work, EVIDENCE provides a unique view of human struggles, tragedies, and triumphs with a particular focus on the culture and history of African Americans and the African diaspora. EVIDENCE tours widely in the United States and internationally, performing in theaters, teaching master classes, holding residencies, and conducting lectures and demonstrations for individuals of all ages, bringing arts education and cultural connections to hundreds of local communities and tens of thousands of audience and community members worldwide.

October 10–12, 2024

Trajal Harrell

Trajal Harrell first gained international recognition for creating a series of works that brought together the tradition of ballroom voguing—a dance style developed in the late 1980s in Harlem, New York—with early postmodern dance. In his latest work, Harrell combines theoretical and formal ideas from voguing, early modern dance, and Japanese Butoh. Weaving together the links between these disparate dance idioms, he centers the body, exploring the ways in which it becomes a receptacle of memory. Intertwining notions of time and history, his work reveals the multitude of layers that make up the rich tapestry of contemporary dance. Harrell's work has been presented at museums, theaters, festivals, and biennials worldwide. From 2019 to 2024, he was artistic director of the Schauspielhaus Zürich Dance Ensemble, which he founded. In 2023 the Festival d'Automne à Paris presented a "portrait" of Harrell's works, featuring nine of his creations.

October 4–6, 2025

Bill T. Jones

Bill T. Jones is an artist, choreographer, dancer, theater director, and writer. He studied dance at the State University of New York at Binghamton, cofounded American Dance Asylum in 1973, and in 1982 he formed the Bill T. Jones/Arnie Zane Company with his late partner, Arnie Zane. In addition to creating more than 140 works for his own company, he has made commissioned works for companies throughout the United States and Europe, including *Fever Swamp* (1983) and *How to Walk an Elephant* (1985) for the Alvin Ailey American Dance Theater. Over a career spanning more than five decades, he has been recognized with numerous prestigious awards, fellowships, and residencies, including a MacArthur Fellowship (1994), the Kennedy Center Honors (2010), a National Medal of Arts (2013), and the Human Rights Campaign's Visibility Award (2016), and his work on Broadway earned him Tony Awards for best choreography for *Spring Awakening* (2007) and *FELA!* (2010). Jones is currently the artistic director of New York Live Arts, which collaborates with boundary-pushing artists and advocates for their vision, fortifying their creative futures.

November 16, 2024

Ralph Lemon and Kevin Beasley

Ralph Lemon is a choreographer, writer, and visual artist based in New York. His most recent works include *Rant* (2019–), an ongoing performance in collaboration with Kevin Beasley; *Chorus* (2015–18); *Scaffold Room* (2015); *Four Walls* (2012); and *How Can You Stay in the House All Day and Not Go Anywhere?* (2008–10). He is the author of *Come home Charley Patton* (2013), the final in a series of books published by Wesleyan University Press documenting his *Geography Trilogy* (1997–2004), a ten-year international research and performance project examining race, history, memory, and the art world. Lemon is the recipient of three Bessie Awards (1986, 2005, 2016); two Foundation for Contemporary Art Awards (1986, 2012); a Herb Alpert Award in the Arts (1999); a United States Artists Fellowship (2006); a Guggenheim Fellowship (2009); a Doris Duke Performing Artist Award (2012); a National Medal of Arts (2015); a Heinz Family Foundation Award (2018); and a MacArthur Fellowship (2020). In 2022 he received the Bucksbaum Award for his work in that year's Whitney Biennial.

New York–based artist Kevin Beasley's practice spans sculpture, photography, sound, and performance, while centering on materials of cultural and personal significance, from raw cotton harvested from his family's property in Virginia to sounds gathered using contact microphones. Beasley alters, casts, and molds these diverse materials to form a body of work that acknowledges the complex, shared histories of the broader American experience, steeped in generational memories. Beasley has collaborated with Ralph Lemon on numerous performances, including *Dust* (2023); with Darrell Jones, Lemon, and Okwui Okpokwasili at Counterpublic, Saint Louis; and *Rant* (2019–), an ongoing series with Lemon initiated at the Whitney Museum of American Art, New York, with subsequent iterations at the Fórum do Futuro, Palácio dos Correios, Porto, Portugal; the Kitchen, New York; and the Hammer Museum, Los Angeles. Beasley received his BFA from the College for Creative Studies, Detroit, in 2007, and his MFA from the Yale School of Art, New Haven, Connecticut, in 2012.

February 7, 2025

Sarah Michelson

British-born, New York–based choreographer, dancer, and artist Sarah Michelson is known for choreographic work that engages notions of process, physicality, immediacy, and impermanence. Drawing from personal and dance history, her formally rigorous, incisive, often humorous work examines the possibilities afforded by questioning, problematizing, and challenging what dance is and can be, while evincing a devotional commitment to the art form and the efforts of its performers and the broader dance community. Michelson's work has been commissioned and presented by notable institutions, including the Chapter Arts Centre, Cardiff, Wales; Danspace Project, New York; The Kitchen, New York; the Lower Manhattan Cultural Council's River to River Festival, New York; Movement Research, New York; the Museum of Modern Art, New York; On the Boards, Seattle; Performance Space New York; the Walker Art Center, Minneapolis; and the Whitney Museum of American Art, New York.

January 9–11, 2025

Okwui Okpokwasili and Peter Born
Sweat Variant

Sweat Variant describes the collaborative practice of Okwui Okpokwasili and Peter Born, partners in work and life. Since 1996, they have probed the intersection of dance, theater, and visual art to make challenging and rigorous work that explores the many meanings entangled in the bodies of Black women. Striving to achieve a spectacle of radical intimacy, wherein the performers and audience are acknowledged as being locked in a mutual gaze, Sweat Variant builds gestural vocabularies and narrative frameworks that are concerned with the problem of memory in the inherent instability of the construction of a persona. "We hope to activate a space that allows the audience to question who they are looking at and how they are looking," they have stated. "We hope this creates a critical space of wonderment, of uncertainty, and of mystery. It is in this space that we believe we can see each other anew."

February 6–8, 2025

Will Rawls

Will Rawls is a New York–based choreographer, dancer, and writer, whose practice probes the boundaries between dance, language, and other media to investigate the poetics of abstraction, Blackness, and the materiality of time. His work has been presented at, among others, the MCA Chicago; the Momentary, Bentonville, Arkansas; On the Boards, Seattle; the Portland Institute for Contemporary Art, Oregon; the 35a Bienal de São Paulo, Brazil; and Counterpublic 2023, Saint Louis. Rawls has been awarded numerous residencies and fellowships, including a 2017 Guggenheim Fellowship, and he received a Herb Alpert Award in the Arts in 2021. His writing has been published by the Hammer Museum, Los Angeles; the Museum of Modern Art, New York; Museu de Arte de São Paulo; and the journal *Dancing While Black*. He is currently associate professor of choreography in the Department of World Arts and Cultures/Dance at the University of California, Los Angeles.

December 13–15, 2024

Matthew Rushing

Dancer-choreographer Matthew Rushing was born in Los Angeles, California. He was a scholarship student at the Ailey School and a member of Ailey II, joining the Alvin Ailey American Dance Theater in 1992. "I dance out of an overwhelming feeling of necessity," he has said. "Dance is literally a form of life to me, and I can't imagine functioning without it." During his time with the Ailey company, Rushing choreographed four ballets: *Acceptance in Surrender* (2005), a collaboration with Hope Boykin and Abdur-Rahim Jackson; *Uptown* (2009), a tribute to the Harlem Renaissance; *ODETTA* (2014), a celebration of singer, songwriter, and civil rights activist Odetta Holmes; and *Testament* (2020), a tribute to Alvin Ailey's *Revelations* (1960) created with Clifton Brown and Yusha-Marie Sorzano.

November 1–3, 2024

Yusha-Marie Sorzano

Originally from the Republic of Trinidad and Tobago, Yusha-Marie Sorzano is a performing artist, choreographer, educator, and mentor who has worked in concert dance, theater, television, and film. She has been a member of eight acclaimed dance companies, including the Alvin Ailey American Dance Theater (AAADT) and Camille A. Brown and Dancers, and has choreographed works for, among others, the AAADT. She received the New York Public Library's Dance Research Fellowship in 2020, and she is currently the co-artistic director of the Zeitgeist Dance Theatre in Santa Fe, New Mexico. Sorzano has said: "Along [my] journey I began to bridge the rhythms of my native culture—the isolation of the hips and the folkloric dances—with classical concert dance," adding that she realized that "being a complete human is about finding harmony among our many selves, our many distinct languages. This desire to communicate what I believe is a universal experience is at the core of my work."

November 7–9, 2024

Jawole Willa Jo Zollar

Kansas City, Missouri–born Jawole Willa Jo Zollar is an award-winning choreographer and dancer whose movement vocabulary mixes elements from postmodern, modern, and Africanist dance styles. In 1984, Zollar founded Urban Bush Women (UBW)—a Brooklyn, New York–based performance ensemble dedicated to exploring the use of cultural expression as a catalyst for social change. In addition to the works she has created for UBW, Zollar has produced work for the Alvin Ailey American Dance Theater, Philadanco, Taylor Mac, and others. "Movement is the foundation of life," she has said. "Dance takes this human imperative to an expressive imperative that supports our ability to make meaning and deepen our understanding of this world."

January 17–19, 2025

As of June 28, 2024

ARTWORKS

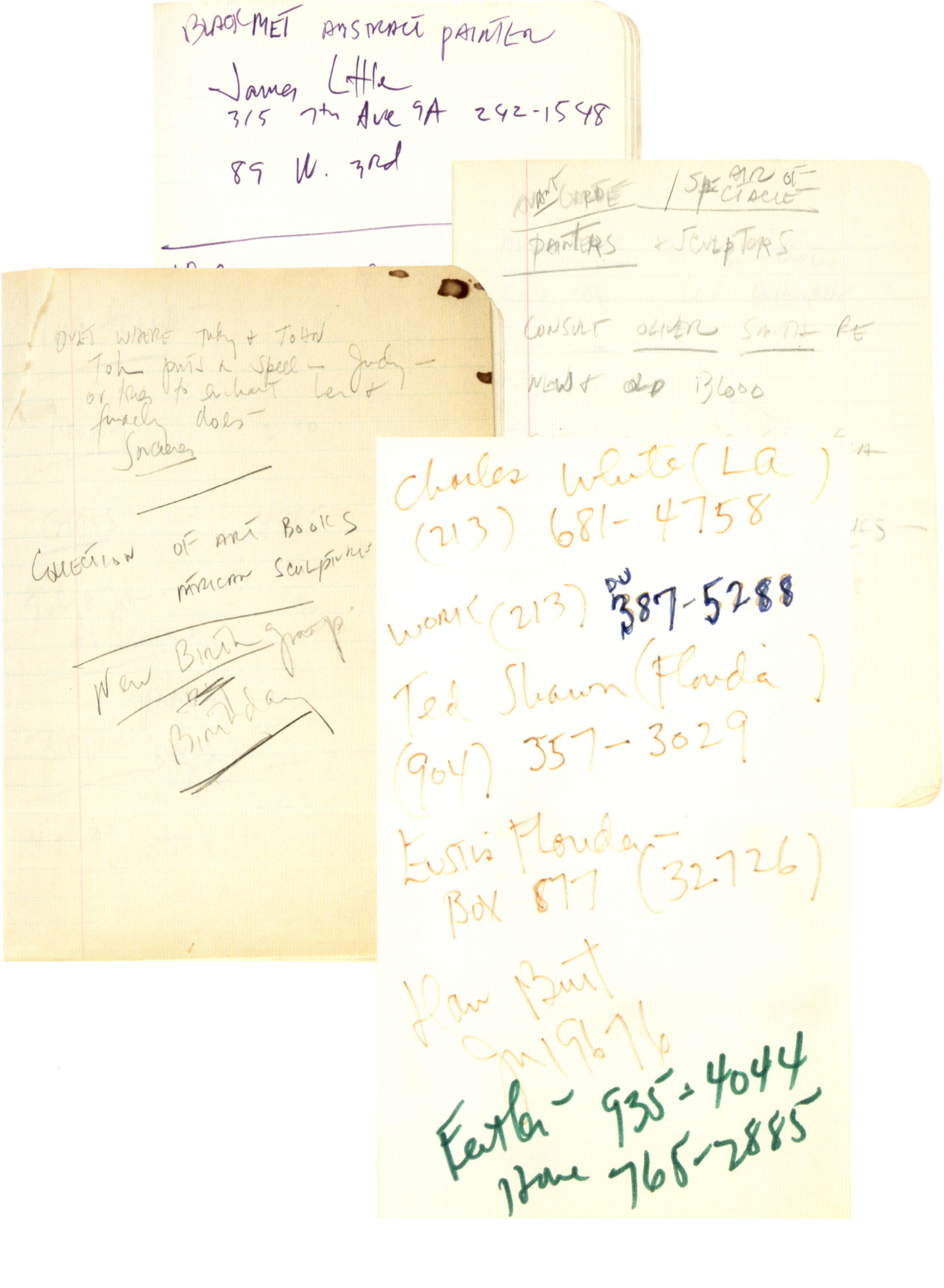

BLACK MET ABSTRACT PAINTER
James Little
315 7th Ave 9A 242-1548
89 W. 3rd

AVANT GARDE / SPEC AIR OF SPECTACLE
PAINTERS + SCULPTORS

CONSULT OLIVER SMITH RE
NEW & OLD BLOOD

OVER WHERE Toby + John
John puts a spell — Judy —
or tries to inherit Ten+
finally does —
Sincere

Collection of art books
African sculpture

New Birth group
Birthday

Charles White (LA)
(213) 681-4758
Work (213) DU 387-5288
Ted Shawn (Florida)
(904) 357-3029
Eustis Florida —
Box 877 (32726)
How But
SN1976
Eartha — 935-4044
Diane 765-2885

Alvin Ailey saw the art of dance as a synthesis of genre and form, once stating in a televised interview, "Modern dance just seemed to encapsulate all my ideas. There was movement. There was color. There was painting, there was this sculpture, and there was the pulling it all together into a meaningful, expressive art form." The visual arts as such were an abiding source of curiosity and inspiration for the choreographer. Mentions of artists abound in Ailey's notebooks, letters, and personal collections, and he actively encouraged his company's dancers to visit museums and other cultural institutions while on tour.

Edges of Ailey pays homage not only to this lifelong commitment to the arts but also to Ailey's pioneering repertory model in modern dance. From the outset, he wanted his company to serve as a platform for Black dancers and choreographers: in other words, he did not want to achieve and create alone. Ailey's generosity, a pillar of his creative method, informs the robust selection of artworks on the following pages and assembled alongside the materials of the Ailey archive and repertory in the exhibition space, in addition to the pendant performance program featuring the Ailey company and new commissions or restaged works by leading choreographers.

These artworks—encompassing the mediums of painting, sculpture, photography, drawings, prints, and video—are staged in the exhibition in a dynamic cross-viewing experience, whereby histories of art are inflected and enlivened through the mutual prism of Ailey and dance. Along the walls and on bespoke islands and systems of support, the artworks are carefully presented in an installation of red: a color that nods to Ailey's "blood memories," the theater interiors in which we typically see Ailey's dances, and the pews and carpet often found in Black churches. This art has been made before, during, and after Ailey's lifetime (1931–1989), bookended by Robert Duncanson's painting *View of Cincinnati, Ohio from Covington, Kentucky* (ca. 1851) and works newly created for the exhibition, inspired by Ailey, his legendary dance *Cry*, Katherine Dunham, or the Black dancing body more generally. Although some artists and subjects can be directly traced to Ailey—including Dunham, Marian Anderson, James Baldwin, Romare Bearden, Carmen de Lavallade, Hector Hyppolite, Geoffrey Holder, Judith Jamison, and James Little—the vast majority share and amplify the themes found in Ailey's dances.

The artworks thus are causal, connective, and constellatory in equal measure, expanding upon the cardinal themes in Ailey's life and work: a southern imaginary bridging the United States, Brazil, Haiti, and the larger Caribbean, and West Africa; the endurance of Black spirituality through candomblé, vodou, and the Black church; the conditions and profound effects of Black migration to the western and northern United States; the ongoing struggle for an intersectional Black liberation; the central importance of Black women; his creative mainstay of collaboration with other artists; the sweeping arc of Black music; and the myriad representations of Blackness in dance—along with meditations on dance after Ailey.

Individually and collectively considered, these concerns have been central to Black art, creativity, and culture for nearly two centuries. Through these juxtapositions of genre, history, and geography, Blackness *appears* as integral and indivisible from any American narrative. The presence of Ailey—whether through his life or his creative preoccupations—becomes the very means through which this statement is given sight, sense, and possibility.

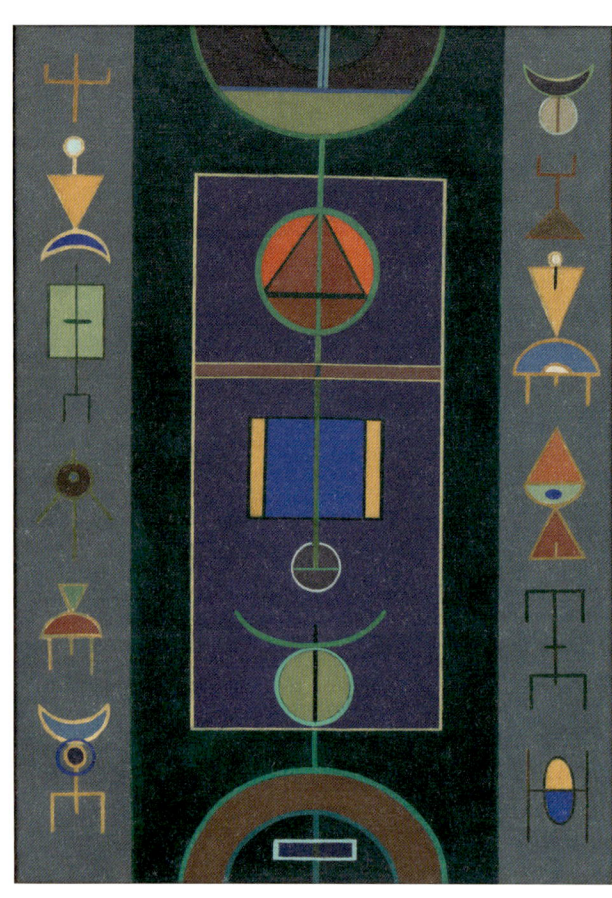
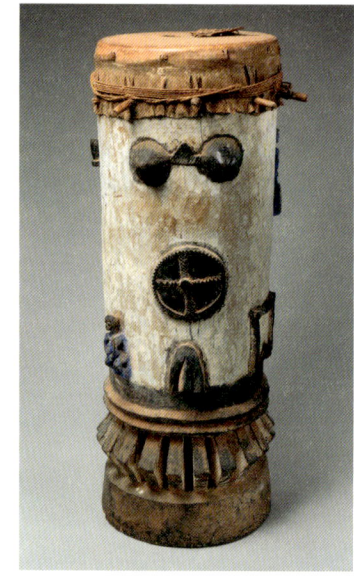
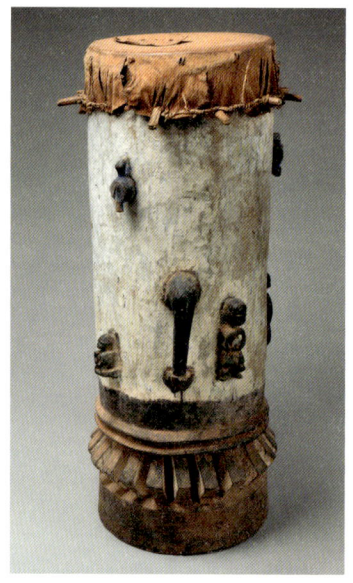

Clockwise from top left:

Rubem Valentim, *Untitled*, 1956–62. Oil on canvas, 27⅝ × 19¾ in. (70.2 × 50.2 cm). The Museum of Modern Art, New York; gift of Patricia Phelps de Cisneros through the Latin American and Caribbean Fund in honor of Lissette Stancioff, 876.2016

Fon peoples, *Female Drum* and *Male Drum*, 19th–20th century. Wood, hide, pigment, cane, and cord, diameter: 20¼ in. (148.6 × 51.4 cm) each. The Metropolitan Museum of Art, New York; gift of Robert H. and Ruth S. Smith, 1982, 1982.495.1–2

Hector Hyppolite, *The Congo Queen*, 1946. Enamel, oil, and graphite pencil on cardboard, 20 × 27⅝ in. (50.9 × 70.1 cm). The Museum of Modern Art, New York; gift of Mr. and Mrs. Walter Bareiss, 852.1956

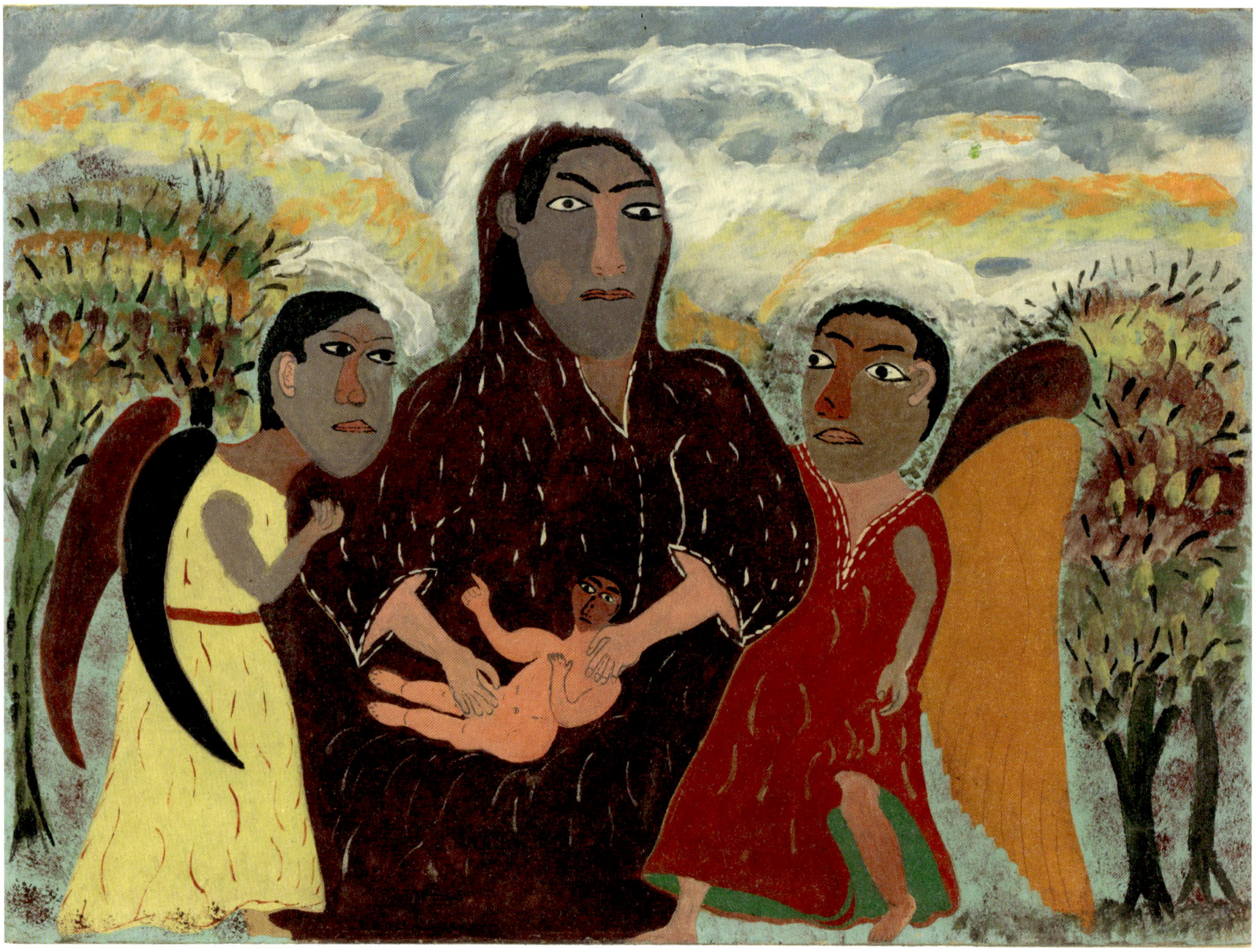

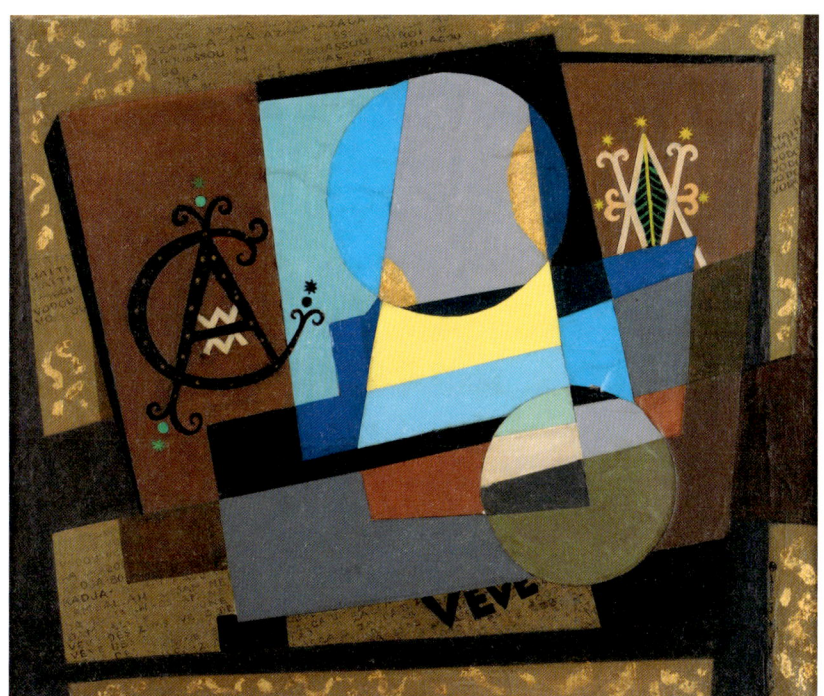

Clockwise from top left:

Loïs Mailou Jones, *Veve Voudou II*, 1963. Mixed media, 21⅛ × 25¼ in. (53.7 × 64.1 cm). Howard University Gallery of Art, Washington, DC; gift of Loïs Mailou Jones Pierre-Noël Trust

David Driskell, *Festival Bahia*, 1985. Gouache and mixed media on paper, 24¼ × 30 in. (61.5 × 76.2 cm). Estate of David Driskell; courtesy DC Moore Gallery, New York

David Driskell, *Bahian Ribbons*, 1987. Acrylic on canvas, 20 × 24 in. (50.8 × 61 cm). Estate of David Driskell; courtesy DC Moore Gallery, New York

Noah Purifoy, *Untitled*, 1970. Wood, leather, brass, and copper, 49⅜ × 28⅝ × 21¼ in. (125.4 × 72.7 × 54 cm). Whitney Museum of American Art, New York; purchase, 71.170

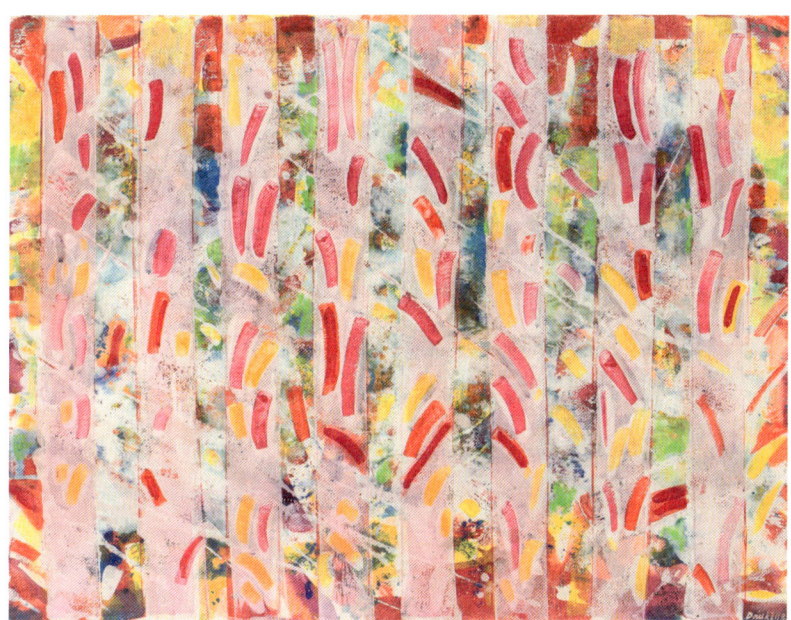

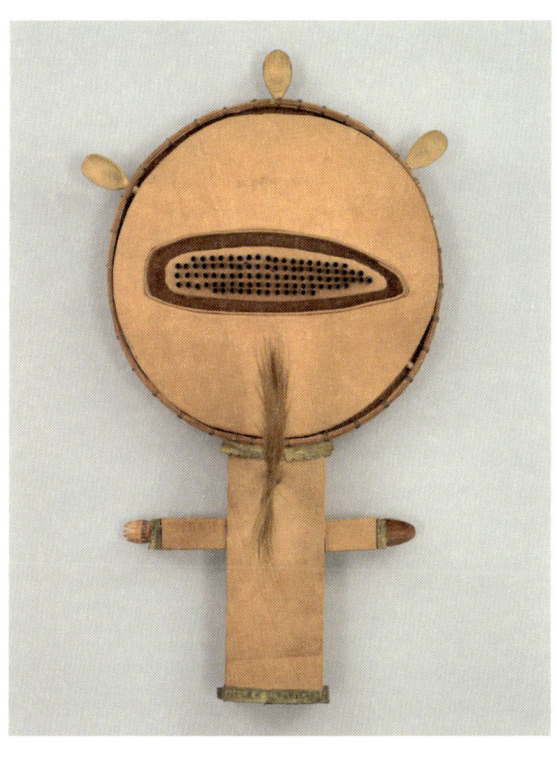

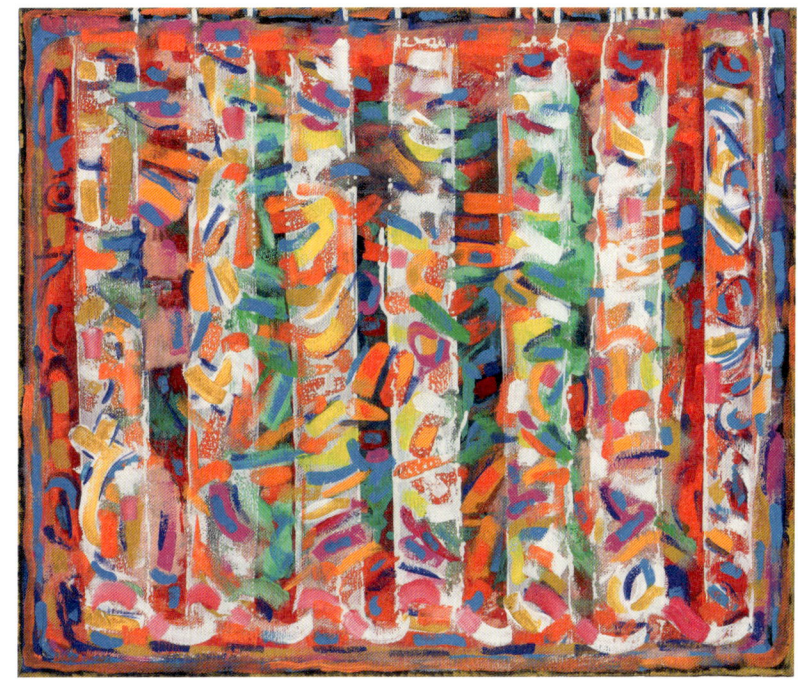

333

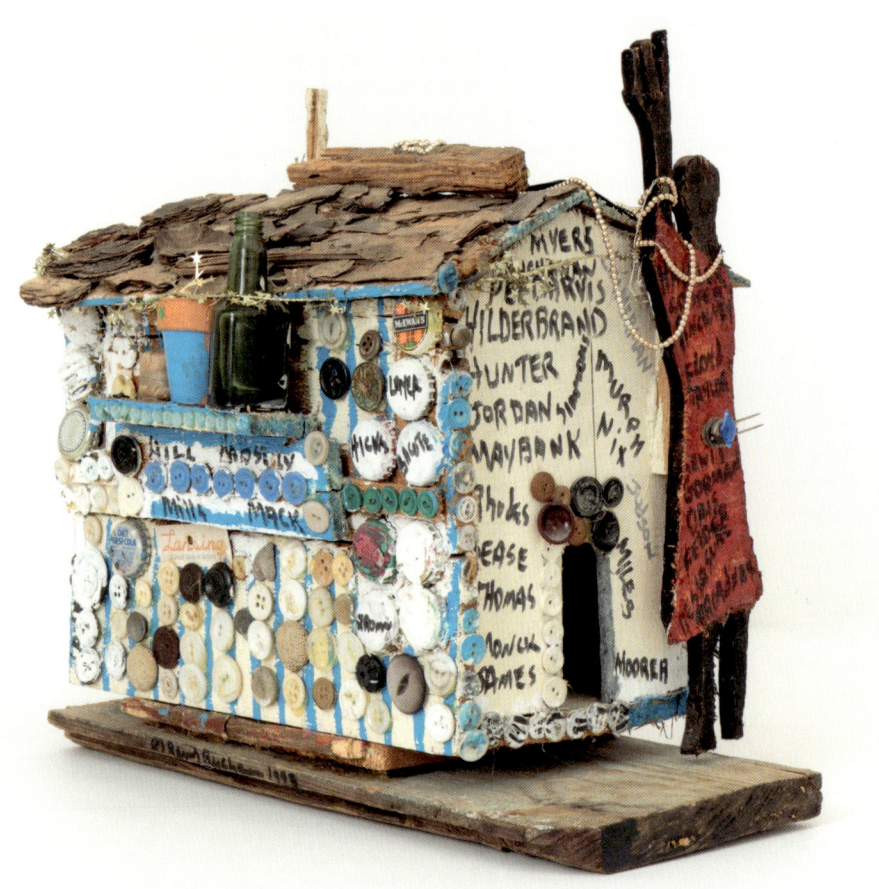

Clockwise from top left:

Beverly Buchanan, *Orangeburg County Family House*, 1993. Paint, marker, garland, necklace, wood chips, bark, buttons, bottle caps, license plate, film canister, thumbtacks, clay pot, glass bottle, thread, and glue on wood, 14 ¼ × 14 ¾ × 10 ½ in. (36.2 × 37.5 × 26.7 cm). Private collection

Kevin Beasley, *Haze*, 2023. Polyurethane resin, raw Virginia cotton, marker transfer, and fiberglass, 55 ½ × 74 × 2 ½ in. (141 × 188 × 6.4 cm). Casey Kaplan Gallery, New York

Al Loving, *Untitled*, ca. 1975. Mixed media, 66 × 74 in. (167.6 × 188 cm). Collection of Beth Rudin DeWoody

John Biggers, *Sharecropper*, 1945. Oil on canvas, 24 × 18 in. (61 × 45.7 cm). Los Angeles County Museum of Art; purchased with funds from the Ducommun and Gross Endowment and the Robert H. Halff Endowment, M.2022.41

Carrie Mae Weems, *Untitled*, from the series *Sea Islands*, 1992. Gelatin silver print, 19 ⅜ × 19 ⅜ in. (49.2 × 49.2 cm). Whitney Museum of American Art, New York; gift of Carrie Mae Weems and P.P.O.W., 97.97.1

Thornton Dial, *Shadows of the Field*, 2008. String, twine, synthetic cotton batting, wood, burlap, sheet metal, cloth rags, nails, staples, and enamel on canvas on wood, 79 × 105 × 5 in. (200.7 × 266.7 × 12.7 cm). The Metropolitan Museum of Art, New York; gift of Souls Grown Deep Foundation from the William S. Arnett Collection, 2014, 2014.548.4

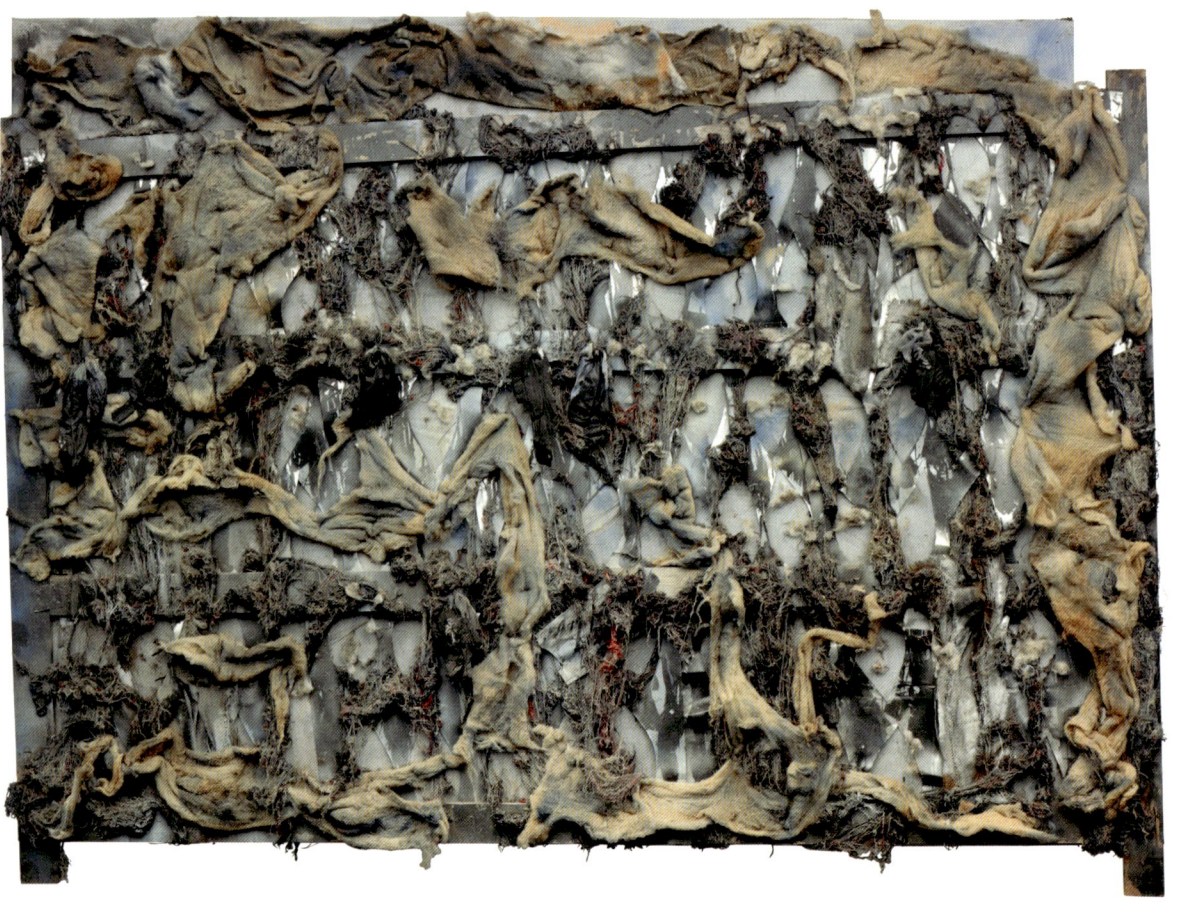

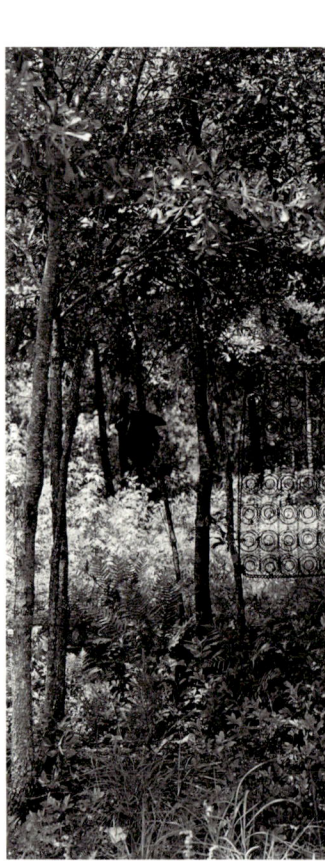

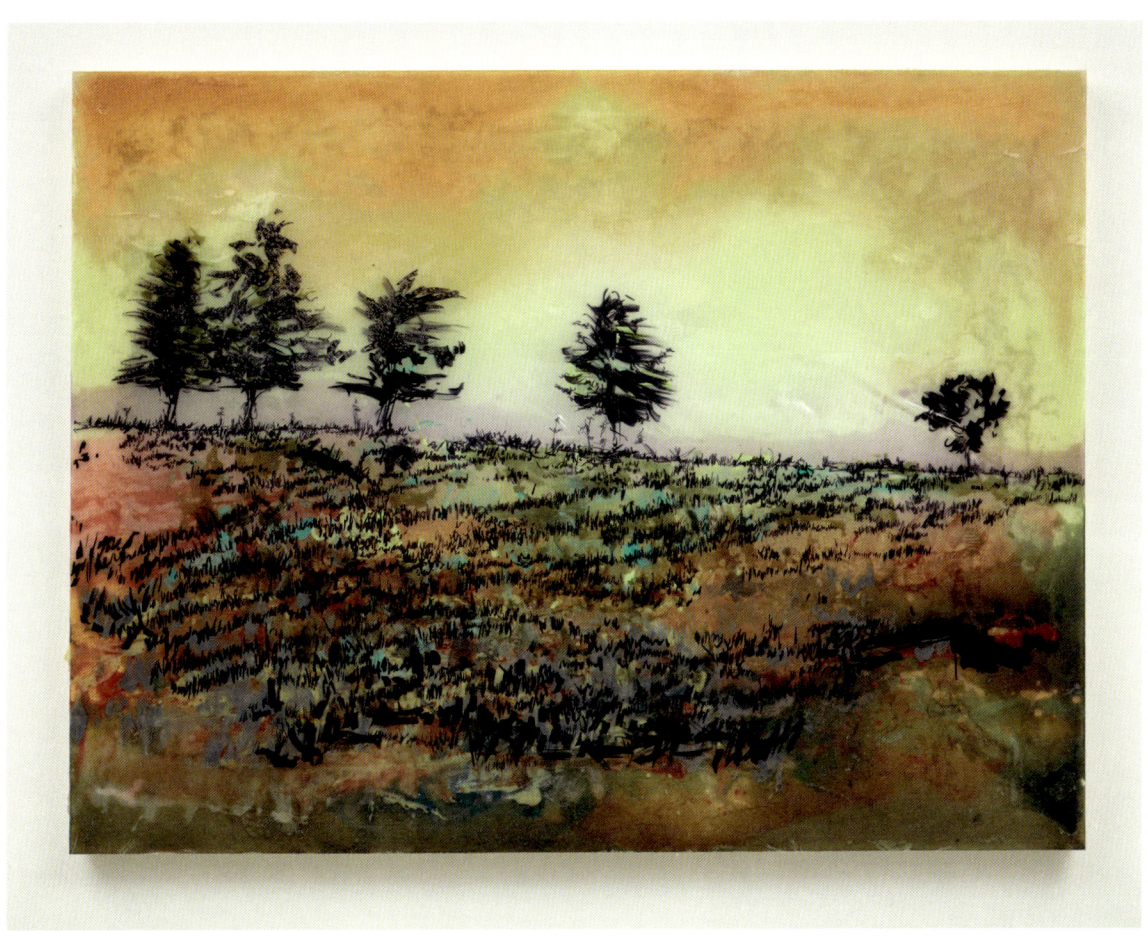
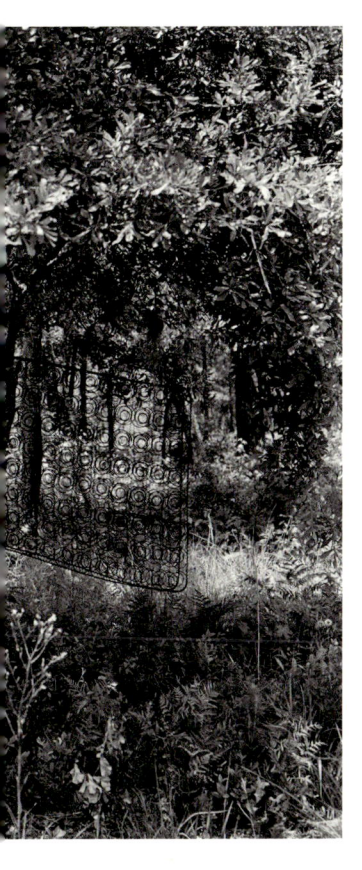
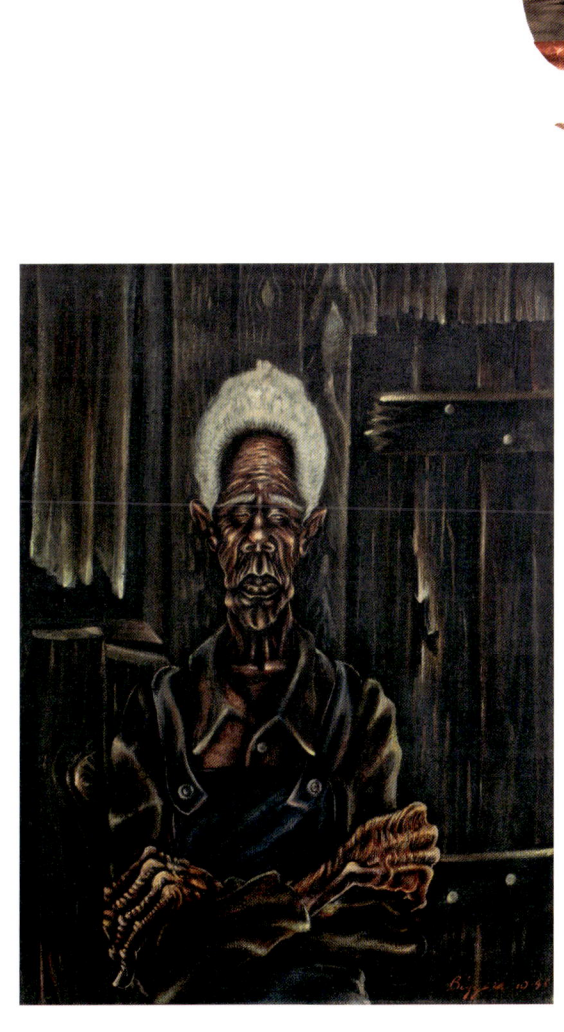

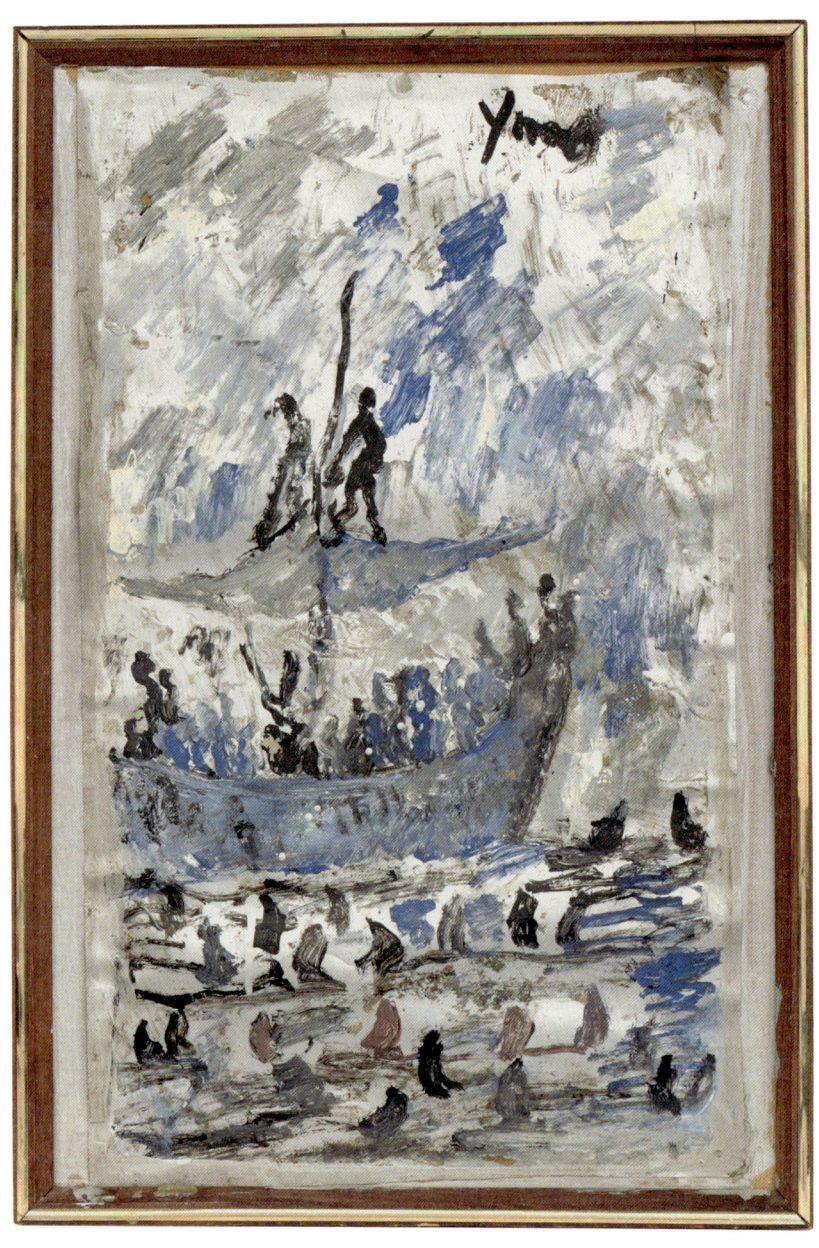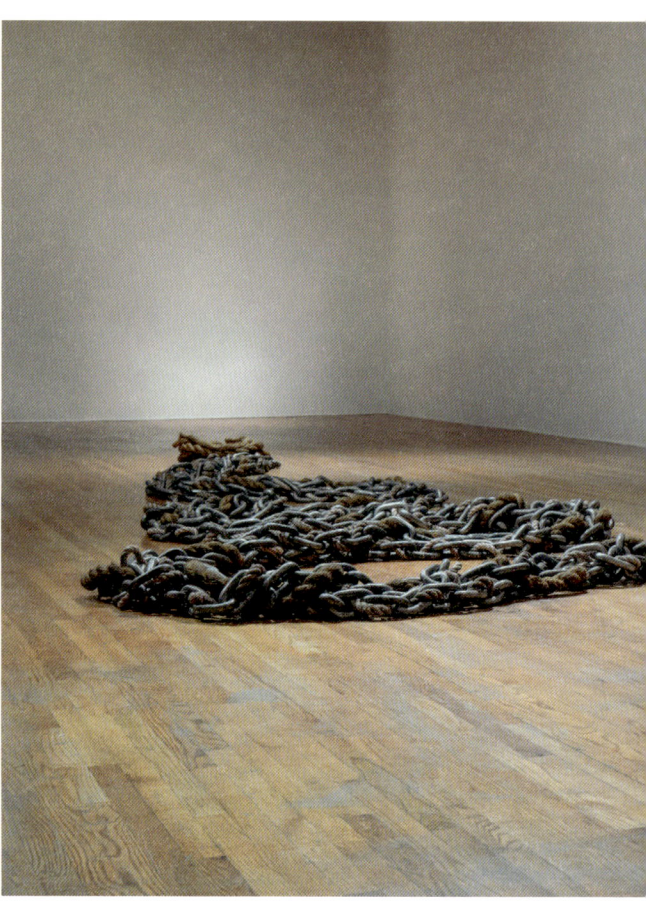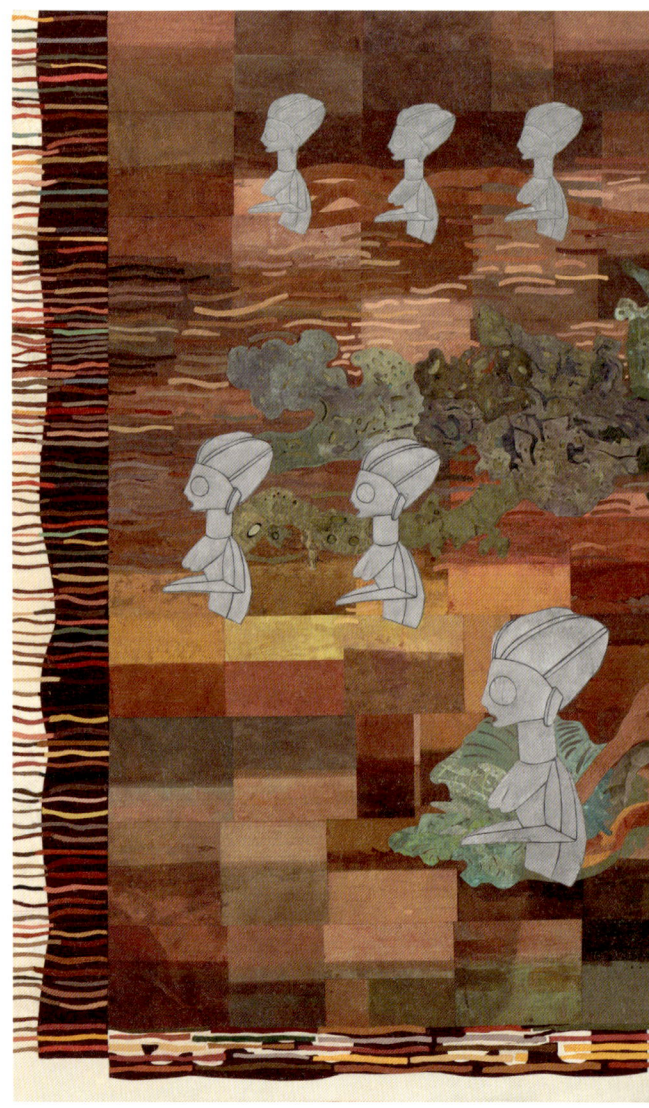

Clockwise from top left:

Purvis Young, *I Love Your America*, late 1970s. Paint on mylar, mounted on found painting, 25¼ × 17¼ in. (64.1 × 43.8 cm). Souls Grown Deep Foundation

Maren Hassinger, *River*, 1972/2011. Mixed-media installation with steel chains and rope, 7 × 89 × 358 in. (17.8 × 226.1 × 909.3 cm). The Studio Museum in Harlem, New York; gift of the artist, 2012.34

Purvis Young, *Ocean*, 1975. Paint and wood on Masonite, 16 × 14¼ in. (40.6 × 36.2 cm). The Metropolitan Museum of Art, New York; gift of Souls Grown Deep Foundation from the William S. Arnett Collection, 2014, 2014.548.19

Alma Thomas, *Mars Dust*, 1972. Acrylic on canvas, 69¼ × 57⅛ in. (175.9 × 145.1 cm). Whitney Museum of American Art, New York; purchase, with funds from The Hament Corporation, 72.58

Ellen Gallagher, *Ecstatic Draught of Fishes*, 2022. Oil, pigment, wax, palladium leaf, and paper on canvas, 89¾ × 118⅛ in. (228 × 300 cm). Whitney Museum of American Art, New York; gift of The George Economou Collection, 2023.74

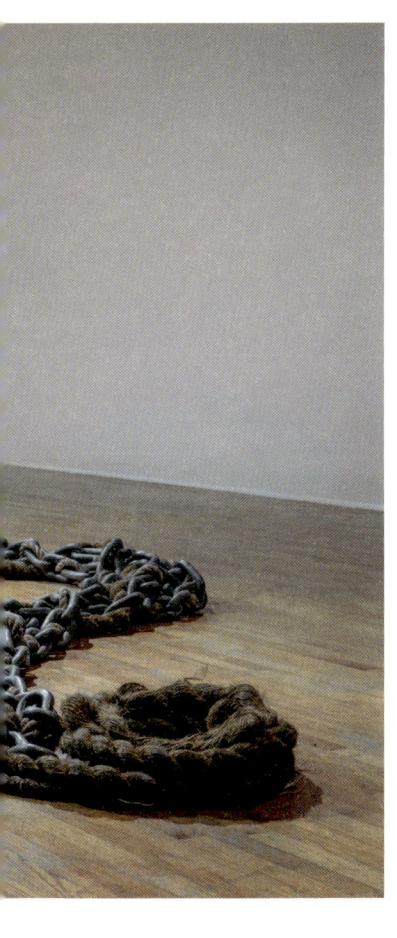
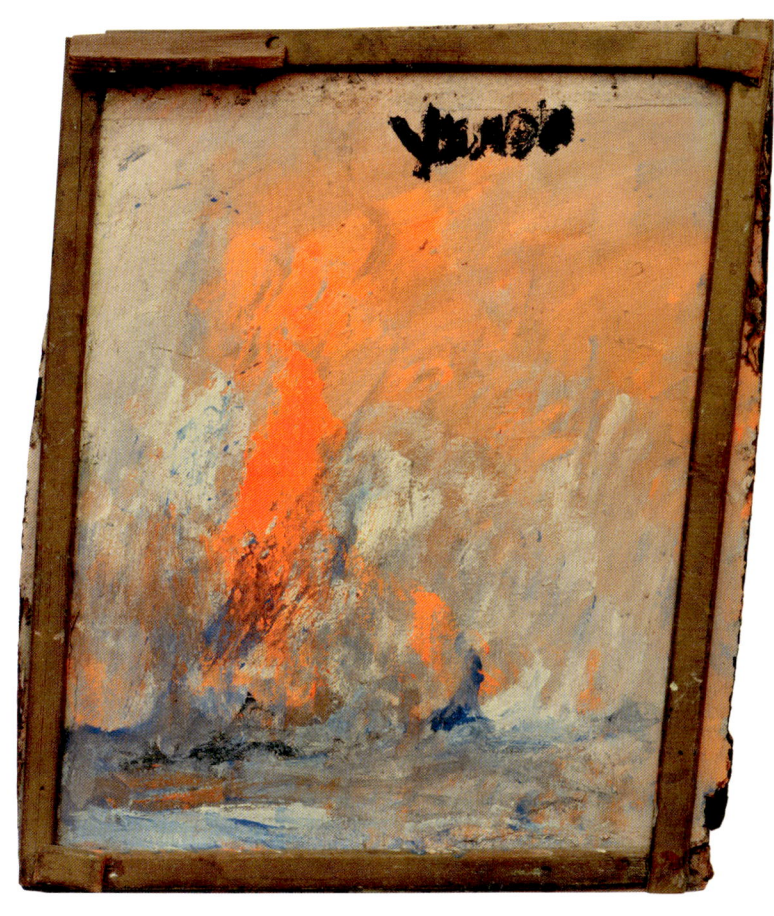
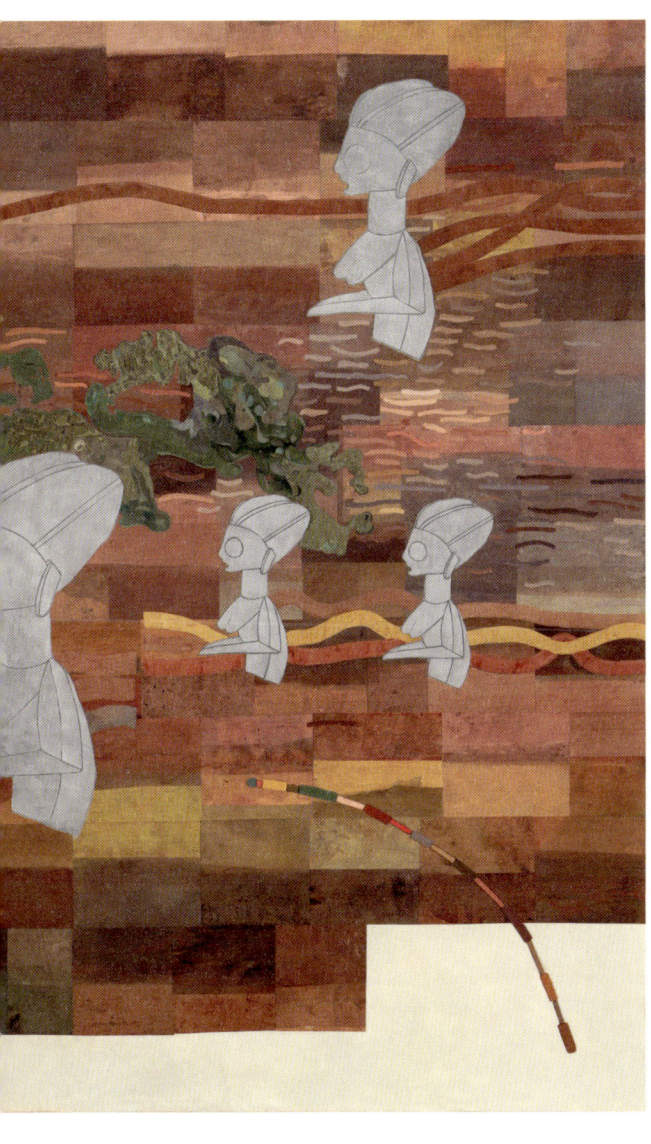
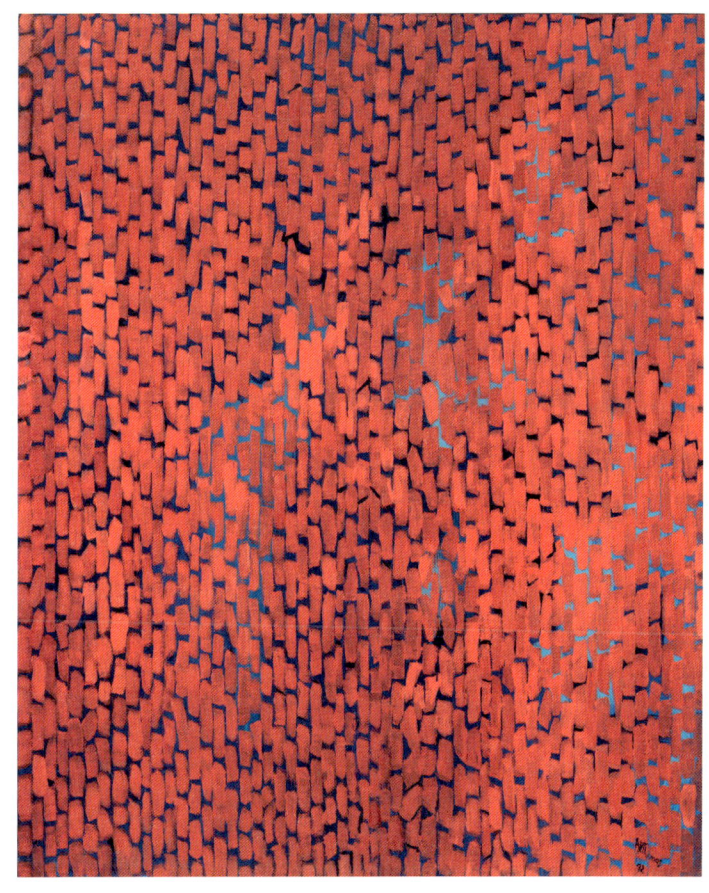

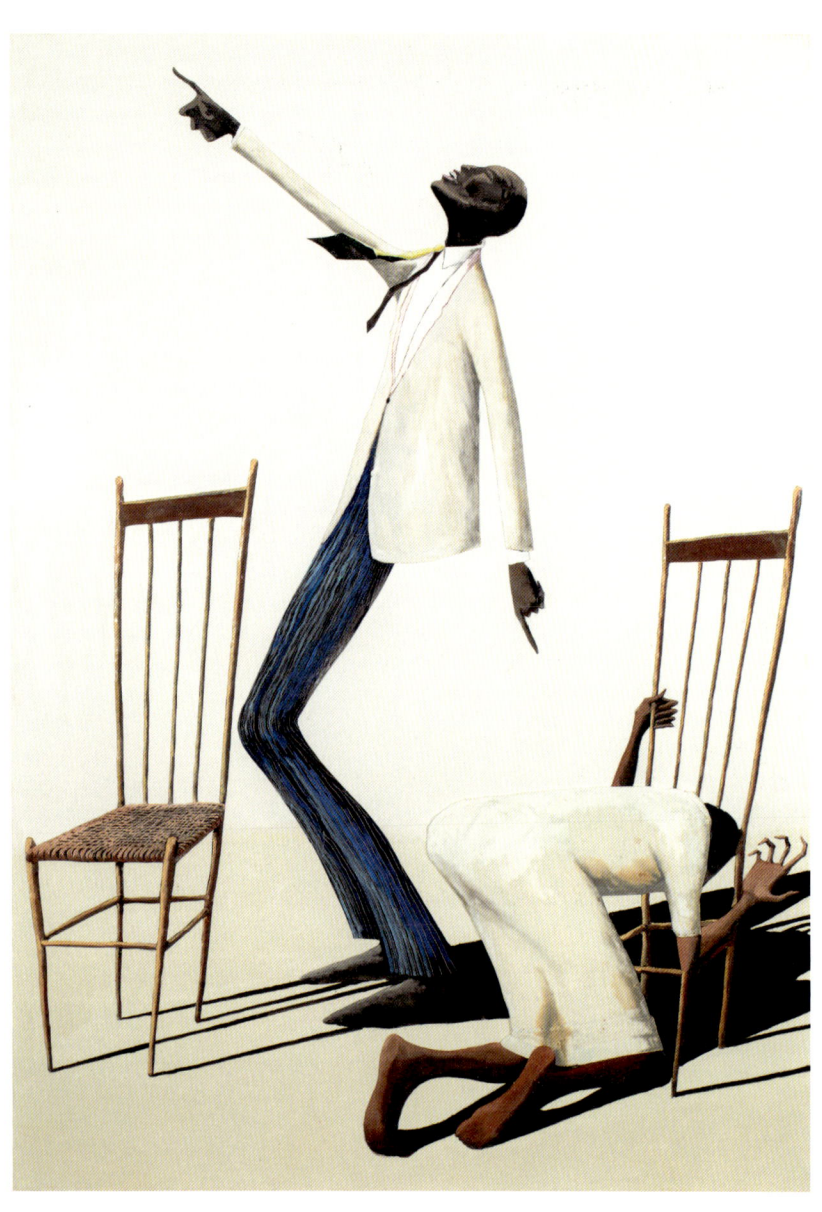
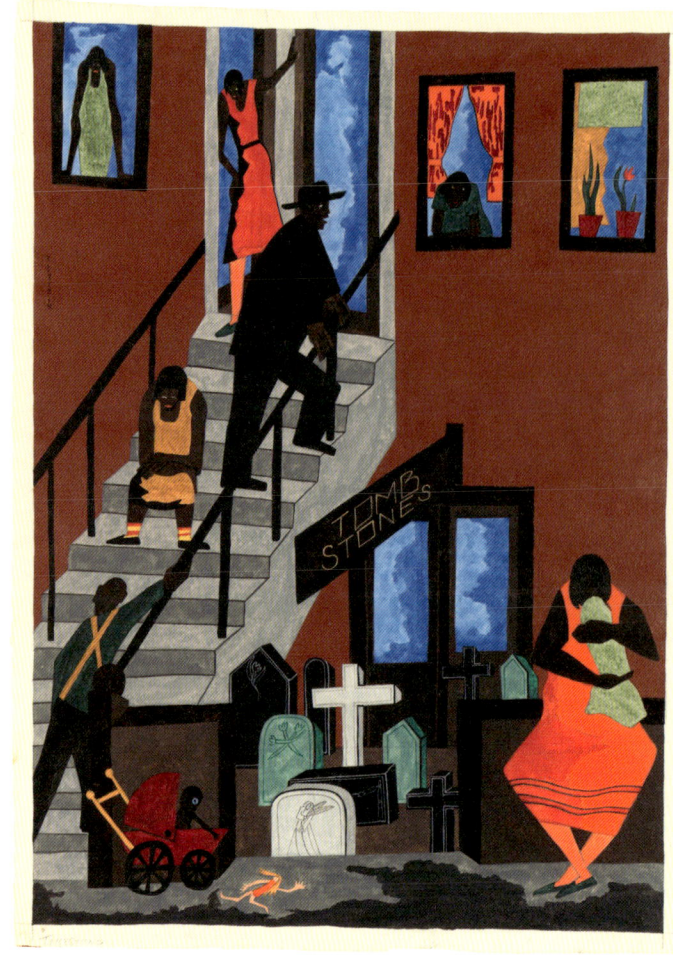
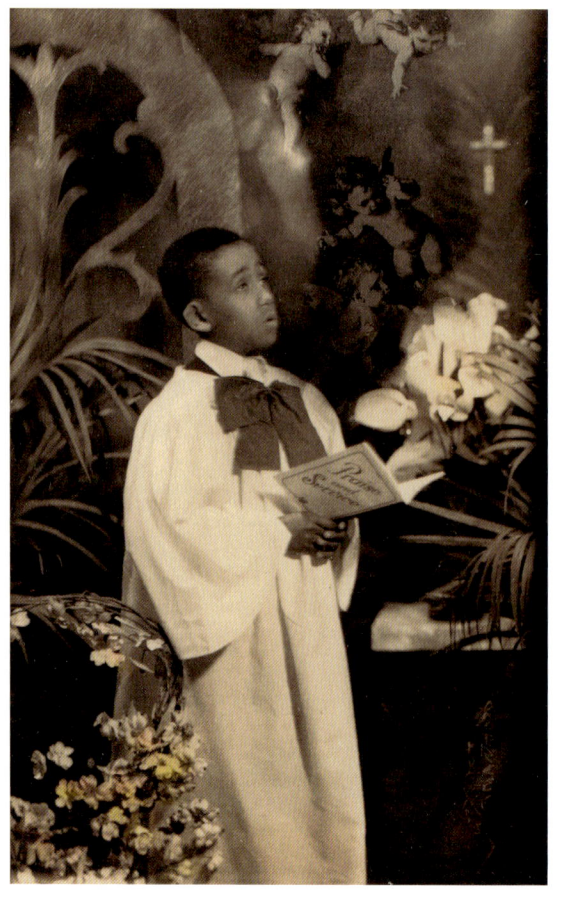

Clockwise from top left:

Benny Andrews, *The Way to the Promised Land (Revival Series)*, 1994. Oil on canvas with painted fabric collage, 72 × 50¾ in. (182.9 × 128.9 cm). Michael Rosenfeld Gallery

Jacob Lawrence, *Tombstones*, 1942. Opaque watercolor on paper, 30⅞ × 22¹³⁄₁₆ in. (78.4 × 57.9 cm). Whitney Museum of American Art, New York; purchase, 43.14

Charles White, *Preacher*, 1952. Pen and ink and graphite pencil on board, 22¹³⁄₁₆ × 29¹⁵⁄₁₆ in. (57.9 × 76 cm). Whitney Museum of American Art, New York; purchase, 52.25

Rotimi Fani-Kayode, *Every Moment Counts (Ecstatic Antibodies)*, 1989. Chromogenic print, 47¼ × 47¼ in. (120 × 120 cm). Autograph, London, and Hales Gallery, New York

James Van Der Zee, *Choir Boy*, 1937. Gelatin silver print, 8 × 5 in. (20.3 × 12.7 cm). The Studio Museum in Harlem, New York; gift of The Sandor Family Collection, Chicago, 2000.11.13

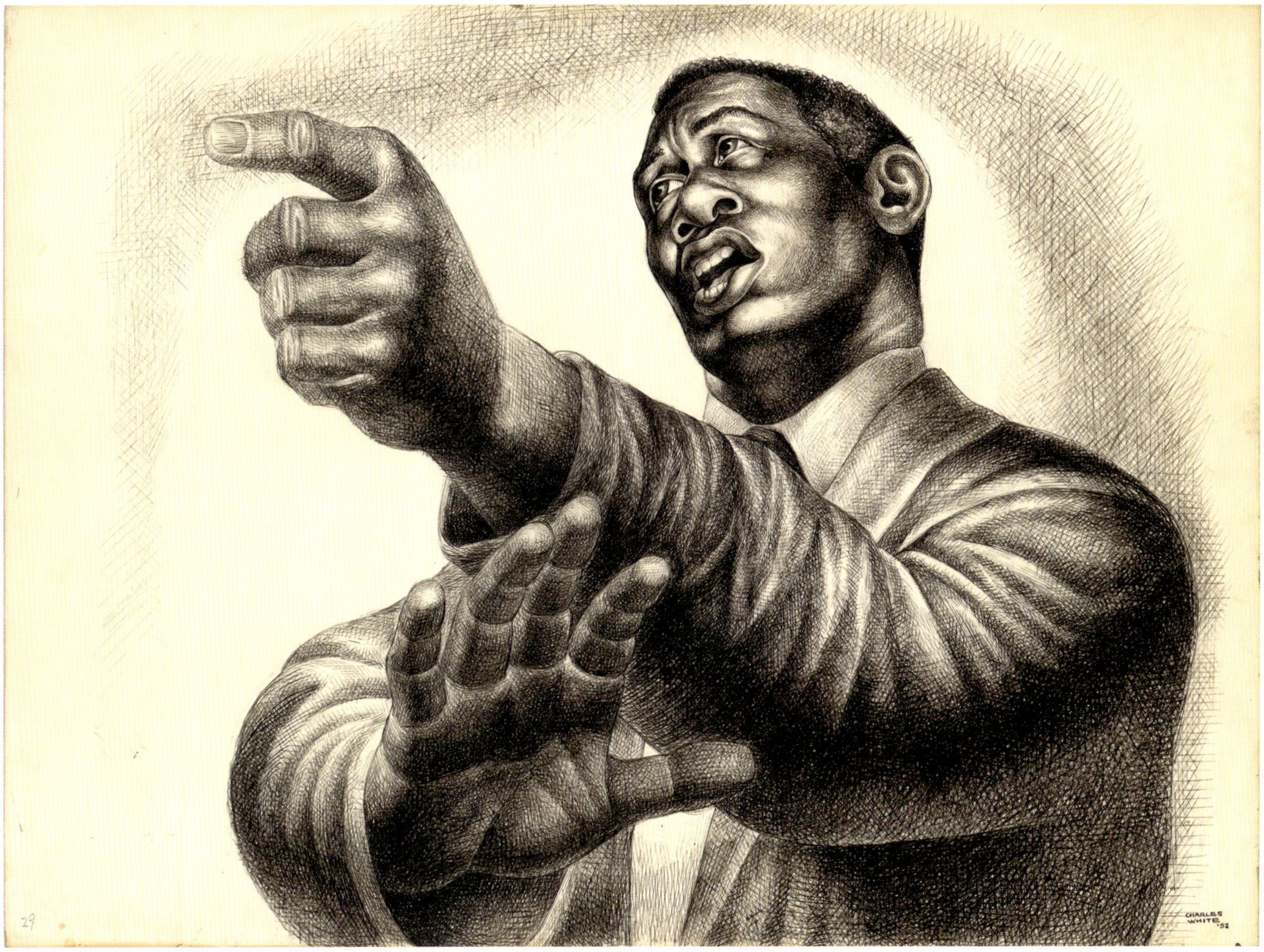

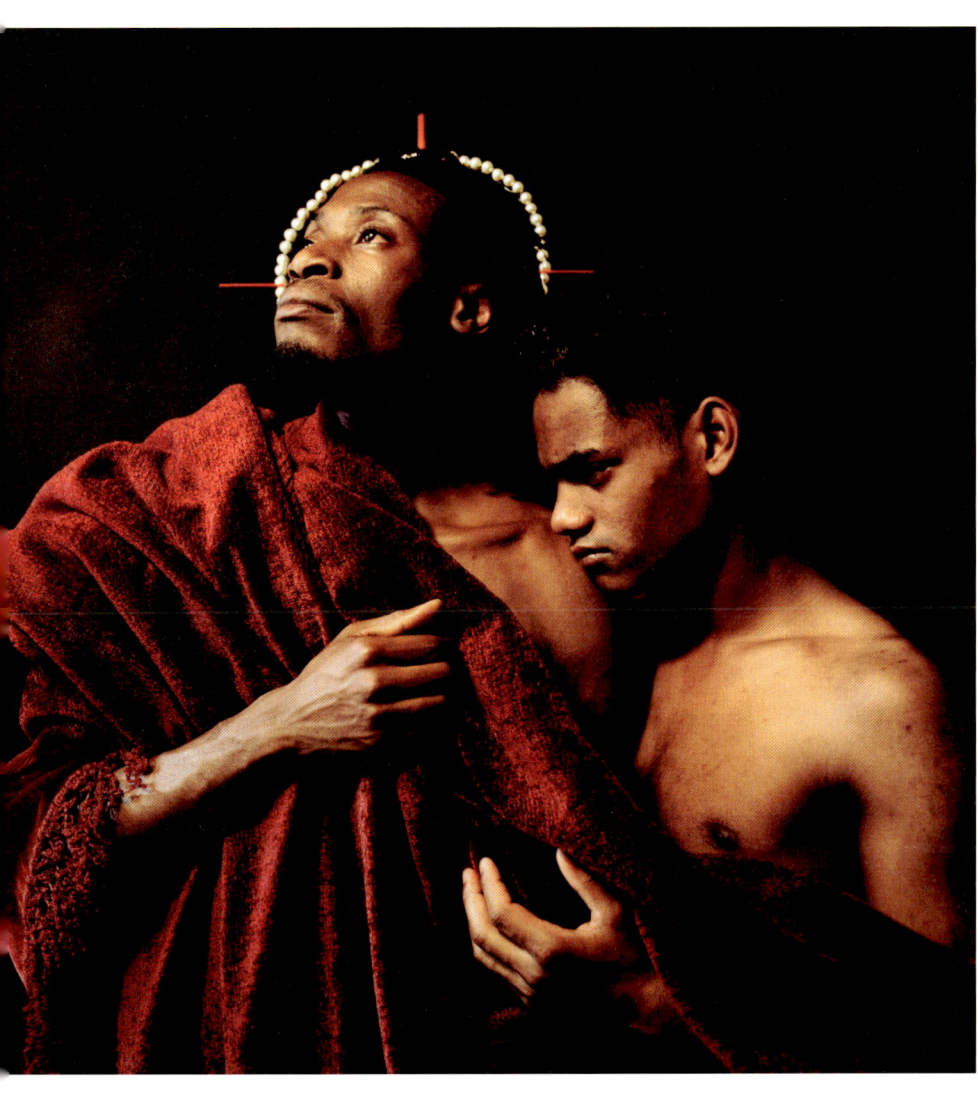

Clockwise from top left:

Clementine Hunter, *Cane River Baptism*, ca. 1950–56. Oil on paperboard, 19 × 23⅞ in. (48.3 × 60.7 cm). The Johnson Collection, Spartanburg, South Carolina

Paul Waters, *Beautiful Life*, 1969. Oil on cut linen collage on canvas, 46 × 60 in. (116.8 × 152.4 cm). Eric Firestone Gallery, New York

Horace Pippin, *Knowledge of God*, 1944. Oil on canvas, 21 × 29½ in. (53.3 × 24.9 cm). Collection of Leslie Miller and Richard Worley

Palmer Hayden, *Spirituals (Dreams)*, ca. 1935. Watercolor and graphite pencil on paper, 14¹¹⁄₁₆ × 9½ in. (37.3 × 24.1 cm). Whitney Museum of American Art, New York; purchase, with funds from the Drawing Committee, 2015.270a–b

Meta Vaux Warrick Fuller, *Te Adoremus Domine*, 1921. Painted plaster, 14¾ × 13½ in. (35.6 × 34.3 cm). Danforth Art Museum, Framingham, Massachusetts; gift of the Meta V.W. Fuller Trust, 2006.282

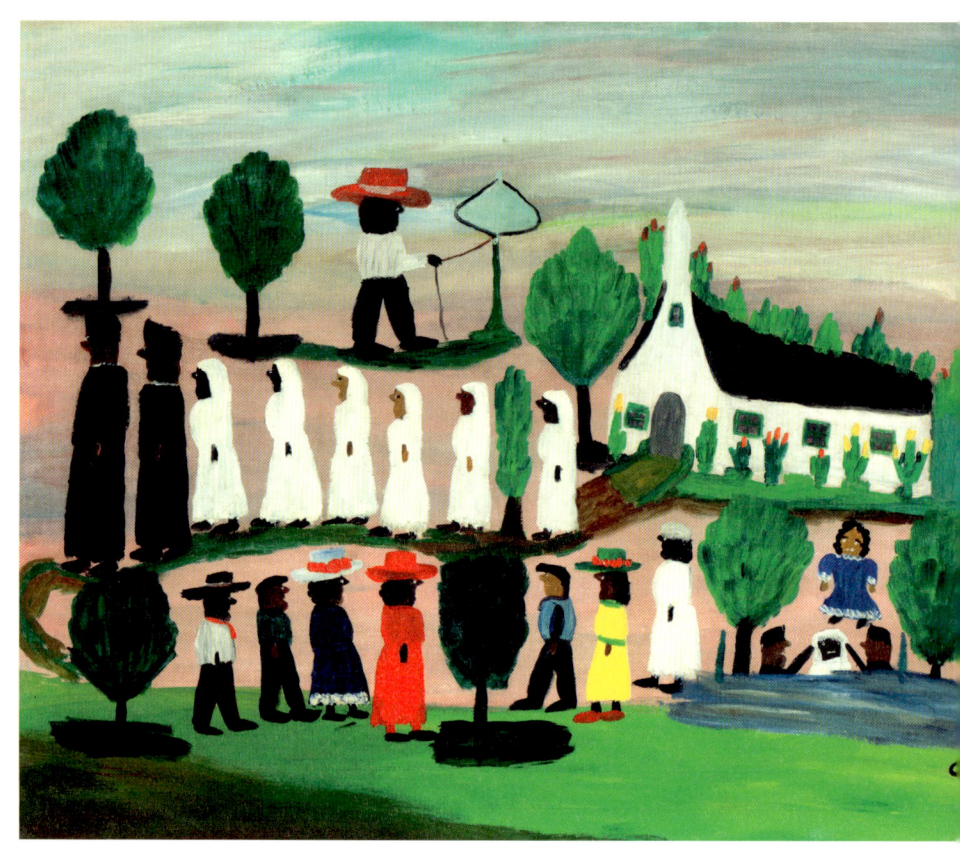

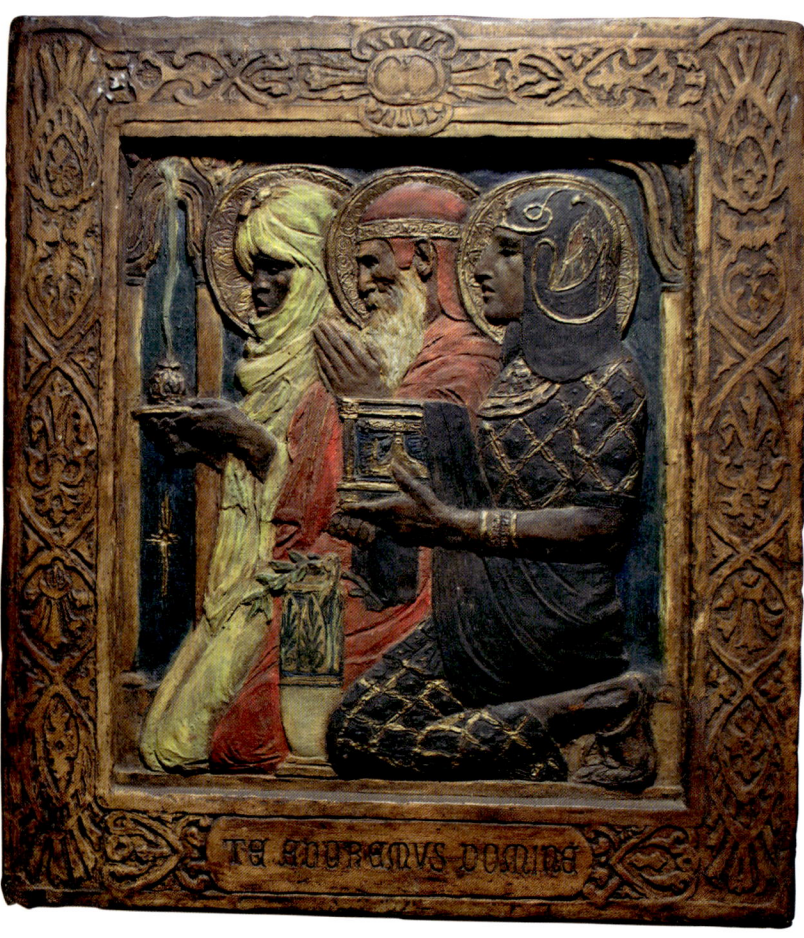

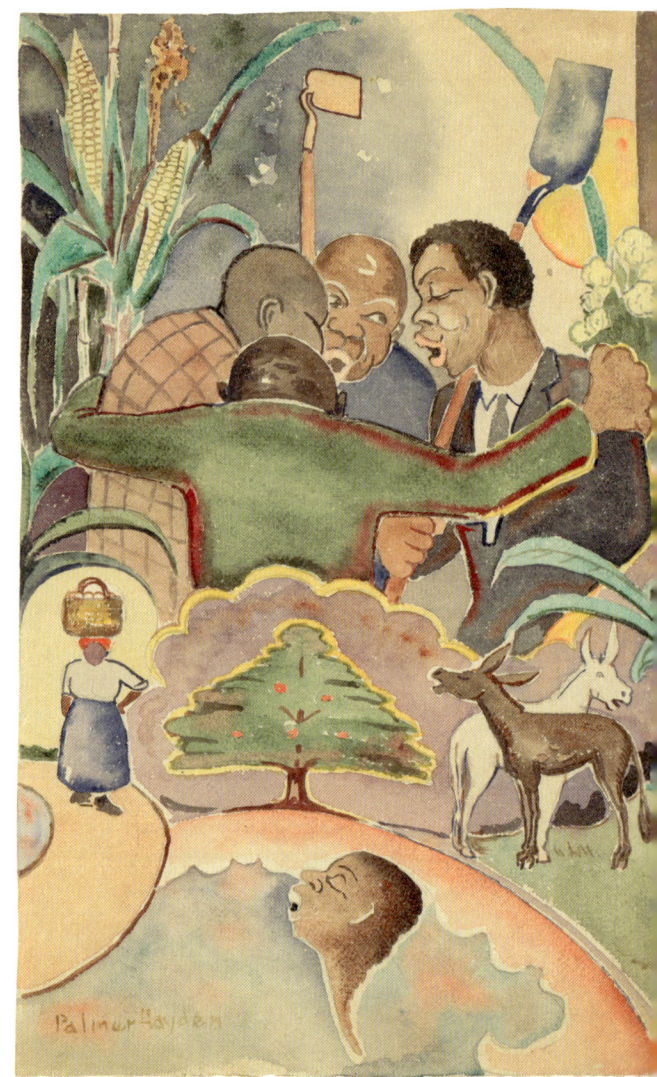

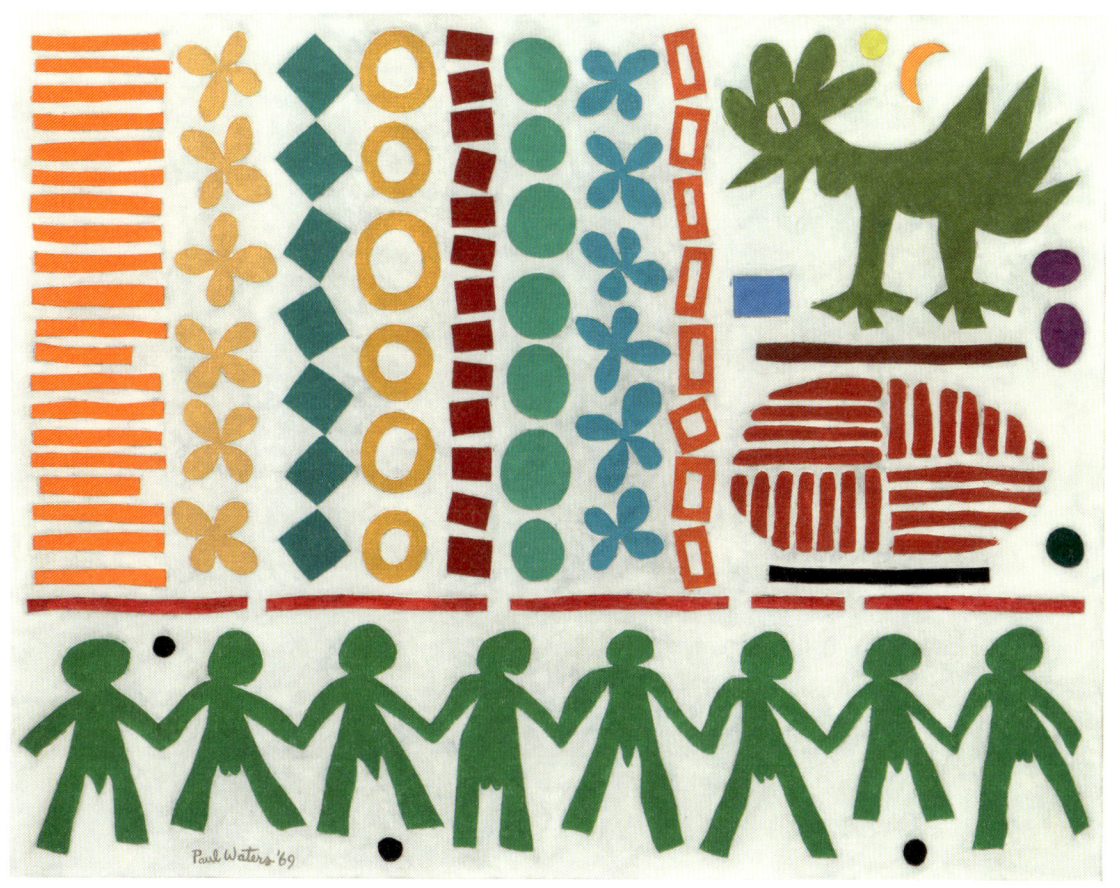

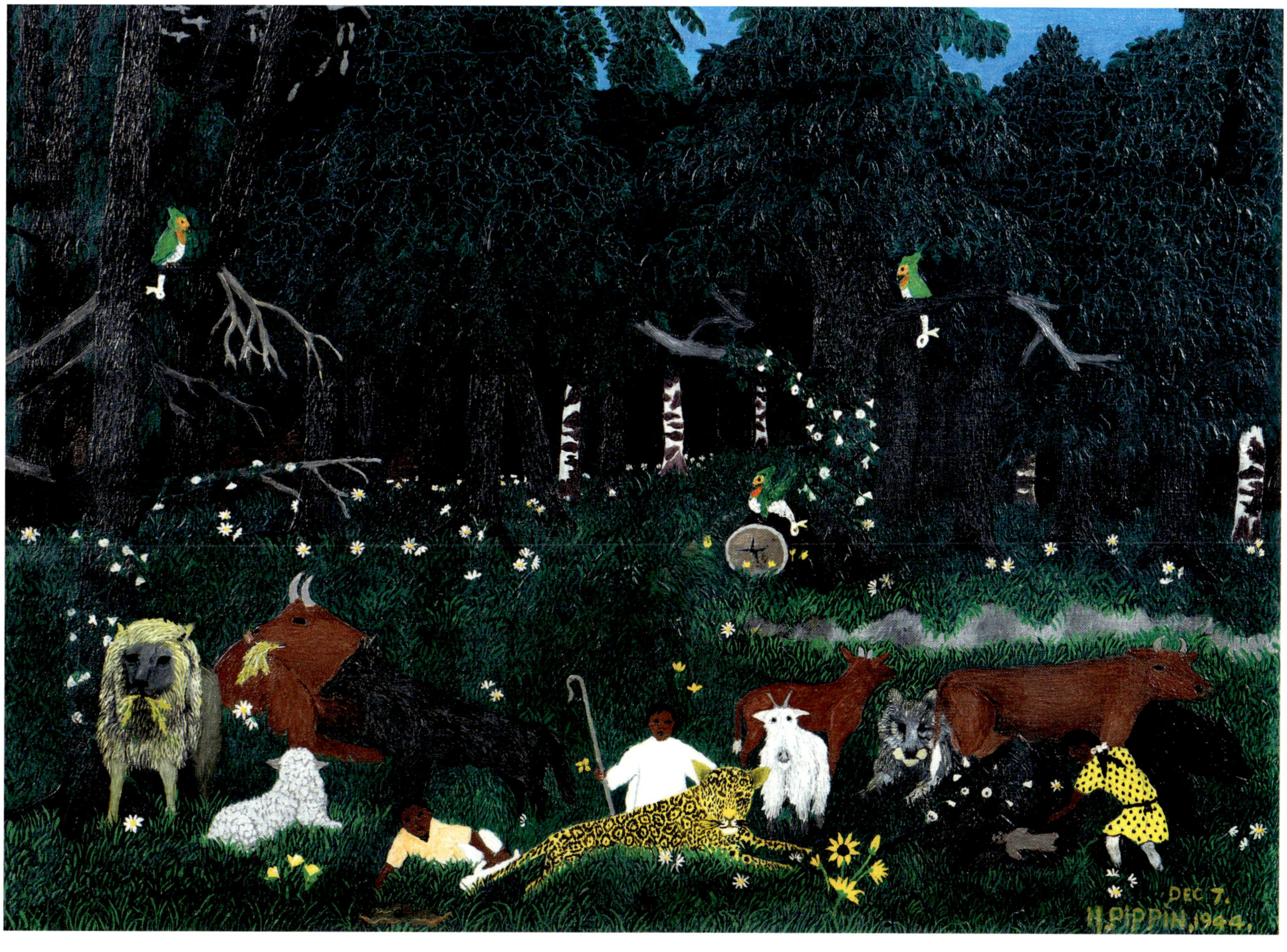

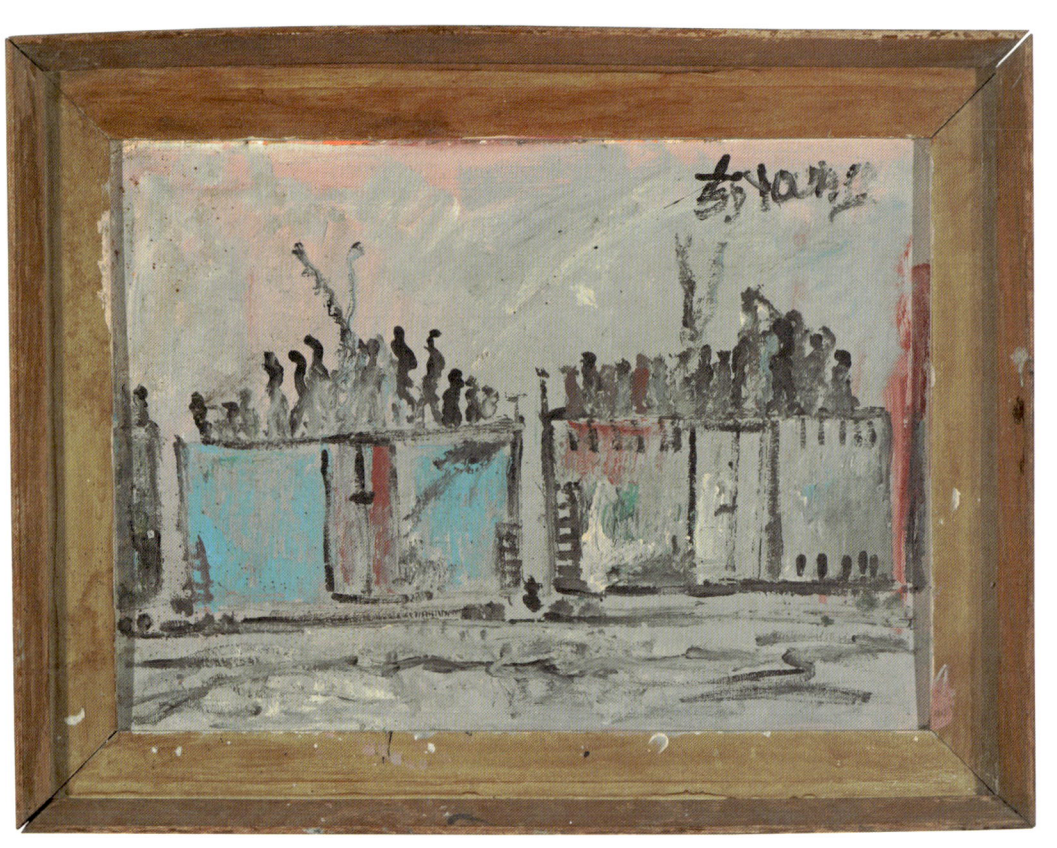
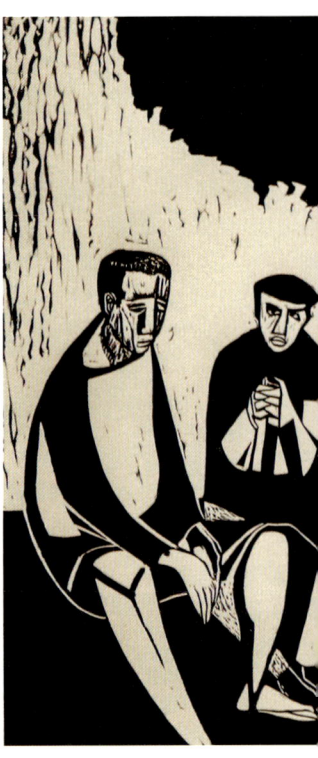
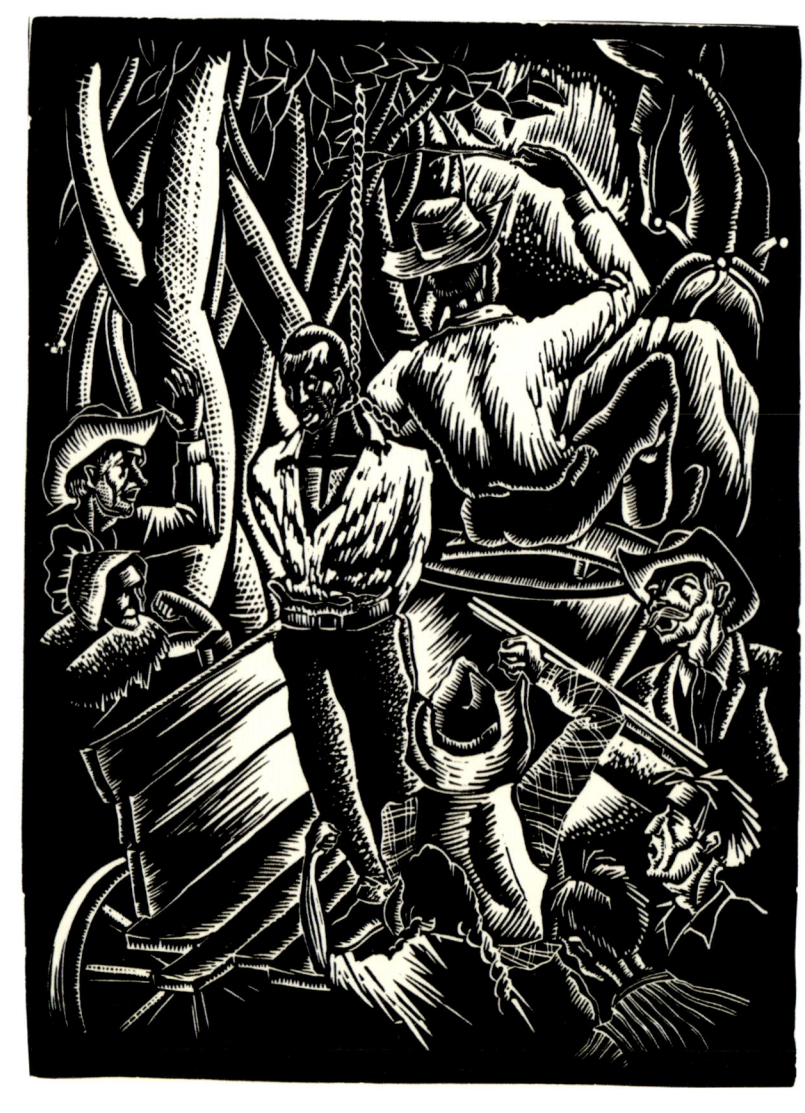

Clockwise from top left:

Purvis Young, *Black People Migrating West*, late 1970s. Paint and poster board, with wood frame, 21¼ × 28¼ in. (54 × 71.8 cm). High Museum of Art, Atlanta; museum purchase, and gift of the Souls Grown Deep Foundation from the William S. Arnett Collection, 2017.80

Samella Lewis, *Migrants*, 1968. Linocut on paper, 17¼ × 24 in. (43.8 × 61 cm). The Johnson Collection, Spartanburg, South Carolina

Martin Puryear, *The Rest*, 2009–10. Bronze, 45¾ × 35⁵⁄₁₆ × 20⅝ in. (116.2 × 89.7 × 52.4 cm). Whitney Museum of American Art, New York; gift of Gretchen and John Berggruen, 2014.350

William H. Johnson, *Moon over Harlem*, ca. 1943–44. Oil on plywood, 28½ × 35¾ in. (72.5 × 90.8 cm.). Smithsonian American Art Museum, Washington, DC; gift of the Harmon Foundation, 1967.59.57

Hale Aspacio Woodruff, *Giddap*, 1935 (printed 1996). Linoleum cut with chine-collé, 12 × 9 in. (30.5 × 22.9 cm). Whitney Museum of American Art, New York; gift of E. Thomas Williams, Jr. and Auldlyn Higgins Williams, 98.22.4

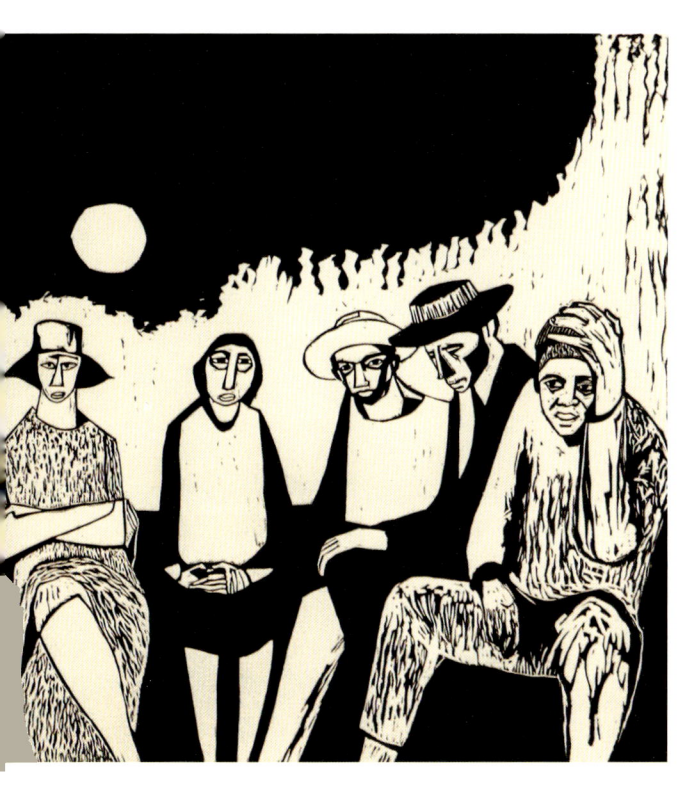
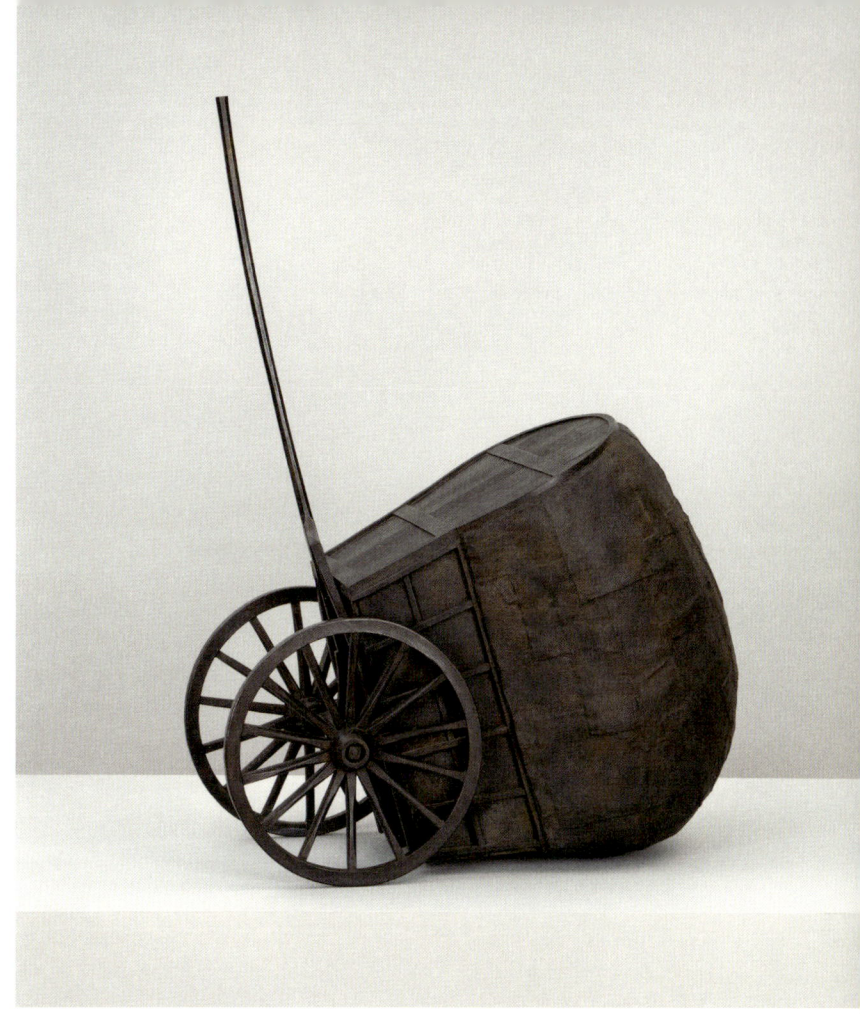

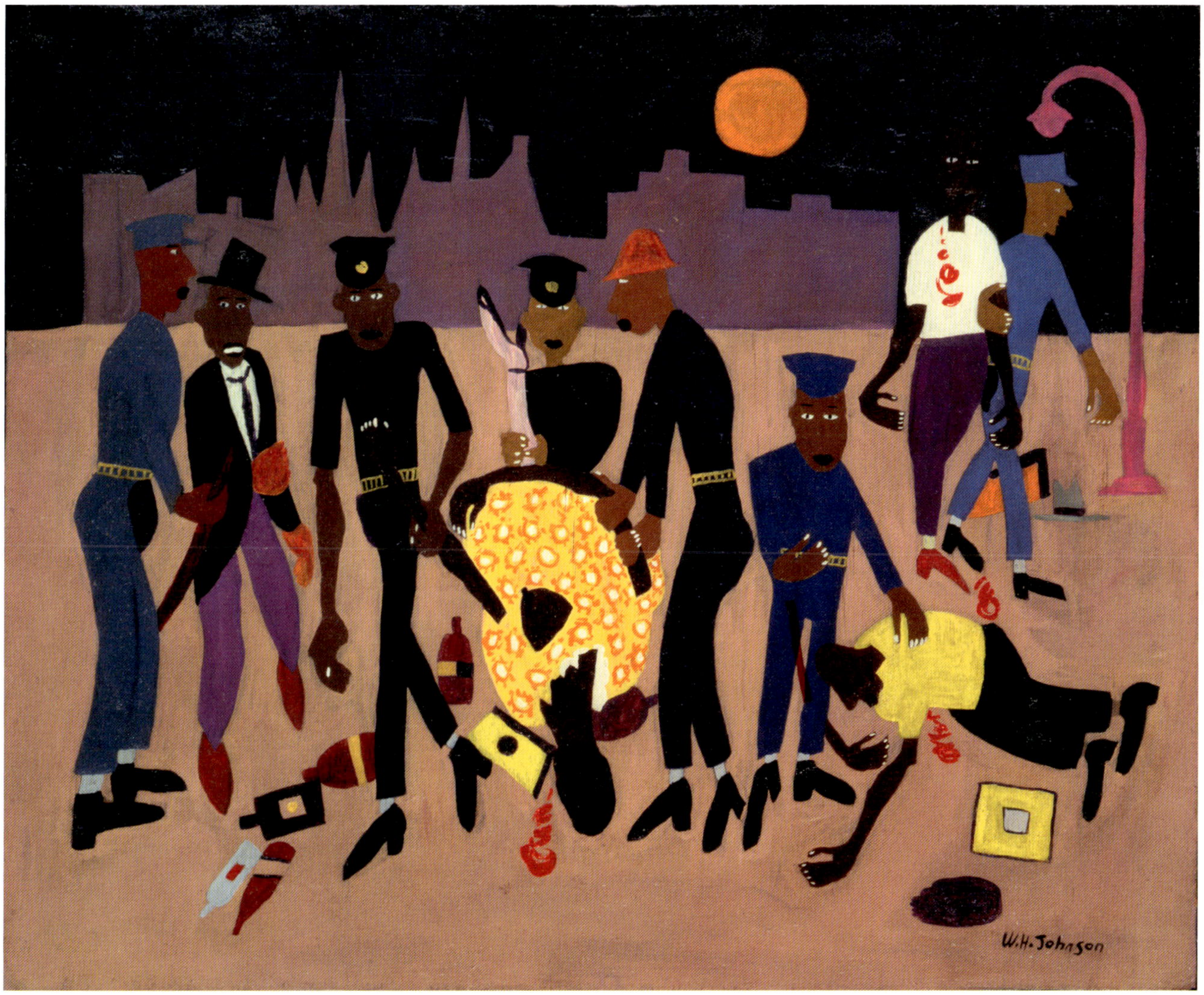

343

Clockwise from below:

Robert Duncanson, *View of Cincinnati, Ohio from Covington, Kentucky*, ca. 1851. Oil on canvas, 25 × 36 in. (63.5 × 91.4 cm). Cincinnati Museum Center

Thomas Nast, *Emancipation of the Negroes—The Past and the Future (from "Harper's Weekly")*, 1863. Wood engraving, 14 5/8 × 20 11/16 in. (37.2 × 52.6 cm). The Metropolitan Museum of Art, New York; Harris Brisbane Dick Fund, 1929, 29.88.4(10)

Meta Vaux Warrick Fuller, *Mold for Crusaders for Freedom*, 1962. Plaster with mold release agent, diameter: 36 in. (91.4 cm). Danforth Art Museum, Framingham, Massachusetts; gift of the Meta V.W. Fuller Trust, 2006.310

Melvin Edwards, *Cup of?*, from the series *Lynch Fragment*, 1988. Steel, 12 7/8 × 6 3/4 × 9 1/2 in. (32.7 × 17 × 24 cm). The Museum of Modern Art, New York; purchase, 243.1990

Melvin Edwards, *Katutura*, from the series *Lynch Fragment*, 1986. Steel, 11 3/4 × 5 7/8 × 4 7/8 in. (30 × 15 × 12.3 cm). The Museum of Modern Art, New York; purchase, 242.1990

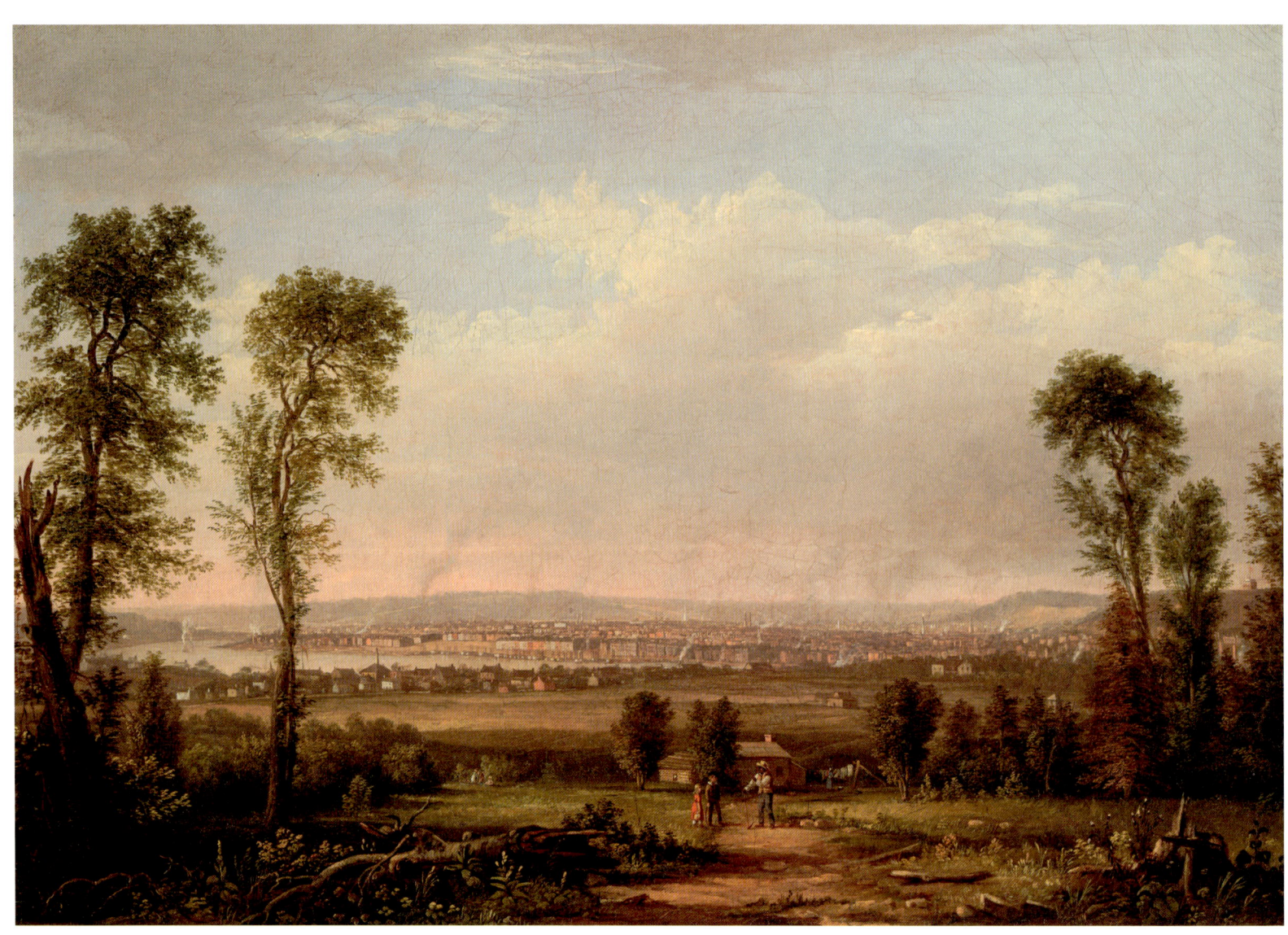

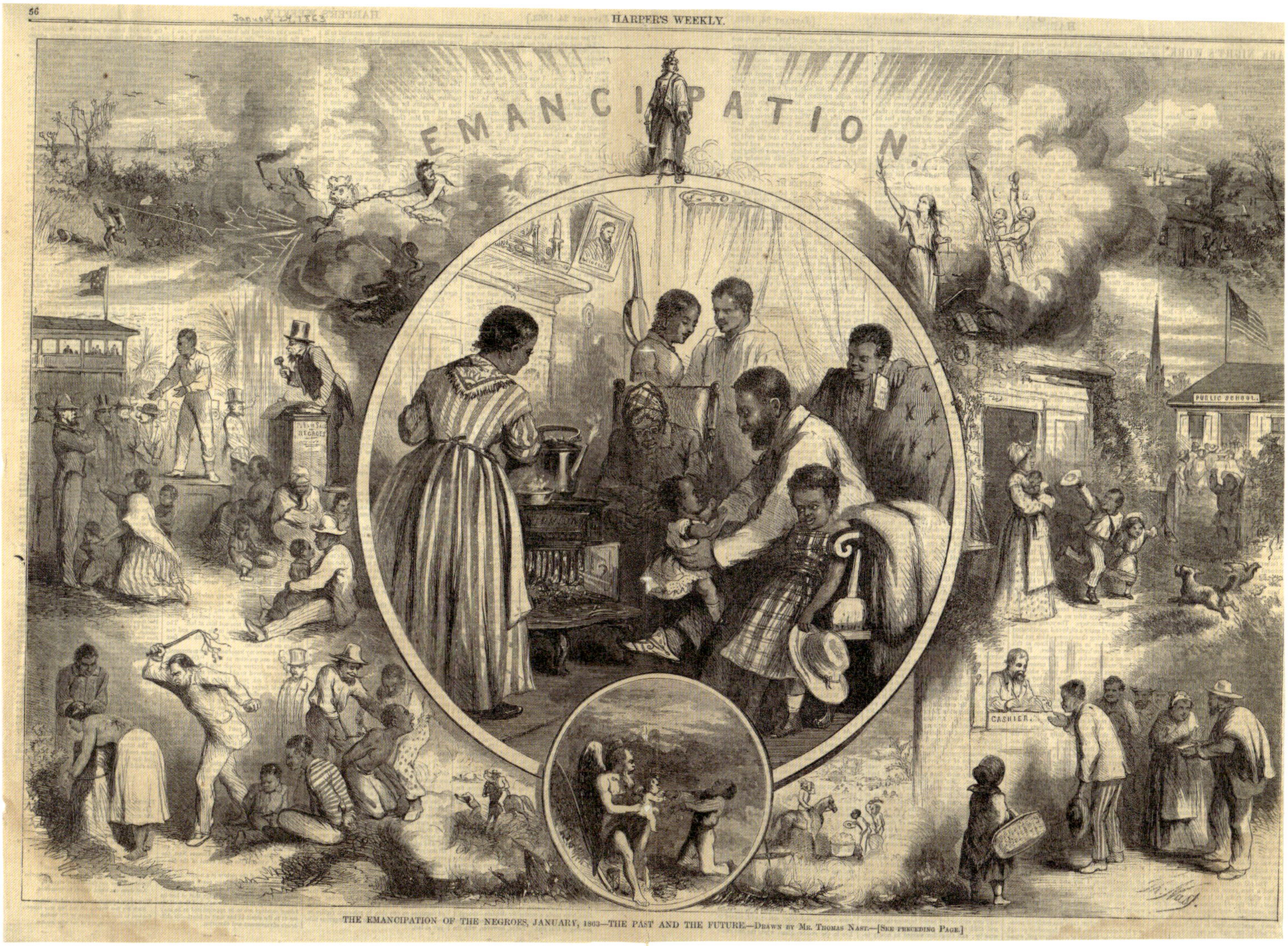

THE EMANCIPATION OF THE NEGROES, JANUARY, 1863—THE PAST AND THE FUTURE—Drawn by Mr. Thomas Nast.—[See preceding Page.]

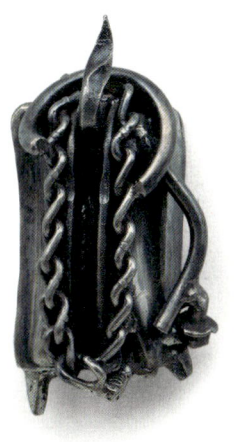

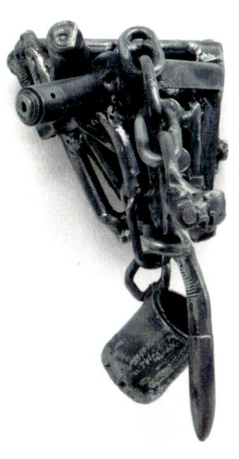

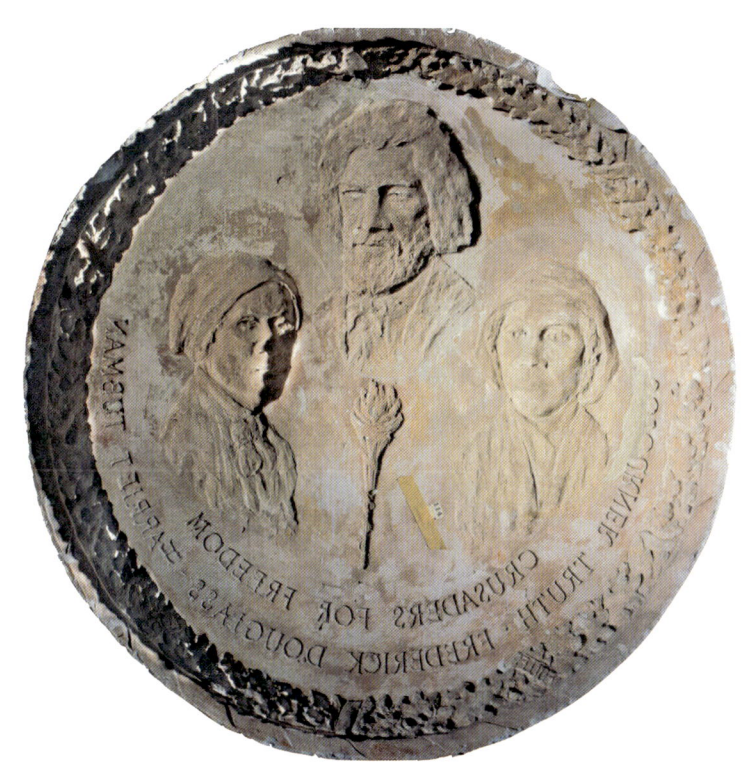

345

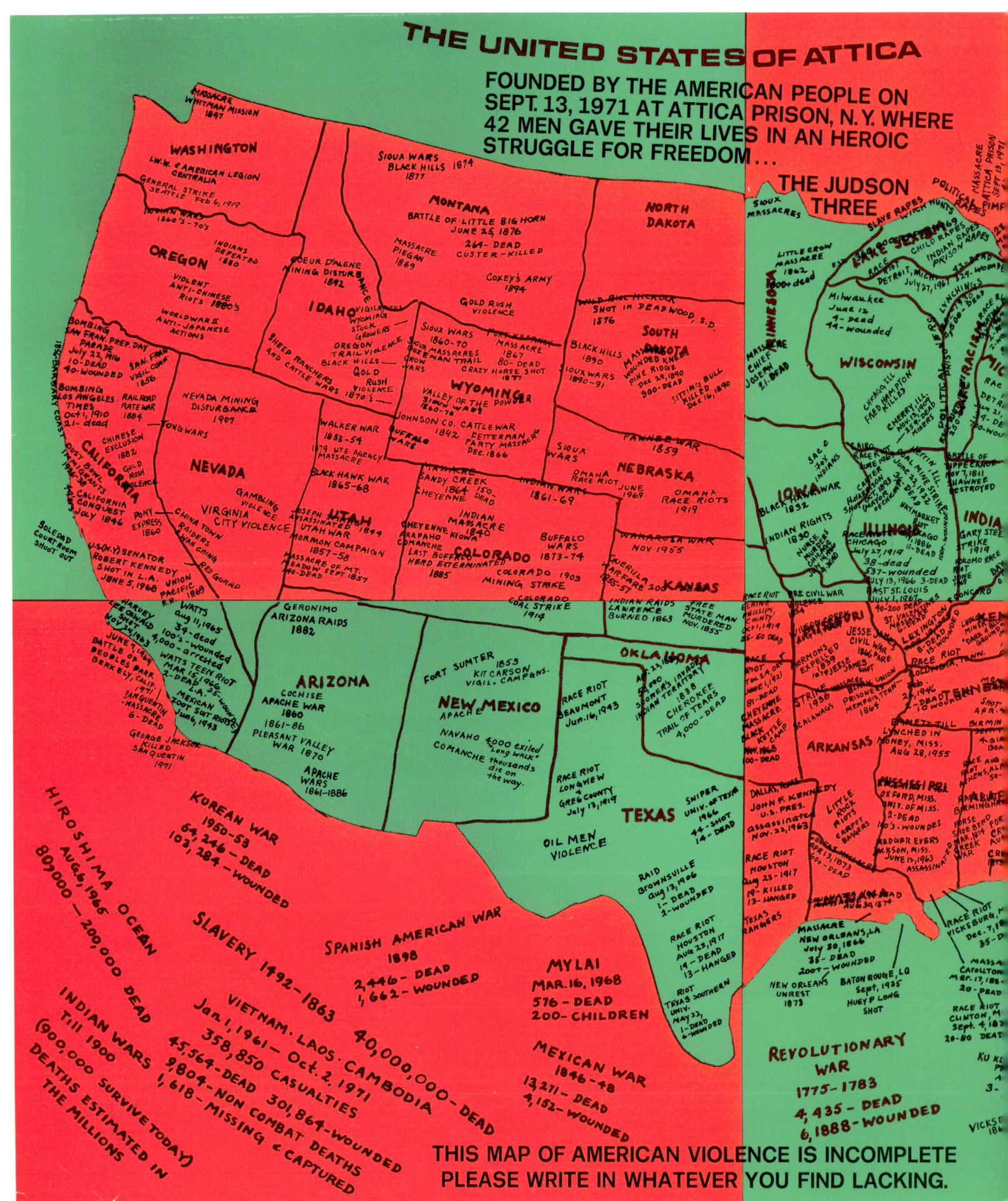

Faith Ringgold, *United States of Attica*, 1971. Offset lithograph, 21 3/8 × 27 3/16 in. (54.3 × 69.1 cm). Whitney Museum of American Art, New York; gift of ACA Galleries in honor of Faith Ringgold, 2017.163

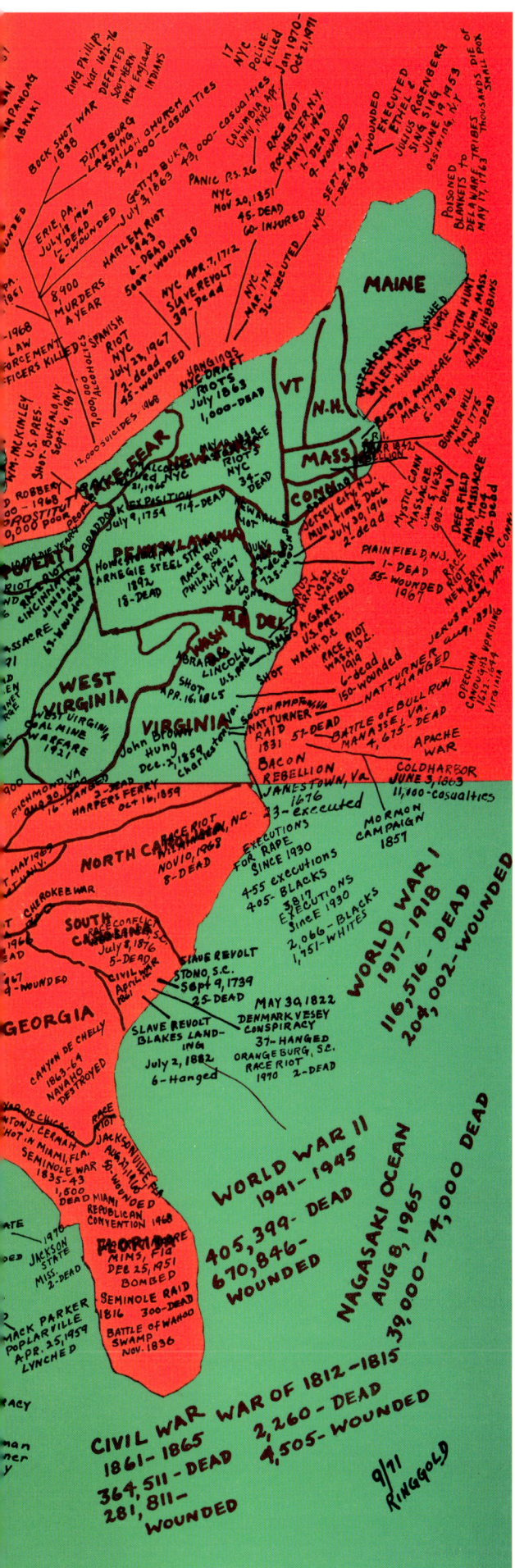
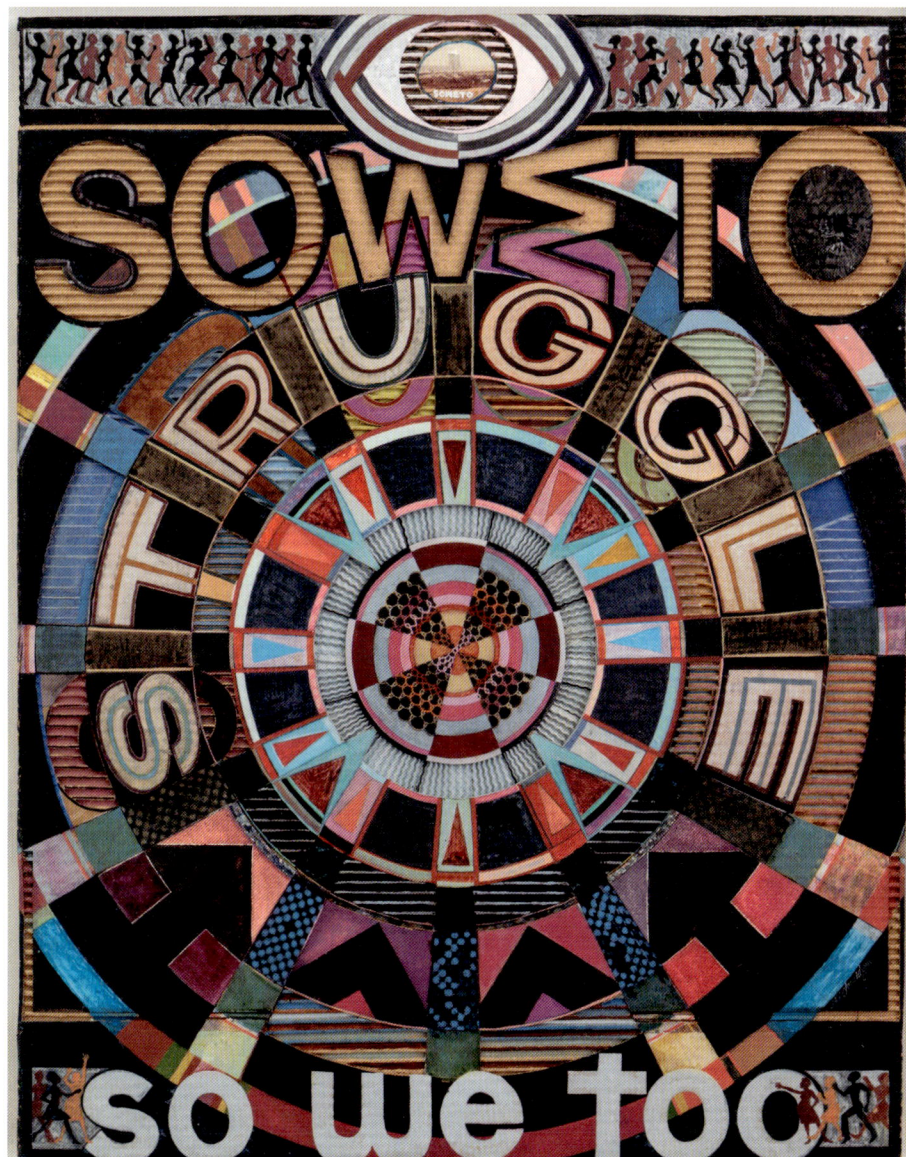
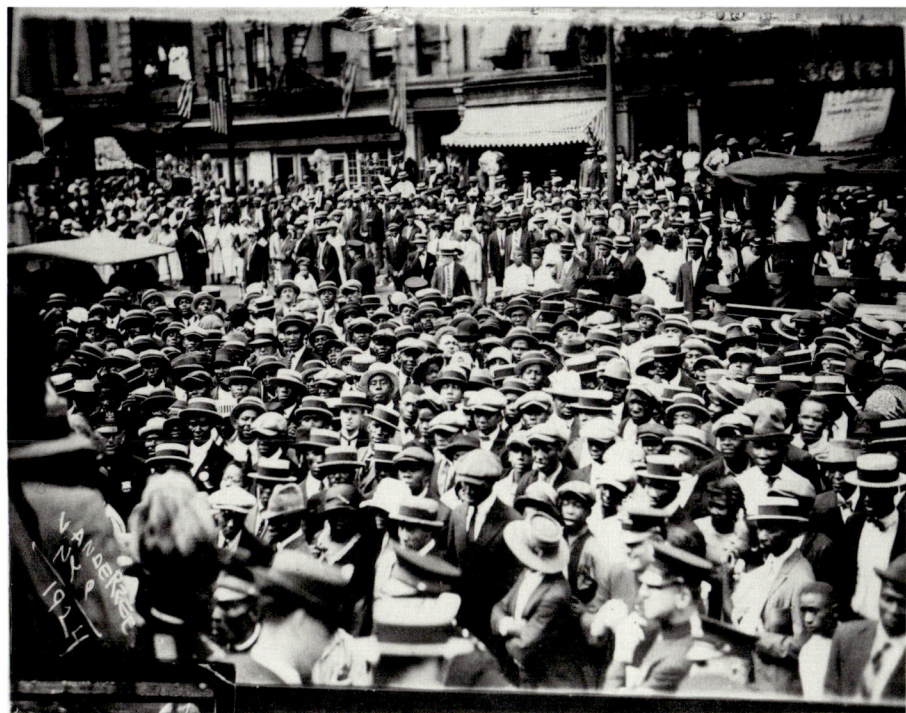

Jeff Donaldson, *Soweto/So We Too*, 1979. Mixed media, 39 × 30½ in. (99.1 × 77.5 cm). Collection of Beth Rudin DeWoody

James Van Der Zee, *Marcus Garvey Rally*, 1924. Gelatin silver print, 7⅛ × 9⅜ in. (18.1 × 23.8 cm). Whitney Museum of American Art, New York; gift of Manny and Skippy Gerard, 2003.416

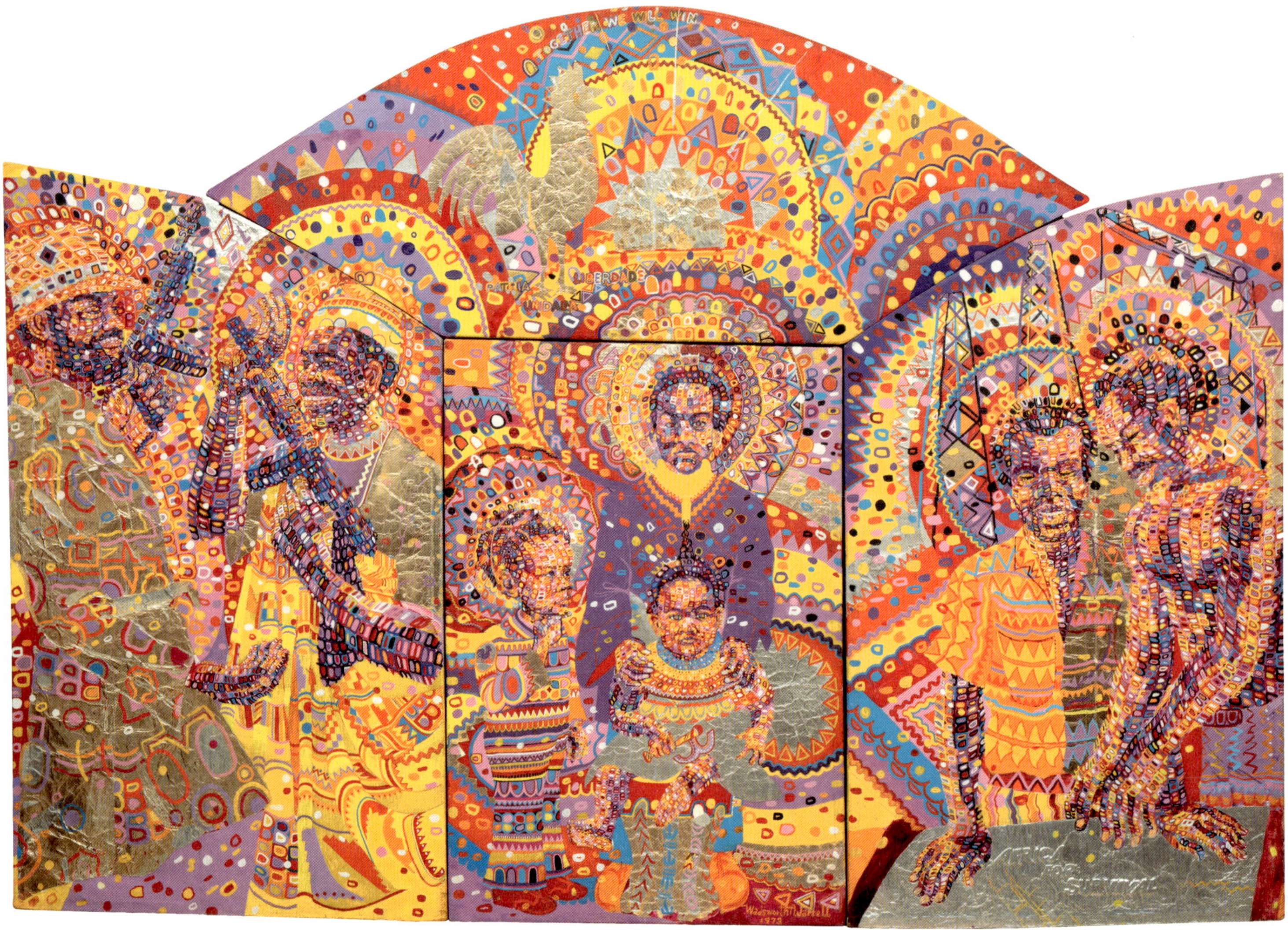

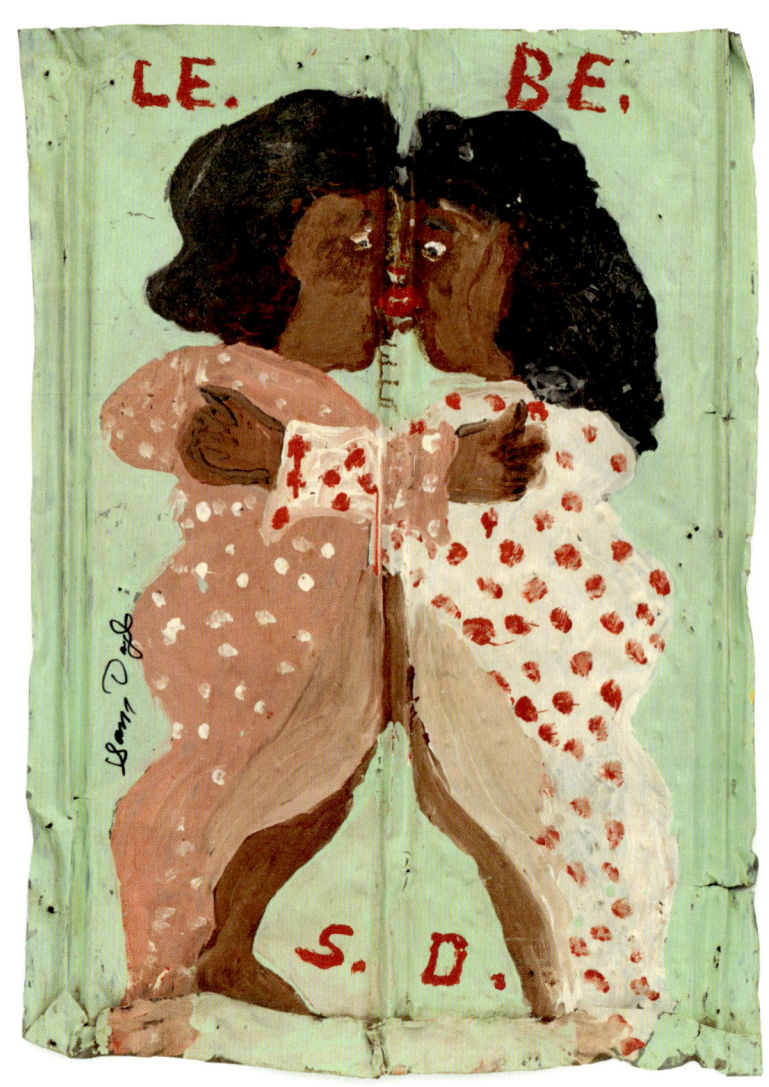

Clockwise from top left:

Wadsworth Jarrell, *Together We Will Win*, 1973. Acrylic and foil on canvas, 60 × 84 in. (152.4 × 213.4 cm). Jenkins Johnson Gallery, San Francisco

Sam Doyle, *Frank Capers*, 1970. Paint and marker on wood, 33 × 20¼ in. (83.8 × 51.4 cm). Souls Grown Deep Foundation

Joe Overstreet, *Purple Flight*, 1971. Acrylic on constructed canvas with metal grommets and cotton rope, dimensions variable. Eric Firestone Gallery, New York

Theaster Gates, *Minority Majority*, 2012. Decommissioned fire hoses and vinyl on plywood, 66 × 111½ × 3¾ in. (167.6 × 283.2 × 9.5 cm). Whitney Museum of American Art, New York; gift of Barbara and Michael Gamson, 2016.262

Sam Doyle, *LeBe*, 1970s. Paint on tin, 37½ × 26¾ in. (95.3 × 67.9 cm). Souls Grown Deep Foundation

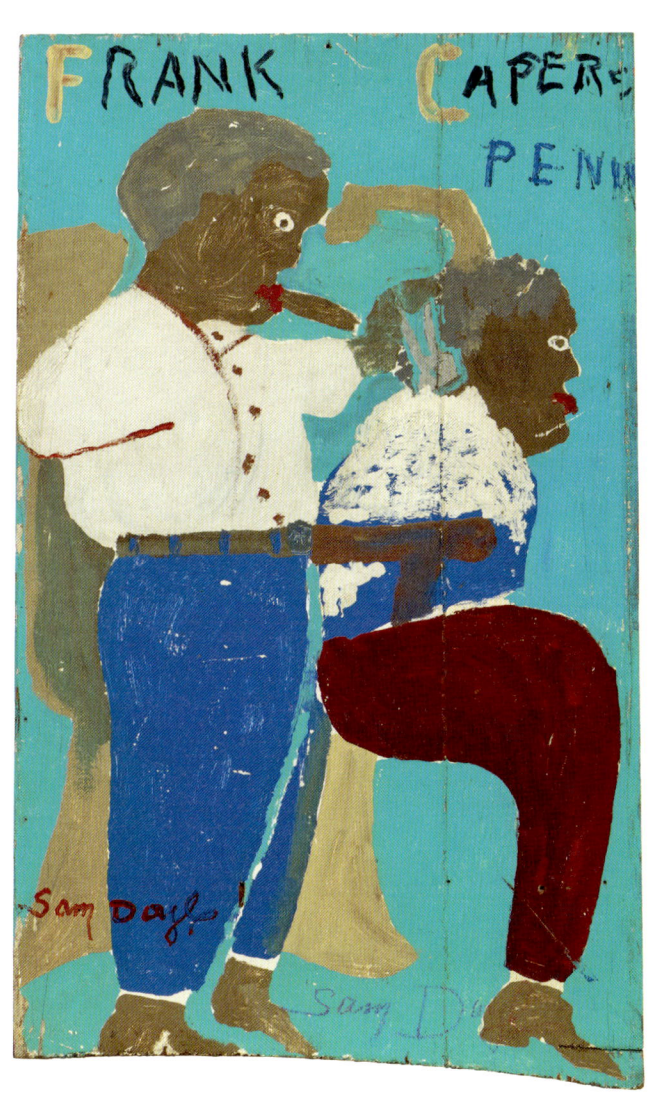
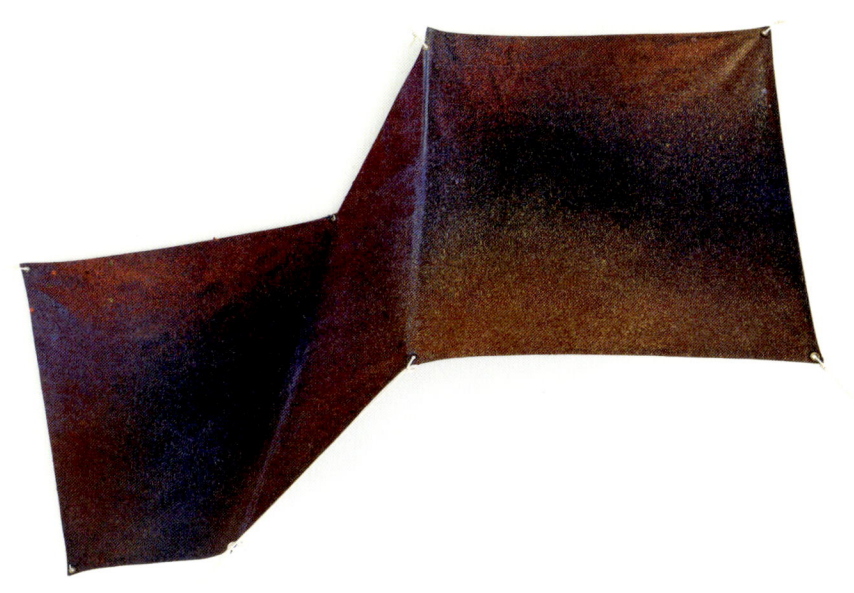
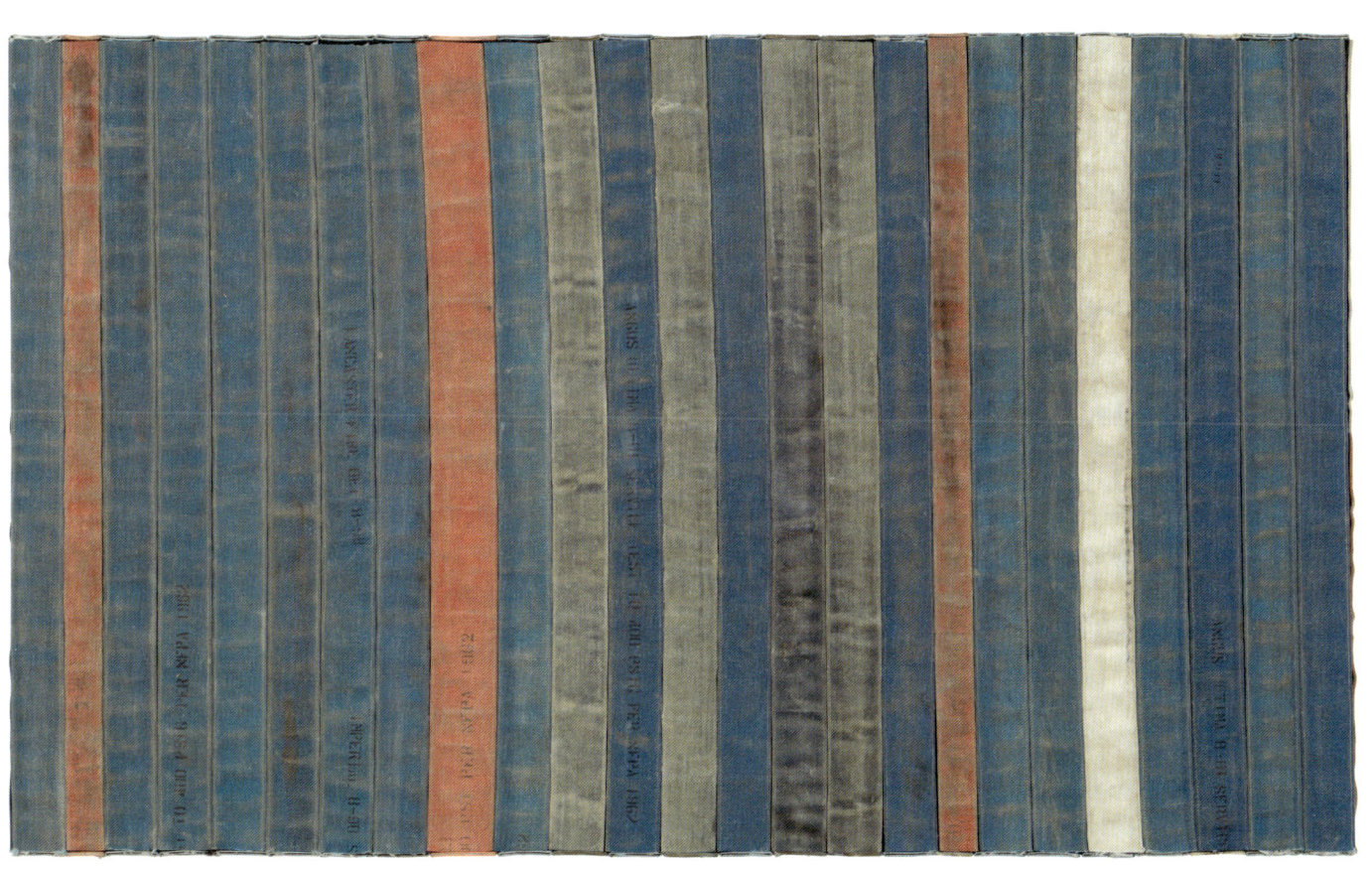

349

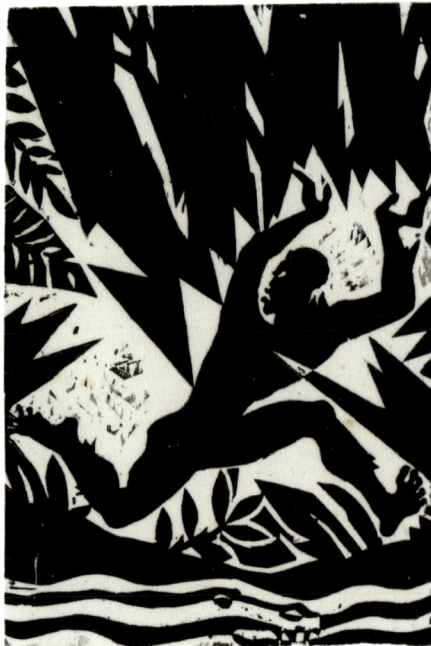

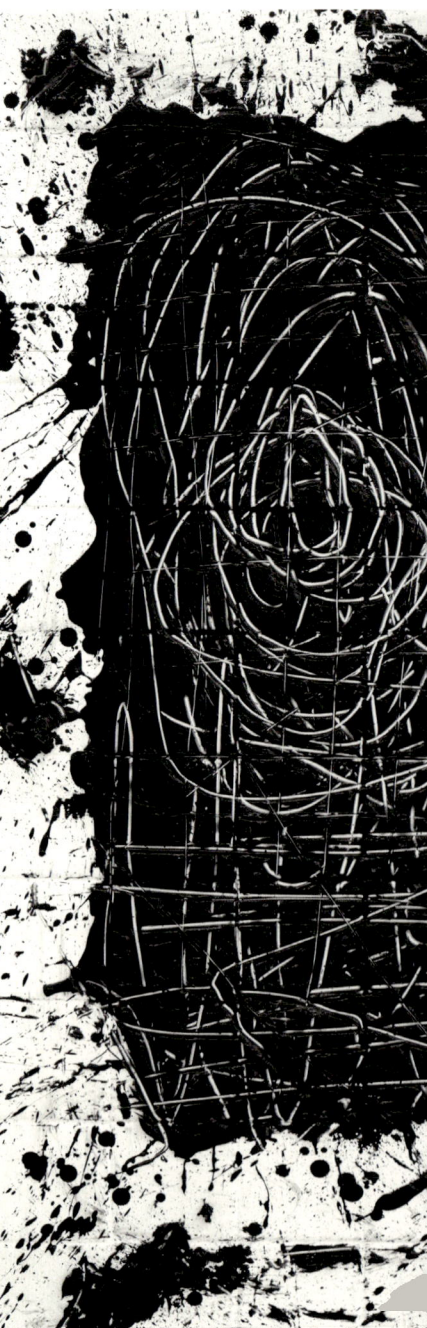

Sam Gilliam, *Untitled (Black)*, 1978. Acrylic, yarn, and cut canvas on stained canvas, 89¾ × 120½ in. (228 × 306.1 cm). Whitney Museum of American Art, New York; gift of Suzanne and Bob Cochran, 94.161

James Little, *Stars and Stripes*, 2021. Oil and wax on linen, 72¼ × 72¼ in. (183.5 × 183.5 cm). Whitney Museum of American Art, New York; purchase, with funds from Marcia Dunn and Jonathan Sobel, 2022.207

Clockwise from top right:

David Hammons, *Untitled*, 1992. Human hair, wire, metallic mylar, sledgehammer, plastic beads, string, metal food tin, panty hose, leather, tea bags, and feathers, dimensions variable. Whitney Museum of American Art, New York; purchase, with funds from the Mrs. Percy Uris Bequest and the Painting and Sculpture Committee, 92.128a–z

Glenn Ligon, *Stranger in the Village #12*, 1998. Enamel, oil, acrylic, gesso, coal dust, and glitter on cotton, 96 × 72⅛ in. (243.8 × 183.2 cm). Whitney Museum of American Art, New York; gift of the artist and purchase, with funds from Joanne Leonhardt Cassullo and the Dorothea L. Leonhardt Fund at the Communities Foundation of Texas and the Painting and Sculpture Committee, 98.55

Rashid Johnson, *Untitled Anxious Men*, 2016. Ceramic tile, black soap, and wax, 47½ × 34¼ in. (120.7 × 87 cm). Collection of the artist

Aaron Douglas, *Flight*, 1926. Woodcut, 8 × 5½ in. (20.3 × 14 cm). Whitney Museum of American Art, New York; promised gift of Crystal McCrary and Raymond J. McGuire to the Whitney Museum of American Art, New York, and The Studio Museum in Harlem, P.2022.3.2

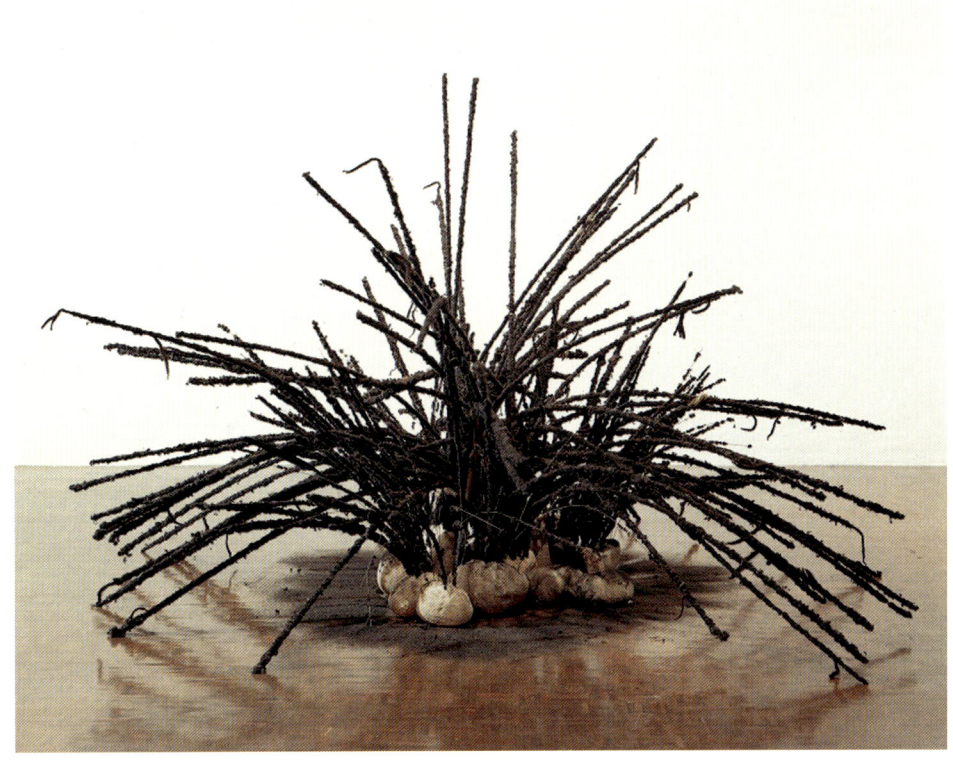
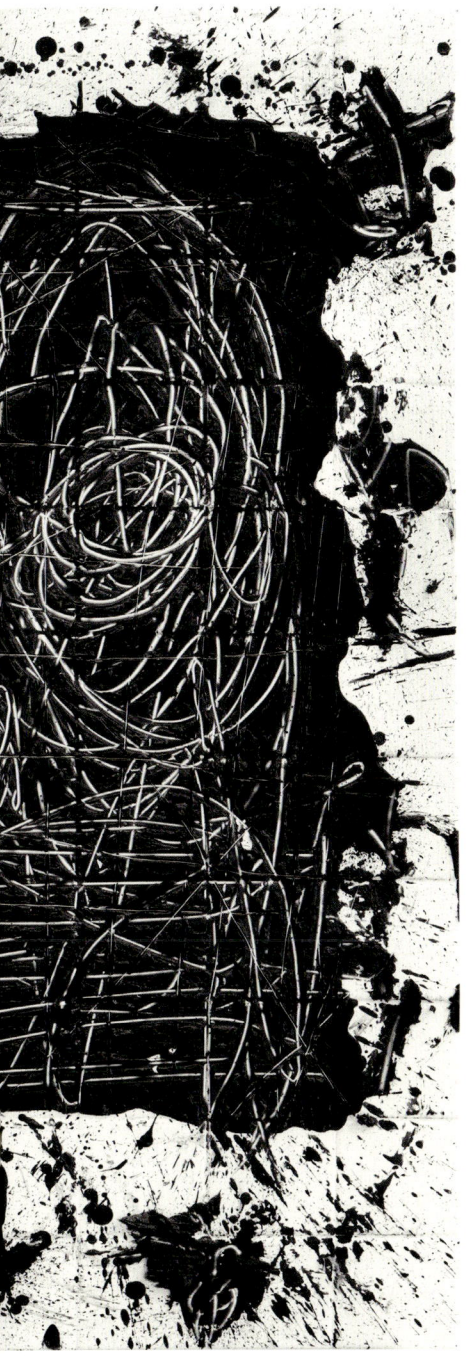

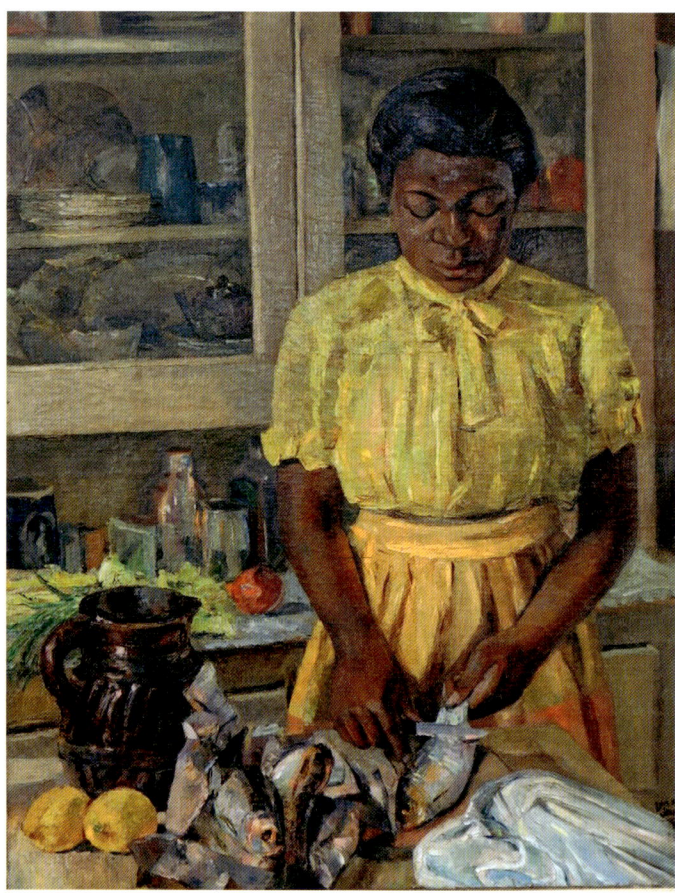

Clockwise from top left:

Loïs Mailou Jones, *Jennie*, 1943. Oil on canvas, 35¾ × 28¾ in. (90.8 × 73 cm). Howard University Gallery of Art, Washington, DC; gift of the IBM Corporation

Emma Amos, *Judith Jamison as Josephine Baker*, 1985. Acrylic on canvas, 100 × 32 in. (254 × 81.3 cm). Ryan Lee Gallery, New York

Mickalene Thomas, *Clarivel Face Forward Gazing*, 2024. Rhinestones, acrylic, and oil on canvas mounted on wood panel, 96 × 144 in. (243.8 × 365.8 cm). Collection of the artist

Beauford Delaney, *Marian Anderson*, 1965. Oil and egg tempera emulsion on canvas, 63 15/16 × 51 5/16 × 1½ in. (162.4 × 130.3 × 3.8 cm). Virginia Museum of Fine Arts, Richmond; J. Harwood and Louise B. Cochrane Fund for American Art, 2012.277

Geoffrey Holder, *Portrait of Carmen de Lavallade*, 1976. Oil on canvas with artist frame, 60 × 40 in. (152.4 × 101.6 cm). Collection of Jordan Roth and Richie Jackson

Mary Lovelace O'Neal, *Race Woman Series #7*, 1990s. Mixed media on canvas, 84 × 60 in. (213.4 × 152.4 cm). Jenkins Johnson Gallery, San Francisco

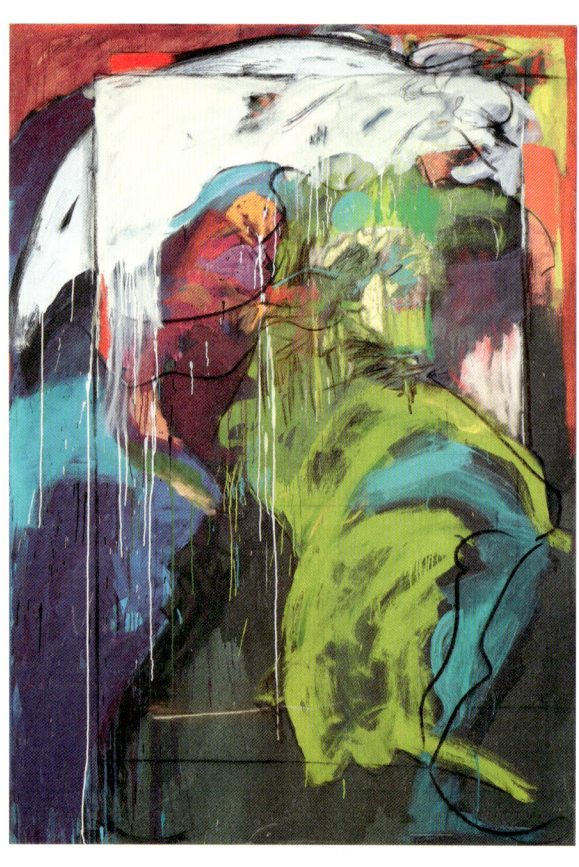

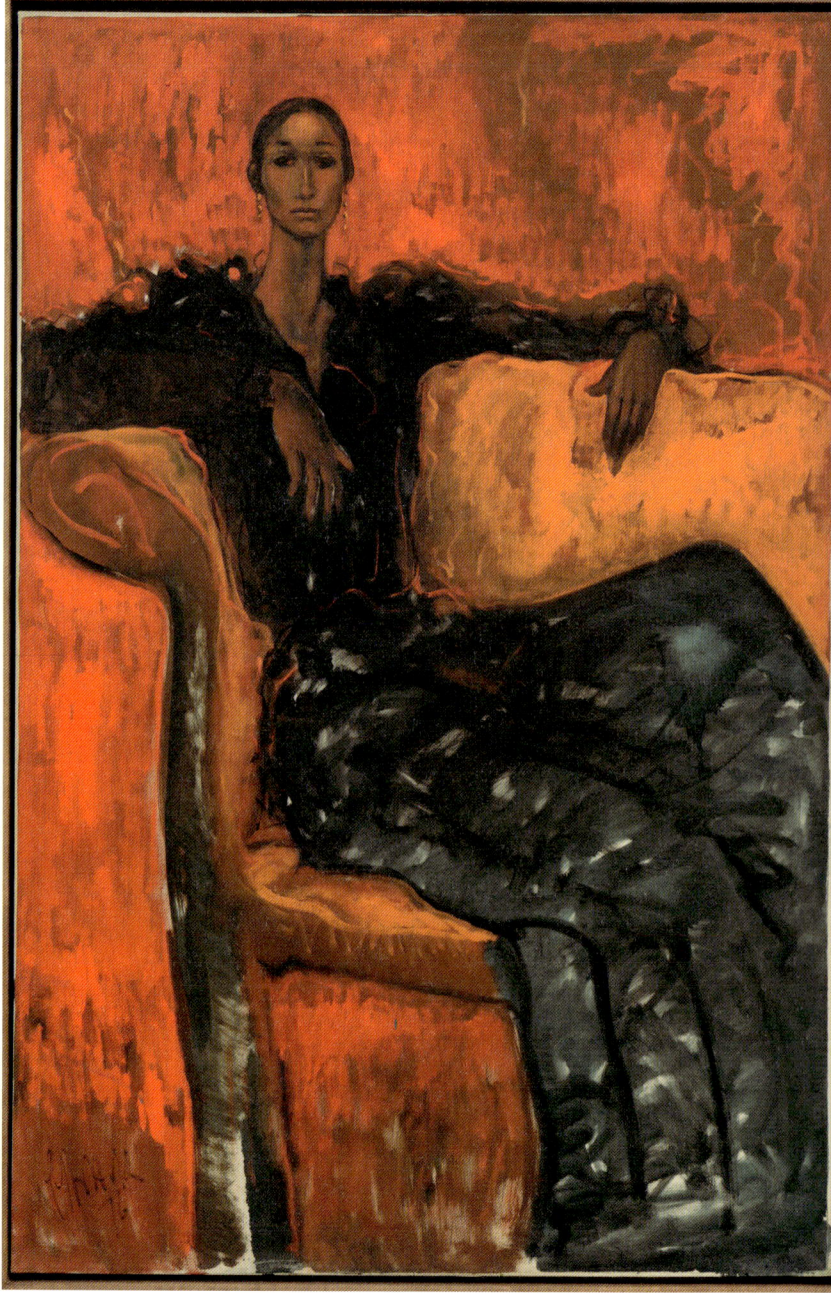

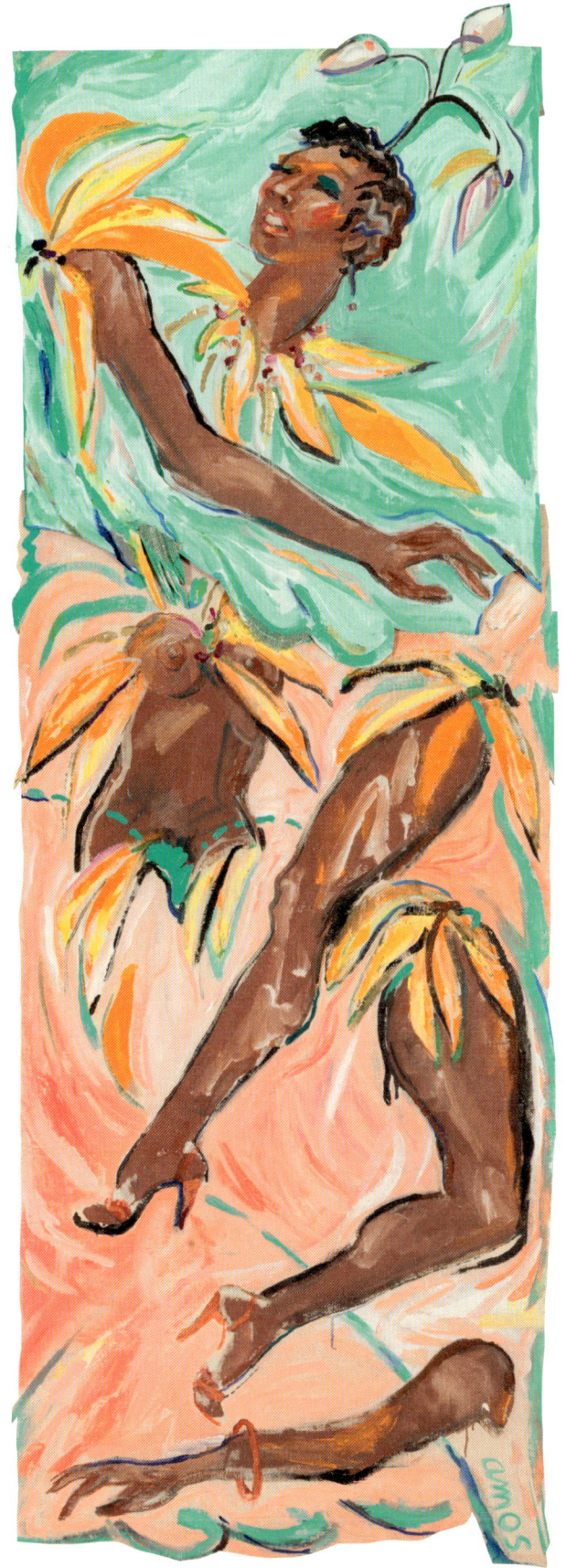
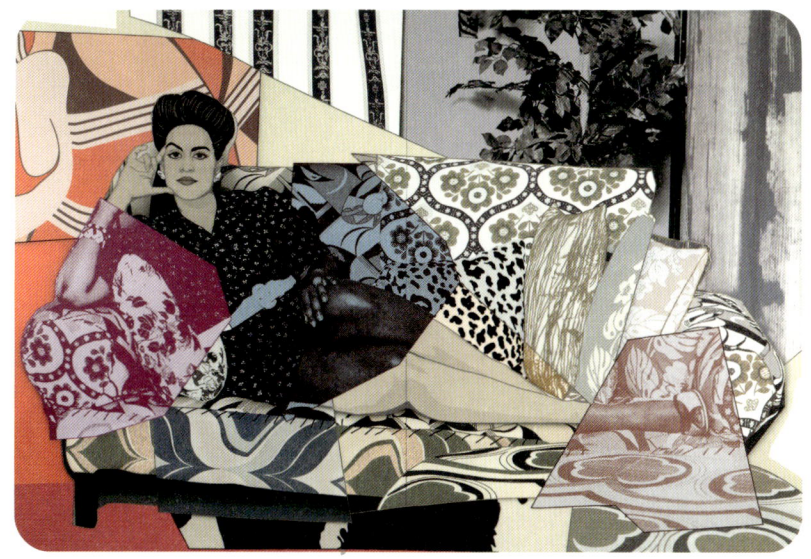
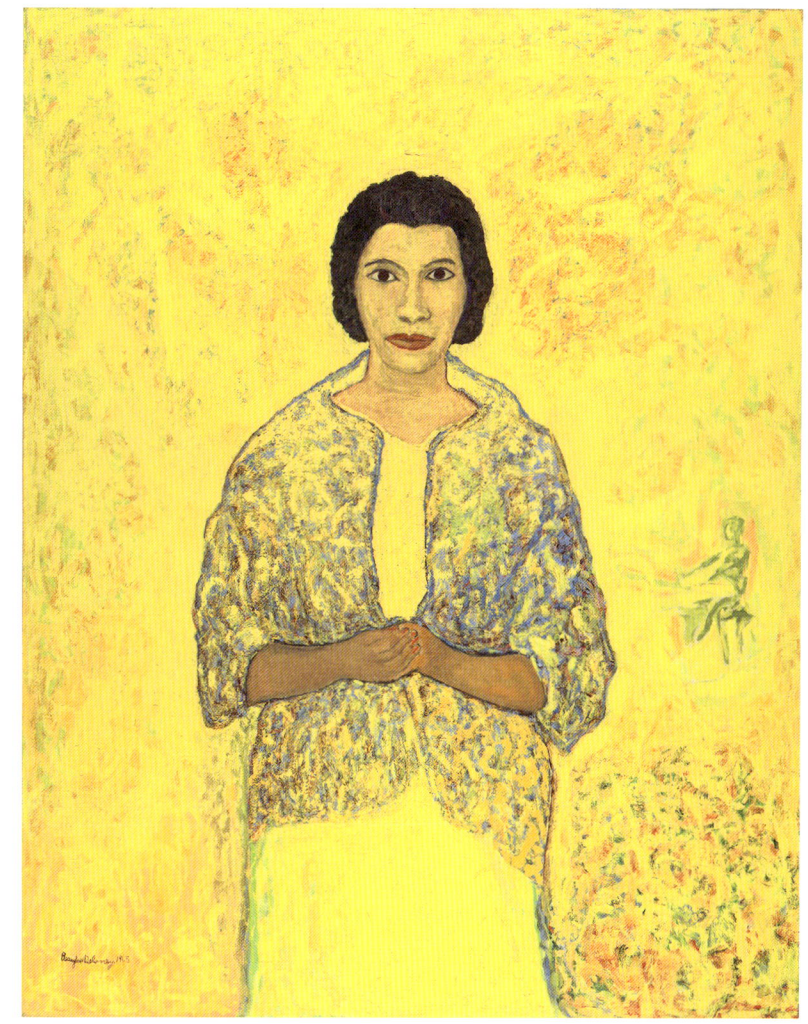

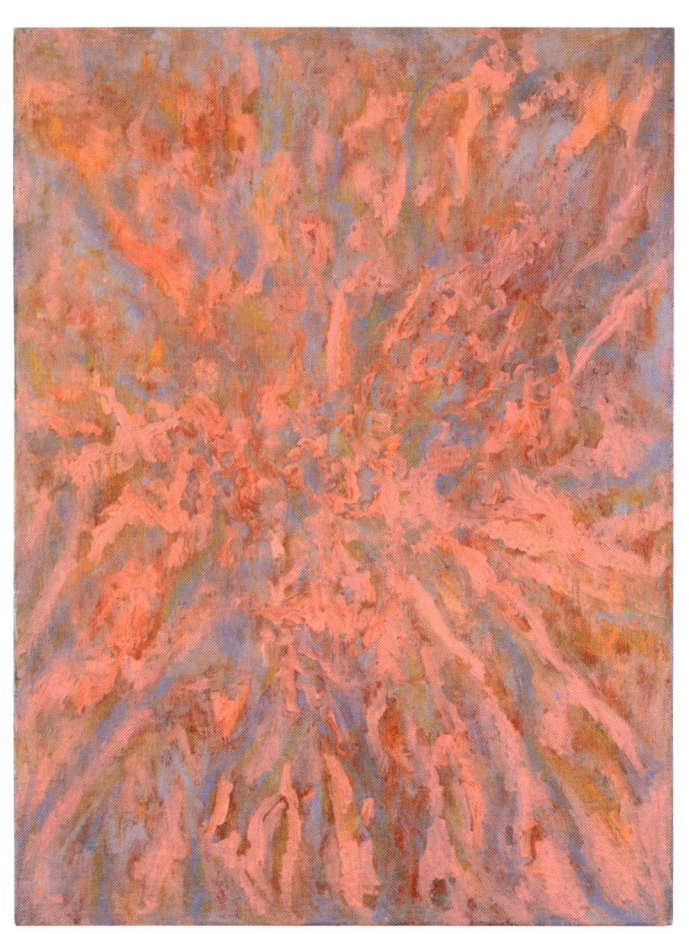
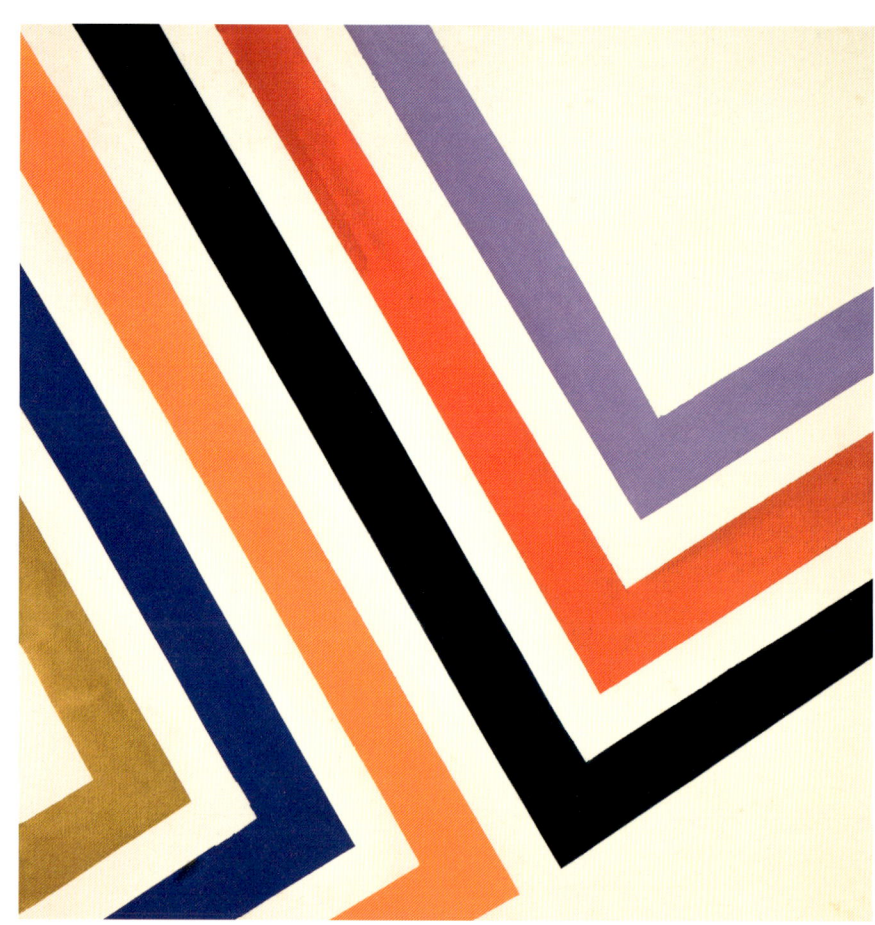
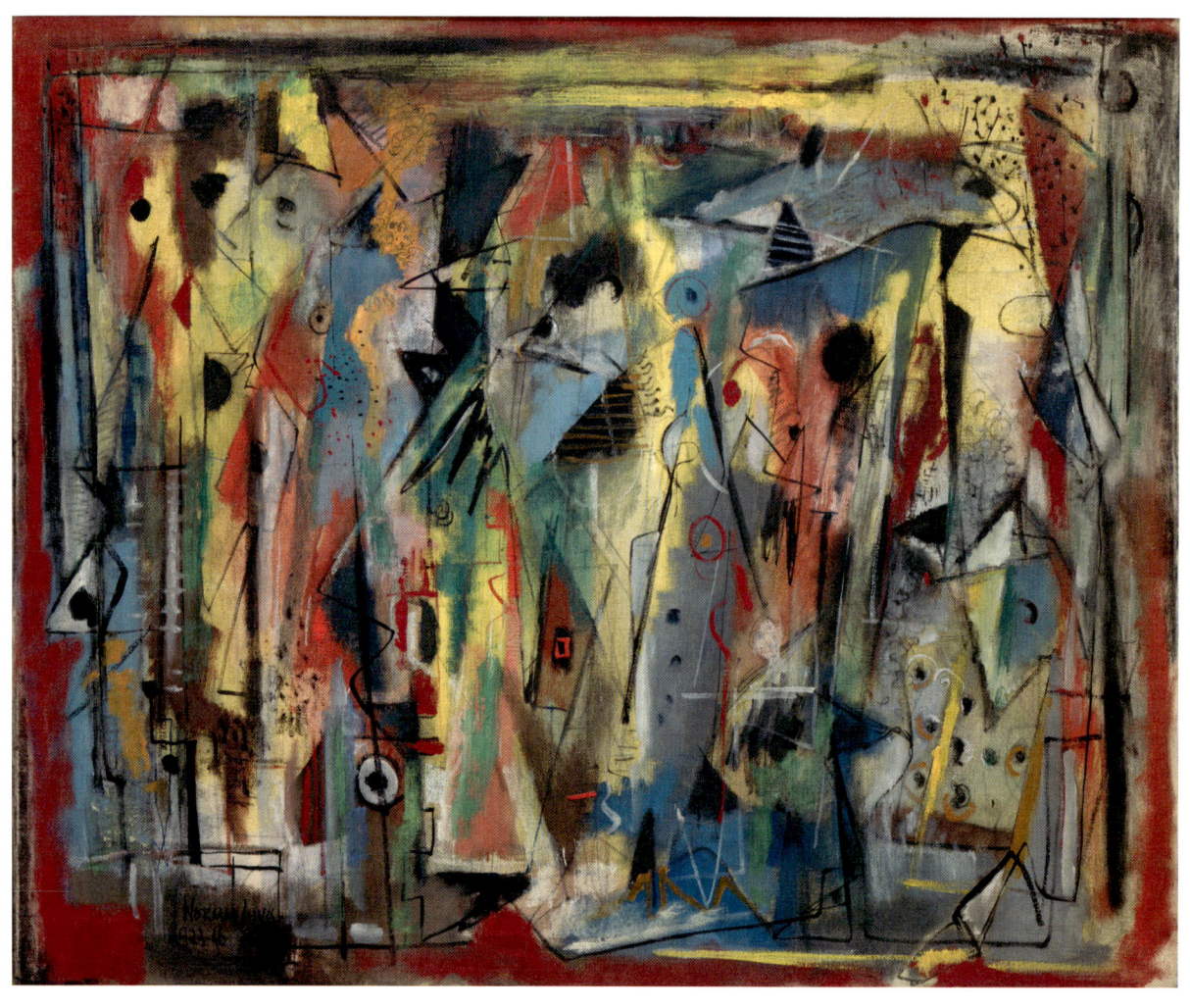

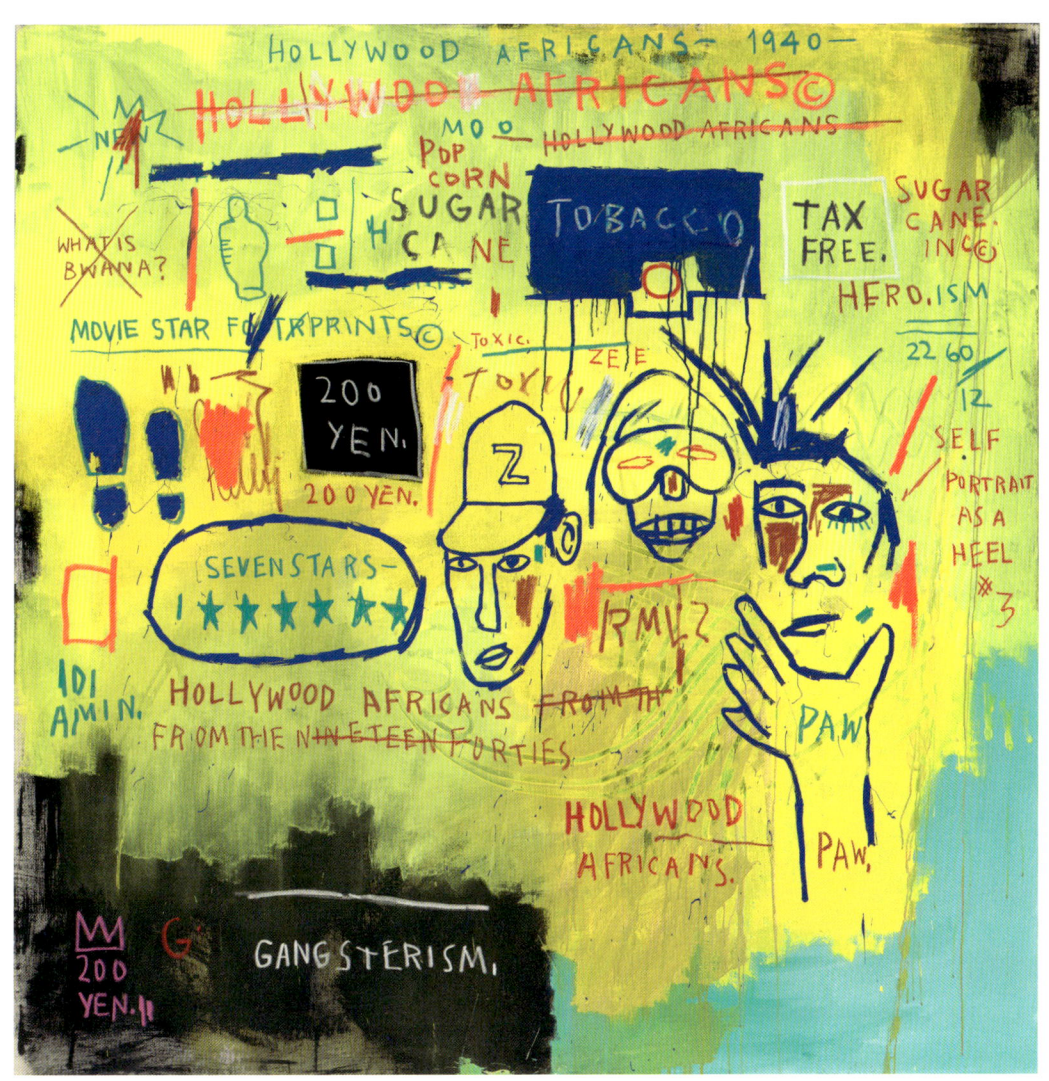

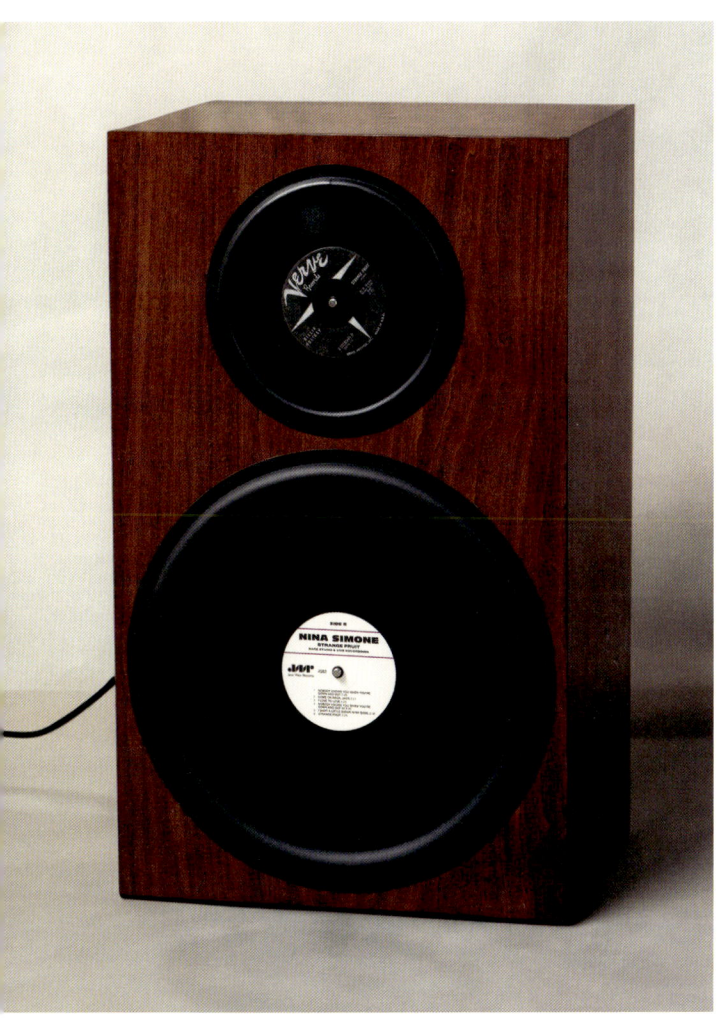

Clockwise from top left:

Beauford Delaney, *Charlie Parker Yardbird*, 1958. Oil on canvas, 39½ × 29½ in. (100.3 × 74.9 cm). Smithsonian American Art Museum, Washington, DC; gift of the James F. Dicke Family, 2013.89.3

Sam Gilliam, *Swing 64*, 1964. Acrylic on canvas, 37 9/16 × 37 1/8 × 1½ in. (95.4 × 94.3 × 3.8 cm). Collection of Beth Rudin DeWoody

Jean-Michel Basquiat, *Hollywood Africans*, 1983. Acrylic and oil stick on canvas, 84 1/16 × 84 in. (213.5 × 213.4 cm). Whitney Museum of American Art, New York; gift of Douglas S. Cramer, 84.23

Charles Gaines, *Sound Box: Nina Simone and Billie Holiday*, 2021. Poplar, vinyl records, rubber, felt, MP3 player, and rechargeable battery, 25½ × 15½ × 12 in. (64.8 × 39.4 × 30.5 cm). Collection of Beth Rudin DeWoody

Norman Lewis, *Phantasy II*, 1946. Oil on canvas, 28 1/8 × 35 7/8 in. (71.4 × 91.2 cm). The Museum of Modern Art, New York; gift of The Friends of Education of The Museum of Modern Art, 528.1998

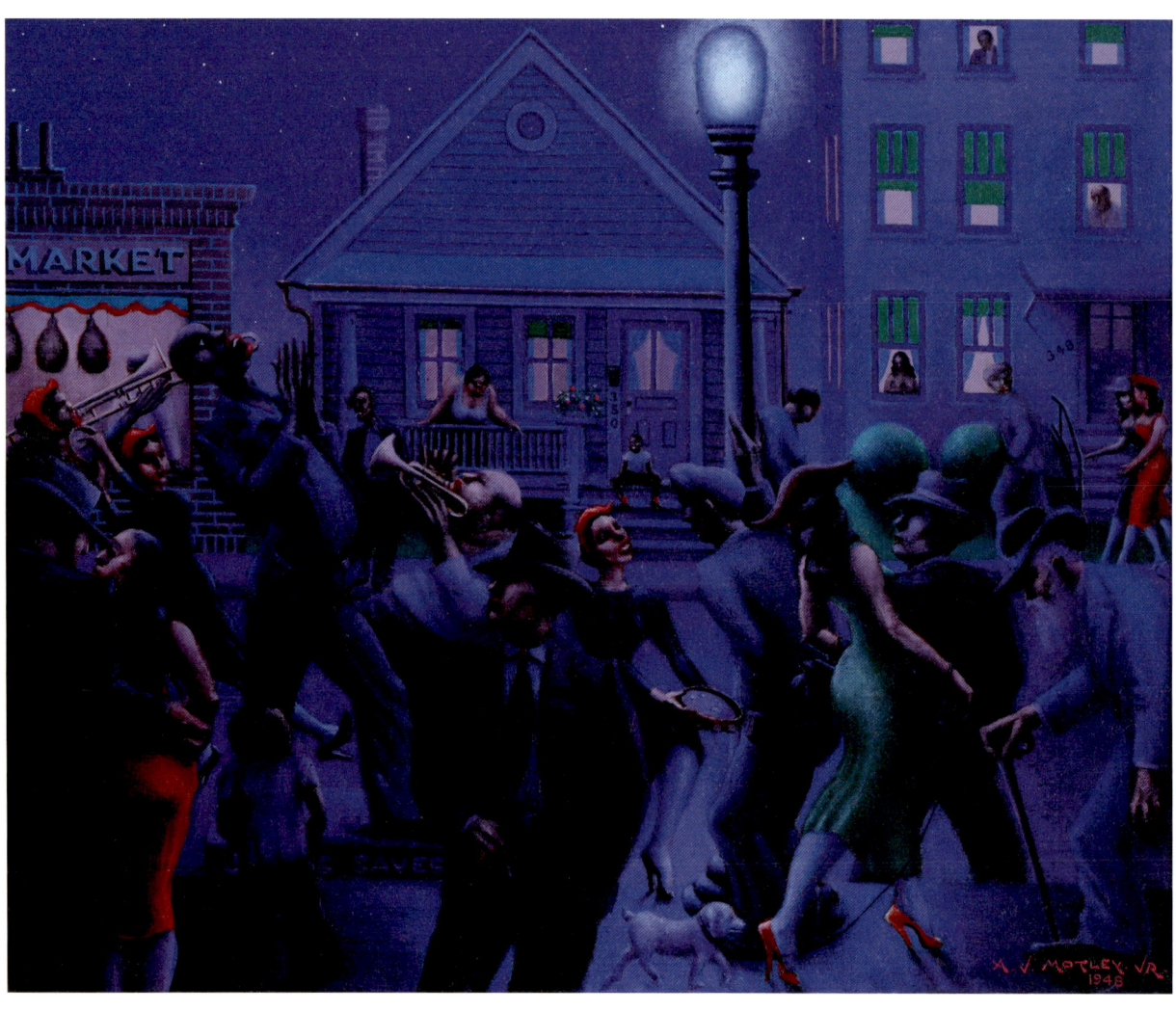
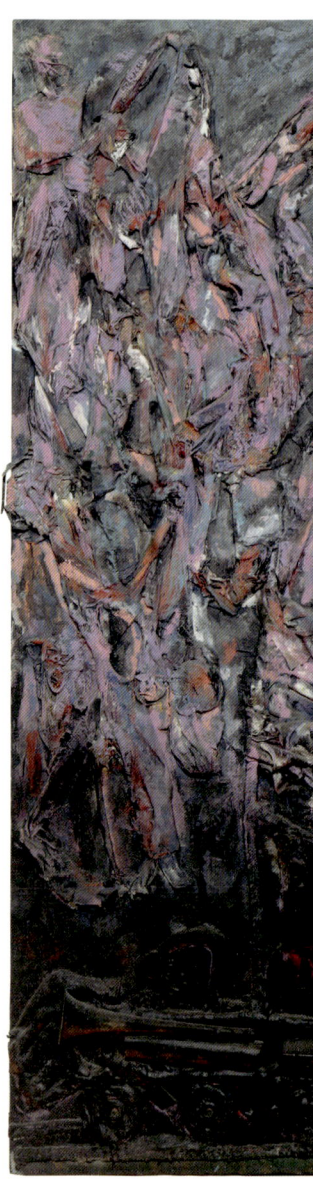
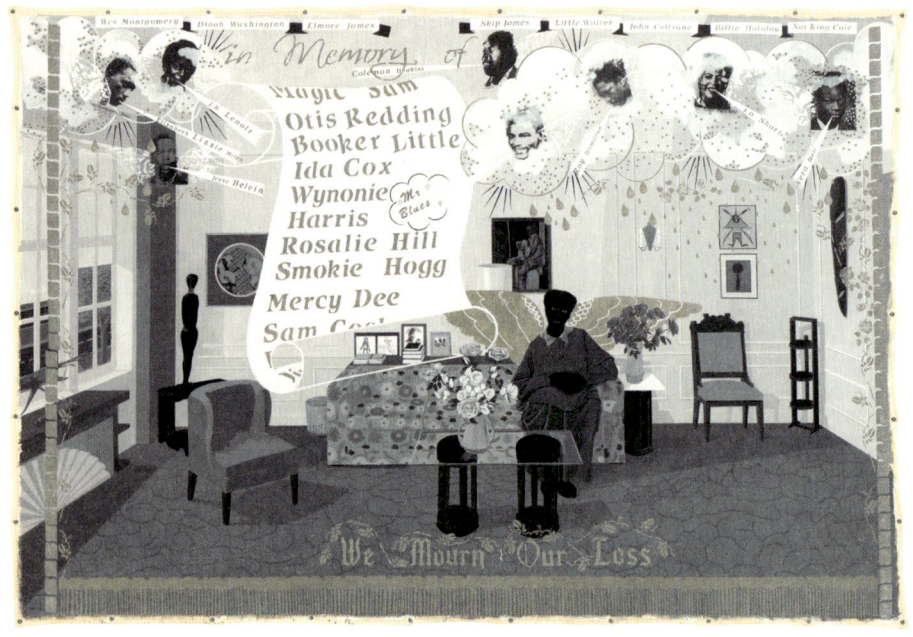
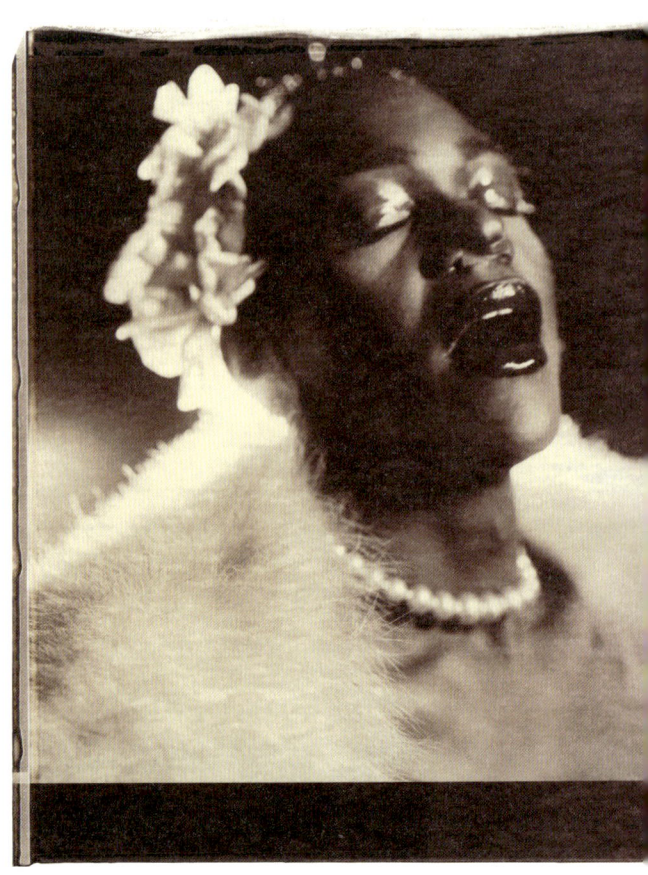

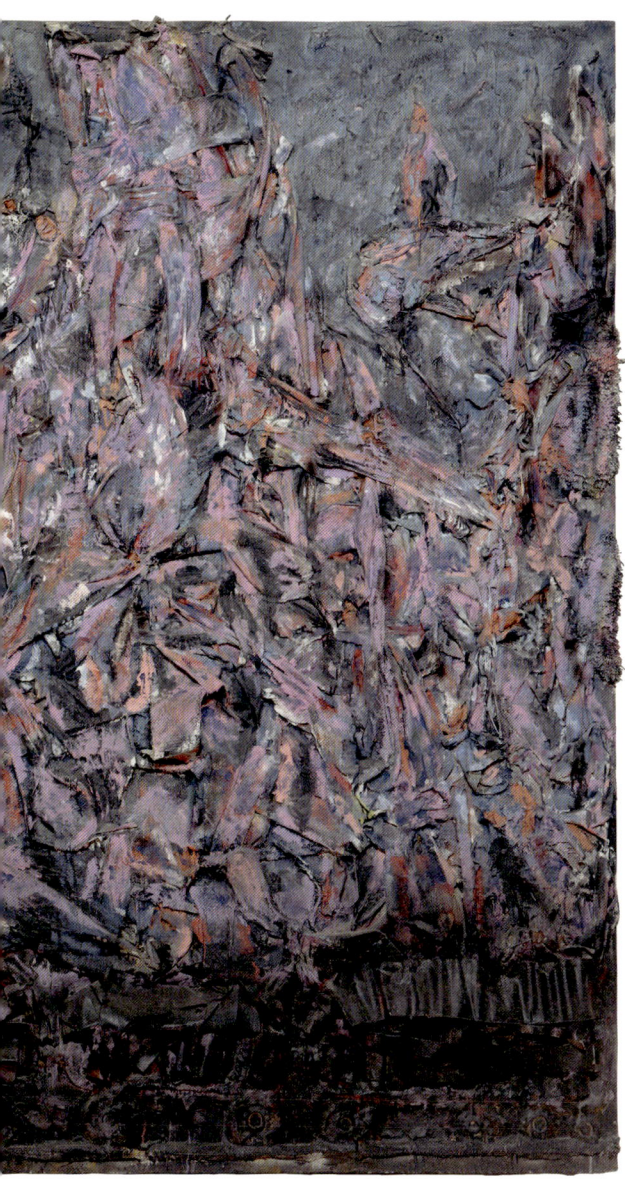

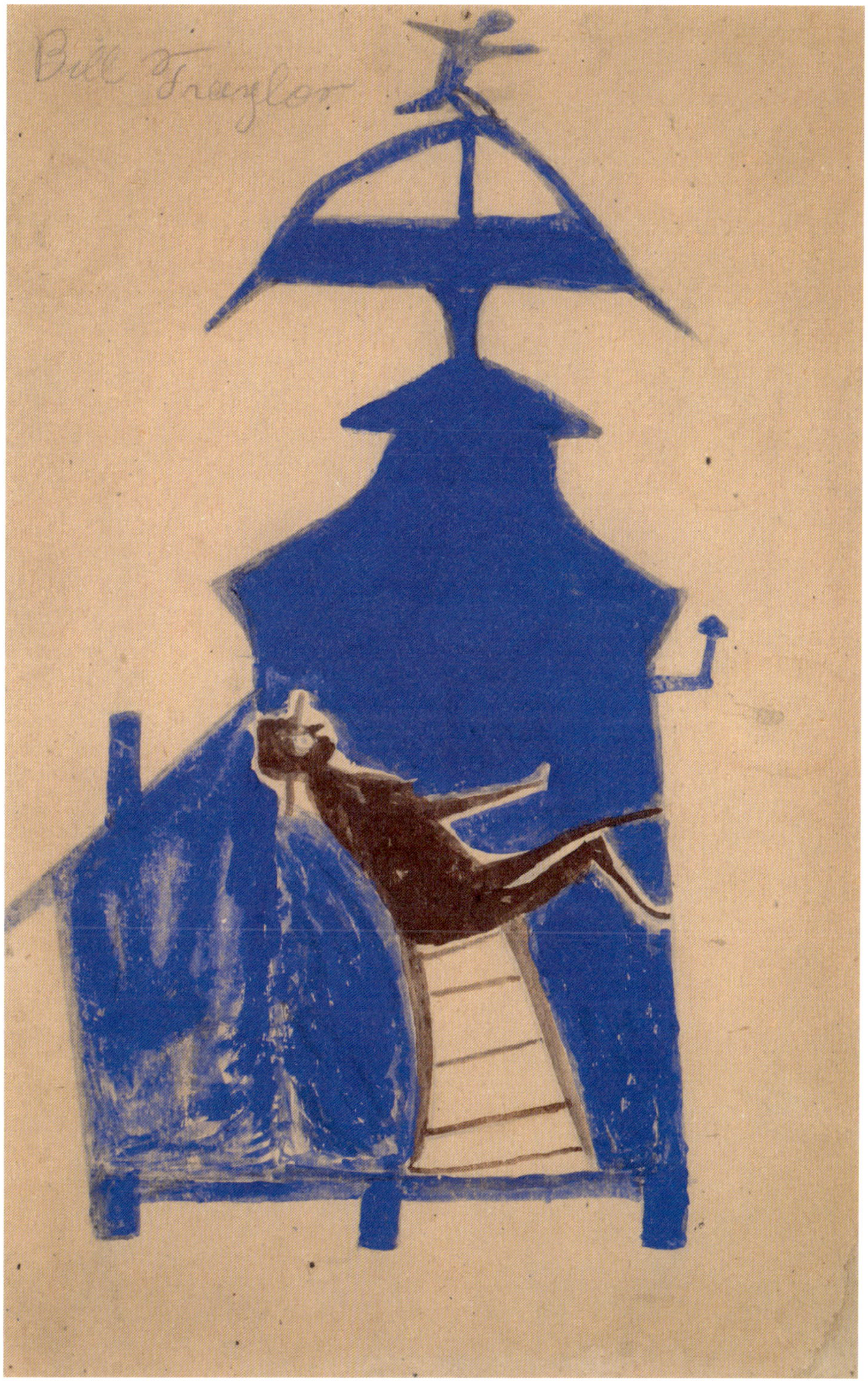

Clockwise from top left:

Archibald John Motley, Jr., *Gettin' Religion*, 1948. Oil on linen, 32 × 39 7/16 in. (81.3 × 100.2 cm). Whitney Museum of American Art, New York; purchase, Josephine N. Hopper Bequest, by exchange, 2016.15

Thornton Dial, *Soul Train*, 2004. Clothing, tin, rope carpet, bicycle horn, oil, enamel, spray paint, and epoxy on canvas, mounted on wood, 71 × 71 1/2 × 5 in. (180.3 × 181.6 × 12.7 cm). Hood Museum of Art, Dartmouth College, Hanover, New Hampshire: purchased through the Evelyn A. and William B. Jaffe 2015 Fund, 2021.11.3

Bill Traylor, *Untitled (Man in a Blue House)*, n.d. Graphite pencil and poster paint on paperboard, 17 1/4 × 11 3/8 in. (43.8 × 28.9 cm). The Johnson Collection, Spartanburg, South Carolina

Lyle Ashton Harris, *Billie #21*, 2002. Dye diffusion transfer print (Polaroid), 24 × 20 in. (61 × 50.8 cm). Whitney Museum of American Art, New York; purchase, with funds from the Photography Committee, 2002.563

Kerry James Marshall, *Souvenir IV*, 1998. Acrylic, glitter, and screenprint on paper on tarpaulin, with metal grommets, 107 5/8 × 157 1/2 in. (273.4 × 400.1 cm). Whitney Museum of American Art, New York; purchase, with funds from the Painting and Sculpture Committee, 98.56

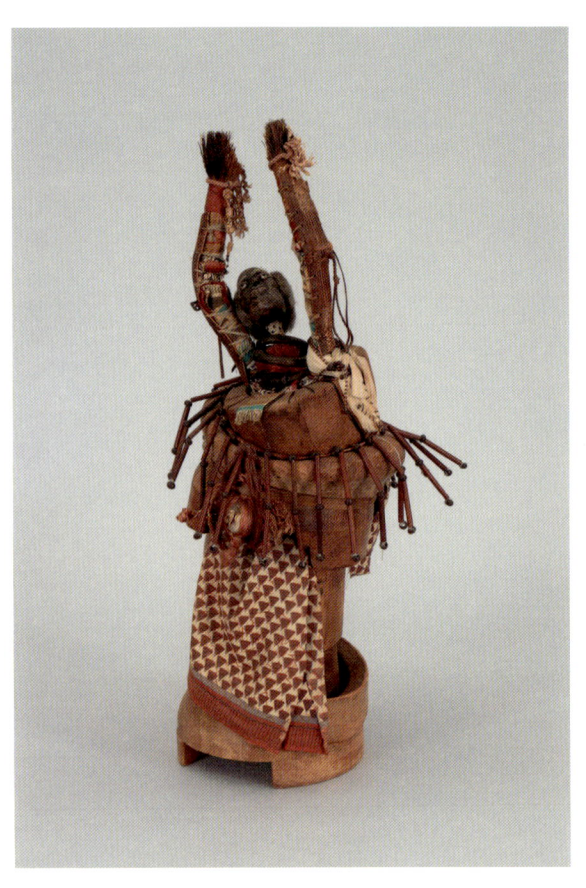
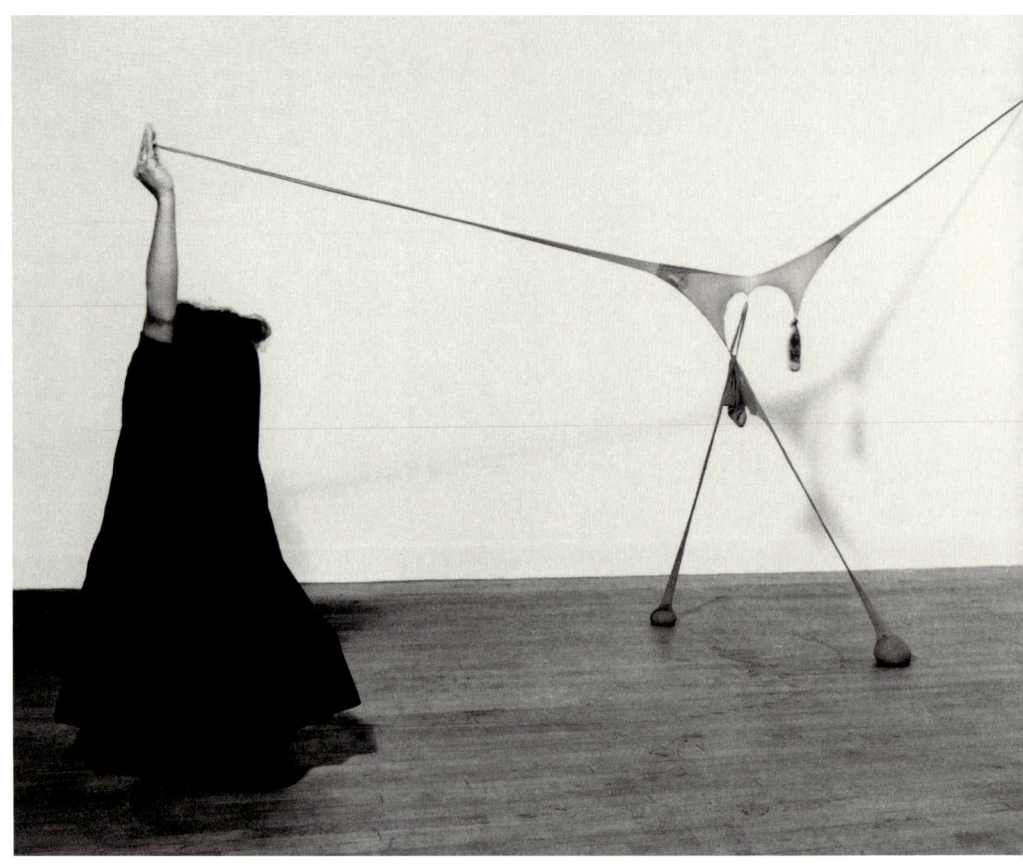
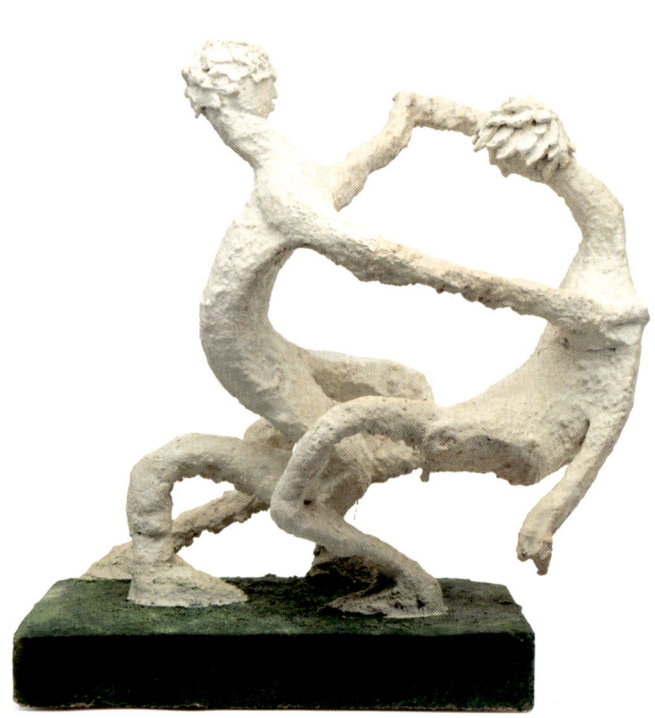
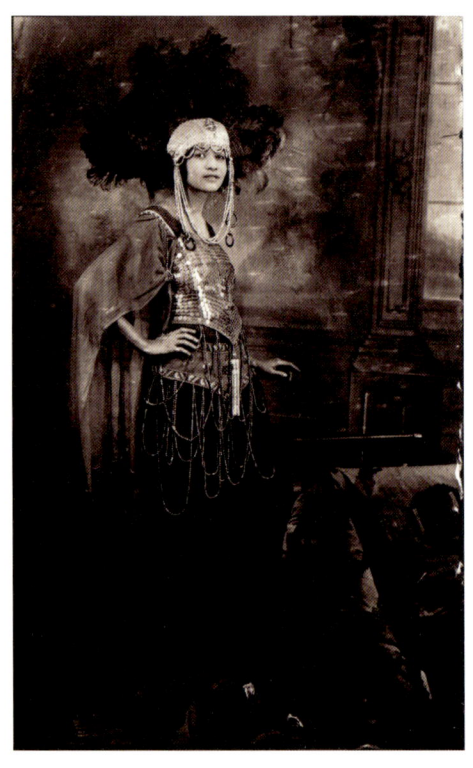
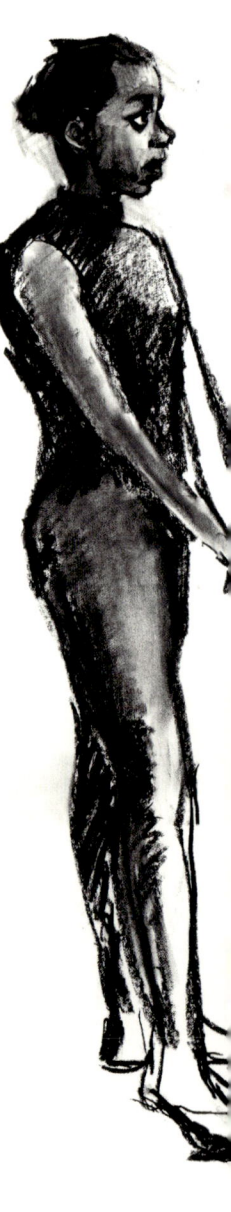

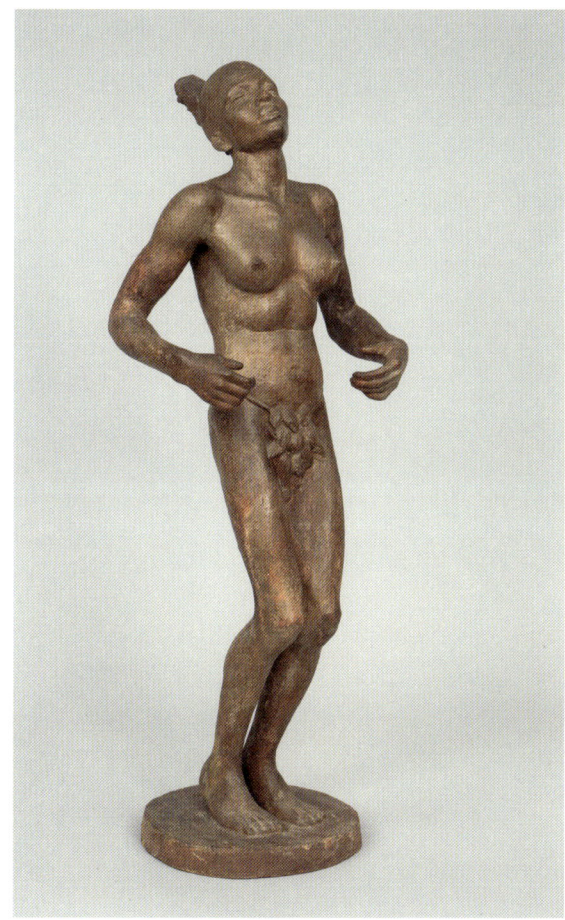
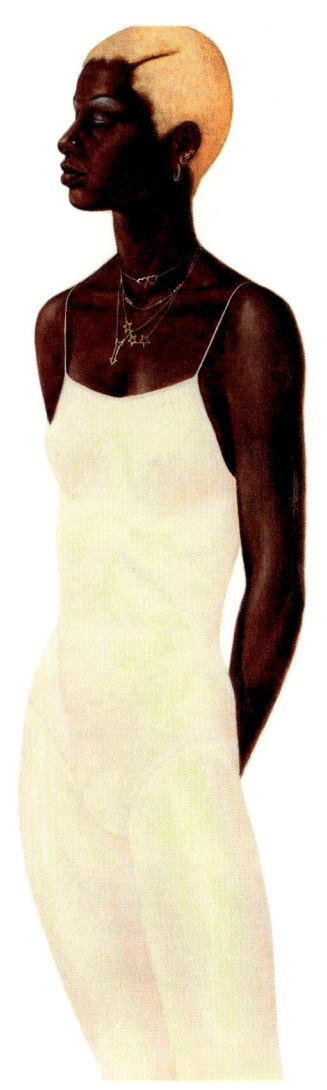
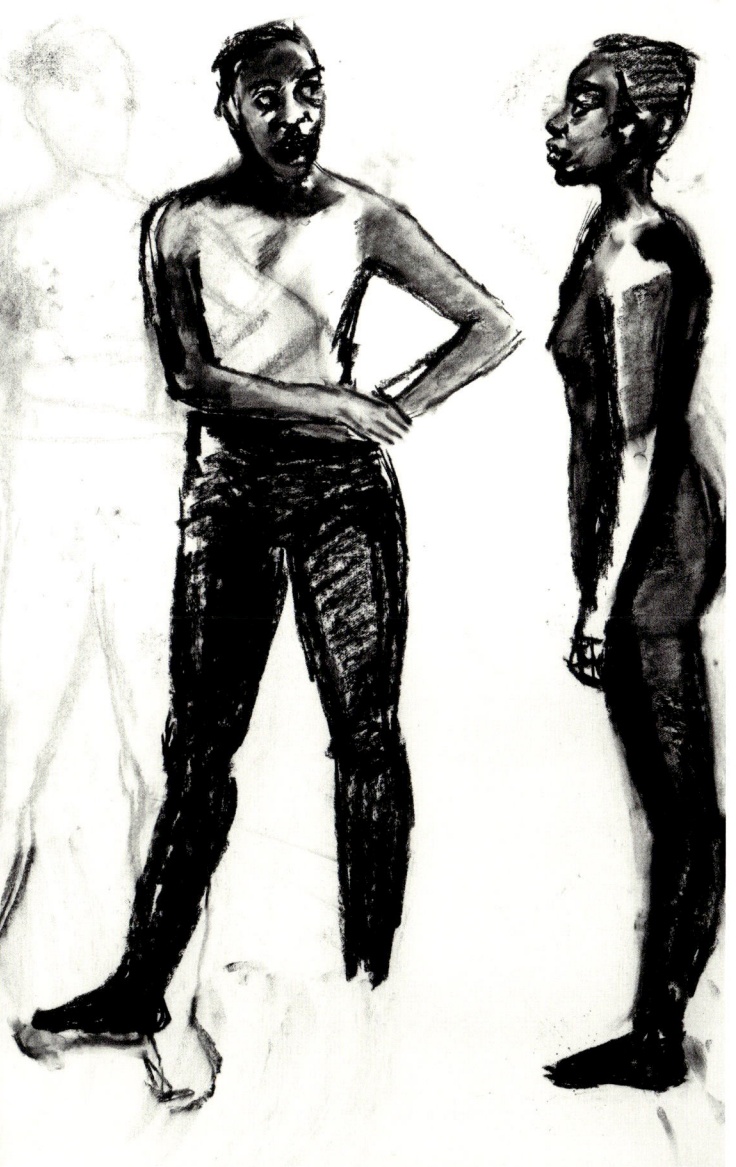

Clockwise from top left:

John Outterbridge, *The Elder, Ethnic Heritage Series*, 1971–72. Wooden hat forms, fabric, wooden beads, twine, metal, paint, and human hair, 28¼ × 11⅞ × 11⅜ in. (71.8 × 30.2 × 28.9 cm). Whitney Museum of American Art, New York; purchase, with funds from David Cancel and an anonymous donor, 2022.189

Senga Nengudi, *Studio Performance with R.S.V.P.*, 1976. Gelatin silver print, 30 × 40 in. (76.2 × 101.6 cm). The Museum of Modern Art, New York; Committee on Media and Performance Art Funds, 1120.2014

Richmond Barthé, *African Dancer*, 1933. Plaster, 42¾ × 16⅞ × 14¼ in. (108.6 × 42.9 × 36.2 cm). Whitney Museum of American Art, New York; purchase, 33.53

Barkley Hendricks, *Dancer*, 1977. Oil on canvas, 47⅞ × 36 in. (121.6 × 91.4 cm). Collection of Jeff and Leslie Fischer

Lynette Yiadom Boakye, Not yet titled, 2024. Collection of the artist; courtesy Corvi-Mora, London, and Jack Shainman Gallery, New York

James Van Der Zee, *Dancer*, 1925. Gelatin silver print, 6¾ × 4¹⁵⁄₁₆ in. (17.1 × 12.5 cm). Whitney Museum of American Art, New York; gift of an anonymous donor, 2001.38

Eldren Bailey, *Dancers*, 1960s. Concrete, plaster, and paint, 29½ × 29 × 17 in. (74.9 × 73.7 × 43.2 cm). Souls Grown Deep Foundation

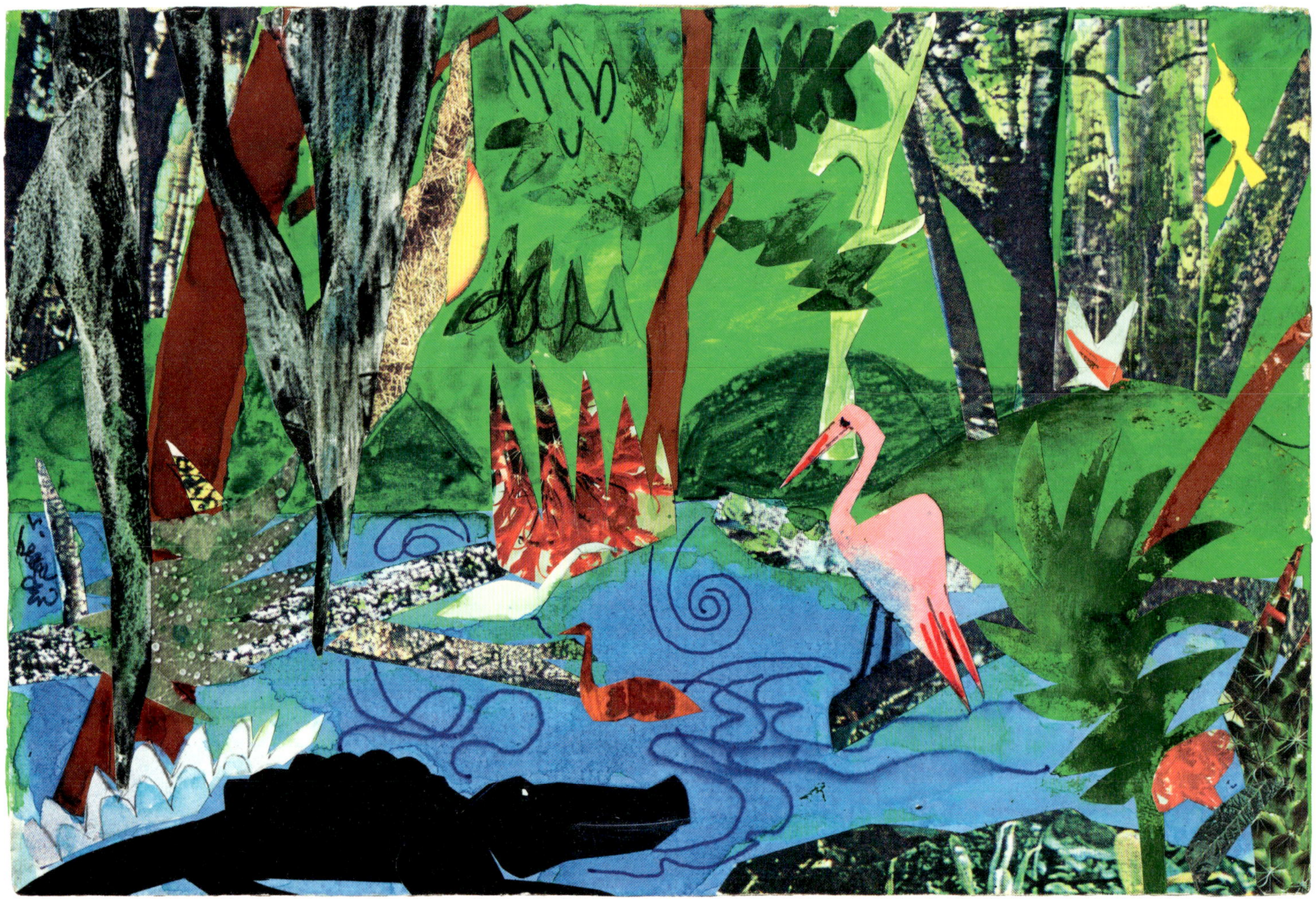

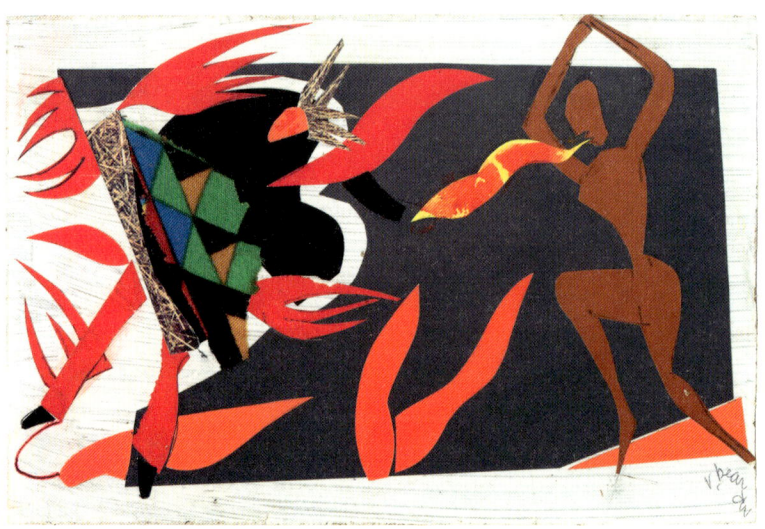

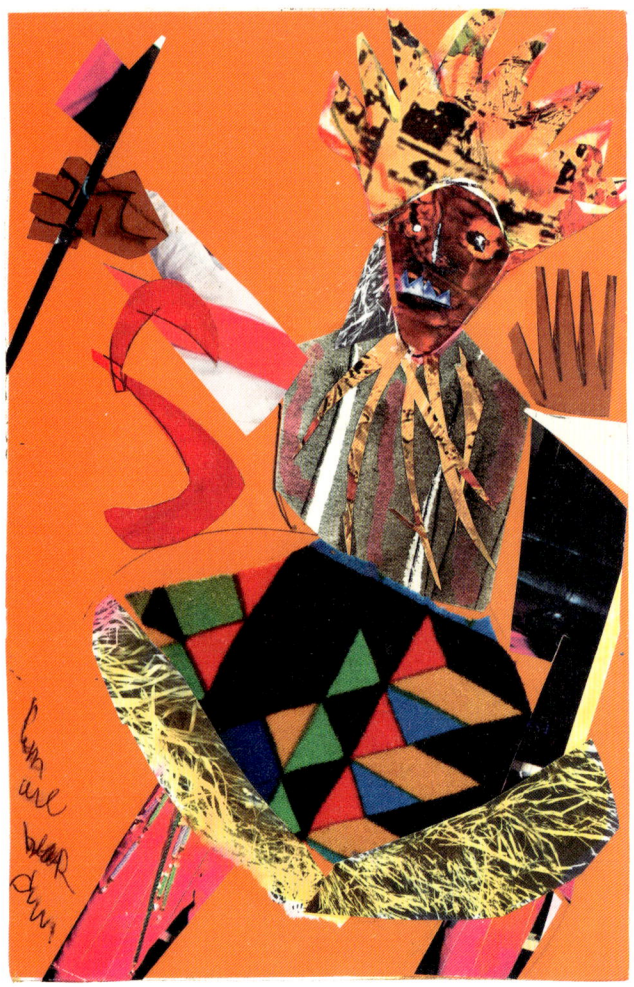

Clockwise from top:

Romare Bearden, *The Bayou*, from the series *Bayou Fever*, 1979. Collage, ink, pencil, and acrylic on fiberboard, 6 × 9 in. (15.2 × 22.9 cm). Estate of Romare Bearden and DC Moore Gallery

The Buzzard and the Snake (The Conjur Woman), from the series *Bayou Fever*, 1979. Collage on fiberboard with attached string and safety pin, 9 × 6 in. (22.9 × 15.2 cm). Estate of Romare Bearden and DC Moore Gallery

The Conjur Woman, from the series *Bayou Fever*, 1979. Collage and acrylic on fiberboard, 6 × 9 in. (15.2 × 22.9 cm). Estate of Romare Bearden and DC Moore Gallery

The Hatchet Man, from the series *Bayou Fever*, 1979. Collage, acrylic, and pencil on fiberboard, 9 × 6 in. (22.9 × 15.2 cm). Estate of Romare Bearden and DC Moore Gallery

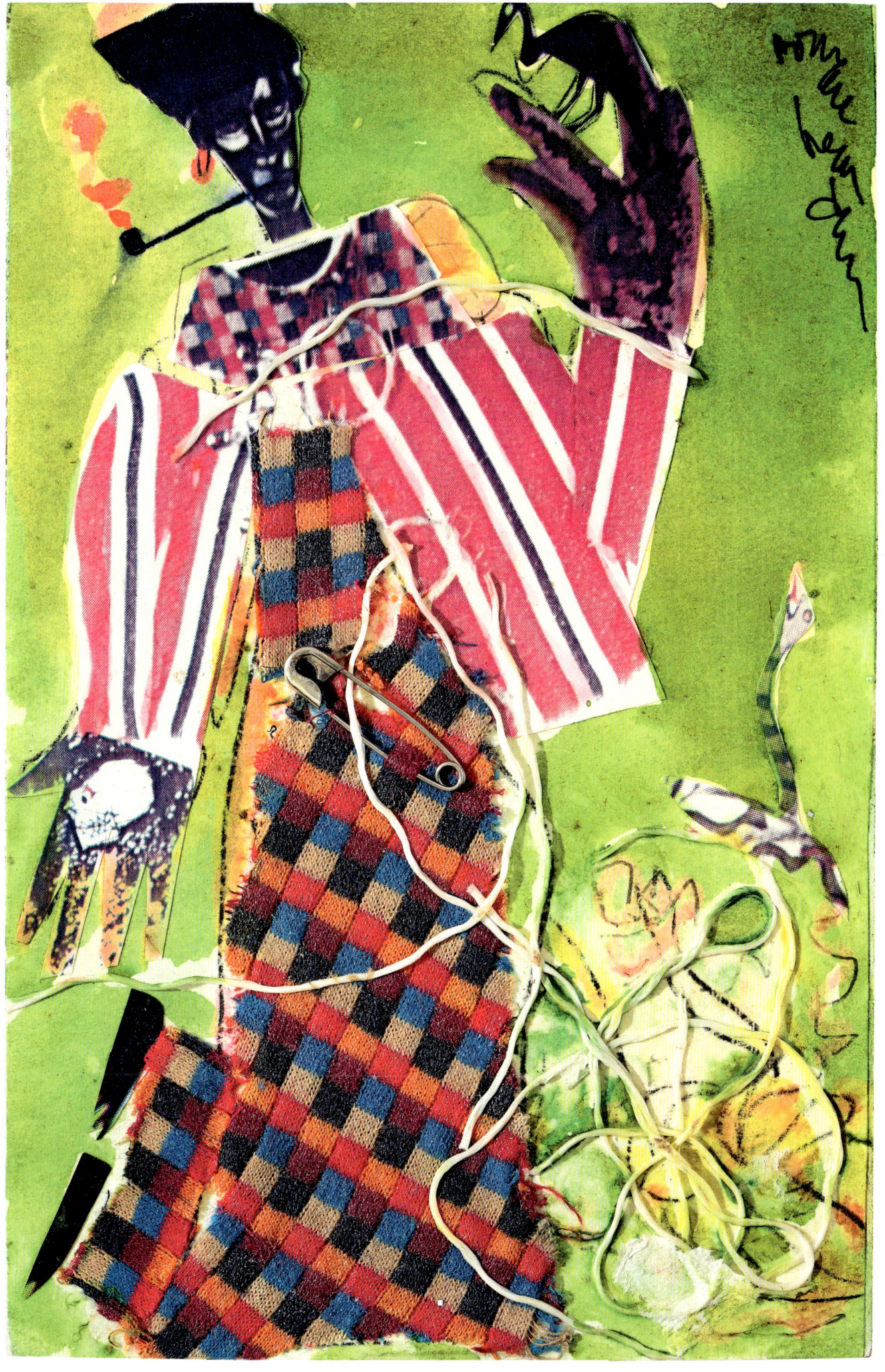

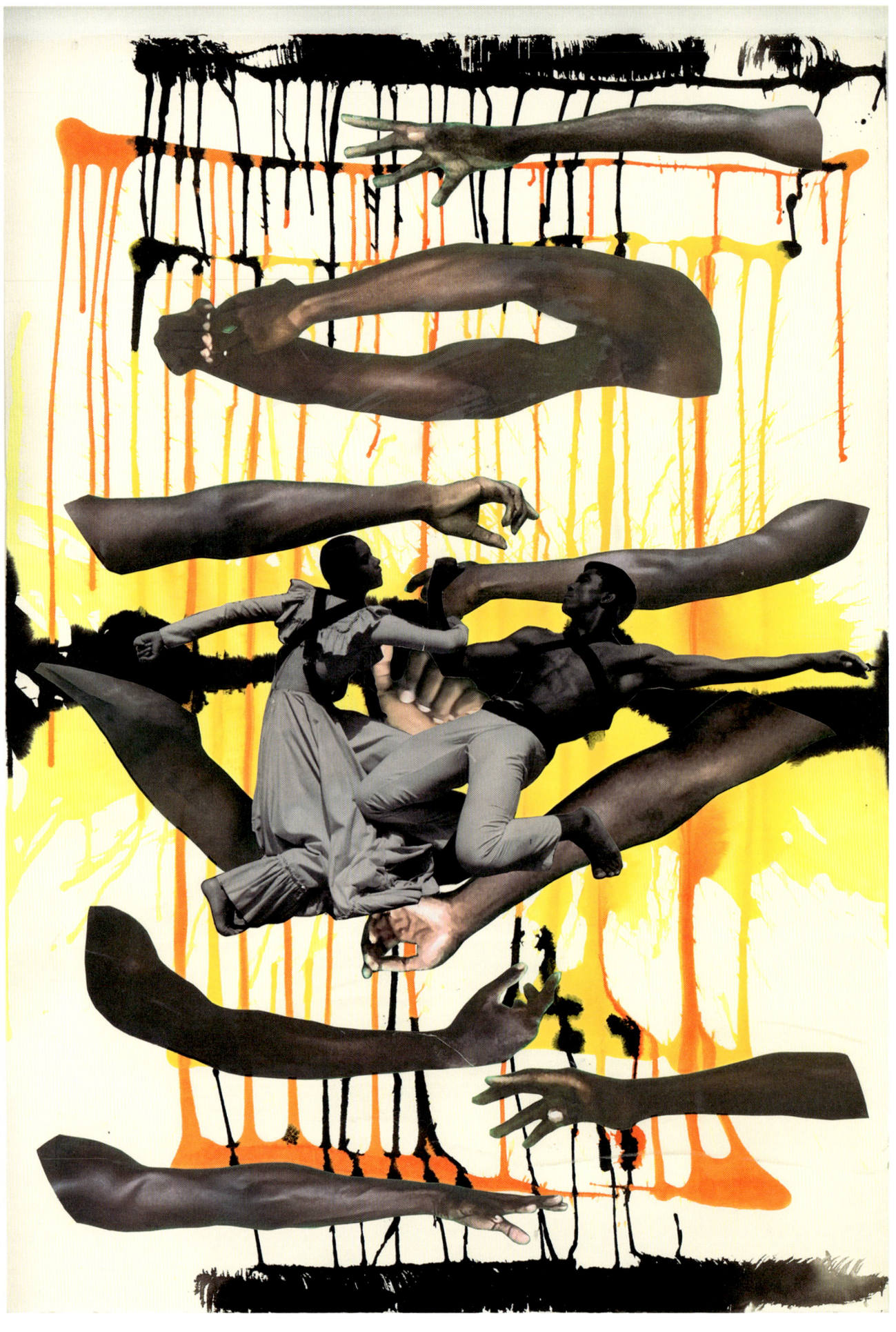

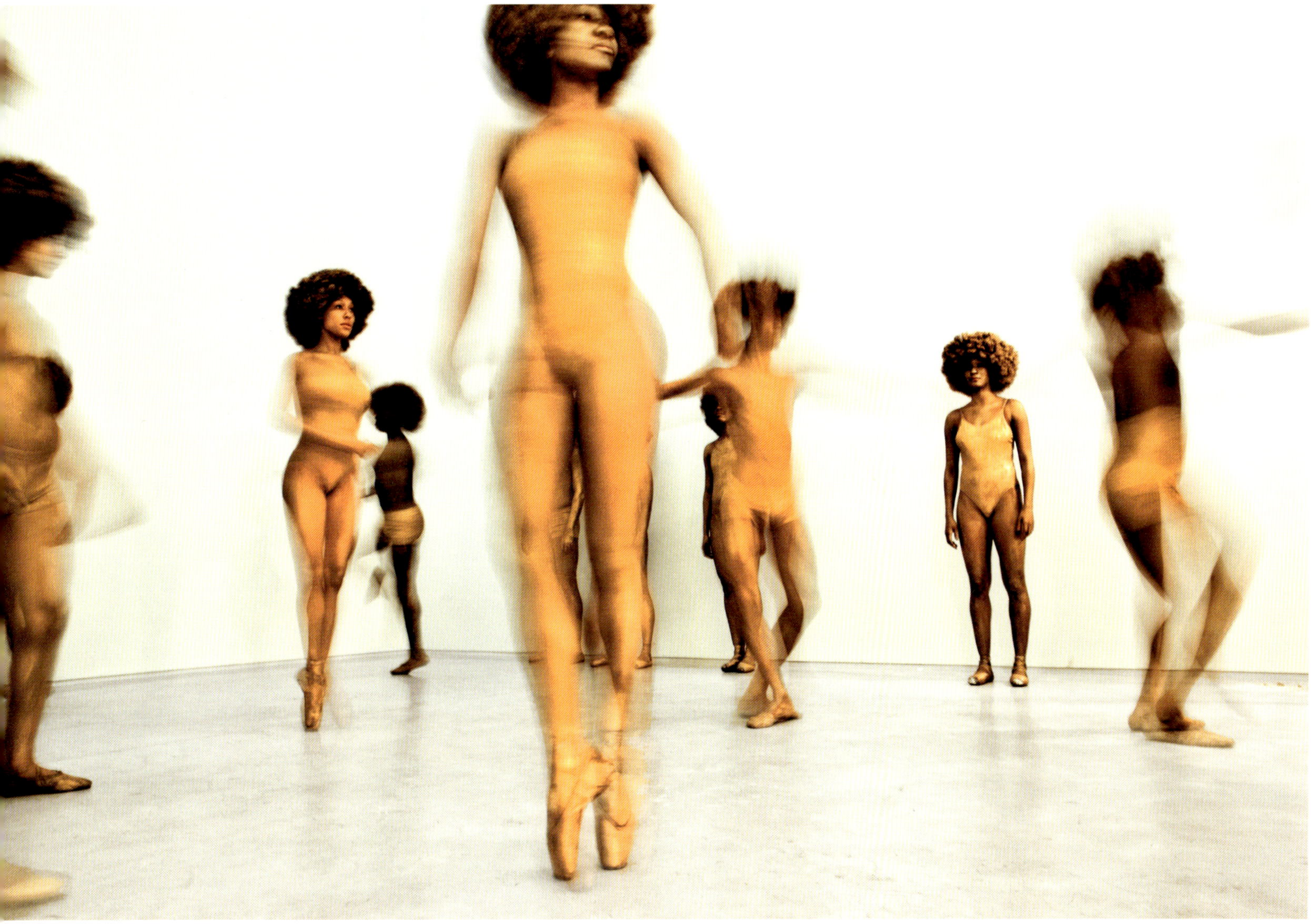

Clockwise from left:

Kandis Williams, *Black Box, 4 points: Horton, Ailey, McKayle contractions and expansions of drama from vernacular—arms outstretched and entangle*, 2021. Xerox collage and ink on paper, 41½ × 29½ in. (105.4 × 74.9 cm). Mohn Family Trust

Lorna Simpson, *Momentum*, 2011. Two-channel video installation, color, sound; 6:56 min., looped. Collection of the artist

Ralph Lemon, *Ailey Dancing Revelations*, 2024. Oil stick on paper, 8 × 8 in. (20.3 × 20.3 cm). Collection of the artist

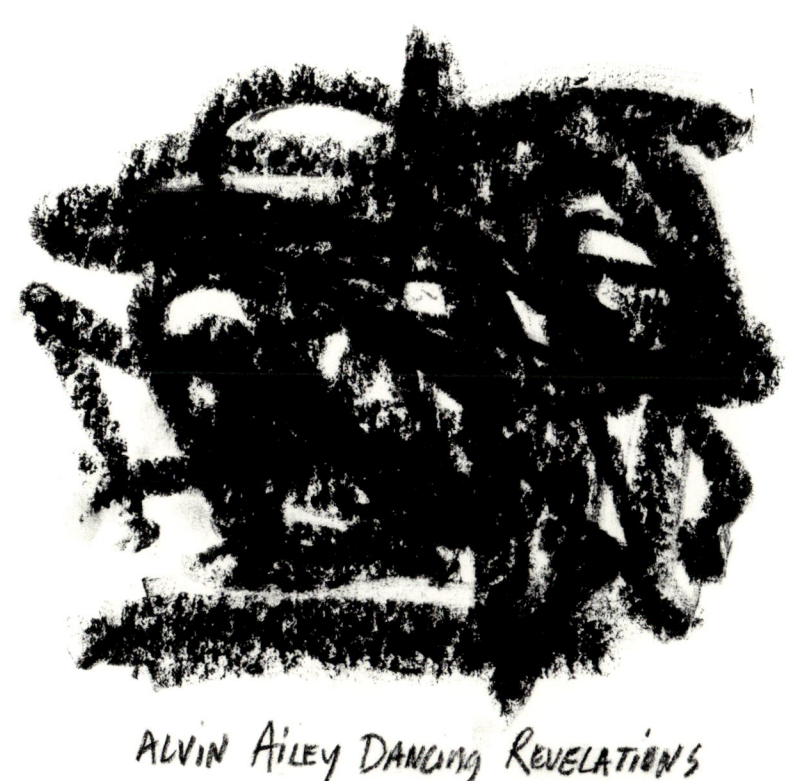

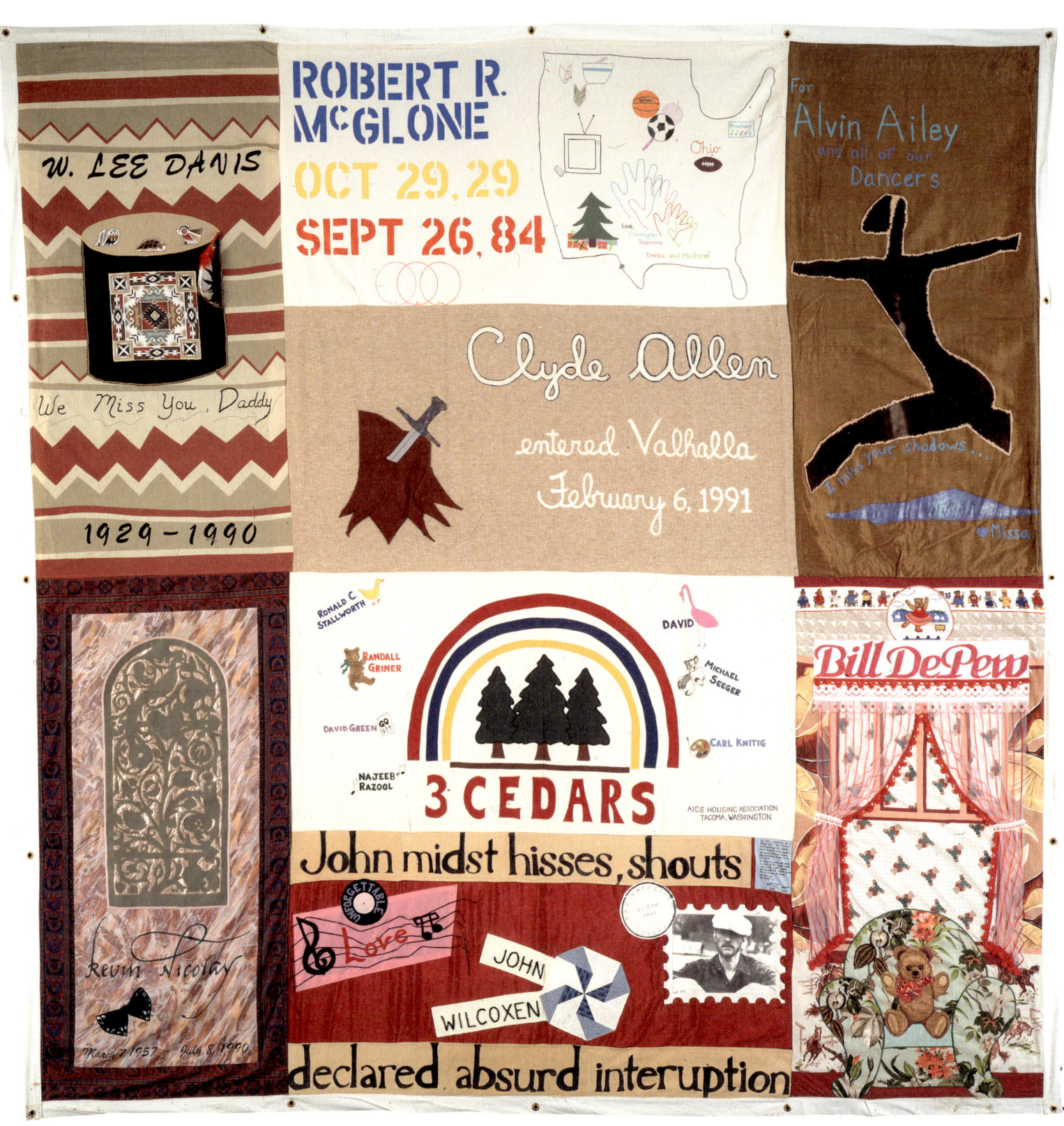

Makers unknown, *Alvin Ailey panel of AIDS Memorial quilt*, 1987. Mixed media, 144 × 144 in. (365.8 × 365.8 cm). National AIDS Memorial, San Francisco

Appendix: Choreography and Dancers

ALVIN AILEY CHOREOGRAPHY, 1954–88

According to St. Francis, 1954, premiere, Wilshire Ebell Theater, Los Angeles (performed by the Lester Horton Dance Theater)

Morning Mourning, 1954, premiere, Wilshire Ebell Theater, Los Angeles (performed by the Lester Horton Dance Theater)

La Création du Monde, 1954, premiere, San Diego (performed by the Lester Horton Dance Theater); 1960, premiere (second version, as *Creation of the World*) (performed by Alvin Ailey and Matt Turney); 1962, premiere (third version), Delacorte Theater, New York

Blues Suite, 1958, premiere, Kaufmann Concert Hall, 92nd Street Y, New York

Ode and Homage, 1958, premiere, Kaufman Concert Hall, 92nd Street Y, New York

Redonda, 1958, premiere, Kaufman Concert Hall, 92nd Street Y, New York

Ariette Oubliée, 1958, premiere, Kaufmann Concert Hall, 92nd Street Y, New York

Cinco Latinos, 1958, premiere, Kaufman Concert Hall, 92nd Street Y, New York

Mistress and Manservant, 1959, premiere, Delacorte Theater, New York (performed by the Shirley Broughton Dance Company)

Carmen Jones (summer stock), 1959, Hudson Celebration Theatre-in-the-Park, New York

Revelations, 1960, premiere, Kaufman Concert Hall, 92nd Street Y, New York

Sonera, 1960, premiere, Kaufmann Concert Hall, 92nd Street Y, New York

African Holiday (theatrical revue), 1960, Apollo Theater, New York

Jamaica (summer stock), 1960, Lambertville Theater in the Round, New Jersey

Dark of the Moon (play), 1960, Lenox Hill Playhouse, New York (production by the Equity Library Theater)

Knoxville: Summer of 1915, 1960, premiere, Clark Center for the Performing Arts, West Side YWCA, New York

Three for Now–Modern Jazz Suite, 1960, premiere, Clark Center for the Performing Arts, West Side YWCA, New York

Roots of the Blues, 1961, premiere, Tenth Annual Boston Arts Festival

Gillespiana, 1961, premiere, location unknown (most likely Clark Center for the Performing Arts, West Side YWCA, New York)

Hermit Songs, 1961, premiere, location unknown (most likely Clark Center for the Performing Arts, West Side YWCA, New York)

Been Here and Gone, 1962, premiere (Southeast Asia tour)

Feast of Ashes, 1962, premiere, Teatro Nacional de São Carlos, Lisbon, Portugal (performed by the Joffrey Ballet); 1974, company premiere, Hackensack, New Jersey

Labyrinth, 1963, premiere, Brooklyn Academy of Music

Reflections in D, 1963, premiere, Brooklyn Academy of Music

My People: First Negro Centennial, 1963, premiere, Arie Crown Theater, Chicago

Rivers, Streams, Doors, 1963, premiere, International Music Festival, Rio de Janeiro

The Twelve Gates, 1964, premiere, Jacob's Pillow Dance Festival, Becket, Massachusetts

Ariadne, 1965, premiere, Opéra Comique, Paris (performed by the Harkness Ballet)

Macumba, 1966, premiere, Gran Teatre del Liceu, Barcelona (performed by the Harkness Ballet)

El Amor Brujo, 1966, premiere, Festival du Marais, Paris (performed by the Harkness Ballet)

Antony and Cleopatra (opera), 1966, Metropolitan Opera House, Lincoln Center, New York (production by the Metropolitan Opera)

Riedaiglia, 1967, premiere, broadcast on Swedish television

Quintet, 1968, premiere, Edinburgh International Festival, Scotland

Diversion No. 1, 1969, premiere, Greek Theatre, Los Angeles

Masekela Langage, 1969, premiere, Connecticut College, New London; 1969, premiere (second version), Brooklyn Academy of Music

La Strada (Broadway musical), 1969, Lunt-Fontanne Theater, New York

Streams, 1970, premiere, Brooklyn Academy of Music

Gymnopedies, 1970, premiere, Brooklyn Academy of Music

The River, 1970/1978/1981, premiere, New York State Theater, Lincoln Center (performed by the American Ballet Theatre); 1978, premiere (second version), National Theatre, Washington, DC (performed by the Ballet Internacional de Caracas); 1981, company premiere, New York City Center

Archipelago, 1971, premiere, ANTA Theatre, New York

Flowers, 1971, premiere, ANTA Theatre, New York

Choral Dances, 1971, premiere, New York City Center

Cry, 1971, premiere, New York City Center

Mass: A Theatre Piece for Singers, Players, and Dancers (musical theater), 1971, John F. Kennedy Center for the Performing Arts, Washington, DC (choreography performed by Ailey dancers)

The Mingus Dances, 1971, premiere, New York City Center (performed by the Joffrey Ballet)

Mary Lou's Mass, 1971, premiere, New York City Center

Myth, 1971, premiere, New York City Center

Lord Byron (opera), 1972, Juilliard, New York (production by the Juilliard American Opera Center)

The Lark Ascending, 1972, premiere, New York City Center

Shaken Angels, 1972, premiere, Tenth New York Dance Festival, Delacorte Theater, New York (performed by Bonnie Mathis and Dennis Wayne)

Carmen (opera), 1972, Metropolitan Opera House, Lincoln Center, New York (production by the Metropolitan Opera)

Sea Change, 1972, premiere, John F. Kennedy Center for the Performing Arts, Washington, DC (performed by the American Ballet Theatre)

Love Songs, 1972, premiere, New York City Center

Four Saints in Three Acts (opera), 1973, Vivian Beaumont Theater, Lincoln Center, New York (production by the Metropolitan Opera at the Forum)

Hidden Rites, 1973, premiere, New York City Center

The Blues Ain't, 1974, broadcast as part of the CBS television special *Ailey Celebrates Ellington*

Night Creature, 1974, broadcast as part of the CBS television special *Ailey Celebrates Ellington*

The Mooche, 1974, broadcast as part of the CBS television special *Ailey Celebrates Ellington*

Praise God and Dance (Sacred Concert), 1974, broadcast as part of the CBS television special *Ailey Celebrates Ellington*

Sonnet for Caesar, 1974, broadcast as part of the CBS television special *Ailey Celebrates Ellington*

Such Sweet Thunder, 1974, broadcast as part of the CBS television special *Ailey Celebrates Ellington*

Night Creature, 1975, premiere, New York City Center

The Mooche, 1975, premiere, New York City Center

Black, Brown and Beige, 1976, premiere, New York City Center

Pas de Duke, 1976, premiere, New York City Center

Three Black Kings, 1976, premiere, Artpark, Lewiston, New York

Passage, 1978, premiere, New York City Center

Shigaon! Children of the Diaspora, 1978, premiere, Israel (performed by the Bat-Dor Dance Company)

Solo for Mingus, 1979, premiere, New York City Center

Memoria, 1979, premiere, New York City Center

Phases, 1980, premiere, New York City Center

Spell, 1981, premiere, New York City Center

Landscape, 1981, premiere, New York City Center

Satyriade, 1982, premiere, New York City Center

Au Bord du Précipice, 1983, premiere, Palais Garnier, Paris (performed by the Paris Opera Ballet); 1984, company premiere (as *Precipice*), Metropolitan Opera House, Lincoln Center, New York

Escapades, 1983, premiere, Reggio Emilia, Italy (performed by Aterballetto)

Isba, 1983, premiere, New York City Center (performed by Ailey II)

Can't Slow Down, 1983, premiere, New York City Center

For 'Bird'—With Love, 1984, premiere, Folly Theater, Kansas City, Missouri

Caverna Magica, 1986, premiere, Royal Theatre, Copenhagen, Denmark (performed by the Royal Danish Ballet); 1986, company premiere, New York City Center

Witness, 1986, premiere, Royal Theatre, Copenhagen, Denmark (performed by the Royal Danish Ballet); 1986, company premiere, Lyric Theater, Kansas City, Missouri

Survivors, 1986, premiere, Lyric Theater, Kansas City, Missouri

La Dea della Acqua, 1988, premiere, La Scala, Milan (performed by La Scala Opera Ballet)

Opus McShann, 1988, premiere, Folly Theater, Kansas City, Missouri

ALVIN AILEY AMERICAN DANCE THEATER DANCERS, 1958–89

The dancers listed below were members of the Alvin Ailey American Dance Theater during Alvin Ailey's lifetime. The following dates indicate their time with the company. Ailey's years as a dancer in the company are also included below.

Loretta Abbott: 1963–68
Charles Adams: 1974–78
Alvin Ailey: 1958–65
Sarita Allen: 1975–84, 1989–95
Barbara Alston: 1959; 1963
Christopher Aponte: 1974–75
Adrienne Armstrong: 1985–91
Takako Asakawa: 1964–66
Consuelo Atlas: 1966–71
Carl Bailey: 1980–91
Marilyn Banks: 1977–96
Thea Nerissa Barnes: 1972–75
Mary Barnett: 1965–66
Don Bellamy: 1989–94, 1994–98
April Berry: 1980–89
Yemina Ben-Gal: 1959–61
Marla Bingham: 1977–78
Shirley Black-Brown: 1979–80
Frederick Bratcher: 1975
Enid Britten: 1967–68, 1974–78
Glen Brooks: 1963–64
Roman Brooks: 1979–84
Kevin Brown: 1980–91
Ronald Brown: 1978–84
Delores Browne: 1960
Cubie Burke: unknown
Eileen Bushman: 1958
Alistair Butler: 1977–81
Sergio Cal: 1975–77
Leu Camacho: 1960
Donato Capozzoli: 1963
Kevin Carlisle: 1959–61
William Chaison: 1972–73
Marie Dominique Chaize: 1984, 1985, or 1986
Debora Chase: 1981–92
Raquelle Chavis: 1987–94
Masazumi Chaya: 1972–88
Daniel Clark: 1979–84
Hope Clarke: 1964–65
Harvey Cohen: 1968–69
Georgia Collins: 1961–62, 1964–65
Otis Daye: 1979–80
Mario Delamo: 1969–70
Carmen de Lavallade: 1961–62
Gary Deloatch: 1978–88
Joan Derby: 1960
Merle Derby: 1959–61
Betsy Dickerson: 1960
Patricia Dingle: 1978–84
Ulysses Dove: 1973–81
Robert DuMee: 1958
Ronald Dunham: 1970–71
Michael Ebbin: 1972–73
Charles Epps: 1982–86
Lynn Elam: 1980–81
George Faison: 1967–69
Louis Falco: 1962–63
Ronni Favors: 1977–81
Cliff Fears: 1958
Valerie Feit: 1975–76
Julius Fields: 1958, 1963
Alphonso Figueroa: 1970–71
Jay Fletcher: 1960
Neisha Folkes: 1981–91
Gene GeBauer: 1960
Ray Gilbert: 1962
Frank Glass: 1958
Ralph Glenmore: 1981–88
Miguel Godreau: 1965–70
Meg Gordon: 1975–76
Altovise Gore: 1962–63
Connie Greco: 1961–62
Paul Grey: 1978–80
Marey Griffith: 1983–85, 1986–88
Lavinia Hamilton: 1958
William Hansen: 1969
Lee Harper: 1971–72
Raymond Harris: 1988–89
Nicky Harrison: 1978–79
Avind Harum: 1970
Dana Hash: 1988–95
Thelma Hill: 1960–64
Nat Horne: 1959–60, 1962
Paul Hoskins: 1972–73
Herman Howell: 1959–60
Christopher Huggins: 1983–88
Carmen Hylton: 1963–64
Judith Jamison: 1965–81
Bobby Johnson: 1969–70
Tommy Johnson: 1958
Wesley Johnson III: 1988–92
Melvin Jones: 1973–80
Mari Kajiwara: 1969–85
Norman Kauahi: 1981–85
Linda Kent: 1968–74
Christina Kimball: 1972–73
Barbara Koval: 1981–83
Beth Lane: 1983–86
Cristyne Lawson: 1958
Keith Lee: 1970
Lea Levin: 1965
Bernard Lias: 1975
Anita Littleman: 1975–76
William Louther: 1964–65
Edward Love: 1972–74
Max Luna III: 1985–89
Aubrey Lynch II: 1989–93
Rosamond Lynn: 1971–72
Deborah Manning: 1981–94
Minnie Marshall: 1959–60, 1962, 1964
Diane Maroney: 1977
Donald Martin: 1961–63
Audrey Mason: 1958–59
Clover Mathis: 1971–74
John Medeiros: 1968–69, 1970
Leonard Meek: 1986–88, 1991–97
Sharrell Mesh: 1978–88
Eleanor McCoy: 1967–68
Keith McDaniel: 1977–84
Hector Mercado: 1970–75
Jan Mickens: 1960
Sharron Miller: 1967–68
Jodi Moccia: 1974–78
Steven Mones: 1977–78
Charles Moore: 1958–62
Ella Thompson Moore: 1960–62
Elbert Morris: 1967–68
Delila Moseley: 1975
Christa Mueller: 1972–74
Michele Murray: 1963–65, 1968–70
Milton Myers: 1978–80
Charles Neal: 1958–59
Rodney Nugent: 1982–88
Michihiko Oka: 1972–78
Richard Orbach: 1979–80
Nat Orr: 1981–85
Ernest Pagnano: 1968–69
Miriam Pandor: 1960–61
Carl Paris: 1975–79

John Parks: 1970–74
Kenneth Pearl: 1970–75
Cynthia Penn: 1974–75
Stanley Perryman: 1980–84
Joan Peters: 1964–65
Michael Peters: 1966, 1968–69
Toni Pierce: 1984–85, 1991–98
Harold Pierson: 1958–59
Margaret Pihl: 1989–91
Dennis Plunkett: 1972–73
Barbara Pouncie: 1980–90
Robert Powell: 1965–66
Don Price: 1958
Lucinda Ransom: 1963–66
Gail Reese: 1971–72
Dwight Rhoden: 1988–94
Desmond Richardson: 1987–94
Doreen Richardson: 1958–60
Danita Ridout: 1978–82
Jonathan Riseling: 1986–88
Alma Robinson: 1968–69
Mabel Robinson: 1958
Renee Robinson: 1981–2012
Paul R. Roman: 1960–61
Freddy Romero: 1968, 1971–73
Renee Rose: 1968–71
Kelvin Rotardier: 1963–75
Elizabeth Roxas: 1985–97
Alton Ruff: 1959–61
David St. Charles: 1984–92
Ruthlyn Salomons: 1985–90
Mariko Sanjo: 1962–63
Dana Sapiro: 1972–74
Leland Schwantes: 1970–72
Ramon Segarra: 1970–71
Geri Seignious: 1962–63
Desiree Sewer: 1986–2001
Maxine Sherman: 1977–84
Beth Shorter: 1974–79
Michele Simmons: 1976–77
Joy Smith: 1960
Stephen Smith: 1985–91
Warren Spears: 1974–77
Linda Spriggs: 1977–81
Estelle Spurlock: 1971–81
Sally Stackhouse: 1962–64
David St. Charles: 1984–92
Rosemary Stevenson: 1963–64
Gregory Stewart: 1981–84
Carol Straker: 1983–84
Danny Strayhorn: 1968–69
Lynne Taylor: 1967–68
Barbara Anne Teer: 1962–63
Ilene Tema: 1958
Glen Tetley: 1959–61
Nasha Thomas: 1986–98
Claude Thompson: 1958–59, 1961–62
Clive Thompson: 1965–67, 1970–80
Ella Thompson: 1960–62
Mel Tomlison: 1977–78
Sally Trammel: 1970
Joyce Trisler: 1964
James Truitte: 1960–68
Marvin Tunney: 1976–77
Matt Turney: 1959–60
Andre Tyson: 1985–94
Desiree Vlad: 1986–2001
Jacqueline Walcott: 1958–59
Lynne Dell Walker: 1971–72
Sylvia Waters: 1968–75
Elbert Watson: 1973–77
Melinda Welty: 1985–86
Myrna White: 1961–62, 1963–64
Dereque Whiturs: 1986–91

Dudley Williams: 1964–2003
Liz Williams: 1958, 1965, 1967
Broderick Wilson: 1983–84
Lester Wilson: 1963–64
Morton Winston: 1964–67, 1970–71
Donna Wood: 1972–86
Peter Woodin: 1973–79
Sara Yarborough: 1970–75, 1977–78
Tina Yuan: 1972–77

Checklist of the Exhibition

ARCHIVES

The eighteen-screen, moving-image montage that forms the surround for *Edges of Ailey* was created by Josh Begley and Kya Lou with Adrienne Edwards. Source material was primarily drawn from the holdings of the Alvin Ailey Dance Foundation, consisting of newly digitized interviews, concert recordings, rehearsal footage, performances for the camera, and other television programs in addition to other contextual source material.

Time-based media content elsewhere in the exhibition was drawn from the following sources (in chronological order): Dwight Godwin (director), Martha Graham in *Primitive Mysteries*, 1931; Katherine Dunham, *Urban Social Dance, Jamaica Fieldwork*, 1936; Ted Shawn, *Nobody Knows the Trouble I've Seen*, 1938; Dwight Godwin (director), Martha Graham, *El Penitente*, ca. 1940; *The March of Time*, "Upbeat in Music" [outtake], 1943; Maya Deren, Talley Beatty (directors), *A Study in Choreography for Camera*, 1945; Ann Barzel (director), Katherine Dunham in *Shango*, 1947; Katherine Dunham, *Negro Ballet*, 1948; Pearl Primus, *Spirituals*, 1950; Jean Negulesco (director), *Lydia Bailey*, 1952; Otto Preminger (director), *Carmen Jones*, 1954; Alex Runciman (director), *Fandango*, December 17, 1955; Katherine Dunham, *Washer Woman*, 1956; Paul Godkin (director), *The United States Steel Hour: A Drum Is a Woman*, 1957; *The Steve Allen Show*, February 19, 1958; Clark Jones (director), *Perry Como's Kraft Music Hall*, September 30, 1959; Katherine Dunham, *Choros* [1947], 1960; Katherine Dunham, *Cumbia* [1947], 1960; Martha Myers (director), *A Time to Dance*, "Ethnic Dance—Roundtrip to Trinidad," 1960; Joe Layton (director), *Porgy and Bess*, 1961; Katherine Dunham at home in Martissant, Haiti, 1962; *Meet the Professor*, June 29, 1962; Allen Shaw (director), *Tribute to Lester Horton*, July 28, 1963; William Greaves (director), *The First World Festival of Negro Arts*, 1966; Robert Drew (director), *On the Road with Duke Ellington*, 1974; Martha Graham, technique video, 1975; Nelson E. Breen (director), *Bearden Plays Bearden*, 1980; James Briggs Murray (director), *An African American Dance Forum*, 1990; and Terry Carter (director), and Katherine Dunham on *Shango*, 2002.

Selected correspondence, notes, journals, posters, programs, and brochures were drawn from the following archives: Allan Gray Family Personal Papers of Alvin Ailey, Black Archives of Mid-America in Kansas City, Missouri; The Antonio Archives; Alvin Ailey Dance Foundation; Beinecke Rare Book and Manuscript Library, Yale University, New Haven, Connecticut; Jacob's Pillow Archives, Becket, Massachusetts; Library of Congress, Washington, DC; The Metropolitan Opera, New York; Museum of the City of New York; The New York Public Library; Stuart A. Rose Manuscript, Archives, and Rare Book Library, Emory University, Atlanta; and Chapin Library, Williams College, Williamstown, Massachusetts.

The following moving image data visualizations commissioned by the Whitney Museum of American Art were created by Kate Elswit and Harmony Bench (Moving Data), with Antonio Jiménez-Mavillard and Tia-Monique Uzor.

"Generations of Embodied Knowledge: The Alvin Ailey American Dance Theater's Dance Artists, 1958–2023" data visualization from the *Radical Accounting* series, 2024. Color and video, 4 min.

"Global Architectures: The Alvin Ailey American Dance Theatre, City by City and Year by Year, 1958–89" data visualization from the *Radical Accounting* series, 2024. Color and video, 4 min.

"Repertory as Living Dance Museum: The Alvin Ailey American Dance Theater's Performance History, 1958–89" data visualization from the *Radical Accounting* series, 2024. Color and video, 4 min.

ARTWORKS

Terry Adkins
Other Bloods (from The Principalities), 2012. Drum, rope, zebra pelt, and parachute, 62 × 19 × 12 in. (157.5 × 48.3 × 30.5 cm). Paula Cooper Gallery, New York

Emma Amos
Judith Jamison as Josephine Baker, 1985. Acrylic on canvas, 100 × 32 in. (254 × 81.3 cm). Ryan Lee Gallery, New York

Benny Andrews
The Way to the Promised Land (Revival Series), 1994. Oil on canvas with painted fabric collage, 72 × 50¾ in. (182.9 × 128.9 cm). Michael Rosenfeld Gallery

Ellsworth Ausby
Untitled, 1970. Painted wood, 82 × 34 × 24 in. (208.3 × 86.4 × 61 cm). Eric Firestone Gallery, New York

Eldren Bailey
Dancers, 1960s. Concrete, plaster, and paint, 29½ × 29 × 17 in. (74.9 × 73.7 × 43.2 cm). Souls Grown Deep Foundation

Richmond Barthé
African Dancer, 1933. Plaster, 42¾ × 16⅞ × 14¼ in. (108.6 × 42.9 × 36.2 cm). Whitney Museum of American Art, New York; purchase, 33.53

Jean-Michel Basquiat
Hollywood Africans, 1983. Acrylic and oil stick on canvas, 84 1/16 × 84 in. (213.5 × 213.4 cm). Whitney Museum of American Art, New York; gift of Douglas S. Cramer, 84.23

Romare Bearden
Selection of twenty-one collages from the series *Bayou Fever*, 1979. Collage and acrylic on fiberboard, dimensions variable. Estate of Romare Bearden; courtesy DC Moore Gallery, New York

Kevin Beasley
Haze, 2023. Polyurethane resin, raw Virginia cotton, marker transfer, and fiberglass, 55½ × 74 × 2½ in. (141 × 188 × 6.4 cm). Casey Kaplan Gallery, New York

John Biggers
Sharecropper, 1945. Oil on canvas, 24 × 18 in. (61 × 45.7 cm). Los Angeles County Museum of Art; purchased with funds from the Ducommun and Gross Endowment and the Robert H. Halff Endowment, M.2022.41

Beverly Buchanan
White Shacks, 1987. Wood and paint, 14 × 13 × 18 in. (35.6 × 33 × 45.7 cm). Collection of Beth Rudin DeWoody

Orangeburg County Family House, 1993. Paint, Sharpie, garland, necklace, wood chips, bark, buttons, bottle caps, license plate, film canister, thumbtacks, clay pot, glass bottle, thread, and glue on wood, 14¼ × 14¾ × 10½ in. (36.2 × 37.5 × 26.7 cm). Private collection

Tom's House, 1995. Wood and tin, 15 × 9½ × 16¼ in. (38.1 × 24.1 × 41.3 cm). Whitney Museum of American Art, New York; gift of Alexandra Wheeler, 2019.427

Lillington, NC Harnett Co., 2007. Acrylic on foamcore, 8½ × 10½ × 11 in. (21.6 × 26.7 × 27.9 cm). Brooklyn Museum; William K. Jacobs, Jr. Fund, 2017.32.2

Family Tree House, 2009. Cedar and acrylic paint, 17 × 10 × 14½ in. (43.2 × 25.4 × 36.8 cm). Collection of Cameron Art Museum, Wilmington, North Carolina; Claude Howell Endowment for the purchase of North Carolina Art

Old Colored School, 2010. Wood and paint, 20¼ × 14¾ × 18½ in. (51.4 × 37.5 × 47 cm). The Metropolitan Museum of Art, New York; Hortense and William A. Mohr Sculpture Purchase Fund, 2017, 2017.270a,b

House from Scraps, 2011. Wood and copper, 18½ × 20½ × 17 in. (47 × 52.1 × 43.2 cm). Nevada Museum of Art, Reno; purchase, with funds from deaccessioning, 2020.14.01

Elizabeth Catlett
I have always worked hard in America, 1946 (printed 1989), from the series *The Negro Woman*, 1946–47 (retitled *The Black Woman*, 1989). Linoleum cut, 8¾ × 6 1/16 in. (22.2 × 15.4 cm). Whitney Museum of American Art, New York; purchase, with funds from the Print Committee, 95.190

In Harriet Tubman I helped hundreds to freedom, 1946 (printed 1989), from the series *The Negro Woman*, 1946–47 (retitled *The Black Woman*, 1989). Linoleum cut, 9⅛ × 7 1/16 in. (23.2 × 17.9 cm). Whitney Museum of American Art, New York; purchase, with funds from the Print Committee, 95.194

In Phillis Wheatley I proved intellectual equality in the midst of slavery, 1946 (printed 1989), from the series *The Negro Woman*, 1946–47 (retitled *The Black Woman*, 1989). Linoleum cut, 9⅛ × 6 1/16 in. (23.2 × 15.4 cm). Whitney Museum of American Art, New York; purchase, with funds from the Print Committee, 95.196

In the fields . . ., 1946 (printed 1989), from the series *The Negro Woman*, 1946–47 (retitled *The Black Woman*, 1989). Linoleum cut, 9 × 6 1/16 in. (22.9 × 15.4 cm). Whitney Museum of American Art, New York; purchase, with funds from the Print Committee, 95.191

I am the Negro woman, 1947 (printed 1989), from the series *The Negro Woman*, 1946–47 (retitled *The Black Woman*, 1989). Linoleum cut, 5 3/16 × 4 in. (13.2 × 10.2 cm). Whitney Museum of American Art, New York; purchase, with funds from the Print Committee, 95.189

In Sojourner Truth I fought for the rights of women as well as Negroes, 1947 (printed 1989), from the series *The Negro Woman*, 1946–47 (retitled *The Black Woman*, 1989). Linoleum cut, 8⅞ × 5 15/16 in. (22.5 × 15.1 cm). Whitney Museum of American Art, New York; purchase, with funds from the Print Committee, 95.195

Karon Davis
Not yet titled, 2024. Mixed media, height: 74 in. (188 cm). Collection of the artist; courtesy Salon 94

Roy DeCarava
Langston Hughes, 1955 (printed 1995). Gelatin silver print, 12 15/16 × 9⅞ in. (32.9 × 25.1 cm). Whitney Museum of American Art, New York; purchase, with funds from the Photography Committee, 98.12.4

Coltrane and Elvin, 1960. Gelatin silver print, 9 15/16 × 12⅞ in. (25.2 × 32.7 cm). Whitney Museum of American Art, New York; purchase, with funds from the Photography Committee, 98.12.3

Elvin Jones, 1961. Gelatin silver print, mounted on board, 12 11/16 × 8¾ in. (32.2 × 22.2 cm). Whitney Museum of American Art, New York; gift of Sherry DeCarava, 2014.134

Beauford Delaney
Charlie Parker Yardbird, 1958. Oil on canvas, 39½ × 29½ in. (100.3 × 74.9 cm). Smithsonian American Art Museum, Washington, DC; gift of the James F. Dicke Family, 2013.89.3

Marian Anderson, 1965. Oil and egg tempera emulsion on canvas, 63 15/16 × 51 5/16 × 1½ in. (162.4 × 130.33 × 3.81 cm). Virginia Museum of Fine Arts, Richmond; J. Harwood and Louise B. Cochrane Fund for American Art, 2012.277

Thornton Dial
Soul Train, 2004. Clothing, tin, rope carpet, bicycle horn, oil, enamel, spray paint, and epoxy on canvas, mounted on wood, 71 × 71½ × 5 in. (180.3 × 181.6 × 12.7 cm). Hood Museum of Art, Dartmouth College, Hanover, New Hampshire: purchased through the Evelyn A. and William B. Jaffe 2015 Fund, 2021.11.3

Shadows of the Field, 2008. String, twine, synthetic cotton batting, wood, burlap, sheet metal, cloth rags, nails, staples, and enamel on canvas on wood, 79 × 105 × 5 in. (200.7 × 266.7 × 12.7 cm). The Metropolitan Museum of Art, New York; gift of Souls Grown Deep Foundation from the William S. Arnett Collection, 2014, 2014.548.4

Jeff Donaldson
Soweto/So We Too, 1979. Mixed media, 39 × 30½ in. (99.1 × 77.5 cm). Collection of Beth Rudin DeWoody

Aaron Douglas
Bravado, 1926. Woodcut, 8 × 5½ in. (20.3 × 14 cm). Whitney Museum of American Art, New York; promised gift of Crystal McCrary and Raymond J. McGuire to the Whitney Museum of American Art, New York, and The Studio Museum in Harlem, P.2022.3.1

Flight, 1926. Woodcut, 8 × 5½ in. (20.3 × 14 cm). Whitney Museum of American Art, New York; promised gift of Crystal McCrary and Raymond J. McGuire to the Whitney Museum of American Art, New York, and The Studio Museum in Harlem, P.2022.3.2

Surrender, 1926. Woodcut, 8 × 5½ in. (20.3 × 14 cm). Whitney Museum of American Art, New York; promised gift of Crystal McCrary and Raymond J. McGuire to the Whitney Museum of American Art, New York, and The Studio Museum in Harlem, P.2022.3.3

Head of a Boy (Portrait of Langston Hughes), 1957. Woodcut, 4⅞ × 4 in. (12.4 × 10.2 cm). The Johnson Collection, Spartanburg, South Carolina

Sam Doyle
Frank Capers, 1970. Paint and marker on wood, 33 × 20¼ in. (83.8 × 51.4 cm). Souls Grown Deep Foundation

Frip, St. Helena's Best, 1970s. Paint on roofing tin, 43⅛ × 52 in. (109.5 × 132.1 cm). High Museum of Art, Atlanta; T. Marshall Hahn Collection, 1997.66

LeBe, 1970s. Paint on tin, 37½ × 26¾ in. (95.3 × 67.9 cm). Souls Grown Deep Foundation

David Driskell
Festival Bahia, 1985. Gouache and mixed media on paper, 24¼ × 30 in. (61.5 × 76.2 cm). Estate of David Driskell; courtesy DC Moore Gallery, New York

Bahian Ribbons, 1987. Acrylic on canvas, 20 × 24 in. (50.8 × 61 cm). Estate of David Driskell; courtesy DC Moore Gallery, New York

Robert Duncanson
View of Cincinnati, Ohio from Covington, Kentucky, ca. 1851. Oil on canvas, 25 × 36 in. (63.5 × 91.4 cm). Cincinnati Museum Center

Melvin Edwards
Katutura, from the series *Lynch Fragment*, 1986. Steel, 11¾ × 5⅞ × 4⅞ in. (30 × 15 × 12.3 cm). The Museum of Modern Art, New York; purchase, 242.1990

Cup of?, from the series *Lynch Fragment*, 1988. Steel, 12⅞ × 6¾ × 9½ in. (32.7 × 17 × 24 cm). The Museum of Modern Art, New York; purchase, 243.1990

Utonga, from the series *Lynch Fragment*, 1988. Steel, 8⅛ × 13½ × 9 in. (20.6 × 34.3 × 22.9 cm). The Metropolitan Museum of Art, New York; gift of Clara Diament Sujo, 1991, 1991.71

Chitungwiza, 1989, from the series *Lynch Fragment*. Steel, 11⅛ × 10¼ × 10⅜ in. (28.5 × 26 × 27.2 cm). The Museum of Modern Art, New York; purchase, 245.1990

Rotimi Fani-Kayode
Adebiyi, ca. 1989. Chromogenic print, 24 3/16 × 23¾ in. (61.4 × 60.3 cm). Solomon R. Guggenheim Museum, New York; purchased with funds contributed by the Photography Council, 2017.34

Every Moment Counts (Ecstatic Antibodies), 1989. Chromogenic print, 47¼ × 47¼ in. (120 × 120 cm). Walther Collection, London

Fon peoples
Female Drum, 19th–20th century. Wood, hide, pigment, cane, and cord, diameter: 20¼ in. (148.6 × 51.4 cm) each. The Metropolitan Museum of Art, New York; gift of Robert H. and Ruth S. Smith, 1982, 1982.495.2

Male Drum, 19th–20th century. Wood, hide, pigment, cane, and cord, diameter: 20¼ in. (148.6 × 51.4 cm) each. The Metropolitan Museum of Art, New York; gift of Robert H. and Ruth S. Smith, 1982, 1982.495.1

Charles Gaines
Sound Box: Nina Simone and Billie Holiday, 2021. Poplar, rubber, felt, MP3 player, rechargeable battery, speaker, remote control, and vinyl records, 25½ × 15½ × 12 in. (64.8 × 39.4 × 30.5 cm). Collection of Beth Rudin DeWoody

Ellen Gallagher
Ecstatic Draught of Fishes, 2022. Oil, pigment, wax, palladium leaf, and paper on canvas, 89¾ × 118⅛ in. (228 × 300 cm). Whitney Museum of American Art, New York; gift of The George Economou Collection, 2023.74

Theaster Gates
Minority Majority, 2012. Decommissioned fire hoses and vinyl on plywood, 66 × 111½ × 3¾ in. (167.6 × 283.2 × 9.5 cm). Whitney Museum of American Art, New York; gift of Barbara and Michael Gamson, 2016.262

Sam Gilliam
Swing 64, 1964. Acrylic on canvas, 37 9/16 × 37⅛ × 1½ in. (95.4 × 94.3 × 3.8 cm). Collection of Beth Rudin DeWoody

Untitled (Black), 1978. Acrylic, yarn, and cut canvas on stained canvas, 89¾ × 120½ in. (228 × 306.1 cm). Whitney Museum of American Art, New York; gift of Suzanne and Bob Cochran, 94.161

David Hammons
Delta Spirit, 1985. Pen and ink on paper, 6 1/16 × 9 in. (15.4 × 22.9 cm). Whitney Museum of American Art, New York; purchase, with funds from the Jack E. Chachkes Endowed Purchase Fund and the List Purchase Fund, 2020.118

Untitled, 1992. Human hair, wire, metallic mylar, sledgehammer, plastic beads, string, metal food tin, panty hose, leather, tea bags, and feathers, dimensions variable. Whitney Museum of American Art, New York; purchase, with funds from the Mrs. Percy Uris Bequest and the Painting and Sculpture Committee, 92.128a–z

Lyle Ashton Harris
Billie #21, 2002. Dye diffusion transfer print (Polaroid), 24 × 20 in. (61 × 50.8 cm). Whitney Museum of American Art, New York; purchase, with funds from the Photography Committee, 2002.563

Maren Hassinger
River, 1972/2011. Mixed-media installation with steel chains and rope, 7 × 89 × 358 in. (17.8 × 226.1 × 909.3 cm). The Studio Museum in Harlem, New York; gift of the artist, 2012.34

Palmer Hayden
Spirituals (Dreams), ca. 1935. Watercolor and graphite pencil on paper, 14 11/16 × 9½ in. (37.3 × 24.1 cm). Whitney Museum of American Art, New York; purchase, with funds from the Drawing Committee, 2015.270a–b

Barkley Hendricks
Dancer, 1977. Oil on canvas, 47⅞ × 36 in. (121.6 × 91.4 cm). Private collection

Geoffrey Holder
Portrait of Carmen de Lavallade, 1976. Oil on canvas with artist frame, 60 × 40 in. (152.4 × 101.6 cm). Collection of Jordan Roth and Richie Jackson

Lonnie Holley
Sharing the Struggle, 2018. Wood rocking chairs and fire hoses, 50 × 45 × 50 in. (127 × 114.3 × 127 cm). Collection of Beth Rudin DeWoody

Clementine Hunter
Cane River Baptism, ca. 1950–56. Oil on paperboard, 19 × 23⅞ in. (48.3 × 60.7 cm). The Johnson Collection, Spartanburg, South Carolina

Hector Hyppolite
The Congo Queen, 1946. Enamel, oil, and graphite pencil on cardboard, 20 × 27⅝ in. (50.9 × 70.1 cm). The Museum of Modern Art, New York; gift of Mr. and Mrs. Walter Bareiss, 852.1956

Wadsworth Jarrell
Revolutionary (Angela Davis), 1972. Screenprint, 25 13/16 × 32½ in. (65.6 × 82.6 cm). Whitney Museum of American Art, New York; purchase, with funds from Kenneth Alpert, 2020.152

Together We Will Win, 1973. Acrylic and foil on canvas, 60 × 84 in. (152.4 × 213.4 cm). Jenkins Johnson Gallery, San Francisco

Rashid Johnson
Untitled Anxious Men, 2016. Ceramic tile, black soap, and wax, 47½ × 34¾ in. (120.7 × 88.3 cm). Collection of the artist

William H. Johnson
Street Life, Harlem, ca. 1939–40. Oil on plywood, 45⅝ × 38⅝ in. (116.0 × 98.0 cm). Smithsonian American Art Museum, Washington, DC; gift of the Harmon Foundation, 1967.59.674

At Home in the Evening, ca. 1940. Oil on canvas, 52¾ × 47 in. (134 × 119.4 cm). Collection of halley k harrisburg and Michael Rosenfeld

Moon over Harlem, ca. 1943–44. Oil on plywood, 28½ × 35¾ in. (72.5 × 90.8 cm.). Smithsonian American Art Museum, Washington, DC; gift of the Harmon Foundation, 1967.59.57

Loïs Mailou Jones
Africa, 1935. Oil on canvas board, 23⅞ × 19⅞ in. (60.6 × 50.5 cm). The Johnson Collection, Spartanburg, South Carolina

Jennie, 1943. Oil on canvas, 35¾ × 28¾ in. (90.8 × 73 cm). Howard University Gallery of Art, Washington, DC; gift of the IBM Corporation

Veve Voudou II, 1963. Mixed media, 21⅛ × 25¼ in. (53.7 × 64.1 cm). Howard University Gallery of Art, Washington, DC; gift of Loïs Mailou Jones Pierre-Noël Trust

Marche-Haiti, 1982. Watercolor, 26 × 32 in. (66 × 81.3 cm). Howard University Gallery of Art, Washington, DC; gift of Floyd W. Coleman

Jacob Lawrence
Tombstones, 1942. Opaque watercolor on paper, 30⅞ × 22¹³⁄₁₆ in. (78.4 × 57.9 cm). Whitney Museum of American Art, New York; purchase, 43.14

Figure Study, ca. 1970. Ink and pencil on paper, 24 × 18 in. (61 × 45.7 cm). Collection of Beth Rudin DeWoody

Ralph Lemon
Ailey Dancing Revelations, 2024. Oil stick on paper, 8 × 8 in. (20.3 × 20.3 cm) each. Collection of the artist

Untitled (Miles Davis), 2006. Ink and watercolor on paper, 5¼ × 7¼ in. (13.3 × 18.4 cm). Hudgins Family

Not yet titled, 2024. Mixed media, 7½ × 5¾ in. (19 × 14.6 cm). Collection of the artist

Norman Lewis
Jazz, 1943–44. Lithograph on wove paper, 14⅜ × 11¼ in (36.5 × 28.6 cm). Estate of the artist; courtesy Michael Rosenfeld Gallery, New York

Phantasy II, 1946. Oil on canvas, 28⅛ × 35⅞ in. (71.4 × 91.2 cm). The Museum of Modern Art, New York; gift of The Friends of Education of The Museum of Modern Art, 528.1998

Samella Lewis
Migrants, 1968. Linocut on paper, 17¼ × 24 in. (43.8 × 61 cm). The Johnson Collection, Spartanburg, South Carolina

Glenn Ligon
Stranger in the Village #12, 1998. Enamel, oil, acrylic, gesso, coal dust, and glitter on cotton, 96 × 72⅛ in. (243.8 × 183.2 cm). Whitney Museum of American Art, New York; gift of the artist and purchase, with funds from Joanne Leonhardt Cassullo and the Dorothea L. Leonhardt Fund at the Communities Foundation of Texas and the Painting and Sculpture Committee, 98.55

James Little
Stars and Stripes, 2021. Oil and wax on linen, 72¼ × 72¼ in. (183.5 × 183.5 cm). Whitney Museum of American Art, New York; purchase, with funds from Marcia Dunn and Jonathan Sobel, 2022.207

Antonio Lopez and Juan Ramos
Slideshow of Studio 54, 1977. Slide projection, dimensions variable. The Antonio Archives

Al Loving
Untitled, ca. 1975. Mixed media, 66 × 74 in. (167.6 × 188 cm). Collection of Beth Rudin DeWoody

Makers unknown
Alvin Ailey panel of AIDS Memorial quilt, 1987. Mixed media, 144 × 144 in. (365.8 × 365.8 cm). National AIDS Memorial

Kerry James Marshall
Souvenir IV, 1998. Acrylic, glitter, and screenprint on paper on tarpaulin, with metal grommets, 107⅝ × 157½ in. (273.4 × 400.1 cm). Whitney Museum of American Art, New York; purchase, with funds from the Painting and Sculpture Committee, 98.56

Archibald John Motley, Jr.
Gettin' Religion, 1948. Oil on linen, 32 × 39⁷⁄₁₆ in. (81.3 × 100.2 cm). Whitney Museum of American Art, New York; purchase, Josephine N. Hopper Bequest, by exchange, 2016.15

Thomas Nast
Emancipation of the Negroes—The Past and the Future (from "Harper's Weekly"), 1863. Wood engraving, 14⅝ × 20¹¹⁄₁₆ in. (37.2 × 52.6 cm). The Metropolitan Museum of Art, New York; Harris Brisbane Dick Fund, 1929, 29.88.4(10)

Senga Nengudi
R.S.V.P., 1975. Nylon mesh and sand, 82½ × 113½ × 4½ in. (209.6 × 288.3 × 11.4 cm). Museum of Contemporary Art, Los Angeles; purchase, with funds provided by the Acquisition and Collection Committee, 2005.35

Studio Performance with R.S.V.P., 1976. Gelatin silver print, 30 × 40 in. (76.2 × 101.6 cm). The Museum of Modern Art, New York; Committee on Media and Performance Art Funds, 1120.2014

Mary Lovelace O'Neal
Race Woman Series #7, 1990s. Mixed media on canvas, 84 × 60 in. (213.4 × 152.4 cm). Jenkins Johnson Gallery, San Francisco

John Outterbridge
The Elder, Ethnic Heritage Series, 1971–72. Wooden hat forms, fabric, wooden beads, twine, metal, paint, and human hair, 28¼ × 11⅞ × 11⅜ in. (71.8 × 30.2 × 28.9 cm). Whitney Museum of American Art, New York; purchase, with funds from David Cancel and an anonymous donor, 2022.189

Joe Overstreet
Purple Flight, 1971. Acrylic on constructed canvas with metal grommets and cotton rope, dimensions variable. Eric Firestone Gallery, New York

Jennifer Packer
Not yet titled, 2024. Collection of the artist

Gordon Parks
Music—That Lordly Power, 1993. Gelatin silver print, 19⅜ × 14 in. (49.2 × 35.6 cm). Gordon Parks Foundation

Horace Pippin
Cabin in the Cotton, ca. 1931–37. Oil on cotton, mounted on Masonite, 20 × 33½ in. (51 × 85 cm). The Art Institute of Chicago; purchased with funds provided by Thomas F. Pick and Mary P. Hines in memory of their mother Frances W. Pick, 1990.417

Knowledge of God, 1944. Oil on canvas, dimensions unknown. Collection of Leslie Miller and Richard Worley

School Studies, 1944. Oil on fabric, 24⅛ × 30³⁄₁₆ in. (61.2 × 76.6 cm). National Gallery of Art, Washington, DC; gift of Mr. and Mrs. Meyer P. Potamkin in honor of the Fiftieth Anniversary of the National Gallery of Art, 1991.42.1

Noah Purifoy
Untitled, 1970. Wood, leather, brass, and copper, 49⅜ × 28⅝ × 21¼ in. (125.4 × 72.7 × 54 cm). Whitney Museum of American Art, New York; purchase, 71.170

Martin Puryear
The Rest, 2009–10. Bronze, 45¾ × 35⁵⁄₁₆ × 20⅝ in. (116.2 × 89.7 × 52.4 cm). Whitney Museum of American Art, New York; gift of Gretchen and John Berggruen, 2014.350

Faith Ringgold
United States of Attica, 1971. Offset lithograph, 21⅜ × 27³⁄₁₆ in. (54.3 × 69.1 cm). Whitney Museum of American Art, New York; gift of ACA Galleries in honor of Faith Ringgold, 2017.163

Betye Saar
I've Got Rhythm, 1972. Mechanical metronome with wood case, plastic toy, American flag pin, paint, and paper collage, 8⁹⁄₁₆ × 4⁷⁄₁₆ × 4⁷⁄₁₆ in. (21.7 × 11.3 × 11.3 cm). Whitney Museum of American Art, New York; purchase, with funds from the Painting and Sculpture Committee, 99.87a–b

Lorna Simpson
Momentum, 2011. Two-channel video installation, color, sound; 6:56 min., looped. Collection of the artist

Alma Thomas
Mars Dust, 1972. Acrylic on canvas, 69¼ × 57⅛ in. (175.9 × 145.1 cm). Whitney Museum of American Art, New York; purchase, with funds from The Hament Corporation, 72.58

Mickalene Thomas
Clarivel Face Forward Gazing, 2024. Rhinestones, acrylic, and oil on canvas, mounted on wood panel, 96 × 144 in. (243.8 × 365.8 cm). Collection of the artist

Blaise Tobia
Ellsworth Ausby rehearsal, 1978. Archival inkjet print, 6 × 9 in. (15.2 × 22.3 cm). Courtesy the artist

Documentation of Ellsworth Ausby Performance, Union Square, 1978. Archival inkjet print, 6 × 9 in. (15.2 × 22.3 cm). Courtesy the artist

Bill Traylor
Untitled (Man in a Blue House), n.d. Graphite pencil and poster paint on paperboard, 17¼ × 11⅜ in. (43.8 × 28.9 cm). The Johnson Collection, Spartanburg, South Carolina

Rubem Valentim
Untitled, 1956–62. Oil on canvas, 27⅝ × 19¾ in. (70.2 × 50.2 cm). The Museum of Modern Art, New York; gift of Patricia Phelps de Cisneros through the Latin American and Caribbean Fund in honor of Lissette Stancioff, 876.2016

James Van Der Zee
Marcus Garvey Rally, 1924. Gelatin silver print, 7⅛ × 9⅜ in. (18.1 × 23.8 cm). Whitney Museum of American Art, New York; gift of Manny and Skippy Gerard, 2003.416

Dancer, 1925. Gelatin silver print, 6¾ × 4¹⁵⁄₁₆ in. (17.1 × 12.5 cm). Whitney Museum of American Art, New York; gift of an anonymous donor 2001.38

Choir Boy, 1937 Gelatin silver print, 8 × 5 in. (20.3 × 12.7 cm). The Studio Museum in Harlem, New York; gift of The Sandor Family Collection, Chicago, 2000.11.13

Carl Van Vechten
Portraits of Alvin Ailey, 1955. Beinecke Rare Book and Manuscript Library, Yale University, New Haven, Connecticut

Kara Walker
African/American, 1998. Linoleum cut on paper, 45⅞ × 60½ in. (116.5 × 153.7 cm). Whitney Museum of American Art, New York; promised gift of the Fisher Landau Center for Art, P.2010.339

Meta Vaux Warrick Fuller
Mother and Child (Secret Sorrow), ca. 1914. Bronze, 5¾ × 5 × 5 in. (14.6 × 12.7 × 12.7 cm). Danforth Art Museum, Framingham, Massachusetts; gift of Mrs. Robert MacPherson, 1975.16

Te Adoremus Domine, 1921. Painted plaster, 14¾ × 13½ in. (35.6 × 34.3 cm). Danforth Art Museum, Framingham, Massachusetts; gift of the Meta V.W. Fuller Trust, 2006.282

Mold for Crusaders for Freedom, 1962. Plaster with mold release agent, diameter: 36 in. (91.4 cm). Danforth Art Museum, Framingham, Massachusetts; gift of the Meta V.W. Fuller Trust, 2006.310

Paul Waters
Beautiful Life, 1969. Oil on cut linen collage on canvas, 46 × 60 in. (116.8 × 152.4 cm). Eric Firestone Gallery, New York

Carrie Mae Weems
Untitled, from the series *Sea Islands*, 1992. Gelatin silver print, 19⅜ × 19⅜ in. (49.2 × 49.2 cm). Whitney Museum of American Art, New York; gift of Carrie Mae Weems and P.P.O.W., 97.97.1

Untitled, from the series *Sea Islands*, 1992. Gelatin silver print, 19⁹⁄₁₆ × 19⁹⁄₁₆ in. (49.7 × 49.7 cm). Whitney Museum of American Art, New York; gift of Carrie Mae Weems and P.P.O.W., 97.97.2

Untitled, from the series *Sea Islands*, 1992. Gelatin silver print, 19⅛ × 19⅛ in. (48.6 × 48.6 cm). Whitney Museum of American Art, New York; gift of Carrie Mae Weems and P.P.O.W., 97.97.3

Charles White
Preacher, 1952. Pen and ink and graphite pencil on board, 22¹³⁄₁₆ × 29¹⁵⁄₁₆ in. (57.9 × 76 cm). Whitney Museum of American Art, New York; purchase, 52.25

Kandis Williams
Black Box, 4 points: Horton, Ailey, McKayle contractions and expansions of drama from vernacular —arms outstretched and entangle, 2021. Xerox collage and ink on paper, 41½ × 29½ in. (105.4 × 74.9 cm). Mohn Family Trust

Hale Aspacio Woodruff
African Headdress, ca. 1931–46 (printed 1996). Linoleum cut with chine-collé, 6 × 4 in. (15.2 × 10.2 cm). Whitney Museum of American Art, New York; gift of E. Thomas Williams, Jr. and Auldlyn Higgins Williams, 98.22.1

Coming Home, ca. 1931–46 (printed 1996). Linoleum cut with chine-collé, 9¹⁵⁄₁₆ × 7¹⁵⁄₁₆ in. (25.2 × 20.2 cm). Whitney Museum of American Art, New York; gift of E. Thomas Williams, Jr. and Auldlyn Higgins Williams, 98.22.3

Old Church, ca. 1931–46 (printed 1996). Linoleum cut with chine-collé, 6⁷⁄₁₆ × 9 in. (16.4 × 22.9 cm). Whitney Museum of American Art, New York; gift of E. Thomas Williams, Jr. and Auldlyn Higgins Williams, 98.22.5

Relics, ca. 1931–46 (printed 1996). Linoleum cut with chine-collé, 8⅛ × 11¹⁄₁₆ in. (20.6 × 28.1 cm). Whitney Museum of American Art, New York; gift of E. Thomas Williams, Jr. and Auldlyn Higgins Williams, 98.22.6

Trusty on a Mule, ca. 1931–46 (printed 1996). Linoleum cut with chine-collé, 7¹⁵⁄₁₆ × 10¹⁄₁₆ in. (20.2 × 25.6 cm). Whitney Museum of American Art, New York; gift of E. Thomas Williams, Jr. and Auldlyn Higgins Williams, 98.22.8

Blind Musician, 1935/1998. Woodcut, 6 × 4¹⁄₁₆ in. (15.2 × 10.3 cm). Whitney Museum of American Art, New York; gift of Auldlyn Higgins Williams and E. Thomas Williams, Jr., 2004.631

By Parties Unknown, 1935 (printed 1996). Linoleum cut with chine-collé, 12 × 9 in. (30.5 × 22.9 cm). Whitney Museum of American Art, New York; gift of E. Thomas Williams, Jr. and Auldlyn Higgins Williams, 98.22.2

Giddap, 1935 (printed 1996). Linoleum cut with chine-collé, 12 × 9 in. (30.5 × 22.9 cm). Whitney Museum of American Art, New York; gift of E. Thomas Williams, Jr. and Auldlyn Higgins Williams, 98.22.4

Sunday Promenade, 1939 (printed 1996). Linoleum cut with chine-collé, 9⁹⁄₁₆ × 7¹¹⁄₁₆ in. (24.3 × 19.5 cm). Whitney Museum of American Art, New York; gift of E. Thomas Williams, Jr. and Auldlyn Higgins Williams, 98.22.7

Lynette Yiadom-Boakye
Fly Trap, 2024. Oil on canvas, two-panels, 78¾ × 51⅛ in. (200 × 130 cm) each. Collection of the artist; courtesy the artist; Corvi-Mora, London; and Jack Shainman Gallery, New York

A Knave Made Manifest, 2024. Oil on linen, 78¾ × 70⅞ in. (200 × 180 cm). Collection of the artist; courtesy Corvi-Mora, London, and Jack Shainman Gallery, New York

Purvis Young
Ocean, 1975. Paint and wood on Masonite, 16 × 14¼ in. (40.6 × 36.2 cm). The Metropolitan Museum of Art, New York; gift of Souls Grown Deep Foundation from the William S. Arnett Collection, 2014, 2014.548.19

Black People Migrating West, late 1970s. Paint and poster board, with wood frame, 21¼ × 28¼ in. (54 × 71.8 cm). High Museum of Art, Atlanta; museum purchase, and gift of the Souls Grown Deep Foundation from the William S. Arnett Collection, 2017.80

Here I Come, Freedom, late 1970s. Paint on mylar, mounted on found painting, 31½ × 27 in. (80 × 68.6 cm). Souls Grown Deep Foundation

I Love Your America, late 1970s. Paint on mylar, mounted on found painting, 25¼ × 17¼ in. (64.1 × 43.8 cm). Souls Grown Deep Foundation

Love Dance, ca. 1991. House paint on mylar, mounted on wood, with wood frame, 96½ × 43 in. (245.1 × 109.2 cm). Souls Grown Deep Foundation

Our Father, 1997. Paint on Masonite and wood, mounted on wood, 64¾ × 48 in. (164.5 × 121.9 cm). Currier Museum of Art, Manchester, New Hampshire; Scheier Fund and gift of the Souls Grown Deep Foundation, 2021.52

As of June 15, 2024

Lenders to the Exhibition

Allan Gray Family Personal Papers of Alvin Ailey, Black Archives of Mid-America in Kansas City, Missouri

Alvin Ailey Dance Foundation

The Antonio Archives

The Art Institute of Chicago

Autograph, London

Estate of Romare Bearden

Beinecke Rare Book and Manuscript Library, Yale University, New Haven, Connecticut

Brooklyn Museum

Cameron Art Museum, Wilmington, North Carolina

Casey Kaplan Gallery, New York

Chapin Library, Williams College, Williamstown, Massachusetts

Cincinnati Museum Center

Corvi-Mora, London

Currier Museum of Art, Manchester, New Hampshire

Danforth Art Museum, Framingham, Massachusetts

Karon Davis

DC Moore Gallery, New York

Beth Rudin DeWoody

Eric Firestone Gallery, New York

Jeff and Leslie Fischer

The Gordon Parks Foundation, Pleasantville, New York

Hales Gallery, New York

halley k harrisburg and Michael Rosenfeld

High Museum of Art, Atlanta

Hood Museum of Art, Dartmouth College, Hanover, New Hampshire

Howard University Gallery of Art, Washington, DC

Hudgins Family

Jack Shainman Gallery, New York

Jacob's Pillow Archives, Becket, Massachusetts

Jenkins Johnson Gallery, San Francisco

The Johnson Collection, Spartanburg, South Carolina

Rashid Johnson

Ralph Lemon

Library of Congress, Washington, DC

Los Angeles County Museum of Art

Crystal McCrary and Raymond McGuire

The Metropolitan Museum of Art, New York

The Metropolitan Opera, New York

Michael Rosenfeld Gallery, New York

Leslie Miller and Richard Worley

Mohn Family Collection

The Museum of Contemporary Art, Los Angeles

The Museum of Modern Art, New York

Museum of the City of New York

The National AIDS Memorial, San Francisco

National Gallery of Art, Washington, DC

Nevada Museum of Art, Reno

The New York Public Library

Jennifer Packer

Paula Cooper Gallery, New York

Jordan Roth and Richie Jackson

Ryan Lee Gallery, New York

Salon 94

The Schomburg Center for Research in Black Culture, The New York Public Library

Lorna Simpson

Smithsonian American Art Museum, Washington, DC

The Solomon R. Guggenheim Museum, New York

Souls Grown Deep Foundation, Atlanta

Stuart A. Rose Manuscript, Archives, and Rare Book Library, Emory University, Atlanta

The Studio Museum in Harlem

Mickalene Thomas

Blaise Tobia

Virginia Museum of Fine Arts, Richmond

Whitney Museum of American Art, New York

Lynette Yiadom-Boakye

Private collections

Whitney Museum of American Art Board of Trustees

Chairman Emeritus
Leonard A. Lauder

Honorary Chairman
Flora Miller Biddle

Chairman
Richard M. DeMartini

President
Fern Kaye Tessler

Chairs of the Executive Committee
Robert J. Hurst
Anne-Cecilie Engell Speyer

Vice Chairmen
Gaurav K. Kapadia
Nancy Poses
Paul C. Schorr, IV

Vice Presidents
Miyoung Lee
Julie Ostrover
Robert Rosenkranz

Secretary
Laurie M. Tisch

Treasurer
Bennett Goodman

Alice Pratt Brown Director
Scott Rothkopf, ex officio

Judy Hart Angelo
Paul Arnhold
Jill Bikoff
Leslie Bluhm
Neil G. Bluhm
David Cancel
David Carey
Joanne Leonhardt Cassullo
Nancy Carrington Crown
Pamella G. DeVos
Beth Rudin DeWoody
Fairfax N. Dorn
Marcia Dunn
Lise Evans
Michael Gamson, ex officio
Victor F. Ganzi
Henry Louis Gates, Jr.
Katja Goldman
Susan K. Hess
Michael E. Kassan
Neal K. Katyal
Claudia Laviada
Jonathan O. Lee
Stephanie March
Raymond J. McGuire
Julie Mehretu
Brooke Garber Neidich
John C. Phelan
Scott Resnick
Jen Rubio
Thomas E. Tuft
Ku-Ling Yurman
David Zalaznick

Honorary Trustees
Joel S. Ehrenkranz
James A. Gordon
Gilbert C. Maurer
Peter Norton
Adam D. Weinberg, Director Emeritus

In Memoriam
Melva Bucksbaum
B.H. Friedman
Philip H. Geier, Jr.
Brendan Gill
Sondra Gilman Gonzalez-Falla
Susan Morse Hilles
Michael H. Irving
Emily Fisher Landau
Thomas H. Lee
Roy R. Neuberger
Robert W. Wilson

Past Chairmen
Flora Miller Biddle
Neil G. Bluhm
Susan K. Hess
Robert J. Hurst
Leonard A. Lauder
Howard Lipman
Flora Whitney Miller
Brooke Garber Neidich
David Solinger
Laurie M. Tisch
Thomas E. Tuft

Founder
Gertrude Vanderbilt Whitney

As of July 1, 2024

Whitney Museum of American Art
Staff

Sepand Abootorab
Nadia Abudi
Jehad Abu-Hamda
Alondra Acevedo Garcia
Becky Acosta
Elena Adasheva-Klein
Casper Aguila Morales
Aimen Ali
Stephanie Alifano
Liam Allan
Gina Allen
Fidel Alleyne
Heather Allison
Scarlet-Frances Alonzo
Adrienne Alston
Andrea Ambro
Charles Amorosso
Casey Amspacher
Alyssa Andrews
Marilou U. Aquino
Shelissa Aquino
Juan Aranda
Santiago Arango
Angelica Arbelaez
Morgan Arenson
Idehen Aruede
Rafael Ayala
Allegra Baker
Nicolette Balmer
Wendy Barbee-Lowell
Whitney Barnes
Paula Bauer
Bernadette Beauchamp
Michael Beiser
Max Rose Bell
Harry Benjamin
Caitlin Bermingham
Christopher Bernu
Theda Berry

Nora Bethune
Casey Betts
Maria Bevilacqua
Taylor Beyrer
Anna Bida
Amy Nicole Black
Ivy Blackman
Marvin Blugh
Sivan Bogan
Gregg Bordowitz
Kelly Borges
Adelle Bortz
Katherine Braun
Corey Braxton
Sam Breed
Colin Brooks
Mitsuko Brooks
Algernon Brown
Carolina Brown
Dalvin Brown
Lisa Brown
Reagan Brown
Kyle Brumsted
Kyle Brunette
Jason Buccieri
Tom Burckhardt
E Richard Burgos
Garfield Burton
Laura Busby
Anne Byrd
Pablo Caines
Adrian Cameron
Savannah Campbell
Annie Canning
Jane Carey
David Carrero
Diana Carvajal
Trista Casanas Ford
Maeve Cavadini
Natalee Cayton
Emily Cazares
Lexander Chacin
Sunil Chaddha
Derrick Charles
Inde Cheong
Lauren Abigail Cheung
Beatriz Cifuentes
Janet Clancy
João Paulo Coelho e Castro
Bojana Coklyat
Aseeli Coleman
Jesse Colon
Nicky Combs
Spencer Compton
Kim Conaty
Andrew Cone
Errol Coore
Brenna Cothran
Heather Cox
Mary Creed
David Critides
Haley Cummings
Anton Davis
Monica Adame Davis
Scott Davis
Lawrence DeBlasio
Monserrate DeLeon
Margo Delidow
Ophelia Deng
Marcia Diaz Claudio
Rowan Diaz-Toth
Yolanda Dixon
Angela Dizon
sage donahue
Marisa Donovan
Sarika Doppalapudi
Isaac Dunne

John Dyer
Kasim Earl
Adrienne Edwards
Sarah Ehtisham
Shanique Emelife
Joanna Epstein
David Ertel
Gabriel Esparza
Natalia Sofia Espinoza
Nakai Falcon
Thursday Farrar
Ezra Feldman
Joel Fennell
Desiree Fermin
Meghan Ferrucci
Judine Fiddler
Dalaeja Foreman
Sarah Fortini
Angel Fosuhene
Ryan Fox
Emilie Foy
Debora Francis
William Francis
Samuel Franks
Denis Frederick
Annie French
Melinda Freudenberger
Eve Frohm
Emma Gabel
Kendall Galant
Behrang Garakani
Steven Garcia
Viridiana Garcia Choy
Karina Garcia Labrana
Donald Garlington
John Gasper
John Gaudio
Jesse Gelaznik
Ronnie George
Alana Giarrano
Michael Gibbons
Gabrielle Giles
Bonnie Glover
Brian Glover
Reina Gochez
Claire Golder
Jennie Goldstein
Nora Gomez-Strauss
Amber Gonzalez
Lucas Gonzalez
Jonathan Gorman
Caitlin Green
Hilary L. Greenbaum
Olivia Gregory
Steven Grimaldi
Kaylee Grippando
Jennifer Groch
Nicole Grullon
Marcela Guerrero
Peter Guss
Abigail Hack
Rita Hall
Alec Harris
Tara Hart
Barbara Haskell
Andrew Hawkes
Maura Heffner
William Hempel
Araya Henry
Elizabeth Henschen
Lawrence Hernandez
Megan Heuer
Jonathan Heutmaker
Rebecca Hickey
Rujeko Hockley
Nicholas S. Holmes
Michael Honigsberg

Aya Horikoshi
Charlotte Houngbedji
Andreas Huang
Ashley Hudson
Ronald Hudson
Jared Huggins
Felicia Huguley
Beth Huseman
Scout Hutchinson
Chrissie Iles
Gina Im
Junichiro Ishida
Luccas Israel
Carlos Jacobo
Emily Jacoby
Armando Jaramillo Garcia
Jesse Jenkins
Nic Jerabek
Jennifer Jhagroo
Alyssa Johnson
Julia McKenzie Johnson
Caitlin Jones
Charles Joseph
Joel Kaplan
Alexandra Karpovich
Faith Kaufman
William Kennedy
Tim Kerins
Christopher Ketchie
Thomas Killie
Leslie King
Daniel Kingery
Tom Koehler
Ashley Kok
Thomas Kotik
Tim Kovolenko
Joanna Kozak
Timothy Kuffner
Hayley Kuhlmann
Josephine Kunkle-Schoen
Courtney Kupferschmidt
Denise Kupferschmidt
Caroline LaCava
Midrene Lamy
Sandy LaPorte
Annalisa LaPuma
Martha LaRose
Joe Laureiro
Dixie Law
Meredith Lawhead
Deanna Lee
Eunice Lee
Heeae Lee
Sang Lee
Emma LeHocky
Doyle Lewis
Paul Li
David Liburd
Benjamin Lipnick
David Lisbon
Brian Lloyd
Robert Lomblad
Kelly Long
Joel Lopez
Iris Loughran
Eleanor Lovinsky
Brianna Lowndes
Angie Lu
Joshua Lubin-Levy
Kiersten Lukason
Jonita Luti
Jason Lutz
Douglas Madill
Drew Madland
Kenneth Madore
Damien Marchese
Alexis Markopoulos

Keyahna Marks
Genevieve Martinez
Wilmer Martinez
John Martins
Kyla Mathis-Angress
Noel McCarthy
James McKnight
Molly McLaughlin
Emma McMillan
Elissa Medina Mejia
Lourdes Mejia
Chanell Melendez
Bridget Mendoza
Marek Milde
Graham Miles
Zack Millicent
Atticus Moorman
David Morales
Robert Morales
Michael Morrissey
Victor Moscoso
Majida Mugharbel
Lane Muniz
Meer Musa
Micah Musheno
Sara Nadal-Melsio
Jared Nangle
Daniel Nascimento
David Neary
Will Neer
Malaika Newsome
Alice Nguyen
Giulia Nicita
Maria Pignataro Nielsen
William Norton
James Nunez
Jaison O'Blenis
Megan O'Brien
Colin O'Con
Bradon O'Connell
Bridget O'Keefe
Arden Orth
Justin Antonio Ortiz
Nelson Ortiz
Vada Ortiz
Ahmed Osman
Julian Osti
Nicky Ozir
Angela Rose Paccione
Luis Padilla
Alexander Page
Debbie Page
Kimie Page
Rose Pallone
Jacqueline Panama
Noam Parness
Max Parry-McDonell
Christiane Paul
Andrew Pazmino
Sasha Peck
Chelsey Pellot
Natasha Pereira
Roberto Perez
Daniel Peterson
Hubert Peterson
Jason Phillips
Laura Phipps
Timothy Pickerill
Angelo Pikoulas
Laura Pitt
Anna Piwowar
Carla Posner
Eliza Proctor
Laura Protzel
Joe Quartararo
Emma Quaytman
Georgina Quintana

Will Raines
Ashley Reese
Robert Reese
Julie N. Rega
Andryck Requena
Gregory Reynolds
Gene Riftin
Belen Rincon
Felix Rivera
Nina Roberts
Melissa Robles
Salvatore Roccaforte
Clare Roche
Anibal Rodriguez
Mario Rodriguez
Victor Ignacio Rodriguez
Clara Rojas-Sebesta
Antonio Rosa
Joshua Rosenblatt
Nicole Rosengurt
Amy Roth
Scott Rothkopf
Angela Rubin
CJ Salapare
Laura Salomon
Kevin Sanchez
Leonel Sanchez
Awa Sanogo
Vincent Santiago
Cythali Sapuis
Bermet Sargazakova
Lynnette Sauer
Lisa Saunders
Drew Sawyer
Lynn E. Schatz
Laura Schwarz
Elizabeth Schweitzer
Cristina Scorza
Peter A. Scott
Shawnace Seegars
Monica Sekaquaptewa
David Selimoski
Jason Senquiz
Leslie Sheridan
Irene Shifman
Dyeemah Simmons
David Simpson
Elizabeth Skalka
Elisabeth Skjaervold
Matthew Skopek
James Skuldt
Roxanne Smith
Daniel Smith
Madeline Smith
Nathan Smith
Michele Snyder
Mary-Jean Sobiesiak
Elizabeth Soland
Cree Solomon
Barbi Spieler
Susan Steinfield
Minerva Stella
Natalia Sterling
Emily Stoller-Patterson
Emilie Sullivan
Charley Summers
Rabinda Surujnath
Denis Suspitsyn
Elisabeth Sussman
Jo Tam
Adin Tannin
Alonso Tapia-Benitez
Andres Tawil
Melanie Taylor
Joseph Teliha
Eva Tenby
Ellen Tepfer

Darlene Thevenin
Alex Tonetta
Matthew Torres
Ana Torres-Hurtado
Julius Treadway
Aislinn Tucker
David Tufino
Tiaalea Tupuola
Beth Turk
Jorge Ulrich
Khaleiah Vasquez
Matthew Vega
Yuyu Vega
Eric Vermilion
Andrew Viola-Lopez
Christopher Voegels
Cynthia Vogt
Eva Von Schweinitz
Tate Waddell
Farris Wahbeh
David Walker
Patrick Walsh
Rowan Walter
Audrey Wang
Sunny Wang
Vivian Wang
Audrey Warne
Caroline Webb
Rachael Wehrle
Maggie Wei
Erika Wentworth
Joshua Wertheimer
Jason Wimbish
Henry Witherow-Culpepper
Marcia Witter
Michael Woodward
Elliot Degrassi Yokum
Christine Zheng
Andrea Zlotowitz
Connie Zuo
Alex Zylka

As of June 28, 2024

Index

Note: Unattributed works accompanied by dates are works choreographed by Alvin Ailey. Page numbers in italic type indicate illustrations.

A

AAADT. *See* Alvin Ailey American Dance Theater
Abbott, Loretta, 109, 110, *140*
Abraham, Kyle, 14, 45, 323, 325
According to St. Francis (1954), 126, 366
Adelphi University, 143
Adler, Stella, 15, 134
aesthetics. *See* Africanist aesthetics; Black aesthetics; queer of color aesthetics
African diaspora. *See* Black/African diaspora
African Holiday (theatrical revue, 1960), 131, 366
Africanist aesthetics, 49–50, 51n6, 54, 80. *See also* Black aesthetics
Afternoon Blues (1953), 126
Agee, James, 134
AIDS, 21, 39–40, 77–78, 80, 83, 98, 149, *364*
Ailey (film), 111
Ailey, Alvin. *See also* choreography
    acting studies and roles of, 17, 40, 134, 135
    Algarin and, 67–69
    awards and honors for, 44, 68, 117, 140, 141, 142, *142*, 143, 144, 145, 148, 149
    and the Black Church tradition, 17, 59–60, 64–66, 74, 101, 122, 131
    "blood memories" of, 14, 18, 22, 53–54, 62, 66, 77, 78, 83, 86, 92n6, 331
    comments on dance, 12, 14, 17–20, 69–70, 72n14, 135, 153, 331
    death of, 21–22, 39, 80, 149, *149*
    early dance experience of, 17–18, 26n26
    gay/queer identity of, 20–22, 39–40, 67, 101–2, 104–5, 115, 117, 122, 126, 138, 140, 144
    influences and inspirations on/for, 15, 17, 18, 37, 55, 65, 73, 87, 93–94, 112, 126, 131, 148, 331
    mental health of, 88, 135, 144, 145, 148
    notebooks and writing of, 12, 15, 19, 20, 22, 74, 85–90, *86*, *88*, *89*, *91*, 113, 115, 118, 153, *276*, *278*, *230–319*, *322*, *330*
    personal life of, 17, 39–41, 55–56, 64, 68, 111, 122, 144 (*see also* gay/queer identity of; Texas childhood of)
    poems of, 15 (*see also* notebooks and writing of)
    range of arts practiced by, 22
    short stories of, 15, 18, (*see also* notebooks and writing of)
    Texas childhood of, 17, 18, 41, 53–54, 62, 74, 77, 94, 122
Ailey, Alvin, Sr. (father of Ailey), 122, 143
Ailey Arts In Education and Community Programs, 324
AileyCamp, 149, 324
Ailey Celebrates Ellington (television special), 143
Ailey Celebrates Ellington festival, 143, *143*
Ailey Extension program, 14, 119, 323, 324
Ailey School, 14, 45, 79, 87, 94, 141, 145, 323, 324, 326
Ailey II, 14, 32, 53, 71, *71*, 80, 98, 100n14, 143, 323, 324, 326
A.I.M by Kyle Abraham, 323, 325
Alexander, Amos, 122–23
Alexander, Michelle, 77
Algarin, Miguel, 67–69, 71, 112, 144
Nuyorican Nights (with Miguel Piñero), 144
Allan Gray Family Personal Papers of Alvin Ailey, 12, 94, 277. *See* Gray, Allan
Allen, Debbie, 103
Alvin Ailey American Dance Theater (AAADT)
    awards and honors for, 149
    critical responses to, 42, 44, 54, 57n3, 65, 70, 88–90, 100n16, 105, 115–16, 130, 135, 140, 142, 145
    dancers for, 94, *95*, *96*, 368–69
    experience of teaching about, 47–50
    financial difficulties of, 33, 35, 68, 138, 140, 141, 142, 145
    founding of, 18, 21, 130
    goals of, 19
    locations of studios/headquarters, 68, 109, 141, 142, 144, 149
    membership flow, 95, 96
    names of, 100n3, 131, 142
    overview of, from exhibition schedule, 324
    performance locations in cities, *97*
    performance locations in New York metropolitan area, *98*, foldout
    racial integration of, 19
    repertory of, 18, 35, 48–49, 78–80, 82, 98–99, 100n17, 110, 114, 130, 153, 323, foldout
    teaching methods of, 17, 19, 36, 87, 103, 111
    touring of, 98, foldout
Alvin Ailey American Dance Theater, The (book), 144
Alvin Ailey Dance Foundation Collection, 277
Alvin Ailey: Memories and Visions (television special), 143
Alvin Ailey panel of AIDS Memorial quilt (makers unknown), *364*
Alvin Ailey Repertory Ensemble. *See* Ailey II
Alvin Ailey Student Workshop, 100n14, 143
American Ballet Company, 141
American Ballet Theatre, 30, 141, 142, 148
American dance, 19, 49, 59, 68, 79–80, 87
American Dance Asylum, 325
American Dance Center, New York, 144
American Dance Festival, 135, 141, 148
American Dance Festival Award, 148
American Dream, 89
American Guild of Musical Artists (AGMA), 33
Americanness
    Ailey and, 49, 85–89
    Blackness and, 22, 62
    in the 1980s and 1990s, 78
American Psychiatric Association, 21
American South, 22, 41, 60–61, 126, 138, 144. *See also* Black South
Amos, Emma, *Judith Jamison as Josephine Baker*, *353*
Amos 'n' Andy Music Hall (television show), 127
Anderson, Marian, 15, 22, 331
    portrait of, *353*
Anderson, Paquita, 130
Andrews, Benny, *The Way to the Promised Land (Revival Series)*, *338*
Angelou, Maya, 21, *124*, 126, 130
ANTA Theatre, New York, 141–42
Anthony, Mary, 109
anti-Blackness, 45, 47, 56, 78, 105
Anti-Drug Abuse Act (1986), 77
Antony and Cleopatra (opera, 1966), 139–40, 367
Archipelago (1971), 142, *209*, 367
Ariadne (1965), 139, 140, 367
Ariette Oubliée (1958), 131, 366
Arlen, Harold, 40
Armstrong, Louis, 42
Arnold, Horace, 134
Arts for the Handicapped, 145
Asakawa, Takako, 32, *140*
Ashford, Nick, 72n21
Astaire, Fred, 123
Aterballetto of Reggio Emilia, 145
Atlas, Consuelo, 75, 139, *140*, *141*
Atomic Energy Commission, 126
Au Bord du Précipice (1983/1984; later called *Precipice*), 85–86, 88–90, 145, *262*, 367
Award of Honor in Arts and Culture (New York), 143

B

Bailey, A. Peter, 148
Bailey, Eldren, *Dancers*, *358*
Bailey, Pearl, 40, *41*, 123, 127

Bakhtin, Mikhail, 80
Balanchine, George, 66n31, 79–82, 112, 113, 127, 131
Baldwin, James, 15, 21–22, 32, 40, 106, 331
Ball, Dorothy, 122
Ballard, Horace D., dance shoes of, *64–65*
ballet. *See* classical ballet
Ballet Folklórico de México, *140*, 141
Ballet Frankfurt, 79
Ballet Russe de Monte Carlo, 17, 41, 123
Baraka, Amiri (formerly LeRoi Jones), 20, 21
Barber, Samuel, 139
Bard College, 143
Barnes, Clive, 31
Barnett, Mary, 148
Barthé, Richmond, *African Dancer*, 359
Bartók, Béla, 145
Baryshnikov, Mikhail, 143, *143*
Basquiat, Jean-Michel, *Hollywood Africans*, 355
Bat-Dor, 144
Battle, Robert, 14, 94, 96
Beame, Abraham, 143
Bearden, Romare, 22, 143, 144, 331
 Bayou, The, from the series *Bayou Fever*, 360
 Bayou Fever series, 144
 Buzzard and the Snake (The Conjur Woman), The, from the series *Bayou Fever*, 361
 Conjur Woman, The, from the series *Bayou Fever*, 360
 Hatchet Man, The, from the series *Bayou Fever*, 360
Beasley, Kevin, 14, 323, 326
 Haze, 335
Beatty, Talley, 30, 32, 35, 81, 99, 114, 130, 138, 140
 Black Belt, 140
 Road of the Phoebe Snow, *63*, 143
 Southern Landscape (1947), 18
 Stack-Up, 114
Been Here and Gone (1962), 1*82–85*, 366
Begley, Josh, 14
Béjart, Maurice, 32
Belafonte, Harry, 40, 130, 148
Belafonte, Julie, 148
Bench, Harmony, *Dunham's Data: Katherine Dunham and Digital Methods for Dance Historical Inquiry*, 93–94
Benjamin, Fred, 33
Bernstein, Leonard, 126
 Mass: A Theatre Piece for Singers, Players, and Dancers, 32, 142
Berry, April, *148*
Beyoncé, 45
Biggers, John, *Sharecropper*, *335*
Bill T. Jones/Arnie Zane Company, 325
Billy Rose Theatre, New York, 32, 141
Black, Brown and Beige (1976), 143, *243*, 367
Black aesthetics, 48, 50, 59, 78–80. *See also* Africanist aesthetics
Black/African diaspora, 12, 17, 42, 48, 59, 65, 78–79, 93, 111, 139
Black Archives of Mid-America, Kansas City, Missouri, 12, 94, 277
Black Arts Movement, 19, 117
Black Church tradition, 17, 22, 53, 59–66, 74, 101, 122, 131, 331
Black dance, 47–50, 56, 68, 78, 80, 85, 106, 277
Black dancers and performers
 Ailey's legacy for, 14, 45
 experiences of, 17, 33, 40
 promotion of, 19
Black Exodus (dance company), 110
Black experience. *See also* Blackness
 Ailey's work as expression of, 12, 14, 17, 19, 22, 39, 41, 49, 53–56, 85, 87, 99, 143
 in American society, 19
 critical commentary on, 19–20
 dichotomy or double nature of, 61–62
 and gay/queer culture, 21–22, 39, 45, 49, 77, 79, 83
Blackness. *See also* anti-Blackness; Black experience

 AAADT and, 107
 and Americanness, 22, 62
 exploration of Ailey's work as exploration of, 48–50
 popular associations with, 18, 19
Black Panther Party, 141
Black Power, 21
Black South, 53–56, 118. *See also* American South
Black study, 49, 55–56, 115
Blackwell, Charles, 29, 131
Blarney Stone, New York, 67
blood memories, 14, 18, 22, 53–54, 62, 66, 77, 78, 83, 86, 92n6, 331
Blues Ain't, The (1974), 367
blues music, 61–62, 87, 102, 139
Blues Suite (1958), 29, 32, 37, 55, 65, 99, 102, 107, 110, 113, 115, 116, 130, 131, *132–33*, 148, 153, *156–59*, 366
body/bodies. *See also* blood memories
 Black, 56
 the blues and, 61
 dance and, 17, 22, 40, 44, 50, 69, 72n14, 73, 87–88
 meanings conveyed through, 48, 50, 54–56, 90
 soul/spirit in relation to, 62, 78
Bord, Marilyn "Mickey," 130, 131
Born, Peter, 14, 323, 326
Borough of Manhattan Community College, 148, 149
Boucourechliev, André, 142
Bowne, William, 26n26
Boykin, Hope, 327
Brand, Dionne, 11–12, 77
Britten, Benjamin, 142
Broadway, 18, 31, 32, 40, 66n31, 69, 71, 94, 97, 116, 126, 127, 128, 130, 131, 134, 141, 144
Brook, Peter, 40, 127
Brooklyn Academy of Music, New York, 32–33, 53, 135, 141
Brooklyn Museum, New York, 71, *71*, 72n21
Brooks, Daphne, 19
Broughton, Shirley, 131
Brown, Clifton, 327
Brown, James, 61–62
Brown, Ronald K., 323, 325
Buchanan, Beverly, *Orangeburg County Family House*, 334
Buchanan, Patrick, 84n6
Bureau of Educational and Cultural Affairs Historical Collection, University of Arkansas, 94
Butler, John, 30, 134
Byrd, Donald (choreographer), 77–83, 99
 Shards, *76*, 77–78, 80–83, *81*
Byrd, Donald (musician), 145

C

Call Me by My Rightful Name (off-Broadway play), 134
calypso, 73, 127, 130
Calypso Heat Wave (film), *124*
Camille A. Brown and Dancers, 327
Canto al Diablo (formerly *Rite*), from *Cinco Latinos* (1958), 131
Can't Slow Down (1983), 145, 367
Capezio Dance Award, 68, 144
Capote, Truman, 40, 127
Carefree Tree, The (Broadway play), 127
Caribbean Calypso Carnival (revue), 130
Carmen (opera, 1972), 142, 367
Carmen Jones (film), 18, 127
Carmen Jones (summer stock, 1959), 131, 366
Carouthers, Nettie, 122
Carroll, Diahann, 40, *40*, 127, 145
Carter, Jimmy, 143, 144
Cathedral of Saint John the Divine, New York, 149
Catholicism, 17
Catlett, Elizabeth, *I have given the world my songs*, *60–61*
Caverna Magica (1986), 148, *267–69*, 367
Cedar Crest College, 142
Century of Negro Progress Exposition (Chicago,

1963), 138
Cernovitch, Nicholas "Nick," 32, 131
Césaire, Aimé, 42
Chambers-Letson, Joshua, 22
Chase, Debora, *83*
Chase-Hicks, Debora, 104
Chaya, Masazumi, *28*, 142, 145, 149
Choral Dances (1971), 142, *215*, 367
choreography
 Ailey's, 18–20, 22–23, 36, 42, 55, 65, 69, 85–91, 102, 104, 105, 112–13, 117, 127, 130, 153
 Ailey's support of others', 30, 35, 86, 99, 114, 130, 138
 and "the break," 79–82
 of Byrd and Dove, 78–83
 commercial venues for, 18
 of *Cry*, 44
 deconstruction in, 79–81
 invited choreographers for *Edges of Ailey* exhibition, 323, 325–27
Chouteau, Yvonne, 123
Christian A. Johnson Endeavor Foundation, 145
Cinco Latinos (1958), 130, 131, *131*, 366
City Center. *See* New York City Center
City Center American Dance Season, 142
City University of New York (CUNY), 148; Graduate Center, 112
civil rights movement, 21, 138
Clark, Hope, 138
Clark, Michael, 79
Clark Center for the Performing Arts, New York, 31, 98, 109, 134, 135, 138, 141
Clarke, Ivy, 31, 141, 142, 143
classical ballet, 18–19, 78–79, 81–82
Clerc, Florence, 90
Clifton, Lucille, "won't you celebrate with me," 56, 57n8
Cold War, 21, 118
Cole, Jack, 15, 18, 112, 113, 123, 126, *128*, 130, 131
Collins, Georgia, 134, *135*
Collins, Janet, 143
Coltrane, Alice, 43
Committee for the Negro in the Arts, 130
Complexions Contemporary Ballet, 83
conceptualism, 64–66
Connecticut College, 115, 135, 141
Connecticut Dance Festival, 32
Conversations on Black Dance: Black Choreographers in Film, Fideo, Broadway (video series), 148
Cook, Susan, 144
Cooper, Calvin (half-brother of Ailey), 123, 142
Cooper, Fred (stepfather of Ailey), 123, *123*
Cooper, Lula (née Cliff) [mother of Ailey], 40, 102, 122–23, *122*, 142, 149, *149*
 letter to Ailey, *279*
Costen, Melva Wilson, 74
Cox, Aimee Meredith, 45, 50
Crane, Hart, 15
Création du Monde, La (1954/1960/1962) [second version as *Creation of the World*], 131, 135, 366
Croft, Clare, 49, 86
Crum, Ted, 123
Cry (1971), 31, 43–44, 64, 98, 99, 102, 104, 107, 116, 142, 153, *216–21*, 331, 367
Cullen, Countee, 15
culture wars, 77–78, 84n6
Cunningham, Merce, 11, 15, 18, 32, 39, 55, 65, 66n31, 79, 81, 110, 112, 127, *129*, 140
CUNY. *See* City University of New York
C. W. Post Campus, Long Island University, 148

D

dance. *See also* American dance; Black dance; choreography; classical ballet; modern dance
 Ailey's comments on, 12, 14, 17–20, 69–70, 72n14
 archival and representational issues in, 14–15, 78, 93–101

Index 381

and the body, 17, 22, 40, 44, 50, 69, 72n14, 73
Dance Center of the YM-YWHA, East Ninety-Second Street, New York, 29, 94, 98, 126, 130, 131
dance companies, 102–3
Dance Company, A, 323
Dance Magazine, 110, 139, 143, 144
dancers, data on, 94, *95*, *96*, 368–69. *See also* Black dancers and performers
Dance Theatre of Harlem, 111, 127, *129*
Dark of the Moon (play, 1960), 131, 366
Dash, Sarah, 43
Davis, Karon, 22
Davis, Ossie, *133*
Dawn, Marpessa, 42
"Day Is Past and Gone, The," from *Revelations* (1960), 104
Debussy, Claude, 131
DeFrantz, Thomas, 19, 48, 49, 88, 112
  Dancing Revelations: Alvin Ailey's Embodiment of African American Culture, 149
Delacorte Theater, Central Park, New York, 138, 142
Delaney, Beauford
  Charlie Parker Yardbird, 354
  Marian Anderson, 353
de Lavallade, Carmen, 15, 17, 22, 30, 31, 40, 109, 112, 118, 123, 126, *126*, 127, *127*, *129*, 130, 131, 134, *134*, 135, *135*, 136, *137*, 138, 144, *144*, 331
  portrait of, *352*
DeLoatch, Gary, 148
de Mille, Agnes, *The Four Marys*, 30
Denard, Michaël, 90
Denishawn company, 18
Denishawn School of Dancing and Related Arts, 65
Derby, Joan, 131
Derby, Marie, 131
Derrida, Jacques, 12
Destiné, Jean-Léon, 131
Dial, Thornton
  Shadows of the Field, 334
  Soul Train, 356–57
diaspora. *See* Black/African diaspora
Dietrich, Marlene, 40, 127
Ding Dong Bell (summer stock), 134
disco, 67, 69–70, 102, 115, 144
Diversion No. 1 (1969), 141, 367
Dixon-Gottschild, Brenda, 49, 51n6, 78, 80
Donaldson, Jeff, *Soweto/So We Too*, 347
Dorfman, Michael, 138, 139
Douglas, Aaron, *Flight*, 350
Douglas, Inez, 122
Dove, Ulysses, 77–80, 82–83, 90, 99, 110, 145
  Episodes, 77–78, *79*, 82–83, *83*
  Vespers, 110
Doyle, Sam, *Frank Capers*, 349
Driskell, David
  Bahian Ribbons, 333
  Festival Bahia, 333
Du Bois, W. E. B., 60, 61
Duncan, Isadora, 87, 123, 141
Duncanson, Robert, *View of Cincinnati, Ohio from Covington, Kentucky*, 22, 331, *344*
Dunham, Katherine, 15, *16*, 17, 18, 19, 22, 39, 55, 65, 79, 87, 93–95, 99, 110–12, 123, *124*, 127, 131, *139*, 148, *148*, 149, 331
  Barrelhouse, 148
  Choros, 99, 142, 148
  dancers affiliated with, *95*
  L'Ag'Ya, *124*, 148
  Shango, 148
  Southland, 117
  Tropical Revue, 17, 41, 73, 123, *123*
Dunning, Jennifer, 40, 84n22
  Alvin Ailey: A Life in Dance, 149
Dupont, Patrick, 88, 89, 145
Duvall, Robert, 134
Dyson, Torkwase, 64

E

Earl, Maggie, 122
Eastman, Julius, 21
Edinburgh International Festival, Scotland, 42, 140
Edwards, Adrienne, 59, 64, 112, 323
Edwards, Melvin
  Cup of?, from the series *Lynch Fragment*, 345
  Katutura, from the series *Lynch Fragment*, 345
Egier, Lars, 140
El Amor Brujo (1966), 139, 367
El Cigaro, from *Cinco Latinos* (1958), 131
"Elijah Rock," from *Revelations* (1960), 30
Ellington, Duke, 15, 17, 20, 42, 102, 112, 123, *125*, 131, 135, 138, 141, 143, 144
Ellington, Mercer, 143
Elswit, Kate, *Dunham's Data: Katherine Dunham and Digital Methods for Dance Historical Inquiry*, 93–94
Eng, Frank, 26n26, 86, 126–27
English, Darby, 64
Englund, Richard, 31
enslaved people, religious practices of, 59–60
ephemera, *108*, *123*, *124*, *127*, *134*, *137*, *139*, *140*, *141*, *142*, *143*, *144*, *145*, *148*, *149*
Escapades (1983), 145, 367
Étoile d'Or, 141
Etter, E. L., 122
Evans, Linda-Denise, 104
Evans, Walker, *Negro Church*, *58*
EVIDENCE, 323, 325

F

Faison, George, 99, 115, 144
Falco, Louis, 143
Fani-Kayode, Rotimi, *Every Moment Counts (Ecstatic Antibodies)*, 339
Favors, Ronni, 14
Feast of Ashes (1962/1974), 135, *186*, 367
Fehl, Fred, 75
  "Revelations": Judith Jamison, Consuelo Atlas, and Kelvin Rotardier, 74–75
Feibleman, Peter, *Tiger Tiger Burning Bright*, 40, 135, 138
Feld, Eliot, 32, 141
Feld Ballet, 148
Fellini, Federico, 141
Ferguson, Roderick, 80
Feuer, Donya, 109
5th Dimension (singing group), 141
Figueroa, Alfonso, *141*
Fiorucci, *68*, 71
First Baptist Church of Artesia, California, 149
First World Festival of Negro Arts (Dakar, Senegal), 41–42, 139
"Fix Me, Jesus," from *Revelations* (1960), 30, 104, 114
Flack, Roberta, 15, 144
Flowers (1971), 88, 114, 142, *210–14*, 367
Fon peoples, *Female Drum and Male Drum*, 332
Fontaine, Lon, 126
For 'Bird'—With Love (1984), 148, *266*, 367
Forsythe, William, 79–80, 82
Fosse, Bob, 112
Four Saints in Three Acts (opera, 1973), 142, *232–33*, 367
Francis of Assisi, Saint, 126
Fuller, Meta Vaux Warrick
  mold for *Crusaders for Freedom*, 345
  Te Adoremus Domine, 340

G

Gaines, Charles, *Sound Box: Nina Simone and Billie Holiday*, 355
Gallagher, Ellen, *Ecstatic Draught of Fishes*, 336–37
García Lorca, Federico, 135
Gary, Ja'Tovia, 61

Gates, Henry Louis, Jr., 60
Gates, Theaster, *Minority Majority*, 349
gay/queer culture. *See also* AIDS
  Ailey and, 20–22, 39–40, 67, 101–2, 104–5, 115, 117, 122, 126, 138, 140, 144
  Black, 21–22, 39, 45, 49, 77, 79, 83
  Black Church tradition and, 60
  and the blues, 61
  in the dance world, 66n31, 79, 80
  Nuyorican Poets Café and, 67
  queer gesture and, 67, 69, 71
  societal role/place of, 20–21, 40
  Studio 54 and, 67
  and virtuosity, 80
gender, Black Church tradition and, 60. *See also* gay/queer culture
George Faison, *Tilt*, 65
George Washington Carver Junior High School, Los Angeles, 123
Gillespiana (1961), 134, *178–79*, 366
Gillespie, Dizzy, 134
Gilliam, Sam
  Swing 64, 354
  Untitled (Black), 350
Glück, Louise, "Parable," 61
God, 60–61, 64, 73, 74, 101, *141*
Godreau, Miguel, 139, *140*, 144
Godunov, Alexander, 144
Goldman, Carl, 140, 142
Goldoni, Lelia, 126, *126*, *127*
gospel music, 62, 102. *See also* spirituals
Gould, Norma, 26n26
Graham, Martha, 15, 18, 19, 39, 54, 55, 79, 86–87, 110, 112, 118, 127, *129*, 131, 140
  Blood Memory (autobiography), 18
Grand Prix Italia, 140
Gray, Allan, 145, 148. *See also* Allan Gray Family Personal Papers of Alvin Ailey
Greaves, William, *First World Festival of Negro Arts*, 42, *43*
Greco, Connie, 19, 134, *135*
Green, Jacqueline, 104
Grinage, Leslie, 134
Gymnopedies (1970), 141, *204*, 367

H

Hackett, Joan, 134
Hairston, William, 138
Haizlip, Ellis, 143, 149
Hall, Stuart, 48, 50
Halprin, Anna, 126
Hammond, Bill, 33
Hammons, David, *Untitled*, 351
Hampton, Fred, 115, 141
Hampton Institute (now Hampton University), 18
Handel Medallion, 149
Hansberry, Lorraine, 15, 21
  A Raisin in the Sun, 40
Hanson Place Central United Methodist Church, New York, 141
Harkarvy, Benjamin, 31
Harkness, Rebekah, 135, 138, 139, 140, 153
Harkness Ballet, 139, 140, 142
Harkness Foundation Dance Festival, 138
Harlem Renaissance, 21, 327
Harney, Stefano, 55–56
Harper, Wes, 131
Harrell, Trajal, 14, 323, 325
Harris, Jacquelin, 104
Harris, Lyle Ashton, *Billie #21*, 356
Harris, Rennie, 117
  Lazarus, 117
Harum, Avind, *141*
Hash, Dana, *81*
Hassan II, king of Morocco, 144
Hassinger, Maren, *River*, 336–37

Hathaway, Donny, 15, 142
Hayden, Palmer, *Spirituals (Dreams)*, 340
Helms, Jesse, 78
Hemphill, Essex, 21
 "When My Brother Fell," 23
Hendricks, Barkley, *Dancer*, 359
Hendrix, Jimi, 15, 89
Hendryx, Nona, 43
Hermit Songs (1961), 65, 134, *180–81*, 366
Hidden Rites (1973), 102, 142, *234–35*, 367
High School of Performing Arts, New York, 31
Hill, Thelma, 109, 134, *135*
hip-hop, 79, 83, 102, 117
Hirabayashi, Kazuko, 110
Hoffman, Dustin, 134
Holder, Geoffrey, 22, 30, 31, 99, 127, 130, 331
 Portrait of Carmen de Lavallade, 352
Holiday, Billie, 15, 123
Holley, Lonnie, *Sharing the Struggle*, 348
Holly, Ellen, *138*
Hollywood, 18, 116, 123, 126, 141
Holm, Hanya, 127, *129*
Holmes, Odetta, 327
Holtz, Alwin, 139, 140, 141
Holtz, Edele, 131, 134, 139, 141
Home, Nat, 131
homosexuality. *See* gay/queer culture
Hønningen, Mette, 148
hooks, bell, 49
Horne, Lena, 40, *41*, 123, *128*, 130, *133*
Horton, Lester, 15, 17–18, 26n26, 29, 35, 40–41, 54, 55, 64, 65, 69, 72n6, 79, 82, 86–87, 99, 103, 111, 112, 118, 123, 124, *125*, 126, *126*, 130–31, 134, 138, 140, 142, 148, 153
 To José Clemente Orozco, 138
 Liberian Suite, 143
House of Flowers (Broadway musical), 18, 40, *40–41*, 94, *95*, 99, 127, *127*, 130
Hoving, Lucas, 140
Hughes, Langston, 15, 21, 40, 42, 60, 127, *128*, 134
 Black Nativity, 29, 31–32, 134
 Jerico-Jim Crow, 138
Humphrey, Doris, 18, 127, *128*, 142
Hunter, Clementine, *Cane River Baptism*, 340
Hyppolite, Hector, 22, 331
 The Congo Queen, 332

I

"I Been 'Buked," from *Revelations* (1960), 30, 47, 81, 83, 119
"I Been 'Buked and I Been Scorned" (gospel song), 122
"Instruction: How to Play Drums" (Ailey, poem), 42. *See also* Ailey, Alvin; notebooks and writing of
Isba (1983), 145, *264–65*, 367
"I Wanna Be Ready," from *Revelations* (1960), 114

J

Jackson, Abdur-Rahim, 327
Jacob's Pillow, Becket, Massachusetts, 18, 126–27, *126*, *127*, 131, *132*, 134, *134*, 138
Jamaica (Broadway musical), 18, 29, 40, *41*, 94, *95*, *128*, 130, *130*, 131, *133*
Jamaica (summer stock, 1960), 131, 366
James, Ashley, 64
Jamison, Judith, 22, *28*, 31, 32, 43–44, 72n21, *75*, 94, *96*, 99, 104, 110, 139, *140*, 141, 142, 143, *143*, 144, 149, 331
 portrait of, 353
Jarrett, Keith, 69, 102
jazz, 79, 139
Jazz City (film), 107
jazz dance, 18, 79, 134
Jenkins, Ella, 73–74
Joan Weill Center for Dance, New York, 324

Joffrey, Robert, 135, 143, 153
Joffrey Ballet, 135, 142, 144
John F. Kennedy Center for the Performing Arts, Washington, DC, 142, 143
Johnson, Louis, 30, 32, 35, 99, 127, 130
 Lament, 138
Johnson, Lyndon B., 141
Johnson, Martha, 30
Johnson, Rashid, *Untitled Anxious Men*, 350–51
Johnson, William H., *Moon over Harlem*, 343
Jolivet, André, 139
Jones, Benjamin, 135, 138
Jones, Bill T., 14, 40, 99, 114, 115, 323, 325
 Fever Swamp, 145, 148
Jones, Darrell, 326
Jones, Grace, 72n21
Jones, Kellie, 64
Jones, LeRoi. *See* Baraka, Amiri
Jones, Loïs Mailou
 Jennie, 352
 Veve Voudou II, 333
Joplin, Janis, 89, 114, 142
Jowitt, Deborah, 57n3
Jude, Charles, 90
Judson Dance Theater, 11, 112
Juilliard Dance Theater, 72n6
Juilliard School, New York, 31

K

Kajiwara, Mari, *141*, 145, *147*
Kansas City Friends of Alvin Ailey, 145, 148, 149
Katselas, Milton, 134
Kawasumi, Misaye, 126
Keith, Naima J., 64
Kelly, Gene, 123
Kennedy, John F., 89, 134
Kennedy Center Honors, 44, 117, 148, *149*
Kent, Linda, *141*
King, Alonzo, 79
King, Martin Luther, Jr., 89, 135, 138, 140, 143
King, Monty, 127
Kirstein, Lincoln, 11, 66n31, 113, 131, 143
Kisselgoff, Anna, 65
Knapp, Albert, 149
Knoxville: Summer of 1915 (1960), 134, 140, *174*, 366
Kolodney, William, 131
Koltun, Marion, 14
Kosuth, Joseph, "1975," 64
Krawitz, Herman, 143

L

Labelle (band), 43
LaBelle, Patti, 43
Labyrinth (1963), 135, *187*, 367
La danse en Révolution (program in honor of French Revolution), 149
La Dea della Acqua (1988), 148, 367
Lamp unto My Feet (television series), 30, 134
Landscape (1981), 145, *259–60*, 367
Lang, Pearl, 131, 141
Lark Ascending, The (1972), 32, 102, 142, *228–30*, 367
La Scala Opera Ballet, 148
La Strada (Broadway musical, 1969), 141, 367
Latham, Jacqueline, 143
Lathrop, Waelland, 126
Laveau, Marie, 144
Lawrence, Jacob, *Tombstones*, 338
Lawson, Cristyne, 127, 130, *131*, 143
Lee, Ming Cho, 139
Lemon, Ralph, 14, 323, 326
 Ailey Dancing Revelations, 363
Lenox Hill Hospital, New York, 149
Leonardo da Vinci, 63
Lester Horton Dance Group, 26n26
Lester Horton Dance Theater, 17–18, 26n26, 40,

72n6, *123*, *125*, 126–27, *127*, 132
Lewis, Norman, *Phantasy II*, 354
Lewis, Samella, *Migrants*, 342–43
Lewitzky, Bella, 17, 26n26, 126
LGBTQI+ community. *See* gay/queer culture
Library of Congress, Washington, DC, 12, 94, 277
lighting, 69, 71
Ligon, Glenn, *Stranger in the Village #12*, 351
Limón, José, 35, 86, 110, 131, 140
Lincoln, Abbey, 102
Lincoln Center, New York, 70, 141, 143
Little, James, 331
 Stars and Stripes, 350
Logan, Joshua, 135
Longhorne, Bruce, 134
Long Island University, 148
Lopez, Antonio, 71
 Arrow, *70*, 71
 David, *68–69*, 71
 Pat, *70*, 71
Lord Byron (opera, 1972), 367
Los Angeles City College, 126
Lou, Kya, 14
Loudières, Monique, 90
Louther, William, 138
Love Songs (1972), 62, 99, 142, *231*, 367
Loving, Al, *Untitled*, 335
Luna, Max, *81*
Lydia Bailey (film), 126

M

Macumba (1966), 138, 139, 367
Magic of Katherine Dunham, The (tribute show), 99, 148, *148*
 rehearsal for, 14, *14–15*
Mandela, Nelson, 148
Mandela, Winnie, 148
Manning, Deborah, 104
Manning, Susan, 18
Mapplethorpe, Robert, *Black Book*, 77–78
Markham, Dewey "Pigmeat," 123
Marshall, Kerry James, *Souvenir IV*, 356
Marshall, Minnie, 30, 109, 134, *134*
Martin, Don, 134, *135*
"Mary, Don't You Weep," from *Revelations* (1960), 30
Mary Lou's Mass (1971), 142, *224–25*, 367
Masekela, Hugh, 141
Masekela Langage (1969), 102, 110, 115–17, 141, *194–97*, 367
Maslow, Sophie, 142
Mass: A Theatre Piece for Singers, Players, and Dancers (musical theater, 1971), 32, 142, *222–23*, 367
Mathis, Bonnie, 142
Maxon, Normand, 130, 131
Mazo, Joseph H., 144
McCarthyism, 117
McCullers, Carson, 127
McDaniel, Keith, *146*
McGregor, Wayne, 79
 Chroma, 117
McIntyre, Dianne, *Ancestral Voices*, 143
McKayle, Donald, 19, 29, 30, 31, 32, 35, 81, 99, 130
 Rainbow Round My Shoulder, 18, 32, 148
McKnight, Anne, 149
McNeil, Claudia, 40, *138*
McReynolds, David, 126
McShann, Jay, 148
Memoria (1979), 65, 68–69, 99, 102, 104, 144, *254–55*, 367
Merce Cunningham Dance Company, 141
metaphor, 59–66
Metropolitan Museum of Art, New York, 45
Metropolitan Opera, New York, 139, 142, 145
Michael's dance studio, New York, 127, 131
Michelson, Sarah, 14, 323, 326
Milhaud, Darius, 127

Index 383

Mills, Stephanie, 72n21
Mingus, Charles, 142, 144
Mingus Dances, The (1971), 142, 144, 367
Mistress and Manservant (1959), 131, 366
Mitchell, Arthur, 39, 127, 139
Mitchell, Jack, 129
 "Episodes": Dwight Rhoden, Renee Robinson, Desmond Richardson, and Debora Chase, 83
 "Episodes": Renee Robinson and Desmond Richardson, 79
 "Episodes": The Company, 83
 Portrait of Alvin Ailey, 64–65
 "The Road of the Phoebe Snow": Dudley Williams, 63
 "Shards": André Tyson and Dana Hash, 81
 "Shards": Desmond Richardson, 76
 "Shards": Max Luna, Dwight Rhoden, Desmond Richardson, and Dereque Whiturs, 81
modern dance. *See also* American dance
 Ailey and, 17, 19, 48, 50, 65, 68–70, 86–88, 99, 148, 331
 Black/African diaspora, 277
 Black/Africanist, 50, 68
 dancers' training in, 55, 79, 82
 eclipse of, 102
 first company devoted to, 17
 non-Western influences on, 112
 postmodern choreography incorporating, 79, 81
modernism, 40, 42, 60, 64, 65, 66n31, 86, 88, 113, 117. *See also* modern dance
Monroe, Marilyn, 42
Montalbán, Ricardo, 130, *133*
Mooche, The (1974/1975), 143, *240–42*, 367
Moore, Charles, 134, 135, *135*
Moore, Marlon Rachquel, 60
Morales, Mio, 82
Morning Mourning (1954), 126, 366
Morrison, Jim, 89, 145
Morrison, Toni, 21, 74
Moses, Gilbert, 138
Moten, Fred, 23, 39, 55–56, 64, 79–80
Motley, Archibald John, Jr., *Gettin' Religion*, 356
Mumford, Kevin, 21
Muñoz, José Esteban, 67, 69
Murray, Albert, 87
Murray, Michele, *141*
Myers, Milton, 110, 143
My People: First Negro Centennial (1963), 138, 367
Myth (1971), 142, *226–27*, 367

N

Nardal, Jeanne and Paulette, 42
Nast, Thomas, *Emancipation of the Negroes—The Past and the Future (from "Harper's Weekly")*, 345
National Association for the Advancement of Colored People, 143
National Association of Schools of Dance, 145
National Council on the Arts, 141
National Endowment for the Arts, 78, 140
National Medal of Arts, 149
Nazism, 17
Nengudi, Senga, *Studio Performance with R.S.V.P.*, 358
New Dance Group, 29, 31, 109, 127, *128*
New Jim Crow, 77–78, 84n7
New Orleans Champagne Supper Club, San Francisco, 126
Newton, Huey P., 21
New York City Ballet, 11, 66n31, 127
New York City Center, 43, 68–70, 112, 117, 141, 142, 143, 144, 145, 148, 325
New York Hospital/Cornell Medical Center, White Plains, NY, 145
New York Live Arts, 325
New York Public Library for the Performing Arts, 94
New York State Theater, Lincoln Center, New York, 143

New York Times (newspaper), 31, 65, 70, 142, 145, 149
Nicholas brothers, 123
Night Creature (1974/1975), 20, 102, 107, 112, 114–15, 143, *236–39*, 367
Nijinsky, Vaslav, 112, 126
Nikolais, Alwin, 140
92nd Street YM-YWHA, New York. *See* Dance Center of the YM-YWHA, East Ninety-Second Street, New York
Nixon, Richard, 84n7
Nkrumah, Kwame, 42
nonperformance, 39–40
Nureyev, Rudolf, 90
Nuyorican Poets Cafè, New York, 67, 69, 112, 119, 144
Nyro, Laura, 42–43, 102

O

Obama, Barack, 149
Ode and Homage (1958), 130, 366
Odetta. *See* Holmes, Odetta
Oka, Michihiko, 31, *147*
Okpokwasili, Okwui, 14, 323, 326
Oliver, Valerie Cassel, 64
O'Neal, Mary Lovelace, *Race Woman Series #7*, 352
Opera House, Paris, 32
Opus McShann (1988), 148, *272–73*, 367
Outterbridge, John, *The Elder, Ethnic Heritage Series*, 358
Overstreet, Joe, *Purple Flight*, 349

P

Packer, Jennifer, 22
Palais des Sports, Paris, 32
Parham, Ernest, 29, 94, 130
 Trajectories, 130
Paris Opera Ballet, 88, 90, 145
Parker, Charlie "Bird," 15, 148
Parker, Edwin Huntington, *141*
Parks, John, 110
Pas de Duke (1976), 102, 143, *244–45*, 367
Passage (1978), 144, *252–53*, 367
Pendergrass, Teddy, 72n21
Perez, Rudy, 99, 113
Perryman, Al, 110
Person, Melanie, 14
Peter Born/Sweat Variant, 323
Phases (1980), 145, *256–57*, 367
Phelan, Peggy, 14
Philadanco, 327
Philip Morris (company), 148
Pierson, Harold, *131*
Pimsleur, Susan, 131, 138, 139
Piñero, Miguel, *Nuyorican Nights* (with Miguel Algarín), 144
Pippin, Horace, *Knowledge of God*, 341
Plesent, Stanley, 143
politics, Ailey's work and, 14, 17, 19, 21, 66, 85–86, 90, 115–19
Pomare, Eleo, 113, 114
popping, 82
Popwell, Albert, 127
Porgy and Bess (television broadcast), 134
POSE (television show), 71
postmodernism, 69, 79–81
Pouncie, Barbara, 104
Powell, Adam Clayton, 104
Praise God and Dance (Sacred Concert) (1974), 367
Precipice. *See Au Bord du Précipice*
Premice, Josephine, *133*
Presidential Medal of Freedom, 149
Price, Leontyne, 15
Primus, Pearl, 15, 99, 110, 112, *128*, 130, 143, *143*
Princeton University, 142
Purifoy, Noah, *Untitled*, 333
Puryear, Martin, *The Rest*, 343

Q

Quashie, Kevin, 19, 22, 50
queerness. *See* gay/queer culture
queer of color aesthetics, 83
queer of color critique, 80
Quintet (1968), 20, 42, 88, 102, 117, 140, *192–93*, 367

R

Rainer, Yvonne, 44
Ravel, Maurice, 131, 145
Rawls, Will, 14, 45, 323, 326
Reagan, Nancy, 44
Reagan, Ronald, 44, 77–78, 80, 117, 148
Redonda (1958), 130, 366
Reed, Briana, 104
Reflections in D (1963), 135, *188–91*, 367
Reinhart, Charles, 141
religion. *See* Black Church tradition; Catholicism; God
repertory companies, 35
Revelations (1960), 18, 29–32, 37, 39, 41–44, *43*, *46*, 47–50, 53–56, 65, 73–74, 79–81, 87, 99, 102, 105, 107, 110–14, 116–19, 131, 134, *136*, 138, 141, 143, *147*, 153, *160–73*, 327, 366
Revelations (Ailey autobiography), 148
Reynolds, Newell, 26n26
Rhoden, Dwight, 79, 81, *81*, 82–83, *83*
Ricci, José, 130
Richardson, Desmond, *76*, 78, 79, *81*, 82–83, *83*, 84n22
Richardson, Dorene, 109, 130
Richie, Lionel, 145
Riedaiglia (1967), 140, 367
Riedel, Georg, 140
Riggs, Marlon, 21
"Right On Be Free," from *Cry* (1971), 43
Ringgold, Faith, *United States of Attica*, 346–47
Rink, Bennett, 14
Rios, Augustine "Augie," *133*
Rite, from *Cinco Latinos* (1958), 131
River, The (1970/1978/1981), 102, 141, 143, 148, *205–8*, 367
Rivers, Streams, Doors (1963), 138, 367
Roach, Joseph, 14
Roach, Max, 102, 145
Robbins, Jerome, 66n31
Robinson, Bill, 123
Robinson, Renee, 79, *83*, 104
"Rocka My Soul in the Bosom of Abraham," from *Revelations* (1960), 110
Rockefeller Foundation, 140, 141
Rodríguez, Juana María, 71
Roots of the Blues (1961), 99, 134, 135, *175–77*, 366
Rose Hills Memorial Park, Whittier, California, 149
Ross, Herbert, 127
Rotardier, Kelvin, 75, 135, *140*, 143
Royal Ballet, 325
Royal Danish Ballet, 148
Rubell, Steve, 71
Rushing, Matthew, 14, 323, 326–27
Russell, Legacy, 64
Russia, 33–34
Rustin, Bayard, 21, 104
Rutgers University, 68

S

Saint-Subber, Arnold, 127
Sanasardo, Paul, 109
 Metallics, 138
Sanders, Pharoah, 43, 145
San Francisco State College, 126
Saroyan, William, *Two by Saroyan*, 134
Satterwhite, Jacolby, *A Metta Prayer* (2023), 44, 45
Satyriade (1982), 145, *261*, 367
Sayyed-Gaines, Bahiyah, 104

Schauspielhaus Zürich Dance Ensemble, 325
School of American Ballet, 11
Schrager, Ian, 71
Schwantes, Leland, *141*
Scripps, Samuel H., 148
Sea Change (1972), 142, 367
Second Great Awakening, 60
Sedgwick, Eve Kosofsky, 20–21
Segal, Lewis, 81
Sellers, Brother John, 134, 135
Senghor, Léopold Sédar, 42, 139
Serrano, Andres, *Piss Christ*, 78
Shaked, Nizan, 65
Shaken Angels (1972), 142, 367
Sharpe, Christina, 73–74
Shawn, Ted, 15, 18, 65, 99, 112, 123, 127
    Kinetic Molpai, 142
Shigaon! Children of the Diaspora (1978), 144, 367
Shook, Karel, 123, 127, 129
Show Boat (Broadway musical), 130
Shultz, George, 149
Shurtleff, Michael, 134
Sibley, O'Shae, *44*, 45
Simone, Nina, 142
Simpson, Lorna, *Momentum*, *363*
Simpson, Valerie, 72n21
Sims, Linda Celeste, 104
Sing, Man, Sing! (Broadway musical), 40
Sing, Man, Sing (roadshow), 130
Sirmans, Franklin, 64
Smallwood, Owana Adiaha, 104
Smith, Barbara, 21
Smith, Bessie, 15
Smith, Hale, 144
Smith, Lowell, 111
Smith, Ming, *Farewell to Alvin Ailey*, *149*
Smith, Tracy K., "Wade in the Water," 74
Sokolow, Anna, 35, 86, 99, 140
    Rooms, 138
Solo for Mingus (1979), 144, 367
Solomon R. Guggenheim Foundation, 140
Sonera (1960), 131, 366
"A Song for You," from *Love Songs* (1972), 22, 62–64
Sonnet for Caesar (1974), 367
Sontag, Susan, 59
Sophisticated Ladies (Broadway musical), 144
Sorzano, Yusha-Marie, 14, 323, 327
soul, 61–62, 65, 78
South. *See* American South; Black South
Soviet Union, 33–35, 41, 118, 141
Special International Program for Cultural Presentations, 134
Spell (1981), 144, *258*, 367
Spingarn Medal, *142*, 143
spirituals, 22, 60, 61–62, 73–74, 102
Spurlock, Estelle, *147*
Squadron, Howard, 143
Stamatiou, Constance, 104
St. Denis, Ruth, 18, 65, 123, 131, 142
Stravinsky, Igor, 142
Streams (1970), 32, 53–56, 57n3, 99, 116, 118–19, 141, 142, *198–203*, 367, foldout
street dance, 79, 82, 110
Strindberg, August, 131
Student Nonviolent Coordinating Committee, 138
Studio 54, New York, 20, *24–25*, 26, 67, 71, 72n21, 143
Studio 54: Night Magic (exhibition), 71, *71*
Such Sweet Thunder (1974), 367
Survivors (1986), 102, 107, 148, *271*, 367
Sweat Variant, 326

T

Tallchief, Maria, 123
Tamiris, Helen, 18
    Negro Spirituals, 18
Tannenbaum, Allan, *Fiorucci Dancers at Studio 54*, *68*, 71
Taplin, Hattie, 122, 131
Taylor, Diana, 17
Taylor, Paul, 32, 140
Taylor Mac, 327
Ted Shawn and His Men Dancers, *Negro Spirituals*, 18
Terry, Walter, 127
Tetley, Glen, *Mountain Way Chant*, 135
Thomas, Alma, *Mars Dust*, 337
    Clarivel Face Forward Gazing, 353
Thomas, Mickalene, 22
Thomas, Nasha, 104
Thomas Jefferson High School, Los Angeles, 123
Thompson, Clive, 139
Thompson, Ella, 134, *134*, 135, *135*
Thompson, Robert Farris, 51n6
Thomson, Virgil, *Four Saints in Three Acts*, 142
Three Black Kings (1976), 143, *246–51*, 367
Three by Three (television special), 148
Three for Now—Modern Jazz Suite (1960), 134, 366
Trammps (band), 71
Traylor, Bill, *Untitled (Man in a Blue House)*, *357*
Trisler, Joyce, 68, 72n6, 99, 104, 110, 126, *126*, *127*, 138, 144
    Journey, 138
True Vine Baptist Church, Rogers, Texas, 74
Truitte, James "Jimmy," 17, 30, 35, 99, 109–10, 111, *126*, 126, 127, 134, *134*, *136*, 138, 140, *140*
    Variegations, 138
Turney, Matt, 131
Tutu, Desmond, 148
Twelve Gates, The (1964), 138, 367
Tyson, André, *81*

U

Ukraine, 33
United Nations Peace Medal, 145
universalism, of Ailey's works, 19, 49, 65, 86, 115
University of California, Los Angeles, 64, 68, 126
University of Cincinnati, 111
Urban Bush Women Choreographic Center Initiative, 114, 327
US Congress, 149
US Embassy in the Soviet Union, 33
US State Department, 33, 41, 49, 114, 116–18, 140, 141

V

Valentim, Rubem, *Untitled*, *332*
Van Der Zee, James
    Choir Boy, *338*
    Dancer, *358*
    Marcus Garvey Rally, *347*
Van Vechten, Carl, 39, 127
    Alvin Ailey, 12, *13*, 20, *20–21*, *38*, 39
    Hard Time Blues, 128, *128*
    Langston Hughes, 128, *128*
    Carmen de Lavallade, 129, *129*
virtuosity, 19, 23, 39–41, 45, 48–50, 53, 77–83, 112
Vivian Beaumont Theater, New York, 142
vodou, 17, 144
Voices of East Harlem, 43
Vulpian, Claude de, 90

W

"Wade in the Water," from *Revelations* (1960), 30, 41, 73–74, 104, 115
Wadsworth, Jarrell, *Together We Will Win*, *348*
Walnut Street Theater, Philadelphia, 30
Waters, Paul, *Beautiful Life*, *341*
Waters, Sylvia, *28*, 53, 80, 87, 110, 140, *141*, 149
Wayne, Dennis, 142
Weems, Carrie Mae, *Untitled*, *334–35*
Weidman, Charles, 118, *128*
White, Charles, *Preacher*, *339*
White, Myrna, *134*
Whitley, Zoé, 64
Whitney Museum of American Art, New York, 112
Whiturs, Dereque, *81*
Widman, Anneliese, 31
Williams, Dudley, 21, 31, 32, 35, 54, 62–64, *63*, 72n21, 94, 99, 131, 138, 145, *147*
Williams, Kandis, *Black Box, 4 points: Horton, Ailey, McKayle contractions and expansions of drama from vernacular—arms outstretched and entangle*, *362*
Williams, Lavinia, 98
Williams, Mary Lou, 105, 142
Williams, Ralph Vaughan, 102, 142
Williams, Tennessee, 15, 126
Williamson, Terrion L., 19–20
Winston, Morton, *140*
Witness (1986), 148, *270*, 367
Wolf Trap/American University Summer Program, 110
Wood, Donna, 94, 104, *146*, *147*
Woodruff, Hale Aspacio, *Giddap*, *342*
World Dance Festival (New York, 1959), 131
Wright, Eric, 14

X

X, Malcolm, 89

Y

Yarborough, Sara, 98
Yerushaimy, Netta, *Paramodernities*, 112
Yiadom-Boakye, Lynette, 22
    not yet titled, *358–59*
Young, Purvis
    Black People Migrating West, *342*
    I Love Your America, *336*
    Ocean, *337*
Young Friends of Alvin Ailey (benefit concert), 72n21
Yuan, Tina, *147*

Z

Zane, Arnie, 325
Zeffirelli, Franco, 139
Zeitgeist Dance Theatre, 327
Zollar, Jawole Willa Jo, 14, 110, 323, 327

Photography Credits

In reproducing the images contained in this publication, the publisher obtained the permission of rights holders whenever necessary and possible. All reasonable efforts have been made to credit the copyright holders, photographers, and sources when known; if any errors or omissions are noted, please contact the publisher so that corrections can be made in subsequent editions.

Many images were generously provided by the Alvin Ailey Dance Foundation. Images from the Alvin Ailey Dance Foundation with unknown photographers are as follows: endpapers (front), pp. 2–4, 16, 52, 127 (left), 126 (center), 126 (right), 130 (top left), 131 (top center), 135, 136, 137, 138 (center), 138 (right), 139 (center), 139 (right), 140, 141 (center), 141 (right), 142 (right), 143 (left), 143 (center), 144 (center), 145 (left), 145 (right), 146 (top left), 147 (bottom row), 148 (left), 149 (left), 154–55, 162, 168, 170, 171, 172, 173, 175, 178, 179, 182, 183, 184–85, 190, 191, 192–93, 200–1, 202–3, 210–11, 212, 213, 220–21 (top center), 258, 261. Additional image credits are listed individually below.

p. 4: courtesy Alvin Ailey Dance Foundation; photograph by Raul Aguilar. p. 10: Allan Gray Family Personal Papers of Alvin Ailey (AC10), Black Archives of Mid-America; photograph by Gabe Hopkins. p. 13: courtesy the Van Vechten Trust and Beinecke Rare Book and Manuscript Library, Yale University. pp. 14–15: courtesy Alvin Ailey Dance Foundation; photograph by Sandy Geis. pp. 20–21: courtesy the Van Vechten Trust and Beinecke Rare Book and Manuscript Library, Yale University. pp. 24–25: courtesy The Antonio Archives. p. 28 (top): courtesy Alvin Ailey Dance Foundation; photograph by Lois Greenfield. p. 28 (center): courtesy Alvin Ailey Dance Foundation; photographs by Sandy Geis. p. 28 (bottom): courtesy Alvin Ailey Dance Foundation; photographs by Sandy Geis. p. 38: courtesy the Van Vechten Trust and Beinecke Rare Book and Manuscript Library, Yale University. pp. 40–41: Photograph by Zinn Arthur. p. 41: © The New York Public Library for the Performing Arts; photograph by Friedman-Abeles. p. 43: courtesy William Greaves Productions Inc. p. 44: courtesy Jacolby Satterwhite. p. 46: courtesy Alvin Ailey Dance Foundation; photograph by Paul Kolnik. p. 58: Photograph by Walker Evans. © Walker Evans Archive, The Metropolitan Museum of Art. p. 60: © 2024 Elizabeth Catlett Artists Rights Society (ARS), NY. p. 63: © Alvin Ailey Dance Foundation and Smithsonian Institution; photographs by Jack Mitchell. pp. 64–65 (top): courtesy Horace D. Ballard. pp. 64–65 (bottom): © Alvin Ailey Dance Foundation and Smithsonian Institution; photograph by Jack Mitchell. p. 68 (bottom): © Allan Tannenbaum; photograph by Allan Tannenbaum. pp. 68–69 (top), 70: courtesy The Antonio Archives. p. 71: Alvin Ailey American Dance Theater and Red Is Dancing. pp. 74–75: courtesy Harry Ransom Center, The University of Texas at Austin; photograph by Fred Fehl. pp. 76, 79, 81, 82–83, 83: © Alvin Ailey Dance Foundation and Smithsonian Institution; photographs by Jack Mitchell. pp. 86, 88–89, 91: courtesy Allan Gray Family Personal Papers of Alvin Ailey (AC10), Black Archives of Mid-America; photographs by Gabe Hopkins. pp. 95, 96, 97, foldout: Harmony Bench and Kate Elswit. p. 108: courtesy Allan Gray Family Personal Papers of Alvin Ailey (AC10), Black Archives of Mid-America; photograph by Gabe Hopkins. pp. 122–23: courtesy Alvin Ailey Dance Foundation; photographs by Jason Mandella. p. 124 (top left): courtesy Prints and Photographs Division, NYWT&S Collection, LC-DIG-ppmsca-05791, Library of Congress; photograph by Phyllis Twachtman. p. 124 (top middle): Jerome Robbins Dance Division, The New York Public Library for the Performing Arts; photographer unknown. p. 124 (top right): courtesy Missouri Historical Society Photographs and Prints Collection; photographer unknown. p. 124 (bottom row): courtesy Columbia Pictures. p. 125 (top row): courtesy Geoffrey Holder and Carmen de Lavallade Papers, Stuart A. Rose Manuscript, Archives, and Rare Book Library, Emory University; photographer unknown. p. 125 (bottom left): photograph by Charles "Teenie" Harris, © Carnegie Museum of Art/Charles "Teenie" Harris Archive/Getty Images. p. 125 (bottom center): Photographs and Prints Division, Schomburg Center for Research in Black Culture, The New York Public Library. p. 125 (bottom right): Magazine Photograph Collection, Prints and Photographs Division, LC-DIG-ds-08301; photograph by Charlotte Brooks; Library of Congress. p. 126 (left): courtesy Geoffrey Holder and Carmen de Lavallade Papers, Stuart A. Rose Manuscript, Archives, and Rare Book Library, Emory University; photograph by Larry Stevens. p. 127 (center): courtesy Alvin Ailey Dance Foundation; photograph by Jason Mandella. p. 127 (right): courtesy Geoffrey Holder and Carmen de Lavallade Papers, Stuart A. Rose Manuscript, Archives, and Rare Book Library, Emory University; photograph by Zinn Arthur. p. 128 (top left): courtesy the Van Vechten Trust and Beinecke Rare Book and Manuscript Library, Yale University; photograph by Carl Van Vechten. p. 128 (top center): New Dance Group Collection, Library of Congress; photographer unknown. p. 128 (top right): Jerome Robbins Dance Division, The New York Public Library for the Performing Arts; photographer unknown. p. 128 (bottom right): Jerome Robbins Dance Division, The New York Public Library for the Performing Arts; photographer unknown. p. 128 (bottom center): courtesy the Van Vechten Trust and Beinecke Rare Book and Manuscript Library, Yale University; photograph by Carl Van Vechten. p. 128 (bottom left): © The New York Public Library for the Performing Arts; photograph by Friedman-Abeles. p. 129 (top left): © 2024 Imogen Cunningham Trust/www.ImogenCunningham.com; photograph by Imogen Cunningham. p. 129 (top center): courtesy Library of Congress; photograph by Herta Moselsio. p. 129 (top right): courtesy the Van Vechten Trust and Beinecke Rare Book and Manuscript Library, Yale University; photograph by Carl Van Vechten. p. 129 (bottom left): courtesy Dance Theatre of Harlem; photograph by Henry Grossman. p. 129 (bottom right): Barbara and Willard Morgan photographs and papers, UCLA Library Special Collections. p. 130 (top center): courtesy Alvin Ailey Dance Foundation; photograph by Will Rapport. p. 131 (top left): courtesy The Donald McKayle Legacy/Lea Vivante McKayle/Dennis Nahat; photograph by Esta McKayle. p. 131 (top right): courtesy Alvin Ailey Dance Foundation; photograph by Normand Maxon. p. 132 (top row): MS Thr 482 Box 64: Interior-box 62, Houghton Library, Harvard University. p. 132 (bottom row), 133 (bottom row): MS Thr 482 Box 58: Interior-box 26, Houghton Library, Harvard University. p. 133 (top row): © The New York Public Library for the Performing Arts; photograph by Friedman-Abeles. pp. 134 (left), 134 (center): courtesy Alvin Ailey Dance Foundation; photographs by Jason Mandella. p. 134 (right): courtesy Alvin Ailey Dance Foundation and Jacob's Pillow Archive; photograph by John Lindquist. © Houghton Library, Harvard University. p. 138 (left): © The New York Public Library for the Performing Arts; photograph by Friedman-Abeles. pp. 139 (left), 141 (left), 142 (center), 143 (right), 144 (left): courtesy Alvin Ailey Dance Foundation; photographs by Jason Mandella. p. 144 (right): courtesy Alvin Ailey Dance Foundation; photograph by Lois Greenfield. p. 145 (center): courtesy Alvin Ailey Dance Foundation; photographs by Jason Mandella. pp. 146 (top right), 146 (bottom row), 147 (top row): courtesy Donna Wood. p. 148 (center): courtesy Alvin Ailey Dance Foundation; photographs by Jason Mandella. p. 148 (right): courtesy Alvin Ailey Dance Foundation; photograph by Sandy Geis. p. 149 (center): courtesy Ming Smith. p. 149 (right): courtesy Alvin Ailey Dance Foundation; photograph by Jason Mandella. p. 152: Allan Gray Family Personal Papers of Alvin Ailey (AC10), Black Archives of Mid-America, Kansas City; photograph by Gabe Hopkins. pp. 156–57: © Alvin Ailey Dance Foundation and Smithsonian Institution; photographs by Jack Mitchell. pp. 158, 159: courtesy Alvin Ailey Dance Foundation; photograph by Paul Crowley. pp. 160–61: © Alvin Ailey Dance Foundation and Smithsonian Institution; photographs by Jack Mitchell. p. 163: © Anthony Crickmay/Victoria and Albert Museum; photograph by Anthony Crickmay. p. 164: courtesy Alvin Ailey Dance Foundation; photographs by Zoe Dominic. p. 165: courtesy Alvin Ailey Dance Foundation; photograph by John van Lund. pp. 166–67: courtesy Alvin Ailey Dance Foundation; photograph by Rosemary Winckley. p. 169: courtesy Alvin Ailey Dance Foundation; photographs by Zoe Dominic. p. 174: courtesy Harry Ransom Center, The University of Texas at Austin; photograph by Fred Fehl. pp. 176, 177, 180, 181: © Alvin Ailey Dance Foundation and Smithsonian Institution; photographs by Jack Mitchell. p. 186: courtesy Harry Ransom Center, The University of Texas at Austin; photograph by Fred Fehl. p. 187: Photograph by Jack Mitchell/Getty Images. p. 188: courtesy Alvin Ailey Dance Foundation; photograph by Beatriz Schiller. p. 189: courtesy Alvin Ailey Dance Foundation; photographs by Zoe Dominic. pp. 194, 195, 196–97, 198–99, 204: courtesy Harry Ransom Center, The University of Texas at Austin; photographs by Fred Fehl. p. 205: courtesy Alvin Ailey Dance Foundation; photographs by William Hilton. pp. 206–7: courtesy Alvin Ailey Dance Foundation; photograph by Johan Elbers. p. 208: courtesy Alvin Ailey Dance Foundation; photograph by Haruhisa Yamaguchi. p. 209: © New York Public Library; photograph by Martha Swope. p. 214: courtesy Alvin Ailey Dance Foundation; photograph by Rosemary Winckley. p. 215: courtesy Harry Ransom Center, The University of Texas at Austin; photograph by Fred Fehl. pp. 216–17: courtesy Alvin Ailey Dance Foundation; photograph by Marion-Valentine. pp. 218, 219: courtesy Alvin Ailey Dance Foundation; photographs by R. Faligant. p. 220 (top left): courtesy Alvin Ailey Dance Foundation; photograph by Larry Farrow. p. 220 (bottom left), 244: courtesy Alvin Ailey Dance Foundation; photographs by Donald Moss. p. 220 (bottom right): courtesy Alvin Ailey Dance Foundation; photograph by Don Middleton. pp. 220–21 (top center): courtesy Alvin Ailey Dance Foundation; photographer unknown. p. 221 (bottom left): courtesy Alvin Ailey Dance Foundation; photograph by Arne Folkedal. p. 221 (top right): © Alvin Ailey Dance Foundation and Smithsonian Institution; photographs by Jack Mitchell. p. 221 (bottom right): courtesy Alvin Ailey Dance Foundation; photograph by Johan Elbers. pp. 222, 223: courtesy the Kennedy Center Archives; photographs by Fletcher Drake. pp. 224–25: courtesy Harry Ransom Center, The University of Texas at Austin; photograph by Fred Fehl. pp. 226–27: courtesy Alvin Ailey Dance Foundation; photograph by Kenn Duncan. pp. 228–29: courtesy Alvin Ailey Dance Foundation; photograph by Johan Elbers. p. 230: courtesy Alvin Ailey Dance Foundation; photograph by Paul Goode. p. 231: courtesy Alvin Ailey Dance Foundation; photograph by Rosemary Winckley. pp. 232, 233: Allan Gray Family Personal Papers of Alvin Ailey (AC10), Black Archives of Mid-America, Kansas City, Missouri; photographs by Louis Mélançon. pp. 234, 235: courtesy Harry Ransom Center, The University of Texas at Austin; photographs by Fred Fehl. p. 236: courtesy Alvin Ailey Dance Foundation;

photographs by William Hilton. p. 237: courtesy Alvin Ailey Dance Foundation; photograph by Roberto Aguilar. pp. 238–39, 240, 241: courtesy Harry Ransom Center, The University of Texas at Austin; photograph by Fred Fehl. pp. 242: courtesy Alvin Ailey Dance Foundation; photograph by Johan Elbers. p. 243: courtesy Alvin Ailey Dance Foundation; photograph by Susan Cook. p. 245: courtesy Alvin Ailey Dance Foundation; photograph by Beatriz Schiller. p. 246: courtesy Alvin Ailey Dance Foundation; photograph by Jack Vartoogian. p. 247: courtesy Alvin Ailey Dance Foundation; photograph by Johan Elbers. pp. 248–49: courtesy Alvin Ailey Dance Foundation; photograph by Jack Vartoogian. pp. 250–51: courtesy Alvin Ailey Dance Foundation; photograph by Randy Masser. pp. 252–53: courtesy Alvin Ailey Dance Foundation; photograph by Johan Elbers. pp. 254, 255: courtesy Alvin Ailey Dance Foundation; photographs by Jack Vartoogian. pp. 256, 257: courtesy Alvin Ailey Dance Foundation; photographs by William Hilton. pp. 259, 260: © Alvin Ailey Dance Foundation and Smithsonian Institution; photographs by Jack Mitchell. p. 262: courtesy Alvin Ailey Dance Foundation; photograph by Francette Levieux. p. 263: courtesy Alvin Ailey Dance Foundation; photograph by John Markowski. pp. 264–65: courtesy Alvin Ailey Dance Foundation; photograph by David Seelig. p. 266: Los Angeles Herald Examiner Photo Collection/Los Angeles Public Library; photograph by Leo Jarzomb. pp. 267, 268–69, 270: courtesy Alvin Ailey Dance Foundation; photographs by Jack Vartoogian. p. 271: courtesy Alvin Ailey Dance Foundation; photograph by Johan Elbers. pp. 272–73: © Alvin Ailey Dance Foundation and Smithsonian Institution; photographs by Jack Mitchell. pp. 276, 278, 279, 280, 281, 282, 283, 284, 285, 286–87, 288, 289, 290–91, 292, 293, 294, 295, 296, 297, 298, 299, 300, 301, 302, 303, 304, 305, 306, 307, 308: Allan Gray Family Personal Papers of Alvin Ailey (AC10), Black Archives of Mid-America, Kansas City, Missouri; photographs by Gabe Hopkins. p. 309: Alvin Ailey Dance Foundation Collection, Music Division, Library of Congress. pp. 310, 311: Allan Gray Family Personal Papers of Alvin Ailey (AC10), Black Archives of Mid-America, Kansas City, Missouri; photographs by Gabe Hopkins. pp. 312, 313, 314, 315, 316, 317, 318, 319: Alvin Ailey Dance Foundation Collection, Music Division, Library of Congress. pp. 322, 330: Allan Gray Family Personal Papers of Alvin Ailey (AC10), Black Archives of Mid-America, Kansas City, Missouri; photographs by Gabe Hopkins. p. 332: Fon peoples: © The Metropolitan Museum of Art. Image courtesy Art Resource, NY. p. 332: Hector Hyppolite, © The Museum of Modern Art/Licensed by SCALA/Art Resource, NY. p. 332: Rubem Valentim, © The Museum of Modern Art/Licensed by SCALA/Art Resource, NY; courtesy Instituto Rubem Valentim. p. 333: David Driskell, © The Estate of David C. Driskell; courtesy DC Moore Gallery. p. 333: Loïs Mailou Jones, Howard University Gallery of Art/Licensed by Art Resource, NY. p. 333: Noah Purifoy, © Noah Purifoy Foundation. p. 334: Beverly Buchanan; courtesy the Beverly Buchanan Estate and Andrew Edlin Gallery. p. 334: Thornton Dial, © The Estate of Thornton Dial; image courtesy Pitkin Studio/Art Resource, NY. pp. 334–35: Carrie Mae Weems, © Carrie Mae Weems. p. 335: Kevin Beasley, © Kevin Beasley. Courtesy the artist and Casey Kaplan; photograph by Jason Wyche. p. 335: John Biggers, © Estate of John Biggers. Courtesy Michael Rosenfeld Gallery. p. 335: Al Loving, courtesy the Estate of Al Loving and Garth Greenan Gallery. p. 336: Purvis Young, © 2024 The Larry T. Clemons Collection/Artists Rights Society (ARS), NY; photograph by Pitkin Studio; courtesy Souls Grown Deep Foundation. pp. 336–37: Ellen Gallagher, © Ellen Gallagher. pp. 336–37: Maren Hassinger, courtesy The Studio Museum in Harlem and Susan Inglett Gallery. p. 337: Alma Thomas, © 2024 Estate of Alma Thomas (courtesy the Hart Family)/Artists Rights Society (ARS), NY. p. 337: Purvis Young, © 2024 The Larry T. Clemons Collection/Artists Rights Society (ARS), NY; photograph by Pitkin Studio/Art Resource, NY. p. 338: Benny Andrews, © Benny Andrews Estate, Courtesy Michael Rosenfeld Gallery. p. 338: Jacob Lawrence, © 2024 The Jacob and Gwendolyn Knight Lawrence Foundation, Seattle/Artists Rights Society (ARS), NY. p. 338: James Van Der Zee, © James Van Der Zee Archive, The Metropolitan Museum of Art. p. 339: Rotimi Fani-Kayode, © Rotimi Fani-Kayode. Courtesy Autograph. p. 339: Charles White, © The Charles White Archives. p. 340: Palmer Hayden, © Hayden Family Revocable Art Trust. p. 340: Clementine Hunter, © Cane River Art Corporation; image courtesy The Johnson Collection, Spartanburg, South Carolina. p. 340: Meta Vaux Warrick Fuller, © Meta V. W. Fuller Trust; image courtesy the Danforth Art Museum. p. 341: Horace Pippin, photograph by Gavin Ashworth; courtesy Leslie Miller and Richard Worley. p. 341: Paul Waters, © Paul Waters. Courtesy Eric Firestone Gallery. p. 342: Hale Aspacio Woodruff, © 2024 Estate of Hale Woodruff/Licensed by VAGA at Artists Rights Society (ARS), NY. p. 342: Purvis Young, © 2024 The Larry T. Clemons Collection/Artists Rights Society (ARS), NY. Courtesy High Museum of Art. pp. 342–43: Samella Lewis, © 2024 Samella Lewis/Licensed by VAGA at Artists Rights Society (ARS), NY. p. 343: William H. Johnson, © William H. Johnson. Smithsonian American Art Museum/Art Resource, NY. p. 343: Martin Puryear, © Martin Puryear. Courtesy Matthew Marks Gallery. p. 344: Robert Duncanson, courtesy Cincinnati Museum Center. p. 345: Melvin Edwards, © Melvin Edwards © The Museum of Modern Art/Licensed by SCALA/Art Resource, NY. p. 345: Thomas Nast, courtesy Metropolitan Museum of Art. p. 345: Meta Vaux Warrick Fuller, © Meta V. W. Fuller Trust. Image courtesy the Danforth Art Museum. pp. 346–47: Faith Ringgold, © 2024 Faith Ringgold/Artists Rights Society (ARS), NY. p. 347: Jeff Donaldson, courtesy the Estate of Jeff Donaldson and Kravets Wehby Gallery. p. 347: James Van Der Zee, © James Van Der Zee Archive, The Metropolitan Museum of Art. p. 348: Wadsworth Jarrell, courtesy the artist and Jenkins Johnson Gallery. pp. 348, 349: Sam Doyle, courtesy Souls Grown Deep Foundation. p. 349: Joe Overstreet, © 2024 Joe Overstreet/Artists Rights Society (ARS), NY. p. 350: Aaron Douglas, © 2024 Heirs of Aaron Douglas/Licensed by VAGA at Artists Rights Society (ARS), NY. p. 350: Sam Gilliam, © 2024 Estate of Sam Gilliam/Artists Rights Society (ARS), NY. p. 350: James Little, © Courtesy James Little and Kavi Gupta. pp. 350–51: Rashid Johnson, courtesy the artist. p. 351: David Hammons, © David Hammons/Artists Rights Society (ARS), NY. p. 351: Glenn Ligon, © Glenn Ligon; courtesy the artist, Hauser and Wirth, Regen Projects, Thomas Dane Gallery, and Galerie Chantal Crousel; photograph by Jason Mandella. p. 352: Loïs Mailou Jones, © The Loïs Mailou Jones Pierre-Noël Trust. Image courtesy Howard University Gallery of Art/Licensed by Art Resource, NY. p. 352: Geoffrey Holder, courtesy the Estate of Geoffrey Holder and James Fuentes Gallery; photograph by Shark Senesac. p. 352: Mary Lovelace O'Neal, courtesy the artist and Karen Jenkins-Johnson. p. 353: Emma Amos, © Emma Amos; courtesy Ryan Lee Gallery. p. 353: Beauford Delaney, © Estate of Beauford Delaney by permission of Derek L. Spratley, Esquire, Court Appointed Administrator. Courtesy Virginia Museum of Fine Arts, Richmond. p. 353: Mickalene Thomas, © Mickalene Thomas. p. 354: Beauford Delaney, © Estate of Beauford Delaney by permission of Derek L. Spratley, Esquire, Court Appointed Administrator. Courtesy Michael Rosenfeld Gallery. p. 354: Sam Gilliam, © 2024 Estate of Sam Gilliam/Artists Rights Society (ARS), NY. p. 354: Norman Lewis, © Estate of Norman Lewis; Courtesy Michael Rosenfeld Gallery. © The Museum of Modern Art/Licensed by SCALA/Art Resource, NY. p. 355: Jean-Michel Basquiat, © The Estate of Jean-Michel Basquiat. Licensed by Artestar. p. 355: Charles Gaines, © Charles Gaines. Courtesy the artist and Hauser and Wirth. p. 356: Archibald John Motley Jr., © Valerie Gerrard Browne. p. 356: Lyle Ashton Harris, © Lyle Ashton Harris. p. 356: Kerry James Marshall, © Kerry James Marshall. Courtesy the artist and Jack Shainman Gallery. pp. 356–57: Thornton Dial, © Estate of Thornton Dial. Courtesy Hood Museum of Art, Hanover, New Hampshire. p. 357: Bill Traylor, courtesy The Bill Traylor Family Foundation. Image courtesy The Johnson Collection, Spartanburg, South Carolina. p. 358: John Outterbridge, © Courtesy the Estate of the artist and Tilton Gallery. p. 358: Senga Nengudi, courtesy the artist, Sprueth Magers, and Thomas Erben Gallery. p. 358: Eldren Bailey, Jacqueline Ford and the family of Eldren Bailey; photograph by Stephen Pitkin/Pitkin Studio, courtesy Souls Grown Deep Foundation. p. 358: James Van Der Zee, © James Van Der Zee Archive, The Metropolitan Museum of Art. p. 359: Barkley Hendricks, © Barkley L. Hendricks. Courtesy the Estate of Barkley L. Hendricks and Jack Shainman Gallery. pp. 358–59: Lynette Yiadom Boakye, courtesy the artist, Corvi-Mora, and Jack Shainman Gallery. pp. 360–61: © 2024 Romare Bearden Foundation/Licensed by VAGA at Artists Rights Society (ARS), NY. p. 362: Kandis Williams, © Kandis Williams; courtesy the Mohn Family Foundation. p. 363: Lorna Simpson, © Lorna Simpson. Courtesy the artist and Hauser and Wirth; photograph by Yosra El-Essawy. p. 363: Ralph Lemon, courtesy the artist; photograph by Brent Wahl. p. 364: image courtesy the National AIDS Memorial. Endpapers (back): courtesy The Antonio Archives.

This book was published on the occasion of the exhibition *Edges of Ailey*, organized by the Whitney Museum of American Art in collaboration with the Alvin Ailey Dance Foundation and curated by Adrienne Edwards, Engell Speyer Family Senior Curator and Associate Director of Curatorial Programs, with Joshua Lubin-Levy, Curatorial Research Associate, and CJ Salapare, Curatorial Assistant, Whitney Museum of American Art.

Whitney Museum of American Art, New York
September 25, 2024–February 9, 2025

The lead sponsor of the exhibition is the Jerome L. Greene Foundation.

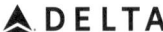

This exhibition is also sponsored by

BANK OF AMERICA

DELTA

Leadership support is provided by the Ford Foundation.

Ford Foundation

Generous support is provided by Judy Hart Angelo and the Arnhold Family | Arnhold Foundation.

Major support is provided by the Barbara Haskell American Fellows Legacy Fund, the Horace W. Goldsmith Foundation, Anne-Cecilie Engell Speyer and Rob Speyer, the Whitney's National Committee, and Clara Wu Tsai.

Significant support is provided by The Holly Peterson Foundation, The Keith Haring Foundation Exhibition Fund, and the National Endowment for the Arts.

Additional support is provided by A4 Arts Charitable Trust, the Adam D. Weinberg Artists First Fund, Candace and Rick Beinecke, Kevin Gan and Benjamin Blad, Elizabeth Marsteller Gordon, The Harkness Foundation for Dance, Sharon and John Hoffman, Nancy Magoon, and an anonymous donor.

Curatorial research and travel for this exhibition were funded by an endowment established by Rosina Lee Yue and Bert A. Lies, Jr., MD.

Support is also provided by the Marshall Weinberg Fund for Performance, endowed in honor of his parents, Anna and Harold Weinberg, who taught him the meaning of giving.

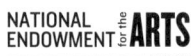

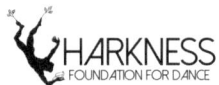

Generous support for the catalogue is provided by the Mellon Foundation.

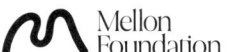

Copyright © 2024 Whitney Museum of American Art

Additional copyright notices and photography credits can be found on page 386.

All rights reserved. No part of this book may be reproduced or transmitted in any form or by any means, electronic or mechanical, including photocopy, recording or other information storage and retrieval system, or otherwise without written permission from the publisher.

Whitney Museum of American Art
99 Gansevoort Street
New York, NY 10014
whitney.org

Distributed by
Yale University Press
302 Temple Street
P.O. Box 209040
New Haven, CT 06520-9040
yalebooks.com

Project manager: Beth Huseman
Editor: Sarah Noreika
Designer: Garrick Gott
Production: The Production Department
Researcher: Katerina Fong
Proofreader: Beth Turk
Indexer: David Luljak
Separations: Altaimage, New York
Printing: Meridian Printing, East Greenwich, RI

Typeset in Tatsuro and Caslon Doric

About the type
Tré Seals started the Vocal Type foundry to increase diversity in a field where Black representation is about 3.5 percent. Seals notes that each typeface he designs "highlights a piece of history from a specific underrepresented race, ethnicity, or gender"—from the Civil Rights Movement to other acts of political resistance. Nearly thirty years before Martin Luther King, Jr. marched with "I AM A MAN" signs, Tatsuro Matsuda commissioned and installed a sign that read, "I AM AN AMERICAN" on his family's storefront. The typeface Tatsuro is based on this iconic sign.

Printed on 135 gsm GardaPat Kiara
and 104 gsm Accent Opaque
Printed and bound in the United States

Cataloging-in-Publication Data is on file with the Library of Congress.

ISBN 978-0-300-27884-2

Jacket (front): Side-turned portrait of Alvin Ailey, 1962. Photograph by Jack Mitchell. © Alvin Ailey Dance Foundation and Smithsonian Institution. Jacket (back): Alvin Ailey and others backstage at *Jamaica*, n.d. Photographs by Gus Dinizulu. Courtesy Nana Yao Opare Dinizulu and Alvin Ailey Dance Foundation

Cover: Alvin Ailey at Jacob's Pillow, Becket, Massachusetts, 1959. Photograph by John Lindquist. Courtesy Jacob's Pillow Dance Festival Archives © Houghton Library, Harvard University

Endpapers (front): *Revelations*, n.d. Photographer unknown. Courtesy Alvin Ailey Dance Foundation. Endpapers (back): Studio 54, 1977. The Antonio Archives. Courtesy The Antonio Archives

Title page: Alvin Ailey in profile, n.d. Photographer unknown. Courtesy Alvin Ailey Dance Foundation.

p. 4: Alvin Ailey with company members, n.d. Photograph by Raul Aguilar. Courtesy Alvin Ailey Dance Foundation.

p. 152: Alvin Ailey, page from Notebook #100 [721], "The River," ca. 1970, Allan Gray Family Personal Papers of Alvin Ailey (AC10), Series 3: Notebooks, folder 129, Black Archives of Mid-America, Kansas City, Missouri.

p. 276: Alvin Ailey, cover of Notebook #29 [651], "Ailey Daily," October 17, 1974, Allan Gray Family Personal Papers of Alvin Ailey (AC10), Series 3: Notebooks, folder 56, Black Archives of Mid-America, Kansas City, Missouri.

p. 322: Alvin Ailey, page from Notebook #6 [728], "Untitled," n.d., Allan Gray Family Personal Papers of Alvin Ailey (AC10), Series 3: Notebooks, folder 33, Black Archives of Mid-America, Kansas City, Missouri.

p. 330 (clockwise from top left): Alvin Ailey, page from Notebook #52 [710], "Untitled," n.d., Allan Gray Family Personal Papers of Alvin Ailey (AC10), Series 3: Notebooks, folder 79, Black Archives of Mid-America, Kansas City, Missouri. Alvin Ailey, page from Notebook #40 [666], "Four Saints," n.d., Allan Gray Family Personal Papers of Alvin Ailey (AC10), Series 3: Notebooks, folder 67, Black Archives of Mid-America, Kansas City, Missouri. Alvin Ailey, page from Notebook #7 [690], "Untitled," n.d., Allan Gray Family Personal Papers of Alvin Ailey (AC10), Series 3: Notebooks, folder 34, Black Archives of Mid-America, Kansas City, Missouri. Alvin Ailey, page from Notebook #61 [743], "Untitled," n.d., Allan Gray Family Personal Papers of Alvin Ailey (AC10), Series 3: Notebooks, folder 88, Black Archives of Mid-America, Kansas City, Missouri.

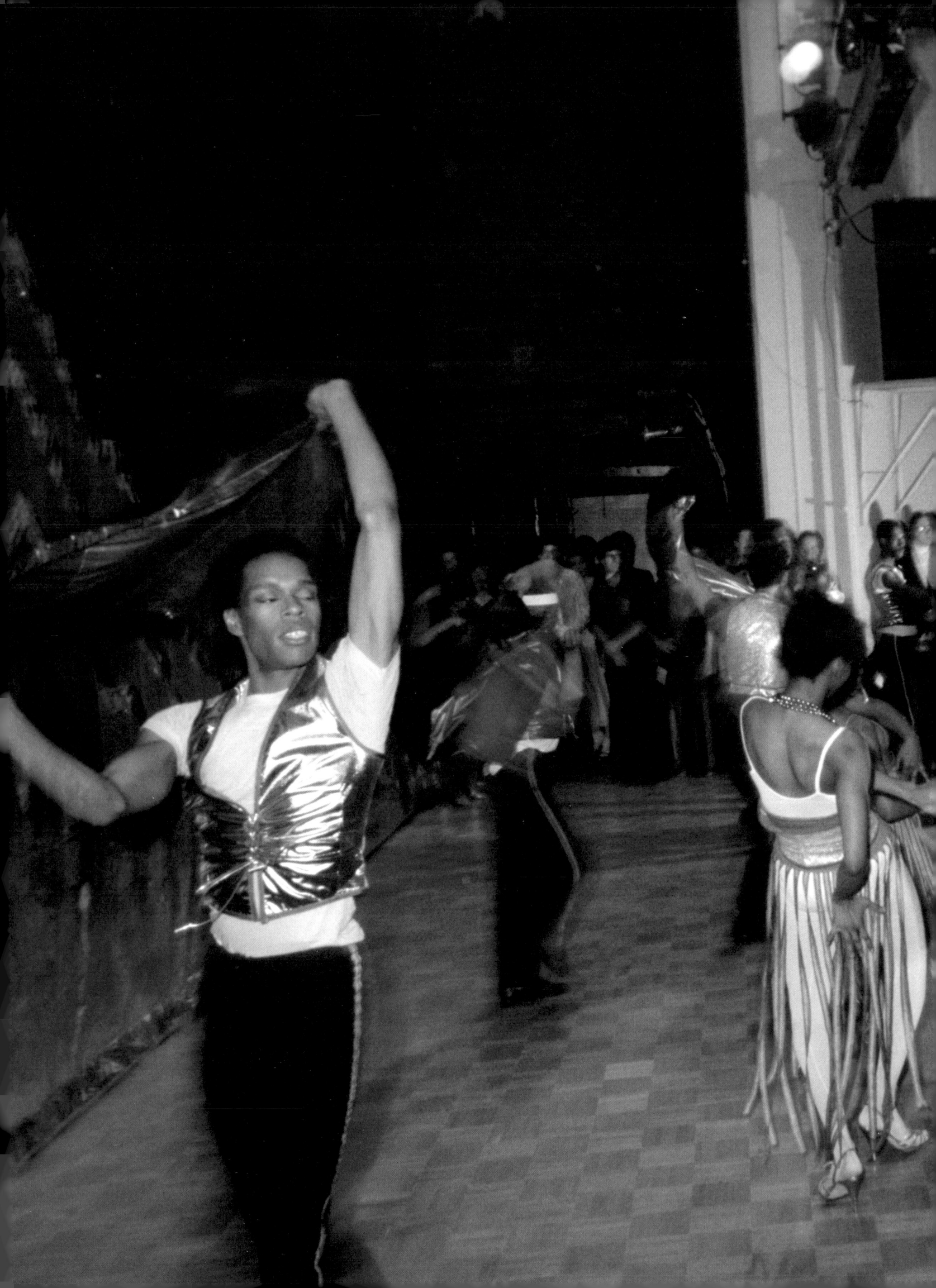